The
PORTABLE
MBA
in
ENTREPRENEURSHIP

The

PORTABLE
MBA
in
ENTREPRENEURSHIP

FOURTH EDITION

Edited by

William D. Bygrave, DBA and
Andrew Zacharakis, PhD

WILEY

John Wiley & Sons, Inc.

For general information on our other products and services or for technical support, please contact our Customer Care Department within the United States at (800) 762-2974, outside the United States at (317) 572-3993 or fax (317) 572-4002.

Wiley also publishes its books in a variety of electronic formats. Some content that appears in print may not be available in electronic books. For more information about Wiley products, visit our web site at www.wiley.com.

ISBN 978-0-470-48131-8

Printed in the United States of America.

10 9 8 7 6 5 4

Contents

Complete List of Downloadable Materials for *The Portable MBA in Entrepreneurship*

Online Only:

Online and in this book:

Preface to the Fourth Edition

As we write the fourth edition, the United States and world have gone through economic upheaval. Unemployment, foreclosures, government bailouts to the financial and auto sectors have created volatility and uncertainty. Yet, while the period has been bleak, we expect the future to be bright. The one truth for the United States—and for more and more nations as entrepreneurship has taken hold globally—is that world-changing new ventures often are born at the depth of economic upheavals. During the Great Depression, Boeing emerged and changed the nature of aerospace; IBM was founded during the Long Depression (1872–1896); and many great companies opened shop during recessions, including Hyatt and Burger King during the 1957–1958 recession, FedEx during the 1973 oil embargo, and CNN and MTV during the 1980–1981 recession. Thus, entrepreneurship is even more important to economic recovery and ongoing health for countries worldwide. We hope that this book will inspire the next generation of great entrepreneurs and companies.

Today, U.S. small businesses—firms with 500 or fewer employees—employ slightly more than 50 percent of the labor force and generate approximately half of the nonfarm private gross domestic product (GDP). If the small business sector of the U.S. economy were a nation, its GDP would rank third in the world behind the non-small-business sector of the United States and the entire economy of Japan, and far ahead of the entire economies of China, Germany, the United Kingdom, France, and Italy.

Not only are small businesses the engine for job creation, they are also a powerful force for innovation. They employ 39 percent of all high-tech workers and produce approximately 14 times more patents per employee than large firms. Since the publication of the third edition, a multitude of new, world-changing companies have been started. Facebook, Skype, and Twitter, among others, are changing the way we communicate and interact with each other. And large existing companies that are entrepreneurial continue to create and rejuvenate their businesses. No example is better than Apple, which since 2003 has launched the iPhone and iTouch. Close to 50 million units have been sold in its first 18 months.

No doubt about it, entrepreneurship is what America does best, bar none. No other advanced industrial nation comes close. U.S. entrepreneurial companies created the personal computer, biotechnology, fast food, and overnight package delivery industries; transformed the retailing industry; overthrew AT&T's telecommunications monopoly; revitalized the steel industry; invented the integrated circuit and the microprocessor; founded the nation's most profitable airline; and the list goes on.

Is it any wonder that more and more people are choosing to be entrepreneurs? Entrepreneurship courses and programs have proliferated in the past 10 years. It is estimated that more than 2,000 U.S. colleges and universities, or about two-thirds of the total, have at least one course in entrepreneurship. It is possible to study entrepreneurship in certificate, associates, bachelors, masters, and PhD programs. Every business student, regardless of their career plans, needs to understand the role of entrepreneurship in the economy. Today, a business education without an entrepreneurship component is as incomplete as medical training without obstetrics.

The Portable MBA in Entrepreneurship is a book for would-be entrepreneurs, people who have started small firms and who want to improve their entrepreneurial skills, and others who are interested in entrepreneurship, such as bank loan officers, lawyers, accountants, investors, and consultants—indeed, anyone who wants to get involved in the birth and growth of an enterprise. The chapters are written by leading authorities on new business creation, including professors, entrepreneurs, and consultants with extensive experience in teaching the art and science of starting and growing a venture. These authors practice what they teach. They have started businesses, served on boards of venture capital funds, been on boards of directors and boards of advisers of entrepreneurial companies, raised start-up and expansion capital, filed patents, registered companies, and, perhaps most important of all, have created new products and many new jobs. What's more, they are tireless champions of entrepreneurship. They believe that entrepreneurs are crucial to America's economic well-being.

We would like to thank all the chapter authors for their contributions, as well as our research assistants, Mark Itskovitz, R. Gabriel Shih, and Henry McGovern. We hope you enjoy this book.

WILLIAM D. BYGRAVE
ANDREW ZACHARAKIS
Arthur M. Blank Center for Entrepreneurship
Babson College
May 2009

About the Contributors

Abdul Ali is the President's Term Chair and an associate professor of marketing at Babson College. Earlier he taught at the University of Maryland in College Park and at Syracuse University. He served as Chair of the Marketing Division for six years (2000 to 2006) at Babson College. Dr. Ali's teaching and research interests include new product management, entrepreneurial marketing, marketing research methods, marketing strategy, and marketing high-tech products. His work has appeared in *Management Science*, the *Journal of Product Innovation Management, Managerial and Decision Economics*, the *Journal of Business Research*, and *Marketing Letters*. He and two co-authors produced *A Casebook for Business Statistics: Laboratories for Decision Making*, published by John Wiley & Sons. He also co-authored a chapter each on entrepreneurial marketing in two books edited by William Bygrave and Andrew Zacharakis.

William D. Bygrave, D.Phil., MBA, is a professor emeritus at Babson College. Dr. Bygrave joined the Center for Entrepreneurial Studies at Babson College in 1985 and directed it from 1993 to 1999. He was also the director of the annual Babson College–Kauffman Foundation Entrepreneurship Research Conference in 1994–1995 and 2001–2003. He teaches and researches entrepreneurship, specifically financing of start-up and growing ventures. In 1997, he and Michael Hay at the London Business School started the Global Entrepreneurship Monitor (GEM), which examines the entrepreneurial competitiveness of nations. He is a member of the board of trustees of Babson College.

Dr. Bygrave has founded a venture-capital-backed high-tech company, managed a division of a New York Stock Exchange–listed high-tech company, co-founded a pharmaceutical database company, and been a member of the investment committee of a venture capital firm. He was the 1997 winner of the Ernst & Young Entrepreneur of the Year award in the supporter category for New England.

He has written more than 100 papers on topics that include venture capital, entrepreneurship, nuclear physics, hospital pharmaceuticals, and philosophy of science. He is also co-editor of *Entrepreneurship* (2007); *The Venture Capital Handbook* (1999); *The Portable MBA in Entrepreneurship* (third edition, 2003); *The Portable MBA in Entrepreneurship Case Studies* (second edition, 1997); *Realizing Enterprise Value* (1993); and *Frontiers of Entrepreneurship Research*; he was also an editor of *Entrepreneurship Theory and Practice*. He has served on the review boards of three entrepreneurship journals. Translations of his books have been published in Chinese, Japanese, Spanish, and Bahasa Indonesia. Areas of expertise include entrepreneurship, new venture creation, informal investment, and venture capital.

Elizabeth J. (Betsy) Gatewood, PhD, has been the director of the University Office of Entrepreneurship & Liberal Arts at Wake Forest University since 2004. She served as the Jack M. Gill Chair of Entrepreneurship and director of the Johnson Center for Entrepreneurship & Innovation at Indiana University from 1998 to 2004. She was the executive director of the Gulf Coast Small Business Development Center Network, an organization providing training and consulting services to entrepreneurs and small business owners in the 32 counties of the greater Houston region, from 1989 to 1998. Dr. Gatewood founded the Center for Business and Economic Studies at the University of Georgia and served as its director from 1983 to 1989.

She is a member of the Diana Project, a research study of women business owners and equity capital access, which won the FSF-NUTEK International Award for scientific work of outstanding quality and importance in the field of entrepreneurship. Dr. Gatewood serves on the board of directors of Delta Apparel, Inc. (AMEX:DLA) and on the Advisory Board for Spring Mill Ventures, a venture capital firm of the Village Ventures network. She is a past chair of the Entrepreneurship Division of the Academy of Management. She received the 1996 Advocate Award for outstanding contributions to the field of entrepreneurship from the Academy of Management. She holds a BS in psychology from Purdue University and an MBA with a concentration in finance and a PhD in business administration with a specialty in strategy from the University of Georgia.

H. David Hennessey, PhD, is Professor of Marketing and International Business at Babson College. After gaining his undergraduate degree in economics and business administration at Norwich University, Northfield, Vermont, and an MBA from Clark University, Worcester, Massachusetts, Dr. Hennessey worked as a senior marketing analyst for the American Can Company. He then became marketing director for Interpace Corporation, based in New Jersey. He completed his PhD at New York University and joined Babson College in 1982. He has taught courses on global marketing, marketing strategy, sales management strategy, and foundations of management and entrepreneurship, and written numerous articles and case studies. He has co-authored *Global Marketing Strategies* (6th edition, 2004, with Jean-Pierre Jeannet); *Global Marketing: An Interactive Approach* (2nd edition, 2006, with Jean-Pierre Jeannet and Kate Gillespie); *Global Account Management* (2004, with Jean-Pierre Jeannet); and *How to Write a Marketing Plan* (3rd edition, 1996, with Robert J. Kopp).

Dr. Hennessey has had executive and MBA teaching experience in programs at Babson College, Ashridge, IMD International, Rotterdam School of Management (RSM) Erasmus, and Helsinki School of Economics and Business Administration, as well as in Costa Rica, France, Holland, Germany, Switzerland, Finland, Hong Kong, and Japan. Participants are from many companies—for example, Electrolux, Unilever, IBM, Procter & Gamble, Investment Company Institute (ICI), Novartis, BBC, Cable and Wireless, BT Group, Compaq, Unisys, Philips, and Nokia.

Professor Hennessey is the faculty director of the Evening MBA program at Babson College. He served as faculty director for the Irving Oil marketing program and the GTECH Corporation growth program.

Joseph S. Iandiorio is a partner in the law firm of Iandiorio Teska & Coleman in Waltham, Massachusetts. The firm specializes in patents, trademarks, copyrights, trade secrets, licensing, litigation of intellectual property matters, employee and consultant contracts, confidential disclosure agreements, and other related areas of intellectual property. Mr. Iandiorio has over 45 years of experience, including a period as an examiner in the U.S. Patent and Trademark Office. He is actively involved in fostering the creation and growth of small businesses and high-technology companies. He was chosen as the Small Business Administration's Lawyer Small Business Advocate of the Year. He has been director and treasurer of the Massachusetts Technology Development Corporation, a venture capital fund; chairman and director of the Smaller Business Association of New England; a member of the Massachusetts Small Business Advisory Council and of the Science and Technology Advisory Board; and a member of the board of trustees of National Small Business United.

Donna J. Kelley, PhD, is an associate professor of entrepreneurship at Babson College, and holds the David H. Park 1991 Term Chair in Entrepreneurship. Donna teaches courses in entrepreneurship, corporate entrepreneurship, and entrepreneurship in Asia. She has published research on innovation and entrepreneurial activities in technology-based start-ups and large established organizations in the United States and Asia. Her research has been published in the *Journal of Business Venturing, Entrepreneurship: Theory & Practice*, the *Journal of Product Innovation Management*, *IEEE Transactions on Engineering Management*, *Human Resource Management*, and others.

Dr. Kelley received her PhD from Rensselaer Polytechnic Institute. Her early career involved work as a chemist in the graphics and industrial/consumer cleaning products industries. Her entrepreneurship experience involves founding a health fitness business and joining the management team of a computer hardware start-up, responsible for finance and operations. She was also a founding team member and a founding board member of a Chinese-immersion public charter school. She is a board member of the Global Entrepreneurship Research Association (GERA), the oversight organization for the Global Entrepreneurship Monitor (GEM), and she was a member of the GEM Korea research team.

Richard P. Mandel, JD, is associate professor of law at Babson College, where he teaches a variety of courses in business law and taxation and serves as associate dean of the Undergraduate School. He has previously served as acting dean of the Undergraduate School at Babson and as chair of its Finance Division. Mr. Mandel is also of counsel to the law firm of Bowditch and Dewey, of Worcester, Boston, and Framingham, Massachusetts, where he specializes in the corporate, tax, and securities law issues of small businesses. Mr. Mandel has written a number of articles regarding the legal issues of small businesses and is a frequent contributor to the Portable MBA series. He holds an AB in political science and meteorology from Cornell University and a JD from Harvard Law School.

Edward P. Marram, PhD, is senior lecturer at Babson College. His academic experience includes serving as director of the Entrepreneurial Center at Babson College, where he was instrumental in developing cooperative programs with the Entrepreneurial Department, the Executive Center, the Olin School of Engineering, and Intel, as well as others. He has taught entrepreneurship at Babson College, Harvard University, Olin School of Engineering, and Northeastern University, as well as at INSEAD in Fontainebleau, France, and at Flanders School of Business in Belgium; he has served as entrepreneur-in-residence at Babson College since 1990. In 1989 he was made a

Price-Babson College Fellow and in 1992 was awarded the Edwin M. Appel Prize "For Bringing Entrepreneurial Vitality to Academics in the True Spirit of the Price-Babson College Fellows Program." Dr. Marram has taught business practices to faculty, graduate students, and entrepreneurs in the United States, in South America, and in both Eastern and Western Europe, and has lectured on entrepreneurial education to Polish faculty members and entrepreneurs at the University of Warsaw, worked with Slovenian entrepreneurs and educators, and developed executive training programs in Scotland and at INSEAD in France.

Dr. Marram's business/entrepreneurial experience includes being the founder, chief executive officer, and chairman of the board of Geo-Centers, Inc., a high-technology professional services firm, until its acquisition by SAIC, Inc. in October 2005. During his tenure as head of Geo-Centers, the company grew to over $200 million in revenue. Under Dr. Marram's leadership, Geo-Centers established an in-house Research and Development Center to provide, for the global scientific community, a place for cutting-edge collaborations with the world's finest scientists and engineers with a mission to transition research into applications and products.

He holds BS and MS degrees from the University of Massachusetts and a PhD in physics from Tufts University.

Heidi Neck, PhD, is the Jeffry A. Timmons Professor of Entrepreneurial Studies at Babson College. She is the faculty director of the Babson Symposium for Entrepreneurship Educators (SEE), where she works to improve the pedagogy of entrepreneurship education because venture creation is the economic growth engine of society. Her research interests include social entrepreneurship, entrepreneurship education, and creativity. She has contributed numerous book chapters, published research monographs, and refereed articles in such journals as the *Journal of Small Business Management*, *Entrepreneurship Theory and Practice*, and the *International Journal of Entrepreneurship Education*. She is on the editorial board of *Entrepreneurship Theory and Practice* and *Academy of Management Learning & Education*. Recognized for her contributions to innovative teaching and curriculum developments, she has received numerous awards, including Babson's Deans' Award for Excellence in Teaching and the Gloria Appel Prize for entrepreneurial vitality in academe. Dr. Neck completed her PhD in strategic management and entrepreneurship from the University of Colorado at Boulder in 2001. She holds a BS in marketing from Louisiana State University and an MBA from the University of Colorado, Boulder.

Mark P. Rice, PhD, currently the Frederic C. Hamilton Professor for Free Enterprise at Babson College, served as the Murata Dean of the F. W. Olin Graduate School of Business at Babson College from 2001 to 2007. He also has an appointment as Professor of Technology Entrepreneurship at Babson's sister school, the Olin College of Engineering. His research on corporate innovation and entrepreneurship has been published widely in academic and practitioner journals, including *Sloan Management Review*, *Organization Science*, *R&D Management*, the *Journal of Marketing Theory and Practice*, *IEEE Engineering Management Review*, *Academy of Management Executive*, and *California Management Review*. Dr. Rice consults and teaches in the areas of innovation management, sales/marketing development, technology strategy, new business incubation, and entrepreneurship. He is co-author of *Radical Innovation: How Mature Companies Can Outsmart Upstarts*, which was published by Harvard Business School.

Professor Rice previously served as director of the nationally recognized RPI Incubator Program and as co-founder and director of the Severino Center for Technological Entrepreneurship at Rensselaer Polytechnic Institute. He has been a director and chairman of the National Business Incubation Association, which honored him in 1998 with its Founder's Award. With Dr. Jana Matthews, he co-authored *Growing New Ventures—Creating New Jobs: Principles and Practices of Successful Business Incubation*.

In 2002 Dr. Rice received the Edwin M. and Gloria W. Appel Entrepreneurship in Education Prize. He holds BS and MS degrees in mechanical engineering and a PhD in management from Rensselaer Polytechnic Institute.

Joel M. Shulman, PhD, CFA, CMA, is an associate professor of entrepreneurship at Babson College. He has a PhD in finance along with Chartered Financial Analyst (CFA) and Certified Management Accountant (CMA) designations. He previously directed the Shulman CFA Review Program, which provided training for more than 12,000 investment professionals in over 100 countries throughout the world. He is the author or a co-author of numerous academic articles and books, including *Getting Bigger by Growing Smaller*, *Encyclopedia of Business*, *Leasing for Profit*, *Alternatives to Conventional Financing*, *Planning Cash Flow*, *How to Effectively Manage Corporate Cash*, *A Manager's Guide to Financial Analysis*, *The Job of Corporate Controller*, and *How to Manage and Evaluate Capital Expenditures*. Dr. Shulman has consulted for small entrepreneurial firms and large corporations, including Coldwell Banker, Ford Motor Company, Freddie Mac, Kmart, Merrill Lynch, Salomon Brothers, Sears, and Unisys. He has also consulted for the World Bank, assisting with the development of capital markets in Central Asia and republics of the former Soviet Union.

Kathleen Seiders, PhD, is an associate professor of marketing and Hillenbrand Distinguished Fellow at the Carroll School of Management, Boston College. Prior to her academic career, she had a 10-year career in food retailing. Her research has been published in journals that include the *Journal of Marketing*, *Sloan Management Review*, *Academy of Management Executive*, the *Journal of Retailing*, *Annals of Internal Medicine*, and the *Journal of Public Policy & Marketing*. She received best article awards for "Understanding Service Convenience" (*JM*) and "Obesity and the Role of Food Marketing" (*JPP&M*). Dr. Seiders is president of the Academic Council of the American Marketing Association. She has appeared on *60 Minutes* and *CBS Morning News*, and has commented on many topics for NPR's *Marketplace*, *All Things Considered*, and *Morning Edition*.

Stephen Spinelli Jr., PhD, a leading authority on entrepreneurship, is president of Philadelphia University. He joined the university in September 2007 and launched a strategic planning process aimed at distinguishing the institution as the model for professional university education in the twenty-first century. Under his leadership, Philadelphia University's commitment to active, collaborative, and real-world education grounded in the liberal arts has shaped its signature learning approach and formed the basis of its developing College of Design, Engineering and Commerce, where a unique curriculum is being created around achieving innovation. A dedicated educator, Dr. Spinelli teaches a popular MBA course in entrepreneurship.

Previously, Dr. Spinelli spent 14 years at Babson College, where he was vice provost for entrepreneurship and global management, chair of the Entrepreneurship Division, director of the Arthur M. Blank Center for Entrepreneurship, the Alan Lewis Chair in Global Management, and chair of the entrepreneurship task force.

He has consulted for major corporations, and his work has appeared in numerous professional journals. He has been featured in the *Chronicle of Higher Education*, the *Wall Street Journal*, *BusinessWeek*, the *Financial Times*, and *Entrepreneur*. He has authored business cases and co-authored *Business Plans That Work*, *Franchising: Pathway to Wealth Creation*, *How to Raise Capital*, *Never Bet the Farm*, *Entrepreneurship: The Engine of Growth*, and *New Venture Creation for the 21st Century*.

Dr. Spinelli co-founded Jiffy Lube International and was chairman/CEO of American Oil Change Corporation, pioneering the quick-lube industry. He holds a PhD in economics from Imperial College, University of London; an MBA from Babson College; and a BA in economics from McDaniel College.

Kirk Teska is the managing partner of the Waltham, Massachusetts–based intellectual property law firm Iandiorio Teska & Coleman. The firm specializes in patents, trademarks, copyrights, trade secrets, licensing, litigation of intellectual property matters, employee and consultant contracts, confidential disclosure agreements, government contracts, and other related areas of intellectual property. Mr. Teska has 18 years of intellectual property law experience. He secures and litigates patents in nearly all areas of engineering, including optics, circuits, mechanical systems, processor-based systems, composites, computer software, the Internet, and business methods.

Mr. Teska taught patent law at the Franklin Pierce Law Center and for nine years has taught classes as an adjunct professor at Suffolk University Law School. He is a regular columnist for *Mass High Tech* and *Lawyers Weekly*, where his columns "Patent Watch" and "IP Litigation Watch" appear monthly.

Mr. Teska has written articles for and has been published in *Trial* magazine, the *Computer Law Reporter*, the *Boston Business Journal*, *Mass High Tech*, *Bottom Line Business*, *Proceedings*, the *Journal of the Patent and Trademark Office Society*, *IEEE Spectrum*, *New England In-House*, the *ACC Docket*, *Mechanical Engineering* magazine, *Contract Management* magazine, and *The Freeman|Ideas on Liberty*. He was also a director of the Smaller Business Association of New England (SBANE) and a past chairman of the IEEE Entrepreneurs' Network.

His book *Patent Savvy* was published in the fall of 2007 by Nolo Press.

Andrew Zacharakis, PhD, is the John H. Muller Jr. Chair in Entrepreneurship and the director of the Babson College Entrepreneurship Research Conference, the leading academic conference on entrepreneurship worldwide. He previously served as chair of the entrepreneurship department and as acting director of the Arthur M. Blank Center for Entrepreneurship at Babson College. In addition, he served as president of the Academy of Management, Entrepreneurship Division, an organization with 1,800 members. His primary research areas include the venture capital process and entrepreneurial growth strategies. Dr. Zacharakis is the co-author of five books: *The Portable MBA in Entrepreneurship*, *Business Plans That Work*, *How to Raise Capital*, *Entrepreneurship:*

The Engine of Growth, and a textbook titled *Entrepreneurship.* He has been interviewed in newspapers nationwide, including the *Boston Globe*, the *Wall Street Journal*, and *USA Today.* He has also appeared on the *Bloomberg Small Business Report* and been interviewed on National Public Radio.

Dr. Zacharakis has taught seminars at leading corporations, such as Boeing, MetLife, Lucent, and Intel. He has also taught executives in countries worldwide, including Spain, Chile, Costa Rica, Mexico, Australia, China, Turkey, and Germany. He received a BS (finance/marketing), University of Colorado; an MBA (finance/international business), Indiana University; and a PhD (strategy and entrepreneurship/cognitive psychology), University of Colorado. Professor Zacharakis actively consults with entrepreneurs and small business start-ups. His professional experience includes positions with the Cambridge Companies (investment banking/venture capital), IBM, and Leisure Technologies.

The Entrepreneurial Process

William D. Bygrave

How This Chapter Fits into a Typical MBA Curriculum
The entrepreneurial process is an introductory lecture at the start of a new venture course in MBA programs. It gives an overview of the importance of entrepreneurship in the economy. Then it sets the table for the semester by giving an outline of the content of the course, which comprises the entrepreneurial process from conception to birth of a new venture and its early growth. This chapter includes understanding entrepreneurial attributes and skills, finding and evaluating opportunities, and gathering resources to convert opportunities into businesses. Students learn how to weigh up entrepreneurs and their plans for new businesses.

In this book, as in most MBA new ventures courses, the focus is on entrepreneurs and how they start new companies. Major areas of concentration include the following: searching the environment for new venture opportunities; matching an individual's skill with a new venture; evaluating the viability of a new venture; and financing, starting up, and operating a new venture.

Who Uses This Material in the Real World—and Why It Is Important
Would-be entrepreneurs hoping to start a new venture and novice entrepreneurs with fledgling businesses get a summary of the essential ingredients of successful entrepreneurship from reading this chapter. The book gives them deep insights into how to start and grow a viable business. The material is important because this book is a manual on best entrepreneurial practices spelled out by leading experts who teach and mentor entrepreneurs.

Introduction

This is the age of entrepreneurship. It is estimated that as many 500 million persons worldwide were either actively involved in trying to start a new venture or were owner-managers of a new business in 2008.[1] More than a thousand new businesses are born every hour of every working day in the United States. Entrepreneurs are driving a revolution that is transforming and renewing economies worldwide. Entrepreneurship is the essence of free enterprise because the birth of new businesses gives a market economy its vitality. New and emerging businesses create a very large proportion of innovative products and services that transform the way we work and live, such as personal computers, software, the Internet, biotechnology drugs, and overnight package deliveries. They also generate most of the new jobs. Since the mid-1990s, small businesses have created 60 to 80 percent of net new jobs. In 2005—the most recent year with data—companies with fewer than 500 employees created 979,102 net new jobs or 78.9 percent, while large companies with 500 or more employees added 262,326 net new jobs or 21.1 percent.

If the small business sector of the U.S. economy were a nation, its GDP would rank third in the world behind the U.S. medium- and big-business sector and the entire economy of Japan, and far ahead of the economies of Germany, the United Kingdom, France, Italy, and China.[2]

There has never been a better time to practice the art and science of entrepreneurship. But what is entrepreneurship? Early in the 20th century, Joseph Schumpeter, the Moravian-born economist writing in Vienna, gave us the modern definition of an *entrepreneur* as the person who destroys the existing economic order by introducing new products and services, by creating new forms of organization, or by exploiting new raw materials. According to Schumpeter, that person is most likely to accomplish this destruction by founding a new business but may also do it within an existing one.

But very few new businesses have the potential to initiate a Schumpeterian gale of creation-destruction as Apple computer did in the computer industry. The vast majority of new businesses enter existing markets. In *The Portable MBA in Entrepreneurship*, we take a broader definition of entrepreneurship than Schumpeter's. Ours encompasses everyone who starts a new business. Our entrepreneur is the person who perceives an opportunity and creates an organization to pursue it. And the entrepreneurial process involves all the functions, activities, and actions associated with perceiving opportunities and creating organizations to pursue them. Our entrepreneur's new business may, in a few rare instances, be the revolutionary sort that rearranges the global economic order as Wal-Mart, Fedex, and Microsoft have done, and amazon.com, eBay, and Google are now doing. But it is much more likely to be of the incremental kind that enters an existing market.

The Changing Economy

General Motors (GM) was founded in 1908 as a holding company for Buick. On December 31, 1955, General Motors became the first American corporation to make over $1 billion in a year. At one point it was the largest corporation in the United States in terms of its revenues as a percent of GDP. In 1979, its employment in the United States peaked at 600,000. In 2008 GM reported a loss of $30.9 billion and burned through $19.2 billion of cash. In a desperate attempt to save the company in February 2009, GM announced plans to reduce its total U.S. workforce from 96,537 people in 2008 to between 65,000 and 75,000 in 2012. By March 2009, GM, which had already received $13.4 billion of bailout money from the U.S. government, was asking an additional $16.6 billion. The Obama Administration forced GM's CEO, Rick Wagoner, to resign; his replacement, Fritz Henderson, said that bankruptcy was a real possibility. On June 1, GM filed for bankruptcy.

Wal-Mart was founded by Sam Walton in 1962. For the year ended January 31, 2008, Wal-Mart had record sales of $374.5 billion, record earnings of $22 billion, and record free cash flow of $5.4 billion. During 2008, Wal-Mart added 191 supercenters in the United States and opened its 3,000th international unit. Wal-Mart is the world's largest corporation, with 1.4 million associates in the United States.

> *We're all working together; that's the secret. And we'll lower the cost of living for everyone, not just in America, but we'll give the world an opportunity to see what it's like to save and have a better lifestyle, a better life for all. We're proud of what we've accomplished; we've just begun.*

—Sam Walton (1918–1992)

An *entrepreneur* is someone who perceives an opportunity and creates an organization to pursue it.

The *entrepreneurial process* involves all the functions, activities, and actions associated with perceiving opportunities.

Is the birth of a new enterprise just happenstance and its subsequent success or demise a haphazard process? Or can the art and science of entrepreneurship be taught? Clearly, professors and their students believe that it can be taught and learned because entrepreneurship is the fastest growing new field of study in American higher education. It was estimated that more than 2,000 U.S. colleges and universities—approximately two-thirds of the total—were teaching entrepreneurship in 2009.

That transformation in higher education—itself a wonderful example of entrepreneurial change—has come about because a whole body of knowledge about entrepreneurship has developed during the past three decades or so. The process of creating a new business is well understood. Yes, entrepreneurship can be taught. However, we cannot guarantee to produce a Bill Gates or a Donna Karan, any more than a physics professor can guarantee to produce an Albert Einstein, or a tennis coach a Venus Williams. But give us students with the aptitude to start a business, and we will make them better entrepreneurs.

Critical Factors for Starting a New Enterprise

We will begin by examining the entrepreneurial process (see Exhibit 1.1). What we are talking about here are the factors—personal, sociological, and environmental—that give birth to a new enterprise. A person gets an idea for a new business through either a deliberate search or a chance encounter. Whether he decides to pursue that idea depends on factors such as his alternative career prospects, family, friends, role models, the state of the economy, and the availability of resources.

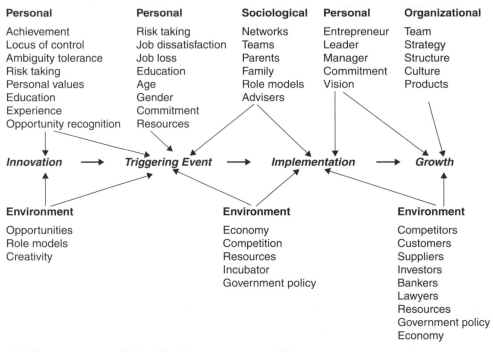

Exhibit 1.1   A Model of the Entrepreneurial Process

Source: Carol Moore, "Understanding Entrepreneurial Behavior," in J. A. Pearce II and R. B. Robinson, Jr., eds., *Academy of Management Best Paper Proceedings*, Forty-sixth Annual Meeting of the Academy of Management, Chicago (1986).

There is almost always a triggering event that gives birth to a new organization. Perhaps the entrepreneur has no better career prospects. For example, Melanie Stevens was a high school dropout who, after a number of minor jobs, had run out of career options. She decided that making canvas bags in her own tiny business was better than earning low wages working for someone else. Within a few years she had built a chain of retail stores throughout Canada. Sometimes the person has been passed over for a promotion, or even laid off or fired. Howard Rose had been laid off four times as a result of mergers and consolidations in the pharmaceutical industry, and he had had enough of it. So he started his own drug packaging business, Waverly Pharmaceutical.

Tim Waterstone founded Waterstone's book stores after he was fired by W. H. Smith. Ann Gloag quit her nursing job and used her bus driver father's $40,000 severance pay to set up Stagecoach bus company with her brother; they exploited legislation deregulating the UK bus industry. Jordan Rubin was debilitated by Crohn's disease when he invented a diet supplement that restored his health; he founded a company, Garden of Life, to sell that diet. Noreen Kenny was working for a semiconductor company and could not find a supplier to do precision mechanical work; she launched her own company, Evolve Manufacturing Technologies, to fill that void. The Baby Einstein Company was started by Julie Aigner-Clark when she discovered that there were no age-appropriate products available to help her share her love of art, classical music, language, and poetry with her newborn daughter.

For other people, entrepreneurship is a deliberate career choice. Babson College specializes in teaching entrepreneurship to undergraduates and MBA students. Many of them have chosen the school because they know that they want to start their own ventures rather than work for someone else. Some of them launch their ventures while they are still students and continue full-time with them as soon as they graduate. Others go and work for someone else for a few years to gain experience before they launch their ventures. A recent survey of Babson alums found that 40 percent of those who had studied entrepreneurship in college had launched one or more full-time businesses.

Origins of Home Depot

Bernie Marcus was president of the now-defunct Handy Dan home improvement chain, based in California, when he and Arthur Blank were abruptly fired by new management. That day and the months that followed were the most pivotal period in his career, he says. "I was 49 years old at the time and I was pretty devastated by being fired. Still, I think it's a question of believing in yourself. Soon after, we [Blank and Marcus] started to realize that this was our opportunity to start over," says Marcus.

Marcus and Blank happened upon a 120,000-square-foot store called Homeco, operating in Long Beach, California. The two instantly realized that the concept—an oversize store, packed with merchandise tagged with low prices—had a magical quality. They wanted to buy the business, but it was essentially bankrupt. Marcus and Blank talked Homeco owner Pat Farah into joining them in Atlanta and the trio, along with Ron Brill, began sketching the blueprint for Home Depot.

Source: Bernie Marcus and Arthur Blank with Bob Andleman, *Built from Scratch*. New York: Times Business, Random House, 1999.

A survey by ACNielsen International Research in July 2005 found the following:

- Approximately 58 percent of Americans say they've dreamed of starting a business and becoming their own boss.
- The most common reason for wanting to start a business is to increase one's personal income (66 percent of respondents), followed by increased independence (63 percent).
- The primary barriers to starting a business are insufficient financial resources (cited by 49 percent of respondents) and satisfaction with their current situation (29 percent).

Source: http://www.forbes.com/businesswire/feeds/businesswire/2005/07/21/businesswire20050721005296r1.html.

Where do would-be entrepreneurs get their ideas? More often than not it is through their present line of employment or experience. A 2002 study of the *Inc.* 500—comprising "America's [500] fastest growing companies"—found that 57 percent of the founders got the idea for their new venture in the industry they worked in and a further 23 percent in an industry related to the one in which they were employed. Hence, 80 percent of all new high-potential businesses are founded in industries that are the same as, or closely related to, the one in which the entrepreneur has previous experience. That is not surprising, because it is in their present employment that they will get most of their viable business ideas.

Some habitual entrepreneurs do it over and over again in the same industry. Joey Crugnale, himself an *Inc.* 500 Hall of Famer and an *Inc.* Entrepreneur of the Year, became a partner in Steve's Ice Cream during his early twenties. He eventually took over Steve's Ice Cream and created both a national franchise of some 26 units and a new food niche, gourmet ice creams. In 1982, Crugnale started Bertucci's, where gourmet pizza was cooked in wood-fired brick, and built it into a nationwide chain of 90 restaurants. Then he founded Naked Restaurants as an incubator to launch his innovative dining concepts. The first one, the Naked Fish, opened in 1999 and brought his wood-fired grill approach to a new niche: fresh fish and meats with a touch of Cubanismo. The second, Red Sauce, which opened in 2002, serves moderately priced authentic Italian food somewhat along the lines of Bertucci's.

Others do it over and over again in related industries. In 1981, James Clark, then a Stanford University computer science professor, founded Silicon Graphics, a computer manufacturer with 1996 sales of $3 billion. In April 1994, he teamed up with Marc Andreessen to found Netscape Communications. Within 12 months, its browser software, Navigator, dominated the Internet's World Wide Web. When Netscape went public in August 1995, Clark became the first Internet billionaire. Then in June 1996, Clark launched another company, Healthscape, to enable doctors, insurers, and patients to exchange data and do business over the Internet with software incorporating Netscape's Navigator.

Much rarer is the serial entrepreneur such as Wayne Huizenga, who ventures into unrelated industries: first in garbage disposal with Waste Management, next in entertainment with Blockbuster Video, then in automobile sales with AutoNation. Along the way he was also the original owner of the Florida Marlins baseball team, which won the World Series in 1997.

What are the factors that influence someone to embark on an entrepreneurial career? As with most human behavior, entrepreneurial traits are shaped by personal attributes and environment.

Personal Attributes

At the start of the entrepreneurial 1980s, there was a spate of magazine and newspaper articles that were titled "Do You Have the Right Stuff to Be an Entrepreneur?" or words to that effect. The articles described the most important characteristics of entrepreneurs and, more often than not, included a self-evaluation exercise to enable readers to determine if they had the right stuff.

Those articles were based on flimsy behavioral research into the differences between entrepreneurs and nonentrepreneurs. The basis for those exercises was the belief, first developed by David McClelland in his book *The Achieving Society,* that entrepreneurs had a higher need for achievement than nonentrepreneurs, and that they were moderate risk takers. One engineer almost abandoned his entrepreneurial ambitions after completing one of those exercises. He asked his professor at the start of an MBA entrepreneurship course if he should take the class, because he had scored very low on an entrepreneurship test in a magazine. He took the course, however, and wrote an award-winning plan for a business that was a success from the very beginning.

Today, after more research, we know that there is no neat set of behavioral attributes that allow us to separate entrepreneurs from nonentrepreneurs. It turns out that a person who rises to the top of any occupation, whether it be an entrepreneur or an administrator, is an achiever. Granted, any would-be entrepreneur must have a need to achieve, but so must anyone else with ambitions to be successful.

It does appear that entrepreneurs have a higher internal locus of control than nonentrepreneurs, which means that they have a higher desire to be in control of their own fate. This has been confirmed by many surveys which have found that entrepreneurs say that independence is their main reason for starting their businesses.

By and large, we no longer use psychological terms when talking about entrepreneurs. Instead we use everyday words to describe their characteristics. The most important characteristics of successful entrepreneurs are shown in Exhibit 1.2.

Dream	Entrepreneurs have a vision of what the future could be like for them and their businesses. And, more important, they have the ability to implement their dreams.
Decisiveness	They don't procrastinate. They make decisions swiftly. Their swiftness is a key factor in their success.
Doers	Once they decide on a course of action, they implement it as quickly as possible.
Determination	They implement their ventures with total commitment. They seldom give up, even when confronted by obstacles that seem insurmountable.
Dedication	They are totally dedicated to their businesses, sometimes at considerable cost to their relationships with friends and families. They work tirelessly. Twelve-hour days, and seven-day work weeks are not uncommon when an entrepreneur is striving to get a business off the ground.
Devotion	Entrepreneurs love what they do. It is that love that sustains them when the going gets tough. And it is love of their product or service that makes them so effective at selling it.
Details	It is said that the devil resides in the details. That is never more true than in starting and growing a business. The entrepreneur must be on top of the critical details.
Destiny	They want to be in charge of their own destiny rather than dependent on an employer.
Dollars	Getting rich is not the prime motivator of entrepreneurs. Money is more a measure of success. They assume that if they are successful they will be rewarded.
Distribute	Entrepreneurs distribute the ownership of their businesses with key employees who are critical to the success of the business.

Exhibit 1.2 The 10 Ds

Environmental Factors

Perhaps as important as personal attributes are the external influences on a would-be entrepreneur. It's no accident that some parts of the world are more entrepreneurial than others. The most famous region of high-tech entrepreneurship is Silicon Valley. Because everyone in Silicon Valley knows someone who has made it big as an entrepreneur, role models abound. This situation produces what Stanford University sociologist Everett Rogers called Silicon Valley fever.[3] It seems as if everyone in the valley catches that bug sooner or later and wants to start a business. To facilitate the process, there are venture capitalists who understand how to select and nurture high-tech entrepreneurs, bankers who specialize in lending to them, lawyers who understand the importance of intellectual property and how to protect it, landlords who are experienced in renting real estate to fledgling companies, suppliers who are willing to sell goods on credit to companies with no credit history, and even politicians who are supportive.

Role models are very important because knowing successful entrepreneurs makes the act of becoming one yourself seem much more credible.

Would-be entrepreneurs see role models primarily in the home and at work. Indeed, if you have a close relative who is an entrepreneur, it is more likely that you will have a desire to become an entrepreneur yourself, especially if that relative is your mother or father. At Babson College, more than half of the undergraduates studying entrepreneurship come from families that own businesses; and half of the *Inc.* 500 entrepreneurs in 2005 had a parent who was an entrepreneur.[4] But you don't have to be from a business-owning family to become an entrepreneur. Bill Gates, for example, was following the family tradition of becoming a lawyer when he dropped out of Harvard and founded Microsoft. He was in the fledgling microcomputer industry, which was being built by entrepreneurs, so he had plenty of role models among his friends and acquaintances. The United States has an abundance of high-tech entrepreneurs who are household names. One of them, Ross Perot, was so well known that he was the presidential candidate preferred by one in five American voters in 1992.

Some universities are hotbeds of entrepreneurship. For example, Massachusetts Institute of Technology (MIT) has produced numerous entrepreneurs among its faculty and alums. Companies with an MIT connection transformed the Massachusetts economy from one based on decaying shoe and textile industries into one based on high technology. According to a 2009 MIT study, *Entrepreneurial Impact: The Role of MIT*, which analyzes the economic effect of MIT alumni–founded companies, if the active companies founded by MIT graduates formed an independent nation, their revenues would make that nation at least the seventeenth largest economy in the world.[5] The overall MIT entrepreneurial environment, consisting of multiple education, research, and social network institutions, contributes to this outstanding and growing entrepreneurial output. Highlights of the findings include:

- An estimated 6,900 MIT alumni companies with worldwide sales of approximately $164 billion are located in Massachusetts alone and represent 26 percent of the sales of all Massachusetts companies.

- Some 4,100 MIT alumni–founded firms are based in California, and generate an estimated $134 billion in worldwide sales.

- States currently benefiting most from jobs created by MIT alumni companies are Massachusetts (estimated at just under one million jobs worldwide), California (estimated at 526,000 jobs), New York (estimated at 231,000 jobs), Texas (estimated at 184,000), and Virginia (estimated at 136,000).

The neighborhood of East Cambridge adjacent to MIT was termed "The Most Entrepreneurial Place on Earth" by *Inc.* magazine.[6] Roughly 10 percent of Massachusetts software companies and approximately 20 percent of the state's 280 biotechnology companies are headquartered in that square mile.

It is not only in high-tech that we see role models. Consider these examples:

- It has been estimated that half of all the convenience stores in New York City are owned by Koreans.

- It was the visibility of successful role models that spread catfish farming in the Mississippi delta as a more profitable alternative to cotton.

- The Pacific Northwest has more microbreweries than any other region of the United States. However, that might change if Oregon's politicians enact their proposal to increase the tax on a barrel of beer by a whopping 1,900 percent in 2009.[7]

- Hay-on-Wye, a tiny town in Wales with 1,500 inhabitants, has 39 second-hand bookstores. It claims to be the "largest used and antiquarian bookshop in the world." It all began in 1961 when Richard Booth, an Oxford graduate, opened his first bookstore.

African Americans make up 12 percent of the U.S. population, but owned only 4 percent of the nation's businesses in 1997.[8] One of the major reasons for a relative lack of entrepreneurship among African Americans is the scarcity of African-American entrepreneurs, especially store owners, to provide role models. A similar problem exists among Native Americans. Fortunately this situation is improving: According to the 2002 census, African Americans owned 5.2 percent of the nation's businesses.[9]

Other Sociological Factors

Besides role models, entrepreneurs have other sociological factors that influence them. Family responsibilities play an important role in the decision whether to start a company. It is, relatively speaking, an easy career decision to start a business when a person is 25 years old, single, and without many personal assets and dependents. It is a much harder decision when a person is 45 and married, has teenage children preparing to go to college, a hefty mortgage, car payments, and a secure, well-paying job. And at 45 plus, if you fail as an entrepreneur, it will not be easy to rebuild a career working for another company. But despite the risks, plenty of 45-year-olds are taking the plunge; in fact, the median age of the CEOs of the 500 fastest-growing small companies, the *Inc.* 500 in 2004, was 43 (range 26 to 54), and the median age of their companies was six years.[10]

Another factor that determines the age at which entrepreneurs start businesses is the trade-off between the experience that comes with age and the optimism and energy of youth. As you grow older you gain experience, but sometimes when you have been in an industry a long time, you know so many pitfalls that you are pessimistic about the chance of succeeding if you decide to go out on your own. Someone who has just enough experience to feel confident as a manager is more likely to feel optimistic about an entrepreneurial career. Perhaps the ideal combination is a beginner's mind with the experience of an industry veteran. A beginner's mind looks at situations from a new perspective, with a can-do spirit.

Twenty-seven-year-old Robert Swanson was a complete novice at biotechnology but convinced that it had great commercial potential. His enthusiasm combined with Professor Herbert Boyer's unsurpassed knowledge about the use of recombinant DNA to produce human protein. They just assumed that Boyer's laboratory bench work could be scaled up to industrial levels. Looking back, Boyer said, "I think we were so naïve, we never thought it couldn't be done." Together they succeeded and started a new industry.

Marc Andreessen had a beginner's mind in 1993 when, as a student and part-time assistant at the National Center for Supercomputing Applications (NCSA) at the University of Illinois, he developed the Mosaic browser and produced a vision for the Internet that until then had eluded many computer industry veterans, including Bill Gates. When Andreessen's youthful creativity was joined with James Clark's entrepreneurial wisdom earned from a dozen or so years as founder and chairman of Silicon Graphics, it turned out to be an awesome combination. Their company, Netscape, distributed 38 million copies of Navigator in just two years, making it the most successful new software introduction ever.

Before leaving secure, well-paying, satisfying jobs, would-be entrepreneurs should make a careful estimate of how much sales revenue their new businesses must generate before they will be able to match the income that they presently earn. It usually comes as quite a shock when they realize that if they are opening a retail establishment, they will need annual sales revenue of at least $600,000 to pay themselves a salary of $70,000 plus fringe benefits such as health care coverage, retirement pension benefits, and long-term disability insurance. Six hundred thousand dollars a year is about $12,000 per week, or about $2,000 per day, or about $200 per hour, or $3 per minute if the business is open six days a week, 10 hours a day.

Entrepreneurs will also be working much longer hours and bearing much more responsibility if they become self-employed. A sure way to test the strength of a marriage is to start a company that is the sole means of support for your family. For example, 22.5 percent of the CEOs of the *Inc.* 500 got divorced while growing their businesses. On a brighter note, 59.2 percent got married and 18.3 percent of divorced CEOs remarried.[11]

When they actually start a business, entrepreneurs need a host of contacts, including customers, suppliers, investors, bankers, accountants, and lawyers. So it is important to understand where to find help before embarking on a new venture. A network of friends and business associates can be of immeasurable help in building the contacts an entrepreneur will need. They can also provide vital human contact, because opening one's own business can be a lonely experience for anyone who used to work in an organization with many fellow employees.

Fortunately, today there are more organizations than ever before to help fledgling entrepreneurs. Often that help is free or costs very little. The Small Business Administration (SBA) has Small Business Development Centers in every state; it funds Small Business Institutes; and its Service Core of Retired Executives provides free assistance to entrepreneurs. Many colleges and universities also provide help. Some are particularly good at writing business plans, usually at no charge to the entrepreneur. There are more than 1,000 incubators in the United States where fledgling businesses can rent space, usually at a very reasonable price, and spread some of their overhead by sharing facilities such as copying and fax machines, secretarial help, answering services, and so on. Incubators are often associated with universities, which provide free or inexpensive counseling. There are numerous associations where entrepreneurs can meet and exchange ideas.

Evaluating Opportunities for New Businesses

Let's assume you believe you have found a great opportunity for starting a new business. How should you evaluate its prospects? Or, perhaps more importantly, how will an independent person such as a potential investor or a banker rate your chances of success?

The odds of succeeding appear to be stacked against you, because according to small business folklore, only one business in ten will ever reach its tenth birthday. This doesn't mean that nine out of ten of the estimated three million businesses that are started every year go bankrupt.[12] During the first six months of 2008, at the onset of the recession, there were 31,458 business bankruptcies and liquidations—a 47 percent increase over the 21,389 figure for the same period in 2007.[13] Even in the severest recessions, the number of businesses filing for bankruptcy or liquidation in the United States has never yet surpassed 100,000 in any year. In an average year, the number is about 50,000. So what happens to the vast majority of the ones that do not survive 10 years? Most just fade away: They are started as part-time pursuits (more than 50 percent of all U.S. businesses are part-time, and 77 percent of all businesses have no employees) and are never intended to become full-time businesses.

The odds that your new business will survive may not be as long as they first appear to be. If you intend to start a full-time, incorporated business, the odds that the business will survive at least eight years with you as the owner are better than one in four; and the odds of its surviving at least eight years with a new owner are another one in four. So the eight-year survival rate for incorporated start-ups is about 50 percent.[14]

But survival may not spell success. Too many entrepreneurs find that they can neither earn a satisfactory living in their businesses nor get out of them easily because they have too much of their personal assets tied up in them. The happiest day in an entrepreneur's life is the day the doors are opened for business. For unsuccessful entrepreneurs, an even happier day may be the day the business is sold—especially if most personal assets remain intact. What George Bernard Shaw said about a love affair is also apt for a business: Any fool can start one, it takes a genius to end one successfully.

How can you stack the odds in your favor so that your new business is a success? Professional investors, such as venture capitalists, have a talent for picking winners. True, they also pick losers, but a start-up company funded by venture capital has, on average, a four in five chance of surviving five years—better odds than for the population of start-up companies as a whole. By using the criteria that professional investors use, entrepreneurs can increase their odds of success. Very few businesses—perhaps no more than one in a thousand—will ever be suitable candidates at any time in their lives for investments from professional venture capitalists. But would-be entrepreneurs can learn a lot by following the evaluation process used by professional investors.

There are three crucial components for a successful new business: the opportunity, the entrepreneur (and the management team, if it's a high-potential venture), and the resources needed to start the company and fuel its growth. They are shown schematically in Exhibit 1.3 in the basic Timmons framework. At the center of the framework is a business plan, in which the three basic ingredients are integrated into a complete strategic plan for the new business. The parts must fit together well. It's no good having a first-rate idea for a new business if you have a second-rate management team. Nor are ideas and management any good without the appropriate resources.

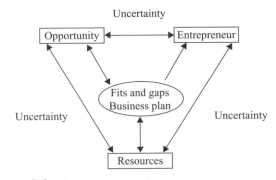

Exhibit 1.3 Uncertainty

Source: Jeffry A. Timmons, *New Venture Creation*
(Homewood, IL: Richard D. Irwin, 2001)

The crucial ingredients for entrepreneurial success are a superb entrepreneur with a first-rate management team and an excellent market opportunity.

The crucial driving force of any new venture is the lead entrepreneur and the funding management team. Georges Doriot, the founder of modern venture capital, used to say something like this: "Always consider investing in a grade A man with a grade B idea. Never invest in a grade B man with a grade A idea." He knew what he was talking about. Over the years he invested in about 150 companies, including Digital Equipment Corporation (DEC), and watched over them as they struggled to grow. But Doriot made his statement about business in the 1950s and 1960s. During that period there were far fewer start-ups each year; U.S. firms dominated the marketplace; markets were growing quickly; there was almost no competition from overseas; and most entrepreneurs were male. Today in 2009, in the global marketplace with ever-shortening product life cycles and low growth or even negative growth for some of the world's leading industrial nations, the crucial ingredients for entrepreneurial success are a superb entrepreneur with a first-rate management team and an excellent market opportunity.

Frequently I hear the comment that success in entrepreneurship is largely a matter of luck. That's not so. We do not say that becoming a great quarterback, or a great scientist, or a great musician, and so on, is a matter of luck. There is no more luck in becoming successful at entrepreneurship than in becoming successful at anything else. In entrepreneurship, it is a question of recognizing a good opportunity when you see one and having the skills to convert that opportunity into a thriving business. To do that, you must be prepared. So in entrepreneurship, just like any other profession, *luck is where preparation and opportunity meet.*

In entrepreneurship, as in any other profession, luck is where preparation and opportunity meet.

In 1982, when Rod Canion proposed to start Compaq to make personal computers, there were already formidable established competitors, including IBM and Apple. By then literally hundreds of companies were considering entering the market or had already done so. For instance, in the same week of May 1982 that DEC announced its ill-fated personal computer, four other companies introduced PCs. Despite the competition, Ben Rosen of the venture capital firm Sevin Rosen Management Company invested in Compaq. Started initially to make transportable PCs, the company quickly added a complete range of high-performance PCs and grew so fast that it soon broke Apple's record for the fastest time from founding to listing on the Fortune 500.

What did Ben Rosen see in the Compaq proposal that made it stand out from all the other personal computer start-ups? The difference was Rod Canion and his team. Rod Canion had earned a reputation as an excellent manager at Texas Instruments. Furthermore, the market for personal computers topped $5 billion and was growing at a torrid pace. So Rosen had found a superb team with a product targeted at an undeveloped niche, transportable PCs, in a large market that was growing explosively. By 1994, Compaq was the leading PC manufacturer, with 13 percent of the market.

The Opportunity

Perhaps the biggest misconception about an idea for a new business is that it must be unique. Too many would-be entrepreneurs are almost obsessed with finding a unique idea. Then, when they believe they have it, they are haunted by the thought that someone is just waiting to steal it from them. So they become super secretive. They are reluctant to discuss it with anyone unless that person signs a nondisclosure agreement. That in itself makes it almost impossible to evaluate the idea. For example, many counselors who provide free advice to entrepreneurs refuse to sign nondisclosure agreements.

Generally speaking, these super-secret, unique ideas are big letdowns when the entrepreneur reveals them to you. Among the notable ones I have encountered were "drive-through pizza by the slice," "a combination toothbrush and toothpaste gadget," and "a Mexican restaurant in Boston." One computer programmer telephoned me and said that he had a fantastic new piece of software. Eventually, after I assured him that I was not going to steal his idea, he told me his software was for managing hairdressing salons. He was completely floored when I told him that less than a month previously another entrepreneur had visited my office and demonstrated a software package for exactly the same purpose. Another entrepreneur had an idea for fluoride-impregnated dental floss. Not three months later, on a visit to England, I found the identical product in Boots—Britain's largest chain of drug stores and a major pharmaceutical manufacturer.

I tell would-be entrepreneurs that almost any idea they have will also have occurred to others. For good measure I point out that some of the most revolutionary thoughts in the history of mankind occurred to more than one person almost simultaneously. For instance, Darwin was almost preempted by Wallace in publishing his theory of evolution; Poincaré formulated a valid theory of relativity about the same time Einstein did; and the integrated circuit was invented in 1959 first by Jack Kilby at Texas Instruments, and then independently by Robert Noyce at Fairchild a few months later.

So the idea per se is not what is important. In entrepreneurship, ideas really are a dime a dozen. Developing the idea, implementing it, and building a successful business are the important things. Alexander Fleming discovered penicillin by chance but never developed it as a useful drug. About 10 years later Ernst Chain and Howard Florey unearthed Fleming's mold. They immediately saw its potential. Working in England under wartime conditions, they soon were treating patients. Before the end of World War II, penicillin was saving countless lives. It was a most dramatic pharmaceutical advance and heralded a revolution in that industry.

> **The idea per se is not what is important. In entrepreneurship, ideas really are a dime a dozen. Developing the idea, implementing it, and building a successful business are the important things.**

Customer Need

Many would-be entrepreneurs call me up and tell me that they have an idea for a new business, and ask if they can come to see me. Unfortunately, it is impossible to see all of them, so I have developed a few questions that allow me to judge how far along they are with their idea. By far the most telling question is, "Can you give me the names of prospective customers?" Their answer must be very specific. If they have a consumer product—let's say it's a new shampoo—I expect them to be able to name buyers at different chains of drug stores in their area. If they are unable to name several customers immediately, they simply have an idea, not a market.

There is no market unless customers have a real need for the product—a proven need rather than a hypothetical need in the mind of a would-be entrepreneur. In a few rare cases it may be a revolutionary new product, but it is much more likely to be an existing product with improved performance, price, distribution, quality, or service. Simply put, customers must perceive that the new business will be giving them better value for their money than existing businesses do.

Timing

Time plays a crucial role in many potential opportunities. In some emerging industries, there is a definite window of opportunity that opens only once. For instance, about 35 years ago, when VCRs were first coming into household use in the United States, there was a need for video stores in convenient locations where viewers could pick up movies on the way home from work. Lots of video retail stores opened up on main streets and in shopping centers. They were usually run by independent store owners. Then the distribution of videos changed. National chains of video stores emerged. Supermarket and drug store chains entered the market. Then the technology changed and VCR cassettes were replaced by DVDs, which are much less bulky. Now you can get DVDs via postal mail, download them via the Internet, or pick them up at vending machines and conventional video stores. Today, the window of opportunity for starting an independent video store is closed.

In other markets, such as high-quality restaurants for example, there is a steady demand that, on average, does not change much from year to year, so the window of opportunity is always open. Nevertheless, timing can be important, because when the economy turns down as it did in 2008–2009, those kinds of restaurants are usually hit harder than lower-quality ones, so the best time to open one is during a recovering or booming economy.

If the window of opportunity appears to be very brief, it may be that the idea is a consumer fad that will quickly pass away. It takes a very skilled entrepreneur indeed to make money out of a fad. Consider the fate of Atkins Nutritionals, Inc.

The late Dr. Robert J. Atkins built a business around the low-carbohydrate, high-protein diet that bears his name. The 1992 and 1999 editions of his book, *Dr. Atkins' New Diet Revolution*, sold more than 10 million copies worldwide. The book is among the top 50 best-selling books ever published and was on the *New York Times* best-seller list for five years. His company, Atkins Nutritionals, Inc., branched out into selling 250 food products (nutrition bars, shakes, bake mixes, breads) and nearly 100 nutritional supplements (antioxidants, essential oils) in more than 30,000 outlets. Sales rapidly ramped up at the beginning of the 2000s. Demand was boosted in 2003 by a widely publicized article in the May edition of the influential *New England Journal of Medicine* reporting that subjects on a low-carb, high-protein diet not only lost weight but also—and perhaps more importantly—had an increase in good cholesterol levels and a decrease in triglycerides, which was contrary to expectations. In October 2003 Goldman Sachs & Company and Boston-based Parthenon Capital LLC bought a majority stake in the firm for an estimated $700 million.

At the peak of the low-carb, get-thin-quick craze in January 2004, 9.1 percent of the U.S. population claimed to be on the diet. There were 16 national distributors of low-carb products. National supermarkets introduced low-carb products. Food manufacturers rushed to promote low-carbohydrate products. The diet was so popular that it was partially blamed for the bankruptcy of Interstate Bakeries, the producer of Twinkies and Wonder Bread. Then the fad faded fast. By 2005 only 2.2 percent of Americans were on low-carb diets. The fall was so precipitous that manufacturers were caught with bloated inventories. Surplus low-carb products were being shipped to Appalachian food banks. For the year ended 2004, Atkins Nutritionals lost $341 million. In August 2005, it filed for Chapter 11 with liabilities of $325 million.

Most entrepreneurs should avoid fads or any window of opportunity that they believe will only be open for a very brief time, because it inevitably means that they will rush to open their business, sometimes before they have time to gather the resources they will need. Rushing to open a business without adequate planning can lead to costly mistakes.

The Entrepreneur and the Management Team

Regardless of how right the opportunity may seem to be, it will not make a successful business unless it is developed by a person with strong entrepreneurial and management skills. What are the important skills?

First and foremost, entrepreneurs should have experience in the same industry or a similar one. Starting a business is a very demanding undertaking indeed. It is no time for on-the-job training. If would-be entrepreneurs do not have the right experience, they should either go out and get it before starting their new venture or find partners who have it.

Some investors say that the ideal entrepreneur is one who has a track record of being successful previously as an entrepreneur in the same industry and who can attract a seasoned team. Half of the CEOs of the *Inc.* 500 high-growth small companies had started at least one other business before they founded their present firms. When Joey Crugnale acquired his first ice cream shop in 1977, he already had almost 10 years in the food service industry. By 1991, when Bertucci's brick oven pizzeria went public, he and his management team had a total of more than 100 years experience in the food industry.

They had built Bertucci's into a rapidly growing chain with sales of $30 million and net income of $2 million.

Without relevant experience, the odds are stacked against the neophyte in any industry. An electronics engineer told me that he had a great idea for a chain of fast-food stores. When asked if he had ever worked in a fast-food restaurant, he replied, "Work in one? I wouldn't even eat in one. I can't stand fast food!" Clearly, he would have been as miscast as a fast-food entrepreneur as Crugnale would have been as an electronics engineer.

True, there are entrepreneurs who have succeeded spectacularly with no prior industry experience. Anita Roddick of The Body Shop, Ely Callaway of Callaway Golf, and as already mentioned, Wayne Huizenga of Blockbuster Video and AutoNation are notable examples. But they were the exceptions that definitely do not prove the rule.

Second to industry know-how is management experience, preferably with responsibility for budgets, or better yet, accountability for profit and loss. It is even better if a would-be entrepreneur has a record of increasing sales and profits. Of course, we are talking about the ideal entrepreneur. Very few people measure up to the ideal. That does not mean they should not start a new venture. But it does mean they should be realistic about the size of business they should start.

Twenty years ago, two 19-year-old students wanted to start a travel agency business in Boston. When asked what they knew about the industry, one replied, "I live in California. I love to travel." The other was silent. Neither of them had worked in the travel industry, nor had anyone in either of their families. They were advised to get experience. One joined a training program for airline ticket agents; the other took a course for travel agents. They became friends with the owner of a local Uniglobe travel agency who helped them with advice. Six months after they first had the idea, they opened a part-time campus travel agency. In the first six months they had about $100,000 of revenue and made $6,000 of profit but were unable to pay themselves any salary. In that way, they acquired experience at no expense and at low risk. Upon graduation, one of them, Mario Ricciardelli, made it his full-time job and continued building the business and gaining experience at the same time. In 2009, after many bumps in the road, the business—now named Studentcity.com—is one of the largest student travel businesses in the world.

Resources

When Stanford graduate students Larry Page and Sergey Brin started Google in 1996, other search engines were already well established and backed with relatively huge resources. Unbelievable as it may seem, Page and Brin financed their fledgling venture for two years with nothing more than their credit cards. To keep costs to a minimum they started the business in Larry's dorm room. And even when they raised a million dollars of funding in 1998, they didn't move into a fancy office in Silicon Valley; instead they moved their operations into a friend's garage to keep expenses as low as possible.

Frugality such as Page and Brin's is essential in the early days of a venture when cash is very scarce. And it often continues long after a venture is successful. Bill Gates, for example, continued to fly coach class for years after Microsoft became a big success.

> *Entrepreneurial frugality* means
>
> - Low overhead.
> - High productivity.
> - Minimal ownership of capital assets.

Determining Resource Needs and Acquiring Resources

In order to determine the amount of capital that a company needs to get started, an entrepreneur must determine the minimum set of essential resources. Some resources are more critical than others. The first thing an entrepreneur should do is assess what resources are crucial for the company's success in the marketplace. What does the company expect to do better than any of its competitors? That is where it should put a disproportionate share of its very scarce resources. If the company is making a new high-tech product, technological know-how will be vital. Then its most important resource will be engineers and the designs they produce. Therefore, the company must concentrate on recruiting and keeping excellent engineers, and safeguarding the intellectual property that they produce, such as engineering designs and patents. If the company is a retail shop, the critical factor is most likely to be location. It makes no sense to choose a site in a poor location just because the rent is cheap. Choosing the wrong initial location for a retail store can be a fatal mistake, because it's unlikely that there will be enough resources to relocate.

When Southwest Airlines started up, its strategy was to provide frequent, on-time service at a competitive price between Dallas, Houston, Austin, and San Antonio. To meet its objectives, Southwest needed planes that it could operate reliably at low cost. It was able to purchase four brand-new Boeing 737s—very efficient planes for shorter routes—for only $4 million each because a recession had hit the airlines particularly hard and Boeing had an inventory of unsold 737s. From the outset, Southwest provided good, reliable service and had one of the lowest costs per mile in the industry. Today, Southwest is the most successful domestic airline, while two of its biggest competitors when it started out, Braniff International and Texas International, have gone bankrupt.

Items that are not critical should be obtained as thriftily as possible. The founder of Burlington Coat, Monroe Milstein, likes to tell the story of how he obtained estimates for gutting the building he had just leased for his second store. His lowest bid was several thousand dollars. One day he was at the building when a sudden thunderstorm sent a crew of laborers working at a nearby site to his building for shelter from the rain. Milstein asked the crew's foreman what they would charge for knocking down the internal structures that needed to be removed. The foreman said, "Five." Milstein asked, "Five what?" The foreman replied, "Cases of beer."

> *I was very lucky to have grown up in this industry. I did everything coming up—shipping, supply chain, sweeping floors, buying chips, you name it. I put computers together with my own hands. As the industry grew up, I kept on doing it.*
>
> —Steve Jobs, 2000[15]

A complete set of resources includes everything that the business will need. A key point to remember when deciding to acquire those resources is that a business does not have to do all its work in-house with its own employees. It is often more effective to subcontract the work. That way it need not own or lease its own manufacturing plant and equipment. Nor does it have to worry about recruiting and training production workers. Often, it can keep overhead lower by using outside firms to do work such as payroll, accounting, advertising, mailing promotions, janitorial services, and so on.

Even start-up companies can get amazingly good terms from outside suppliers. An entrepreneur should try to understand the potential suppliers' marginal costs. Marginal cost is the cost of producing one extra unit beyond what is presently produced. The marginal cost of the laborers who gutted Milstein's building while sheltering from the rain was virtually zero. They were being paid by another firm, and they didn't have to buy materials or tools.

A small electronics company was acquired by a much larger competitor. The large company took over the manufacturing of the small company's products. Production costs shot up. An analysis revealed that much of the increase was due to a rise in the cost of purchased components. In one instance, the large company was paying 50 percent more than the small company had been paying for the same item. It turned out that the supplier had priced the item for the small company on the basis of marginal costs and for the large company on the basis of total costs.

Smart entrepreneurs find ways of controlling critical resources without owning them. A start-up business never has enough money. It should not buy what it can lease. It must be resourceful. Except when the economy is red-hot, there is almost always an excess of capacity of office and industrial space. Sometimes a landlord will be willing to offer a special deal to attract even a small start-up company into a building. Such deals may include reduced rent, deferral of rent payments for a period of time, and building improvements at low cost or even no cost. In some high-tech regions, there are landlords who will exchange rent for equity in a high-potential start-up.

When equipment is in excess supply, it can be leased on very favorable terms. A young database company was negotiating a lease with IBM for a new minicomputer when its chief engineer discovered that a leasing company had identical secondhand units standing idle in its warehouse. It was able to lease one of the idle units for one-third of IBM's price. About 18 months later, the database company ran out of cash. Nevertheless, it was able to persuade the leasing company to defer payments, because by then there were even more minicomputers standing idle in the warehouse, and it made little economic sense to repossess one and add it to the idle stock.

Google

Google founders Larry Page and Sergey Brin bought a terabyte of disks at bargain prices and built their own computer housings in Larry's dorm room, which became Google's first data center. Unable to interest the major portal players of the day, Larry and Sergey decided to make a go of it on their own. All they needed was a little cash to move out of the dorm—and to pay off the credit cards they had maxed out buying a terabyte of memory. So they wrote up a business plan, put their Ph.D.

plans on hold, and went looking for an angel investor. Their first visit was with a friend of a faculty member.

Andy Bechtolsheim, one of the founders of Sun Microsystems, was used to taking the long view. One look at their demo and he knew Google had potential—a lot of potential. But though his interest had been piqued, he was pressed for time. As Sergey tells it, "We met him very early one morning on the porch of a Stanford faculty member's home in Palo Alto. We gave him a quick demo. He had to run off somewhere, so he said, 'Instead of us discussing all the details, why don't I just write you a check?' It was made out to Google Inc. and was for $100,000."

The investment created a small dilemma. Since there was no legal entity known as "Google Inc.," there was no way to deposit the check. It sat in Larry's desk drawer for a couple of weeks while he and Sergey scrambled to set up a corporation and locate other funders among family, friends, and acquaintances. Ultimately they brought in a total initial investment of almost $1 million.

On September 7, 1998, more than two years after they began work on their search engine, Google Inc. opened its door in Menlo Park, California. The door came with a remote control, as it was attached to the garage of a friend who sublet space to the new corporation's staff of three. The office offered several big advantages, including a washer and dryer and a hot tub. It also provided a parking space for the first employee hired by the new company: Craig Silverstein, now Google's director of technology.

Source: Excerpted from "Google History," http://www.google.com/corporate/history.html.

Start-up Capital

You have reached the point where you have developed your idea; you have carefully assessed what resources you will need to open your business and make it grow; you have pulled all your strategies together into a business plan; and now you know how much start-up capital you will need to get you to the point where your business will generate a positive cash flow. How are you going to raise that start-up capital?

There are two types of start-up capital: debt and equity. Simply put, with debt you don't have to give up any ownership of the business, but you have to pay current interest and eventually repay the principal; with equity you have to give up some of the ownership to get it, but you may never have to repay it or even pay a dividend. So you must choose between paying interest and giving up some of the ownership.

What usually happens, in practice, depends on how much of each type of capital you can raise. Most start-up entrepreneurs do not have much flexibility in their choice of financing. If it is a very risky business without any assets, it will be impossible to get any bank debt without putting up some collateral other than the business's assets—most likely that collateral will be personal assets. Even if entrepreneurs are willing to guarantee the whole loan with their personal assets, the bank will expect them to put some equity into the business, probably at least 25 percent of the amount of the loan.

The vast majority of entrepreneurs start their businesses by leveraging their own savings and labor. Consider how Apple, one of the most spectacular start-ups of all time, was funded. Steven Jobs and Stephen Wozniak had been friends since their school days in Silicon Valley. Wozniak was an authentic computer nerd. He had tinkered with computers from childhood, and he built a computer that won first prize in a science fair. His SAT math score was a perfect 800, but after stints at the University of Colorado, De Anza College, and Berkeley, he dropped out of school and went to work for Hewlett-Packard. His partner, Jobs, had an even briefer encounter with higher education: After one semester at Reed College, he left to look for a swami in India. When he and Wozniak began working on their microcomputer, Jobs was working at Atari, the leading video game company.

Apple soon outgrew its manufacturing facility in the garage of Jobs's parents' house. Their company, financed initially with $1,300 raised by selling Jobs's Volkswagen and Wozniak's calculator, needed capital for expansion. They looked to their employers for help. Wozniak proposed to his supervisor that Hewlett-Packard should produce what later became the Apple II. Perhaps not surprisingly, he was rejected. After all, he had no formal qualification in computer design; indeed, he did not even have a college degree. At Atari, Jobs tried to convince founder Nolan Bushnell to manufacture Apples. He, too, was rejected.

However, on the suggestion of Bushnell and Regis McKenna, a Silicon Valley marketing ace, they contacted Don Valentine, a venture capitalist, in the fall of 1976. In those days, Jobs's appearance was a hangover from his swami days. It definitely did not project the image of Doriot's grade A man, even by Silicon Valley's casual standards. Valentine did not invest. But he did put them in touch with Armas Markkula, Jr., who had recently retired from Intel a wealthy man. Markkula saw the potential in Apple, and he knew how to raise money. He personally invested $91,000, secured a line of credit from Bank of America, put together a business plan, and raised $600,000 of venture capital.

The Apple II was formally introduced in April 1977. Sales took off almost at once. Apple's sales grew rapidly to $2.5 million in 1977 and $15 million in 1978. In 1978, Dan Bricklin, a Harvard business student and former programmer at DEC, introduced the first electronic spreadsheet, VisiCalc, designed for the Apple II. In minutes it could do tasks that had previously taken days. The microcomputer now had the power to liberate managers from the data guardians in the computer departments. According to one source, "Armed with VisiCalc, the Apple II's sales took off, and the personal computer industry was created." Apple's sales jumped to $70 million in 1979 and $117 million in 1980.

In 1980, Apple sold some of its stock to the public with an initial public offering (IPO) and raised more than $80 million. The paper value of their Apple stock made instant millionaires out of Jobs ($165 million), Markkula ($154 million), Wozniak ($88 million), and Mike Scott ($62 million), who together owned 40 percent of Apple. Arthur Rock's venture capital investment of $57,000 in 1978 was suddenly worth $14 million, an astronomical compound return of more than 500 percent per year, or 17 percent per month.

By 1982, Apple IIs were selling at the rate of more than 33,000 units a month. With 1982 sales of $583 million, Apple hit the Fortune 500 list. It was a record. At five years of age, it was at that time the youngest company ever to join that exclusive list.

Success as spectacular as Apple's has seldom been equaled. Nonetheless, its financing is a typical example of how successful high-tech companies are funded. First, the entrepreneurs develop a prototype with sweat equity and personal savings. *Sweat equity* is ownership earned in lieu of wages. Then a wealthy investor—sometimes called an informal investor or business angel—who knows something about the entrepreneurs, or the industry, or both, invests some personal money in return for equity. When the company is selling product, it may be able to get a bank line of credit secured by its inventory and accounts receivable. If the company is growing quickly in a large market, it may be able to raise capital from a formal venture capital firm in return for equity. Further expansion capital may come from venture capital firms or from a public stock offering.

Would-be entrepreneurs sometimes tell me that they did not start their ventures because they could not raise sufficient money to get started. More often than not, they were unrealistic about the amount of money that they could reasonably have expected to raise for their start-up businesses. I tell them that many of the best companies started with very little capital. For example, 50 percent of companies on the 2008 list of *Inc.* 500 companies were started with less than $25,000; 87 percent of all the companies on the list were funded with money from the entrepreneurs themselves; 19 percent with money from family and friends; 17 percent from bank loans; and only 3 percent with venture capital, which is by far the rarest source of seed-stage investment.[16] It is estimated that at most only 1 in 10,000 of all new ventures in the United States have venture capital in hand at the outset, and only 1 in 1,000 get venture capital at any stage of their lives.

The vast majority of new firms will never be candidates for formal venture capital or a public stock offering. Nevertheless, they will have to find some equity capital. In most cases, after they have exhausted their personal savings, entrepreneurs will turn to family, friends, and acquaintances (see Exhibit 1.4). It can be a scary business. Entrepreneurs often find themselves with all their personal net worth tied up in the same business that provides all their income. That is double jeopardy, because if their businesses fail, they lose both their savings and their means of support. Risk of that sort can be justified only if the profit potential is high enough to yield a commensurate rate of return.

Profit Potential

The level of profit that is reasonable to expect depends on the type of business. On average, U.S. companies make about 5 percent net income. Hence, on one dollar of revenue, the average company makes five cents profit after paying all expenses and taxes. A company that consistently makes 10 percent is doing very well, and one that makes 15 percent is truly exceptional. Approximately 50 percent of the *Inc.* 500 companies make 5 percent or less; 13 percent of them make 16 percent or more. Profit margins in a wide variety of industries for companies both large and small are published by Robert

Exhibit 1.4 Relationship of Investor to Entrepreneur

	All Nations	**United States**
Close family member	40%	44%
Other relative	11%	6%
Work colleague	10%	9%
Friend/neighbor	28%	28%
Stranger	9%	7%
Other	2%	6%
	100%	100%

Source: Information extracted from the Global Entrepreneurship Monitor 2002 data set, www.gemconsortium.org.

Morris Associates. Therefore it is possible for entrepreneurs to compare their forecasts with the actual performance of similar-size companies in the same industry.

Any business must make enough profit to recompense its investors (in most cases that means the entrepreneur) for their investment. It must be profit after all normal business expenses have been accounted for, including a fair salary for the entrepreneur and any family members who are working in the business. A common error in assessing the profitability of a new venture is to ignore the owner's salary. Suppose someone leaves a secure job paying $50,000 per year plus fringe benefits and invests $100,000 of personal savings to start a new venture. That person should expect to take a $50,000 salary plus fringe benefits out of the new business. Perhaps in the first year or two, when the business is being built, it may not be possible to pay $50,000 in actual cash; in that case, the pay that is not actually received should be treated as deferred compensation to be paid in the future.

In addition to an adequate salary, the entrepreneur must also earn a reasonable return on the $100,000 investment. A professional investor putting money into a new, risky business would expect to earn an annual rate of return of at least 40 percent, which would be $40,000 annually on a $100,000 investment. That return may come as a capital gain when the business is sold, as a dividend, or as a combination of the two. But remember that $100,000 compounding annually at 40 percent grows to almost $2.9 million in 10 years. When such large capital gains are needed to produce acceptable returns, big capital investments held for a long time do not make any sense unless very substantial value can be created, as occasionally happens in the case of high-flying companies, especially high-tech ones. In most cases, instead of a capital gain, the investor's return will be a dividend, which must be paid out of the cash flow from the business.

The cash flow that a business generates is not to be confused with profit. It is possible, indeed very likely, that a rapidly growing business will have a negative cash flow from operations in its early years even though it may be profitable. That may happen because the business may not be able to generate enough cash flow internally to sustain its ever-growing needs for working capital and the purchase of long-term assets such as plant and equipment. Hence, it will have to borrow or raise new equity capital. So it is very important that a high-potential business intending to grow rapidly make careful cash-flow projections so as to predict its needs for future outside investments. Future equity investments will dilute the percentage ownership of the founders, and if the dilution becomes excessive, there may be little reward remaining for the entrepreneurs.

Biotechnology companies are examples of this; they have a seemingly insatiable need for cash infusions to sustain their R&D costs in their early years. Their negative cash flow, or *burn rate*, sometimes runs at $1 million per month. A biotechnology company can easily burn up $50 million before it generates a meaningful profit, let alone a positive cash flow. The expected future capital gain from a public stock offering or sale to a large pharmaceutical company has to run into hundreds of millions of dollars, maybe into the billion-dollar range, for investors to realize an annual return of 50 percent or higher, which is what they expect to earn on money invested in a seed-stage biotechnology company. Not surprisingly, to finance their ventures, biotechnology entrepreneurs as a group have to give up most of the ownership. A study of venture capital–backed biotechnology companies found that after they had gone public, the entrepreneurs and management were left with less than 18 percent of the equity, compared with 32 percent for a comparable group of computer software companies.

As has already been mentioned, the vast majority of businesses will never have the potential to go public. Nor will the owners ever intend to sell their businesses and thereby realize a capital gain. In that case, how can those owners get a satisfactory return on the money they have invested in their businesses? The two ingredients that determine return on investment are (1) amount invested and (2) annual amount earned on that investment. Hence, entrepreneurs should invest as little as possible to start their businesses and make sure that their firms will be able to pay them a dividend big enough to yield an appropriate annual rate of return. For income tax purposes, that so-called dividend may be in the form of a salary bonus or fringe benefits rather than an actual dividend paid out of retained earnings. Of course, the company must be generating cash from its own operations before that dividend can be paid.

For entrepreneurs, happiness is a positive cash flow. The day a company begins to generate cash is a very happy day in the life of a successful entrepreneur. In 2008, Microsoft generated $1.8 billion of cash flow from operations every month—almost $2,900 per second on the basis of a five-day working week, 8 hours per day. No wonder Bill Gates and Steve Ballmer were smiling a lot.

> **For entrepreneurs, happiness is a positive cash flow.**

Ingredients for a Successful New Business

The great day has arrived. You found an idea, wrote a business plan, and gathered your resources. Now you are opening the doors of your new business for the first time, and the really hard work is about to begin. What are the factors that distinguish winning entrepreneurial businesses from the also-rans? Rosabeth Kanter prescribed Four Fs for a successful business,[17] a list that has been expanded into the Nine Fs for entrepreneurial success (see Exhibit 1.5).

Exhibit 1.5   The Nine Fs

Founders	Every startup company must have a first-class entrepreneur.
Focused	Entrepreneurial companies focus on niche markets. They specialize.
Fast	They make decisions quickly and implement them swiftly.
Flexible	They keep an open mind. They respond to change.
Forever-innovating	They are tireless innovators.
Flat	Entrepreneurial organizations have as few layers of management as possible.
Frugal	By keeping overhead low and productivity high, entrepreneurial companies keep costs down.
Friendly	Entrepreneurial companies are friendly to their customers, suppliers, and employees.
Fun	It's fun to be associated with an entrepreneurial company.

First and foremost, the founding entrepreneur is the most important factor. Next comes the market. This is the "Era of the Other," in which, as Regis McKenna observed, the fastest-growing companies in an industry will be in a segment labeled "Others" in a market share pie chart. By and large, they will be newer entrepreneurial firms rather than large firms with household names; hence specialization is the key. A successful business should focus on niche markets.

The rate of change in business gets ever faster. The advanced industrial economies are knowledge based. Product life cycles are getting shorter. Technological innovation progresses at a relentless pace. Government rules and regulations keep changing. Communications and travel around the globe keep getting easier and cheaper. And consumers are better informed about their choices. To survive, let alone succeed, a company has to be quick and nimble. It must be fast and flexible. It cannot allow inertia to build up.

Look at retailing: Woolworths in the United Kingdom and Circuit City in the United States went bankrupt in 2008–2009; and historical U.S. giants such as Sears and Kmart are on the ropes, while nimble competitors dance around them. Four of the biggest retailing successes are Les Wexner's The Limited, the late Sam Walton's Wal-Mart, Bernie Marcus and Arthur Blank's Home Depot, and Jeff Bezos' Amazon.com. Entrepreneurs such as these know that they can keep inertia low by keeping the layers of management as few as possible. Tom Peters, an authority on business strategy, liked to point out that Wal-Mart had three layers of management, whereas Sears had ten when Wal-Mart displaced Sears as the nation's top chain of department stores. "A company with three layers of management can't lose against a company with ten. You could try, but you couldn't do it!" says Peters. So keep your organization flat. It will facilitate quick decisions and flexibility, and keep overhead low.

Small entrepreneurial firms are great innovators. Big firms are relying increasingly on strategic partnerships with entrepreneurial firms in order to get access to desirable R&D. It is a trend that is well under way. Hoffmann-La Roche, hurting for new blockbuster prescription drugs, purchased a majority interest in Genentech and bought the highly regarded biotechnology called PCR (polymerase chain reaction) from Cetus for $300 million. Eli Lilly purchased Hybritech. In the 1980s, IBM spent $9 billion a year on research and development, but even that astronomical amount of money could not sustain Big Blue's commercial leadership. As its market share was remorselessly eaten away by thousands of upstarts, IBM entered into strategic agreements with Apple, Borland, Go, Lotus, Intel, Metaphor, Microsoft, Novell, Stratus, Thinking Machines, and other entrepreneurial firms for the purpose of gaining computer technologies.

IBM

When it introduced the first personal computer in 1981, IBM stood astride the computer industry like a big blue giant. Two suppliers of its personal computer division were Intel and Microsoft. Compared with IBM, Intel was small and Microsoft was a midget. By 2002, Intel's revenue was $26.8 billion and Microsoft's was $28.4 billion. Between 1998 and 2002 Microsoft's revenue increased 86 percent while IBM's stood still. In 2002, IBM—the company that invented the PC—had only 6 percent of the worldwide market for PCs. In 2005, IBM announced that it was selling its PC division to Lenovo, the leading Chinese manufacturer of PCs. Today, it was Microsoft's Windows operating system and Intel's microprocessors—the so-called WINTEL—that shaped the future of information technology.

When it comes to productivity, the best entrepreneurial companies leave the giant corporations behind in the dust. According to 2008 computer industry statistics, Dell's revenue per employee was $693,000, Microsoft's was $630,000, while Hewlett-Packard's was $369,000, and IBM's was $260,000. Of course, Dell subcontracts more of its manufacturing, but this does not explain all the difference. Whether you hope to build a big company or a small one, the message is the same: Strive tirelessly to keep productivity high.

But no matter what you do, you probably won't be able to attain much success unless you have happy customers, happy workers, and happy suppliers. That means you must have a friendly company. It means that everyone must be friendly, especially anyone who deals with customers.

"The most fun six-month period I've had since the start of Microsoft," is how Bill Gates described his astonishing accomplishment in reinventing his 20-year-old company to meet the threat posed by Internet upstarts in the mid-1990s. In not much more than six months of Herculean effort, Microsoft developed an impressive array of new products to match those of Netscape. Having fun is one of the keys to keeping a company entrepreneurial. If Microsoft's product developers had not been having fun, they would not have put in 12-hour days and sometimes overnighters to catch up with Netscape.

Most new companies have the Nine Fs at the outset. Those that become successful and grow pay attention to keeping them and nurturing them. The key to sustaining success is to remain an entrepreneurial gazelle and never turn into a lumbering elephant and finally a dinosaur, doomed to extinction.

Notes

1. P. D. Reynolds, W. D. Bygrave, E. Autio, and M. Hay, Global Entrepreneurship Monitor—2002 Summary Report, www.gemconsortium.org. The 500 million number for 2008 was based on an extrapolation from the estimate published in 2002.
2. This is based on GDPs and actual currency exchange rates in 2008.
3. E. M. Rogers and J. K. Larsen, *Silicon Valley Fever: Growth of High-Technology Culture* (New York: Basic Books, 1984).
4. *Inc. 500*, September 2005.
5. Excerpted from http://web.mit.edu/newsoffice/2009/kauffman-study-0217.html.
6. *Inc.*, March 1, 1990.
7. "This Tax Is for You: A Levy on Joe Six Pack," *Wall Street Journal*, April 15, 2009, http://online.wsj.com/article/SB123976316293519743.html?mod=googlenews_wsj.
8. http://www.census.gov/Press-Release/www/2001/cb01-54.html.
9. http://www.census.gov/Press-Release/www/releases/archives/cb05_108_table.xls.
10. *Inc. 500* 25:12 (2004).
11. *Inc. 500* 22:15 (2000).

12. For more information on start-ups and failures, refer to William Dennis, "The Shape of Small Business," NFIB foundation, www.nfib.com/object/PolicyGuide2.html.

13. American Bankruptcy Institute. http://www.abiworld.org/AM/Template.cfm?Section= Home&TEMPLATE=/CM/ContentDisplay.cfm&CONTENTID=54478.

14. Detailed information on survival rates can be found in the following articles and books: R. J. Boden Jr., 2000. "Analysis of Business Dissolution by Demographic Category of Business Ownership" (2000), http://www.sba.gov/advo/research/rs204tot.pdf; Bruce A. Kirchhoff and Bruce D. Phillips, 1989, "Innovation and Growth Among New Firms in the U.S. Economy," *Frontiers of Entrepreneurship Research* (Wellesley, MA: Babson College, 1989), 173–188; Bruce A. Kirchhoff, *Entrepreneurship and Dynamic Capitalism* (Westport, CT: Praeger, 1994); Bruce D. Phillips and Bruce A. Kirchhoff, 1989, "Formation, Growth, and Survival: Small Firm Dynamics in the U.S. Economy," *Small Business Economics* 1:65–74.

15. *BusinessWeek*, February 6, 2006, 66.

16. *Inc.*, September 2008.

17. R. M. Kanter, *Change Masters: Innovation and Entrepreneurship in the American Corporation* (New York: Simon and Schuster, 1985).

2

Idea Generation

Heidi M. Neck

How This Chapter Fits into a Typical MBA Curriculum

Creativity is a necessary ingredient for idea generation. Though creativity is taking a more visible role in graduate management education, it continues to remain peripheral. However, I polled a few of my MBA students, past and present, and asked them: How does creativity fit into an MBA curriculum? My favorite response was from Jennifer Green, Babson College MBA 2007:

An MBA curriculum will fill your toolbox. Creativity allows you to imagine what can be built.

An MBA curriculum will hand you work to do. Creativity allows you to imagine new ways of getting the work done.

An MBA curriculum will encourage teamwork and shared accountability. Creativity allows you to consider different ways to allocate the work and effective tools to hold each other accountable.

An MBA curriculum will present you with difficult problems and possible solutions. Upon graduation, creativity allows you to think through difficult situations and apply the most appropriate combination of solutions.

An MBA curriculum will ask more of you than you can deliver. Upon graduation, creativity allows you to deliver more than what is asked of you.

Who Uses This Material in the Real World—and Why It Is Important

The entrepreneurship process begins with ideas for new products, services, processes, business models, organizations, or markets. The ability to solve problems with unique and novel solutions is not just a start-up task—creation is a continuous process through the life of an organization. It is a necessary antecedent of not only emergence but growth, diversification, and renewal. Oftentimes in the real world the immediate takes precedence over the important; survival has a higher priority than creation; operations overpower imagination. Those who recognize the significance of creativity are also those who understand that creativity is present in everyone but it must be unleashed, cultivated, and continuously trained. This chapter addresses three creative competencies that need to be developed in order to be a master idea generator: play, improvisation, and observation. Together these help develop a free and imaginative mind, allowing one to see a wealth of possibilities.

Helena, Montana—August 5, 1949

Idea: The Escape Fire

The profession of smoke jumping began in 1941. Firefighters known as smoke jumpers parachute into remote forest fire locations to contain the blaze as quickly as possible. Originally thought to be a young, adventurous, and immortal group, young smoke jumpers beat the odds on many occasions. But the history of this elite group of men within the United States Forestry Service was forever changed during the summer of 1949.

On August 5, 1949, 13 of 15 smoke jumpers perished fighting a devastating fire that burned 4,500 acres in Mann Gulch near Helena, Montana. At 4:00 pm on August 5, 15 smoke jumpers parachuted in to fight what was then a class C fire, indicating a small burn of 10 to 99 acres. Upon landing, the men descended the mountain toward the Missouri River in hopes of digging a fire-line to prevent the fire from spreading.

The winds were high, the land dry. With all variables in place (wind, temperature, fuels, topography) a rare occurrence happened. The fire "blew up" and began racing up the mountain toward the smoke jumpers. At 5:45 pm the crew turned around to trek back up the hill away from the fire, but the fire was gaining momentum. At 5:53 the fire foreman, Wag Dodge, instructed his men to drop all tools and run for their lives up the hill. However the hill was a 76 percent grade mountain and the men needed to run approximately three-quarters of a mile to reach a possible ridge for safety.

The fire was gaining ground; the men were losing ground. Dodge, as the story goes, stopped and began to light a fire in front of the approaching inferno. He waved his men, who were on average 30 feet away from him, to join him. Dodge's men could not comprehend what he was asking them to do so they kept running. The idea: Dodge lit a fire to burn the fuel from the brush covered terrain. After the burn he would lie down on the burnt ground and the large fire would jump over him. What became known as the "escape fire" worked. Norman Maclean, in his highly acclaimed book, *Young Men and Fire*, recounts the moment of ideation:

> *Of course, Dodge had the Smokejumper's knowledge that if you can't reach the top of the hill you should turn and try to work back through burned-out areas in the front of a fire. But with the flames of the fire solid and a hundred yards deep Dodge had to invent the notion that he could burn a hole in the fire. Perhaps, though, his biggest invention was not to burn a hole in the fire but to lie down in it. Perhaps all he could patent about his invention was the courage to lie down in his fire. Like a lot of inventions, it could be crazy and consume the inventor. His invention, taking as much guts as logic, suffered the immediate fate of many other inventions—it was thought to be crazy by those who first saw it. Somebody said, "To hell with that," and they kept going, most of them to their deaths.*

> —Norman Maclean, *Young Men and Fire* (Chicago: University of Chicago Press, 1992), 106.

And most did die. Dodge survived because of his escape fire, and two others were able to make it to a ridge of open rock. Today the escape fire is common practice in open areas when no other options for survival exist.

Source: Much of the information in this section was sourced from Norman Maclean's *Young Men and Fire* (Chicago: University of Chicago Press, 1992).

Boston, Massachusetts—1806

Idea: Ice Harvesting

Frederic Tudor, a young 22-year-old Bostonian, had an idea. He was going to harvest pond, river, and lake ice during the harsh winter months of New England. His venture idea was cutting ice in the form of blocks from Fresh Pond in Cambridge, Massachusetts, and then shipping the ice to warmer, southern climates. Investors declined to be involved and he was ridiculed by the Boston business elite.

> The idea was considered so utterly absurd by the sober minded merchants as to be the vagary of a disordered brain, and few men would have been willing to stand the scoffs and sneers from those whose assistance it was necessary to obtain, to aid [Frederic] in his enterprise. . . . Merchants were not willing to charter their vessels to carry ice. The offices declined to insure and sailors were afraid to trust themselves with such a cargo.*

The novel idea was not simply creating a business using the raw materials of a Boston winter, but he had to also create ways to cut ice, ship ice, and store ice for long periods in warmer climates and in hulls of ships. Ships from the southern United States brought cotton to Massachusetts but nothing was coming out of Massachusetts back to the South. As a result, ship owners made no money on the trip south and, without the weight of inventory, they had to store rocks in the hull to give the ship the ballast necessary for stability.

Ship owners did not want to partner with Tudor because they feared the ice would melt and harm the ship, so he bought his own ship to prove ice could be shipped. After a successful first voyage, there was never a need for Tudor to buy additional ships, and other ship owners agreed to work with the ice cargo. He experimented with various forms of insulation, including sawdust, to prevent the ice from melting too much. The insulation was sufficient to maintain the ballast even though a portion of the ice melted each trip.

Tudor created the North American ice industry. Though he did not know it at the time, Frederic Tudor paved the way for the electric refrigeration industry that

*This quote is from Gavin Weightman's *The Frozen Water Trade* (New York: Hyperion, 2003), p. 27. Weightman was quoting Frederic Tudor's brother-in-law, Robert Gardiner, in his writing, *Early Reflections*. Robert Gardiner worked closely with Tudor in the ice harvesting business. He often took care of the home operations in Boston when Frederic Tudor was traveling to customer ports.

(continued)

emerged in the early 1900s—a century after Tudor's spark of an idea. Dubbed the "ice king" of "the frozen water trade," Tudor achieved success and shipped to ports such as Cuba and Calcutta as well as U.S. cities of Charleston, Savannah, and New Orleans. But his idea of harvesting ice should not overshadow his creative, or what we would call today *guerrilla* marketing and selling techniques. For example, he gave away ice free, knowing that even the average consumer would be hooked.†
He introduced the refreshing nature of ice in drinks, ice cream, and the benefits of ice to food preservation. Tudor's creation of an ice industry for the masses grew in importance.

The techniques created by Tudor's venture that made ice harvesting both efficient and profitable engendered competition throughout the late 1800s in Maine, Wisconsin, New York, and Pennsylvania. Competition became interesting in that the ice source became part of the brand. Ice from the far north was perceived as cleaner than, say, ice harvested from the Hudson River in New York City.‡

If you ever wondered why the United States is so dependent on ice for cold drinks when compared to other countries, especially European countries, now you know!

---

†Jason Zasky, "Cool Customer: Frederic Tudor and the Frozen Water Trade," http://failuremag.com/index.php/feature/article/cool_customer/.

‡Gavin Weightman's book *The Frozen Water Trade* (New York: Hyperion, 2003) was a great reference source in writing this section on Frederic Tudor.

Paths of Idea Generation

The stories of the escape fire and the ice industry represent two paths of idea generation—the *alertness* path and the *search* path, as highlighted in Exhibit 2.1.[1] Alert ideas tend to be identified in a more spontaneous, less calculated way, whereas the search process is deliberate and more purposeful because the creator is using her existing knowledge in a specific domain as a platform for idea generation.

Frederic Tudor identified the ice water trade through a unique level of alertness. By historical accounts it seems that Frederic Tudor was constantly scanning the environment for new ideas.[2] Before he stumbled on the ice idea, he tried his hand at business in commodities such as pimento, nutmeg, flour, sugar, tea, candles, cotton, and silk. But none of these ventures provided the life he wanted. Being part of Boston society, he observed that the wealthy elite already enjoyed the luxury of ice, and he thought it could become a commodity of the masses on a much grander scale. The idea was risky, as indicated by the ridicule of family, friends, and potential business partners. Additionally, Frederic Tudor had no knowledge of the ice industry, which required a significant amount of learning. Entrepreneurs who generate ideas outside their previous experience, as in the case of Frederic Tudor, face a greater risk of failure. In other words, Tudor's skill and ability level were not well suited to the idea generated. Ideas generated along this path are not doomed; rather, they are just more difficult to execute and identify.

By contrast, the story of Wag Dodge creating an escape fire to survive the Mann Gulch fire of 1949 was representative of an idea generated through search. It is often

Exhibit 2.1 Idea Generation Paths

	Alertness	Search
Idea stimuli	Environment	Information channel
Source of differentiation	Learning	Knowledge
Process	Spontaneous	Deliberate
Basis of discovery	Subconscious	Conscious
Fit with entrepreneur	Typically poor	Typically strong
Venture decision	Risky	Uncertain

perceived that a search process is an extensive and lengthy process, but this is not always the case. Ideas generated through search are often found in *information channels*—a place where one searches for ideas. For example, if I wanted to identify new methods of survival in fighting forest fires, I could research various methods of survival used in some of the most vicious fires of our time. Where the research is published or housed is an information channel. But in the Mann Gulch story, Dodge's information channel was his own mind. He was able to quickly generate the idea of lying down in a burned escape fire because he already had knowledge that working through burned out areas was a path out of a fire. He knew this but did not know previously that lying down in a burned area would cause the fire to leap over him. According to Maclean's research, when Dodge was asked if he had ever learned about setting an escape fire, Dodge responded, "Not that I know of. It just seemed the logical thing to do."[3]

Admittedly it is difficult to separate idea generation into such either-or thinking. It is very likely that an idea you are thinking about at this very moment may have characteristics of both paths. The path differentiation is simply an organizing framework—a way to codify and present the information to you, the reader, and to illustrate that there is no one identifiable path. The most important thing is that you do generate ideas, but this requires creativity and we all have it.

Creativity researchers often discuss the 3 Bs of where new ideas are generated: bathtub, bed, and bus. The notion of an "aha" or "eureka" moment, however, is a myth. Keith Sawyer, in his book *Explaining Creativity: The Science of Human Innovation*, discusses results of a study where he reviewed notebooks, manuscripts, and historical records of famous individuals such as the Wright brothers, Charles Darwin, Jackson Pollock, and others to demystify the creative process. He found that "creativity happens not with one brilliant flash but in a chain reaction of many tiny sparks while executing an idea. . . . Even when an idea seems sudden, our minds have actually been working on it all along."[4]

Creativity is difficult to define because of its elusive, mysterious, and somewhat enigmatic nature. It is one of those things that you just know when you see it, but you know it only *after* you see it. The "why didn't I think of that" syndrome occurs when you see great yet simple inventions such as the paper clip, Post-it Note, Slinky, Frisbee, or the ballpoint pen. Consider Bette Nesmith Graham, who created Liquid Paper in the 1950s and later sold it to Gillette in 1979 for $47.5 million. Bette was a secretary in the 1950s, working to support her son after being divorced. Admittedly a poor typist, Bette felt the frustration of making one mistake after another with no simple solution for correction. Bette was an aspiring artist and knew that when artists made mistakes while painting on canvas, they covered the mistake by painting over the error with the color of the canvas. So she thought the same process would work on white paper to cover typing mistakes, and it did. I know what you are thinking. "That's creative. Why didn't I think of that?"

For better or for worse, we do know creativity when we see it, yet there are different degrees of creativeness. The conceptual definition of creativity:

> **"A product or response will be judged as creative to the extent that (a) it is both a novel and appropriate, useful, correct or valuable response to the task at hand, and (b) the task is heuristic rather than algorithmic."[5]**

The latter part of the definition simply implies that the path to a solution is not known or clearly defined because the word *algorithmic* implies a set of rules that must be followed in order to maintain the integrity of the solution. Assuming the task is heuristic and focusing on novelty, value, and usefulness, a classification of ideas emerge.

Degree of novelty implies newness and uniqueness of an idea, while *value and usefulness* imply that a significant group of people will adopt the idea, buy the product, accept the solution, or some variation on this theme. In pure product terms, an *innovation* is high on both novelty and usefulness—there is a market. (See Figure 2.2.) Though *inventions* have an incredibly high degree of novelty, especially if patentable, unless there is a market for the invention it will likely live on a shelf collecting dust over an extended period of time. If an invention does find a market, then it moves to the innovation category. For example, Liquid Paper was originally invented by Bette Graham Nesmith, but once to market it emerged as a highly valued innovation.

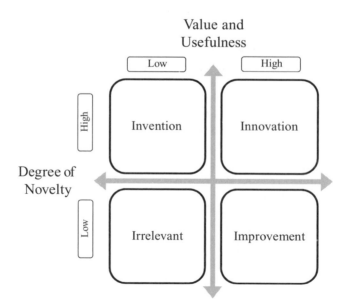

Exhibit 2.2   Idea Classification Matrix

Most ideas that hit the market fall into the *improvement* category. A whitening agent is added to toothpaste; boot-cut jeans replace flared jeans; wheels are added to suitcases; cameras are built into cellular phones. These are all improvements—enhancements to existing products that lack a high degree of novelty (this does not mean zero novelty), but the market readily accepts the improvement.

Finally there are the *irrelevant* ideas that are neither novel nor useful. Coors Brewing Company introduced bottled water using Rocky Mountain spring water. Irrelevant. Maxwell House introduced prebrewed coffee in a half-gallon milk style carton. Irrelevant. And, of course, the "New Coke" with a formula that differed from the classic—definitely irrelevant. But irrelevance, invention, or innovation is difficult to forecast. For fun, take a moment and Google "Pet Rock"—an irrelevant idea on the surface, but within six months of its introduction it became an iconic product in 1975. Have you heard of the Snuggie? Introduced in 2008, the Snuggie is a fleece blanket with arms. In its first three months on the market over four million units were sold. How would you classify the Snuggie?

The Entrepreneur and Creativity

Though there is little disagreement that creativity is important to entrepreneurship, not enough attention is given to creativity in traditional MBA programs. The typical entrepreneurship course often assumes the opportunity is in place, and students develop acute skills in opportunity analysis—market, financial, and industry analyses. Though these are necessary and important skills, the business environment today requires the development of creativity skills because entrepreneurial action is not necessarily intended for jobs that exist today—it is for future jobs and for businesses needed to create the jobs. The entrepreneur who understands the need for a balance of analytical and creative processes will be much more competitive in the new and uncertain environments of today. The creative entrepreneur has a better ability to navigate uncharted waters, anticipate change, play offense, and create the future. One hurdle in developing the creative entrepreneur is the false perception that creativity is a born trait rather than a developed skill. Consider the so-called attributes of the creative person in Exhibit 2.3.[6]

The attributes of the creative person are not much different than attributes of the entrepreneur. Jeffry Timmons and Stephen Spinelli, authors of one of the best selling

---

Exhibit 2.3   Attributes of Creative Individuals

- Open to experience
- Observant
- Reconciles apparent opposites
- Tolerant with ambiguity
- Selective
- Needs and assumes autonomy
- Self-reliant
- Willing to take calculated risks
- Persistent
- Not subject to group standards and control
- Thinks in images
- Sensitive to problems
- Generates a large number of ideas
- Flexible
- Original
- Responsive to feelings
- Open to unconscious phenomena
- Motivated
- Free from fear of failure
- Able to concentrate
- Independent in judgment, thought, and action

MBA textbooks, *New Venture Creation*, list 40 attributes of entrepreneurs grouped under seven themes: commitment and determination; courage; leadership; opportunity obsession; tolerance of risk, ambiguity, and uncertainty; creativity, self-reliance, and adaptability; and motivation to excel.[7] Just about every attribute of the creative person from Exhibit 2.3 can be found within one of these themes. As a result, two conclusions can be drawn.

First, entrepreneurs are creative individuals. Empirical support is found from a study published in 2008. Data were collected from 40 graduate students enrolled in entrepreneurship programs. The control group consisted of another 38 students enrolled in other graduate programs. Those enrolled in entrepreneurship programs scored higher on personal creativity than those students from other programs. Thus, personal creativity had a strong influence on entrepreneurial intentions—that is, intentions to start a business.[8]

My second conclusion is that attributes of creative individuals and attributes of entrepreneurs are so similar that even attempting to define a set of predetermined characteristics is a futile exercise. Researching the unique traits of entrepreneurs started in 1967 and continues today,[9] yet there is little scientific evidence that separates an entrepreneur from a good manager. So I give little credence to the traits approach with respect to creativity and/or entrepreneurship. Both are about behavior, and behaviors can be learned. In particular, creativity is inherent in all individuals; it makes us human; and it is a process. If my proposition is correct, then creativity can be unleashed even in the most adamant person who thinks, "I'm not creative in any way, shape, or form!"

Dead Poets Society, a now classic film released in 1989, is a timeless coming-of-age story about a group of young men attending a college preparatory school called Welton. Central to the story is their teacher, Mr. Keating, played by Robin Williams. Mr. Keating is a newly hired teacher at Welton and throughout the movie he challenges the school structure, known for its tradition, conformity, and academic rigor. Keating attempts to use the medium of an English class not only to facilitate the boys' learning of poetry but also to catapult them on a path of self-discovery. Given his unorthodox teaching methods and associated ideology, the movie dramatizes the influence Keating had on changing the mindset and behavior of a particular group of boys who constituted "The Dead Poets Society."

One magical clip from the movie illustrates how creativity can be unleashed even in the most reluctant creator. Mr. Keating assigns the students to each write their own piece of original poetry to read aloud during class. One student, Todd Anderson, played by Ethan Hawke, is portrayed as timid, insecure, and lacking self-confidence. He works tirelessly to create a poem but his own self-doubt creates a cognitive roadblock. Todd shows up for class without a poem. When Mr. Keating discovers that Todd did not complete the assignment, he brings him to the front of the class and points to a picture of the famous poet, Walt Whitman, hanging above the chalkboard. Part of the scene unfolds as follows.

Keating: The picture of Uncle Walt up there. What does he remind you of? Don't think. Answer. Go on. (*Keating begins to circle around Todd.*)

Todd: A m-m-madman.

Keating: What kind of madman? Don't think about it. Just answer again.

Todd: A c-crazy madman.

Keating: No, you can do better than that. Free up your mind. Use your imagination. Say the first thing that pops into your head, even if it's total gibberish. Go on, go on.

Todd: Uh, uh, a sweaty-toothed madman.

Keating: Good God, boy, there's a poet in you, after all. There, close your eyes. Close your eyes. Close 'em. Now, describe what you see. (*Keating puts his hands over Todd's eyes and the two of them begin to slowly spin around.*)

Todd: Uh, I-I close my eyes.

Keating: Yes?

Todd: Uh, and this image floats beside me.

Keating: A sweaty-toothed madman?

Todd: A sweaty-toothed madman with a stare that pounds my brain.

Keating: Oh, that's excellent. Now, give him action. Make him do something.

Todd: H-His hands reach out and choke me.

Keating: That's it. Wonderful. Wonderful. (*Keating removes his hands from Todd but Todd keeps his eyes closed.*)

Todd: And, and all the time he's mumbling.

Keating: What's he mumbling?

Todd: M-Mumbling, Truth. Truth is like, like a blanket that always leaves your feet cold. (*The students begin to laugh and Todd opens his eyes. Keating quickly gestures for him to close them again.*)

Keating: Forget them, forget them. Stay with the blanket. Tell me about that blanket.

Todd: Y-Y-Y-You push it, stretch it, it'll never be enough. You kick at it, beat it, it'll never cover any of us. From the moment we enter crying to the moment we leave dying, it will just cover your face as you wail and cry and scream. (*Todd opens his eyes. The class is silent. Then they begin to clap and cheer.*)[10]

Take a moment and view the clip of this scene on YouTube (http://www.youtube.com/watch?v=DmNyv2Pddg4). I guarantee that it is worth the three minutes of your time.

Like Todd, it is easy for us to feel paralyzed at times when asked to do something perceived as creative. All of a sudden our thinking becomes limited and we get stuck based on what we know, and have trouble embracing what we *could* know. Consider the popular image in Exhibit 2.4.[11] Try to draw four straight lines through all nine dots without lifting your pen from the paper.

Exhibit 2.4   Nine-Dot Exercise (Downloadable) Copyright © 2010 by William D. Bygrave and Andrew Zacharakis. To download this form for your personal use, please visit www.wiley.com/go/portablembainentrepreneurship.

The nine-dot exercise illustrates how limited our thinking can be. If you had difficulty completing the exercise, the most likely culprit was your mind being blocked by the imaginary boundaries the dots created. Too often it is assumed that to complete the exercise we have to stay within the lines, as if we were children coloring. If you were unsuccessful on your first attempt, try the exercise again. This time, however, try to view the image beyond the "box" of dots. If you are still having trouble, the solution to the exercise can be found in the endnotes at the end of this chapter.[12]

Creating false boundaries limits our thinking, as does another culprit: habit. Try one more exercise. Following are five sentences with concealed colors. Can you identify the color in each sentence?

1. The new law hit everybody's wallet pretty hard.
2. You can always catch Rome on your way back from Naples.
3. Newspaper editors decided to go on strike.
4. A big, old, hungry dog appeared at our door every morning.
5. The cab lacked proper brakes to stop at the intersection.[13]

We view the world in such a way simply because it is habit, but we must work to train our mind's eye to be more flexible. Did you get the correct answers: white, chrome, red, gold, and black, respectively?

1. The new la**w hit e**verybody's wallet pretty hard.
2. You can always cat**ch Rome** on your way back from Naples.
3. Newspape**r ed**itors decided to go on strike.
4. A bi**g**, **old**, hungry dog appeared at our door every morning.
5. The ca**b lack**ed proper brakes to stop at the intersection.

Knowing that creativity can be developed and unleashed, and knowing that every human being is creative, why do many of us find it incredibly difficult to let our creativity flow? There are several emotional roadblocks to creativity. James Adams, author of *Conceptual Blockbusting*, identified six roadblocks: (1) fear, (2) no appetite for chaos, (3) preference for judging over generating ideas, (4) dislike for incubating ideas, (5) perceived lack of challenge, and (6) inability to distinguish reality from fantasy.[14] Fear is by far the most significant roadblock and it hits us from two angles—the starting point of creating (ideas in) and the finishing line of sharing what you created (ideas out). As you can imagine, being surrounded by such fear can only lead to a feeling of being boxed in or even paralyzed. Exhibit 2.5 highlights what I call the *fear factor* and its causes.

To illustrate how the fear factor invades our lives, let me tell you a story about Max. He's a recent graduate of a top MBA program and is currently working for a small start-up with high growth potential. The focus of the company—let's call it AppTech—is rapid prototyping of new cell phone applications such as those used for the iPhone. When Max interviewed with AppTech he was told the available position was for a market analyst. The company was looking for candidates with a background in competitive benchmarking, industry analysis, and market forecasting. Max was excited about the prospect of working at AppTech because this was right in line with what he wanted to do. Max interviewed

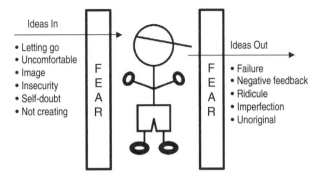

Exhibit 2.5   The Fear Factor

well, was offered the job with a competitive salary, accepted the job, and started a week later. But as with any emerging start-up, all team members are required to wear multiple hats. Two weeks into his job Max was told that he was needed on the creative development team—*the* team responsible for generating new ideas for cell phone applications. Max's first thought? "I'm not creative. I even hated coloring in kindergarten."

Max entered a room where the other members of the creative development team were meeting. Jill had a background in graphic design; Simon was a video game developer; Wanda was a summer intern working on her degree in anthropology. Louis, the final team member, was absent from the meeting. He was a freelance photographer, and a few of his photos taken while on safari in Africa were being included in an exclusive art show in London. Louis was to be out of the office for two weeks and Max was assigned to take his place. The team welcomed Max and they began a simple brainstorming exercise. The group decided on the objective of the session: to brainstorm applications that relate to productivity in personal and professional lives. Max immediately froze and could not think of one idea to share—the fear factor had invaded.

Max was thrown into a new environment and asked to participate on a project that he had no experience with. By habit he self-screened every idea that entered his head. The group encouraged him to just throw out any idea that came to mind, no matter how big, small, funny, or mundane. Still, Max allowed nothing through. He was a market analyst, after all, professionally educated and serious. Historically, success had come naturally to him, but now he was faced with an unprecedented challenge. And his biggest fear at this juncture was that he could not generate any ideas. Such pressure does not provide a relaxed mindset conducive for idea generation.

But this was just half of the battle. Not only was his brain blocked by fear, disallowing new ideas to emerge, but his mind's eye had already jumped minutes ahead into the future, seeing the potential outcome after sharing an idea, any idea.

Wait! Max finally has an idea—a to-do list that is networked among iPhone users so all members of a family can add to or electronically scratch tasks off the list as they are completed. Max tries very hard to speak about his idea but he encounters another wall of fear. He begins to question himself: "What if they laugh at the idea? What if they roll their eyes? What if the idea is already out there? Or what if they think it's a good idea but it fails miserably?" I wonder how many great ideas like Max's have never left the minds of the creator? The fear factor can be devastating and controlling. Recognize it; face it; and help others do the same.

A More Creative Mind for a Challenging World

In a very compelling book called *A Whole New Mind*, author Daniel Pink discusses an imperative we are facing in the new millennium. The twentieth century was one dominated by left-brain thinking, but circumstances of today require right-brain (or what he refers to as *right-directed*) thinking. In other words, we need to cultivate our creative minds. Exhibit 2.6 highlights basic differences between left- and right-brain thinking.

The notion that our brain is split into two distinct hemispheres was theorized by Roger Sperry and Robert Ornstein in the 1960s. Their work significantly advanced our understanding of how the brain works. Sperry proved that each hemisphere has distinct functions (as outlined in Exhibit 2.6) and that the left hemisphere controls the right side of our body while the right hemisphere controls the left side of our body. Ornstein studied the amount of time people used one side of the brain versus the other. He found that when individuals are trained to employ one side only, the other side was virtually unused and could not be used. Yet, when the underutilized side was forced to work with the dominant side, task effectiveness increased.[15] Think about your own daily activities. What percent of your activities require left- versus right-brain thinking?

Pink recognizes three forces that are mandating the move to more right-brain thinking; he calls these abundance, Asia, and automation, but they can also be referred to as affluence, globalization, and technology, respectively. Pink, speaking in American-centric prose, reasonably claims that we are an abundant society so we are now becoming more concerned with meaning over accumulation. Most of the work that has historically been done by the white-collar workforce is representative of left-brain thinking, and these activities are now being outsourced to Asia at a lower cost or they are being performed

Exhibit 2.6   Brain Orientation Comparison

Left-Brain Thinking	Right-Brain Thinking
Detail oriented	Big-picture oriented
Forms strategies	Presents possibilities
Logic	Intuition
Rational	Emotional
Analytical	Synthesizing
Verbal	Spatial
Quantitative processing	Nonverbal processing
Talking	Drawing
Writing	Manipulating objects
Objective	Subjective
Linear	Creative
Directive	Experiential
Words	Symbols
Language	Images
Reasoning	Dreaming

by computers at a faster rate. He argues that we are entering a new age called the "Conceptual Age," an age that requires us to use both right- and left-brain thinking in order to develop talent that technology cannot do better, faster, or cheaper. To reach this conclusion, Pink codifies the type of worker that was needed throughout various ages. The eighteenth century was the agricultural age and needed farmers. We entered the nineteenth century and witnessed the birth of industrialization, where the factory worker became essential labor. The twentieth century created a knowledge worker for the information age. And now, the conceptual age requires what Pink calls "creators and empathizers," which requires a different way of thinking—a more whole-brain approach that emphasizes the right hemisphere of the brain.

Using both sides of the brain seems like a contradiction. Is it possible to develop and use both hemispheres? Can we exist with such neuro-conflict? A challenge is perceived when we are encouraged to be both objective and subjective, or rational and emotional, or even to talk and draw at the same time. These are exigent paradoxes.

Earlier in this chapter I argued against traits to separate the creative from the non-creative or the entrepreneurs from general managers. My rationale was to avoid putting individuals in boxes, especially if the box was labeled "lacks creativity." Mihaly Csikszent-mihalyi conducted a study between 1990 and 1995 to dig deeper into the creative mind. He and his research team identified 91 people they considered to be "exceptional" in their field. Study participants included scientists, artists, business executives, political figures—all over 60 years of age. What he found was that a creative individual had con-flicting traits. He acknowledged, of course, that for every trait there is an opposite trait, but what he found most remarkable was that while conflicting traits are rarely found in the same person, he found them to be present among his study participants.[16] The traits represented poles (see Exhibit 2.7) and Csikszentmihalyi noted:

> . . . without the second pole, new ideas will not be recognized. And without the first, they will not be developed to the point of acceptance. Therefore, the novelty that survives to change a domain is usually the work of someone who can operate at both ends of these polarities—and that is the kind of person we call "creative."[17]

What perhaps is more interesting is that the conflicting traits of Exhibit 2.7 are strikingly similar to the characteristics of left- and right-brain thinking in Exhibit 2.6, which only amplifies the position that in a conceptual age that demands more creative individuals, a whole-minded approach is desirable if not essential.

Toward Idea Generation Mastery

Every person is creative but not every creative technique will work for all people. The best advice I can give is to experiment with many techniques, but sharing such tech-niques is not my primary purpose here. Idea generation requires training, ongoing practice, and application; and the willingness to engage and use ideation techniques demands a frame of mind conducive for creative thinking. Without such a mindset, your participating in idea generation techniques is mostly an exercise in futility rather than creativity. Practice, however, is required for the mindset as well. You don't get off that easy!

Exhibit 2.7   Csikszentmihalyi's Polarity of Creative Individuals

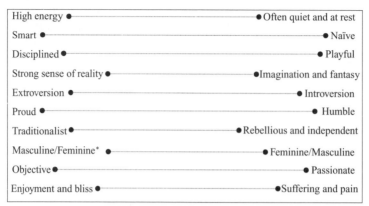

High energy ●	● Often quiet and at rest
Smart ●	● Naïve
Disciplined ●	● Playful
Strong sense of reality ●	● Imagination and fantasy
Extroversion ●	● Introversion
Proud ●	● Humble
Traditionalist ●	● Rebellious and independent
Masculine/Feminine* ●	● Feminine/Masculine
Objective ●	● Passionate
Enjoyment and bliss ●	● Suffering and pain

Adapted from Csikszentmihalyi, Mihaly (1996) *Creativity Flow and the Psychology of Discovery and Invention*. HarperCollins: New York.

Idea generation mastery requires competency building in three areas: play, improvisation, and observation. These building blocks serve two purposes—to set mood and assist in creative output. Not only will play, improvisation, and observation create a psychological environment for idea generation, they will also serve as broad, higher-level ideation techniques.

Before proceeding, I want to mention the concept of *brainstorming*, because the process is naturally associated with idea generation and it may appear odd as an obvious omission from this chapter. Alex Osborn created the concept of brainstorming in 1953. He stated, "In the average person, judgment grows automatically with years, while creativity dwindles unless consciously kept up."[18] The problem with the current form of brainstorming is that it is commonplace. We do it almost on a daily basis and it has become habit. So the act of sitting in a room and coming up with ideas is not new and does not need to be discussed here, but let's not lose sight of the four fundamental tenets of brainstorming created by Alex Osborn in 1953:[19]

1. Criticism and judgment are not allowed.
2. Wild ideas are welcome.
3. Focus on quantity rather than quality.
4. Improve on the ideas of others or connect individual ideas for new ideas.

These principles of brainstorming should be present in any and all forms of idea generation, whether specific or broad. The process of *ideation* is not synonymous with a process of *opportunity identification*. Opportunity immediately connotes the presence of economic and social value in the world of entrepreneurship, while ideation is the antecedent of opportunity identification. In many respects an opportunity is an idea judged as good. In the famous words of Nobel Prize winner Linus Pauling, "The best way to have a good idea is to have lots of ideas."

The three major building blocks are described next. I will give a brief description of each concept, its relationship to idea generation, and a *prescription*—medicine for your mind so you can begin developing and using both sides of your brain in order to become master idea generators.

Building Block 1: Play

Play is incredibly important to the creative process, and the creative process is essential to idea generation, if not *the* essential part. The problem, however, is that we (the adults) tend to associate play with childhood, a time of freedom and imagination where minutes turned into hours, backyards transformed into magical faraway kingdoms, living rooms were reconfigured into tent cities, swimming pools became uncharted waters littered with sunken treasure, and stuffed animals sat at attention waiting for the assignment from the young seven-year-old teacher. These childhood images are indicative of a type of play called *sociodramatic* play, a form of play based on imagination and fantasy. Two other forms of play are *functional* play (integrating with one's environment) and *constructive* play (creating and building something).[20] The Strong National Museum of Play highlights six elements that are present in all forms of play: anticipation, surprise, pleasure, understanding, strength, and poise. Engaging in play, according to the museum, sharpens our minds, helps us grow, keeps us healthy, and boosts our creativity.[21]

The elements of play are fun and the outcomes seem quite attractive, so why don't we play as adults? Sure, we play with our kids or nieces and nephews, but we don't engage in play for the sake of play. I'll even admit that I use other people's children as an excuse to play with Play-Doh, build something out of lots of Legos, tell crazy and unbelievable stories, or run down the beach flying a kite pretending to be carrying an important message to the citizens in the faraway galaxy somewhere named Raynemore. Given our preconceived notion of what play is, even though many forms of play exist, for adults and for education a new, more palatable form of play has emerged called *serious play*. Serious play is simply using play or gaming in an educational context. Serious play is reflected in the words of Sara Lawrence-Lightfoot, sociologist and expert on school culture and learning. She said, "Learning is at its best when it is deadly serious and very playful at the same time."[22]

Adults do engage in play, but not the childhood form that we so often associate with play. Mihaly Csikszentmihalyi researched various people engaged in different forms of play (e.g., dancers, chess masters, mountain climbers) and identified qualities that make play enjoyable. He found that during play a person is only able to concentrate on a limited "stimulus field" where they are transcended to a new environment that allows the player to only exist in the moment, unable to grasp problems outside of the stimulus field.[23] This state of being, according to Csikszentmihalyi, is called "flow" and is often experienced through play. He states:

> Flow denotes the holistic sensation present when we act with total involvement. It is the kind of feeling after which one nostalgically says: "that was fun," or "that was enjoyable." It is the state in which action follows upon action according to an internal logic which seems to need no conscious intervention on our part. We experience it as a unified flowing from one moment to the next, in which we feel in control of our actions, and in which there is little distinction between self and environment; between stimulus and response; or between past, present and future.[24]

Play Prescription

You are probably expecting a prescription such as go create an imaginary world in your backyard, or draw a picture of the world and show it to your best friend! Well, feel free to do this, but I have another suggestion. Go play a video game of your choice. Consider playing the bass guitar in Xbox's Rock Band or traveling the fantasy world in Wii's Super Mario Galaxy. For a bit of extreme play consider experiencing the Web 2.0 world of online, collaborative gaming such as creating your own world in The Sims or assuming the identity of your own superhero in City of Heroes, which is one of the most popular games played by adults. Before cringing at the idea of playing a massive, multiplayer online video game, you may be surprised to learn that the average age of a gamer is 30 years old. Go play!

Dr. Merrilea Mayo, director of Future Learning Initiatives at the Ewing Marion Kauffman Foundation, identified several game features that contribute to enhanced learning environments. By analyzing video-gaming research from various authors she concluded that video games foster self-efficacy, collaboration, user-directed exploration, and continuous feedback.[25] These gaming features also contribute to enhanced creativity. Improving self-efficacy leads to a greater belief in one's ability; collaboration requires group-based problem-solving; user-directed exploration incites tolerance of ambiguity and curiosity; and continuous feedback provides real-time learning to apply as one moves forward through the game. In many of the multiplayer collaborative gaming environments that exist today, beating the computer is not possible. Virtual worlds have emerged that depend on the movements of the players, where gaming is redefined as purposeful and creative engagement to achieve desired outcomes.

Building Block 2: Improvisation

When I say *improvisation* I am referring to theatrical improvisation. Even though many of the same principles apply to other forms of improvisation, such as jazz improvisation, my lens is purely from a theatrical perspective. The modern form of theatrical improvisation was developed to help actors solve problems on stage. Rather than halting a performance because lines were forgotten or something on the set was misplaced or simply missing, actors could improvise and the audience would not recognize any irregularity. The skill of theatrical improvisation has become its own art form, leading to the proliferation of improvisation style comedy clubs and the popular television show *Whose Line Is It Anyway?* hosted by Drew Carey, which ran from 1998 to 2006.

Improvisation is connected to forms of play previously discussed. The difference, however, is that the output of free play is fun and enjoyment. Given that improvisation is naturally funny, it also is connected to fun and enjoyment, yet the focus is on creating scenes and building stories with very limited physical resources.

Perceived as an art form without rules, improvisation actually does have a few guiding rules for actors on stage. A minimum structure increases the flexibility of the artist. Successful improvisation actors understand the importance of (1) listening to others without prejudgment, (2) trusting that the group (not the individual actor) will solve a particular problem, (3) building on a storyline in creative but useful ways, (4) letting go of the need to control a situation, and (5) thinking quickly and acting under pressure to maintain momentum.

The number one obstacle, however, is self-doubt, because improvisation requires one to create on the spot while being fully exposed. In other words, there is no time for planning; whatever comes out of your mouth must be used to contribute to the scene. As a result, many individuals who go through improv training acquire a heightened sense of self and a greater tolerance for failure. Remember the fear factor previously discussed in this chapter? Improvisation skills help to eliminate the fear factor, allowing ideas to flow freely in order to create scenes and build stories.

The Second City is the premiere training ground for theatrical improvisation. Second City Chicago has trained some of the finest comedic talent of this generation, such as Tina Fey, Bonnie Hunt, Mike Myers, Chris Farley, and Nia Vardalos. In 2004 Anne Libera, the artistic director of the Second City Training Center, authored *The Second City Almanac of Improvisation*, a truly masterful inside view of the art and skill of improvisation—The Second City style. At the end of each major section of the book is a list of helpful guidelines for those aspiring to master the art form. Some of these guidelines, reproduced in Exhibit 2.8, are particularly applicable to idea generation.[26]

Improvisation Prescription

A popular improvisation exercise is called "Yes, And." The essence of this exercise is very representative of improvisation doctrine. The power of *yes* in conversation cannot be

Exhibit 2.8   Select Improvisation Guidelines from The Second City

- To improvise is to expand and heighten the discoveries in the moment.
- Avoid preconceived ideas. Start each improv like a blank canvas waiting to be covered with details.
- Move action forward by adding to the last moment, not sideways by trying to wedge your idea into the fray.
- Be alert. Listen very hard to everything outside of yourself.
- Everything is important. Everything matters.
- Try not to invent. Try to discover.
- Show, don't tell.
- Think of all your possibilities or think of all the availabilities.
- Improvising is a bit like Zen archery. One must misdirect oneself to be on target.
- Incorporate the moments of discovery from the past into the institution of the future.
- Playful, direct, codeveloped ideas, information, or dreams will always be far hipper than one person's alone.
- Try to bring a brick rather than a cathedral to improv.
- Be aware of patterns; play with them.
- Treat absurd notions seriously.
- It is not a matter of setting out to "make things," but of letting the improvisation determine what will become.
- Follow the process and the product will follow.
- The less you plan, the more you will discover, and the more you plan the less you will discover.
- If you follow a fantasy long enough it becomes real.
- If you are always turning something into something you can never see what is becoming.

understated. It connotes positivity, acceptance, and a willingness to participate. We have all experienced a conversation that flowed as follows:

Jason: I have a great idea for a new way of making beer that will significantly reduce the energy used to brew beer. I want to create and market an instant beer-making powder.

Walter: Seriously? No way. The real beer enthusiasts will never go for it. The beer will never taste right. What do you think Heather?

Heather: It's an interesting idea but are you sure it hasn't already been developed? I feel like my brother tried such a powder a couple of years ago.

In a conversation such as the one among Jason, Walter, and Heather, a negative tone immediately emerges, with the result that either consciously or subconsciously, Jason's mind will likely shut down, instantly limiting his freedom to explore, create, and ideate. Furthermore, Walter and Heather offer little assistance in moving the idea forward because their focus is on judgment rather than building on Jason's original idea.

The "Yes, And" exercise does not allows words or phrases such as "Yes, but" or "No," or even just "But." If Jason, Walter, and Heather were following the rules of the "Yes And" exercise, their conversation may have gone something like this:

Jason: I have a great idea for a new way of making beer that will significantly reduce the energy used to brew beer. I want to create and market an instant beer-making powder.

Walter: Yes, and each powder packet could produce beer equivalent to one pint.

Heather: Yes, and given that it's a powder I bet supplements could be added to lessen hangover symptoms.

By forcing each response to begin with "Yes, and," a positive tone and new ideas emerge. It is a simple yet powerful exercise. Find a friend or a group of friends and play "Yes, And" to find a unique solution to a problem or create a new product idea. Be specific in your objective. For example, don't just say "Let's create a new product." The exercise works better with a clearer objective such as, "Let's create a new game to replace Trivial Pursuit." Remember, every time a participant speaks they must begin with the words, "Yes, and."

Improvisation exercises and games run the gamut of simple to complex. The more complex exercises that you see at improv comedy clubs require intense training, but the skills developed through improv apply to everything we do in life. So if you want to expand your world, open your mind, feel freer to create, acquire greater self-confidence, improve your listening skills, and learn to think quickly on your feet, then consider signing up for a theatrical improvisation course. Amateur courses are offered all around the world and not only for aspiring actors. Improvisation as a part of the corporate training repertoire is quite popular today, so if you do sign up don't be surprised when you are surrounded by entrepreneurs, salespeople, public speakers, doctors, educators, or even chefs.

Building Block 3: Observation

Earlier I cited Daniel Pink's work and his conception of workers in the twenty-first century as creators and empathizers. I bring this point up again now because observation is a vehicle for developing empathy, understanding lives and situations in the context you are studying.

Ethnography is a research method grounded in observation. The methodology was made popular in culture anthropology studies. The difference between ethnography and other forms of qualitative research is that the researcher is in the environment for an extended amount of time. The popular colloquialism "going native" helps describe ethnography because oftentimes the researcher becomes a part of the culture she is investigating. But going native is only one form of ethnography.

There is a continuum of observation, which is presented in Exhibit 2.9.[27] Some forms of ethnographic observation, as seen in this exhibit, encourage the researcher to participate in events rather than simply watch events. Participating and observing are both important because in both situations you are living in the environment that you are studying. You are observing daily and often mundane activities in order to understand a culture, create solutions to specific problems, or make lives better. For example, anthropologist Jane Goodall lived among chimpanzees in Tanzania to study family and social interaction.

Ethnography has emerged recently as a popular tool for design and new product development. Cemex, a Mexico-based international cement manufacturer, created a unique program called *Patrimonio Hoy* ("property today"). Cemex wanted to enter the market of poor rural Mexicans who spent 10 or more years building their homes in a very piecemeal, do-it-yourself fashion as cash and materials became available. Through the Patrimonio Hoy program, home owners could finance the cost of materials over a 70-week period. By paying $1,000 over 70 weeks, home owners purchased materials delivered at phased intervals as well as services from architects and inspectors. Homes were built faster and cheaper than ever before, which significantly changed the lives of rural Mexicans.

What is most interesting to this discussion on ethnography is how Cemex generated the Patrimonio Hoy idea. The company sent a group of architects, salespeople, and construction workers to live in different poor, rural neighborhoods for months to acquire a deeper understanding of why and how homes were built in this market.

IDEO, an international product design firm with offices throughout the United States, Europe, and Asia, uses a design approach that includes observation, prototyping, building, and storytelling. The "Grocery Cart Challenge" was popularized in an ABC *Nightline* episode that aired on July 13, 1999. *Nightline* challenged an IDEO team to redesign the shopping cart in 10 days. A fascinating story unfolded. IDEO heavily relied on observation as a data gathering method and stimulus to generate new ideas for the redesign. IDEO designers went shopping, watching consumers load carts with items and navigate crowded aisles. They noticed how children sat in the carts and leaned outside the cart to touch items on the shelves. Safety became a variable in need of change as did ease of navigation. Furthermore, the team talked to grocery store managers, cashiers, stockers, and others, where they learned how fast a grocery cart can travel when left outside in a windstorm and how many carts are stolen from the premises on an annual basis.

All of this information significantly contributed to the redesign: Wheels with a 360-degree turning radius, a safer child seat with a play surface to keep children engaged inside the cart, removable modular baskets, and other features created a completely redesigned, award-wining grocery cart that would not have been possible without observation.

Exhibit 2.9   Observation Continuum

Observation Type	Description	Example
Active participant observation (going native)	Researcher is a full participant in the world being studied and is able to behave and act just as others do.	A researcher chooses to study poverty and homelessness. She abandons her home, throws away all credit cards, and lives on the streets for two years without a job, income, or housing.
Moderate participant observation	Researcher strikes an equal balance between observation and participation but never really will be an accepted member of the culture or activity being studied. The goal is to gain acceptance so one can acquire a more intimate understanding of what is being observed and studied.	A researcher wants to study the culture of poker players. She attends tournaments as an accepted fan (observer) and later may enter a tournament because she's learned the game. She interacts with players, asks questions, and briefly participates in the life of poker players but never tries to master the skill of poker playing.
Passive participant observation	Present at the scene of action but does not interact, engage, or participate with research subjects or activities. The researcher is in observation mode at the scene.	A person is thinking about starting a new coffee shop. He sits in a Starbucks and counts people passing through, what they purchase, and how they use the space they are in.
Observation only (no participation)	The researcher has no involvement or interaction with people or activities studied—not even present at the scene.	A person watches reality television shows to assess the treatment and portrayal of women.

Observation Prescription

Yes, it seems simple and intuitive, so why don't we practice observation more often? First, we think we are already observant, so we observe only what we allow ourselves to see or what has become "normal" or "natural" for us to see. Second, we don't necessarily know what to look for, and we think we must observe something extraordinary. The irony

Exhibit 2.10   Observation Dimensions

	Dimension	Description
1	Space	The physical place or places
2	Actor	The people involved
3	Activity	A set of related acts people do
4	Object	The physical things that are present
5	Act	Single actions that people do
6	Event	A set of related activities that people carry out
7	Time	The sequencing that takes place over time
8	Goal	The things people are trying to accomplish
9	Feeling	The emotions felt and expressed

Source: Adapted from James Spradley, *Participant Observation* (Orlando, FL: Harcourt Brace, 1980), 58–61.

is that you should observe the mundane, the everyday activities or motions. The goal of observation is to develop empathy for those you are watching, but empathy only emerges from truly understanding what the person is going through, as if you were going through the same thing.

Pick a people-gathering place to observe for a minimum of two hours. This could be a coffee shop, restaurant, bus depot, subway station, church, classroom, hair salon, car dealership—any place you want. Prior to observing you need a plan—a list of observation guidelines. The guidelines you establish in advance will help you focus your observation so that you are better able to collect significant and relevant data. Exhibit 2.10 offers a list of dimensions that can be observed. These dimensions can help codify your observations while you are in the field. The nine dimensions guide your observations so that you notice the environment, who is there, what they are doing, the artifacts being used, and so on.

For everything you observe, record notes—lots of notes. Do not discount the relevance of any piece of data. Take the time and observe movement, actions, processes, that the average observer would not notice. I bet that if you lifted your eyes right now from these pages, you would immediately observe things you have never seen before in your current space. You are already training your eyes to see the world from a different perspective!

After observing a people-gathering space for two hours, review your field notes and add to them any thoughts that have emerged since the observation. Next, write down at least 15 new ideas for products and services based on your notes. They do not have to be complete ideas, but through this exercise you should be able to see the power of observation in the idea generation process.

Connecting Play, Improvisation, and Observation

The three competencies of idea generation—play, improvisation, and observation—are each important but together they represent a powerful and symbiotic relationship that forms the foundation for idea generation mastery (Exhibit 2.11). Play is about fun and enjoyment; improvisation relates to creating and building; and through observation we seek to understand and identify meaning or significance. When play is combined with improvisation there is a freedom that emerges; when play intersects with observation, that freedom turns to imagination; and when skills of improvisation are used with skills

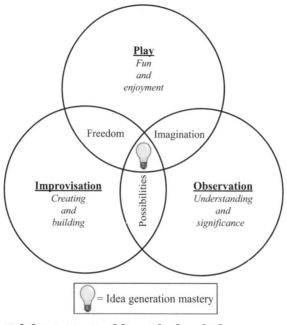

Exhibit 2.11   Building Blocks of Idea Generation

of observation, a plethora of possibilities surface. Freedom plus imagination plus possibilities equals innumerable novel and useful ideas. An individual, particularly an adult, who can develop the core competencies of play, improvisation, and observation and use them in a deeply interconnected way will be a master idea generator. Enjoy the journey!

New Eyes for New Futures

The purpose of this chapter is to identify the building blocks of idea generation that can be developed and trained over time. Creativity is something we are *all* born with, but it must be cultivated with care and intention. The work is tiring but fun, exhausting but invigorating, scary but exciting, uncomfortable but comfortable. Remember, the most creative people work both ends of the spectrum, embrace contrast, and know that both the left and right hemispheres of the brain need to be utilized.

"It is not the strongest of species that survives, nor the most intelligent; it is the one that is the most adaptable to change." This famous quote attributed to Charles Darwin, 1809–1882, highlights humanity as a creative and evolving force. Without our human ability to be creative and generate ideas, where would we be as a society? As entrepreneurs we must embrace and develop this fuzzy, ambiguous, nonlinear, and sometimes frustrating skill known as creativity. It is time to play, to observe, to improvise in order to develop a new frame of mind for a new future. The world needs you to generate new ideas that generate value!

As a point of departure I would like to leave you with a technique that is essential to any creativity tool kit. I am a believer in images and portraying information in a visual and concise way, so I can see connections, disconnections, redundancies, and gaps, and

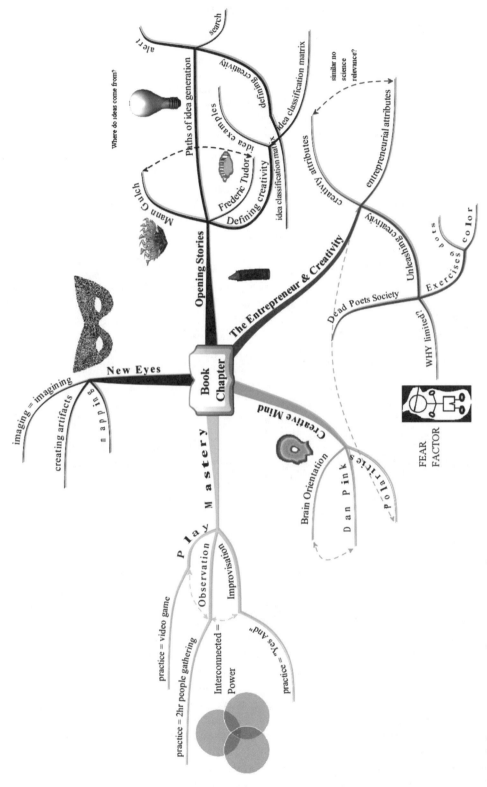

Exhibit 2.12   Mind Map Example

49

simply be more imaginative. Text, though useful, is too much part of our daily rituals. It helps us very little to view the world in a unique way; text gives us all the same lens. Have you ever written a paper and then gone back to proofread the paper—probably multiple times? You were certain that you had caught and fixed all the typos, yet when you got the paper back from a teacher or editor you saw that you had missed many other mistakes. "But," you might say to yourself, "I read through that paper at least ten times. How could I have missed those?"

When you are with the same material for an extended amount of time you are unable to see the irregularities, to see things afresh. To generate ideas I encourage you to experiment with mind-mapping—a visual, nonlinear depiction of data using hierarchies, associations, categories, colors, symbols, and pictures. Mind mapping is a powerful idea generation tool.

Exhibit 2.12 is a mind map I created *before* writing this chapter. I used Tony Buzan's software call iMindMap.[28] All mind maps start with a central image, and in my case this was a book. Following the central image clockwise, starting with "Opening Stories," you can see the visual outline of my chapter, how it flows, and how it unfolds. Simple words and pictures are used to capture thoughts on how I wanted the chapter to unfold.

The first version of the map was very different than the one you see here. I reconfigured sections, added branches, and deleted branches. New ideas emerged as I began mapping, and by viewing the map on one page I was able to determine where I needed a new story or when to connect a later concept to an earlier concept. Finally, by looking at my mind map I'm sure you can better recall the contents of this chapter. Thus, mind mapping is a tool for creating, problem solving, organizing, note taking, and outlining. The next time you have to create something (a proposal, a report, a book chapter) or have a problem to solve, try mind mapping and see how much more productive you become.

Downloadable Resources for this chapter available at www.wiley.com/go/portablembainentrepreneurship

Ideaspace Exercise
Nine-Dot Exercise

Notes

1. Many classifications exist in the entrepreneurship and creativity literatures. For example, Sharon Alvarez and Jay Barney use the terminology *Discovery Theory* and *Creation Theory* in their working paper, "Discovery & Creation: Alternative Theories of Entrepreneurial Action." My classification is supported by their work but my interest in this chapter is on idea generation only and not necessarily entrepreneurial action that is defined, according to Alvarez and Barney, "as any activity entrepreneurs might take—from initially identifying opportunities, to assembling resources to exploit opportunities, to generating and appropriating the economic profits created by exploiting opportunities—to produce new products or services" (p. 5). As a result of our different foci, my classification scheme differs in some contexts but is also inspired by the work of Israel Kirzner (1985).

2. Proceedings of the Massachusetts Historical Society, 1933. http://www.iceharvestingusa.com/Frederic%20Tudor%20Ice%20King.html.

3. Norman Maclean, *Young Men and Fire* (Chicago: University of Chicago Press, 1992), 101.

4. Time Magazine Online Jan 8 2006 The Hidden Secrets of the Creative Mind http://www.time.com/time/magazine/article/0,9171,1147152,00.html.

5. T. Amabile, *Creativity in Context* (Boulder, CO: Westview Press, 1996), 35.

6. Attributes from John J. Kao, *Entrepreneurship, Creativity & Organization* (London: Prentice-Hall, 1989), 15–16. His list is compiled from the work of E. Raudsepp, "Profile of the Creative Individual," *Creative Computing*, August 1983; and A. Roe, "Psychological Approaches to Creativity in Science," in M. A. Coler and H. K. Hughes, eds., *Essays on Creativity in the Sciences* (New York: New York University, 1963).

7. J. Timmons and S. Spinelli, *New Venture Creation*, 8th ed. (Boston: McGraw-Hill, 2009), 47.

8. D. Y. Hamidi, K. Wennberg, and H. Berglund, "Creativity in Entrepreneurship Education," *Journal of Small Business and Enterprise Development* 15(2): 301–320.

9. See David McClelland's work in the 1960s and John B. Miner, *The 4 Routes to Entrepreneurial Success* (Berrett-Koehler, 1996).

10. From final script of the theatrical release of Dead Poets Society, reproduced at http://www10.pair.com/crazydv/weir/dps/script.html.

11. E. Raudsepp and G. Hough, *Creative Growth Games* (New York: Jove Publications, 1977). The nine-dot exercise is referred to as "Breaking Out" and is found on page 29. Solution is on page 113.

12. Ibid., 113.

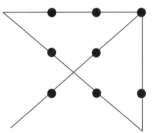

13. Ibid., 18–19.

14. James Adams, *Conceptual Blockbusting*, 4th ed. (Cambridge, MA: Perseus, 2001), 45.

15. Carol Kinsey Goman, *Creativity in Business: A Practical Guide for Creative Thinking*, rev. ed. (Cengage Learning, 2000).

16. Mihaly Csikszentmihalyi, *Creativity: Flow and the Psychology of Discovery and Invention* (New York: Harper Collins, 1996).

17. Ibid., 76.

18. Alex Osborn, *Applied Imagination: Principles and Procedures of Creative Problem Solving* (Buffalo, NY: Creative Education Foundation, 2001), 41.

19. Ibid., 156.

20. Sandra Stone works in childhood education. Her articles introduced the three forms of play and she states they are based on Piaget's 1962 cognitive levels of play, but his forms of play do not follow Stone's exact terminology. I choose to use Stone's work because her description of the play forms has the most relevance to my work here. Important citations include S. J. Stone, "Integrating Play into the Curriculum," *Childhood Education* 72(2): 104–107; and J. Piaget, *Play, Dreams, and Imitation in Childhood* (New York: Norton, 1962).

21. http://www.museumofplay.org/about_play/index.html.

22. Finding this quote is attributed to Suzanne De Castell and Jennifer Jenson, who wrote the article "Serious Play" in the *Journal of Curriculum Studies* 35(6): 649–665. The Lawrence-Lightfoot quote was in Y. Kafai, *Minds in Play: Computer Game Design as a Context for Children's Learning* (Hillsdale, NJ: Erlbaum, 1995), 314.

23. M. Csikszentmihalyi, "Play and Intrinsic Rewards," *Journal of Humanistic Psychology* 15:41–63.

24. Ibid., 43.

25. Merrilea Mayo, "Want to Truly Scale a Learning Program? Try Gaming," *Kauffmann Thoughtbook 2009* (Kansas City, MO: Kauffman Foundation, 2009), 26–31.

26. Anne Libera, *The Second City Almanac of Improvisation* (Evanston, IL: Northwestern University Press, 2004). Guidelines are reproduced from pages 23, 24, 57, 82, 83, 101, 104, 132, 160, and 161.

27. Adapted from James Spradley, *Participant Observation* (Orlando, FL: Harcourt Brace, 1980), 58–61. The chart reproduced here was created as part of an assignment description in classes co-taught with my colleagues Dennis Ceru and Steve Schiffmann.

28. Tony Buzan invented mind mapping and his software is one of the most tested softwares on the market.

3

Opportunity Recognition, Shaping, and Reshaping

Andrew Zacharakis

How This Chapter Fits into a Typical MBA Curriculum

Entrepreneurship is all about opportunity. Would-be entrepreneurs often have one of two things on their minds: "How do I come up with a good business idea?" (Chapter 2) and "Is this idea big enough to make a successful business?" This chapter focuses on evaluating ideas and assessing whether they are indeed good opportunities. As such, most entrepreneurship courses devote some time to this question. Opportunity recognition most commonly occurs in introductory entrepreneurship courses and provides the foundation for follow-on courses in business planning, entrepreneurial marketing, entrepreneurial finance, and so forth. While an idea is necessary to entrepreneurship, it isn't sufficient. To have a successful entrepreneurial endeavor, your idea needs to be an opportunity.

Who Uses This Material in the Real World—and Why It Is Important

Entrepreneurship occurs on several levels. Entrepreneurs who are creating new ventures either within an existing organization (corporate entrepreneurship) or as a stand-alone venture need to assess the nature of the opportunity so that they can build a successful business model. Existing corporations continuously search and scan the environment for new opportunities that their company can pursue. While businesspeople can haphazardly fall into a successful opportunity, you have a better chance of success by searching, shaping, and reshaping the opportunity. Thus, it isn't too far-fetched to say that all businesses follow opportunity recognition processes to a certain degree.

From Glimmer to Action: How Do I Come Up with a Good Idea?

Belief in your idea is a great thing. But first step back and ask a more important question: "Is this idea an *attractive* opportunity?" Moving from an idea to a viable opportunity is an iterative process. Entrepreneurs need to conduct a series of tests—what we refer to as market tests—to identify interesting ideas and then see whether they are viable opportunities. Each test is an escalation of commitment, an important step to successfully launching the venture. So the process of recognizing, shaping, and reshaping an opportunity combines thought and action to take the idea from formulation to execution.

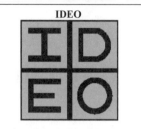

You may not have heard of them but, chances are, they've designed a product you own. Based in Palo Alto, California (with offices around the world), IDEO was founded in 1991 through the merger of three design firms. In the time since they've been in business, IDEO and its eclectic band of employees have designed products and solutions ranging from Apple's first mouse to a shifting mechanism for Caterpillar to a supply chain innovation called "chimney stacking" for Kraft.

IDEO helps various companies design products, services, and customer experiences.

www.ideo.com/work/clients

Exhibit 3.1 IDEO

Both are critical as you embark on your entrepreneurial adventure. In this chapter, we lay out the opportunity recognition process from the very beginning and move through opportunity shaping and reshaping.

All good opportunities start with the customer. Most often, entrepreneurs come across opportunities by noting that there is some product or service they would like but can't find. This is your first interaction with a customer—yourself. To validate this idea, you need to go further by gathering stimuli. IDEO, a very successful product innovation company (see Exhibit 3.1), does this through a process called *customer anthropology*, in which the IDEO team goes out and observes the customer in action in their natural environment and identifies their pain points.[1] For example, in an ABC *Nightline* segment about IDEO, the team went to a grocery store to better understand how customers shop and, more specifically, how they use a shopping cart. The team's mission was to observe, ask questions, and record information. They did not ask leading questions in hopes that the customer would validate a preconceived notion of what that shopping cart should be. Instead the questions were open-ended.

Beware the leading question. As an entrepreneur who is excited about your concept, you may find it all too easy to ask, "Wouldn't your life be better if you had concept X?" or "Don't you think my product/service idea is better than what exists?" While this might be a direct way to validate your idea, it requires that people answer honestly and that they understand exactly what they need. Most people like to be nice and they want to be supportive of new ideas, until they actually have to pay money for them. In addition, many times people can't envision your product/service until it actually exists, so their feedback may be biased. During the *gathering stimuli* phase, act as if you were Dian Fossey observing mountain gorillas in Africa—just *observe*. Ideally, you'll gather stimuli as a team so that you have multiple interpretations of what you have learned. Through this process you will hopefully identify an opportunity.

The next phase in the IDEO process is to *multiply stimuli*. Here, the team members report back on their findings and then start brainstorming on the concept and how to improve upon the solution. As was highlighted in Chapter 2, the comedy improv process can facilitate idea generation. A group of actors (usually three to four) pose a situation to the audience and then let the audience shout out the next situation or reply that one actor is to give to another. From these audience suggestions, the actors build a hilarious skit. The key to success is to always say "Yes, and . . ." Doing so allows the skit to build upon itself and create a seamless and comical whole. Likewise, multiplying stimuli requires that the team take the input of others and build upon it. Be a bit wild-eyed in this process. Let all ideas, no matter how far-fetched, be heard and built upon, because even if you don't incorporate them into the final concept, they might lead to new insights that are ultimately important to the product's competitive advantage.

Remember that "yes and . . ." means that you build upon the input of your colleagues. All too often in a group setting it is easy to say, "That won't work because . . ." These kinds of devil's advocate debates, while important in the later phases of business development, can prematurely kill off creative extensions in this early phase. Also beware of "Yes, but . . ." statements, which are really just another way of saying, "Your idea won't work and here's why . . ." The key to this phase of development is to generate as many diverse ideas as possible.

As you go through this multiplication stage, *brain-writing* is a useful technique to avoid prematurely squashing interesting extensions. The process is like brainstorming, but the focus is on written rather than verbal communication. The biggest shortcoming of brainstorming is that it opens up the opportunity for the most vocal or opinionated members of the group to dominate the conversation and idea generation process. In contrast, brain-writing ensures that everyone has a chance to contribute ideas. To start, the team identifies a number of core alternative variations to the central idea (or, if you have a disparate team, as you might for an entrepreneurship class, use each member's favored idea). Put the core ideas onto separate flip-chart sheets and attach them to the wall. Then the team and trusted friends, or classmates, go around and add "Yes, and . . ." enhancements to each idea. Keep circulating among the flip-chart sheets until everyone has had an opportunity to think about and add to each idea. At the end of that cycle, you'll have several interesting enhancements to consider. Instead of publicly discussing the ideas, have everybody vote on the three to five they like best by placing different color Post-it Notes on the sheets. In essence, this is another market test in which your team and other interested parties are gauging the viability of the idea.[2]

Once you've narrowed the field to the idea and features you think have the most potential, the next step is to create customer concepts. In other words, build a simple mock-up of what the product will look like. This helps the team visualize the final product and see which features/attributes are appealing, which are detrimental, and which are nice to have but not necessary. Keep in mind that this mock-up doesn't need to be functional; it is just a tool to solidify what everybody is visualizing and to help the team think through how the product should be modified.

When your team is developing a service, your mock-up won't necessarily be a physical representation, but some kind of abstract modeling of what you hope to achieve. For example, the initial mock-up for a restaurant is often just a menu. Entrepreneurs who want to take the research process even further will often test the product or service in a low-cost way. Wally Amos was the first African-American talent agent for William Morris. In building his clientele, Wally would greet potential clients with chocolate chip cookies. The cookies were a hit and Wally continually refined and tested variations of his recipe. In 1975, Wally decided to sell his cookies and so the Famous Amos Chocolate Chip Cookie store was born.[3] Wally's process allowed him to get a reaction to the recipes and think through how to modify them to better suit customer expectations and tastes. This process allows for rapid-fire prototyping of ideas, and it also provides the luxury of failing early and often before making substantial investments in a bricks-and-mortar establishment.

Quite often at this stage people overdevelop the product and incorporate every bell and whistle that the team has come up with during the brainstorming process. This is fine—but the next and last step is to *optimize practicality,* when the team will identify those features that are either unnecessary, impractical, or simply too expensive.

This is the phase in which it is important to play devil's advocate. As the IDEO developers state, it is a time for the grown-ups to decide which features are the most important to optimize. If the previous steps have gone well, the team has learned a tremendous amount about what the customer may want, and that means they have a deeper understanding of the features/attributes that create the greatest value for the customer.

BigBelly Solar used this approach to transform a great idea into a winning solution. Founder Jim Poss and his team determined that the most important attributes of their solar-powered trash-compacting receptacles were durability (the bins were in public places and rough treatment or vandalism was a real threat), size (the receptacle couldn't be overly large or it wouldn't fit in the public places intended, and the bags couldn't weigh too much when filled), and price (the higher up-front purchase cost had to be offset by the reduced trips to collect trash, so the receptacle would pay for itself within a year). Understanding these basic parameters helped Jim's team refine their original design. For durability, they found that sheet metal was a cost-effective casing, that a Lexan plastic cover on the solar panel prevented vandalism and accidental chipping, and so forth. They went through a similar process to determine the right size. These steps helped them design a product that the customer would want, at a price the customer was willing to pay.[4]

The entire idea generation process is iterative. At each of the four steps we've presented, you learn, adjust, and refine. You start to understand the critical criteria that customers use in their purchase decision and the pain points in building your product or delivering your service. This process allows you to identify and refine your idea with relatively little cost, compared to the costs you would have incurred if you'd immediately opened your doors for business with what you mistakenly believed to be the most important attributes. Nonetheless, up to this point you still don't know whether your idea, which is now very robust and well thought out, is a viable opportunity.

Is Your Idea an Opportunity?

While the idea generation process helps you shape your idea so that it is clearer and more robust, it is only part of the process. The difference between venture success and failure is a function of whether your idea is truly an opportunity. Before quitting your

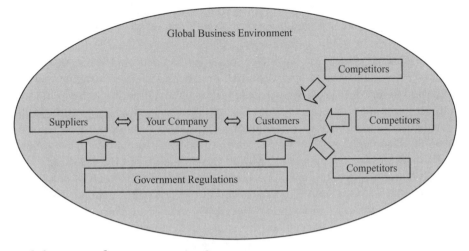

Exhibit 3.2   The Opportunity Space

job and investing your own resources (as well as those of your family and friends), spend some time studying the viability of your idea. There are five major areas you need to fully understand prior to your launch: (1) customers, (2) competitors, (3) suppliers and vendors, (4) the government, and (5) the broader global environment (see Exhibit 3.2). We'll discuss each of these areas in turn.

The Customer

Who is your customer? This broad question, the first you must answer, can be problematic. For instance, you might be tempted to think, if you're hoping to open a restaurant, that anyone who would want to eat in a restaurant is your customer. In other words, just about everyone in the world except for the few hundred hermits spread out across the country. But you need to narrow down your customer base so that you can optimize the features most important to your customer. So a better question is, who is your *core* customer? Understanding who our primary customer is allows us to better direct our efforts and resources to reach that customer.

We can further refine this definition. Starting with your initial definition, break your customers down into three categories: primary target audience (PTA), secondary target audience (STA), and tertiary target audience (TTA). Most of your attention should focus on the PTA. These are the customers you believe are most likely to buy at a price that preserves your margins, and with a frequency that reaches your target revenues. For example, imagine that you are opening a fast casual Thai restaurant. The sector is growing, even during an economic downturn, as consumers seek less expensive food that does not sacrifice quality.[5] Fast casual restaurants usually have larger footprints (more square feet) than fast-food restaurants and food court outlets. Thus, you want a customer willing to pay a bit more than a fast-food customer for perceived higher quality. A wise location might be a destination mall with outlets like Barnes and Noble, Pottery Barn, and other stores that attract middle-income and higher-income shoppers. Your PTA, in this situation, might be soccer moms (30 to 45 years old, with household incomes ranging from $50,000 to $150,000). These women tend to shop, watch what they eat, and enjoy ethnic food

During the investigation stage, you would focus your attention on better understanding your PTA. How often do they shop? How often do they eat out? What meals are they more likely to eat outside the home? What other activities do they participate in besides shopping and dining out? What you are collecting is information about things like income and ethnicity (demographics), and about personality traits and values (psychographics[6]). Both categories help you design and market your product or service.

During the launch phase, you would design the décor in a manner that most appeals to the PTA. You would create a menu that addresses their dietary concerns and appeals to their palette. During operations, you would market towards your PTA and train your employees to interact with them in an appropriate and effective manner. Note that the efforts across the three stages of your venture (investigation, launch, and operations) are different than they would be if you were launching a fast-food restaurant or a fancy sit-down French restaurant, because your target audience is different.

While you should focus most of your attention to your PTA, the STA group also deserves attention. The PTA may be your most frequent, loyal customers, but to increase your revenues you'll want to bring in some of your STA as well. In the restaurant example, your STA may be men with similar demographics as your PTA, older couples who are active and near retirement age, and younger yuppie post-college working professionals (see the box describing the demographics of fast casual customers). These groups are likely to find your restaurant appealing, but may not attend with the same frequency (possibly more on weekends or during the dinner hour versus lunch). Your STA may also be part of your growth strategy. For instance, after you get past your first two to three restaurants, you may choose to expand your menu or your location profile (urban centers, for instance). Understanding which STA is the most lucrative helps you make better growth decisions.

Fast Casual Demographics

The growth in the fast casual segment is due to the generation of consumers who grew up on fast food and won't eat it anymore, plus aging baby boomers looking for healthier alternatives and who can afford to pay a little more for better quality. Moreover, the price of a meal in a moderately priced restaurant has dropped and is now only 25 percent more than the price of a meal purchased in a grocery store and prepared at home, making dining out an economically viable alternative. Fast casual is also now competing evenly on price with upscale grocery stores that offer expensive ready-to-eat meals. According to *Fast Casual* magazine online, the 2009 Fast Casual State of the Industry Report shows 18 percent growth in the fast casual restaurant industry from 2007 to 2008 in spite of the challenging economic environment. Other fast casual demographics and psychographics:

1. The 18 to 34 age group is most likely to opt for fast casual and makes up 37 percent of the traffic at such outlets.

2. A newly emerging segment of fast casual consumers is married, dual income couples with no kids (known as *DINKs*). These DINKs range in age from 35 to 54, and 38 percent own a home worth $100,000 to $199,000. They make up 28 percent of the customer base.

3. Fifteen percent of fast casual customers were under 18.

4. Casual dining is too slow for kids; parents don't want to eat fast food.

5. Fast casual restaurants offer teens on dates a destination their parents are comfortable with that does not serve alcohol.

6. Casual dining has now become an event, not a spur-of-the-moment dining decision.

Sources: E-Business Trends (Food and Beverage), August 21, 2002, http://www.army.mil/cfsc/documents/business/trends/E-TRENDS-8-21-02.doc; "Fast-Casual Restaurant Trends Forecast 2009" webinar, http://www.fastcasual.com/white_paper.php?id=1648; Fred Minnick, "Knowing Your Customer," *Fast Casual* magazine, May 30, 2006, http://www.fastcasual.com/article.php? id=5120&na=1&prc=43

Finally, your TTA requires a little attention. During the investigation and launch stage, you shouldn't spend much time on the TTA. However, once you begin operating, a TTA may emerge that has more potential then you originally realized. Keeping your eyes and ears open during operations helps you adjust and refine your opportunity to better capture the most lucrative customers. In our Thai restaurant example, you might find that soccer moms aren't your PTA, but that some unforeseen group emerges, such as university students. If you segment your customer groups throughout the three stages as we have outlined, you'll be better prepared to adapt your business model if some of your preconceptions turn out to be incorrect.

We've said it's important to understand your audience's demographics and psychographics. Part of your investigation phase should include creating customer profiles. Exhibit 3.3 provides a sampling of the types of demographics and psychographics that might be used in describing your customer.

Exhibit 3.3   Common Demographic/Psychographic Categories

Demographics	Psychographics
Age	Social group (e.g., white collar, blue collar, etc.)
Gender	Lifestyle (e.g., mainstream, sexual orientation, materialistic, active, athletic, etc.)
Household income	
Family size/family life cycle	Personality traits (worriers, type A's, shy, extroverted, etc.)
Occupation	
Education level	Values (liberal, conservative, open-minded, traditional, etc.)
Religion	
Ethnicity/heritage	
Nationality	
Social class	
Marital status	

Trends

Customers aren't static groups that remain the same over time. They evolve, they change, they move from one profile to another. In order to best capture customers, you need to spot trends that are currently influencing their buying behavior and that might influence it in the future. When considering trends, look at broader macro trends and then funnel down to a more narrow focus on how those trends affect your customer groups. Trends might also occur within customer groups that don't affect the broader population.

One of the most influential trends in the macro environment within the United States over the past 50 years has been the life cycle of the baby boom generation. Born between 1946 and 1964, the country's 77.6 million baby boomers are usually married (69.4 percent), well educated (college graduation rates hit 19.1 percent at the end of the boomer generation, compared to just 6 percent for prior generations), and active (46 percent of boomers exercise regularly).[7] What links them as a generation is the experience of growing up in post–World War II America, a time of tremendous growth and change in this nation's history.

Since they represent such a large percentage of the U.S. population, it is no wonder that they have created numerous new categories of products and services. For example, in the 1950s the disposable diaper industry emerged and then exploded to the point where today it has $4.32 billion in sales. In the late 1950s and through the 1960s, the rapidly growing population created a need for large numbers of new schools, which in turn led to a building frenzy. (Now you know why so many schools were named after former President John F. Kennedy.) In the late 1960s and 1970s, the rock and roll industry exploded. Then in the 1980s, as these baby boomers became parents, a new car category was created (the minivan) which saved Chrysler from bankruptcy. In the 1990s the boomers were in their prime working years, and new investment categories emerged to help them plan for their retirement and their children's college educations. Today, as the boomers age, we see growth in pharmaceuticals and other industries related to the more mature segment. According to one market research firm, "boomers are expected to change America's concepts of aging, just as they have about every previous life stage they have passed through."[8] How does this macro trend influence your idea?

Numerous macro trends affect the potential demand for your product or service. Trends create new product/service categories, or emerging markets, that can be especially fruitful places to find strong entrepreneurial opportunities. The convergence of multiple trends enhances the power of an opportunity like the Internet boom. First the PC became common in the workplace, and as a result many Americans grew comfortable using it. That led to a proliferation of PCs in the home, especially for children and teenagers who used it for school, work, and video games. While the Internet had been available for decades, the development by Tim Berners Lee of the World Wide Web system of hyperlinks connecting remote computers, followed by the development of the Mosaic Web browser (the precursor to Netscape and Explorer), and the proliferation of Internet service providers like Prodigy and AOL, created huge opportunities for commerce online. From the very first domain name—symbolics.com—assigned in 1985, the Web has evolved into an integral component of the modern economy. Even though many dot-coms failed, others have established themselves as profitable household names, like eBay and Amazon. That many of these successful businesses have become *multibillion*-dollar companies in less than a decade speaks to the incredible power of convergent trends.

Trends also occur in smaller market segments and may be just as powerful as macro trends; in fact, they may be precursors to larger macro trends. For example, according to Packaged Facts, a market research consultancy, the market for religious products (including blockbuster movies, pop music, clothing, books, and even games and toys) will reach $6 billion in annual sales by 2013.[9] This represents 21 percent annual growth from the $5.6 billion sold in 2004. Indeed, major companies are capitalizing on this market. At the end of 2005 Starbucks announced it would be featuring a quotation on its coffee cups from Rick Warren, pastor and best-selling author of *The Purpose Driven Life,* which includes the line, "You were made by God and for God, and until you understand that, life will never make sense."[10] While the quote is just one of many that the company featured on its coffee cups, you can rest assured that the decision to include it was a calculated move to make the company's products more appealing to the growing Christian market.

Another important trend is the changing demographics of the U.S. population. By many estimates, in 2030 nearly one in four United States residents will be a Hispanic if current trends hold.[11] With the incredible growth in both size and purchasing power of this untapped market, it's no wonder that companies are scrambling to serve emerging opportunities. The past decade has seen a proliferation of media outlets targeting the Spanish-speaking U.S. population, and since some pundits believe the Hispanic population could emerge as the next middle class, it's likely more and more companies will find ways to capture this enormous demographic.

Trends often foretell emerging markets and suggest when the window of opportunity for an industry is about to open. Exhibit 3.4 lists some influential trends over the past 50 years. However, it is the underlying convergence of trends that helps us measure the power of our ideas and whether they are truly opportunities.

How Big Is the Market?

Trends suggest increasing market demand. Thus, one of the questions that distinguish ideas from opportunities asks whether there is sufficient market demand to generate the level of revenues necessary to make this an exciting career option. As mentioned in Chapter 1, an entrepreneur typically needs the new venture to generate a minimum of $600,000 per year in revenue to meet market rates on a forgone salary of $70,000 plus benefits. While this level might make a nice mom-and-pop store, many entrepreneurs

Exhibit 3.4   Important Trends over the Past 50 Years

Trend	Impact
Baby boom generation	Pampers, rock and roll, television, minivans, real estate, McMansions, and so on.
Personal computing	Internet, media on demand, electronic publishing, spreadsheets, electronic communication
Obesity	Drain on health care system, growth of diet industry, changes in food industry, health clubs, home gyms
Dual-income households	Child care, home services—landscaping, house cleaning, prepared foods

are interested in creating something bigger. The larger your goals, the more important are your market demand forecasts.

To accurately gauge your demand, start at the larger macro market and funnel demand down to your segment and your geographic location. Granted, as you expand, you'll likely move beyond your segment and your geographic origins, but the most critical years for any venture are its first two. You need to be certain that you can survive the startup, and that means you need to be confident of your base demand.

Let's go back to our Thai fast casual restaurant example to begin to understand how large our market demand might be. Exhibit 3.5 steps through the demand forecast. It is best to start with the overall market size—in this case, the size of the entire restaurant industry in the U.S. Next, segment the industry into relevant categories. We are interested in both the relative size of the fast casual segment as well as the size of the ethnic segment. It would be ideal to find the size of the fast casual ethnic (or better yet, Thai) segment, but as you narrow down to your opportunity there is likely to be less information because you may be riding new trends that suggest future demand that has yet to materialize.

Finally, during your initial launch, you'll likely have some geographic focus. Extrapolate your overall market data so that it captures your geographic market. In this case, we took the population of the towns within a five-mile drive along the major thoroughfare on which our restaurant would be located and multiplied that percentage of the state population by the total spent in the state (Massachusetts). Basically, for this last step you should try to assess the number of soccer moms in your geographic reach. The U.S. census makes this very easy as it breaks out demographics by town. Thus, it appears that there are roughly 14,000 soccer moms in this target market.

Market Size Today and into the Future

While it is important to size your market today, you'll also need to know how big it will be in the future. If you are taking advantage of trends, your market is likely growing. Attractive opportunities open up in growing markets because there is more demand than supply, and a new firm doesn't need to compete on price. In the early years when the firm is going through a rapid learning curve, operational expenses will be proportionately higher than in later years when the firm has established efficient procedures and systems. Market growth also means that your competitors are seeking all the new customers entering the market rather than trying to steal customers away from you.

Projecting growth is notoriously difficult, but you can make some educated guesses by looking at trends and determining overall market size, as previously described. Then make some estimates of what type of market penetration you might be able to achieve and how long it will take you to get there. If all else fails, the easiest thing to do is verify past growth. As trend analysis tells us, past growth is usually correlated with future growth, which means you can make reasonable estimates based on historical numbers. The *S curve* is a powerful concept that highlights the diffusion of product acceptance over time.[12] When a product or innovation is first introduced, few people are aware of it. Typically, the firm has to educate consumers about why they need this product and the value it offers. Hence, the firm concentrates its efforts on early adopters. It is expensive to develop the right concept and educate the consumer, but the firm can offset this cost somewhat by charging a high price.

As customers react to the concept, the company and other new entrants learn and modify the original product to better meet customer needs. At a certain point (designated

Exhibit 3.5   Market Size for Thai Fast Casual Restaurant

Overall amount spent on dining out projected for 2007	**$491.2 Billion[a]**
Size of market segments	
Full service restaurants	**$181.6 Billion[b]**
Quick service restaurants (including fast casual)	**$150.1 Billion**
Cafeterias, grills, and buffets	**$5.4 Billion**
Social caterers	**$6.1 Billion**
Snack and nonalcoholic beverage bars	**$20.2 Billion**
Bars and taverns	**$15.8 Billion**
Market share for ethnic restaurants	**$163.7 Billion[c]**
Market share by region	
New England	**$23.1 Billion[d]**
Middle Atlantic	**$54.1 Billion**
South Atlantic	**$81.2 Billion**
East North Central	**$61.4 Billion**
East South Central	**$21.5 Billion**
West North Central	**$25.8 Billion**
West South Central	**$44.5 Billion**
Mountain	**$28.9 Billion**
Pacific	**$73.4 Billion**
Massachusetts	
Overall restaurant sales	**$11.7 Billion[e]**
Ethnic	**$245.7 Million[f]**
Natick (we are opening in Natick shopping district)	**$234 Million[g]**
Massachusetts population 6.4M	
Natick population 32K	
Framingham population 67K	
Wellesley population 29K	
Soccer Moms (women ages 30–45) 14K	**$19 Million**

[a]R. Ebbin, B. Grindy, H. Riehle, D. Roach, and T. Smith "Restaurant Industry Sales Trends in Recent Years," *2007 Restaurant Industry Forecast*. National Restaurant Association, 2007: 38.
[b]Ibid.
[c]"Fullservice Steams Ahead", *Restaurants USA*, October 2001. This article estimates that ethnic food accounts for one-third of total restaurant sales, so we multiplied the total industry size by one-third.
[d]R. Ebbin, B. Grindy, H. Riehle, D. Roach, and T. Smith, "Projected Growth in State and Regional Economic Indicators," *2007 Restaurant Industry Forecast*, National Restaurant Association, 2007: 38.
[e]Ibid.
[f]Based on 2.1% fast casual market share estimate from ThinkEquity Partners, LLC, *Company Note: Chipotle Mexican Grill*, February 16, 2006. Accessed via Investext Plus, Babson College Horn Library, Babson Park, MA, March 4, 2005, http://web3.infotrac.galegroup.com/itw/.
[g]http://quickfacts.census.gov/qfd/states/25000.html

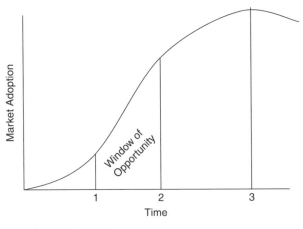

Exhibit 3.6   S Curve

on the vertical line 1 in Exhibit 3.6), customer awareness and demand exceeds supply and the market enters a fast growth phase. During this time (designated between points 2 and 3 in Exhibit 3.6), a dominant design emerges and new competitors enter to capture the emerging market. Typically, demand exceeds supply during this phase, meaning that competitors are primarily concerned with capturing new customers entering the market. After point 3, market demand and supply equalize, putting price pressure on the companies as they fight to capture market share from each other. Finally, innovations push the product towards obsolescence and overall demand declines.

While it is hard to say what market size indicates the window is opening and what size indicates it is closing, research suggests that markets become attractive around $20 million in revenue. Demand and supply tend to equalize around $1 billion.

Frequency and Price

Market size and growth are important, but we also need to think about how often our average customer buys our product or service and how much he is willing to pay. Ideally, our product or service would have perfectly inelastic demand; the customer would pay any price to have it. For a product with elastic demand, the quantity demanded will go down if the price goes up, and vice versa. Inelasticity results in the opposite—whether prices increase or decrease, the demand for the product stays stable. Consider front row seats for your favorite baseball team or theater production. Nearly everyone would like to sit in the front row, but most of us can't or don't because the price is too high. However, if the price were lowered by a certain amount we might be more than happy to buy the tickets. This is an example of elastic demand—as the price decreases, demand for that product increases.

In contrast, consider gasoline. People who rely on a car to get to work have little choice but to pay the prices charged at the pump. If prices go down they are unlikely to buy more gas, and if prices go up they will still need to buy enough gas to get to work and run errands. While not perfectly inelastic, the demand for gasoline is relatively inelastic. In reality, there will almost always be elasticity in customer demand, and our price will be a function of that elasticity. We need to determine the optimal price that encourages regular purchases, accounts for the value inherent in our product, and allows us to earn an attractive margin on the sale. These three variables are highly correlated, and an imbalance would hurt the profitability and even the viability of the firm.

In a classic mistake, some entrepreneurs use a penetration pricing strategy. They reason that in order to pull customers from existing alternatives, the firm needs to price lower than the competition. Then, once the product is able to gain acceptance and market share, the company can raise prices to increase gross margins and better reflect underlying value. There are a number of flaws in this logic. First, as we've noted, attractive ventures are often launched in emerging markets where demand exceeds supply. This means that price is relatively inelastic. Consumers want the product and are willing to pay a premium for it. Second, many new products are designed to be better than existing alternatives. These products offer greater value than competitive products and the price should reflect this greater value, especially since it usually costs more to add the features that led to it. Third, price sends a signal to the customer. If a product with greater value is priced lower than or at the same price as competing products, customers will interpret that signal to mean it isn't as good, despite claims that it has greater value.

Fourth, even if customers flock to the low-priced product, this rapid increase in demand can sometimes cause serious problems for a start-up. Demand at that price may exceed your ability to supply, resulting in stock-outs. Consumers are notoriously fickle and are just as likely to go to a competitor as wait for your backlog to catch up.[13] Finally, these same customers may resist when you try to recapture value by raising prices in the future. They will have developed an internal sense of the value of your product, and they may take this opportunity to try other alternatives. The last thing you want is a business built around customers who are always searching for the lowest price. These will be the first people to leave you when a competitor finds a way to offer a lower price.

The Internet boom and bust saw many poor pricing decisions. Internet firms entered the market at very low price points. Take kozmo.com, for example. Many thought the company's revolutionary approach to delivering things like groceries and videos would change the way people shopped, but in the end, the value proposition was too good to be true. The company was delivering goods at a cost higher than it was charging. The total ticket for a simple order of a few sodas, a bag of chips, and a candy bar might be only $7, but kozmo.com was paying as much as $10 to the person who had to find those items and then deliver them. The venture capital–backed company burned through almost all its cash before it finally recognized the flaw of its pricing logic, but by then it was too late.[14]

Webvan is an eerily similar example. In its attempt to deliver groceries directly to consumers, the company failed to adapt its business model to the extremely thin gross profit margins of the grocery business. Webvan offered to deliver groceries free of charge, but the labor costs of deliveries, along with the warehousing needs of a large-scale grocery delivery operation, were such that the company was losing money on almost every order. Webvan burned through $1 billion in cash before failing.[15] This underscores one of the primary rules of economics: You shut down the business if the price you are charging can't cover the direct costs of the good or service.

Peapod (http://www.peapod.com), a company that survived in the online local delivery segment, made the decision to go after a profitable opportunity in the marketplace. In 2000, Peapod partnered with food provider Royal Ahold, parent company of Stop & Shop and Giant Foods. This "clicks and bricks" strategy allowed Peapod to position itself as a lifestyle solution for those with busy schedules. Peapod offers a select 8,000 items—far fewer than the over 200,000 items found in partnering grocery stores. Peapod limits orders to a $60 minimum, and its delivery fee decreases as the size of the order increases. Peapod can claim that its average order size is $150 and its sales enjoyed a greater than 25 percent year-over-year growth rate in 2008.

The argument many unsuccessful Internet entrepreneurs made at the time was that the number of eyeballs looking at a site was more important than profitability, which firms figured would come later as they developed a critical mass of customers. These firms reasoned that they could charge lower prices than brick-and-mortar outlets (traditional stores that the customer had to physically visit) because they didn't have the overhead costs of renting or buying so many store locations. Furthermore, Internet companies could serve a larger volume of customers via a single web site than a chain of stores could serve in thousands of physical locations. For the most part, these strategies failed due to a number of reasons.

First, the Internet firms continued reducing prices to the point where they weren't generating a positive gross margin. The continued decrease in price was a function of competition. New online firms that were basically identical started to appear. For instance, do you remember the difference between pets.com and petopia.com? Traditional retailers responded by adding web sites as an additional channel of distribution. Toys "R" Us was able to enter the online market and secure new customers at one-tenth the cost of Toys.com due to higher name recognition.

Finding the right price to charge is difficult. It requires understanding your cost structure. You cannot price under your costs of goods sold (COGS) for an extended period of time unless you have lots of financing (and are certain that access to financing will continue into the future). Thus, your minimum price should be above your COGS. Some firms look at their costs to produce a unit of the product, and then add a set percentage on top of that cost to arrive at the price. This is called *cost-plus pricing*, and the problem is that it may set your price lower or higher than the underlying value in your product or service. For example, if you price at 40 percent above marginal cost, that may result in your product being a great value (software usually has gross margins of 70 percent or better) or drastically overpriced (groceries often have gross margins in the 20 percent range).

A better approach is to assess market prices for competing products. For instance, consider GMAT test preparation courses that help students strengthen their business school applications. At the time of this writing, a quick scan of Kaplan and Princeton Review reveals that prices for their classroom GMAT programs are $1,449 and $1,249, respectively. Given the similarities of the content, structure, and results of these programs, it is no surprise that their prices are comparable. The slight difference reflects the differences in marketing and operational strategy as well as value customers perceive in the services. Over the years, Kaplan and Princeton Review have gained deep insight into what parents will pay. For an entrepreneur entering this marketplace, Kaplan and Princeton Review provide a starting point in deciding what price can be charged. The entrepreneur would adjust his price based on the perceived difference in value of the offering.

Many entrepreneurs claim they have no direct competition so it is impossible to determine how much customers might pay. In such cases, which are very rare, it is essential to understand how customers are currently meeting the need that you propose to fill. Assess how much it costs them to fulfill this need and then determine a price that reflects the new process plus a premium for the added value your product delivers.

Margins

For new ventures, research suggests that gross margins of 40 percent are a good bench-mark that distinguishes more attractive from less attractive opportunities. It is important to have higher gross margins early in the venture's life, because operating costs during the early years are disproportionately high due to learning curve effects. For instance, no matter how experienced they are in the industry, your team will incur costs as you train yourselves and new hires. Over time, the team will become more efficient and the associated costs of operations will reach a stability point.

Another reason for keeping margins high is that the new venture will incur costs prior to generating sales associated with those costs. For instance, well before you are able to generate any leads or sales, you will need to hire sales people and invest time and money training them. Even if you are a sole proprietorship, you will incur costs associated with selling your product or service before you receive any cash associated with the sale. For instance, you may have travel expenses like airline tickets or gasoline for your car, and infrastructure expenses like a new computer and office furniture. This lag between spending and earning creates a strain on cash flows, whether you are a one-person shop or a growing enterprise, and if your margins are thin to begin with, it will be harder to attract the investment needed to launch.

It typically takes three to five years for a firm to reach stability and for operating costs to stabilize. At this point strong firms hope to achieve net income as a percentage of sales of 10 percent or better. If the net income margin is lower, it will be hard to generate internal cash for growth or to attract outside investors, to say nothing about generating returns for the founding team.

The exceptions to this rule are businesses that can generate high volumes. During the 1980s and 1990s many new ventures sought to replicate the Wal-Mart concept. Staples, Office Max, Home Depot, and Lowes are good examples. Gross margins on these businesses range from as low as 10 percent to 33 percent, and net income margins range from 1.8 to 6.5 percent. However, the stores do such enormous volumes that they are still able to generate huge profits. For example, in the 12-month period ending on January 31, 2008, Wal-Mart posted profits of $12.7 billion, more in profits than the vast majority of all U.S. companies had in sales, and it was able to do so because it generated $278 billion in sales during the same period. While Wal-Mart's net profit margin of 3.3 percent is small by most measures, its sales and profit numbers are clear indicators that its business strategy is working.

The performance of these big companies suggests another kind of industry structure that can be very attractive—fragmented industries. Prior to the launch of Staples and Home Depot, people filled their office supply and hardware needs through mom-and-pop companies. These small enterprises served small geographic regions and rarely expanded beyond them. The big-box stores entered these markets and offered similar goods at much lower prices against which mom-and-pop firms couldn't compete.

While entering a fragmented industry and attempting to consolidate it, as big-box stores do, can create huge opportunities, the financial and time investments required are substantial. For instance, Arthur Blank and Bernard Marcus founded Home De-pot in 1978 in the Atlanta area. While its individual stores had enormous sales and profit potential, the company needed significant up-front capital for the initial building costs and inventory; it raised venture capital, followed by $7.2 million from its 1981 public offering (which translates to $17 million in 2008 dollars). Almost 10 years later,

Thomas Stemberg founded Staples and followed a nearly identical path in office supplies. Here again, the start-up costs were enormous and the company relied heavily on its founders' experience in retailing. Staples raised $33.83 million in venture capital before it went public in April 1989, raising $51.3 million.[16] The bottom line is that such opportunities are rarer than in emerging markets and require a team with extensive industry experience and access to venture capital or other large institutional financing resources.

Reaching the Customer

Reaching the customer can be very difficult, even for the most experienced entrepreneur. Take the example of the founder of Gourmet Stew.[17] After completing her MBA, she spent many years with one of the top three food producers in the country, where she gained a deeper understanding about the industry. In the 1980s, she joined a small food start-up company that developed a new drink concept that became widely successful and was ultimately acquired by Kraft Foods. Still a young woman, she cashed out and started her own venture, Gourmet Stew. Its first product was beef stew in a jar, like Ragu spaghetti sauce. The product tasted better than competitors like Hormel Stew (in a can). However, despite her extensive entrepreneurial and industry experience and even though her product tasted better, the entrepreneur couldn't overcome one obstacle: how to reach the customer.

Stew in a jar is usually distributed in grocery stores, but this is a very difficult market to enter on a large scale. The industry is consolidated and mature, with only 19 chains throughout the entire country. Large product and food companies like Procter & Gamble and General Mills control much of the available shelf space, due to their power and ability to pay the required slotting fees (that is, the fees supermarket chains charge suppliers for providing shelf space within their stores). Grocery stores also have an incentive to deal with fewer rather than more suppliers because it improves their internal efficiency.

Given these factors, companies that sell only a few products, such as Gourmet Stew, have a difficult time accessing large chain stores. And, even though smaller chains may find a unique product like Gourmet Stew appealing, it costs one-product companies more to distribute through these channels, since they have to deal with multiple vendors instead of sealing a few large distribution agreements. Alternatively, Gourmet Stew could work with a large food brokerage company, but that would mean giving a portion of its margins to the brokerage. With all these options, the economics of distribution makes it almost impossible to generate a decent margin on this type of company.

One of the most overlooked keys to entrepreneurial success is distribution. How *do* you reach the customer? While Gourmet Stew might have been able to reach the customer through alternative distribution channels, like the Internet, these are likely to generate lower sales volume and higher marketing expenses, because you have to educate the customer not only about what your product is, but also about where to find it.

It is important to understand the entire value chain for the industry you are competing in. You need to lay out the distribution of your product from raw materials all the way to the end consumer. Exhibit 3.7 captures the value chain for Gourmet Stew. From the exhibit, we can see the respective gross margins of the players—note that their net income margins would be much lower based upon their operating costs. The higher gross margins of the grocery stores indicate their relative power. Consider whether there is a variation on your business idea that would allow you to enter the portion of the value

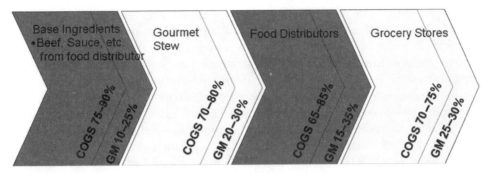

Exhibit 3.7 Value Chain (Downloadable) Copyright © 2010 by William D. Bygrave and Andrew Zacharakis. To download this form for your personal use, please visit www.wiley.com/go/portablembainentrepreneurship.

Source: Information for this value chain was gathered from financial data on sample industry companies found at http://biz.yahoo.com/ic/340.html and linked pages.

chain where greater margins are available. In sum, you must understand the entire value chain in order to determine where opportunities to make a profit might exist.

While Gourmet Stew wasn't successful gaining distribution, the accompanying box shows how a small food company, Stacy's Pita Chips, can slowly gain distribution and build momentum to the point where it achieves a successful harvest for the entrepreneurs.

Stacy's Pita Chips

Gaining Widespread Distribution

Stacy's Pita Chips didn't start out as a snack food maker. Instead, Stacy Madison, a social worker by training, and Mark Andrus, a psychologist, wanted to open a restaurant. Their first venture was a small food cart that sold pita bread wraps in downtown Boston. They were instantly successful and soon had long lines of hungry customers waiting for their freshly made wraps. Some of these potential customers tired of waiting in line and would give up before placing an order. To minimize the number of lost customers, Stacy and Mark started serving seasoned pita chips, baked from the bread they had left at the end of each day. The pita chips were a hit. In addition to great roll-up sandwiches, customers had a delicious incentive while they waited in line. Eventually, the couple was running two businesses and had to make a choice. They chose the pita chips, figuring they'd be able to gain national growth more rapidly. A new venture was born.

Even though Stacy and Mark had a great product, the question was, how could they reach the end consumer en masse? Most people buy chips in the grocery store, but getting space in the snack aisle is nearly impossible. Large distributors sell to grocery stores and they are only interested in products that their buyers (the grocery stores) want. Recognizing this problem, Stacy decided that there was another way into this channel: Stacy's would place its chips in the natural food aisle and the

(continued)

in-store delis. Stacy and Mark attended trade shows and made direct contact with grocery stores, sold them on their product, and secured trial placements in the stores. Stacy supplied display racks for her chips to each store and worked hard to increase consumer awareness by offering sample chips to shoppers.

Without a distributor, Stacy's Pita Chips often shipped their product via UPS. But once they secured 10 or more stores in a particular geographic region, they went to the stores and asked who distributed snacks to them. The stores often contacted the distributors on Stacy's behalf, asking them to handle the product for them. Stacy noted, "Having customers that the distributor sold to gave us leverage. They wanted to carry our products because we created customer demand for them." Once Stacy's had a few large distributors in line, the company had gained momentum and other stores and distributors wanted to carry the product. In 2005, Stacy's hit $60 million* in sales and Frito-Lay, the largest snack food maker in the world, finalized the acquisition of the company in January 2006.

Source: Compiled from a personal interview with Stacy Madison, March 22, 2006.

*"ETC.," *Brandweek*, November 28, 2005, http://www.brandweek.com/bw/esearch/article_display.jsp?vnu_content_id=100157082.

The Competition

Would-be entrepreneurs often say, "I have a great idea, and the best part is, there's *no competition*." If that were true, then as long as you have a customer, you have a license to print money. However, most nascent entrepreneurs turn out to be defining their competition too narrowly. For example, an overly optimistic entrepreneur might suggest that Gourmet Stew has no competition because there are no other companies producing stew in a jar. That doesn't account for Hormel canned stew (direct competition). It doesn't account for the multitude of frozen pizzas and other prepared foods that customers can bring home from the grocery store (more direct competition). It also ignores the customers' options of preparing their own secret recipe for stew (indirect competition) or going out to eat (substitute). In other words, Gourmet Stew's competition isn't just stew in a jar; it is all the other businesses competing for a share of the consumer's stomach. Entrepreneurs ignore these competitors and substitutes at their peril.

To fully identify the competition, start with the customer. How is the customer currently fulfilling the need or want you intend to fill? You must identify direct competitors, indirect competitors, and substitutes. The number and strength of your competition mirrors the market structure. In a mature market, the industry is likely consolidated and the power of existing competitors is strong. From the Gourmet Stew example, the industry is highly consolidated. Five major prepared food companies control 57 percent of the market: Nestlé S.A., Kraft Foods Inc., Unilever, Frito-Lay North America, Inc., and Cargill, Inc.[18] Entering this market is difficult, as we saw earlier, because the major competitors control the primary channel of distribution.

Even if you successfully enter the market, the strength of the competition enables them to retaliate. Competitors can lower prices to a point that makes it difficult for new ventures to compete due to economies of scale and scope. They can spend more on their advertising campaign and other marketing expenditures and increase their visibility due to greater resource reserves or easier access to capital. The good news is that many times, strong competitors won't bother with new start-ups because they're so small that they aren't noticeable, or because they don't seem threatening in either the short or medium term. However, entrepreneurs should plan for contingencies just in case the larger competitors retaliate earlier than expected.

When markets are emerging, such as the market for video game consoles, fewer products compete for customers, primarily because demand exceeds supply. The main struggle within these markets is trying to find and own the dominant design that will become the customer favorite. The classic example of convergence towards a dominant design is the personal computer operating system. In the early years, there were a multitude of potential operating systems that ran computers ranging from Apple to Tandy Radio Shack. In the 1970s, Digital Research Inc.'s CP/M system looked to be the dominant system, until the company's founder, Gary Kildall, apparently blew off a meeting with IBM officials looking for an operating system for the company's new personal computer. IBM then approached Microsoft, which had bought Q-DOS from Seattle Computer Products for the foundation of its MS-DOS system. Tandy Radio Shack, meanwhile, created a proprietary system, TRSDOS, for its own computers. Exhibit 3.8 shows some of the competing systems, when they were designed, and when they went out of business. Note that by the late 1980s DOS controlled 85 percent of the marketplace, Apple had 7 percent, and all others were also-rans.[19]

What this means is that firms in emerging markets have to work feverishly to design a better product and to communicate its benefits to customers, because your competition is doing the same. DOS became the dominant operating system primarily because it was included in the most popular PC at the time, the IBM PC. As PC design converged toward the IBM design, existing PC manufacturers and new manufacturers alike adopted the Microsoft DOS platform. This example highlights the evolution of most marketplaces. Once a dominant design is in place, the market moves rapidly to maturity.

Emerging markets are characterized by *stealth* competitors. Entrepreneurs often believe their idea is so unique that they will have a significant lead over would-be competitors. But just as your venture will operate under the radar as it designs its products, builds its infrastructure, and tests the product with a few early beta customers, so will a number of other new ventures likely be at similar stages of development. While it is relatively easy to conduct due diligence on identifiable competition, it is extremely

Exhibit 3.8   Operating Systems Move to Dominant Design

Operating System	Year Introduced	Year it Failed
Tandy/Radio Shack TRS-DOS	1977	1987
Apple DOS	1978	1983
Digital Research Inc. CP/M	1976	1983
Seattle Computer Co QDOS	1980	1981
Microsoft MS DOS	1981	1995
Microsoft Windows	1983	
Apple Macintosh OS	1984	

difficult to learn about competition that isn't yet in the marketplace. Thus, it is imperative for new ventures to scan the environment to identify and learn about stealth competition.

There are several sources of intelligence you can tap. It is probable that your competition is using similar inputs, and thus similar suppliers, to the ones you are using. As you interview your potential suppliers, make sure to query them about similar companies with whom they are working. While the suppliers may not divulge this information, more often than not, they don't see it as a conflict of interest to do so. Outside professional equity capital can also help you determine competitors. Angel investors and venture capitalists see many deals and have knowledge about how an industry is developing even if they haven't actually funded one of your stealth competitors. Again, you can talk to professional investors about who they see as strong emerging competitors.

Furthermore, a number of widely available databases track and identify companies that receive equity financing. PriceWaterhouseCoopers publishes *MoneyTree*, which allows you to screen new investments by industry, region, and VCs making the investment.[20] *VentureWire* is one of many daily e-mail newsletters published by Dow Jones that tracks current deals—and the best part is that *VentureWire Alert* is free.[21] The smart entrepreneur will diligently monitor his industry and use these resources, as well as many others, to avoid being surprised by unforeseen competition. An excellent source of industry gossip is trade shows.

While your direct competition is most relevant to your success, you also should spend some time understanding why your target customer is interested in your indirect competitors and substitutes. As you increase your knowledge of the total marketplace, you will start to understand the key success factors (KSFs) that distinguish those firms that win from those that lose. Key success factors are the attributes that influence where the customer spends money. If we think once again about Gourmet Stew, customers base their food purchasing decisions on a number of factors, including taste, price, convenience (time to prepare and serve), availability (the distribution channel issue discussed earlier), and healthy attributes of the food, among other factors. As you gather data on these factors, constructing a competitive profile matrix to identify the relative strength of each will help you decide how to position your venture into the marketplace (see Exhibit 3.9). Gauge how well each of your competitors is doing by tracking their revenues, gross margins, net income margins, and net profits. Note that we don't yet know what the figures are for Gourmet Stew because it has yet to hit the marketplace. Likewise, homemade stew is the creation of the consumer, who buys all the ingredients separately at the grocery store.

As we examine the competitive profile matrix, we understand our competitors' strategy and which customers they are targeting. Hormel, for example, is targeting price-sensitive, convenience-minded consumers. Typical customers might include a male living on his own, college students, or others who don't have the time or desire to cook but are living on a budget. Homemade stew, by contrast, falls in the domain of the person who enjoys cooking and has more time. The stay-at-home parent may have the time to shop for all the ingredients and to cook the stew from scratch, or weekend gourmets might like to create something special for guests or family. Gourmet Stew might appeal to families where both parents work outside the home. They want quality food but don't have the time to cook it from scratch and are not as sensitive to prices. Lastly, DiGiorno pizza (a higher-quality pizza) is targeting families who want something in the freezer for those nights when they just don't have time to cook.

Exhibit 3.9   Competitive Profile Matrix (Downloadable) Copyright © 2010 by William D. Bygrave and Andrew Zacharakis. To download this form for your personal use, please visit www.wiley.com/go/portablembainentrepreneurship.

	Gourmet Stew	Hormel	Homemade	DiGiorno Pizza
Taste	Good	Fair	Excellent	Fair
Price	High $3.50	Medium $1.89	Low	Very high $6.50
Convenience	High	High	Low	High
Availability	Low	High	High	High
Healthy	Medium	Low	High	Medium
Revenues		<$135 million*		$500 million*
Gross margins		23.7%*		34.9%*
Net income margins		16.5%*		Loss*
Net profit		22.3 million*		

*Financial figures for Hormel and DiGiorno are for the whole company, not just the product.

While there are many more competitors than the ones we have highlighted, it is often best to pick a few representative competitors rather than to highlight every potential company. The matrix is a tool to help you understand the competitive landscape by drilling down deep on a few key competitors. Although you'll want to be aware of every potential competitor and substitute, focusing on a few in-depth will help you devise a successful strategy.

From this information, we can start to get the broad guidelines of our competitors' strategies—for example, Hormel is pursuing a low-cost strategy—and what might be an appropriate strategy for our firm. Gourmet Stew might pursue a differentiation strategy of better quality at a higher price. Moreover, considering the difficulties of entering the distribution channels, we might focus on a niche strategy. Maybe we could access health-oriented grocery stores like Whole Foods. Understanding the marketplace helps us formulate a strategy that can help us succeed.

Vendors/Suppliers

Understanding the customers and competition is critical to determining whether your idea is indeed an opportunity, but other factors also need consideration. Referring back to the value chain we created for Gourmet Stew (see Exhibit 3.7), you'll notice that suppliers are providing commodity goods such as beef, vegetables, and other food products. These types of vendors usually have limited power, which means that more of the ultimate gross margin in the chain goes to Gourmet Stew. A sudden rise in the market price of beef, however, could have a negative impact on your margins even though your power over suppliers is strong. A diversified offering that includes vegetarian stew, for example, can guard against such problems.

In other instances, your suppliers can have tremendous power and that will directly affect your margins. For example, Microsoft as the dominant operating system and core software provider, and Intel as the dominant microprocessor supplier, have considerable power over PC manufacturers. Microsoft has gross margins of 81 percent and Intel has gross margins of 55 percent,[22] whereas the average gross margins for PC manufacturers are between 8 and 33 percent.[23] Putting aside the strong competition in the mature PC market for a moment, the fact that suppliers have so much power lessens the opportunity potential for entrepreneurs entering the PC market unless they find an innovation to supplant the Intel chip or the Microsoft operating system.

Government

For the most part, the U.S. government is supportive of entrepreneurship. Taxes are lower than in most nations in the world, the time required to register a new business is shorter, and the level of regulations is generally lower. However, in certain industries, government regulation and involvement are significantly higher, such as in pharmaceuticals and medical devices. For example, consider a start-up company that produces a new drug therapy that more quickly and effectively treats hypertension. In order to bring this product to market, you would have to guide your product through FDA approval. The approval process is often lengthy, with a median time to approval of 19 months before the product can be brought to market.[24] During this time the start-up company is incurring costs with no revenue to offset the negative cash flows, increasing the time to reach breakeven and also the amount of money at risk if the venture fails.

While the up-front time and expense is an entry barrier that reduces potential future competition, your company benefits only if the product proves successful in gaining both FDA approval and adoption by doctors. Thus, as an entrepreneur, you need to be aware of government requirements and their impact on your business. If the requirements are stringent, such as getting FDA approval, and the potential margins you can earn are relatively low, it is probably not a good opportunity. In the case just described, the stents command a very high margin so the company can more than recoup its investment if it successfully navigates FDA approval and secures wide doctor adoption.

Global Environment

As the world marketplace becomes global, your opportunity is increasingly strengthened by looking overseas. What international customers fit within your PTA, STA, and TTA? How easy is it to reach them? When might you go international? On the flip side, you also need to be aware of your international competitors. Have they entered your market yet? When might they? It is increasingly common for entrepreneurial firms to use an outsourcing strategy, which means you may need to evaluate international vendors and their relative power.

In today's global economy, new entrepreneurial firms often should consider expansion at their inception. Advances in logistics, technology, and manufacturing have allowed smaller and younger firms to compete globally. Firms that look globally from the outset often have tightly managed organizations, innovative products, and strong networks for marketing. They also have more aggressive growth strategies, use more distribution channels, and have more experienced management teams. They don't simply export, but instead choose foreign direct investment in the countries in which they seek to operate. With their global reach, they can introduce innovative products to new markets, giving them an advantage over start-ups that operate only in the domestic sphere. They also may operate in industries that are globally integrated from the start.[25]

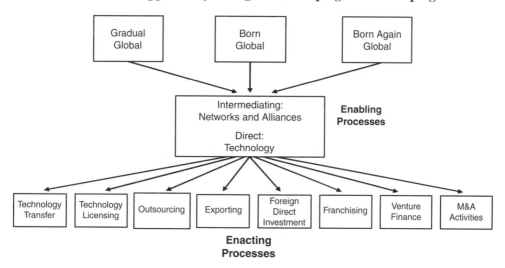

Exhibit 3.10   The Entrepreneurial Firm International Expansion Process

According to a study by the United Nations, there are more than 60,000 multinational firms, many of which are *micro-nationals*. As the number of multinationals continues to grow, their average size continues to shrink.[26] In another study, Shrader and colleagues estimate that one-third of all small manufacturing firms derive at least 10 percent of their revenues from foreign sources.[27] Unfortunately for a new venture, going global increases risk and costs money. Dickson provides a model that illustrates when and how entrepreneurial ventures go after global opportunities.[28] (See Exhibit 3.10.)

Dickson notes that there are three types of global entrepreneurial firms. The first he calls *gradual globals*. These firms enter international markets in stages in order to reduce their risk. During their initial entry, gradual globals will enter countries similar to their domestic market and use processes that require lower costs and commitment, such as exporting. Over time, they will enter more, and increasingly dissimilar, countries. Gradual globals will also expand their entry modes, moving from exporting to foreign direct investment (FDI), for example.

For these gradual globals, the opportunity assessment is carefully balanced by assessing the risks and rewards. The second category of entrepreneurial firms is *born global*. These firms plan to enter international markets right from the outset. They see the global opportunity as inherent to their business strategy.

The final category is *born-again globals*. These firms have been operating only domestically, but some event triggers them to move rapidly into new international markets, such as an unsolicited order from abroad. These firms could be described as tactically opportunistic; they take a more reactive approach to global operations. Although there is a lot of debate about which type of firm is more likely to succeed globally, entrepreneurs need to think about international business opportunities from day one.

Dickson suggests that entrepreneurs pursue enabling strategies, given that new ventures are resource constrained. For instance, they can use intermediaries to reduce needed resources or use low-cost methods, such as the Internet, that enable them to make contact with potential international partners. In many cases, entrepreneurs can tap their existing networks, such as employees, investors, vendors, or customers, to facilitate international entry. One of your vendors, for instance, may have distribution in another country that you can use on a variable cost basis. You might also pursue alliances with other companies. Faxes and the Internet enable entrepreneurs to directly access international markets in a low-cost manner. You can market to firms worldwide by simply putting up a Web page. You can proactively manage relationships overseas by using the Internet and e-mail. The toy designers at Kidrobot communicate with their subcontractors from afar, electronically sending their plans and product changes to China.[29] Whatever the enablers you use, it is easier today to enter global markets than ever before.

Dickson's model moves from enablers to enacting processes. There are eight primary means to expand globally, each representing a possible avenue to opportunity:

1. *Technology transfer (joint venture).* When firms choose to enter the global market, they may need to decide whether to sell their technology or produce it abroad themselves. Producing technology overseas can involve significant risk and investment. Instead, having a partner firm in the target country or region that can produce and distribute your product can reduce your entry costs. The costs of technology development and production often lead young firms to build alliances and joint partnerships and to focus on niche markets.[30] However, there is a risk you'll lose control of the technology, because the partner firm will gain insight into how you produce the product.

2. *Technology licensing.* Perhaps the most common means to enter a foreign market is to secure an agent to represent the company abroad. Here the entrepreneur may decide that he is better off letting a foreign company produce and sell the product, perhaps rebranded under its own name, and taking a royalty as compensation. Licensing reduces risk from an operational perspective. While this is an excellent means of generating revenue and conserving resources, it is also a lost opportunity to extend your own brand into new markets.

3. *Outsourcing.* Outsourcing allows businesses to handle key attributes of their products while handing over the responsibility for development and manufacturing to a subcontractor. The outsourced production may be sent back to the company's home country for sale.

4. *Exporting.* The cheapest and easiest way to enter new markets is to sell from your headquarters. However, as always, there are trade-offs. It is harder to establish a critical mass within the country if you don't have anyone on the ground, and, as mentioned earlier, you may incur additional costs in after-sales support. Your customers also may have difficulty contacting you or providing information about the market and their needs. You incur the transportation costs and risks of getting your products through the target country's customs. A second alternative is to hire a sales rep in the target country. The advantages are that sales reps have deep knowledge of the country and presumably a strong network they can leverage in selling the product. However, agency theory suggests there are risks to consider.[31] First, it is difficult for you to confirm that agents are as skilled as they might claim (this risk is referred to as *adverse selection*). Second, it is difficult to ensure that the agent is honoring the contract (which is referred to as *moral hazard*).

5. *Foreign direct investment (FDI).* Under this strategy, companies set up a physical presence in the countries of interest, whether in the form of a sales office, retail outlets, production facilities, or something else. The start-up retains control of the

assets and facilities, an issue that can prove expensive. The primary means of FDI are acquiring foreign assets and building and expanding current facilities overseas. FDI is usually beyond the means of most early stage companies. French clothing line Chloe tested the Chinese market by exporting the product first through retail stores. Once it learned that Chinese customers liked the product, it started to establish its own retail outlets in Beijing and then Shanghai. It plans to branch out slowly from those locations.[32] Similarly, Jeff Bernstein started Emerge Logistics by using China's bureaucratic red tape and the unwillingness of American companies to invest in Chinese facilities to his advantage. Bernstein's logistics company stocks three overseas warehouses with industrial parts for clients like Daimler Chrysler and Gates Rubber.[33]

6. *Franchising.* Some see franchising as a low-risk method of entering a foreign market because it allows the firm to license an operational system. Yet there can be difficulties in monitoring the international franchisee and ensuring that it protects the company's brand (moral hazard). Until recently the Chinese as a whole had a dim view of franchises. The media in China highlighted several news stories about franchise owners receiving payment but failing to provide services. And as a parent company, KFC had difficulties in convincing its franchisees in China to collectively bargain in order to receive lower prices from suppliers.[34]

7. *Venture financing.* According to Dickson, venture capital is both an enabling and an enacting mechanism. What he means is that the available capital and expertise provided by VCs may enable a firm to go international using any of the previously mentioned means to enter a market. However, research suggests that venture capital often leads to mergers and acquisitions with foreign companies.

8. *Mergers and acquisitions (M&A).* For some businesses, buying an overseas firm may be the most efficient manner to enter a foreign market. You gain an instant presence in the country with an established infrastructure. Mergers and acquisitions also allow an entrepreneurial company to grow and expand quickly. Some research shows that firms that use acquisitions for expansion have a higher survival rate than those that choose a start-up.[35] The capital required means that the firm must secure venture capital or go public; thus, this method is beyond the means of most early stage entrepreneurs.

As the world becomes increasingly connected, entrepreneurs need to look beyond their home borders to see whether they can expand on their initial opportunity. While it is more difficult to enter and operate in a country you are not familiar with, technology and increasing trade are reducing the knowledge gap. As research points out, more and more entrepreneurs are becoming global early in their companies' lives. As an entrepreneur you need to be aware of your options, and the Dickson model provides a solid framework for understanding them.

The Opportunity Checklist

Exhibit 3.11 summarizes the concepts we have covered in this chapter. Use it to evaluate whether your idea is a strong opportunity, or to evaluate several ideas simultaneously to see which one has greater promise. While your opportunity would ideally fit entirely in the middle column under "Better Opportunities," there will be some aspects where it is weak. Examine the weak aspects and see how you can modify your business model to strengthen them. In the end, of course, the goal is to be strong in more areas than you are weak.

"I Don't Have an Opportunity"

After doing a thorough analysis, some entrepreneurs conclude that the marketplace isn't as large or accessible, or competition is much greater than they expected, and they quickly reach the conclusion that they should abandon their dreams. But in fact, if you analyze every aspect of the business, and if you do your assessment completely, you'll always find a reason for the business to fail. There is no perfect business. There will be areas of weakness in any business model, and it is human nature to amplify those weaknesses until they seem insurmountable. Step back, take a second look, and ask yourself two questions: How can you modify your business model so that it isn't as weak in those aspects? And what can go *right* as you launch your business?

> "Analysis and criticism are of no interest to me unless they are a path to constructive, action-bent thinking. Critical type intelligence is boring and destructive and only satisfactory to those who indulge in it. Most new projects—I can even say every one of them—can be analyzed to destruction."
>
> —Georges Doriot, founder of the modern venture capital industry

The entrepreneurial process is one of continuous adjustment. Many times entrepreneurs stick stubbornly to an idea as it was originally conceived. After a thorough customer and competitive analysis, you need to find ways to modify the business concept so that it better matches the needs of your customer and so that it has advantages over your competitors. The more you learn about the opportunities that exist for your product, the more you must refine your business plan. For instance, as you open your doors and customers come in and provide feedback, you'll find more ways to improve your business model. If you ignore feedback and remain stuck to your initial concept as you originally visualized it (and possibly as you wrote it up in your plan), you are more likely to fail. The business planning process is ongoing, and you'll learn more about your opportunity every step along the way. Therefore, to prematurely abandon your concept after some negative feedback from your analysis is a mistake unless the negatives far outweigh the positives in Exhibit 3.11.

Ruth Owades, who founded Calyx and Corolla (a direct flower delivery service from the growers to your home), persisted in launching a mail order catalog called *Gardener's Eden* for unique gardening tools even though the initial analysis suggested it would be difficult to break even in the first year.[36] While Ruth envisioned her business as seasonal—customers would order gardening supplies during the spring planting season—she found she had two seasons: People also used the catalog during the Christmas season for gifts. She also found that the amount people would spend per order was higher than expected, making the dynamics of the business much more robust than she initially imagined.

Exhibit 3.11   Opportunity Checklist (Downloadable) Copyright © 2010 by William D. Bygrave and Andrew Zacharakis. To download this form for your personal use, please visit www.wiley.com/go/portablembainentrepreneurship.

Customer	Better Opportunities	Weaker Opportunities
Identifiable	PTA	STA
Demographics	Clearly defined and focused	Fuzzy definition and unfocused
Psychographics	Clearly defined and focused	Fuzzy definition and unfocused
Trends		
Macro market	Multiple and converging	Few and disparate
Target market	Multiple and converging	Few and disparate
Window of opportunity	Opening	Closing
Market structure	Emerging/fragmented	Mature/decline
Market size		
How many	PTA	STA
Demand	Greater than supply	Less than supply
Market growth		
Rate	20% or greater	Less than 20%
Price/frequency/value		
Price	GM > 40%	GM < 40%
Frequency	Often and repeated	One time
Value	Fully reflected in price	Penetration pricing
Operating expenses	Low and variable	Large and fixed
NI margin	10% or greater	<10%
Volume	Very high	Moderate
Distribution		
Where are you in value chain?	High margin, high power	Low margin, low power
Competition		
Market structure	Emerging	Mature
Number of direct competitors	Few	Many
Number of indirect competitors	Few	Many
Number of substitutes	Few	Many
Stealth competitors	Unlikely	Likely
Key success factors		
Relative position	Strong	Weak
Vendors		
Relative power	Weak	Strong
Gross margins they control in value chain	Low	High
Government		
Regulations	Low	High
Taxes	Low	High
Global environment		
Customers	Interested and accessible	Not interested or accessible
Competition	Nonexistent or weak	Existing and strong
Vendors	Eager	Unavailable

Your prelaunch analysis is just a starting point. You need to understand the variables in your business model, how they might be greater or less than you initially imagine, and what that might mean for your business. In the next chapter we define and examine business models—how you make money and what it costs to generate revenues.

Conclusion

All opportunities start with an idea. We find the ideas that most often lead to successful businesses have two key characteristics: First, they are something that the entrepreneur is truly passionate about; second, the idea is a strong opportunity as measured on the opportunity checklist. To be sure of having a strong opportunity, entrepreneurs need a deep understanding of their customer, preferably knowing the customer by name. Better opportunities will have lots of customers currently (market size) with the potential for even more customers in the future (market is growing). Furthermore, these customers will buy the product frequently and pay a premium price for it (strong margins). Thus, entrepreneurs need to be students of the marketplace. What trends are converging, and how do these trends shape customer demand today and into the future?

Savvy entrepreneurs also recognize that competitors, both direct and indirect, are vying for the customers' attention. Understanding competitive dynamics helps entrepreneurs shape their opportunity to reach the customer better than the competition can. As this chapter points out, the entrepreneurial environment is holistic and fluid. In addition to the customer and competition, entrepreneurs need to understand how they source their raw materials (suppliers) and what government regulations mean to their business. If all these elements—customers, competitors, suppliers, and government—are favorable, the entrepreneur has identified a strong opportunity. The next step is successfully launching and implementing your vision.

Downloadable Resources for this chapter available at www.wiley.com/go/portablembainentrepreneurship

Value-Chain Exercise
Competitive Profile Matrix
Opportunity Checklist

Notes

1. *Pain points* are those aspects of a current product or service that are suboptimal or ineffective from the customer's point of view. Improving on these factors or coming up with an entirely new product or service that eliminates these points of pain can be a source of competitive advantage.
2. If you are interested in learning more about brain-writing, visit http://litemind.com/brainwriting/
3. http://www.wallyamos.com/about/index.html
4. W. Bygrave and C. Hedberg, *Jim Poss Case* (Babson Park, MA: Babson College, 2004), available through http://www3.babson.edu/ESHIP/research-publications/Jim-Poss.cfm.
5. Paul Barron, "The Year Ahead: 7 Take-to-the-Bank Predictions," *Fast Casual Magazine*. December 2008–January 2009, 33.

6. Psychographic information categorizes customers based upon their personality and psychological traits, lifestyles, values, and social group membership. It helps you understand what motivates customers to act in the ways they do, and is important because members of a specific demographic category can have dramatically different psychographic profiles. Marketing strictly based on demographic information will be ineffective because it ignores these differences. Our use of soccer mom captures both the demographic and psychographic attributes of a broad customer profile.

7. Packaged Facts, *The U.S. Baby Boomer Market: From the Beatles to Botox*, 3rd ed. (Rockville, MD: Packaged Facts, November 2002), 8–10.

8. Ibid., 7.

9. Ibid., 2.

10. C. Grossman, "Starbucks Stirs Things Up with a God Quote on Cups," *USA Today*, October 19, 2005, http://www.usatoday.com/life/2005-10-19-starbucks-quote_x.htm.

11. K. Rives, "U.S. Hispanics Expected to Fill Baby Boomer Labor Gap," Hispanic Business .com, March 3, 2006, http://www.hispanicbusiness.com/news/newsbyid.asp?id=29151& cat=Headlines&more=/news/more-news.asp.

12. R. Brown, "Managing the 'S' Curves of Innovation," *Journal of Consumer Marketing* 9(1): 61–72.

13. Backlog is the sales that have been made but not fulfilled due to lack of inventory to finalize the sale.

14. J. Slaton, "Webvan, Kozmo—RIP. Money Lessons We've Learned from the Last Mile Failures," SFGate.com, July 21, 2001.

15. K. Maney, "Founder of Webvan Grocery Store Tries Again with Online Newsstand," *USA Today*, July 23, 2003, B1, B3.

16. VentureWeb Xpert "Staples. Company Profile." VentureXpert. June 17, 2009. Thomson. Babson College Horn Library, Babson Park, MA. 18 August 2008.

17. The name of the company and entrepreneur are disguised.

18. General rankings for food sales found at http://biz.yahoo.com/ic/profile/340_1349.html.

19. J. Reimer, "Total Share: 30 Years of Personal Computer Market Share Figures," Ars Technica, December 14, 2005, http://arstechnica.com/articles/culture/total-share.ars.

20. http://www.pwcmoneytree.com/moneytree/index.jsp.

21. www.djnewsletters@dowjones.com.

22. http://biz.yahoo.com/ic/ind_index.html.

23. http://msnmoney.com.

24. http://www.fda.gov/downloads/AboutFDA/CentersOffices/CDER/WhatWeDo/UCM078985 .pdf.

25. P. McDougall, B. Oviatt, and R. Shrader, "A Comparison of International and Domestic New Ventures," *Journal of International Entrepreneurship*, 2003.

26. http://money.cnn.com/magazines/business2/business2_archive/2006/07/01/8380230/index .htm.

27. R. Shrader, B. Oviatt, and P. McDougall, "How New Ventures Exploit Trade-offs among International Risk Factors: Lessons for the Accelerated Internationalization of the 21st Century," *Academy of Management Journal* 43(6): 1227–1247.

28. P. Dickson, "Going Global" in A. Zacharakis and S. Spinelli, eds., *Entrepreneurship*, vol. 2 (Greenwich, CT: Praeger Publishers, 2006), 155–177.

29. M. Copeland and A. Tilin, "The New Instant Companies: Cheap Design Tools, Offshore Factories, Free Buzz Marketing. How Today's Startups are Going from Idea to $30 Million Hit—Overnight," *Business 2.0*, June 6, 2005 (5): 82–94.

30. L. Eden, E. Levitas, and R. Martinez, "The Production, Transfer and Spillover of Technology: Comparing Large and Small Multinationals as Technology Producers," *Small Business Economics* 9(1): 53–66.
31. A. L. Zacharakis, "Entrepreneurial Entry into Foreign Markets: A Transaction Cost Perspective," *Entrepreneurship: Theory and Practice*, 21(3): 23–39.
32. L. Movius, "Chloe Launches in China," *WWD* 190(137) (December 29, 2005).
33. R. Flannery, "Red Tape," *Forbes* 171 (5) (March 3, 2003): 97–100.
34. L. Chang, "From KFC to Beauty Spas, Chinese Are Embracing Franchises—As Maturing Retail Market Moves Past Fraudsters, Chain Stores Take Root," *Wall Street Journal*, April 18, 2002.
35. F. Vermeulen, and H. Barkema, "Learning through Acquisitions," *Academy of Management Journal* 44(3): 457–476.
36. H. Stevenson, R. Von Werssowetz, and R. Kent, *Ruth Owades, Case 383051* (Watertown, MA: Harvard Business School, 1982).

4

Entrepreneurial Marketing

Abdul Ali and Kathleen Seiders

How This Chapter Fits into a Typical MBA Curriculum
The topics covered in this chapter are appropriate for an advanced elective course in a typical MBA curriculum. This chapter is designed to provide a strategic as well as tactical decision-making perspective in entrepreneurial marketing. The specific focus throughout this chapter will be on the following topic areas:

- The application of basic marketing principles and the entrepreneurial marketing mix.
- Critical early stage marketing decisions.
- Practical, cost-effective marketing approaches for start-ups and smaller companies.
- The use of research to keep pace with rapidly changing consumer needs and evolving competition.
- The importance of product and service quality for entrepreneurs.
- The science and art of entrepreneurial customer focus.
- The solution of typical marketing-related problems that entrepreneurs face.

Who Uses This Material in the Real World—and Why Is It Important?
The materials in this chapter are intended for those who are interested in examining the marketing strategies and methods used by start-up or early stage companies. It provides a practical guide for those who are interested in starting or managing small or medium-size companies. However, managers of larger, more established businesses may be interested to know how to become entrepreneurial in marketing products or services in a more creative, impactful way without breaking the bank. This chapter compares and contrasts conventional marketing with entrepreneurial marketing on multiple fronts.

What Is Marketing?

Marketing's task is to identify and serve customers' needs. In essence, marketing spans the boundaries between a company and its customers. It is marketing that delivers a

---

The authors contributed equally to this chapter and are listed in alphabetical order.

company's products and services to customers, and marketing that takes information about those products and services, as well as about the company itself, to the market. In addition, it is marketing's role to bring information about the customers back to the company.

Although many people relate the term *marketing* to advertising and promotion, the scope of marketing is actually much broader. The American Marketing Association defines marketing as "the activity, set of institutions, and processes for creating, communicating, delivering, and exchanging offerings that have value for customers, clients, partners, and society at large."

Marketing **is the activity, set of institutions, and processes for creating, communicating, delivering, and exchanging offerings that have value for customers, clients, partners, and society at large.**

Marketing practices vary depending on the type of company and the products and services it sells. Marketers of consumer products, such as carbonated soft drinks, use different tools than marketers of business-to-business products, such as network software. Companies in the services sector, such as banks, market differently from companies that sell durable goods, such as automobile manufacturers. Successful entrepreneurs select and optimize the marketing tools that best fit their unique challenges.

Marketing Is Critical for Entrepreneurs

No venture can become established and grow without a customer market. Quite simply, without customers, there is no venture, and the process of acquiring and maintaining customers is at the core of marketing. Entrepreneurs must create the offer (design the product and set the price), take the offer to the market (through distribution), and, at the same time, tell the market about the offer (communications). These activities define the famous four Ps of marketing: product, price, place, and promotion.

Entrepreneurs often are faced with designing the entire *marketing system*—from the product and price to distribution and advertising. Because it is difficult and expensive to bring new products and services to market—even more difficult for new companies—entrepreneurs are faced with the need to be more creative and resourceful in their marketing. Many entrepreneurs must rely on creativity, rather than cash, to create a compelling image in a noisy marketplace.

Any start-up or early stage venture must gain the market's acceptance of its products or services. An important part of this process is building brand awareness, which, depending on the stage of the venture, may be small or even nonexistent. Another key part of gaining market acceptance is differentiating the product or service so the distinctiveness and value of what is being sold is clear to the customer. Beyond gaining initial acceptance, marketing plays a central role in a venture's early growth stages when changes to the original business model may be necessary. Companies focused on market growth must be able to switch gears quickly and attract new and different customer segments.

Entrepreneurs Face Unique Marketing Challenges

Entrepreneurial marketing is different from marketing done by established companies, for a number of reasons. First, entrepreneurial companies typically have limited resources—financial as well as managerial. Just as they rarely have enough money to support marketing activities, they also rarely have proven marketing expertise within the company. Most entrepreneurs do not have the option of hiring experienced marketing managers. Time—as well as money and marketing talent—is also often in short supply. Many entrepreneurs don't have the luxury of conducting marketing research, testing strategies, or carefully designing marketing campaigns.

Most entrepreneurial companies have little or no market share and have a confined geographic market presence. As a result, they enjoy few economies of scale; for example, it is difficult for small companies to make good media buys because their range of advertising is so limited. Entrepreneurs usually are limited in their access to distributors, both wholesalers and retailers. On the customer side, entrepreneurs struggle with low brand awareness and customer loyalty, both of which must be slowly cultivated.

It is clear that entrepreneurs face daunting challenges. Not only is information limited, but decision making can be muddled by strong, personal biases and beliefs. Early stage companies often stumble in their marketing because of a product focus that is excessively narrow. Companies often assume that their products will be embraced by enthusiastic consumers when, in reality, consumer inertia prevents most new products from being accepted at all. Research has shown that common marketing-related dangers for entrepreneurs include overestimating demand, underestimating competitor response, and making uninformed distribution decisions.

Entrepreneurs market to multiple audiences: investors, customers, employees, and business partners. Because none of these bonds is well established for early stage companies, it is imperative that entrepreneurs be both customer-oriented and relationship-oriented. A customer orientation involves understanding the market and where it is going. A relationship orientation is needed to create structural and emotional ties with all stakeholders. Research scholars have defined *entrepreneurial marketing* (EM) as "the proactive identification and exploitation of opportunities for acquiring and retaining profitable customers through innovative approaches to risk management, resource leveraging, and value creation."[1]

Entrepreneurial marketing **is the proactive identification and exploitation of opportunities for acquiring and retaining profitable customers through innovative approaches to risk management, resource leveraging, and value creation.**

In this chapter, we consider entrepreneurial marketing in depth. First, we address market research needed in identifying and assessing opportunities. Next, we focus on developing and implementing marketing strategies that best optimize these opportunities. We also look at how certain marketing skills serve to support a new company's growth.

Market Research and Opportunity

Behind every successful new venture is the story of a business opportunity that was recognized for its potential worth and profitably developed before others realized that potential. Identifying and assessing opportunity are two critical steps that an entrepreneur must take before starting a new venture.

Sometimes, an entrepreneur stumbles upon an opportunity in her daily life. While serendipity may occasionally play a role in identifying an opportunity, more often it is a systematic analysis of the business environment that is required. How does one identify an opportunity that is worth exploiting? Using market research tools and techniques, entrepreneurs can scan the broad macro environment for any shifts or changes that may create new business opportunities. They can interview customers to discover potential unmet needs, consult with experts to size up an opportunity, and seek out business partners to commercialize an idea and transform it into reality. While earlier chapters have dealt with opportunity recognition and criteria for evaluating venture opportunities, we focus here on the role that market research plays in identifying and assessing opportunity.

Acquiring Market Information

An entrepreneur needs to do research to identify and assess an opportunity. Intuition, personal expertise, and passion can take you only so far. Some studies show that good pre-venture market analysis could reduce venture failure rates by as much as 60 percent.[2] But many entrepreneurs tend to ignore negative market information because of their strong commitment to their idea.

We define *market research* as the collection and analysis of any reliable information that improves managerial decisions. Questions that market research can be used to answer include: What changes or disruptions in the broad macro environment are taking place that will create new business opportunities for entrepreneurs? Who would most likely buy my product or service? How big is this new opportunity? For this type of product, what attributes are important to customers? How is customers' willingness to buy influenced by product design, pricing, and communications? Where do customers buy this kind of product? How is the market likely to change in the future?

Both traditional and nontraditional marketing research can be used to assess opportunity. Often entrepreneurs do not conduct extensive marketing research because of time and resource constraints. However, entrepreneurs can overcome some of these constraints by being creative in collecting information.

There are two basic types of market data: *secondary data*, which is gathered from already published sources, like an industry association study or census reports, and *primary data*, which is collected specifically for a particular purpose through surveys, focus groups, or experiments.

A great deal of market information can be acquired from secondary resources. Since secondary research requires less time and money than primary research, we recommend that entrepreneurs first try to find the information with secondary sources. Some successful entrepreneurs use databases at college libraries to collect baseline information about product and geographic markets.

For primary research, entrepreneurs may have faculty members from business schools assign the company's project to a student team. For example, most marketing research

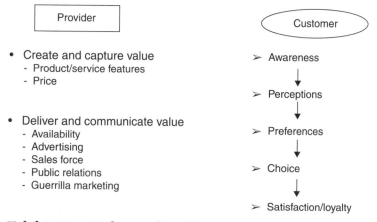

Exhibit 4.1 Understanding the Customer Choice Process

classes are structured so that the students do a real-world project as part of the course requirement. However, quality and time considerations may be such that entrepreneurs will choose marketing research firms for primary research. Some types of primary data can be collected easily, as with personal interviews or focus groups, but the limitations of such data, such as lack of statistical significance, must be recognized.

Appendix A provides a checklist of possible questions that an entrepreneur can address in a customer interview format. Such an interview can be structured as one-on-one or as a focus group. In focus groups, 5 to 10 people, moderated by a discussion leader, are encouraged to express views related to the company's products or services. The focus group has distinct stages and one needs to ask specific questions to get quality information from the group participants.

The proof that an opportunity is worth pursuing is in customers' acceptance of the idea that an entrepreneur wants to sell. Entrepreneurs must understand the customer decision-making process and how they can influence a customer's choice. Exhibit 4.1 provides an illustration of the role marketing tools play in affecting the customer choice process.

Developing and Implementing Marketing Strategy

Any company's marketing strategy must be closely aligned with its resources and capabilities. For an entrepreneurial company, this is particularly important because, with limited resources, there is little room for strategic mistakes or failure. Segmentation, targeting, and positioning are key marketing dimensions that set the strategic framework. We begin this section by discussing these three activities and their role in marketing strategy. Then we examine the widely studied marketing elements known as the *marketing mix*: product, price, distribution (place), and communications (promotion).

Segmentation and *targeting* are the processes used to identify the right customers for a company's products and services. A segment is a group of customers, defined by certain common characteristics which may be demographic or psychographic (commonly called *lifestyle*) in nature. Demographic characteristics include age, education, gender, and income; lifestyle characteristics include descriptors like active, individualistic, risk-taking, and time-pressured. The segmentation process involves identifying the most relevant *bases* (characteristics) for segmentation and then developing segment profiles. It is common practice to define a segment using a combination of demographic and lifestyle characteristics—for example high-income, sophisticated baby boomers. Marketers also segment customers based on where they live (geography), how often they use a product (usage rates), and what they value in a product (product attribute preferences). An industrial market can be segmented with some of the same variables used in segmenting consumer markets such as geography, benefits sought, and usage rate, but it could also be segmented using demographic descriptors such as company size, industrial sector, and purchasing approaches.[3]

Targeting involves comparing the attractiveness of various segments and then selecting the most attractive, which becomes the target segment, also called the target market or primary target audience. Target market definition is essential because it is the means by which companies engage in *customer selection.* The attractiveness of a segment is related to its size, growth rate, and profit potential. Targeting decisions should also be influenced by a company's specific capabilities and longer-term goals. Accurate targeting is important for entrepreneurs: It is not always apparent which customer segment(s) represents the best target market, but because of resource constraints, identifying the appropriate target market early on is critical. Pursuing multiple targets or waiting for one to emerge is an expensive strategy.

To illustrate segmentation and targeting, we offer the example of Nantucket Nectars, the new age beverage company founded by marketing-savvy entrepreneurs Tom Scott and Tom First. Relevant segment characteristics for this company are age, individualism, and health consciousness. In Nantucket Nectar's early days, its primary target market was young, active, health-oriented consumers who enjoyed breaking with conformity by choosing a noncarbonated soft drink alternative.

While segmentation and targeting are performed in relation to a company's customers, *positioning* is performed in relation to competitors. Positioning relates to customers' *perceptions* about the entrepreneur's product. Positioning usually refers to a company's offering relative to certain product attributes—the ones customers care about most. Such attributes often include price, quality, and convenience, all of which can be scaled from high to low. For example, if brands of single-serve beverages were shown on a positioning map with the two dimensions of *price* and *quality*, Nantucket Nectars would be positioned in the high-price, high-quality (upper right) quadrant, whereas a store-brand, canned cola would likely be positioned in a lower-price, lower-quality (lower left) quadrant.

The Marketing Mix

The marketing mix—the four Ps—is often referred to as a set of tools used by a company to achieve marketing-related goals. In fact, the marketing mix is so basic to a company's business model that marketing strategy often defines company or corporate strategy. In this section, we discuss the individual elements of the marketing mix, shown in Exhibit 4.2. Our focus is on the particular challenges of entrepreneurial marketers.

Product Strategy

This element of the marketing mix is often divided into the *core product* and the *augmented product*. The core product is the essential good or service, while the augmented

Exhibit 4.2   Marketing Mix Strategy for an Entrepreneur

product is the set of attributes peripherally related to the product. For example, Dell is a major marketer of personal computers (core product), but it also provides online and telephone service for troubleshooting, repair, and parts replacement (augmented service).

Another way to look at the product variable is in terms of goods and services. Whereas beverages and computers are obviously tangible goods, supermarkets, Internet service providers, and banks are services and offer service products, such as food shopping, Internet connection, and checking accounts. As has been noted for some time, the line between products and services is eroding. Moreover, we live in a services economy, where the majority of the gross national product and new job creation is tied to services. It should be noted that the word *product* may refer to either a service or a good.

In using product strategy, entrepreneurs must pay attention to the strength of the *value proposition* they are offering customers, and ensure that *product differentiation* is maximized and clear to customers. They also should be guided by the *product life cycle* in crafting their strategy, and by *product diffusion theory* in assessing how fast consumers will adopt their products. Finally, from the beginning, entrepreneurs should be obsessively focused on *quality*.

Many entrepreneurs establish companies based on a new product or product line. When a new product is being developed, the company must ensure that an unmet consumer need truly is being addressed—that there is a real *customer value proposition (CVP)*. Customer value is defined as the difference between total customer benefits and total customer costs. A product attribute is not a benefit until consumers buy into the advantage. Entrepreneurs need to know which attributes customers consider important

Exhibit 4.3   Importance/Performance Analysis

| | | Perceived Performance | |
		Poor	Good
Attribute Importance	High	Improve	Maintain
	Low	Monitor	Deemphasize

Source: Adapted from John A. Martilla and John C. James, "Importance-Performance Analysis," *Journal of Marketing*, January 1977, 77–79.

and how customers rate the company's products—and competing products—on each attribute. Exhibit 4.3 can be used to identify the product/service attributes entrepreneurs should consider when designing their offerings.

Product differentiation is important for initial product success as well as for longer-term brand building. In its early days, Maker's Mark, a sixth-generation, family-run Kentucky bourbon producer, leveraged the product attributes that make Maker's Mark unique (wheat instead of rye, six-year fermentation, roller mill, open cooker, and small batch production) to build a distinctive image for the brand. For decades, the company has been able to rely on these product differences to reinforce its quality position.

A framework that has long been used to understand product strategy is the *product life cycle*. The stages of the product life cycle are introduction, growth, maturity, and decline, and theory holds that marketing during each stage will be different. During the introduction stage, marketers must educate the customer and secure distribution. During the growth stage, customer loyalty must be cultivated and the brand must be built. Differentiation is important during maturity, and marketing efficiency is critical during the decline stage. Product life cycle analysis can be used to recognize how marketing requirements differ at each stage of a company's growth.

The marketing challenges that face entrepreneurs are formidable, in part because their companies are operating in the introduction and/or growth stages of both the product and the company life cycle. Consider the example of Stacy's Pita Chip Company, a fast-growing gourmet snack food manufacturer, now owned by Frito-Lay. The company began its marketing efforts in the introduction stage of both the company life cycle, as Stacy's, and the product life cycle, as a producer of pita chips, a product the founders accidentally created by baking pita bread left over from their sandwich cart in downtown Boston. Stacy's faced great obstacles in entering an industry dominated by giants. But by creating a high-energy presence at every major food trade show, where thousands of buyers would taste its distinctive products, Stacy's was able to steadily gain retail customers and shelf space.

An entrepreneur often builds a new venture around an innovative product. In our current business environment, with intense global competition and fast-paced technology development, entrepreneurs face increasing pressure. Even after creating a winning new venture, they must continue to develop new products in order to maintain a profitable market position. New product development is critical for market success. As noted by Professor William Bygrave, entrepreneurship combined with innovation equals success. Naturally, entrepreneurs need to understand new product opportunities and the new product development process if they are to ensure their venture's survival.

Because new products have varying levels of *newness* to both the company and the marketplace, entrepreneurs must make different *risk-return* trade-offs. At one extreme, pioneering or radical innovation represents a technological breakthrough or "new-to-the-world" product. Although pioneering products may be risky investments, they may produce handsome returns. At the other extreme, entrepreneurs may develop *incremental* products which are basically modifications of existing products, or *product line extensions*. Incremental products are less risky to develop but typically produce a more modest return.

Regardless of the type of new products entrepreneurs develop, bringing products to market quickly—by mastering the new product development process—is critical for gaining a competitive advantage. Booz, Allen, and Hamilton identified key stages of the new product development process, as shown in Exhibit 4.4. Developing new products consumes considerable time and financial resources, both of which are in short supply for entrepreneurs. Therefore, entrepreneurs must be flexible and choose the steps that are most instrumental to their specific product development process.

Entrepreneurs who introduce products that are very innovative must be particularly attentive to consumer adoption behavior. Consumer willingness to adopt a new product also is a major factor in the realm of technology products. One way to consider this is to use the *product diffusion curve* (see Exhibit 4.5), which shows customer segments

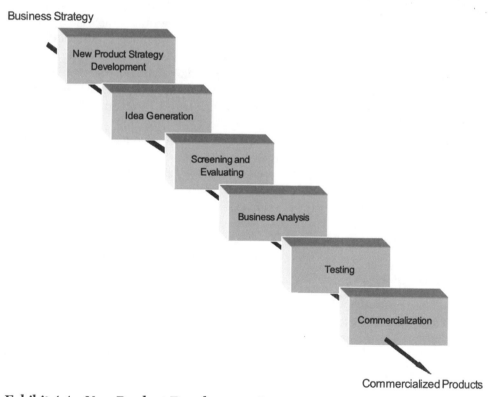

Exhibit 4.4   New Product Development Process

Source: Booz, Allen, and Hamilton, "New Products Management for the 1980s" (New York: Booz, Allen & Hamilton, 1982), 11.

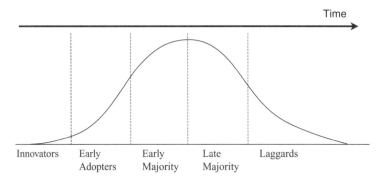

Exhibit 4.5   Product Diffusion Curve (Downloadable) Copyright © 2010 by William D. Bygrave and Andrew Zacharakis. To download this form for your personal use, please visit www.wiley.com/go/portablembainentrepreneurship.

comprised of innovators, early adopters, early majority, late majority, and laggards. A number of factors affect the rate of diffusion, or how fast customers adopt a new product. If a product represents risk or is complex, or is not completely compatible with existing products, then the market usually will adopt it at a fairly slow rate.

Entrepreneurs sometimes err in being overly product focused, concentrating on the product as they conceive it rather than as customers may want it. One way to offset the danger of this mindset is to involve the customer in the design process. Custom Research, a Baldrige National Quality Award–winning marketing research firm, surveys each of its clients prior to beginning a project. This allows the company to learn exactly what the client hopes to gain from its investment. The practice of studying the customer up front not only results in better service quality, but also enables the company to deliver a highly customized product.

Perhaps the most important product attribute for entrepreneurs is quality. Quality of product or service is an imperative, not only because it serves as a powerful differentiator, but because it is needed to gain the recommendation of customers and generate positive word of mouth. Companies with a quality orientation also find it easier to engage in internal marketing: Employees are more enthusiastic and proud about selling high-quality products than products of mediocre quality.

Pricing Strategy

Developing an optimal pricing strategy is a daunting challenge for even the most sophis-ticated entrepreneurial company. Exhibit 4.6 shows various price-setting options.

An entrepreneur incurs many costs in starting a venture. Some are fixed costs, which do not change with volume of production (such as facility, equipment, and salaries), and some are variable costs, which do change with the volume of production (such as raw materials, hourly labor, and sales commissions). The price of a product/service must be higher than its variable cost or an entrepreneur will sustain losses with the sale of each additional unit. In order to operate successfully, an entrepreneurial venture must not only recover both fixed and variable costs but must also make a reasonable profit. The

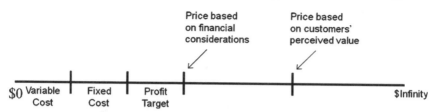

Exhibit 4.6   Pricing Decision for an Entrepreneur (Downloadable)
Copyright © 2010 by Andrew Zacharakis and William D. Bygrave.
To download this form for your personal use, please visit
www.wiley.com/go/portablembainentrepreneurship.

crash of many of the early dot-com businesses bears testimony to this simple financial logic: Many of these companies followed a get-big-fast strategy by aggressively selling their products below cost!

An entrepreneur can set the price of a product/service based on financial considerations. In fact, most entrepreneurs, in setting prices, use a cost-based method, marking up a product based on its cost and a desired profit margin. Another method, often used in conjunction with a mark-up approach, involves matching competitors' prices. A common problem with these methods is that entrepreneurs often price too low, thereby leaving money on the table. Pricing too low can have an effect that often is unanticipated: the impact on the longer-term profitability of the venture. Pricing too high also has a serious downside, as it can create a purchase barrier and limit sales.

So what choices does an entrepreneur have relative to identifying the most appropriate price? An alternative to cost-based and competitive pricing is *perceived value pricing*, which is especially viable for pricing a new or innovative product or service. Entrepreneurs also can pursue strategies that trade off high profit margins for high sales, or vice versa. Determining the full value of a product/service, and then using effective communications to convince target customers to pay for that value, is challenging even for an established company.

If possible, entrepreneurs should approach perceived value pricing with premarket price testing, estimating the number of units that will be purchased at different price points. Two well-known pricing strategies, which represent opposite ends of the pricing spectrum, are price skimming and penetration pricing. *Price skimming* involves high margins and expects to gain limited market share because prices are relatively high. *Penetration pricing* aims to gain high market share with lower margins and relatively lower prices. For entrepreneurs with a product that brings something new to the marketplace, a skimming (or modified-skimming) strategy usually is preferred. Unless channels of distribution are very well established, a penetration strategy, which generally is reserved for mature products, is hard to implement.

Price can be represented in a variety of ways. There are basic price points or price levels which are standardized or fixed, and there is *price promotion*—a valuable tool by which marketers can achieve specific goals, such as introducing a product to a new customer market. Price promotions are short-term and use regular prices as a base to discount from; they provide a way to offer customers good deals. The use of price promotions allows a company to increase sales, reward distributors, gain awareness for a new product, and clear excess inventory.

Price promotions often are necessary to maintain good relationships with distributors: Both wholesalers and retailers must offer price promotions in order to stay competitive. Price promotions also are widely used in business-to-business markets; for example, companies often reward their business customers with volume discounts applied to the ongoing purchase of particular goods and services. Promotions are an important tool for entrepreneurs, who often use them to gain an initial position in the marketplace. Nantucket Nectars used promotions to motivate retailers to make the initial purchases of their products (*trade promotion*) and offered promotions to the retailers' customers to motivate them to try the product (*consumer promotion*).

A common pricing strategy is *price discrimination*, where different prices are charged to different customer segments. Examples of this practice are as varied as the lower prices received by shoppers using store loyalty cards and the differing price structures used to charge airline passengers. *Couponing* is a widely used form of price discrimination that rewards customers who care about receiving a discount but does not reward those who don't care enough to put forth the extra effort to redeem the coupon. Couponing is used by product manufacturers as well as service companies. Coupons for discounts from retailers, rental car companies, and dry cleaners all reflect price discounting in the services sector.

Pricing is important to entrepreneurs not just because it impacts revenue and profit, but also because price plays a role in how consumers perceive a product's position in the market. Price serves as a quality cue to consumers, who often base their quality perceptions on a product's price. This is especially true when a consumer has had limited experience with the product. The *economic perspective* views consumers as rational actors who buy when the perceived benefits of a product exceeds its price. Those who study consumer behavior, however, understand that consumers' *willingness to pay* is affected by a variety of psychological factors. If a price is out of line with a consumer's price expectations, that price might be perceived as unfair.

In summary, entrepreneurs can use some marketplace wisdom relative to pricing. The selling effort of a product must match its price. Price skimming, for example, must be accompanied by a sophisticated, effective selling process. It is easier to lower than to raise prices because customers are resistant to price increases. The more established the differentiation and/or quality of a product or service, the more price insensitive the consumer—if the perceived benefits are valued. Customers also are less price sensitive when products and services are bundled into a single offer because this makes prices more difficult to compare. A good entrepreneur will be aware of both the pricing practices of competing companies and the pricing-related purchase behavior of consumers.

Distribution Strategy

Distribution presents special challenges for entrepreneurs because channels of distribution are often difficult to set up initially. Exhibit 4.7 shows the structure of traditional distribution channels for consumer and business-to-business marketing. While established businesses may introduce new products, price points, and communications strategies, they usually rely on existing channels of distribution. For example, Crest, a Procter & Gamble brand, may introduce a new type of electric toothbrush with a distinctive price position and an innovative advertising campaign, but will use its existing network of wholesalers and retailers to actually distribute the product. Entrepreneurs usually don't have this luxury.

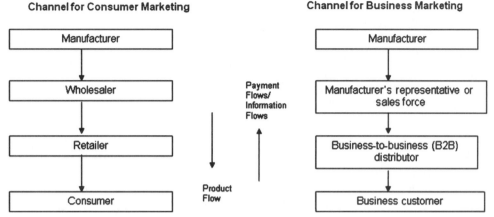

Channel for Consumer Marketing

| Manufacturer |
| Wholesaler |
| Retailer |
| Consumer |

Payment Flows/ Information Flows

Product Flow

Channel for Business Marketing

| Manufacturer |
| Manufacturer's representative or sales force |
| Business-to-business (B2B) distributor |
| Business customer |

Exhibit 4.7   Capabilities Needed to Compete in Electronic Channels

Finding the right channel can be far less difficult than breaking into the right channel. Entrepreneurs who want to market food products, for instance, face enormous barriers when they try to get their products on supermarket shelves. Most supermarkets are national chains that charge large slotting allowances—fees manufacturers must pay to, in effect, lease shelf space. Even when brokers and distributors accept new products into their lines, they may be unwilling to dedicate much effort to selling them when the products are unknown.

Distribution can be problematic for entrepreneurial service companies as well as for those that manufacture goods. Distribution decisions for a service company are often location decisions; because many services require that service providers interact directly with customers, services tend to be decentralized in their implementation. Effective distribution is the availability and accessibility of a service to the company's target customers. As early stage service companies grow, new locations are often the most important means of attracting new customers and increasing sales.

Starbucks is an international services-sector company with thousands of stores; nevertheless, the service is sold locally, and one location may be more or less successful than another. If a Starbucks location is unsuccessful, the company can cancel its lease and open an alternative location in that neighborhood, or focus on locations in other neighborhoods. But if an entrepreneur makes a bad location decision for his first or second or third location, the impact on the business can be deadly because the financial loss can paralyze the company.

Finding the Right Channel Design

Poor distribution decisions have haunted many entrepreneurial companies. Dell Computer, in its early years, became worried about the limitations of its direct model and decided to go into the retail marketplace with its computers. The low product margins and high promotional costs of the new channel took Dell by surprise, and the company lost millions of dollars before it quickly pulled out of the retail channel. Were it not for Michael Dell's brave decision to admit his mistake and execute a fast about-face, Dell might have stumbled fatally trying to make the strategy succeed.

There is a great deal of *interdependency* in a distribution channel: Each channel member has a particular function to perform, and each relies on the others. Entrepreneurs especially are inclined to rely on other companies to fulfill certain distribution tasks. Many companies were able to enter the Internet retailing sector quickly because they could outsource *fulfillment*—warehousing, picking, and delivering the order—to another company, allowing them to maintain *virtual* companies with low fixed costs. There are disadvantages to this kind of outsourcing, though: Quality is hard to control, the information flow between you and your customer is interrupted, and longer-term cost economies are harder to achieve.

Sometimes channel partners don't do what you want or expect them to do. When Nantucket Nectar's founders became frustrated with their distributors' slow progress in getting the brand established, they took over distribution themselves. Like Dell, the company lost millions of dollars trying to change its distribution model, and went back to contracting with distributors after it found more capable partners. Although distribution mistakes such as those made by Dell and Nantucket Nectars early in their company life cycles extract a price, they also teach entrepreneurs what their capabilities are and are not.

Channel Dynamics

Distribution channel strategy includes three types of channel coverage: *intensive, selective*, and *exclusive*. The appropriate strategy depends on the type of product or service that is being sold. *Intensive* coverage is used for consumer goods and other fast-moving products. The carbonated soft drink category is one of the most intensively distributed: It is sold in supermarkets, drug stores, convenience stores, restaurants, vending machines, sporting event concessions, and fast-food outlets. *Selective* distribution involves selecting specific distributors, often limiting selection geographically by establishing a dealer network. Kate Spade sells her handbags and other fashion accessories to high-end department stores but not to mainstream retailers or mass merchandisers. Selective distribution can protect dealers and retailers from competition, while helping manufacturers maintain prices by thwarting price competition. The third coverage strategy, *exclusive* distribution, is often used for luxury products. For some time, Neiman-Marcus had exclusive rights to distribute the Hermes line of very high-end leather goods and fashion accessories.

Channel partnerships or relationships have important implications for entrepreneurs. Often the channel member with the most power will prevail; for this reason, *channel power* is an important concept in distribution strategy. While channel partnerships can speed a young company's growth, preserve resources, and transfer risk, entrepreneurs must be careful not to sacrifice direct relationships with customers. Most important, relationships with channel partners must be carefully managed and monitored over time.

Another widely applied concept, *channel conflict*, refers to situations where differing objectives and turf overlap lead to true disharmony in the channel. Channel conflict was a high-profile phenomenon in the early days of the Internet, when many start-up companies were using the strategy of *disintermediation*—cutting intermediaries out of traditional distribution channels by selling direct. Amazon, the large online bookseller, created conflict between book publishers and distributors and traditional book retailers. Because Amazon could buy in volume and avoid the high occupancy costs retailers pay, it could offer an enormous assortment at deeply discounted prices. Amazon's volume allowed it to negotiate low prices from publishers and wholesalers, who in turn alienated their other customers, the traditional book retailers in the channel.

Entrepreneurs succeed with their distribution strategies when they have a strong understanding of channel economics. Giro, the bicycle helmet company that has helmeted both Greg LeMond and Lance Armstrong—American winners of the Tour de France—gained initial access to the retail channel by offering high margins and selective distribution to selected bike shops. This allowed the company to maintain its premium prices and establish loyalty among experts and cycling enthusiasts.

Current practice reflects a focus on multichannel distribution, which gives a company the ability to reach multiple segments, gain marketing synergies, provide flexibility for customers, save on customer acquisition costs, and build a robust database of purchase information. J.Crew, for instance, has been successful diversifying its store-based business to include strong catalog and online channels. But a multichannel strategy adds operating complexity and demands more resources, so entrepreneurs are advised to approach these opportunities cautiously and be careful that their timing is in line with their capabilities and resources.

Research shows that many of the most serious obstacles to entrepreneurial success are related to distribution. Specifically, entrepreneurs tend to be overly dependent on channel partners and short on understanding channel behavior in their industry. It is critical that entrepreneurs take the time to learn about distribution and make fact-based decisions about channel design and channel partnerships to overcome these threats to good distribution strategy.

Marketing Communications Strategy

Marketing communications involves conveying messages to the market—messages about the company's products and services as well as about the company itself. The marketing communications element of the marketing mix is a mix within a mix: The *communications mix* is defined as advertising, sales promotion, public relations, personal selling, direct marketing, and interactive/Internet marketing. While components of Internet marketing could belong to other traditional categories—online ads to advertising, permission e-mail to direct marketing—we give them a separate category because they represent important and popular new media and methods. The marketing communications mix and some of its key elements are shown in Exhibit 4.8.

The components of the communications mix, like the marketing mix, are often referred to as tools, and the use of these tools by marketers differs substantially across business and industry contexts. To illustrate, consumer product companies' communications often involve mass market approaches, such as advertising and sales promotion, whereas business-to-business companies use more customized, interactive tools, such as personal selling performed by a sales force. Of course, the communications a marketer uses are closely aligned with both the specific type of product the company is attempting to sell and the company's marketing objectives.

It is common marketing wisdom that a variety of tools should be used in marketing any product or service. Because of this focus on multiple methods, and the need to integrate and coordinate these methods, the term *integrated marketing communications* is often used. A range of factors—including cost, timing, and target market—determines the selection of a company's key communications tools. The question a company must answer is, what is the most effective way to communicate with my customers and influence their actions? And the sooner an entrepreneur can answer this, the better.

Exhibit 4.8   Marketing Communications Mix

Two commonly used terms to describe communications strategies are *push* and *pull*. A *push strategy* is one that aims to push a product through the channel using tools such as trade promotions, trade shows, and personal selling to distributors or other channel members. A *pull strategy's* goal is to create end user demand, and rely on that demand to pull the product through the channel. Pull strategies, which are directly targeted to end users, often employ advertising and consumer sales promotions, such as in-store specials. These strategies apply to the sale of both goods and services. Fidelity Investments, for example, can push its mutual funds through brokers or advertise them directly to investors, who then, hopefully, will request them.

Marketing communications is a broad and sophisticated field. Many of the tools that are the most visible are primarily accessible to large companies with deep marketing budgets and in-house marketing talent. This is usually the case for major television and print advertising and high-penetration direct mail campaigns. Probably the greatest breadth of tools exists within the domain of advertising, which includes everything from billboards to web sites to local newspapers to Super Bowl commercials. There also are various direct marketing tools, including catalogs, direct mail and e-mail, telemarketing, and infomercials (vehicles for direct selling). As media becomes more fragmented and technology costs decline, more and more options are available to entrepreneurs.

Advertising

What advertising choices are best for an entrepreneur? Anything that is appropriate, affordable, and measurable or at least possible to evaluate. Entrepreneurs can use traditional major media by focusing on scaled-back options, such as regional editions of national magazines, locally broadcast commercials on cable television stations, and local newspapers and radio stations. Two terms that are frequently mentioned in relation to advertising objectives are *reach*, the percentage of a company's target market that is exposed to an ad campaign within a certain time period, and *frequency*, the number of times a target market member is exposed during that period. A disadvantage for entrepreneurs is that advertising economies of scale are difficult to achieve, at least initially. But tightly targeted campaigns can be conducted efficiently with a focus on cost control.

In addition to regionalized or localized major media, there are a number of minor media options for entrepreneurs. These include classified ads, yellow pages and online information services, brochures, flyers, online bulletin boards, local canvassing (for business-to-business), and educational seminars or demonstrations. As mentioned earlier, most marketing experts support using multiple methods in combination, in part because different methods have particular strengths and weaknesses. But even though the media are varied, the message and the brand image that an entrepreneur wishes to communicate should be strictly consistent.

When selecting media, entrepreneurs match their communications goals to media capabilities. Radio is more targeted and intimate than other advertising media; it allows flexibility for the advertiser, but requires repetition for the message to get through. Television has relatively large reach and is good for demonstrating product benefits, but is usually expensive and involves substantial production costs. Many magazines are well targeted, involving, and have a long shelf life (consider how many times a magazine may be read in a doctor's waiting room). Newspapers are good for geographical targeting and promotional advertising, but have a very short shelf life and are losing ground to online news sites. Infomercials, which may also be considered a direct marketing tool, have high production costs and a short life span, but are persuasive and good for telling the product story. Online advertising, which continues to grow in importance, allows companies to reach a specific desirable customer market and offers good opportunities for measuring ad effectiveness. Brief guidelines for strategic use of advertising media are presented in Exhibit 4.9.

Even entrepreneurs often go to marketing experts for advice about how to execute campaigns and how to frame an effective message. While some early stage companies use established advertising agencies, others contract with freelance marketing professionals, many of whom have experience in the entrepreneurial domain. It is advisable for any entrepreneur to learn the basics of advertising, public relations, direct marketing, and marketing research in order to be able to select and evaluate agencies or individuals brought in to assist a company with its early stage marketing.

Sales Promotion

The three primary types of sales promotion are consumer promotions, trade promotions, and sales force promotions. Consumer promotions are deals that are offered directly to consumers and are used to support a pull strategy. Trade promotions are deals offered to a company's trade or channel partners—such as distributors or retailers—and are used to support a traditional push strategy. Sales force promotions are used by companies to motivate and reward their own sales force or their distributors' sales forces.

There are two basic subtypes of sales promotions: price and nonprice. We discussed price promotions in our section on pricing strategy. Consumer *price* promotions include coupons, rebates, and loyalty rewards; trade price promotions include discounts,

Exhibit 4.9   Strategic Use of Advertising Media

Advertising Medium	Key Factors for Entrepreneurs to Consider
Brochures and flyers	• Allow creative flexibility and focused message. • Production quantity and distribution must be well planned.
Direct mail	• Permits precise targeting and encourages direct response. • Results are measurable and can guide future campaigns.
Infomercials	• Effective for telling a story and communicating or endorsing product benefits. • Costly to produce but measurable and good for collecting data.
Internet communications	• A variety of options, such as banner ads and permission e-mail marketing. • Superior for collecting data and measuring responses.
Magazines	• Can easily be targeted, are involving for readers, and have a long shelf life. • Offer budget flexibility but involve a long lead time.
Newsletters	• Good creative opportunities and maximum control. • Cost factors (time and money) should be carefully considered.
Newspapers	• Best medium for advertising promotions and reaching a geographically based or local market. • Shelf life is fairly short and ads are usually not carefully read.
Outdoor	• Can have strong visual impact and repeat exposure; this medium is believed to offer a high return on investment. • Targeting is difficult because ads are location-bound.
Radio	• Good potential for creativity and connecting with the audience; message can be easily varied. • Excellent for targeting but ads must be repeated to be effective.
Telemarketing	• Interactive communication with one-on-one selling capabilities. • A direct response method that has faced increased regulation because it is seen by many to be intrusive.
Television	• High media and production costs but superior reach; most effective way to present and demonstrate a product. • Commonly used for brand building.
Yellow pages	• An important local medium used as a basic reference by consumers; necessary for credibility. • Low cost but standardized format limits creativity.

Source: Philip Kotler, *Marketing Management*, 11th ed. (Upper Saddle River, N.J.: Prentice Hall, 2003), 601.

allowances, buy-back guarantees, and slotting fees. Types of consumer *nonprice* promotions include product sampling, advertising specialties (such as T-shirts with a brand logo), contests, and sweepstakes. Trade nonprice promotions include trade shows and sales contests.

The effects of sales promotions differ from the effects of advertising. In general, sales promotions produce more immediate, sales-driven results whereas advertising produces a more long-term, brand-building result. Sales promotions have become increasingly popular with companies in the past couple of decades. Online coupons have been embraced by consumers; there are numerous coupon sites that offer a collection of online discount codes that consumers can use when shopping on the Internet. Most of these sites—for example, Fatwallet.com, Couponcode.com, and Retailmenot.com—were started by Web entrepreneurs. In 2008, coupon sites reported 27 million users, a 33 percent increase from the prior year.

Public Relations

Many entrepreneurs derive great value from using public relations as a strategic communications tool. Public relations has two major dimensions: publicity and corporate communications, including public affairs and investor relations. Bill Samuels Jr., the CEO of Maker's Mark bourbon, used a personal connection and an elaborate plan to gain major-league publicity (see accompanying box). And the rest, as they say, is history.

Dave Garino covered the Kentucky area for the Wall Street Journal. *Bill Samuels Jr. discovered that he and Dave had a mutual friend, Sam Walker, with whom Dave had gone to journalism school. Bill knew Dave was going to be in town covering an unrelated story and decided to try a unique approach to persuade him to do a story on Maker's Mark.*

Bill staged an event at the distillery and awarded exclusive rights to cover the show to a local news station. He found out which hotel Dave Garino was staying in and had Sam Walker arrange to meet Dave for cocktails in the hotel's bar. Next, Bill convinced the bartender to turn all the televisions above the bar to the local station that was covering the distillery show. When Dave saw the news footage he asked Sam what Maker's Mark was and why, if there was so much interest in this distillery, he had never heard of it. When Sam replied that it was the local favorite and offered to introduce him to Bill, Dave accepted. Subsequently, Dave and Bill spent three days developing a story that was published on the front page of the Wall Street Journal.

Bill later recalled: "From that one story we received about 50,000 letters inquiring about our product. The phone lines didn't stop ringing for weeks. We had one salesman at the time and we were trying to figure how to best capitalize from all this publicity."

Source: K. Seiders, "Maker's Mark Bourbon" case study and teaching note (Wellesley, MA: Babson College, Arthur M. Blank Center for Entrepreneurial Studies, 1999).

It is often argued that publicity is an entrepreneur's best friend, more valuable than millions of dollars of advertising. This is because PR is perceived as more credible and more objective; a reporter's words are more believable than those of an advertising agency. Also, the argument goes, PR is free! This, of course, is not true—it takes a significant amount of time and effort, sometimes money, and always the ability to leverage connections to generate good PR. If this were not the case, there would not be so many public relations firms charging high fees and battling for the media's attention.

Personal Selling

For companies operating in a business-to-business environment, or those that need to sell into an established distribution channel, personal selling is a core component of the communications mix. Although some companies separate sales and marketing, a company's sales force is often its primary marketing tool. Establishing and managing a sales force requires decisions related to sales force size, training, organization, compensation, and selling approaches.

A sales force is often considered to be a company's most valuable asset. Maintaining a strong sales force is an expensive proposition, though, and start-up companies often face a difficult decision: whether to absorb the expense and sell directly or hire manufacturers' representatives (*reps*, sometimes called *brokers*) to sell the company's products (along with those of other companies) on commission. Reps are advantageous in that they have existing relationships with customers, but a company has more control—and a closer relationship with its customers—if it invests in its own sales force.

A sales force may be organized geographically, by product line, by customer size, or by customer segment or industry. Compensation is usually some mix of base salary and commission, and incentives may be linked to gaining new customers, exceeding sales quotas, or increasing profitability. Current marketing practice places a high value on selecting and retaining customers based on their profit potential to the company. The sales force typically should have access to effective selling materials, credible technical data, and client management software that will ensure an effective and efficient selling process.

Personal selling is an important activity for entrepreneurs on an informal, personal level—through professional networking. Leveraging personal and industry connections is a key success factor, especially in the start-up or early growth stage of the venture. But this is a time consuming and often laborious process, which is often neglected and rarely fully optimized. Giro's founder, Jim Gentes, personally attended top triathlons and other high-profile races across the country, demonstrating his helmets and giving them to the best cyclists. Jim was ahead of his time in understanding the value of endorsements from world-class athletes.

Direct Marketing

Entrepreneurs can implement direct marketing campaigns to be broad-based or to be local or limited in scope. Direct marketing methods include direct mail, catalogs, telemarketing, infomercials, and permission (where consumers elect to opt in) e-mail. The effectiveness of direct media is easy to measure, and these media are ideal for building a database that can be used for future marketing and analysis. Direct marketing is an important tool for communicating with new or existing customers, who can be targeted for mailings that range from thank-you notes to announcements of future promotions.

With the increased use of technology and databases in marketing, and the growing sophistication of the Internet channel, the practice of one-to-one marketing has become pervasive. This type of marketing is interactive and so has qualities similar to personal selling: A company can address a customer on an individual level, factoring in that customer's previous purchasing behavior and other kinds of information, and then respond accordingly. The use of databases allows marketers to personalize communications and design customer-specific messages.

Customer relationship management (CRM) systems are designed to help companies compile and manage data about their customers. While CRM systems are usually large-scale and expensive, an astute entrepreneur can set up a more fundamental system to capture and use customer data to facilitate relationship building. Part of this process involves capturing the right metrics—for example, the *cost of customer acquisition* or the *average lifetime value of a customer*—and knowing how to act on them.

Interactive and Internet Marketing

With the intense activity in new media channels, some radically different arenas have become relevant for marketing. These include chat rooms, blogs, and social networking and messaging sites such as Twitter.com, MySpace.com, Facebook.com, and LinkedIn.com. An interesting phenomenon for marketers is the prominent role of third-party opinion where products and services are concerned—for example, specialized blogs, expert reviews, and user rating services. Sites such as Yelp, Epinions, and TripAdvisor must balance the competing interests of the site users (including volunteer reviewers) and businesses that provide critical advertising revenue.

The third-party sites' influence has produced a problem called *astroturfing*, where companies' employees, agencies, or related individuals, in a deceptive manner express false praise and recommendations for products they wish to protect or promote. Although codes have been established by organizations such as the Blog Council, their lack of enforcement means individual companies are left to enforce their own codes. As one contributor to the RetailWire blog noted, "When access to media is broadened, both the truth and the half-truth become much more available."

Guerrilla Marketing

Guerrilla marketing is a commonly used term that defines marketing activities that are nontraditional, grassroots, and captivating—that gain consumers' attention and build awareness of the company. The practice of guerrilla marketing is often linked to creating a buzz, generating a lot of word of mouth in the marketplace, or even spreading virally in the population. The terms *buzz*, *viral*, or *word of mouth* marketing are usually associated with these unconventional promotional practices.

Entrepreneurs may use all these nontraditional promotion campaigns to get people's attention, especially younger generations who may not pay attention to TV campaigns and print media. Such guerrilla marketing is also attractive to entrepreneurs because they often have to work with a limited or nonexistent budget and traditional media is very expensive. Unfortunately for entrepreneurs, such nontraditional promotional methods are getting the attention of big marketers, as they want to break through the clutter of existing media. BzzAgent, a Boston-based word of mouth marketing agency, has more than 500,000 agents who will try clients' products and then talk about them with their friends, relatives, and acquaintances over the duration of the campaign. It has worked with companies like Anheuser-Busch, General Mills, and Volkswagen. Procter & Gamble's Tremor division has a panel of 350,000 moms and 200,000 teenagers who are asked to talk with friends about new products or concepts that P&G sends them. Some experts, however, suggest that traditional marketers have underused public relations or used it only as an afterthought, thus opening the door for creative guerrilla marketers.

It is easier to define what guerrilla marketing *does* than what it *is*. Guerrilla marketing is heard above the noise in the marketplace and makes a unique impact: It makes people talk about the product and the company, effectively becoming missionaries for the brand. It creates drama and interest and a positive *affect*, or emotion: all pretty amazing results. But in fact, truly good guerrilla marketing is as difficult as (maybe more than) good traditional marketing because many companies are trying to do it, and it is hard to break free from the pack.

Guerrilla marketing may be best understood as guerrilla *tactics* that can be applied to various media or elements of the communications mix rather than as an entirely different communications tool. Guerrilla tactics can be used in advertising (riveting posters in subways) and in personal selling (creative canvassing at a trade show), but they are most often used as a form of PR—as tactics that garner visibility and positive publicity. The president of Maker's Mark practiced guerrilla marketing when he inspired the *Wall Street Journal* reporter to learn and write the story of his bourbon. Nantucket Nectars' Tom and Tom were relentless guerrilla marketers, dressing up like grapes and making a stir on the Cape Cod Highway on Memorial Day weekend as thousands of motorists were stuck in traffic, and sending purple vans to outdoor concerts to distribute free juice before it became common practice. During February and March 2008, Travel Alberta International used ordinary bench seating and some clever photo wraps to put commuters into a momentary paradise (the Great White North version). Eight stations featured the installations, but apparently eight was enough: Visits to skicanadianrockies.com jumped 138 percent in the period.[4]

Much of what is now called *event marketing* is in the realm of guerrilla marketing because it is experiential, interactive, and light-hearted. But as previously noted, guerrilla tactics are becoming more and more difficult to execute because every corporate marketing executive is also trying to succeed at guerrilla marketing, and has a much larger budget. Sony Ericsson Mobile executed a guerrilla marketing campaign in New York City that involved trained actors and actresses pretending to be tourists and asking people passing by to snap a picture with the company's new mobile phone/digital camera product. Deceptive? Yes, but too commonplace a tactic to truly be controversial.

In some cases, however, the results of guerrilla marketing may have an opposite effect. On January 31, 2007, several magnetic light displays in and around Boston, Massachusetts, were mistaken for possible explosive devices and created a terror alert, disrupting the normal city life for a few hours. The suspicious objects were later revealed to be a guerrilla marketing ploy to depict the characters of an animated TV series from the Cartoon Network.[5]

In conclusion, entrepreneurs who create successful marketing strategies must have a clear vision of their goal. They must also understand how one strategic element affects another, because if the marketing mix elements of product, price, distribution, and communications are not perfectly compatible—if the mix is not internally logical—the strategy will not work. Even a good beginning strategy is not enough, however, since the marketplace is dynamic, and entrepreneurial companies, more than mature businesses, are compelled to constantly reevaluate strategy and how it is affecting growth.

Marketing Skills for Managing Growth

It is beyond the scope of this chapter to offer a comprehensive discussion of the next step: the marketing processes and capabilities a young company needs in order to pursue strong growth. However, we suggest that two key areas of focus are *understanding and listening to customers* and *building a visible and enduring brand*.

Understanding and Listening to the Customer

Although intuition-based decision making can work well initially for some entrepreneurs, intuition has its limitations. Entrepreneurs must be in constant touch with their customers as they grow their companies. When a company decides to introduce its second product or open a new location, for example, it needs to be able to determine whether that product or location will be welcomed in the marketplace. Entrepreneurs with a successful first product or location often overestimate demand for the second, sometimes because their confidence encourages them to over-rely on their own intuition.

Entrepreneurs must obtain information that will allow them to understand consumer buying behavior and customer expectations related to product design, pricing, and distribution. They also need information about the best way to communicate with customers and influence their actions. Finally, they need information about the *effectiveness* of their own marketing activities, so they can continue to refine them. Marketers build relationships, in part, by using information to customize the marketing mix. Good entrepreneurial marketers do whatever it takes to build relationships with customers.

Entrepreneurs involved in a high growth strategy often need to continuously find new customer segments to support that growth. Bill Samuels Jr. recognized that for Maker's Mark to grow significantly, a new segment would need to be reached: Drinkers of other types of alcohol would need to be switched to bourbon (and to Maker's Mark) because the bourbon connoisseur market was near saturation. Rather than relying on his own intuition, Samuels studied the consumer market to understand where he would find his new customers and how he would attract them.

There are a number of ways to listen to customers; some involve formal research, and others involve informal systems for soliciting information and scanning the market environment. Leonard Berry cites a portfolio of methods that entrepreneurs can use to build a *listening system*.[6] These include:

- *Transactional surveys* to measure customer satisfaction with the company.
- *New and lost customer surveys* to see why customers choose or leave the firm.
- *Focus group interviews* to gain information on specific topics.
- *Customer advisory panels* to get periodic feedback and advice from customers.
- *Customer service reviews* to have periodic, one-on-one assessments.
- *Customer complaint/comment capture* to track and address customer complaints.
- *Total market surveys* to assess the total market—customers and noncustomers.

Building the Brand

All entrepreneurs face the need for brand building, which involves the dual task of building brand awareness and brand equity. *Brand awareness* is the customer's ability to recognize and recall the brand when provided a cue. Marketing practices that create brand awareness also help shape *brand image*, which relates to how customers perceive the brand. *Brand equity* is the effect of brand awareness and brand image on customer response to the brand. It is brand equity, for example, that spurs consumers to pay a premium price for a brand—a price that exceeds the value of the product's tangible attributes.

Brand equity can be positive or negative. Positive brand equity is the degree of marketing advantage a brand would hold over an unnamed competitor. Negative brand equity is the disadvantage linked to a specific brand. Brand building is closely linked to a company's communications strategy. While brand awareness is created through sheer exposure to a brand—through advertising or publicity—brand image is shaped by how a company projects its identity, through its products, communications, and employees. The customer's actual experience with the brand also has a strong effect on brand image.

Maker's Mark used its communications strategy, implemented through humorous, distinctive print advertising in sophisticated national magazines like *Forbes* and *BusinessWeek*, to create a brand image that would help establish a high-end market for bourbon where none had existed in the past. The company created a likeable, genuine brand personality for its bourbon. Because many of the advertisements were in the form of an open letter from Bill Samuels Jr. to his customers, Samuels was able to represent and personalize the brand.

Conclusion

Marketing is often described as a delicate balance of art and science. Certainly, developing the expertise to be a master marketer is difficult, especially for entrepreneurs who are constantly pulled in a thousand directions. Nevertheless, the task remains: to have customer knowledge and PR mastery; to recognize effective advertising as well as effective experiential promotion. Entrepreneurial marketers must, first and foremost, be able to sell: sell their ideas, their products, their passion, their company's long-term potential. And they must learn the skill of knowing where the market is going, now and into the future.

Early stage companies often find it necessary to scale up or change focus. In these scenarios, competition can be a potent driver of marketing decisions, whether it involves staying under the radar screen of giant companies or buying time against a clone invasion. But successful entrepreneurs will have a strong, focused marketing strategy—a consistent strategy—and therefore will not easily be thrown off course.

Appendix A
Customer Interview

Some important factors to consider in creating a customer interview are:

- To whom should we ask the questions?
- What possible information would be asked for?
- Should the questions be open-ended or structured?
- How should the questions be sequenced?

Following is a sample approach that can be tailored to meet your research needs.

General Outline

- **Opening discussion (introduction and warm-up)**: The researcher introduces himself, briefly describes the research purpose, assures the interviewee about the confidentiality of responses, and states the expected duration of the interview session.
- Opening questions: Think of the last time you purchased or used such a product.
  - What prompted or triggered this activity?
  - What specific activities did you perform to get the product or service?
  - What was the outcome of your shopping experience?
- Current practice:
  - How do you currently purchase or use a product/service of interest?
  - How did you go about deciding what to buy?
  - How frequently do you buy/use this product/service?
  - How much do you buy/use each time?
  - Where do you buy it?
- Familiarity/awareness about product/service: What other products/services/stores have you considered before deciding on the final product/service you bought?
- Important attributes: If you were shopping for such a product, what would you look for? What is important? What characteristic(s) are important to you?
- Perception of respondents:
  - How would you compare different products/services?
  - How highly do you think of the product/service you bought compared with its competitors with respect to these attributes?
- Overall satisfaction or liking toward the product/service: Ask about the interviewee's satisfaction level and preference ranking among competitive products.

Product Demo/Introduction/Description

The purpose of this part of the interview is to get reactions to the new product concept and elicit a response that may identify additional decision drivers.

- What do you like about this idea?
- What do you dislike?
- Does listening to this idea suggest some factors that you would consider important and that we have not discussed so far?
- Does it change the importance you attach to different factors before choosing a product or service?
- Purchase intent for new product or service:
  - What would be the level of interest or willingness of respondents to buy or use this new product/service?
  - At what price?

- How likely is it that you would buy such a product or service?

  a. Would definitely buy.
  b. Would probably buy.
  c. Might or might not buy.
  d. Would probably not buy.
  e. Would definitely not buy.

- How much would you be willing to pay for such a product or service?
- Please note that comparable products are priced at $——. Knowing this, how much would you be willing to pay for such a product or service?
- Media habits:
  - How do you find out about a product or service?
  - What newspapers, magazines, radio programs, TV shows, and so on, do you read, listen to, or watch?

Demographic and Other Information, and Wrap-up

Demographic and personal information should be requested at the end of the interview: city of residence, age, income, occupation, gender, education, and so on. When interviewing potential business clients, ask about the size of their firm (revenue, total full-time staff, R&D staff), resources, experience, skills, and so on.

Ask the interviewee for any final comments or ideas, and thank them for their time.

Downloadable Resources for this chapter available at www.wiley.com/go/portablembainentrepreneurship

Customer Interview
Product Diffusion Curve
Pricing Decision for an Entrepreneur

Notes

1. M. Morris, M. Schindehutte, and R. LaForge, "Entrepreneurial Marketing: A Construct for Integrating Emerging Entrepreneurship and Marketing Perspectives," *Journal of Marketing Theory and Practice*, Fall 2002, 1–19.
2. G. Hills, "Market Analysis and Marketing in New Ventures: Venture Capitalists' Perceptions," in K. Vesper, ed., *Frontiers of Entrepreneurship Research* (Wellesley, MA: Babson College, 1984), 167–182.
3. B. Shapiro and T. Bonoma, "How to Segment Industrial Markets," *Harvard Business Review*, May/June 1984, 104–110.
4. "Heard on the Street: Tales of Guerrilla Marketing," *AdWeek* 49 (36) (December 8, 2008): 12–13.
5. S. Smalley and R. Mishra, "Froth, Fear, and Fury: Cartoon Devices Spur Anti-terror Sweeps; Two Men Are Arrested," *Boston Globe*, February 1, 2007, www.boston.com/news/local/massachusetts/articles/2007/02/01/froth_fear_and_fury/.
6. L. Berry, *Discovering the Soul of Service* (New York: Free Press, 1999), 100–101.

5

Business Planning

Andrew Zacharakis

How This Chapter Fits in a Typical MBA Curriculum

Business planning is often central to teaching entrepreneurship. Entrepreneurship is an iterative cycle between *thinking* and *acting*. If would-be entrepreneurs only think and never *act* on that thinking, then they are what I affectionately term "cocktail entrepreneurs." For any new business or invention that comes around, cocktail entrepreneurs will regale you with tales about how they thought of this idea first and how the company that ultimately launched it "stole" their idea, or some other reason why the entrepreneur didn't *act*. In reality, cocktail entrepreneurs are missing a key component to entrepreneurial success—the ability to *act* on their ideas. Likewise, entrepreneurs who *act* without *thinking* are apt to make more mistakes, and those mistakes are often much more costly than entrepreneurs who are active *thinkers*. Thus, entrepreneurship is an iterative balance between *thinking* and *acting*.

Within most MBA programs, there is a course that is focused on business planning, because it is a means to gain deep learning about the opportunity that you wish to pursue. While most MBA courses focus on producing a formal finished product that the entrepreneur can share with investors or other stakeholders, it is the process that is important. As I tell my students, I don't care whether they produce an actual written document, or just accumulate numerous computer files on areas of importance. But following a formal process can help ensure that you don't miss any important gaps in your planning process. As General Dwight D. Eisenhower famously stated, "In preparing for battle I have always found that plans are useless, but planning is indispensable."[1]

Who Uses This Material in the Real World

Business planning is widely used throughout the business world. Entrepreneurs use business planning to launch nascent ventures, and managers throughout existing organizations use business planning on a regular basis as they anticipate their companies' next moves. Large Fortune 500 companies also see the benefits of business planning. For example, Bert DuMars, vice president of e-business and interactive marketing at Newell Rubbermaid, was tasked with integrating social

Special thanks to Matt Feczko, Michael DiPietro, Dan Goodman, Henry McGovern, and R. Gabriel Shih for their assistance in writing this chapter.

media marketing into well-established products, such as the Sharpe pen. "This is a new area for us and heavy investing (whether dollars, personnel or both) without understanding how, when, and why our consumers would like to engage with us is risky and dangerous for our brands."[2] For Newell Rubbermaid, it would be considered reckless to pursue a new opportunity without the benefit of thoughtful evaluation that is achieved through a well-prepared business plan.

The Story of Your Business

The purpose of business planning is to tell a story—the story of your business. Thorough business planning can establish the fact that there is an opportunity worth exploiting and should then describe the details of how this will be accomplished. During the dot-com boom of the late 1990s, many entrepreneurs and venture capitalists questioned the importance of the business plan. Typical of this hyper-start-up phase are stories like that of James Walker, who generated financing on a 10 day-old company based on "a bunch of bullet points on a piece of paper." He stated, "It has to happen quick in the hyper-competitive wireless-Internet-technology world. There's a revolution every year and a half now."[3] The implication was simple: Business planning took time—time that entrepreneurs didn't have.

April 2000 brought a sobering wake-up call for investors and entrepreneurs who had invested in that dot-com boom. Previously, many entrepreneurs believed that all they needed in order to find investors and go public was a few PowerPoint slides and a good idea. The NASDAQ crash in April dispelled those beliefs as people came to realize that the majority of these businesses never had the potential to produce profits. Today, investors have learned from this lesson and demand well-researched market opportunities and solid business planning. Entrepreneurs have also learned the various benefits of a well-researched plan.

There is a common misperception that business planning is primarily used for raising capital. Although a good business plan assists in raising capital, the primary purpose of the process is to help entrepreneurs gain a deeper understanding of the opportunity they are envisioning. Many would-be entrepreneurs doggedly pursue ideas that will never be profitable because they lack deep understanding of the business model. The relatively little time spent developing a sound business plan can save thousands or even millions of dollars that might otherwise be wasted in a wild goose chase. For example, if a person makes $100,000 per year, spending 200 hours on a business planning process equates to a $10,000 investment in time spent ($50/hour × 200 hours). However, launching a flawed business concept can quickly accelerate into millions in spent capital. Most entrepreneurial ventures raise enough money to survive two years, even if the business will ultimately fail. Assuming the only expense is the time value of the lead entrepreneur, a two-year investment equates to $200,000, not to mention the lost opportunity cost and the likelihood that other employees were hired and paid and that other expenses were incurred. So do yourself a favor and spend the time and money up front.

The business planning *process* helps entrepreneurs shape their original vision into a better opportunity by raising critical questions, researching answers for those questions, and then answering them. For example, one question that every entrepreneur needs to answer is "What is the customer's pain?" Conversations with customers and other trusted advisers assist in better targeting the product offering to what customers need and want. This pre-start-up work saves untold effort and money that an entrepreneur might spend trying to reshape the product after the business has been launched. While all businesses adjust their offerings based upon customer feedback, business planning helps the entrepreneur to anticipate some of these adjustments in advance of the initial launch.

Perhaps the greatest benefit of business planning is that it allows the entrepreneur to articulate the business opportunity to various stakeholders in the most effective manner. The plan provides the background so the entrepreneur can communicate the upside potential and attract equity investment. The business plan provides the validation needed to convince potential employees to leave their current jobs for the uncertain future of a new venture. It is also the instrument that can secure a strategic partner or key customer or supplier. In short, business planning provides the entrepreneur with the deep understanding she needs to answer the critical questions that various stakeholders will ask. Completing a well-founded business plan gives the entrepreneur credibility in the eyes of various stakeholders.

Types of Plans

Business plans can take a number of forms depending upon their purpose. Each form requires the same level of effort and leads to the same conclusions, but the final document is crafted differently depending on who uses it and when they use it. For instance, when you are introducing your concept to a potential investor, you might send them a short, concise summary plan. As the investor's interest grows and she wants to more fully investigate the concept, the investor may ask for a more detailed plan. Although commonly associated with raising capital, a business plan serves so much more than the needs of potential investors. Employees, strategic partners, financiers, and board members all may find use in a well-developed business plan. Most importantly, the entrepreneur herself gains immeasurably from the business planning process as it allows her not only to run the company better, but also to clearly articulate her story to stakeholders who may never read the plan. In conclusion, different consumers of the business plan require different presentation of the work.

If outside capital is needed, a business plan geared towards equity investors or debt providers typically is 25 to 40 pages long. Entrepreneurs need to recognize that professional equity investors (such as venture capitalists) and professional debt providers (such as bankers) will not read the entire plan from front to back. That being the case, the entrepreneur needs to produce the plan in a format that facilitates spot reading. We investigate the major sections that comprise business plans throughout this chapter. My general rule of thumb is that less is more. For instance, I've seen more plans receive venture funding that were closer to 25 pages than 40 pages.

A second type of business plan, the *operational* plan, is primarily for the entrepreneur and her team to guide the development, launch, and initial growth of the venture. There really is no length specification for this type of plan; however, it is common for these plans to exceed 80 pages. The basic organizational format of the two types of plans is the same, but the level of detail tends to be much greater in an operational plan. The creation of this document is where the entrepreneur really gains the deep understanding so important in discerning how to build and run the business. Since this document is typically for internal use only, it may not be published per se, but it might exist virtually on various computer files.

A *dehydrated* business plan is considerably shorter than the previous two, typically no more than 10 pages. The purpose of this plan is to provide an initial conception of the business. As such, it can be used to test initial reaction to the entrepreneur's idea. It is a document that the entrepreneur can share with her confidantes and receive feedback before investing significant time and effort on a longer business planning process.

After entrepreneurs complete the business planning process, I encourage them to come back and rewrite the dehydrated plan (otherwise known as an *expanded executive summary*). This expanded executive summary can be used to attract attention. For instance, entrepreneurs may send it to investors that they have recently met to spur interest and a meeting. It is usually better to send an expanded executive summary rather than a full business plan, as the investor will be more apt to read it. If the investor is interested, she will call the entrepreneur in for a meeting. If the meeting goes well, the investor often then asks for the full business plan.

From Glimmer to Action: The Process

Perhaps the hardest part of business planning is getting started. Compiling the data, shaping it into an articulate story, and producing a finished product can be a daunting task. That being the case, the best way to attack business planning is in steps. First, write a short (less than five pages) summary of your current vision. This provides a road map for you and others to follow as you complete the rest of the planning process. Second, start attacking major sections of the planning process. Although each section interacts and influences every other section, it is often easiest for entrepreneurs to write the product/service description first. This is usually the most concrete component of the entrepreneur's vision. Keep in mind, however, that business planning isn't purely a sequential process. You will be filling in different parts of the plan simultaneously or in whatever order makes the most sense in your mind. Finally, after completing a first draft of all the major sections, it is time to come back and rewrite a shorter, more concise executive summary. Not too surprisingly, the executive summary will be quite different than the original summary because of all the learning and reshaping that the business planning process facilitates.

Wisdom is in realizing that the business plan is a living document. Although your first draft will be polished, most business plans are obsolete the day they come off the presses. That means that entrepreneurs are continuously updating and revising their business plan. Each major revision should be kept and filed, and occasionally looked back upon for the lessons you have learned. Remember, the importance of the business plan isn't the final product, but the learning that is gleaned from writing the novel of your vision. It articulates what you see in your mind, as well as crystallizes that vision for you and your team. It also provides a history, a photo album if you will, of the birth, growth, and maturity of your business. Although daunting, business planning can be exciting and creative, especially if you are working on it with your founding team. So now let us dig in and examine how to effectively conduct the business planning process.

The Story Model

One of the major goals of business planning is to attract various stakeholders and convince them of the potential of your business. Therefore, you need to keep in mind how these stakeholders will interpret your plan. The guiding principle is that you are writing a story.

Exhibit 5.1   Taglines

Nike:	*Just Do It!*
Federal Express:	*When it absolutely, positively has to be there overnight*
McDonald's:	*We love to see you smile*
Cisco Systems:	*Discover all that's possible on the Internet*

All good stories have a theme, a unifying thread that ties the setting, characters, and plot together. If you think about the most successful businesses in America, they all have well publicized themes, summarized in taglines. When you hear these taglines, you instantly gain insight into the business. For example, when you hear the tagline "When it absolutely, positively has to be there overnight," most people connect it to Federal Express and package delivery. In addition, most people think of reliability—the quality that is associated with FedEx. Similarly, "Just do it" is intricately linked to Nike and the image of athletic proficiency (see Exhibit 5.1). A tagline is a sentence, or even a fragment of a sentence, that summarizes the pure essence of your business. It is the theme that every sentence, paragraph, page, diagram, and so on, within your business plan should adhere to, the unifying idea of your story. A useful tip is to put your tagline in a footer that runs on the bottom of every page. As you are writing, if the section doesn't build on, explain, or otherwise directly relate to the tagline, it most likely isn't a necessary component to the business plan. Rigorous adherence to the tagline facilitates writing a concise and coherent business plan.

The key to the story model is capturing the reader's attention. The tagline is the foundation, but in writing the plan you want to create a number of visual catch-points. Too many business plans are text-laden, dense manifestos. Only the most diligent reader will wade through all that text. Help the reader by highlighting different key points throughout the plan. How do you create these catch-points? Some effective techniques include extensive use of headings and subheadings, strategically placed bullet point lists, diagrams, charts, and the use of sidebars.[4] The point is to make the document not only content rich, but visually attractive.

Now, let's take a look at the major sections of the plan (see Exhibit 5.2). Keep in mind that although there are variations, most plans have these components. It is important

Exhibit 5.2   Business Plan Outline

I.	Cover
II.	Executive Summary
III.	Table of Contents
IV.	Industry, Customer, and Competitor Analysis
V.	Company and Product Description
VI.	Marketing Plan
VII.	Operations Plan
VIII.	Development Plan
IX.	Team
X.	Critical Risks
XI.	Offering
XII.	Financial Plan

to keep your plan as close to this format as possible because many stakeholders are accustomed to the format and it facilitates spot reading. If you are seeking venture capital, for instance, you want to facilitate quick perusal because venture capitalists often spend as little as five minutes on a plan before rejecting it or putting it aside for later consideration. If a venture capitalist becomes frustrated with an unfamiliar format, it is more likely that she will reject it rather than try to pull out the pertinent information. Even if you aren't seeking venture capital, the structure given in Exhibit 5.2 is easy for other investors to follow and understand. Furthermore, the sections highlighted provide a road map for questions that you need to consider as you prepare to launch your business.

The Business Plan

We will progress through the sections in the order that they typically appear, but keep in mind that you can work on the sections in any order that you wish.

The Cover

The cover of the plan should include the following information: company name, tagline, contact person and address, phone number, fax number, e-mail address, date, disclaimer, and copy number. Most of the information is self-explanatory, but a few things should be pointed out (see Exhibit 5.3). First, the contact person for a new venture should be the president or another founding team member. I have seen some business plans that failed to include the contact person's name, e-mail, and phone on the cover. Imagine the frustration of an excited potential investor who can't find out how to contact the entrepreneur to gain more information. More often than not, that plan will end up in the rejected pile.

Second, business plans should have a disclaimer along these lines:

> This business plan has been submitted on a confidential basis solely to selected, highly qualified investors. The recipient should not reproduce this plan, nor distribute it to others without permission. Please return this copy if you do not wish to invest in the company.

Controlling distribution is particularly important when seeking investment, especially if you do not want to violate Regulation D of the Securities Exchange Commission (SEC), which specifies that you may only solicit qualified investors (high net worth and income individuals).

The cover should also have a line stating which number copy it is. For example, you will often see on the bottom right portion of the cover a line that says "Copy 1 of 5 copies." Entrepreneurs should keep a log of who has copies so that they can control for unexpected distribution.

Finally, the cover should be eye-catching. If you have a product or prototype, a picture of it can draw the reader in. Likewise, a catchy tagline draws attention and encourages the reader to look further.

Executive Summary

This section is the most important part of the business plan. If you don't capture the reader's attention in the executive summary, it is unlikely that she will read any other parts of the plan. This is just like a book's jacket notes: Most likely, the reader will only buy

THE

HISTORY

SHOPPE™

Making history come to life.

Matthew J. Feczko
13333 Washington Street Suite 33
Wellesley, MA 02481
mfellows@historyshoppe.com

Dated: December 4, 2008

Copy #:   **3 of 5**   Distributed to: Zacharakis

Exhibit 5.3   Sample Business Plan Cover

the book if she is impressed with the notes inside the cover. Therefore, you want to hit your reader with the most compelling aspects of your business opportunity right up front.

Hook the reader. That means having the first sentence or paragraph highlight the potential of the opportunity. "The current market for widgets is $50 million, growing at an annual rate of 20 percent. Moreover, the emergence of mobile applications is likely to accelerate this market's growth. Company XYZ is positioned to capture this wave with its proprietary technology: the secret formula VOOM." This creates the right tone. The first sentence emphasizes that the potential opportunity is huge and that company XYZ has some competitive advantage that enables it to become a big player in this market. Yet I have read too many plans that start with "Company XYZ, incorporated in the state of

Delaware, will develop and sell widgets." Ho-hum. That does not excite me. I don't really care, at this point, that the business is incorporated or that it is a Delaware corporation (aren't they all?). Capture my attention immediately or risk losing me altogether.

Common subsections within the executive summary include:

- Description of opportunity.
- Business concept.
- Industry overview.
- Target market.
- Competitive advantage.
- Business model and economics.
- Team and offering.
- Financial snapshot.

Remember that since this is an executive summary, all of these components are covered in the body of the plan. As such, you will explore them in greater detail as you progress through the sections. Keep it brief here.

Since the executive summary is the most important part of the finished plan, it should be written after you have gained your deep learning by going through all of the other sections. Don't confuse the executive summary included in the plan with the expanded executive summary that I suggested you write as the very first step of the business plan process. Again, the two summaries are likely to be significantly different as the later summary incorporates all the deep learning that you have gained throughout the process. Don't recycle your initial summary. Rewrite it entirely based on the hard work you have done going through the business planning process.

Table of Contents

Continuing the theme of making the document easy to read, a detailed table of contents is critical. It should list major sections, subsections, exhibits, and appendixes. The table provides the reader a road map to your plan (see Exhibit 5.4).

Industry, Customer, and Competitor Analysis

Industry

The goal of this section is to illustrate the business opportunity and how you are going to capture that opportunity. Before you can develop your plot and illustrate a theme, you need to provide a setting or context for your story. A useful framework for visualizing the opportunity is Timmon's Model of Opportunity Recognition.[5] Using the "three Ms" helps quantify an idea and assess how strong an opportunity the idea is.

First, examine *market demand*. If the market is growing at 20 percent or better, the opportunity is more exciting. Second, we look at *market size and structure*. A market that is currently $50 million with $1 billion potential is attractive. This often is the case in emerging markets, those that appear poised for rapid growth and have the potential to change how we live and work. For example, the PC, disk drive, and computer hardware markets of the 1980s were very hot. Many new companies were born and rode the wave of the emerging technology, including Apple, Microsoft, and Intel. In the 1990s, it was anything dealing with the Internet. Google, eBay, and Facebook have leveraged the

Exhibit 5.4   Business Plan Table of Contents

TABLE OF CONTENTS

Internet and changed the way we live. Today, we are seeing important trends in energy and environment that have created a clean technology boom. According to the 2008 Clean Energy Trends Report, revenue from clean technologies grew 40 percent from $55 billion in 2006 to $77 billion in 2007 and is projected to grow to $255 billion by 2017.[6]

Another market structure that tends to have promise is a fragmented market where small, dispersed competitors compete on a regional basis. Many of the big names in retail revolutionized fragmented markets. For instance, category killers such as Wal-Mart, Staples, and Home Depot consolidated fragmented markets by providing quality products at lower prices. These firms replaced the dispersed regional and local discount office supply and hardware stores.

The final M is *margin analysis*. Do firms in the industry enjoy high gross margins (revenues minus cost of goods sold) of 40 percent or greater? Higher margins allow for higher returns, which again leads to greater potential businesses.

The three Ms help distinguish opportunities and as such should be highlighted as early as possible in your plan. Describe your overall industry in terms of revenues, growth, and pertinent future trends. Within this section, avoid discussing your concept—the proposed product or service you will offer. Instead, use dispassionate, arm's-length analysis of the industry with the goal of highlighting a space or gap that is underserved. Thus, how is the industry segmented currently, and how will it be segmented into the future? After identifying the relevant industry segments, identify the segment that your product will target. Again, what are the important trends that will shape the segment into the future?

Customer

Once the plan has defined the market space it plans to enter, the target customer needs to be examined in detail. The entrepreneur needs to define who the customer is by using demographic and psychographic information. The better the entrepreneur can define her specific customers, the more apt she is to deliver a product that the customer truly wants. Although you may argue that everyone who is hungry is a restaurant's customer, such a vague definition makes it hard to market to the core customer. As a middle aged man with a family, I have different eating habits than I did in my twenties. I frequent different types of establishments and expect certain kinds of foods within a certain price range. The entrepreneur needs to understand who her core customer is so that she can create a product that the core customer wants and then market a message to which the core customer responds.

A venture capitalist recently told me that the most impressive entrepreneur is the one who comes into his office and not only identifies who the customer is in terms of demographics and psychographics, but can also name who that customer is by address, phone number, and e-mail address. When you understand who your customer is, you can assess what compels them to buy, how your company can sell to them (direct sales, retail, Internet, direct mail, etc.), how much it is going to cost to acquire and retain that customer, and so forth.

For example, Best Buy has profiled a variety of customers, which serves as an aide to help employees to better understand their customers' needs. "Buzz" is a young urban male who might be interested in video games, whereas "Barry" is an upscale suburban client who wants premium products that are packaged as a total solution.[7] A schedule inserted into the text describing customers on the basic parameters can be very powerful. It communicates a lot of data quickly.

Exhibit 5.5   Competitive Profile Matrix

	THS	Big Box	Amazon	THC Web site	Museum Stores	Specialty Web sites
History book selection	2	3	1	3	4	3
Display of artifacts	1	5	5	5	3	5
History-related gift items	1	5	4	2	1	2
Videos/DVDs	1	4	3	3	5	2
Price	3	2	1	2	3	3
Atmosphere	1	2	5	5	4	5
Employee knowledge	1	4	5	5	2	5
Ease to shop specific item	2	2	1	1	3	4
Ease to browse	1	2	3	3	2	4

Competition

The competition analysis falls directly out of the customer analysis. Specifically, you have previously identified your market segment and described what the customer looks like and what the customer wants. The key factor leading to competitive analysis is what the customer wants in a particular product. These product attributes form a basis of comparison against your direct and indirect competitors. A competitive profile matrix not only creates a powerful visual catch-point, it conveys information regarding your competitive advantage and also the basis for your company's strategy (see Exhibit 5.5). The competitive profile matrix should lead the section and be followed by text describing the analysis and its implications.

In Exhibit 5.5, the entrepreneur rates each competitor (or competitor type) on various key success factors using a five-point scale (with 1 being strong on the attribute and 5 being weak). The entrepreneur has also listed his concept, The History Shoppe (THS), in the matrix. We can see that THS expects to do well on most attributes, except for price. The rationale is that customers are willing to pay a bit more for the added benefit of the THS concept. To this point in his business plan, the entrepreneur has been setting the platform to introduce his concept by using dispassionate analysis of the industry, customer, and competition. By including THS in the matrix, he is foreshadowing the company section.

Finding information about your competition can be easy if the company is public, harder if it is private, and very difficult if the company is operating in stealth mode (it hasn't yet announced itself to the world). Most libraries have access to databases that contain a wealth of information about publicly traded companies (see Exhibit 5.6 for some sample sources), but privately held companies or those stealth ventures represent a greater challenge.

The best way for savvy entrepreneurs to gather competitive information is through their network and via trade shows. Who should be in the entrepreneur's network? First and foremost are the customers the entrepreneur hopes to sell to in the near future. Just as you are (or should be) talking to your potential customers, your existing competition is interacting with the customers every day and your customers are likely aware of the "stealth" competition that is on the horizon. Although many entrepreneurs are fearful

Exhibit 5.6   Sample Source Information for Public/Private Companies

---

Infotrac—Index/Abstracts of journals, general business and finance magazines, market overviews, and profiles of public and private firms.

Dow Jones Interactive—Searchable index of articles from over 3000 newspapers.

Lexis/Nexis—Searchable index of articles.

Dun's Principal International Business—International Business directory.

Dun's One Million Dollar Premium—Database of public and private firms with revenues greater than $1 million or more than 8 employees.

Hoover's Online—Profiles of private and public firms with links to web sites, etc.

Corp Tech—Profiles of high technology firms.

Bridge Information Services—Detailed financial information on 1.4 million international securities that can be manipulated in tables and graphs.

RDS Bizsuite—Linked databases providing data and full-text searching on firms.

Bloomberg—Detailed financial data and analyst reports.

(verging on the brink of paranoia) that valuable information will fall in the wrong hands and lead to new competition that invalidates the current venture, the reality is that entrepreneurs who operate in a vacuum (meaning they don't talk to customers or show up to tradeshows, etc.) fail far more often than those who are talking to everybody they can. Take the risk. Talking allows entrepreneurs to get valuable feedback that enables them to reshape their offering prior to launching a product that may or may not be accepted by the marketplace. So, network not only to find out about your competition, but also to improve your own venture concept.

Company and Product Description

Completing the dispassionate analysis described in the previous section lays the foundation for describing your company and concept. In one paragraph, identify the company name, where it is incorporated, and provide a brief overview of the concept for the company. This section should also highlight what the company has achieved to date; what milestones have you accomplished that show progress?

More space should be used to communicate the product. Again, graphic representations are visually powerful (see Exhibit 5.7). Highlight how your product fits into the customer value proposition. What is incorporated into your product and what value-add do you deliver to the customer? Which of the customer's unmet wants and needs are fulfilled by your offering?

The History Shoppe uses retailing research by Pine and Gilmore that identifies the attributes customers desire in experiential shopping.[8] As shown in Exhibit 5.7, The History Shoppe then illustrates how it meets the needs of the customer in each quadrant (they will have guest speakers, display historical artifacts, sell books and historical merchandise, all in a pleasing atmosphere). The diagram captures The History Shoppe's customer value proposition and explains why THS believes its customers will pay a bit more for its books than they would at Barnes & Noble.

This section should clearly and forcefully identify your venture's competitive advantage. Based upon your competitive analysis, why is your product better, cheaper, faster than what customers currently have access to? Your advantage may be a function of

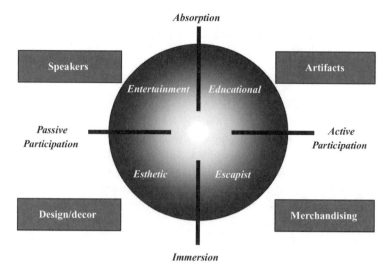

Exhibit 5.7   Customer Value Proposition

proprietary technology, patents, distribution, and so forth. In fact, the most powerful competitive advantages are derived from a bundle of factors, because this makes them more difficult to copy. The History Shoppe, for example, plans on bundling products, museumlike atmosphere, and educated sales personnel (history buffs) with locations near historical sites. Achieving a good fit among all the items in this bundle is what will set your business apart.

Entrepreneurs also need to identify their market entry and growth strategies. Since most new ventures are resource constrained, especially in terms of available capital, it is crucial that the lead entrepreneur establish the most effective way to enter the market. Based upon analysis in the market and customer sections, entrepreneurs need to identify their primary target audience (PTA). Focusing on a particular niche or subset of the overall market allows new ventures to effectively utilize scarce resources to reach those customers and prove the viability of their concept.

The business plan should also sell the entrepreneur's vision for growth because that indicates the true potential for the business. Thus, a paragraph or two should be devoted to the firm's growth strategy. If the venture achieves success in its entry strategy, it will either generate internal cash flow that can be used to fuel the growth strategy or be attractive enough to get further equity financing at improved valuations. The growth strategy should talk about the secondary and tertiary target audiences that the firm will pursue. For example, The History Shoppe plans on building a flagship store in Lexington, Massachusetts (birthplace of the Revolutionary War), and then expanding to other states with strong customer demographics and important historical sites. Other industries might show growth strategies along other dimensions. For instance, technology companies might shift from selling to users who want the best performance (early adopters) to users who want ease of use (mainstream market).

Marketing Plan

To this point, we have described your company's potential to successfully enter and grow in a market place. Now we need to devise the strategy that will allow the company to reach its potential. The primary components of this section include a description of the target market strategy, the product/service strategy, pricing strategy, distribution strategy, advertising and promotion, sales strategy, and sales and marketing forecasts. Let's take a look at each of these subsections in turn.

Target Market Strategy

Every marketing plan needs some guiding principles. Based upon the knowledge gleaned from the customer analysis, entrepreneurs need to target and position their product accordingly. For instance, product strategies often fall on a continuum with the endpoints being rational purchase and emotional purchase. As an example, when I buy a new car, the rational purchase might be a low-cost, reliable car such as the Ford Aspire. However, there is an emotional element as well. I want the car to be an extension of my personality. So, based upon my economic means and self-perception, I might buy a BMW or Audi because of the emotional benefits I derive.

Within every product space, there is room for products measured at different points along this continuum. You may also find other dimensions that define continuums upon which you can classify your marketplace. These tools help entrepreneurs decide where their product fits (or where they would like to position it). Your target market strategy determines the other aspects of the marketing plan.

Product/Service Strategy

Building from the target market strategy, this section of the plan describes how your product is differentiated from the competition. Discuss why the customer will switch to your product and how you will retain customers so that they don't switch to your competition in the future. Incorporating the attributes defined in your customer profile matrix, a product attribute map is a powerful visual to show how your firm compares to the competition. It is best to focus on the two most important attributes, putting one on the x-axis and the other on the y-axis. The map should show that you are clearly distinguishable from your competition on desirable attributes.

Exhibit 5.8 shows the competitive map for The History Shoppe. The two attributes upon which it evaluates competitors are atmosphere (is this a place that people will linger) and focus (broad topic focus or specialized). As you can see from Exhibit 5.8, The History Shoppe plans to have a high level of history specialization and atmosphere,

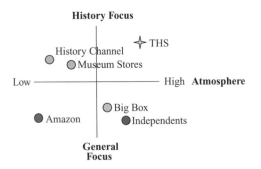

Exhibit 5.8   Competitive Map (Downloadable) Copyright © 2010 by William D. Bygrave and Andrew Zacharakis. To download this form for your personal use, please visit www.wiley.com/go/portablembainentrepreneurship.

placing it in the upper right quadrant. The competitor map identifies how THS plans on distinguishing itself from the competition. THS believes that history specialization and atmosphere will attract history buffs and entice them to return time and again.

This section should also address how you will service the customer. What type of technical support will you provide? Will you offer warranties? What kind of product upgrades will be available and when? It is important to detail all these efforts, as they must all be accounted for in the pricing of the product. Many times, entrepreneurs underestimate the costs of these services, which leads to a drain on cash and ultimately to bankruptcy.

Pricing Strategy

Determining how to price your product is always difficult. The two primary approaches can be defined as a *cost-plus* approach and a *market demand* approach. I advise entrepreneurs to avoid cost-plus pricing for a number of reasons. First, it is difficult to accurately determine your actual cost, especially if this is a new venture with a limited history. New ventures consistently underestimate the true cost of developing their products. For example, how much did it really cost to write that software? The cost would include salaries and benefits, computer and other assets, overhead contribution, and so on. Since most entrepreneurs underestimate these costs, there is a tendency to underprice the product.

Often, I hear entrepreneurs claim that they are offering a low price so that they can penetrate and gain market share rapidly. The problems with a low price are that it may be difficult to raise the price later; it can send a signal of lower quality; demand at that price may overwhelm your ability to produce the product in sufficient volume; and it may unnecessarily strain cash flow.

Therefore, the better method is to canvass the market and determine an appropriate price based upon what the competition is currently offering and how your product is positioned. If you are offering a low-cost value product, price below market rates. Price above market rates if your product is of better quality and possesses many features (the more common case).

Distribution Strategy

This section identifies how you will reach the customer. A company's distribution strategy is more than an operational detail. It can define a company's fortune as much as or more than the company's product. Much of the cost of delivering a product is tied up in its distribution. For example, the e-commerce boom of the late 1990s assumed that the growth in Internet usage and purchases would create new demand for pure Internet companies. Yet the distribution strategy for many of these firms did not make sense. Pets.com and other online pet supply firms were based on a strategy where the pet owner would log on, order the product from the site, and then receive delivery via UPS or the U.S. Postal Service. In theory this works, except that the price the market would bear for this product didn't cover the exorbitant shipping costs of a 40-pound bag of dog food.

It is wise to examine how the customer currently acquires the product. If I buy my dog food at Wal-Mart, then you should probably use primarily traditional retail outlets to sell me a new brand of dog food. This is not to say that entrepreneurs might not develop a multichannel distribution strategy, but if they want to achieve maximum growth, at some point they will have to use common distribution techniques, or reeducate the customer about the buying process (which can be very expensive). If you determine that Wal-Mart is the best distribution channel, the next question becomes whether you can access it. As a new start-up in the dog food industry, it may be difficult to get shelf space at Wal-Mart. That may suggest an entry strategy of boutique pet stores to build brand recognition. The key here is to identify appropriate channels and then assess how costly it is to access them.

Advertising and Promotion

Communicating effectively to your customer requires advertising and promotion. Resource-constrained entrepreneurs need to carefully select the appropriate strategies. What avenues most effectively reach your primary target audience (PTA)? If you can identify your PTA by names, then direct mail may be more effective than mass media blitzes. Try to utilize grassroots techniques such as public relations efforts geared toward mainstream media.

Sheri Poe, founder of Ryka shoes (geared towards women), appeared on the Oprah Winfrey show touting shoes for women, designed by women. The response was overwhelming. In fact, she was so besieged by demand that she couldn't supply enough shoes. Referring again to the dot-com boom of the late 1990s, the soon-to-be-defunct Computer.com made a classic mistake in its attempt to build brand recognition. It blew over half of the venture capital it raised on a series of expensive Super Bowl ads for the January 2000 event ($3 million of $5.8 million raised on three Super Bowl ads).[9]

As you develop a multipronged advertising and promotion strategy, create detailed schedules that show which avenues you will pursue and the associated costs (see Exhibits 5.9 and 5.10). These types of schedules serve many purposes including providing accurate cost estimates, which will help in assessing how much capital you need to raise. These schedules also build credibility in the eyes of potential investors as they demonstrate that you understand the nuances of your industry.

Sales Strategy

This section provides the backbone that supports all of the preceding strategies. Specifically, it illustrates what kind and level of human capital you will devote to the effort. How many salespeople, customer support personnel, and so on do you need? Will these people be internal to the organization or outsourced? If they are internal, will there be a

Exhibit 5.9 Advertising Schedule

Promotional Tools	Budget over One Year
Print advertising	$ 5,000
Direct mail	3,000
In-store promotions	2,000
Tour group outreach	1,000
Public relations	1,000
Total	$ 12,000

Exhibit 5.10 Magazine Advertisements

Publication	Circulation	Ad Price for Quarter Page	Total Budget for Year 1
Lexington Minuteman Newspaper	7,886	$ 500	$4,000
Boston Magazine	1,400,000	$1,000	$1,000

designated sales force or will different members of the company serve in a sales capacity at different times? Again, this section builds credibility if the entrepreneur demonstrates an understanding of how the business should operate.

Sales and Marketing Forecasts

Gauging the impact of the efforts just described is difficult. Nonetheless, to build a compelling story, entrepreneurs need to show projections of revenues well into the future. How do you derive these numbers? There are two methods: the comparable method and the build-up method. After detailed investigation of the industry and market, entrepreneurs know the competitive players and have a good understanding of their history. The *comparable* method models sales forecasts after what other companies have achieved, adjusting for age of company, variances in product attributes, support services such as advertising and promotion, and so forth. In essence, the entrepreneur monitors a number of comparable competitors and then explains why her business varies from those models.

In the *build-up* method, the entrepreneur identifies all the revenue sources and then estimates how much of that revenue type they can generate per day, or some other small time period. For example, The History Shoppe generates revenues from books and artifacts. The entrepreneur would then estimate the average sales price for each category. Then he might estimate the number of people who would come through the store on a daily basis and what percentage would purchase each revenue source. Those estimates can then be aggregated into larger blocks of time (months, quarters, or years) to generate rough estimates, which might be further adjusted based upon seasonality in the retail industry.

The build-up technique is an imprecise method for the new start-up with limited operating history, but it is critically important to assess the viability of the opportunity. It is so important, in fact, that I advise entrepreneurs to use both the comparable and build-up techniques to assess how well they converge. If the two methods are widely divergent, go back through and try to determine why. The deep knowledge you gain of your business model will greatly help you articulate the opportunity to stakeholders, as well as manage the business when it is launched. Chapter 6 provides more detail on how to derive these estimates.

The one thing we know for certain is that these forecasts will never be 100 percent accurate, but the question is the degree of error. Detailed investigation of comparable companies reduces that error. Triangulating the comparable results with the build-up method reduces that error further. The smaller the error, the less likely it is that the company will run out of cash. Rigorous estimates also build credibility with your investors.

Operations Plan

The key in the operations section is to address how operations will add value to your customers. This section details the production cycle, allowing the entrepreneur to gauge the impact on working capital. For instance, when does the company pay for inputs? How long does it take to produce the product? When does the customer buy the product and, more importantly, when does the customer pay for the product? The time from the beginning of this process until the product is paid for will drain cash flow and has implications for financing.

Counterintuitively, many rapidly growing new companies run out of cash even though they have increasing sales and substantial operating profit, because they fail to properly finance the time cash is tied up in the procurement, production, sales, and receivables cycle.

Operations Strategy

The first subsection provides a strategy overview. How does your business win/compare on the dimensions of cost, quality, timeliness, and flexibility? The emphasis should be on those aspects that provide your venture with a comparative advantage.

It is also appropriate to discuss geographic location of production facilities and how this enhances the firm's competitive advantage. Discuss available labor, local regulations, transportation, infrastructure, proximity to suppliers, and so forth. This subsection should also provide a description of the facilities, how the facilities will be acquired (bought or leased), and how future growth will be handled (e.g., renting an adjoining building, etc.). As with all sections detailing strategy, it is imperative that you support your plans with actual data.

Scope of Operations

What is the production process for your product or service? A diagram facilitates the decision of which production aspects to keep in-house and which to outsource (see Exhibit 5.11). Considering that cash flow is king and that resource-constrained new ventures typically should minimize fixed expenses on production facilities, the general rule is to outsource as much production as possible.

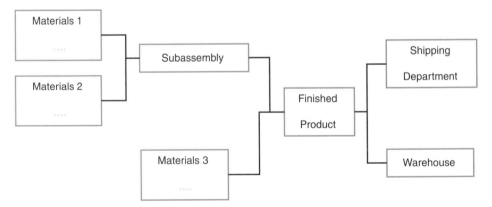

Exhibit 5.11 **Operations Flow (Downloadable) Copyright © 2010 by William D. Bygrave and Andrew Zacharakis. To download this form for your personal use, please visit www.wiley.com/go/portablembainentrepreneurship.**

However, there is a major caveat to that rule: Your venture should control aspects of production that are central to your competitive advantage. Thus, if you are producing a new component with hardwired proprietary technology—let's say a voice-recognition security door entry—it is wise to internally produce that hard-wired component. The locking mechanism, though, can be outsourced to your specifications. Outsourcing the aspects that aren't proprietary reduces fixed costs for production equipment and facility expenditures, which means that you have to raise less money and give up less equity.

The scope of operations should also discuss partnerships with vendors and suppliers. Again, the diagram should illustrate the supplier and vendor relationships by category (or by name if the list isn't too long and you have already identified your suppliers). The diagram helps you visualize the various relationships and strategies to better manage or eliminate them. The operations diagram also helps entrepreneurs to identify personnel needs. For example, the diagram provides an indication of how many production workers might be needed, dependent upon the hours of operations, number of shifts, and so on.

Ongoing Operations

This subsection builds upon the scope of operations by providing details on day-to-day activities. For example, how many units will be produced in a day and what kinds of inputs are necessary? An operating cycle overview diagram graphically illustrates the impact of production on cash flow (see Exhibit 5.12). As entrepreneurs complete this detail, they can start to establish performance parameters, which will help monitor and modify the production process into the future. If this is an operational business plan, the level of detail may include specific job descriptions, but for the typical business plan, this level of detail would be much more than an investor, for example, would need or want to see in the initial evaluation phase.

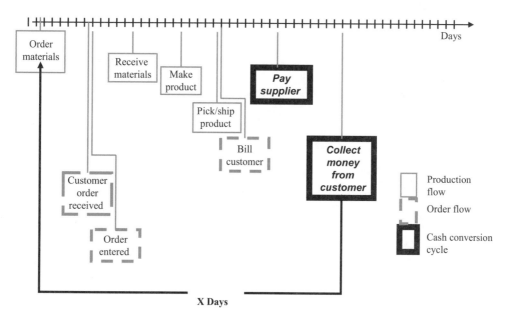

Exhibit 5.12   Operating Cycle

Source: Adapted from work by Professor Bob Eng, Babson College.

Development Plan

The development plan highlights the development strategy and also provides a detailed development timeline. Many new ventures will require a significant level of effort and time to launch the product or service. This is the prologue of your story. For example, new software or hardware products often require months of development. Discuss what types of features you will develop and tie them to the firm's competitive advantage. This section should also talk about patent, trademark, or copyright efforts if applicable.

Development Strategy

What work remains to be completed? What factors need to come together for development to be successful? What risks does the firm face? For example, software development is notorious for taking longer and costing more than most companies originally imagined. Detailing the necessary work and what is required for the work to be considered successful helps entrepreneurs understand and manage the risks involved. After you have laid out these details, a development timeline is assembled.

Development Timeline

A development timeline is a schedule that highlights major milestones and can be used to monitor progress and make changes. Exhibit 5.13 details the steps The History Shoppe needs to take prior to opening its doors. The timeline helps entrepreneurs to track major events and to schedule activities to best execute on those events. It is a good idea to show what has already transpired as well, as of the writing of the business plan. Illustrate which development milestones you have already achieved.

It is also helpful to assign names to the tasks. Who is responsible for ensuring that the milestone is met? As the old adage says, time is money. For every day your product is in development and not on the market, you lose a day's worth of sales. So work hard to meet those deadlines, especially in those industries where speed to market is critical.

Team

Georges Doriot, the father of venture capital and founder of American Research and Development Corporation (the first modern-day venture capital firm), said that he would rather back "an A entrepreneur with a B idea than a B entrepreneur with an A idea." The team section of the business plan is often the section that professional investors read after the executive summary. This section is also critically important to the lead entrepreneur. It depicts the members responsible for key activities and conveys why they are exceptionally skilled to execute on those responsibilities. This section also helps the entrepreneur consider how well this group of individuals will work together. It is well established that ventures started by strong teams tend to succeed at a greater rate.

Team Bios and Roles

Every story needs a cast of characters. The best place to start is by identifying the key team members and their titles. Often, the lead entrepreneur assumes a CEO role. However, if you are young and have limited business experience, it is usually more productive to state that the company will seek a qualified CEO as it grows. In these cases, the lead entrepreneur may assume a chief technology officer role (if she develops the technology) or vice president of business development. However, don't let these options confine you.

Activity	12	11	10	9	8	7	6	5	4	3	2	1	Open Month
10 – 12 Months Prior to Opening	▓		▓										
1. Finalize business plan and financials													
2. Review plans with local bookstores / specialty shop owners	▓												
3. Fill in skill gaps with advisory board			▓										
4. Determine exact location possibilities													
7 – 9 Months Prior to Opening				▓									
5. Register rights to business name				▓									
6. Seek funding from appropriate sources				▓	▓								
7. Update business plan per feedback from potential financiers					▓								
8. Initial contact with product vendors				▓									
9. Contact for POS/inventory vendors and store designers				▓									
4 – 6 Months Prior to Opening							▓						
10. Determine exact store design							▓						
11. Finalize product vendors								▓					
12. Confirm funding									▓				
3 Months Prior to Opening									▓				
13. Finalize store design plans													
14. Open vendor/bank accounts													
15. Place fixture orders										▓			
16. Finalize marketing plan and implement to announce store opening events													
17. Submit merchandise orders with all vendors													
1 Month Prior to Opening										▓			
18. Contact local media regarding placement in local newspapers and magazines										▓			
19. Code merchandise category data in inventory management system											▓		
20. Recruit and train staff													
21. Receive merchandise, fixtures, and complete set-up of store										▓			
Opening Month												▓	
22. "Soft opening" of store to assess customer response, training, and system functioning												▓	
Grand Open Store												▓	

Exhibit 5.13   Launch Timeline (Downloadable) Copyright © 2010 by William D. Bygrave and Andrew Zacharakis. To download this form for your personal use, please visit www.wiley.com/go/portablembainentrepreneurship.

The key is to convince investors that you have assembled the best team possible and that your team can execute on the brilliant concept you are proposing.

A simple, relatively flat organization chart is often useful to visualize what roles you have filled and what gaps remain. It also provides a road map for reading the bios that follow. The bios should demonstrate records of success; if you have previously started a business (even if it failed), highlight the company's *accomplishments*. If you have no previous entrepreneurial experience, discuss your achievements within your last job. For example, bios often contain a description of the number of people the entrepreneur previously managed and, more importantly, a measure of economic success, such as growing division sales by 20-plus percent. The bio should demonstrate your leadership capabilities. To complement this description, resumes are often included as an appendix.

Advisory Boards, Board of Directors, Strategic Partners, External Members

To enhance the team's credentials, many entrepreneurs find that they are more attractive to investors if they have strong advisory boards. In building an advisory board, identify individuals with relevant experience within your industry. Industry experts provide legitimacy to your new business as well as strong technical advice. Other advisory board members may bring other skills, such as financial, legal, or management expertise. Thus, it is common to see lawyers, professors, accountants, and so on, who can assist the venture's growth, on advisory boards. Moreover, if your firm has a strategic supplier or key customer, it may make sense to invite them onto your advisory board. Typically, these individuals are remunerated with a small equity stake and compensation for any organized meetings.

By law, most organization types require a board of directors. This is different from an advisory board (although these members can also provide needed expertise). The board's primary role is to oversee the company on behalf of the investors. Therefore, the business plan needs to briefly describe the size of the board, its role within the organization, and any current board members. Most major investors, such as venture capitalists, will require one or more board seats. Usually, the lead entrepreneur and one or more inside company members (e.g., chief financial officers, vice presidents, etc.) will also have board seats.

Strategic partners may not necessarily be on your advisory board or your board of directors, but they still provide credibility to your venture. In such cases, it makes sense to highlight their involvement in your company's success. It is also common to list external team members, such as the law firm and accounting firm that your venture uses. The key in this section is to demonstrate that your firm can successfully execute the concept. A strong team provides the foundation that conveys assurance your venture will implement the opportunity successfully.

Compensation and Ownership

A capstone to the team section should be a table listing key team members by role, compensation, and ownership equity. A brief description of the table should explain why the compensation is appropriate. Many entrepreneurs choose not to pay themselves in the early months. Although this strategy conserves cash flow, it would misrepresent the individual's worth to the organization. Therefore, the table should contain what salary the employee is due, and then, if deemed necessary, that salary can be deferred until a time when cash flow is strong.

Another column that can be powerful shows what the person's current or most recent compensation was and what she will be paid in the new company. I am most impressed when I see highly qualified entrepreneurs taking a smaller salary than at their previous job. This suggests that the entrepreneur really believes in the upside payoff the company's growth will generate. Of course, the entrepreneur plans on increasing this salary as the venture grows and starts to thrive. As such, the description of the schedule should underscore the plan to increase salaries in the future.

It is also a good idea to hold stock aside for future key hires and to establish a stock option pool for lower-level but critical employees, such as software engineers. Again, the plan should discuss such provisions.

Critical Risks

Every new venture faces a number of risks that may threaten its survival. Although the business plan, to this point, is creating a story of success, there are a number of threats that readers will identify and recognize. The plan needs to acknowledge these potential risks; otherwise investors will believe that the entrepreneur is naive or untrustworthy, and they may therefore withhold investment.

How should you present these critical risks without scaring your investor? Identify the risk and then state your contingency plan (see Exhibit 5.14). Critical risks are critical assumptions, factors that need to happen if your venture is to succeed as currently planned. The critical assumptions vary from one company to another, but some common categories are market interest and growth potential, competitor actions and retaliation, time and cost of development, operating expenses, and availability and timing of financing.

Market Interest and Growth Potential

The biggest risk any new venture faces is that once the product is developed, no one will buy it. Although there are a number of things that can be done to minimize this risk, such as market research, focus groups, and beta sites, it is difficult to gauge overall demand and growth of that demand until your product hits the market. This risk must be stated, but countered with the tactics and contingencies the company will undertake. For example, sales risk can be reduced by an effective advertising and marketing plan or identifying not only a primary target customer but also secondary and tertiary target customers that the company will seek if the primary customer proves less interested.

Exhibit 5.14   Sample Critical Risk

Highly Competitive Industry

The book and DVD industries are highly competitive across many different channels, including superstores, independent bookstores, Internet retailers, book clubs, and specialty stores. Many of these competitors have been in business for many years, have developed significant brand recognition and loyal customers, and have substantial resources to promote their products. We believe the THS concept is in a unique position with its offering of a complete selection of historical merchandise across several product categories and its superior shopping environment. However, unexpected increases in local competition, including Internet competition, alternative delivery methods for books and video, or unanticipated margin pressures caused by irrational pricing by competitors, could have a materially adverse effect on the Company's financial results.

Competitor Actions and Retaliation

Having had the opportunity to work with entrepreneurs and student entrepreneurs over the years, I have always been struck by their firmly held belief that direct competition either didn't exist or that it was sleepy and slow to react. I caution against using this as a key assumption of your venture's success. Most entrepreneurs passionately believe that they are offering something new and wonderful that is clearly different from what is currently being offered. They go on to state that existing competition won't attack their niche in the near future. The risk that this assessment is wrong should be acknowledged.

One counter to this threat is that the venture has room in its gross margins, and cash available to withstand and fight back against such attacks. You should also identify some strategies to protect and reposition yourself should an attack occur.

Time and Cost to Development

As mentioned in the development plan section, many factors can delay and add to the expense of developing your product. The business plan should identify the factors that may hinder development. For instance, as the popularity of mobile device applications grows, there will be an increased demand for software engineers who are skilled in mobile application development. That leads to the risk of hiring and retaining the most qualified professionals. One way to counter the problem might be to outsource some development to the underemployed engineers in India. Compensation, equity participation, flexible hours, and other benefits that the firm could offer might also minimize the risk.

Operating Expenses

Operating expenses have a way of growing beyond expectations. Sales and administration, marketing, and interest expenses are some of the areas that the entrepreneur needs to monitor and manage. The business plan should highlight how these expenses were forecasted (comparable companies and detailed analysis), but also talk about contingencies such as slowing the hiring of support personnel, especially if development or other key tasks take longer than expected.

Availability and Timing of Financing

I can't stress enough how important cash flow is to the survival and flourishing of a new venture. One major risk that most new ventures face is that they will have difficulty obtaining needed financing, both equity and debt. If the current business plan is meant to attract investors and is successful, that isn't a near-term risk, but most ventures will need multiple rounds of financing. If the firm fails to make progress (or to meet key milestones), it may not be able to secure additional rounds of financing on favorable terms. A contingency to this risk is to identify alternative sources that are viable, or strategies to slow the burn rate (how much more cash the company is spending than it is bringing in).

There are a number of other risks that might apply to your business. Acknowledge them and discuss how you can overcome them. Doing so generates confidence in your investors and helps you anticipate corrective actions that you may need to take.

Offering

Based upon the entrepreneur's vision and estimates of the capital required to achieve it, the entrepreneur can develop a "sources and uses" schedule (see Exhibit 5.15). The

Exhibit 5.15   Sources/Uses of Funds Table

Sources of funds			Uses of funds		
Founder	$50,000		Inventory	$94,541	
Friends/family	$200,000	$250,000	Computers, software and office equipment	20,000	
			Leasehold improvements	30,000	
			Furniture and fixtures	51,000	
			Opening Costs	$17,000	
					$212,541
			Working Capital/ Contingencies	$37,459	
					$37,459
Total Sources		**$250,000**	**Total Uses**		**$250,000**

sources section details how much capital the entrepreneur needs and the types of financing, such as equity investment and debt infusions. The *uses* section details how the money will be spent. Typically, the entrepreneur should secure enough financing to last 12 to 18 months. If the entrepreneur takes more capital than needed, she has to give up more equity. If she takes less capital than needed, it may mean that the entrepreneur runs out of cash before reaching milestones that equate to higher valuations.

Financial Plan

If the preceding plan is your verbal description of the opportunity and how you will execute it, the financial plan is the mathematical equivalent. The growth in revenues speaks to the upside of your opportunity. The expenses illustrate what you need to execute on that opportunity. Cash flow statements serve as an early warning system to point out potential problems (or critical risks), and the balance sheet enables monitoring and adjustment of the venture's progress.

That being said, generating realistic financials is one of the most intimidating hurdles that many entrepreneurs face. Chapter 6 goes into detail on how to construct your pro-forma financials.

This section of the business plan should include a description of the key drivers that impact your revenues and costs so that the reader can follow your pro-forma financials. I typically break the description down into four main subsections, after beginning with an overview paragraph that briefly introduces the business model. For example, The History Shoppe might highlight that the projections are based upon one store in year one, growing to three stores by year five. This helps the reader understand the growth in revenues. They might then reiterate the main sources of revenues and any other information that gives a sense of the numbers behind the concept.

The first subsection should discuss the *income* statement. Talk about the factors that drive revenue, such as store traffic, percentage of store visitors that buy, average ticket price, and so forth. It is also important to talk about seasonality and other factors that might cause uneven sales growth. Then discuss the *expense* categories, paying attention to cost of goods sold and major operating expense categories, such as rent, interest expense, and so forth. Based upon your description, the reader should be able to look at and understand the actual financials. The key focus here is to help the reader follow your financials; you don't need to provide the level of detail that an accountant might if they were auditing your company.

The next subsection should discuss the *cash flow* statement. Here you focus on major infusions of cash, such as equity investments and loan disbursements. It is also good to describe the nature of your accounts receivables and payables. How long, for instance, will it be before your receivables convert to cash? If you are spending money on leasehold improvements, plant and equipment, and other items that can be depreciated, you should mention them here. Typically, the discussion of the cash flow statement is quite a bit shorter than the discussion of the income statement.

The final subsection discusses the *balance sheet*. Here you would talk about major asset categories, such as amount of inventory on hand and any liabilities that aren't clear from the previous discussion.

Appendixes

The appendixes can include anything and everything that you think adds further validation to your concept but doesn't fit or is too large to insert in the main parts of the plan. Common inclusions would be one-page resumes of key team members, articles that feature your venture, technical specifications, and so on.

As a general rule, I try to put all exhibits discussed within the written part of the plan on the same page that the exhibit is discussed. This facilitates reading as the reader doesn't have to keep flipping back to the end of the plan to look at an exhibit. However, some exhibits are very large (such as the store layout of The History Shoppe). In such cases, it is acceptable to put large exhibits in the appendix.

Conclusion

The business plan is more than just a document; it is a process, a story. Although the finished product is often a written plan, the deep thinking and fact-based analysis that go into that document provide the entrepreneur with keen insight needed to marshal resources and direct growth. The whole process can induce pain, but it almost always maximizes revenue and minimizes costs as it allows the entrepreneur to better anticipate instead of react. Business planning also provides talking points so that entrepreneurs can get feedback from a number of experts, including investors, vendors, and customers. Think of business planning as one of your first steps on the journey to entrepreneurial success.

Other Resources

A number of resources exist for those seeking help to write business plans. There are numerous software packages, but I find that generally the templates are too confining. The text boxes asking for information drive writers into a dull, dispassionate tone. The best way to learn about business plans is by digging out the supporting data, writing sections as you feel compelled, and circulating drafts among your mentors and advisers.

Nonetheless, I have provided links to some business planning software sites. I also firmly believe that the entrepreneur should read as many other articles, chapters, and books about writing business plans as possible. You will want to assimilate different perspectives so that you can find your own personal voice.

For Further Reading

Bygrave, W., and A. Zacharakis. *Entrepreneurship*. New York: John Wiley & Sons, 2008.

Timmons, J., A. Zacharakis, and S. Spinelli. *Business Plans that Work*. New York: McGraw-Hill, 2004.

Bhide, A. "The Questions Every Entrepreneur Should Ask." *Harvard Business Review*, November/December 1996, 120–130.

Kim, C., and R. Mauborgne. *Blue Ocean Strategy: How to Create Uncontested Market Space and Make the Competition Irrelevant*. Boston: Harvard Business School Press, 2005.

Downloadable Resources for this chapter available at www.wiley.com/go/portablembainentrepreneurship

Competitive Map
Operations Flow
Launch Timeline

Internet Links

Business Plan Preparation Sites

http://www.bplans.com/

http://www.pasware.com/

http://www.brs-inc.com/

http://www.jian.com/

Other Great Sites

http://www.entrepreneurship.org/—The Kauffman Foundation offers a comprehensive site providing a variety of information for entrepreneurs and links to other helpful sites.

http://www.bizmove.com/—The Small Business Knowledge Base is a comprehensive, free resource of small business information packed with dozens of guides and worksheets.

http://www.babson.edu/ESHIP/eship.cfm—The Babson College entrepreneurship site links to different resources of interest to those studying and practicing entrepreneurship.

http://www.nbia.org/—National Business Incubation Association. Business incubators nurture young firms, helping them to survive and grow during the start-up period when they are most vulnerable.

http://www.nfib.com/—The National Federation of Independent Business (NFIB) is the largest advocacy organization representing small and independent businesses in Washington, D.C., and all 50 state capitals—a great resource.

http://www.score.org—The SCORE Association is a national nonprofit association and a resource partner with the U.S. SBA, with 11,500 volunteer members and 389 chapters throughout the United States.

http://www.morebusiness.com/—Comprehensive business resource center providing entrepreneurs with information on start-up, running the business, templates, and so on. This site is updated daily

www.entrepreneur.com—*Entrepreneur* magazine publishes stories on entrepreneurship, management, and opportunities.

Notes

1. The Quotations Page, http://www.quotationspage.com/quote/36892.html, retrieved December 18, 2008.
2. J. Leggio, "Fortune 500 Series: How Newell Rubbermaid Uses Social Media," ZDNet. http://blogs.zdnet.com/feeds/?p=346&page=1, retrieved December 18, 2008.
3. P. Thomas, "Rewriting the Rules: A New Generation of Entrepreneurs Find Themselves in the Perfect Time and Place to Chart Their Own Course," *Wall Street Journal,* May 22, 2000, R4.
4. A sidebar is a visual device that is positioned down the right-hand side of the page that periodically highlights some of the key points in the plan. Don't overload the sidebar, but one or two items per page can draw attention to highlights that maintain reader interest.
5. J. Timmons and S. Spinelli, *New Venture Creation,* 8th ed. (New York: McGraw-Hill/Irwin, 2008).
6. J. Makower, R. Pernick, and C. Wilder, *Clean Energy Trends 2008* (San Francisco: Clean Edge, Inc., 2008).
7. M. Marco, "Leaks: Best Buy's Internal Customer Profiling Document," The Consumerist.com, http://consumerist.com/368894/leaks-best-buys-internal-customer-profiling-document. Created March 18, 2008; retrieved December 19, 2008.
8. B. J. Pine and J. H. Gilmore, *The Experience Economy: Work Is Theatre and Every Business a Stage* (Boston: Harvard Business School Press, 1999).
9. O. Sacirbey, "Private Companies Temper IPO Talk," *IPO Reporter,* December 18, 2000.

6

Building Your Pro Forma Financial Statements

Andrew Zacharakis

How This Chapter Fits into a Typical MBA Curriculum

Creating pro forma financials is central to launching a new business, developing a strategy for an existing business, or buying a business. Thus, you would encounter this topic in a variety of entrepreneurship courses, such as new venture creation and corporate entrepreneurship, as well as courses in strategy. Business planning involves not only a description of your business and its strategy, but also projections on what the plan means to the bottom line. In essence, pro forma financials are the numerical representation of what you are saying in a business plan.

Who Uses This Material in the Real World—and Why It Is Important

Financial projections are used throughout the business world, from the smallest enterprise to the largest multinational. Projecting your financials is typically easier if you have been in business because you can use past performance as an indicator of what might happen in the future. This chapter focuses on the more difficult task of generating financial projections for a nascent venture that has yet to launch or achieve sales. For example, Sean Hackney, founder of Roaring Lion Energy Drink, found making financial projections to be the most difficult task of planning a new business. As a former employee of Red Bull North America, Inc., Hackney had a strong understanding of how he could succeed in the marketplace, and he felt confident enough to try after completing his business plan. Although Hackney succeeded in his business venture, he admitted in an interview with *Entrepreneur* magazine that some of the biggest planning mistakes he made were overestimating projected revenues by 500 percent and underestimating the financial capital required to meet early sales forecasts.[1]

Introduction

Most of the entrepreneurs I have worked with are intimidated by numbers, even after they have gone through the business planning process. The entrepreneurs understand their concept, they even have a good sense of the business model, but ask them to

Spcial thanks to Matt Feczko, Michael DiPietro, Dan Goodman, Michael Collins, Jeff Greenstein, Henry McGovern, and R. Gabriel Shih for their assistance in writing this chapter.

put together pro forma financials or read an income statement and they have panic attacks. A common refrain is that building your financials or understanding them isn't that important because an accountant can always be hired. Although an accountant is a useful adviser, in the prelaunch stage, I strongly believe that the lead entrepreneur needs to understand the numbers inside and out. After all, the lead entrepreneur is the person who will be articulating her vision to potential employees, vendors, customers, and investors. If the entrepreneur is easily stumped by simple questions of profitability or costs, then potential employees, customers, and other important parties to the new venture's success will lose confidence in the lead entrepreneur's ability to execute on the concept. The business plan financial statements serve to bridge the entrepreneur's great idea and what that idea really means in terms of dollars and cents. So, although it can be painful, the lead entrepreneur needs to learn the numbers behind her business. The rewards of gaining this deep insight are often the difference between success and failure.

If for no other reason, the lead entrepreneur needs to understand the numbers so she can decide whether this business has the potential to provide her with a good living. It is too easy to get caught in a trap where a new venture is slowly draining away your investment or where you are working, in real terms, for less than the legally mandated minimum wage. The goal of this chapter is to give you an introduction to entrepreneurial financial planning. Unlike existing businesses that have an operating history, entrepreneurs must develop their financials from scratch. There are no previous trends in revenue and costs that you can use as a basis to project future revenues and costs. Yet the failure to come up with solid projections may cost you your initial investment, as well as that of your investors. This chapter will help you generate sound projections.

Common Mistakes

In preparing this chapter, I sent an e-mail to several acquaintances who are professional equity investors (either angels or venture capitalists). I asked them, "What are the most common mistakes that you see when you review an entrepreneur's business proposal?" In other words, what red flags make you hesitant to believe that the business can survive and succeed? The following six mistakes were consistently cited by the investors.

1. *Not understanding the revenue drivers.* Entrepreneurs need to know what the leverage points are that drive revenues. They need to understand how many customers are likely to see the product, how many of those who see will buy, and how much, on average, they will buy each time. Although every entrepreneur claims that her estimates are conservative, 99 percent of the time, entrepreneurs are overly optimistic in their projections due to a failure to understand the revenue drivers.

2. *Underestimating costs.* If you were to graph the revenue and cost projections of entrepreneurs over time, you would often see revenues growing in a hockey-stick fashion while costs slowly progress upward (see Exhibit 6.1). I often see revenue projections of $15 million after five years on costs of only $5 million. That is unbelievable. When I dig into those numbers, I often see that the firm only has five employees in year 5. That means revenues per employee of $3 million, which is nearly impossible. Often, entrepreneurs underestimate how much infrastructure (i.e., employees, physical assets) they need in order to achieve that level of sales. Entrepreneurs also underestimate the cost of acquiring and retaining customers

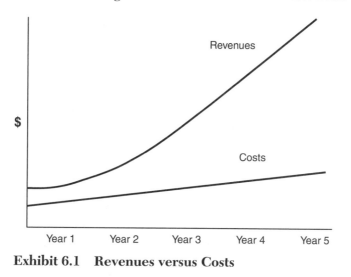

Exhibit 6.1   Revenues versus Costs

(marketing expenditures). Poor projections lead to cash crunches and ultimately failure.

3. *Underestimating time to generate revenues.* Pro forma financials often show sales occurring immediately. Typically, however, a business will incur costs for many months before revenue can be generated. For instance, if you are opening a restaurant, you will incur rent, inventory, and labor costs among others before you generate a dime in revenue. Another red flag is how quickly revenues ramp up. Often, projections show the business at full capacity within the first year. That is rarely realistic.

4. *Lack of comparables.* Investors typically think about the entrepreneur's concept from their knowledge of similar businesses. They will compare your gross margins, net income margins, and other metrics to industry standards and selected benchmark companies. Yet many entrepreneur projections have ratios that far exceed industry standards, and when questioned about this above-average performance, entrepreneurs often can't explain why. You need to understand your business model in relation to the industry and be able to explain any differences.

5. *Top-down versus bottom-up forecasting.* Investors often hear entrepreneurs claim that their revenues represent "only" 3 percent of the market after year 3. The implied assumption is that it is easy to get that 3 percent. Investors know that, although it doesn't sound like much, the trick is how you get to that 3 percent. They want to see the process (cost of acquiring, serving, and retaining the customer). Investors won't believe that you can get 3 percent without causing competitors to take notice and action.

6. *Time to secure financing.* The last pet peeve of investors is that entrepreneurs assume that financing will close quickly. Whether entrepreneurs want to raise $25,000 or $1 million, they project that it will happen in the next month. In reality, it often takes as long as six months to close a round of financing. As my deceased colleague Jeffry Timmons used to say, "Happiness is a positive cash flow." If entrepreneurs are too optimistic about how quickly they can close a round of

financing, they will quickly discover one of the many paths to negative cash flow, which often means they are out of business.

Understanding these pitfalls will help you generate realistic financials and, more importantly, enable you to convincingly articulate your business model so that you can sell your vision to employees, customers, vendors, and investors.

Financial Statement Overview

There are three standard financial statements that you will need to include in your business plan: the income statement, the statement of cash flows, and the balance sheet. Most people first want to know why there are three statements. The reason is simple. Each one provides a slightly different view of the company. Any one alone is only part of the picture. Together they provide a detailed description of the economics of your company.

The first of these statements, the income statement, describes how well a company conducted its business over a recent period of time, typically a quarter (three months) or a year. This indicator of overall performance begins with the company's revenues on the top line. From this accounting of sales, the company's expenses are subtracted. These include:

- Cost of the products that the company actually sold.
- Selling, marketing, and administrative costs.
- Depreciation—the estimated cost of using your property, plant, and equipment.
- Interest on debts.
- Taxes on profits.

The bottom line of the statement (literally) is the company's profits, called *net income*. It is important to realize that the income statement represents a measurement of business performance. It is *not* a description of actual flows of money.

A company needs cash to conduct business. Without it, there is no business. The second financial statement, the statement of cash flows, monitors this crucial account. As the name implies, the statement of cash flows concerns itself exclusively with transactions that involve cash. It is not uncommon to have strong positive earnings on the income statement and a negative statement of cash flows—less cash at the end of the period than at the beginning. Just because you shipped a product does not necessarily mean that you have received the payment for it yet. Likewise, you might have purchased something like inventory or a piece of equipment that will not show up on your income statement until it is consumed or depreciated. There are many noncash transactions that are represented in the income statement.

What is curious (and sometimes confusing to those who have never worked with financial statements before) is the way the statement of cash flows is constructed. It starts with the bottom line (profits) of the income statement and works backwards, removing all of the noncash transactions. For example, since the income statement subtracted out depreciation (the value of using your plant and equipment), the statement of cash flows adds it back in because you don't actually pay any depreciation expense to anybody. Similarly, the cash flow statement needs to include things that you paid for but that were not used that period. For example, you might have paid for product that has not yet sold, or you might have bought a piece of equipment that you will depreciate over time, so you would need to put those items on the cash flow statement. After all of these adjustments, you are left with a representation of transactions that are exclusively cash.

The balance sheet enumerates all of the company's assets, liabilities, and shareholder equity. *Assets* are all the things that the company owns that are expected to generate value over time—things like inventory, buildings, equipment, accounts receivable (money that your customers still owe you), and cash. *Liabilities* represent all the money the company expects to pay eventually. These include accounts payable (money the company owes its suppliers), debt, and unpaid taxes. *Shareholder equity* is the money that shareholders have paid into the company as well as the company's earnings so far. Where the income statement describes a process or flow, the balance sheet is a snapshot of accounts at a specific point in time.

All of your assets come from a liability or from shareholder equity. Therefore, the sum of the asset accounts must equal the sum of the liabilities and shareholder equity account.

$$\text{Assets} = \text{Liabilities} + \text{Shareholder Equity}$$

The assets are shown on the left side of the sheet, with the liabilities and shareholder equity on the right. The balance sheet *always* balances. If your balance sheet does not balance, you have made a mistake.

This is, of course, only a partial treatment of financial statements but it should be enough to understand this chapter. I strongly recommend reading John Tracy's excellent book, *How to Read a Financial Report: Wringing Vital Information Out of the Numbers*, 7th edition (New York: John Wiley & Sons, 2009). It is simple, short, and easy for the novice to quickly learn the basics. The remainder of this chapter will step you through a process to generate your financials.

Building Your Pro Forma Financial Statements

Exhibit 6.2 previews the points we will cover. Think of this as a checklist in developing your financials. Rigorously completing each step will lead to better financial projections and decisions. Underlying these steps are two methods: the build-up method and the comparable method. My advice is to go through all the steps in an iterative fashion so that you not only *know* the numbers, but you *own* the numbers.

Build-up Method

Scientific findings suggest that people make better decisions by decomposing problems into smaller decisions. If you think about the business planning process, you are going through a series of questions that help you answer the big question: Is this an attractive opportunity? Thus, you evaluate the industry, the competition, the customer, and so forth. Based upon that analysis, you decide whether to launch the business. Constructing pro forma financials is part of this process.

The place to start is the income statement. The other two statements are, in part, derived from the income statement. First, identify all of your revenue sources (usually, the various product offerings). Second, identify all of your costs. Once you have the business broken down into its component parts, the next step is to think about how much revenue you can generate in a year, but we can decompose this estimate as well.

**Exhibit 6.2   Financial Construction Checklist (Downloadable) Copyright ©
2010 by William D. Bygrave and Andrew Zacharakis. To download this form
for your personal use, please visit
www.wiley.com/go/portablembainentrepreneurship.**

Build-up Method

1. Identify all your sources of revenues.
2. Determine your revenues for a typical day.
3. Understand your revenue drivers:
    a. How many customers you will serve.
    b. How much product they will buy.
    c. How much they will pay for each product.
4. Validate driver assumptions:
    a. Primary research (talk to customers, attend tradeshows, etc.).
    b. Secondary research (industry reports, company reports, etc.).
5. Recombine. Multiply the typical day by the number of days in a year.
6. Determine cost of goods sold (COGS) for a typical day.
7. Recombine. Multiply COGS by number of days in a year.
8. Determine operating expenses by most appropriate time frame.
9. Refine operating costs.
10. Create preliminary income statement.

Comparable Method

11. Compare revenue projections to industry metrics.
12. Run scenario analysis.
13. Compare common-size cost percentages to industry averages.

Building Integrated Financial Statements

14. Derive monthly income statements for first two years.
15. Create balance sheet.
16. Create cash flow statement.

Final Steps

17. Write two- to three-page description of financial statements.

Revenue Projections

Instead of visualizing what you will sell in a month or a year, break it down into a typical
day. For example, if I were the entrepreneur starting The History Shoppe (as described
in Chapter 5), I would estimate how many customers I might serve in a particular day
and how much they would spend per visit based upon the types of books and artifacts

Exhibit 6.3   Revenue Worksheet

Product/Service Description	Price	Units Sold/Day	Total Revenue
Historical books	$20	75 visitors × 75% × 1.5 books	$1,687.50
Videos	$30	75 visitors × 15% × 1 video	337.50
Maps	$50	75 visitors × 10% × 1 map	375.00
Globes	$100	75 visitors × 5% × 1 globe	375.00
Other (postcards, magazines, etc.)	$5	75 visitors × 20% × 2 items	150.00
Totals			$2,925.00

Assumptions:

Traffic—75 visitors a day
Books—75% of visitors will buy 1.5 books each
Videos—15% of visitors will buy one video each
Maps—10% of visitors will buy one map each
Globes—5% of visitors will buy one globe each
Other—20% of visitors will buy two misc items

50% of sales will happen during Christmas season.
30% of sales will happen during summer tourist season (May through September).

they would buy. Exhibit 6.3 illustrates my process. First, I detail my product mix and the average price for each item. As you can see, I expect to sell books, maps, and other historical artifacts. Second, I estimate the traffic that the store might draw on a typical day. I list my assumptions down at the bottom of the schedule. Then, I estimate how many people who come into the store buy an item and how many items they might buy. The last column gives me total revenue per day by product category.

Exhibit 6.3 highlights critical revenue assumptions, or what might be termed *revenue drivers*. The thought process involved in generating the assumptions enhances your understanding of the business model. Simply put, going through this exercise tells you how you make money. It also helps you understand how you might be able to make *more* money. In other words, what revenue drivers can you influence? The History Shoppe might be able to increase its daily sales by increasing the traffic coming into the store (through advertising), how many people buy, and how much they buy (through up-selling; "Can I get you anything else today?").

Although this thought exercise is invaluable, the estimates are only as good as the assumptions. So how do we strengthen our assumptions? How can we validate the traffic level, the percentage of customers who buy, and so forth? The answer is through research. The first place I would start is by talking to people who know the business. I would talk to bookstore owners, book vendors, mall leasing agents, and others in the industry. A good way to interact with these participants is at industry trade shows. The next thing I would do is visit a number of bookstores and count how many people come in, what percentage of them buy, and how much they spend. Although you might feel conspicuous, there are ways to do this field research without drawing attention to yourself or interfering in the store's business. For example, you might go sit outside a bookstore and watch how many people who walk by enter the store, how many people come out of the store with a package, and so on. Finally, I would also talk to my expected customers, history buffs. I would find out how often they buy history books or other history paraphernalia. I would ask them how much they spend on these items per month and where they currently buy them. By going through several iterations of primary research, you will sharpen your estimates.

In addition to conducting the research yourself, you can seek out secondary sources such as industry reports and web sites. For example, The History Shoppe found great reference books, including Leonard Shatzkin's *The Mathematics of Bookselling: A Monograph* (Ideological Press, 1997) and the *Manual on Bookselling,* edited by Kate Whouley and published by the American Booksellers Association (ABA) in 1996. The ABA also offers a variety of resources online, including their annual *ABACUS Financial Study,* which provides detailed information on all sorts of financial metrics in the industry.

Once you are comfortable that your revenue assumptions are sound, you can then multiply the typical day by the number of days of operation in the year. This exercise gives you yearly revenue estimates. This is a first cut. Clearly, a typical day varies by the time of the year. People do much of their shopping around the Christmas holiday. Therefore, most pro forma projections for new companies typically show monthly income figures for the first two years. This allows the entrepreneur to manage seasonality and other factors that might make sales uneven for the business.

Cost of Goods Sold

Once you have your revenue projections, you next consider costs. On an income statement, we see two categories of costs: cost of goods sold and operating expenses. Cost of goods sold (COGS) is the direct costs of the items sold. For The History Shoppe, COGS is the cost of inventory that is sold in that period. As a first cut, I would assume that COGS for a retail outlet would be around 50 percent (this assumes a 100 percent markup). Since my sales were approximately $3,000 per day, my COGS would be around $1,500.

As with revenue assumptions, I would want to sharpen my COGS assumptions. I would use a schedule similar to the one in Exhibit 6.3 so that I could refine my COGS by product (see Exhibit 6.4). After some investigation at Hoovers.com, I find that the gross margin on books is only 27 percent for the likes of Amazon, Borders, Barnes & Noble, and Books a Million. On other items that I sell, other companies (like Best Buy on videos) have gross margins of around 24 percent. Although these margins are lower than I estimated, these companies have a different business model; high volume, lower margins. The History Shoppe offers a premium shopping experience, meaning highly knowledgeable sales staff and unique historical artifacts. For the time being, I would keep my margin estimates, but would look for further validation as to whether they are achievable. Exhibit 6.4 shows the price per item, the gross margin (revenue minus COGS) per item, the revenues per item (from Exhibit 6.3), and then calculates COGS in dollar terms [Revenue × (1 − COGS)]. Since the gross margins per items differ, we see that the overall gross margin is 44 percent.

Operating Expenses

In addition to direct expenses, businesses also incur operating expenses, such as salaries and general administration (SG&A), rent, marketing, interest expenses, and so forth.

Exhibit 6.4   Costs of Goods Worksheet

Product/Service Description	Price	Gross Margin	Revenue	COGS
Historical books	$20	40%	$1,687.50	$1,012.50
Videos	$30	50%	337.50	168.75
Maps	$50	50%	375.00	187.50
Globes	$100	50%	375.00	187.50
Other (postcards, magazines, etc.)	$5	50%	150.00	75.00
Totals			$2,925.00	$1,631.25

Total Revenue	$2,925.00
COGS	1,631.25
Gross Profit	$1,293.75
Gross Profit Margin	44%

The build-up method forecasts those expenses on a daily, monthly, or yearly basis as appropriate (see Exhibit 6.5). For example, The History Shoppe has been quoted a store rental price of $30 per square foot per year. The space is about 3,000 square feet so we put $90,000 in the yearly expense column. It should be noted that rent will be paid on a monthly basis, so in the final income statement you would show a rent expense of $7,500 in the month-to-month income statement. At this point, however, you are just trying to get a sense of the overall business model and gauge whether this business can be profitable; showing it on a yearly basis is sufficient.

Based upon the first cut, The History Shoppe is projecting operating expenses of approximately $315,000 per year. However, the devil is in the details, as they say, and one problem area is accurately projecting operating costs, especially labor costs. Constructing a head count schedule is an important step in refining your labor projections (see Exhibit 6.6). Although the store is open on average 10 hours per day, you can see from the head count table that Sunday is a shorter day and the store is open 11 hours on the other days. The store operates with a minimum of two employees at all times (including either the assistant manager or store manager). During busier shifts, the number of employees reaches a peak of six people (afternoon shift on Saturday, including both managers). Looking at the calculation below the table, you see that the new wage expense is about $66,000, a bit higher than the first estimate. This *process* of examining and reexamining your assumptions over and over is what leads to compelling financials.

Just as you refined the hourly wage expense, you should work to do the same with other expenses. For example, you can see that The History Shoppe is projecting $12,000 in marketing expenses. Create a detailed schedule of how you plan on spending those advertising dollars. If you refer back to Chapter 5, you see in Exhibit 5.9 that we had already created a schedule of detailed expenses.

This illustrates another point: Financial analysis is really just the numerical expression of your overall business strategy. Everything you write about in your business plan has revenue or cost implications. As I read business plans, my mind is putting together a mental picture of the financial statements, especially the income statement. If the written

**Exhibit 6.5 Operating Expenses Worksheet (Downloadable) Copyright ©
2010 by William D. Bygrave and Andrew Zacharakis. To download this form
for your personal use, please visit www.wiley.com/go/portablembainentre
preneurship.**

Expense	Daily	Monthly	Yearly	Total
Store rent			$90,000	$90,000
Manager salary			$60,000	$60,000
Assistant manager			$40,000	$40,000
Hourly employees	$176			$63,360
Benefits	$21		$12,000	$19,603
Bank charges			$10,530	$10,530
Marketing/advertising		$1,000		$12,000
Utilities		$333		$4,000
Travel			$1,000	$1,000
Dues			$1,000	$1,000
Depreciation		$833		$10,000
Miscellaneous			$4,000	$4,000
				$0
Totals				$315,493

Assumptions:
Rent—3,000 sq. ft. at $30/year = $90,000
Hire 1 manager at $60,000/year
Hire 1 assistant manager at $40,000
Store is open from 9 AM. to 7 PM. daily, so 10 hours per day
Need 2 clerks when open and 1 clerk an hour before and after open:
   2 clerks × 10 hours × $8/hour + 1 clerk × 2 hours × $8/hour
Benefits are 12% of wages and salaries
Bank charges about 1% of sales
Advertising—$1,000/month
Travel—$1,000/year to attend trade shows
Dues—$1,000/year for trade association
Depreciation—$100,000 of leasehold improvements and equipment, depreciated straight line
over 10 years

plan and the financials are tightly correlated, I have much greater confidence that the
entrepreneur knows what she is doing.

The Preliminary Income Statement

Once we have forecasted revenues and expenses, we put them together in an income
statement (see Exhibit 6.7). Looking at Exhibit 6.3, we forecasted average daily sales of
almost $3,000. We need to annualize that figure. I expect the store to be open on average
360 days per year (assuming that the store might be closed for a few days a year, such
as Christmas, Thanksgiving, etc.). Note that I lead with a line called "Total Revenue"
and then show the detail that creates that total revenue line by itemizing the different
revenue categories. COGS are handled in the same manner as revenues; we multiply the
typical day by 360 days to get the annual total.

Exhibit 6.6 Head Count Table

	Mon	Tues	Wed	Thurs	Fri	Sat	Sun	Total
Store hours	10:00–9:00	10:00–9:00	10:00–9:00	10:00–9:00	10:00–9:00	10:00–9:00	11:00–5:00	
Hours open	11	11	11	11	11	11	6	72
Shift 1	9:30–1:30	9:30–1:30	9:30–1:30	9:30–1:30	9:30–1:30	9:30–1:30	10:00–2:00	
Shift 2	1:30–5:30	1:30–5:30	1:30–5:30	1:30–5:30	1:30–5:30	1:30–5:30	1:00–5:00	
Shift 3	5:30–9:30	5:30–9:30	5:30–9:30	5:30–9:30	5:30–9:30	5:30–9:30		
Shift 1 hours	4	4	4	4	4	4	4	
Shift 2 hours	4	4	4	4	4	4	4	
Shift 3 hours	4	4	4	4	4	4	0	
Total Shift Hours	12	12	12	12	12	12	8	80
Staff Head Count								
Shift 1	2	2	1	2	1	4	3	
Shift 2	1	1	0	1	1	4	4	
Shift 3	1	1	1	2	4	4	0	
Total Staff	4	4	2	5	6	12	7	40
Total Hours Worked								
Shift 1	8	8	4	8	4	16	12	
Shift 2	4	4	0	4	4	16	16	
Shift 3	4	4	4	8	16	16	0	
	16	16	8	20	24	48	28	160
Manager	0	0	8	8	8	8	8	40
Assistant Manager	8	8	8	0	8	8	0	40

Total hourly employee hours/week = 160
Hourly rate $8/hour   8
Total wages per week $1,280
Total wages per year $66,560

Exhibit 6.7 Income Statement

Total Revenues	**$1,053,000**	**100%**
Historical books	607,500	
Videos	121,500	
Maps	135,000	
Globes	135,000	
Other	54,000	
Total COGS	**$587,250**	**55.8%**
Historical books	364,500	
Videos	60,750	
Maps	67,500	
Globes	67,500	
Other	27,000	
Gross Profit	**$465,750**	**44.2%**
Operating Expenses		
Store rent	90,000	
Manager salary	60,000	
Assistant manager	40,000	
Hourly employees	66,560	
Benefits	19,987	
Bank charges	10,530	
Marketing/advertising	12,000	
Utilities	4,000	
Travel	1,000	
Dues	1,000	
Depreciation	10,000	
Miscellaneous	4,000	
Total Operating Expenses	**$319,077**	**30.3%**
Earnings from Operations	**$146,673**	**13.9%**
Taxes	**$58,669**	
Net Earnings	**$88,004**	**8.4%**

After adjusting the hourly wages per the head count table (which also means adjusting employee benefits), take the operating expenses table (see Exhibit 6.5) and put it into the income statement. If you believe that you can secure debt financing, put in an interest expense. For the initial forecast, we will leave out interest expense because we are still not certain what amount of financing we need to launch the business. Next, we compute taxes. Make sure to account for federal, state, and city taxes as applicable. Note that in the right-hand column I have calculated the expense percentage of total revenues.

This is called a *common-sized* income statement. Although we have been rigorous in building up our statement, we can further validate by comparing our common-sized income statement to the industry standards.

Comparable Method

How can you tell if your projections are reasonable? The first thing to do is gauge whether your revenue projections make sense, and then see if your cost structure is reasonable. Comparables help you validate your projections.

For instance, a good metric for revenue in retail is sales per square foot. The History Shoppe is projecting sales of $1 million in 3,000 square feet, which equates to $351 per square foot. Secondary research into the average sales per square foot for other bookstores[2] and also into what one or two specific bookstores achieve is a good place to start.[3] For example, $351 is in line with that of independent bookstores ($350/square foot) but higher than Barnes & Noble ($297/square foot). The History Shoppe projection seems reasonable considering that it will be selling certain items (globes, maps, etc.) that have a much higher ticket price than books, but there are a couple of caveats to this estimate.

First, it is likely to take The History Shoppe some time to achieve this level. In other words, the income statement that we have derived might be more appropriate for the second or third year of operation. At that point, The History Shoppe will have built up a clientele and achieved some name recognition. Second, I would want to run some scenario analysis. Does this business model still work if The History Shoppe only achieves Barnes & Noble's sales per square foot ($297)? I would also run a few other scenarios related to higher foot traffic, recession, outbreak of war (sales of books on Islam increased with September 11 and escalating tensions in the Middle East), and so on. Having some validated metrics, such as sales per square foot, helps you run different scenarios and make sound decisions on whether to launch a venture in the first place, and then how to adjust your business model so that the venture has the greatest potential to succeed.

Other metrics that are easily obtainable for this type of establishment include sales per customer, or what is referred to as *average ticket price*. From Exhibit 6.3, The History Shoppe expects sales of $2,925 per day from 75 unique store visitors. That translates into an average transaction per visitor of $39. However, not every visitor will buy, as many people will just come in and browse. In Exhibit 6.3, we assumed that 75 percent of the visitors would buy a book and a lesser percentage of visitors would buy other items. If that percentage holds true, 56 people will actually purchase something each day. Thus, the average receipt becomes $52. This average ticket price is considerably higher than Barnes & Noble's rate of $27.

As with all your assumptions, you have to gauge whether a higher ticket price is reasonable. An entrepreneur might reason that The History Shoppe isn't discounting its books and is also selling higher-priced ancillary goods (e.g., globes, maps, etc.). Run a scenario analysis again to see if The History Shoppe survives if its average ticket price is closer to that of Barnes & Noble. In other words, see what happens to the model overall when you change one of the assumptions—the average selling price, in this case.

After you are comfortable with the revenue estimate, you next need to validate the costs. The best way is to compare your common-sized income statement with the industry averages or some benchmark companies. It is unlikely that your income statement will exactly match the industry averages, but you need to be able to explain and understand the differences.

Exhibit 6.8 looks at the common-sized income statement for The History Shoppe and Barnes & Noble. The first discrepancy appears in the COGS. The History Shoppe projects COGS of 56 percent of revenue whereas Barnes & Noble is projecting 70 percent. Why would Barnes & Noble's COGS be so much higher? Upon further investigation, we find that Barnes & Noble includes occupancy costs (rent, utilities, etc.) in COGS. If we add The History Shoppe's $90,000 rent plus $4,000 in utilities into COGS, COGS becomes 65 percent of revenue—still lower than Barnes & Noble's. However, COGS of 65 percent is in line with the specialty retail industry rate of 67 percent.[4] The reasoning for this discrepancy is similar to that of the higher ticket price. The History Shoppe's COGS is likely lower than Barnes & Noble because it is not a discount book seller (meaning it earns higher margins on every book sold than Barnes & Noble). Additionally, The History Shoppe also sells other retail items (i.e., globes, maps, etc.) that generate higher margins.

Since the gross profit margin is the inverse of COGS—revenue minus COGS—the explanation provided for COGS also holds for gross margin. Barnes & Noble's gross margin is 30 percent, versus 35 percent for The History Shoppe (with rent included in COGS).

When comparing the operating expenses of the two companies, we see that The History Shoppe is projecting operating expenses to be 29 percent of revenue versus 27 percent for Barnes & Noble. However, we must once again adjust for the occupancy expense because The History Shoppe is including occupancy in operating expenses whereas Barnes & Noble includes it in COGS. With that adjustment, The History Shoppe's operating expenses are about 21 percent of revenue, somewhat less than Barnes & Noble's. We would want to investigate to see if we are underestimating the number of employees we will need. Or are we paying lower rent because we aren't in a high profile location? The key is to determine whether our lower costs are reasonable.

Based upon the comparable analysis, it appears that The History Shoppe's projections are reasonable. The History Shoppe's earnings from operations are higher (13.9 percent) than Barnes & Noble's (3.9 percent) and the independent bookstore average (2.5 percent), but that may be explained by the higher gross margins and the fact that we haven't yet included any interest expenses. For example, if we use debt financing for any of our start-up expenses, such as leasehold improvements, we will have an interest expense that would reduce our net income margin to be more in line with the comparable companies.

In this exercise, we have primarily used benchmark companies, but industry averages also provide useful comparable information. Leo Troy's *Almanac of Business and Industrial Financial Ratios,* published by CCH, and *Industry Norms and Key Business Ratios,* published by Dun & Bradstreet, are excellent sources to use as starting points in building financial statements relevant to your industry. Specifically, these sources help entrepreneurs build income statements by providing industry averages for costs of goods sold, salary expenses, interest expenses, and so on. Again, your firm will differ from these industry averages, but going through scenario analysis and understanding your business model, you should be able to explain why your firm differs.

Exhibit 6.8   Comparable Analysis

	The History Shoppe		Barnes & Noble (FY2007) (in millions)		Industry Average
Total Revenues	**$1,053,000**	100%	**$5,410**	100%	100%
Historical books	607,500				
Videos	121,500				
Maps	135,000				
Globes	135,000				
Other	54,000				
Total COGS	**$587,250**	55.8%	**$3,770**	69.7%	60.0%
Historical books	364,500				
Videos	60,750				
Maps	67,500				
Globes	67,500				
Other	27,000				
Gross Profit	**$465,750**	44.2%	**$1,641**	30.3%	40.0%
Operating Expenses					
Store rent	90,000				
Manager salary	60,000				
Assistant manager	40,000				
Hourly employees	66,560				
Benefits	19,987				
Bank charges	10,530				
Marketing/ advertising	12,000				
Utilities	4,000				
Travel	1,000				
Dues	1,000				
Depreciation	10,000				
Miscellaneous	4,000				
Total Operating Expenses	**$319,077**	30.3%	**$1,432**	26.5%	37.5%
Earnings from Operations	**$146,673**	13.9%	**$209**	3.9%	2.5%
Taxes	**$58,669**		**$73**		
Net Earnings	**$88,004**	8.4%	**$136**	2.5%	

Building Integrated Financial Statements

Once you have a baseline income statement, the next step is to construct monthly income and cash flow statements for two years (followed by years 3 through 5 on a yearly basis), and a yearly balance sheet for all five years. Five years is standard for many business plans as it usually takes new firms some time to hit their stride. It takes time to build sales and operate efficiently. Five years also gives the entrepreneur a sense of whether her investment of time and energy will pay off. Can the business not only survive, but provide the kind of financial return to make the opportunity costs of leaving an existing job worthwhile?

The income statement, cash flow statement, and balance sheet are the core statements for managing any business. Changes in one statement affect all others. Understanding how these changes impact your business can mean the difference between survival and failure. Many entrepreneurs will find their business on the verge of failure, even if it is profitable, because they fail to understand how the income statement is related to the cash flow and balance sheet. How is that possible, you might ask?

Entrepreneurs need to finance rapid growth. For example, The History Shoppe needs to buy inventory in advance of selling to its customers. The owner needs to insure that he has enough books and other products on hand that he doesn't lose a sale because a customer is frustrated that the book or globe isn't in stock. Americans are notorious for wanting instant gratification. Yet having inventory on hand drains cash. If The History Shoppe expects sales of $500,000 in December, then it must have $280,000 worth of inventory at the end of November ($500,000 × 56 percent − average COGS). How does The History Shoppe pay for this? Internal cash flow? Vendor financing? Equity? Having strong pro forma financials helps the entrepreneur anticipate these needs far enough in advance so that the appropriate financing can be arranged. Failing to understand the numbers behind the business leads to ruin more often than not.

The preceding example illustrates why a new business wants to show the income statement and cash flow on a monthly basis for the first two years—the most vulnerable period in a new venture's life. It takes time to build up your clientele (lower revenues), learn how to efficiently operate (higher costs), develop a track record so you can secure vendor financing (cash flow implications), understand seasonality (variance in demand), and deal with a plethora of other issues. For instance, monthly projections allow the entrepreneur to anticipate and understand any seasonality that might happen in the business. In addition to the financing issue already discussed, seasonality impacts other key operations and decisions. For example, The History Shoppe will need to hire more salespeople during the Christmas season. Integrated financials can help the entrepreneur plan for that hiring increase.

In sum, it is critical to show the first two years of pro forma projections on a monthly basis because this is when a company is most vulnerable to failure. Monthly forecasts help you understand these issues and prepare for them. For years 3 through 5, yearly projections are sufficient because the further out one goes, the less accurate the projections become. Nevertheless, your longer-term projections communicate your vision of the upside potential of your opportunity. The exercise of going through the projection process is more important than the accuracy of the projections. The process helps you gain a deeper understanding of the business and whether you should pursue the opportunity.

The preceding example indicates how changes in one statement impact other statements. Exhibit 6.9 formally shows how the pro forma financials are integrated. You can see that the income statement drives the balance sheet which drives the cash flow statement (although the cash from financing and uses of cash from the cash flow statement feed back into the balance sheet). I will briefly touch on how to move from our base income statement into a full set of financial pro forma projections, but going into a step-by-step process is beyond the scope of this chapter.

Income Statement

The base income statement we generated for The History Shoppe shows the level of operations that might be achievable in year 3 or 4. Thus, we need to make a number of adjustments to generate the other years. First, we need to create monthly statements for the first two years. That means we need to understand the seasonality of our business and the sales cycle.

One mistake that many entrepreneurs make is showing revenues from the first day they launch the business, but most new businesses incur expenses well in advance of generating revenue. If we think about The History Shoppe, I would consider the business launched soon after the first round of financing is closed. At this point, the entrepreneur can start spending money to establish the business. For instance, he might sign a lease, contract for equipment, and so forth. I advocate showing those expenses as incurred. Thus, The History Shoppe might show expenses for three months (the time to build out the store before opening) before it shows its first revenue.

The next consideration in generating monthly forecasts is seasonality. Revenues in retail are not evenly spread across the 12 months. Exhibit 6.10 estimates how sales might be spread for a retail operation. The make-or-break season for The History Shoppe is Christmas as we see sales jumping dramatically in November and December. Another important season is the tourist season. (The History Shoppe plans to locate near a major Revolutionary War site.) Based upon these projections, it makes sense to lease and build out the retail space in the January to March time frame when sales levels are expected to be low.

Another consideration is how long it will take The History Shoppe to build its clientele and ramp up its revenues. The History Shoppe is projecting sales of $350 per square foot once it hits its optimal operating position. In the first year of operation, that number might be significantly lower, say $200 per square foot, well below the Barnes & Noble average of $297 and the independent bookstore average of $350. In year 2, a reasonable estimate might be that average sales per square foot hit $250, and finally in year 3 they hit the independent bookstore average of $350. Additionally, The History Shoppe is not generating sales for the first three months of year 1 due to the time it takes to build out the store, so we have adjusted the sales accordingly.

Balance Sheet

The balance sheet can be the most difficult to integrate into your other financial statements. For pro forma projections, yearly balance sheets are sufficient. Again, going into great detail is beyond the scope of this chapter, but there are a few items that often cause confusion.

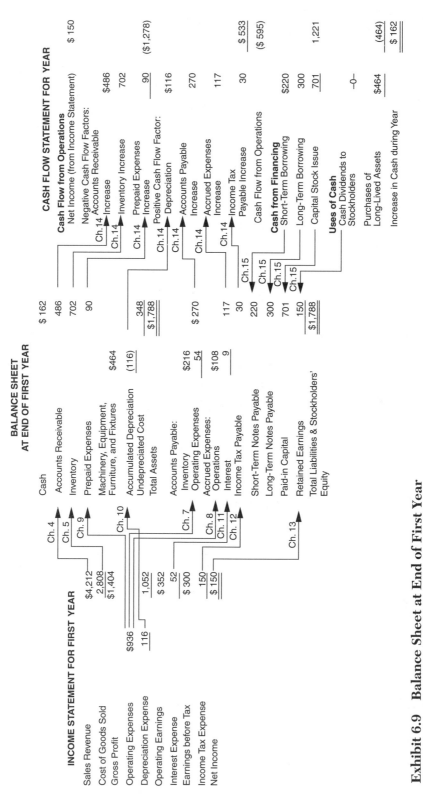

Exhibit 6.9   Balance Sheet at End of First Year

Source: Reprint of Exhibit D from John Tracy, *How to Read a Financial Report,* 2nd ed. (New York: John Wiley & Sons, 1983).

154

Exhibit 6.10 Seasonality Projections (in Thousands)

	Jan	Feb	Mar	Apr	May	Jun	Jul	Aug	Sep	Oct	Nov	Dec	Year
	3%	2%	3%	4%	6%	7%	9%	8%	5%	3%	10%	40%	100%
Year 1	$22.5			$24.0	$36.0	$42.0	$54.0	$48.0	$30.0	$18.0	$60.0	$240.0	$552.0
Year 2	$22.5	$15.0	$22.5	$30.0	$45.0	$52.5	$67.5	$60.0	$37.5	$22.5	$75.0	$300.0	$750.0
Year 3	$31.5	$21.0	$31.5	$42.0	$63.0	$73.5	$94.5	$84.0	$52.5	$31.5	$105.0	$420.0	$1,050.0

First, will your business sell on credit? If so, it will record accounts receivable. Exhibit 6.9 shows how your sales from the income statement drive your accounts receivable on the balance sheet (some portion of those sales), which then drives the accounts receivable increase on the cash flow. While you would record the sale when the customer took possession, you may not actually receive payment until some point in the future. Recording the sale would have a positive impact on your profitability but would not affect your cash flow until the customer actually paid.

If your business is buying equipment, land, or a plant—or, as in the case of The History Shoppe, adding leasehold improvements—you will have an asset of plant and equipment. A common error is to show this as a capital expense, meaning that it appears in full on your income statement the moment you contract for the work. Doing so assumes that you will fully use that equipment within the year (or whatever length of time your income statement covers). To accurately reflect the acquisition of the asset, you show the full outflow of money as it occurs on your cash flow statement and then depreciate the cost per year of life of the asset on your income statement. You would also have an accumulated depreciation line item on your balance sheet showing how much of the asset has been used up. Referring back to Exhibit 6.5, you see that The History Shoppe is projecting leasehold improvements of $100,000 which it expects to use up over 10 years (10,000 per year or $833 per month).

Accounts payable acts in a similar manner to accounts receivable, except that this is a loan to your company from a supplier (see Exhibit 6.9). Once The History Shoppe is able to secure vendor financing on inventory, for example, it will show the COGS as it sells its books, but it may not have to pay a given publisher until later (assuming that the book is a fairly fast moving item). So the expense would show up on your income statement but not on your cash flow statement until you paid for it. Until then, it is held in accounts payable on the balance sheet.

The final problem area is retained earnings. Entrepreneurs know that the balance sheet should *balance*. A common error is to use the retained earnings line to make the balance sheet balance. Retained earnings is actually:

Previous Retained Earnings + Current Period Net Income − Dividends Paid That Period

If you find that your balance sheet isn't balancing, the problem is often in how you have calculated accounts receivable or accounts payable. Balancing the balance sheet is the most frustrating aspect of building your financial pro forma statements. But hardwiring the retained earnings will ultimately lead to other errors, so work through the balancing problem as diligently as possible.

Cash Flow Statement

If you have constructed your financial statements accurately, the cash flow statement identifies when and how much financing you need. I coach the entrepreneurs that I work with to leave the financing assumptions empty until after they see how much the cash flow statement implies they need (see Exhibit 6.11). One of the many benefits of this process is that it will help you determine exactly how much you need so as to protect you from yielding too much equity or too much (or not enough) debt.

Exhibit 6.11 The History Shoppe Cash Flow Statement

	Month 1	Month 2	Month 3	Month 4	Month 5	Month 6
Operating Activities						
Net Earnings	(17,000)	(12,882)	(2,244)	(7,079)	(1,277)	8,394
Depreciation	1,115	1,115	1,115	1,115	1,115	1,115
Working Capital Changes						
(Increase)/Decrease Accounts Receivable	0	(64)	(88)	40	(48)	(80)
(Increase)/Decrease Inventories	(104,562)	(19,605)	32,676	(39,211)	(65,351)	71,886
(Increase)/Decrease Other Current Assets	0	(230)	(316)	144	(172)	(287)
Increase/(Decrease) Accounts Payable and Accrued Expenses	0	3,215	4,421	(2,010)	2,411	4,019
Increase/(Decrease) Other Current Liabilities	0	3,445	4,737	(2,153)	2,584	4,306
Net Cash Provided/(Used) by Operating Activities	(120,446)	(25,005)	40,301	(49,154)	(60,737)	89,354
Investing Activities						
Property and Equipment	(101,000)	0	0	0	0	0
Other						
Net Cash Used in Investing Activities	(101,000)	0	0	0	0	0
Financing Activities						
Increase/(Decrease) Short-Term Debt						0

(continued)

Exhibit 6.11 *(Continued)*

	Month 1	Month 2	Month 3	Month 4	Month 5	Month 6
Increase/(Decrease) Current Portion Long-Term Debt						0
Increase/(Decrease) Long-Term Debt						0
Increase/(Decrease) Common Stock						0
Increase/(Decrease) Preferred Stock						0
Dividends Declared						0
Net Cash Provided/(Used) by Financing	0	0	0	0	0	0
Increase/(Decrease) in Cash	(221,446)	(25,005)	40,301	(49,154)	(60,737)	89,354
Cash at Beginning of Period	0	(221,446)	(246,451)	(206,150)	(255,304)	(316,041)
Cash at End of Period	(221,446)	(246,451)	(206,150)	(255,304)	(316,041)	(226,687)

The History Shoppe cash flow shows some major outlays as the store is gearing up for operation, such as inventory acquisition and equipment purchases. We can also see from the cash flow statement that the business is incurring some expenses prior to generating revenue (−$17,000 listed as net earnings). This net earnings loss is reflected on the company's monthly income statement and is primarily attributable to wage expenses to hire and train its staff.

We can see that in the first six months, the cash position hits a low of −$316,000. This is how much money The History Shoppe needs to raise in order to launch the business. For a new venture, most of the money will likely be in the form of equity from the entrepreneur, friends, and family. However, the entrepreneur may be able to secure some debt financing against his equipment (which would act as collateral if the business should fail). In any event, once we recognize our financing needs, we can devise a strategy to raise the money necessary to start the business. To provide some buffer against poor estimates, The History Shoppe might raise $350,000. This amount would show up on both the cash flow and the balance sheet.

Integrating the Financial Statements

As the preceding discussion implies, it can be difficult to integrate the statements unless you are a CPA and a spreadsheet wizard. Although I have my students go through the spreadsheet creation exercise, I recognize that entrepreneurs may not have the time or aptitude to build their spreadsheets from scratch. If you aren't spreadsheet proficient, I would suggest hiring an accountant. If you are comfortable with spreadsheets but can't create your financial spreadsheets from scratch, I recommend using a fantastic template created by Frank Moyes and Stephen Lawrence at the University of Colorado.[5]

Putting It All Together

Once the financial spreadsheets are completed, a two- to three-page explanation of the financials should be written and it should precede the statements. Although you understand all the assumptions and comparables that went into building the financial forecast, the reader needs the background spelled out. Describing the financials is also a good exercise in articulation. If your reader understands the financials and believes the assumptions are valid, you have passed an important test. If not, work with the reader to understand her concerns. Continuous iterations strengthen your financials and should give you further confidence in the viability of your business model.

The written explanation should have four subheadings: Overview, Income Statement, Cash Flow, and Balance Sheet. The overview section should highlight the major assumptions that drive your revenue and expenses. This section should map to several of the critical risks you identified in your written plan (see Chapter 5). The income statement description goes into more detail as to some of the revenue and cost drivers that haven't been discussed in the overview section. The cash flow description talks about the timing of cash infusions, accounts payable, accounts receivable, and so on. The balance sheet description illustrates how major ratios compare to industry standards and change as the firm grows.

Conclusion

Going through the preceding exercises allows you to construct a realistic set of pro forma financials. It is difficult, but understanding your numbers cold enables you to articulate your business to all stakeholders so that you can build momentum towards the ultimate launch of your business.

Just as I said in Chapter 5 that the business plan is a living document, the financial statements are also a living document. The financials are obsolete immediately after they come off the printer. As you start your launch process, you can further refine your numbers, putting in actual revenues and expenses as they occur and adjusting projections based upon current activity. Once the business is operating, the nature of your financial statements changes: They not only help you assess the viability of your business model, but they also help you gauge actual performance and adjust how you operate based upon that experience.

Although most entrepreneurs tell me that creating the financials induces some pain, they also concede that going through the process is gratifying and rewarding. They learn to master new management skills, build their business, and protect their investment. So dig in.

Additional Resource

Tracy, J. *How to Read a Financial Report: Wringing Vital Signs Out of the Numbers*, 7th ed. New York: John Wiley and Sons, 2009.
This is a classic book on how to create pro forma financial statements and how these statements tie together.

Downloadable Resources for this chapter available at www.wiley.com/go/portablembainentrepreneurship

Pro Forma Financial Statements
Financial Construction Checklist
Operating Expenses Worksheet

Notes

1. Mark Hendricks, "Do You Really Need a Business Plan?" *Entrepreneur*, December 2008, 93–95.
2. 1999 ABACUS Financial Study. American Booksellers Association. http://www.bookweb.org/index.html.
3. Look for publicly traded companies on your favorite database, such as SEC.gov.
4. http://bizstats.com/otherretail.htm.
5. As of the writing of this chapter, you could download the template at http://leeds-faculty.colorado.edu/moyes/html/resources.htm. Hit the "Financial Projections" link.

7

Equity Financing: Informal Investment, Venture Capital, and Harvesting

William D. Bygrave

Where This Chapter Fits into a Typical MBA Curriculum
The first half of an MBA entrepreneurship course deals with entrepreneurs, their opportunities, and how to meld them into a new venture with a business plan. As the would-be entrepreneurs develop their business plans, they make financial projections and discover how much money they will need to launch and grow their businesses. Before they begin searching for start-up funding, they should read this chapter.

Who Uses This Material in the Real World—and Why It Is Important
Most budding entrepreneurs have little if any idea of how entrepreneurs get equity capital to fund their ventures or how successful entrepreneurs harvest their businesses. This chapter teaches them how to value their businesses, and gives them comprehensive information on sources of funding and how to set about raising money from them. Not only is this knowledge vital for novice entrepreneurs before they launch their ventures, it is also valuable for old hands who have built successful businesses and are looking for expansion capital or are harvesting them.

Introduction

You have developed your business idea and have written a business plan in which you have forecast how much money you will need for your new venture. You are now wondering where you will get the initial money to start your business and the follow-on capital to grow it. In this chapter we discuss the mechanics of raising money from informal investors including business angels, venture capitalists, and public stock markets. But first we examine how Jim Poss scraped together the resources to start his business.[1]

Jim Poss, Seahorse Power Company

During his second year of MBA studies, Jim enrolled in Babson College's Entrepreneurship Intensity Track, which is for students who want to develop a new venture that they will run full-time as soon as they graduate. Jim's first product, the BigBelly, is an automatic, compacting trash bin powered by solar energy. The innovative BigBelly dramatically cuts emptying frequency and waste handling costs, trash overflow, and litter at outdoor sites with high traffic and high trash volume. The BigBelly's target end users, such as municipalities and outdoor entertainment venues, face massive volumes of daily trash, and very high collection costs. By the time he graduated in May 2003, Jim had a company, Seahorse Power, and a business plan, and he was developing a prototype.

While still in school, Jim won $1,500 of legal services at an investors' forum by Brown and Rudnick, a leading Boston law firm. Jim used this as part payment for the legal fees associated with his patent application. Jim also invested $10,000 from his own savings in Seahorse Power, and he was awarded $12,500 through the Babson hatchery program. He recruited two unpaid Olin College engineering students to help with the design, manufacture, and testing of the prototype. He developed a cooperative partnership with Bob Treiber and his firm, Boston Engineering, from which he received a "ton of work pro bono" and free space in which to assemble and test the prototype. The Vail Ski Resort ordered a BigBelly and paid Jim the full purchase price ($6,000) in advance. He presold nearly half of the first production run, requiring a 50 percent down payment with each order. Jim's parents invested $12,500. A business angel invested $12,500. Spire Corporation, a 30-year-old publicly traded solar energy company, invested $25,000.

Jim won the Babson College business plan competition, which brought in $20,000 cash, which he shared among the team members—the first compensation that they had ever received from the project; it also brought in $40,000 of services and lots of publicity. Over the next year, Jim raised $250,000 with an A round of private investment from 17 individuals and companies in amounts ranging from $12,500 to $50,000 of convertible debt. By the fall of 2005, Seahorse Power had sold about 100 BigBellys. In November 2005, Jim closed a round of equity investment.

Bootstrapping New Ventures

Jim Poss is a typical example of how an entrepreneur bootstraps a start-up by scraping together resources, including financing, services, material, space, and labor. In Chapter 1 you read about how Steve Jobs and Stephen Wozniak at Apple, and Sergey Brin and Larry Page at Google, raised their capital. Jobs and Wozniak developed their first computer, Apple I, in a parent's garage and funded it with $1,300 raised by selling Jobs's Volkswagen and Wozniak's calculator. They then found an angel investor, Armas Markkula Jr., who had recently retired from Intel a wealthy man. He personally invested $91,000 and secured a line of credit from Bank of America. Sergey Brin and Larry Page maxed out their credit cards to buy a terabyte of storage that they needed to start Google in Larry's dorm room. Then they raised $100,000 from Andy Bechtolsheim, one of the founders of Sun Microsystems, plus approximately $900,000 from family, friends, and acquaintances. Both Apple and Google subsequently raised venture capital and then went public.

There is a pattern in the initial funding of Seahorse Power Corporation, Apple, and Google that is repeated over and over again in almost every start-up. The money comes from the four Fs: First the *founders* themselves dip into their own pockets for the initial capital; next they turn to *family*, *friends*, and *foolhardy* investors (business angels). If their companies grow rapidly and show the potential to be superstars, they raise venture capital, and then they have an initial public offering (IPO) or are acquired by a bigger company. The money from family and friends might be a loan or equity or a combination of both, but when it is raised from business angels, venture capitalists, or with an IPO, it will be equity.

Before they raise money in exchange for equity, it is crucial that entrepreneurs know the value of their companies, so that they know how much equity they will have to give up. Hence, before we discuss the mechanics of raising money, we examine how to value a company.

Valuation

There are four basic ways of valuing a business:

1. Earnings capitalization valuation.
2. Present value of future cash flows.
3. Market-comparable valuation.
4. Asset-based valuation.

No single method is ideal because the value of a business depends, among other things, on the following:

- Opportunity.
- Risk.
- Purchaser's financial resources.
- Future strategies for the company.
- Time horizon of the analysis.
- Alternative investments.
- Future harvest.

Valuation of a small, privately held corporation is difficult and uncertain. It is not public so its equity, unlike that of a public company, has very limited liquidity or probably none at all; hence, there is no way to place a value on its equity based on the share price of its stock. What's more, if it is an existing company rather than a start-up, its accounting practices may be quirky. For instance, the principals' salaries may be set more by tax considerations than by market value. There may be unusual perquisites for the principals. The assets such as inventory, machinery and equipment, and real estate may be undervalued or overvalued. Goodwill is often worthless. There might be unusual liabilities or even unrecognized liabilities. Perhaps the principals have deferred compensation. Is it a subchapter S, a limited liability corporation, or a partnership? If so, tax considerations might dominate the accounting.

When valuing any business, especially a start-up company with no financial history, it is important not to let finance theory dominate over practical rule-of-thumb valuations. In practice, there is so much uncertainty and imprecision in the financial projections that elaborate computations are not justified; indeed, they can sometimes lead to a false sense of exactness.

"The engine that drives enterprise is not thrift, but profit."

—John Maynard Keynes[2]

Earnings Capitalization Method

The value of a company computed with the earnings capitalization method is as follows:

$$\text{Company Value} = \text{Net Income}/\text{Capitalization Rate}$$

This method is precise when valuing an asset where the net income is steady and very predictable but is not useful when valuing a company, particularly a start-up, where the net income is very uncertain. Even for an existing small business it is fraught with problems; for example, should the net income be for the most recent year, or next year's expected income, or the average income for the past five years, or . . . ? Hence, the earnings capitalization method is seldom used for valuing small, privately held businesses.

Present Value of Future Cash Flows

The present value of the company is the present value of the future free cash flows plus the residual (terminal) value of the firm:

$$\mathbf{PV} = \sum_{t=1}^{N} \frac{(\text{FCF}_t)}{(1+K)^t} + \frac{\text{RV}_N}{(1+K)^N}$$

Where

$K = $ cost of capital
$\text{FCF}_t = $ free cash flow in year t
$N = $ number of years
$\text{RV}_N = $ residual value in year N.

Free cash flow can be calculated as follows:

Operating income

− Interest

− Taxes on operating income

+ Depreciation and other noncash charges

− Increase in net working capital

− Capital expenditures (replacement and growth)

− Principal repayments

Free cash flow is cash in excess of what a firm needs to maintain its optimum rate of growth. A rapidly growing, high-potential firm will not generate any free cash flow in its first few years. In fact, its entrepreneurs and investors want it to use excess cash to grow faster. Hence, the value of such a firm is determined entirely by its residual value.

Market-Comparable Valuation (Multiple of Earnings)

This valuation method is the company's net income multiplied by a ratio of the market valuation to net income (a ratio also known as price to earnings, or P/E) of a comparable public company or, preferably, the average for a number of similar public companies. Ideally, the comparable companies should be in the same industry segment as the company that is being valued. If the company being valued is private, then its valuation is usually discounted because its shares are not liquid.

$$\text{Total Equity Valuation} = \text{NI} \times \text{P/E}$$

Where

NI = net income
P/E = price to earnings ratio

For a public company, the total equity valuation is the same as the market capitalization. If we substitute net income per share (EPS) for NI in the preceding formula, we have the price per share instead of market capitalization.

Variations on this method use the operating income before depreciation and amortization (EBITDA) instead of net income, multiplied by the price to EBITDA per share ratio of comparable companies, or simply the operating income multiplied by the price to operating income per share ratio.

The NI × P/E method is the most commonly used technique for valuing rapidly growing companies that are seeking investment from professional investors, such as venture capitalists, or when a company is going public. For a fast-growing company with no free cash flow, NI × P/E is the same as the residual value, RV_N, in the equation in the previous section.

Asset-Based Valuation

There are three basic variations on the asset-based method:

1. Modified (adjusted) book value.
2. Replacement value.
3. Liquidation value.

Modified book value is appropriate for an established company that is stable or just growing slowly. In this case, the value of the company is its book value, which is paid in equity plus retained earnings—or, looked at another way, assets minus liabilities. The problem with taking the book value on the existing balance sheet is that it assumes that accounting records accurately reflect the economic value of the assets and the liabilities. Unfortunately, the accounting of most businesses distorts the economic value of an organization—none more so than private, closely held companies. Hence, adjustments to assets and liabilities are necessary before an accurate value can be determined. The major weakness of this method is that it reflects the past instead of the future. It is static, not dynamic, because it is based on existing assets and liabilities rather than future earnings.

Replacement value is appropriate when someone is considering whether to set up a similar business from scratch or to buy an existing business. *Liquidation value* is appropriate for a business that has ceased to be a going concern. It might be in bankruptcy or simply a business that is for sale but no one is willing to buy it as a going concern. Just as the name implies, the valuation of such a business is the amount someone is willing to pay for the assets.

Example of Market-Comparable Valuation

Following is a simplified illustration of market-comparable valuation, which is the most commonly used method for valuing a potential superstar company that is trying to raise venture capital.

Bug Free Web Software (BFWS), a 12-month old World Wide Web software company, has successfully beta-tested its product and is seeking $4 million of venture capital to go into full-scale production and distribution. BFWS is forecasting sales revenue of $50 million with net income of $5 million in five years. What percent of the equity will the venture capitalists require?

To value this company and estimate the amount of equity that the venture capitalists will need to get their required internal rate of return (IRR), we need the following five figures:

1. Future earnings (NI).
2. Comparable price to earnings ratio (P/E).
3. Amount being invested (at time 0), INV_0.
4. Risk-adjusted cost of capital (IRR).
5. Number of years before the investment will be harvested (N).

BFWS's financial projections forecast that the net income in five years will be $50 million; so NI is $5 million and N is 5. What is the P/E? The P/E will be the average for public companies that are comparable to BFWS. In general, P/E ratios are determined by the rate of growth of a company and the rate of growth of the industry segment that a company is in. This is illustrated in Exhibit 7.1.

In the bottom left-hand corner are companies in slow-growing industries; they grow at approximately the same rate as the industry—for example, automobile manufacturers. If the company is growing faster than the overall industry, its P/E should be higher than the industry average, and vice versa. (Of course, if a company is losing money, its NI is negative so it does not have a positive P/E ratio.) In the upper right-hand corner are rapidly growing companies in high-growth industry segments, which is where BFWS

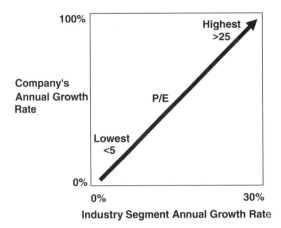

Exhibit 7.1   Price to Earnings

expects to be. As we will see when we come to the section on venture capital later in this chapter, P/E ratios for superstar software/Internet companies in the top right-hand corner are sometimes much higher than 25, but when valuing a very young company such as BFWS with no history of sales and income, venture capitalists will be conservative and use a P/E of approximately 20.

Using BFWS's financial projections, the future value of the company in five years will be as follows:

$$FV_5 = NI_5 \times (P/E)_5 = \$5 \text{ million} \times 20 = \$100 \text{ million}$$

We now want to calculate the percent of the equity that the venture capitalists will need to get their required rate of return (IRR). The expected return depends on the risk involved. In general, the younger the company, the greater is the risk. Exhibit 7.2 shows the expected IRR for the various stages of a company in which the investment is being made.

A *seed stage* company is one with not much more than a concept; a *start-up* company is one that is already in business and is developing a prototype but has not sold it in significant commercial quantities; a *first-stage* company has developed and market-tested a product and needs capital to initiate full-scale production. *Second-stage, third-stage,* and *mezzanine* financing fuels growing companies; and *bridge* financing may be needed to support a company while it is between rounds of financing, often while it waits to go public.

BFWS has a prototype that has successfully passed its beta test and now wants to go into full-scale production; therefore, it is classified as being at the start-up stage where the expected IRR is 60 percent. Now we need to find out what percent of BFWS's equity will be needed by the venture capitalists to meet a 60 percent return. Exhibit 7.3 shows the percent of equity needed to produce a return of 60 percent on a $4 million investment for various future values (from $20 million to $100 million) and holding periods (from two to eight years).

The future value of BFWS is expected to be $100 million in five years; hence the venture capitalist will require 42 percent of BWFS's equity.

The market-comparable valuation formula is as follows:

$$\text{Percent equity} = \frac{INV_0 \times (1 + IRR/100)^N}{NI_N \times (P/E)_N} \times 100$$

Exhibit 7.2   Expected IRR by Stage

Company Stage	Expected Annual Return (IRR)
Seed	80%
Start-up	60%
First-stage	50%
Second-stage	40%
Third-stage/mezzanine	30%
Bridge	25%

Exhibit 7.3 Percent of Equity to Produce a 60 Percent IRR on a $4 Million Investment

Holding Period	Future Value ($ million)				
Years	20	40	60	80	100
2	51%	26%	17%	13%	10%
3	82%	41%	27%	20%	16%
4	NA	66%	44%	33%	26%
5	NA	NA	70%	52%	42%
6	NA	NA	NA	84%	67%
7	NA	NA	NA	NA	NA
8	NA	NA	NA	NA	NA

Applying this formula to BFWS:

$$\text{Percent equity} = \frac{4,000,000 \times (1 + 60/100)^5}{5,000,000 \times 20} \times 100 = 42\%$$

There is a lot of uncertainty in this computation: Will BFWS achieve the net income that it has forecast? If so, will it reach it in five years or will it take longer? Will the price to earnings ratio for comparable public companies be 20 or higher, or will it be lower? Will the window for floating initial public offerings be open in five years or will it be shut and delay BFWS's IPO? Any of these contingencies will affect the IRR when the venture capitalists harvest their investment in BFWS. Occasionally, a venture capital–backed company does better than expected. However, more often than not it does not meet its financial forecast; hence the actual IRR is usually less than expected.

Asset-Based Valuation

In the previous section we looked at how to value a high-growth superstar company with the potential to attract venture capitalists or go public. In this section we will examine how to value an ordinary company that does not have the potential to attract venture capital or go public. Most companies are ordinary rather than glamorous superstars.

Suppose you want to become an entrepreneur by buying out an ordinary business—let's call it XYZ Corporation—that is well established but is in an industry that it growing about as fast as the overall economy and is an average performer. You would probably hope to buy it for its *modified book value*. The balance sheet for XYZ Corporation is shown in Exhibit 7.4. It lists the assets and liabilities as they are reported on the latest financial statements. The reported book value (total shareholder equity) is $5,159,000. In the second column are the adjustments that the accountants make to bring the assets and liabilities to actual market value; the footnotes explain the adjustments. The third column shows the restated numbers, which are the reported values (column 1) plus the adjustments (column 2). The restated book value is $6,309,000. That is probably what the seller will ask for the company.

Exhibit 7.4 XYZ Balance Sheet

Adjusted to Reflect Fair Market Value of Assets and Liabilities ($ Thousands)

Assets	As Reported	Adjustments	Restated	Liabilities	As Reported	Adjustments	Restated
				Capitalized Leases	500		500
Cash	1,500		1,500	Long-Term Debt	600	—	600
Accounts Receivable (net)[a]	3,300	(100)	3,200	Total Liabilities	4,860	100	4,960
Inventory[b]	3,419	450	3,869				
Total Current Assets	8,219	350	8,569	Shareholder Equity			
Land and Buildings[c]	1,000	750	1,750	Capital Stock	500		500
Machinery and Equipment[d]	750	200	950	Retained Earnings[g]	4,659	1,150	5,809
Other Assets[e]	50	(50)	0				
Total Assets	10,019	1,250	11,269	Total Shareholder Equity	5,159	1,150	6,309
Liabilities							
Accounts Payable	1,700		1,700				
Short-Term Debt	1,410		1,410				
Accruals[f]	650	100	750				
TOTAL CURRENT LIABILITIES	3,760	100	3,860	Total Liabilities and Shareholder Equity	10,019	1,250	11,269

RESTATEMENT NOTES:

[a.] Deduct $100K for uncollectible receivables

[b.] LIFO reserve adjustment of inventory of Fair Market Value

[c.] MAI Appraisal of Land & Building reflect value of $1,750K

[d.] Machinery & Equipment Appraisal reflects current market value of $950K

[e.] Other Assets were principally goodwill from expired patents - deduct

[f.] Investigation found accruals unrecorded of an additional $100K

[g.] the net PRE TAX effect of changes in (1) through (6)

Before buying an existing business, the buyer should ask the following critical questions:

- What is the growth rate of the industry?
- Is the company's growth rate above or below the industry average?
- What adjustments need to be made to the income and cash flow statements and to the balance sheet to reflect how the new owners will operate the business?
- How do the adjusted earnings and cash flows compare with industry averages?
- How does the balance sheet compare with industry averages (especially debt to equity)?
- How is the purchase being financed and how will that change the income, cash flow, and balance sheet?
- How will the new owner's strategies affect the company's future performance?

When these questions have been answered, the buyer should make five-year pro forma financial statements and do some sensitivity analysis of the critical factors such as sales revenue, cost of sales, and interest and repayment of both the old debt that the buyer takes over and any new debt that will be added to help finance the purchase of the business.

Financing a New Venture

The first financing for your new business will come from you and your partners if you have any. It will be cash from your savings and probably from your credit card. According to the Global Entrepreneurship Monitor (GEM) study, the average amount of start-up financing for a new business in the United States is $70,000, of which 70 percent is provided by the entrepreneurs themselves.[3] Perhaps you will also contribute tangible assets such as intellectual capital (e.g., software and perhaps patents) and hard assets such as computer equipment. As the company gets under way, you will also be contributing financially to your company by working very long hours for substantially less than the salary that you could get working for someone else; seven-day work weeks and 12-hour days are not unusual for entrepreneurs starting up businesses.

Before you turn to family and friends for start-up money, you should look at all the possibilities of getting funding from other external sources, just as Jim Poss did. Sources might include the following:

- Services at reduced rates (some accounting and law firms offer reduced fees to start-up companies as a way of getting new clients).
- Vendor financing (getting favorable payment terms from suppliers).
- Customer financing (getting down payments in advance of delivering goods or services).
- Reduced rent from a landlord (some landlords, such as Cummings Properties in Massachusetts,[4] offer entrepreneurs reduced rents or deferred rents for the first six months or perhaps a year).
- Starting out in an incubator that offers rent and services below market rates.

- Leasing equipment instead of buying it.
- Government programs such as the SBIR awards for technology companies.

You probably should also talk to a bank officer. But keep in mind that banks expect loans to be secured by assets, which include the assets of the business and its owner or someone else, such as a wealthy parent, who is willing to guarantee the loan with personal assets. The SBA guaranteed loan program is a possibility. In 2008 the SBA program provided approximately $50 million of loans per day to small businesses.[5] However, even if you qualify for an SBA loan you will have to guarantee the loan personally, and the bank granting the loan will expect that at least 33 percent of the start-up financing will be owners' equity, which means that if you want to borrow $70,000 under the SBA program, the owners must have $35,000 invested in the company. The SBA figure of $50 million per day is impressive, but most of that money goes to existing businesses rather than to new companies.

Informal Investors

After you have exhausted all the other potential sources of financing, you should turn to informal investors for help with the initial funding of your new business. Informal investors are by far the biggest source of start-up financing after the entrepreneurs themselves. In the United States, informal investors provide in the region of $100 billion per year to start-up and young businesses.[6] Slightly more than 50 percent of informal investment goes to a relative's business; 28 percent to a friend or neighbor's; 9 percent to a work colleague's; and 7 percent to a stranger's.[7] In this section we look at informal investors, who are mostly inexperienced when it comes to funding start-up companies; in the next section we look at an important subset of informal investors, business angels, who are more sophisticated about dealing with start-up entrepreneurs.

Half of all informal investors in the United States expect to get their money back in two years or sooner, according to the GEM study. This suggests that they regard their financial involvement as a short-term loan instead of a long-term equity investment. We are using the term *investment* loosely in this context because it may be more like a loan rather than a formal investment. Whether it is a loan or an equity investment, the downside financial risk in the worst case is the same because if the business fails, the informal investors will lose all their money.

It is important to make clear to informal investors what the risks are. If you have a business plan you should give them a copy and ask them to read it. But assume that they probably will not read it thoroughly; hence, you should make sure you have discussed the risks with them. A guiding principle when dealing with family and friends is not to take their money unless they assure you that they can afford to lose their entire investment without seriously hurting their standard of living. It may be tempting to borrow from relatives and friends because the interest rate is favorable and the terms of the loan are not as strict as they would be from a bank, but if things go wrong, your relationship might be seriously impaired, perhaps even ended.

How should you treat money that a relative or friend puts into your business in the early days? At the beginning the business has no operating experience and it is very uncertain what the outcome will be; hence, it is extremely difficult—maybe impossible—to place a valuation on the fledgling new venture. It is probably better to treat money from friends and family as a loan rather than an equity investment. As with any loan, you should pay interest, but to conserve cash flow in the first year or two, the interest should be payable in a lump sum at the end of the loan rather than in monthly installments. You should give the loan holders the option of converting the loan into equity during the life of the loan. In that way, they can share in the upside if your company turns out to have star potential with the possibility of substantial capital gains for the investors.

When you are dealing with relatively small amounts of money from relatives and friends, especially close family such as parents and brothers and sisters, it is quite likely that you will not bother to have a formal loan agreement, particularly if you ask them to loan you money when you are under pressure because your business is out of cash. But at a minimum you should record the loan in writing with perhaps nothing more than a letter or a note. If you want something more formal, Virgin Money (formerly Circle Lending) sets up loan agreements for small businesses with informal investors.[8] A documented loan agreement could be important if you subsequently start dealing with professional investors such as sophisticated business angels and venture capitalists.

Business Angels

Informal investors are most likely to be entrepreneurs themselves. In the case of the funding of Apple, Google, and Netscape, and many other companies not as famous, such as Seahorse Power, wealthy entrepreneurs play a key role in the funding of many new ventures. We call those types of informal investors *business angels*.

It is estimated that business angels fund between 30 and 40 times the number of entrepreneurial firms financed by the formal venture capital industry and provide between $20 and $30 billion annually in the United States.[9,10] Angels invest in seed stage and very early stage companies that are not yet mature enough for formal venture capital or where the amount of financing is too small to justify the venture capitalist's costs, including evaluation, due diligence, and legal fees. While venture capital firms are funding proportionately fewer seed and start-up companies, angel investors are funding more. For example, in 2008, venture capitalists invested only $1.5 billion in seed stage and start-up companies out of a total of $28.3 billion that they invested in all U.S. companies.[11]

We do not know how many wealthy persons are business angels. But we do know that SEC Rule 501 states that an "accredited investor" is a person with a net worth of at least $1 million or annual income of at least $200,000 in the most recent two years, or combined income with a spouse of $300,000 during those years. According to Forrester consulting, the number of households in the United States that fit that profile is approximately 630,000.[12] So that is the number of potential business angels qualified to invest in private offerings governed by SEC rules.

Searching for Business Angels

Most nascent entrepreneurs do not know anyone who is a business angel, so how should they search for them? The good news is that today there are formal angel groups. These are angels who have joined together to seek and invest in young companies. Most of them are wealthy entrepreneurs; some are still running their businesses, while others are retired. Angel investor groups have been around for many years, but they started to proliferate in the late 1990s when it seemed as if everyone was trying to make a fortune by getting in early on investments in Internet-related start-ups. The good news is that, although

many angels along with many venture capital firms lost a lot of money on their investments when the Internet bubble burst, angel groups did not disband and they continued
investing in seed and early stage companies, albeit at a much reduced rate. A comprehensive list of angel groups can be found at http://www.inc.com/articles/2001/09/23461.html.
You can also find additional angel groups in your area by searching on the Web.

Angel groups have different ways of selecting potential companies to invest in. A few
groups only consider opportunities that are referred to them, but most angel groups
welcome unsolicited business plans from entrepreneurs. They evaluate the plans and
invite the entrepreneurs with the most promising plans to make a presentation to the
group at one of their periodic (usually monthly) meetings. A few of those presentations
eventually result in investments by some of the angels in the group. Some groups charge
the entrepreneurs a fee to make a presentation and a few even require a fee when an
entrepreneur submits a business plan. The size of each investment by angel groups ranges
from less than $100,000 to as much as $2 million, and in a few instances considerably
more.

As important as angel groups have become, they comprise only a few thousand business
angels compared with hundreds of thousands of business angels who invest on their own.
Hence, entrepreneurs are much more likely to raise money from angels who invest
individually rather than in packs. Unfortunately, individual business angels are very hard
to find. Searching for them requires extensive networking. But, according to Bill Wetzel,
professor emeritus at the University of New Hampshire, who pioneered research into
angel investing and started the first angel investment network, which was the forerunner
of ACE-Net (Angel Capital Investment Network, now Active Capital[13]), "Once you find
one angel investor, you have probably found another half dozen."

Consider how other entrepreneurs found business angels. Steve Jobs and Stephen
Wozniak found Armas Markkula through an introduction by a venture capitalist who
looked at Apple and decided it was too early for him to invest. Sergey Brin and Larry
Page were introduced to Andy Bechtolsheim by a Stanford University faculty member.
Jim Poss worked for Spire Corporation and got to know Roger Little, founder and CEO
of Spire and a leading expert on solar power; he met another of his angel investors at
a wind energy conference sponsored by Brown Rudnick. When a company acquires
financing from a well-known business angel who is a leader in an industry related to the
one that the new company is entering, it sends an important signal to other potential
investors. For instance, once Andy Bechtolscheim had invested in Google, Brin and Page
soon put together $1 million of funding. And Jim Poss's parents said they would invest
only if Roger Little invested.

Types of Business Angels

Business angels have many different objectives and styles of operating. They range from
silent investors who, once they have made their investment, sit back and wait patiently
for results, to others who want to be involved in the operations of the company, either
as a part-time consultant or as a full-time partner in the business. Judith Kautz classifies
business angels in the following categories: entrepreneurial, corporate, professional,
enthusiast, and micromanagement.[14]

Entrepreneurial angels are entrepreneurs who have started their own businesses and
are looking to invest in new businesses. Some of them have realized substantial capital
gains by taking their companies public or merging them with other companies. Others

are still running their businesses full-time and have sufficient income to enable them to be business angels. In general, entrepreneurial angels are the most valuable to the company that they invest in because they are usually knowledgeable about the industry and, just as important, they have built substantial businesses from the ground up, so they understand the challenges that entrepreneurs face. Hence, they can be invaluable advisers and mentors. Armas Markkula is a famous example of a business angel who had made his fortune in two entrepreneurial companies, first Fairchild and then Intel. He had retired at the age of 38 when Steve Jobs and Stephen Wozniak were introduced to him. He invested in Apple; worked with Steve Jobs to write Apple's first business plan; secured a bank line of credit; helped raise venture capital; recruited Michael Scott, Apple's first president; and then became president himself from 1981 to 1983. According to Steve Wozniak, "Steve [Jobs] and I get a lot of credit, but Mike Markkula was probably more responsible for our early success, and you never hear about him."[15]

Corporate angels are managers of larger corporations. They invest from their savings and current income. Some of them are looking to invest in a start-up and become part of the full-time management team. Corporate angels who have built their careers in big, multinational corporations can be a problem for a neophyte entrepreneur because they know a lot about managing companies with vast resources but they have never worked in a small company with very limited resources. Granted, they know a lot about how a big company is run, but how relevant is that to a company that is just starting out on a shoestring?

Here is an example of what might go wrong. A fish importing wholesaler was started and run by two young men. The company grew fast but it ran out of working capital. Two angels, one of them a marketing executive with a huge multinational food company, invested $500,000 on condition that the marketing executive be hired by the young company as its marketing/sales vice president. Very soon there was a clash of cultures; the founders continued to work 12-hour days, while the new vice president was traveling first class and staying in fancy hotels when he made sales trips. Within a year, the business angels took control of the company. The two founders left, and a year later it closed its doors.

Professional angels are doctors, dentists, lawyers, accountants, consultants, and even professors who have substantial savings and incomes and invest some of their money in start-ups. Generally, they are silent partners, although a few of them, especially consultants, expect to be retained by the company as paid advisers.

Enthusiast angels are retired or semiretired entrepreneurs and executives who are wealthy enough to invest in start-ups as a hobby. It is a way for them to stay involved in business without any day-to-day responsibilities. They are usually passive investors who invest relatively small amounts in several companies.

Micromanagement angels are entrepreneurs who have been successful with their own companies and have strong views on how the companies they invest in should be run. They want to be a director or a member of the board of advisers and get regular updates on the operations of the company. They do not hesitate to intervene in the running of the business if it does not perform as expected.

There is no ideal type of business angel. And in general, most entrepreneurs cannot pick and choose because it is so hard to find business angels who are prepared to invest. But an entrepreneur should find out as much as possible about business angels before accepting money from them. A wise angel will carefully investigate the entrepreneur before investing; likewise, a smart entrepreneur will find out as much as possible about a potential business angel. There is probably no better source of information about a business angel than other entrepreneurs in whom the angel has previously invested. So an entrepreneur should ask the business angel if he has invested in other entrepreneurs, and if so would it be okay to talk with them.

Putting Together a Round of Angel Investment

If you are raising a round of investment from business angels you will need a lawyer who is knowledgeable in this area because there are various Securities and Exchange Commission (SEC) rules that you need to comply with. The SEC web site has a good brochure on private placements that you should read.[16] Most private placements by start-up entrepreneurs are made under regulation D, Rule 504, dealing with offerings up to $1 million; fewer are made under Rule 505 dealing with offerings up to $5 million. There is a brief explanation of these in Chapter 10.

The first thing that you will want to do is place a value on your start-up. As discussed earlier in this chapter, it is impossible to arrive at a precise valuation for a seed stage company. Valuations at that stage are more an art than a science. Indeed, the valuation is very subjective, with entrepreneurs placing a substantially higher value than business angels. Informed business angels will determine the value based on similar deals that have recently been made by other angels and venture capital firms. The comparable-market valuation method will probably be used for a back-of-the-envelope estimate to see if the company has a chance of meeting the business angels' required return.

In general, business angels are satisfied with a lower return than venture capitalists because, unlike venture capitalists, they have only minimum operating costs and they do have to pay carried interest on any capital gains. Venture capitalists charge as much as 3 percent per year on the money that they invest, and on top of that they deduct 20 percent—sometimes more—from the capital gain that they pass on to their investors. Hence, to produce a return of 25 percent for their investors, venture capitalists need to get a return of 35 percent or more from their investment portfolio.

According to Wainwright, business angels expect an IRR of 15 to 25 percent with a payback time between five and seven years.[17] An MIT study found that the business angels expected returns between 3:1 and 10:1 on their investments, and that actual returns ranged from losses on 32 percent of their investments to higher than 10:1 on 23 percent of them.[18] The same MIT study found that business angels were evenly split between IPOs and acquisitions as their preferred exit; none preferred a buyback. In practice, 27 percent of business angel investments were exited with an IPO, 35 percent with an acquisition, 5 percent with a buyback, and 32 percent were losses.

While financial returns are very important to business angels, they also invest for nonfinancial reasons, including a desire to give back and mentor budding entrepreneurs, to be involved in start-ups without total immersion, to have fun, to be part of a network of other business angels, to stay abreast of new commercial developments, to be involved with development of products and services that benefit society, and to invest in entrepreneurs without the pressure of being a full-time venture capitalist.[19]

Most angel investments are for preferred stock that is convertible into common stock on a one-to-one ratio. Preferred stock gives investors priority rights over founders' common stock. The priority rights relate to liquidation and voting rights. The potential problem with convertible preferred stock is that it sets a valuation on the stock at the first round. If that valuation turns out to be higher than the venture capitalist's valuation at the second round, negotiations between the venture capitalist and the entrepreneur will be difficult. It might even be a deal breaker.

Jim Poss placed a premoney valuation of $2.5 million on Seahorse Power when he was raising his first round of funding from business angels. He raised $250,000, so the post-money valuation was $2.75 million. Investors would have owned 9.1 percent $(250,000/2,750,000 \times 100)$ of the equity if Jim had issued stock. But instead of stock, he issued convertible debt.

Some seed stage companies that expect to get venture capital investment in later rounds of financing use convertible debt rather than convertible preferred stock. Convertible debt is a bridge loan that converts to equity at the next round of investment, assuming that it is an equity round. Convertible debt securities allow the next round of investors, who are usually venture capitalists, to set the value of the company and provide the first-round angel investors with a discount. Business angels would like to get a 30 percent discount but actual discounts range from 10 to 30 percent. Convertible debt has the advantage over convertible preferred stock because it reduces or eliminates squabbling over the valuation between venture capitalists and the entrepreneur.[20]

The major conditions of a proposed deal are spelled out in a term sheet. Three examples of business angel term sheets can be found in *Venture Support Systems Project: Angel Investors*.[21]

Venture Capital

Raising money from business angels for seed stage and start-up companies is difficult, but getting it from formal venture capitalists is daunting. In 2008, venture capitalists invested in only 3,808 U.S. deals, of which just 327 were seed or start-up stage investments in companies receiving venture capital for the first time. The reality is that a person has a better chance of winning $1 million or more in a lottery than getting seed stage or start-up venture capital.[22] It is extremely rare that entrepreneurs have venture capital in hand when their new businesses begin operating. Too many nascent entrepreneurs waste too much time in a fruitless search for venture capital instead of getting their businesses up and running. For some, failure to raise venture capital becomes an excuse for abandoning their nascent ventures.

It is important to understand that venture capital is almost always invested in companies that are already in business and have demonstrated the potential to become stars, or better yet superstars, in their industry. Venture capital accelerates the commercialization of new products and services; it seldom pays for the initial development of concepts. It is also important to keep in mind that the bulk of venture capital in the United States goes to high-technology-based companies.

Candidates for Venture Capital

Following are the six top factors, in order of importance, that venture capitalists look for when they are evaluating a potential candidate for investment.[23]

1. Management team.
2. Target market.
3. Product/service.

4. Competitive positioning.

5. Financial returns.

6. Business plan.

Management Team

We wrote in Chapter 1 that "the crucial ingredients for entrepreneurial success are a superb entrepreneur with a first-rate management team and an excellent market opportunity." The lead entrepreneur and the management team are by far the most important ingredient to entrepreneurial success. Entrepreneurs should have most of the start-up team identified before they approach venture capitalists. If they are sufficiently impressed with the progress that a start-up company has made, venture capitalists will sometimes help to recruit a key member of the team. They will even help recruit a new CEO if they have reservations about the lead entrepreneur's ability to build a rapidly growing company with the potential to go public. The best venture capitalists have extensive Rolodexes with potential candidates for management positions in their portfolio companies.

> *"...there's plenty of technology, market opportunity, and venture capital, but too few great entrepreneurs and teams [in 2004]."*
>
> —John Doerr, legendary venture capitalist, Kleiner Perkins Caufield & Byers[24]

Target Market

The target market should be fragmented, accessible, and growing rapidly. The Internet triggered a stampede of venture capital investing in the late 1990s because it promised to become a huge market with many different segments; there were no dominant players in the new segments; and the segments were readily accessible to new entrants. In the 2000s, nanotechnology has a similar appeal to venture capitalists; likewise, what is called clean technology.

Product/Service

The product or service should be better than competing products and it should be protected with patents or copyrights. It does not have to be the first product in its market segment. For example, Google was not the first Web search engine; it was simply superior to the existing ones.

Competitive Positioning

There should be no dominant competitor in the market niche, distribution channels should be open, and the company should have an experienced marketing manager with expert knowledge of the market segment. SolidWorks positioned its CAD/CAM software in a niche into which it was difficult for well-established competitors, especially Parametric Technology, to move without cannibalizing their business models.[25]

Financial Returns

The potential financial return is important, but classic venture capital does not depend on sophisticated financial computations. Venture capitalists have a rule of thumb for early and expansion stage companies: They will invest only if the company has the potential to return at least seven times their investment (or, in venture capital jargon, "seven x") in five years. A 7x return in five years produces an IRR of 47.6 percent; a 10x return in five years produces an IRR of 58.5 percent.

Business Plan

Every entrepreneur seeking money from business angels or professional venture capitalists must have a competently written business plan. But it is important to keep in mind that no matter how good a business plan may be, it will not impress investors nearly as much as a product or service that is already being evaluated by customers. Too many entrepreneurs spend too much effort refining and polishing their business plans rather than implementing their business.

Ideal Candidate for Venture Capital

It is said the *ideal* technology-based candidate for its first round of venture capital meets the following criteria:

- CEO/lead entrepreneur has significant management and entrepreneurial experience with demonstrated ability to manage a rapidly growing company in a fast-paced industry segment.
- Vice president of engineering is recognized as a star in the industry.
- Vice president of marketing has a proven track record.
- Some members of the top management team have worked together before.
- The product/service is better than its competitors.
- Intellectual capital such as patents and copyrights are protected.
- The market segment is fragmented, growing rapidly, and expected to be big.
- There are no dominant competitors.
- The company has satisfied customers.
- The company projects sales of $50 million in five years.
- The gross income margin is expected to be better than 60 percent with a net income margin better than 10 percent.
- The amount of investment is between $5 million and $10 million.
- The company has the potential to go public in five years.
- The potential return is 7x or higher.
- The IRR is projected to be 60 percent or higher.

Actual Venture Capital–Backed Companies

Venture capital–backed companies that have IPOs are the cream of the crop. By examining profiles of companies at the time they go public, it is possible to see how the best companies measure up to the ideal. Exhibit 7.5 shows the results of a study of

122 venture-backed companies that went public in the years 1994–1997.[26] This was a period when the stock market indexes were rising, but it was before the Internet bubble that began at the end of 1997 and was over by the beginning of 2001.

The management of those companies came close to the ideal. For instance, half of the top management teams had a combined experience of 114 years or more. Seventy-one percent of the companies had at least one founder with previous start-up experience. And about two-thirds of the companies had two or more founders who had worked together before starting their present venture. These figures held true for all 122 companies combined and for the groups of companies in each of the industry segments (Internet, software, hardware, and semiconductor).

Market and operating performance at the time of the IPO was quite different among the industry segments, as shown in Exhibit 7.5. The industry segments are in order of the maturity from left to right, with the Internet being the least mature and the semiconductor the most mature. Much of the difference between companies in the four industries is explained by the maturity of the industry segment that the companies were in. The Internet market segments were growing much faster the semiconductor ones, likewise the annual growth rate of the sales revenue. There was a big difference between the characteristics of Internet and semiconductor companies.

Internet companies had the least sales revenue at the time of the IPO and the semiconductor companies the most. None of the four segments attained the ideal of at least $50 million in annual sales revenue. Not one of the industry segments met the net income margin of at least 10 percent prescribed for the ideal, but the Internet and software companies exceeded the gross margin requirement of at least 60 percent, while hardware and semiconductor companies fell short. In all segments except the Internet the annualized net income improved dramatically in the quarter before the IPO.

However, despite the shortcomings on sales revenue and net income, the venture capitalists met their hoped-for times return on the first round of venture capital in all industries except semiconductors. And their IRR handily topped their expectations. The median IRR for Internet companies was a whopping 507 percent because they went public only one year after they received their first round of venture capital. In contrast, five years elapsed for semiconductor companies between the first round of venture capital and the IPO. So although the times return in the semiconductor segment was almost 5 compared with just over 7 in the Internet segment, their IRR was only 30.5 percent because the longer that an investment is held, the lower the IRR. It should be noted that the P/E ratios were 70 for the Internet companies that were profitable, 54 for software, 32 for hardware, and 26 for semiconductors. The difference in the P/E ratios mainly explains the differences in market capitalization among the different industry segments.

What does this mean for entrepreneurs who are seeking venture capital? First, there is not one set of ideal criteria for a company. Second, the management team must be excellent. Third, the faster the growth of the industry and the growth of the company, the more likely it is to get the attention of venture capitalists. Fourth, entrepreneurs should focus on sales growth rather than profitability in the first few years, and then show a profitability spurt in the year before the IPO. Fifth, on average, companies are several years old before they get their first venture capital investment.

Exhibit 7.5 Venture Capital–Backed Public Companies

Marketing and Operations	Medians			
	Internet	Software	Hardware	Semiconductor
Market growth rate	135.7%	23.5%	37.5%	15.5%
Annual sales growth trend (all years)	87.0%	54.3%	55.7%	24.7%
Sales growth trend (12 months)	93.3%	45.9%	54.3%	30.1%
Annualized sales revenue	$9,720,000	$23,396,000	$27,268,000	$39,940,000
Gross margin	72.7%	75.6%	39.1%	42.2%
Profit margin	−36.7%	3.4%	−0.5%	7.9%
Net income (last year)	($2,414,530)	$308,000	($639,000)	$1,495,000
Net income (last quarter annualized)	($3,462,921)	$1,644,000	$2,140,000	$3,226,000
R&D ratio	27.0%	18.4%	14.5%	14.6%
Number of employees	124	134	92	213
Financial				
IRR	506.9%	124.8%	148.0%	30.5%
Times return	7.16	6.67	10.71	4.94
Years from first VC investment to IPO	0.96	2.53	4.04	5.00
Time from incorporation to IPO	5	8	7	11
Price/share first round of VC	$1.25	$1.50	$1.13	$2.79
IPO price	$14	$12	$10	$11
P/E ratio	70	54	32	26
Size of IPO	$34,000,000	$27,600,000	$22,320,000	$29,130,000
Market capitalization after IPO	$163,488,290	$105,510,812	$89,244,768	$77,468,542

Dealing with Venture Capitalists

The first big challenge for an entrepreneur is reaching a venture capitalist. It is easy to get names and contact information for almost every venture capital firm; for example, *Pratt's Guide to Private Equity and Venture Capital Sources* boasts that

> ... over 4,400 listings offer contact information, capital under management, recent investments and more, plus four indexes by company, personnel, investment stage, and industry preferences enable users to hone their search and target the ideal firm with a minimum of effort. The Web-based product is continually updated and easy to search.[27]

However, venture capital firms pay much more attention to entrepreneurs who are referred to them than to unsolicited business plans with a cover letter that arrive by mail. Entrepreneurs are referred to venture capitalists by accountants, lawyers, bankers, other entrepreneurs, consultants, professors, business angels, and anyone else in contact with venture capitalists. However, most of them are reluctant to recommend an entrepreneur to a venture capitalist unless they are confident that the entrepreneur is a good candidate for venture capital.

Entrepreneurs should be wary of "finders" who offer to raise venture capital for the entrepreneur. Most venture capitalists do not like dealing with finders because they charge the company a fee based on the amount of money raised—a fee that comes out of the money that the venture capitalist invests in the company. What's more, it's the entrepreneur, not the finder, who has to deal with the venture capitalists.

If the entrepreneur is fortunate enough to find a venture capitalist who would like to learn more about the new business, a meeting will be arranged either at the company's or the venture capital firm's office. The first meeting is usually an informal discussion of the business with one of the partners of the venture capital firm. If the partner decides to pursue the opportunity, he will discuss it with more of the partners in the firm; if they like the opportunity, the entrepreneur will be invited to make a formal presentation to several partners in the firm. This meeting is the crucial one, so it is important to make as good a presentation as possible. Not only are the venture capital partners assessing the company and its product or service, they are also carefully scrutinizing the entrepreneur and other team members to see if they have the right stuff to build a company that can go public.

It the venture capital partners like what they see and hear at this meeting, the venture capital firm will pursue the entrepreneur with the intent to invest in the company. The dealings will be with the venture capital partner who initiated the discussions with the entrepreneur. The venture capital firm will then begin its due diligence on the entrepreneur, other team members, and the company. Entrepreneurs who get to this stage will be evaluated as never before in their lives. It is not unusual for a venture capital firm to check dozens of references on the entrepreneur. Any suggestion of dubious conduct by the entrepreneur will be investigated. After all, the entrepreneur is asking the venture capital firm to trust him with several million dollars that in most cases is not secured by any collateral. All entrepreneurs should get a copy of their credit reports and be prepared to explain any delinquencies.

Entrepreneurs who get to this stage may be wondering if the venture capital firm is the right one for them. There might be a temptation to approach other venture capital firms to see what they might offer. But rather than do that, the entrepreneur should conduct due diligence on the venture capital firm. Entrepreneurs should ask the venture capitalist for a list of the entrepreneurs that the firm has invested in and ask if it is okay to speak with them. Here are some of the things that the entrepreneur should be looking for:

- *Value-added*. The best venture capitalists bring more than money to their portfolio companies.[28] They bring what they call value-added, which includes help with recruiting key members of management, strategic advice, industry contacts, and professional contacts such as accountants, lawyers, entrepreneurs, consultants, other venture capitalists, commercial bankers, and investment bankers.

Venture Capital Is "Relationship" Capital

Brook Byers and Ray Lane talking about how Kleiner Perkins Caufield & Byers helps entrepreneurs:

Brook Byers (referring to Kleiner Perkins Caufield & Byers' network): It's not keiretsu, it's relationship capital.

Ray Lane: Whether you call it a network, a Rolodex, keiretsu, or whatever, it is something that entrepreneurs crave, because they're looking for help. As Brook said, money is not a differentiator in our business, but they're looking for help. Either you have knowledge in their domain, and you can help them get from start-up to a company that actually gets something in the market, or you help them scale through relationships. In this world, at least in the enterprise world, it helps to know somebody.

Source: "SiliconBeat: Q&A with Kleiner Perkins Caufield Byers," *San Jose Mercury News*, November 14, 2004, http://www.siliconbeat.com/entries/2004/11/13/qa_with_kleiner_perkins_caufield_byers.html.

- *Patience*. Some venture capital firms, especially newer ones with relatively inexperienced partners, are more likely to get impatient when a portfolio company fails to meet expectations. Studies of venture capital–backed companies that have not yet gone public or been acquired find that approximately 50 to 60 percent of them have changed CEOs at some time after the first round of venture capital.[29,30] By contrast, only 18 percent of those that have had IPOs have changed CEOs.[31] Another indication of lack of patience is a venture capital firm that is trigger-happy to invoke covenants in the investment agreement, which contains a couple of hundred pages. There are all manner of covenants in those agreements, and it is not unusual for a company to violate one or perhaps more. An experienced venture capitalist will usually waive a covenant unless the violation is so severe that it jeopardizes the viability of the company.
- *Deep pockets*. Will the firm have enough money to invest in follow-on rounds of venture capital if the company needs them? Venture capital firms that have been in business for a long time have established a reputation of producing good returns for their limited partners. Hence, they are able to raise new funds from time to time. In contrast, a young venture capital firm with only one small fund without a

proven track record of producing satisfactory returns for its limited partners will have difficulty raising a second round.

- *Board of directors.* Does the venture capitalist sit on the board and regularly attend meetings? How often does the board meet? And how many boards does the venture capitalist serve on? A rule of thumb is that a venture capitalist should not be on more than a half-dozen boards of portfolio companies.

- *Accessibility.* Is the venture capitalist readily available when the entrepreneur needs advice? Conversely, does the venture capitalist interfere too much in the day-to-day running of the company?

Negotiating the Deal

The valuation of the company is probably the biggest issue that has to be negotiated. Generally, the entrepreneur's valuation is higher than the venture capitalist's. Entrepreneurs can make valuations of the company based on computations like the one earlier in this chapter for BFWS; they can also talk to other entrepreneurs who have recently received venture capital. In general, the venture capitalists have more information about pricing than do the entrepreneurs, because they know the valuations of similar deals that have been recently completed, and those will be the basis for the valuation.

Let's return to BFWS. The entrepreneur's calculations show that the venture capital firm will be looking for 42 percent of the equity after it has put in its $4 million. Hence, the company will be worth $9.42 million ($4 million/0.42) after the money has been invested, or what is called the post-money valuation. So the premoney valuation is $5.42 million ($9.42 million − $4 million).

The venture capitalist knows that comparable deals have been valued at $4 million premoney. Hence, the venture capitalist needs 50 percent of the equity post-money. After negotiations the entrepreneur and the venture capitalist settle for a premoney valuation of $4.5 million for BFWS, which means that the venture capitalist will get 47.1 percent of the equity with a post-money valuation of $8.5 million, and the entrepreneurs and any angel investors who have already put money into BFWS will be left with 52.9 percent. The venture capitalists will expect that a pool of stock will be reserved for key employees who will be hired in the future. The pool will be approximately 15 percent of the issued stock.

The next step is a term sheet that the venture capitalist will provide to the entrepreneur. It will be several pages long and list the main conditions of the deal. Samples of venture capital term sheets can be found on the Web.[32] The term sheet will specify how much money the venture capital firm is investing, how much stock it is getting, a detailed listing of all the stock that has been issued or reserved for stock options before the venture capital is invested, and how much stock will have been issued or reserved for stock options after the venture capital financing. The venture capitalists will in almost every case get convertible preferred stock. The rights of the preferred stock will be spelled out; those will include dividend provisions, liquidation preferences, conversion rights (usually one share of preferred converts to one share of common stock), antidilution provisions, voting rights, and protective provisions.

The term sheet will also have clauses covering information rights, such as a requirement for the company to supply timely unaudited quarterly and audited annual financial statements; board membership; how the venture capital will be used; employment agreements; stock registration rights; and rights that deal with terms under which management can sell stock privately. It will also specify the date when the deal will be closed.

Provisions on the term sheet are subject to negotiations between the entrepreneur and the venture capitalist. But the term sheet will contain a date and time when the venture capitalist's offer will expire unless the entrepreneur has conveyed his acceptance of the offer in writing.

Follow-on Rounds of Venture Capital

It is quite likely that there will be subsequent rounds of venture capital. For instance, in 2008 there were 1,171 first-round venture capital financings and 2,637 follow-on financings in the United States. Let's see what might happen in a second round of financing for BFWS.

Two years after the first round of venture capital, BFWS has met its milestones set out in its business plan, so the venture capitalists are happy. They had expected that the company would go public to raise more money but the IPO window is closed (as it was in 2002 and 2003 after the Internet bubble burst and investors lost their appetite for IPO stocks of not only Internet-related companies but information technology companies in general). BFWS estimates that it needs $6 million to keep it on its rapid growth trajectory for the next two years, when it hopes that the IPO window will again be open.

When a company has met its milestones, its valuation has increased. It is not unusual for venture capitalists to agree to a valuation that is three times what it was at the first round. BFWS will be talking both to its present venture capitalists, who will be eager to invest in a second round, and to other venture capitalists so as to get more than one valuation. We will assume that the deal will be struck at a premoney valuation of three times the post-money valuation of the first round, or $25.5 million (3 × $8.5 million). The post-money valuation will be $31.5 million. So the venture capitalist will get an additional 19 percent of the stock for their $6 million investment at the second round of financing. If all goes well and the IPO window opens up during the next two years, BFWS expects to go public.

Harvesting Investments

When business angels or venture capitalists put money into a business, there has to be a way in which they can realize their investments at a future date. This is called the *exit* or *harvest* for the investor. Essentially, there are three ways in which an investment is exited: an initial public offering, an acquisition, and a buyback of the investor's stock by the company itself. As mentioned earlier in this chapter, an IPO is the exit preferred by most investors because it produces the highest valuation in most but not all cases. An acquisition is the second choice. A buyback is a distant third because in almost every instance it produces a mediocre return.

One of the questions most frequently asked by neophyte entrepreneurs seeking external equity financing is, "Can I buy back the investors' equity?" The answer is, in principle, yes, but in practice it is extremely unlikely. Buybacks are rare because a successful and rapidly growing company needs all the cash that it can get just to keep on its growth trajectory. Hence, it has no free cash to buy out its external investors. A buyback is more likely to be one of the living dead where an IPO or an acquisition is not feasible but

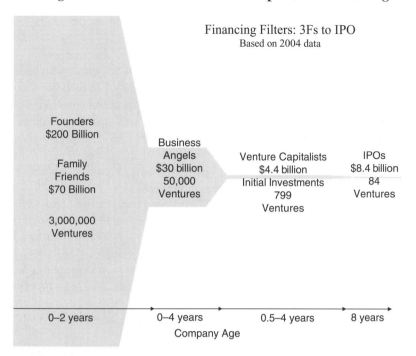

Exhibit 7.6   Financing Filters

somehow the company arranges a refinancing in which it buys back the stock owned by the original investors. Sometimes a venture capital agreement includes a redemption (buyback) clause that allows the venture capital firm to exit its investment by selling it back to the company at a premium if an IPO or acquisition does not occur within a specified time period.

Initial Public Offering

Only a minuscule number of companies raise money with a firm commitment IPO.[33] For example, in an average year, fewer than 100 venture capital–backed companies have IPOs. When this is divided by the number of companies that raise venture capital each year, it turns out that only 10 percent of them ever go public. In 2004, 43 percent of all IPOs were by venture capital–backed companies. Exhibit 7.6 shows the funding filters that most venture capital–backed companies must pass through to get to an IPO.

Without doubt, initial public offerings are glamorous and generally yield the biggest returns for the pre-IPO investors, but in the long run they are not always satisfactory for the entrepreneurs and the management team, for a variety of reasons. Granted, many entrepreneurs such as Bill Gates (Microsoft), Larry Ellison (Oracle), Robert Noyce and Gordon More (Intel), and Bernie Marcus and Arthur Blank (Home Depot) took their companies public and never looked back, but that is not always the case.

Joey Crugnale took his small chain of brick-oven pizza restaurants, Bertucci's, public in 1991 at $13 per share. But he was unable to satisfy Wall Street's appetite for ever-increasing sales and earnings. By 1998 Bertucci's stock, which at one time peaked at $25, was languishing at $6. Crugnale decided that he wanted to take his company private so that he would be free from the continual scrutiny of investors quarter by quarter. He made an offer to buy out the investors for $8 per share. He knew that once he proposed to buy back the company, there was a possibility other companies might bid for it, but he assumed that it was very unlikely because he had founded the company and he ran it.

He soon found out that his assumption was wrong. Quite unexpectedly, New England Restaurant Company handily topped his offer with a bid of $10.50 per share, which Crugnale agonized over but then decided not to make a counteroffer. Crugnale walked away from his baby, Bertucci's, a wealthy man at 46 but with a feeling of loss that he no longer was running the business that he had built from scratch into a chain of 84 restaurants in 11 states and the District of Columbia. He sometimes regrets taking Bertucci's public instead of keeping the company private and building his personal wealth from the cash flow that his restaurants were generating.

Crugnale has subsequently started Cajun-Mexican, Latin fish, and Italian restaurants—each one with several outlets—hoping to repeat his success with Bertucci's. So far that success has eluded him. But he consoles himself with the knowledge that it took several years before Bertucci's was a hit. However, one thing he knows for sure is that his restaurants will not go public: "I have no investors, I own everything myself, so I don't have to answer to anybody. . . . There are no restrictions, and I like that freedom."[34]

Pros and Cons of an IPO

The upside of going public is as follows:

- *Financing*. The principal reason for a public offering is to raise a substantial amount of money that does not have to be repaid. For example, the average amount of money raised by the 83 venture capital–backed companies that floated initial public offerings in 2004 was $101.5 million. The average post-money valuation of the companies was $671.1 million. And on average, the companies sold 16.4 percent of their equity at the IPO.

- *Follow-on financing*. A public company can raise more capital by issuing additional stock in a secondary offering.

- *Realizing prior investments*. Once a company is public, shareholders prior to the IPO know the value of their investment. What's more, their stock is liquid and can be sold on the stock market after the lockup period is over. The lockup period is a length of time after the IPO date (usually 180 days) when the prior shareholders are not permitted to sell any of their stock.

- *Prestige and visibility*. A public company is more visible and has more prestige. This sometimes helps the company with marketing and selling its products, outsourcing, hiring employees, and banking.

- *Compensation for employees*. Stock options presently held by employees or granted in the future have a known value.

- *Acquiring other companies*. A public company can use its shares to acquire other companies

And here is the downside of going public:

- *High expenses*. Expenses associated with going public are substantial. They include legal and accounting fees, printing costs, and registration fees, which can range from $100,000 to $400,000 or more. Those expenses are not recoverable if the company does not actually go public, which happens to about half of the companies that embark on the IPO process but fail to complete it. If the company does go public, the underwriter's commission takes approximately 7 percent of the money raised.

- *Public fishbowl.* When a company goes public, SEC regulations require that it disclose a great deal of information about itself that until then has been private and known only to insiders. That information includes compensation of officers and directors; employee stock option plans; significant contracts such as lease and consulting agreements; and details about operations including business strategies, sales, cost of sales, gross profits, net income, debt, and future plans. The IPO prospectus and other documents that have to be filed with the SEC are in the public domain; they are a gold mine for competitors and others who want to pry into the company's affairs.

  At the peak of the Internet bubble in November 1999, Cobalt Networks went public; its market niche was inexpensive thin servers for small and mid-size organizations. Before the IPO, the inexpensive thin server market had not attracted much competition from big companies such as Dell, IBM, Hewlett-Packard, and Sun Microsystems; however, after Cobalt's spectacular IPO, they became aware that the small niche was growing rapidly. Ten months later, Sun announced that it was acquiring Cobalt.

- *Short-term time horizon.* After an IPO, shareholders and financial researchers expect ever-increasing performance quarter by quarter. This forces management to focus on maximizing short-term performance rather than long-term goals.

- *Post-IPO compliance costs.* To meet SEC regulations, a public company incurs accounting costs that it never had when it was private. Those additional costs can amount to $100,000 or more annually.

- *Management's time.* After an IPO, the CEO and the CFO have to spend time on public relations with the research analysts, financial journalists, institutional investors, other stockholders, and market makers—so-called because they make a market for the company's stock. This is a distraction from their main job, which is running the company for optimum performance. Some public companies have executives whose main job is dealing with investor relations.

- *Takeover target.* A public company sometimes becomes the target of an unwelcome takeover by another company.

- *Employee disenchantment.* A rising stock price boosts the morale of employees with stock or stock options, but when it is sinking, it can be demoralizing—and never more so than when an employee's options go *underwater*, which is when the stock price falls below the options price. Underwater options can make it difficult to motivate and retain key employees.

Process of Going Public

Before a company can have an IPO it must file a registration statement with the SEC. The IPO cannot go forward until the SEC has approved the registration statement. The reason for the SEC's oversight is to ensure that the company's prospectus discloses to the public everything about the company before they decide whether to buy its shares. To avoid delays at the SEC, it is important that the registration statement be as clear as possible when it is filed; otherwise there will be delays as the company negotiates back and forth with the SEC. A delay sometimes wreaks havoc for a company's finances if the

IPO window closes suddenly, as it did when the Internet bubble burst in 2000. Many CEOs who had anticipated using the proceeds from IPOs to finance their companies were unable to float public offerings. Some companies were sold at fire-sale prices, and others shut their doors with huge losses to private investors, especially venture capital firms.

Entrepreneurs with serious aspirations to take their companies public should be far-sighted and run their companies from the beginning as if they will have a future IPO. In practice this means that their accounting firm should be a well-known national accounting firm with lots of clients who have had IPOs; the same goes for its law firm. Of course this is more expensive than starting out with small, local firms, but it will pay off in the long run if there is an IPO or the company is acquired by a public company.

When a company decides it is time to go public, its first step is to select an investment banker. This is where professional advisers such as accounting firms, law firms, and venture capitalists are valuable. Studies have shown that the market capitalization of companies taken public by top underwriters is higher than that of companies taken public by second-tier underwriters. Companies backed by leading venture capital firms and taken public by leading underwriters have the highest market capitalizations.[35]

Leading investment bankers are not shy. They aggressively pursue companies that they would like to take public. When banks are competing for a company's IPO, it is called a *beauty contest* or *bake-off*. They present their credentials to the company's CEO and board of directors and place a preliminary valuation on the company using the market-comparable method (NI × P/E). The company usually selects the underwriter that has had the most success with IPOs of companies in the same industry during the previous few years. More than one underwriter may be chosen; in that case the bank that is managing the IPO is known as the *lead underwriter*, and the other banks participating in the deal are called the *syndicate*.

As soon as the underwriter has been selected, the IPO process begins in earnest with an all-hands meeting in which the key players, including the lead underwriter, accounting and law firms, and company executives, decide what they will do and when. They then prepare the prospectus that contains all the information that the SEC deems that the public needs to know before investing. It includes details of the offering, what the company plans to do with the proceeds, the company's financial history and its future strategy, information on company management, and the company's industry niche, especially its competition. Risks are spelled out in detail. The preliminary prospectus is colloquially called the *red herring* because on the front page is a notice printed in red stating that some information is subject to change, in particular the price per share and the number of shares to be offered.

The preliminary prospectus is filed with the SEC. Then the company waits for the SEC, the National Association of Securities Dealers (NASD), and perhaps state securities organizations to review the documents for any omissions or problems that must be corrected before the IPO can proceed. There is a quiet period that lasts from the moment the company files the preliminary prospectus with the SEC until 25 days after the IPO. During the quiet period the company is forbidden to distribute any information about the company that is not contained in its prospectus.

Once the approval of the preliminary prospectus has been given, the lead underwriter and the CEO embark on a whirlwind tour of leading financial centers such as New York, San Francisco, Los Angeles, Chicago, Boston, and perhaps overseas centers such as London, Paris, Frankfurt, Hong Kong, and Tokyo. The purpose of the tour, or *road show*, is to promote the upcoming IPO and gauge the level of interest from potential investors. During the road show and immediately after, the underwriter builds a book of investors who say they want to buy the stock. The underwriter and the company meet the day before the IPO and use the order book to set the price of the stock and the size of the offering. The more the stock is oversubscribed, the higher the price will be. The underwriter commits to deliver the agreed-upon proceeds to the company, regardless of whether it sells all the stock at the offering price. Hence, there is a tension between the company pushing for a high price and the underwriter wanting to set a price that will enable it to sell all the stock at the offering price. Once the price had been set, stock is distributed to the banks in the syndicate, who then allocate it to their clients.

Setting the offering price is an art, not a science. The underwriter hopes the price at the end of the first day's trading will be about 15 percent higher than the offering price; this is known as the first-day *pop*. The number of shares in the offering multiplied by the pop is known as *money left on the table*; it is the additional amount of money that the company would have received if the offering price had been the same as the first day's closing price. (Academic researchers refer to it as *underpricing*.) During the Internet bubble, when the public's appetite for Internet-related stocks was insatiable, first-day pops of more than 100 percent were not unusual.

There is a lockup period of usually 180 days after the IPO when insiders are prohibited from selling any of their shares. If the share price shoots up and stays there, some companies have a secondary public offering and raise more money, usually before the 180-day lockup expires and the market is flooded by insiders selling shares and depressing the price. Sycamore Networks, for example, raised $284 million at its IPO in October 1999. It had a first-day pop of almost 400 percent. About five months later with the stock about 500 percent above its IPO price, it had a secondary offering and raised about $1.2 billion.

BFWS Goes Public

Two years after raising its second round of venture capital, and five years after it was founded, the IPO window for software companies is open so BFWS decides to go public. It has exceeded its forecasts and has revenue at $75 million with net income of $8.33 million. Revenue is growing at 50 percent per year. It wants to raise $50 million gross with an IPO. Based on the prevailing industry P/E ratio of 30, the investment bank values the company post-IPO at $250 million ($8.33 million × 30). To raise $50 million BFWS will have to sell 20 percent of its equity (50/250 × 100). That leaves the existing stockholders with 80 percent of the company.

Everyone should be happy with the return on their investments. At the IPO price, the $4 million of first-round venture capital is worth $64.8 million (16.2x return and IRR of 100 percent) and the $6 million of second-round venture capital is worth $38.1 million (6.3x return and IRR of 152 percent). The founders and the original investors hold stock worth $72.9 million, and the stock option pool is worth $24.3 million. The company receives the proceeds of $50 million minus the underwriter's 7 percent commission—that is, $46.5 million.

The original founders and stockholders own 29.1 percent of BFWS, the venture capitalists 41.1 percent, the stock option pool 9.7 percent, and the public 20 percent. The percentage of equity remaining in the hands of BFWS's founding entrepreneurs, 29.1 percent, is in line with the 32 percent average for all software companies post-IPO. Had it been a biotech company the average would have been less than 18 percent because in general a biotech company needs much more private equity than a software company to get it from start-up to IPO.[36]

Selling the Company

By far the most common way for investors to realize their investment is by selling the business to another company. As we have already pointed out, some companies that are acquired or merged with other companies simply have not done well enough to be candidates for a public offering. But that is not always the case: Sometimes the acquired company has done well enough to have a public offering but instead the entrepreneur and the board of directors choose to sell the company.

A company is usually bought by a bigger company for strategic reasons, such as when a big pharmaceutical company buys out a young biotech company that has developed a promising drug but lacks the resources and experience to take it through the FDA approval process, and, if the drug is approved, does not have the resources to market it. It is quite likely that the big pharmaceutical company will pay top price to acquire the biotech company.

A Strategic Acquisition: LowerMyBills.com

Matt Coffin started LowerMyBills.com in 1999. His vision was to provide consumers with a free, one-stop Internet destination to obtain better deals on all their recurring monthly expenses including mortgages, utilities, automobile loans, insurance, and credit cards. LowerMyBills.com attracts customers for mortgage lenders and others by advertising on a wide variety of web sites, including the major portals such as Yahoo!, AOL, and MSN. Consumers who click through on mortgage ads, for example, are taken to the LowerMyBills.com web site, where they enter information relevant to the mortgage approval process. This information is then matched against the lending criteria of the clients of LowerMyBills.com, and qualifying leads are passed on to several different lenders. The lenders then contact the consumer, who can choose the most appropriate offer. LowerMyBills.com is paid for every lead passed on to each lender.

In the last quarter of 2001, LowerMyBills.com posted its first profit. By 2005, it had a leading position in the U.S. market. The company, based in Santa Monica, was financed with $12 million first from business angels and venture capital firms. Matt, who still owned 25 percent of the equity, commented:

> By 2004, I knew personally that I was way in the money, but I also knew that I had 99 percent of my net worth tied up in the business. Back when the Internet crashed, I had a bunch of friends that had started online companies that had gone up and come down fast. One guy who had turned down an offer for $700 million went bankrupt a year later.
>
> Investment banks were calling me like crazy to say it was time for us to go public. We looked at the possibility of raising additional capital from new investors—recapitalize with new shareholders so that current stakeholders could get some liquidity. There was also the option of selling to a corporate buyer while staying on in some sort of earn-out arrangement.

The team hired an investment bank, gave nine presentations, and within short order had received eight offers from corporate buyers ranging from two to four hundred million dollars. Private equity firms that were interested in a partial buyout were putting forward valuations that averaged half of what the acquirers were offering. Matt added that his decision was about a lot more than finance:

> Every employee owns stock in this business, and they have worked really hard to get us to this point. We did need some sort of harvest, but I also knew that we still had a lot of growth ahead of us, and every option has its own set of risks and potential ramifications.[37]

Matt was in the enviable position of having a business that was growing rapidly in an industry segment that was expanding extremely fast. LowerMyBills.com had 176 employees. On a pro forma basis, sales in the year ended March 31, 2005, were $120 million with operating profit of $26 million. Clearly, the company could have gone public, but Matt decided to explore being acquired by a strategic partner. In May 2005, LowerMyBills.com was acquired by Experian, a member of GUS plc, the British retail and services group. Here are excerpts from a press release by Experian:

Acquisition of LowerMyBills.com by Experian[38]

GUS plc, the retail and business services group, today [May 5, 2005] announces that Experian has acquired 100% of the share capital of LowerMyBills.com, a leading online generator of mortgage and other loan application leads in the United States.

LowerMyBills.com is complementary to Experian's existing direct-to-consumer activities and operates in large, fast-growing markets. The purchase price is $330 million, plus a maximum performance-related earn-out of $50 million over the next two years. Further strong growth in sales and profit is expected in the current financial year and beyond. The acquisition is being funded from GUS's existing banking facilities. The acquisition is expected comfortably to exceed GUS' financial target of generating a double-digit post-tax return on investment over time.

Don Robert, Chief Executive Officer of Experian, commented:

"This acquisition represents a step-change in building Experian's direct-to-consumer activities. With LowerMyBills.com, we will now assist consumers in making the most cost-effective financial services decisions, while also providing our lender clients with high-quality leads for new borrowers. The strategic fit could not be better and we are delighted to welcome the talented people of LowerMyBills.com to Experian." . . .

Experian is establishing leading positions in various markets in connecting consumers with companies via the Internet. Its strategy is to offer a wide range of products that assist consumers in managing the financial aspects of key life events such as moving into a house or buying a car. Experian enables consumers to find financial products and services that best suit their needs, while helping companies to find new customers quickly and effectively.

As well as LowerMyBills.com, the newly-formed Experian Interactive operation includes Consumer Direct (selling credit reports, scores and monitoring products to consumers) and MetaReward and Affiliate Fuel (both of which generate online leads for clients). . . .

This acquisition is attractive because:

LowerMyBills.com operates in large, fast growing markets. More than 20 million American households take out a new mortgage each year. In 2004, home lenders spent $22 billion on acquiring customers, an amount which has grown by over one-third in the last five years. Of the $22 billion, about $1 billion is currently spent online and this is growing by about 30 percent a year. For example, Experian estimates that the percentage of mortgages originated online will treble between 2003 and 2008.

LowerMyBills.com has a strong market position. LowerMyBills.com is the most visited home loan service on the Internet. In a highly fragmented market, it is one of only two players of scale with its online leads generating more loans than any individual lending institution. It has strong relationships with more than 400 lenders, including five of the top ten mortgage providers in the United States. . . .

Over time, LowerMyBills.com will benefit from the skills, expertise and client relationships within Experian. Consumer Direct, MetaReward and LowerMyBills.com all work in the same Internet space and can share expertise and traffic. Combined, these businesses have more than 29 million visitors to their web sites each month. There are also benefits of LowerMyBills.com working more closely with Experian's Credit business. The introduction of Experian's modeling and analytical capabilities will allow it to improve the quality of leads passed to lenders. Experian will also be able to sell LowerMyBills.com's services to its existing financial services clients, where it has strong relationships.

Why Be Acquired

The acquisition of LowerMyBills.com by Experian is a very good example of what the seller and the acquirer are seeking from a strategic acquisition. Here are the advantages and disadvantages of an acquisition, from the perspective of the seller:

- *Management.* By selling the company rather than going public, the managers can stay focused on what they do best—continuing to build the company—rather than having to spend a lot of time on public relations with the financial community. Also, they probably will not be as driven by quarter-by-quarter results as they would be if the company was public. For example, LowerMyBills.com will have only a tiny effect on GUS's net income; hence, it is likely that LowerMyBills.com can focus on rapid sales growth rather than optimizing quarterly profits for the next few years.

- *Founder and CEO.* Selling a company that the entrepreneur has built from nothing more than an idea into a thriving enterprise can be traumatic for the entrepreneur. Edward Marram, the co-author of Chapter 13 of this book, sold his company, GeoCenters, in 2005. He said his head told him that it was the right thing to do, but his heart told him not to do it. After all, he was selling a company that he started from nothing in 1975 and built into an organization with 1,100 employees. When a company is private, the CEO reports only to a board of directors, but when it is acquired he has to report to a boss; and if the acquirer is a big company, that boss may report to a boss. It can be very frustrating for the CEO/founder, who has been making all the important decisions, to find after the acquisition that his decisions have to be approved by a hierarchy before they can be implemented.

- *Company.* The acquiring company likely has very deep pockets; it will be able to provide capital to the acquired company if it needs it.

- *Investors.* Acquisitions are often paid for in cash rather than stock. Hence, investors get cash immediately upon completion of the deal. This is in contrast to a public offering, where pre-IPO investors have stock that cannot be sold immediately after the offering; Thus, they bear a risk that the stock will go down before they can sell it. Of course, if the company is bought with the acquirer's stock instead of cash, and if there are restrictions on the sale of the stock, there is also risk that the stock price will go down before the investors can sell it.

- *Entrepreneur and employees stock.* If it is a cash transaction, as it was in the LowerMyBills.com acquisition, the entrepreneurs and employees get cash immediately. The potential disadvantage compared to an IPO is that they no longer hold stock so they have no upside potential if the company continues to do well. True, there is usually an earn-out in which additional compensation will be paid in a few years if the company meets targets that are specified at the time of the acquisition. In the case of LowerMyBills.com the earn-out is $50 million, compared with $330 million paid when the acquisition was completed. It is well worth getting the earn-out, but it is only 15.2 percent more, so it might not be enough to motivate employees to stay.

- *Employment agreement.* Key employees will have an employment agreement that forbids them from competing with the company for a specific number of years—usually no more than two—if they leave. That will probably be the same agreement that the employees had with the company before it was acquired. However, the CEO and top management will almost certainly be required to sign new noncompete agreements as part of their employment contracts with the acquirer.

- *Culture.* Initially, the acquirer will not interfere in the management of the company that it has just bought, but eventually it will probably want to put in its own management system and maybe its own executives in a few key positions. When it does that, there is a risk that there will be a clash of cultures.

- *Expenses and commissions.* The expenses and investment banker's commission are substantially lower for an acquisition than for an IPO.

Summary

When an entrepreneur accepts money from a financially sophisticated investor such as a business angel or a venture capitalist, there has to be a future harvest when the investment can be realized. Generally that harvest is when the company is acquired; occasionally, it is when the company goes public. The harvest is primarily for the investors rather than the entrepreneurs. If entrepreneurs are not careful, they can give would-be investors the impression that they themselves are planning to exit the company at the harvest. That is not what professional investors like to hear. They want to invest in entrepreneurs whose vision is to build a business and continue building it after the harvest, not in entrepreneurs who give the impression that they are in it to get rich quick. Remember that Bill Gates made almost all his huge fortune by the appreciation of Microsoft's stock after its IPO; so did Microsoft employees and investors who held on to their stock for many years after the IPO.

After a long negotiation between a Boston area entrepreneur and a venture capitalist for seed stage financing of a medical device company, the venture capitalist asked the entrepreneur, "Where do you personally want to be in ten years' time?" The entrepreneur replied that he hoped that he would have built a $200 million company that was the leader in its market niche and that he would still be the CEO. The venture capitalist immediately shook the entrepreneur's hand and said, "You have your money." The entrepreneur was very surprised because it seemed to him that the venture capitalist had already known about how big the company might become if things went well. So he asked what he had said that triggered the spontaneous decision to invest. The venture capitalist replied: "If you had said, 'retired to a house on the beach in Maine,' we would not have invested. We want entrepreneurs who are focused on building businesses for the long haul, rather than short-term personal wealth." The venture capitalist added, "Congratulations, you have just completed the most difficult selling job that you will ever do. You have convinced a venture capitalist to invest in a seed stage company."

Downloadable Resources for this chapter available at www.wiley.com/go/portablembainentrepreneurship

BFSW Cap Table

Notes

1. *Jim Poss*, a case study published by Babson College. (2004)
2. John Maynard Keynes, *A Treatise on Money* (London: Macmillan and Co., 1933).
3. W. D. Bygrave with M. Cole and M. Quill, *GEM (Global Entrepreneurship Monitor) 2006 Financing Report*, Global Entrepreneurship Monitor; see also W. D. Bygrave with S. A. Hunt, *GEM 2004 Financing Report*.
4. Cummings Properties works with local colleges and universities to promote entrepreneurship. Cummings helps sponsor several local business plan competitions and also provides special rate packages for new business growing out of college programs. The following page contains links to colleges with Cummings Properties sponsorship programs: http://www.cummings.com/how_to_lease_space.htm#entrep.
5. http://www.sba.gov/idc/groups/public/documents/sba_homepage/serv_bud_lperf_grossapproval.pdf
6. W. D. Bygrave and P. D. Reynolds, "Who Finances Startups in the U.S.A.? A Comprehensive Study of Informal Investors, 1999–2003," in *Frontiers of Entrepreneurship Research 2004*, ed. S. Zahra et al. (Wellesley, MA: Babson College).
7. Global Entrepreneurship Monitor 2002 data set, www.gemconsortium.org.
8. See www.virginmoneyus.com. Generally, the process works like this: (1) Identify a lender and agree on financing terms, such as loan amount, interest rate and term; (2) formalize the loan with a legally binding document, such as a promissory note; (3) create a system for repayment that is affordable for you and reassures your lender that the loan will eventually be repaid. By structuring your private financing in a businesslike manner, you will be able to demonstrate to your investors that you are serious about your endeavor.
9. W. E. Wetzel Jr. and J. Freear, "Promoting Informal Venture Capital in the United States: Reflections on the History of the Venture Capital Network," in R. T. Harrison and C. M. Mason (eds.), *Informal Venture Capital: Information, Networks and Public Policy* (Hemel-Hemstead, UK: Woodhead-Faulkner, 1994).
10. Mark Van Osnabrugge and Robert J. Robinson, *Angel Investing: Matching Startup Funds with Startup Companies—A Guide for Entrepreneurs, Individual Investors, and Venture Capitalists* (Cambridge, MA: Harvard Business School, 2000).
11. Press release, National Venture Capital Association, January 24, 2009.
12. F. Wainwright, "Note on Angel Investing," Tuck School of Business at Dartmouth, Center for Private Equity and Entrepreneurship, Case # 5001 (2005).
13. http://activecapital.org/.
14. J. Kautz, "Small Business Notes: Finding an Angel," http://www.smallbusinessnotes.com/financing.html.
15. http://www.failuremag.com/failure_interview.html.
16. http://www.sec.gov/info/smallbus/qasbsec.htm#eod6
17. See note 12.
18. *Venture Support Systems Project: Angel Investors*, release 1.1 (MIT Entrepreneurship Center, February 2000), http://entrepreneurship.mit.edu/Downloads/AngelReport.pdf.
19. Ibid.
20. Ibid.

21. Ibid.

22. http://www.lottery.state.mn.us/qanda.html#0

23. Jagdeep Baccher, Venture Capitalists' Investment Criteria in Technology-Based New Ventures, dissertation, University of Waterloo (2000).

24. "SiliconBeat: Q&A with Kleiner Perkins Caufield Byers," *San Jose Mercury News,* November 14, 2004, http://www.siliconbeat.com/entries/2004/11/13/qa_with_kleiner_perkins_caufield_byers.html.

25. *John Hirschtick and SolidWorks*, case studies published by Babson College.

26. W. D. Bygrave, G. Johnstone, J. Lewis, and R. Ullman, "Venture Capitalists' Criteria for Selecting High-Tech Investments: Prescriptive Wisdom Compared with Actuality," in *Frontiers of Entrepreneurship Research 1998* (Wellesley, MA: Babson College, 1998), www.babson.edu/entrep/fer/papers98/XX/XX_A/XX_A.html.

27. Pratt's Guide to Private Equity & Venture Capital Sources. http://www.thomsonreuters.com/products_services/media/media_products/professional_publishing/deals/pratts_guide

28. J. Rosenstein, A. V. Bruno, W. D. Bygrave, and N. T. Taylor, "CEO Appraisal of Their Boards in Venture Capital Portfolios," *Journal of Business Venturing* 8 (2) (2003): 99–113.

29. J. Rosenstein, A. V. Bruno, W. D. Bygrave, and N. T. Taylor, "How Much Do CEOs Value the Advice of Venture Capitalists on Their Boards?" in *Frontiers of Entrepreneurship Research 1990* (Wellesley, MA: Babson College, 1990).

30. W. D. Bygrave, E. Marram, and T. Scherzer, "Boards of Directors of Venture-Capital-backed Companies," presented at Babson-Kauffman Entrepreneurship Research Conference, Boulder, Colorado, June 2002. Summary published in *Frontiers of Entrepreneurship* 2002 (Wellesley, MA: Babson College, 2002).

31. See note 26.

32. http://www.netpreneur.org/funding/anatomy_term_sheet.pdf

33. In a *firm commitment* IPO, an underwriter guarantees to raise a certain amount of money for a company; in contrast, with a *best efforts* offering, an underwriter does its best to sell as many of the shares as it can at the offering price. Firm commitments are far superior to best efforts offerings. All IPOs that are listed on the NASDAQ, the New York Stock Exchange, and the American Stock Exchange are firm commitment ones. The statistics given in this book refer to firm commitment offerings.

34. Daniel McGinn, "Reinventing Mr. Bertucci," *Boston Globe*, January 18, 2004, http://www.boston.com/news/globe/magazine/articles/2004/01/18/reinventing_mr_bertucci?mode=PF.

35. William D. Bygrave and Jeffry A. Timmons, *Venture Capital at the Crossroads* (Boston, MA: Harvard Business School Press, 1992).

36. Ibid.

37. *Matt Coffin*, a case study published by Babson College, 2005.

38. Excerpted from http://www.experiangroup.com/corporate/news/releases/2005/2005-05-05/.

8

Debt and Other Forms of Financing

Joel M. Shulman

How This Chapter Fits Into a Typical MBA Curriculum

Unlike finance treasurers at Fortune 500 Companies, entrepreneurs at small, growing companies do not have easy access to a wide range of inexpensive financing sources. And when market conditions tighten, as they typically do during economic recessions, the consequences can be fatal for small firms. Entrepreneurs need to be efficient with their working capital requirements and external capital needs. They also need to grow within their means—otherwise they won't survive. MBA students learn about various financing options for entrepreneurs and identify potential pitfalls and solutions. Financing needs are shaped by the type of industry and life cycle of the firm as well as macroeconomic conditions.

Today's funding sources for small businesses are very much affected by changing market influences and dynamic funds' flow changes. Entrepreneurs need to adapt to these altering market forces and plan accordingly. As we've seen in recent years, market forces can move swiftly, with devastating consequence for the ill prepared.

This chapter fits into an MBA curriculum during the first year of study. It allows students to grasp the important consequence of dynamic funding needs in changing market conditions. Tomorrow's business leaders need to have plans in place to fund both rapid changes in asset growth and profit contraction. It's not enough simply to have funds in place for rosy market conditions or steady growth; over an extended period of time, managers must always be wary of sudden shocks to the financial system and how they might affect their companies.

Who Uses This Material—and Why It Is Important

Growth companies require debt and equity capital to expand. Companies that are unable to access funding sources will be unable to expand to their full potential, which may open a window to outside competition. However, companies that grow too fast using heavy amounts of debt may find that a sudden shift in profitability can result in capital flight and corporate upheaval. The most prudent path for growth demands a steady blend of debt and equity capital coupled with managed working capital resources. The lessons may sound simple, but in practice they are not trivial to implement. A financing program using supplier financing and bank debt needs to be balanced with the need to finance some customers with receivable credit.

Ultimately, if an entrepreneurial team is able to provide their value-added service, generating a profit to shareholders, then they will be able to afford their funding sources and grow comfortably in the years ahead. These time-honored lessons do not change with market conditions. They are important to learn now and practice throughout a career.

Entrepreneurs at small, growing firms, unlike finance treasurers at most Fortune 500 companies, do not have easy access to a variety of inexpensive funding sources. In the entire world, only a handful of very large firms have access to funding sources such as asset-backed debt securitizations, A-1 commercial paper ratings, and below-prime lending rates. Most financial managers of small- to medium-size firms are constantly concerned about meeting cash flow obligations to suppliers and employees and maintaining solid financial relationships with creditors and shareholders. Their problems are exacerbated by issues concerning growth, control, and survival. Moreover, their difficulty in attracting adequate funds exists even when firms are growing rapidly and bringing in profits (this is explored later in the chapter). However, when financing from external sources such as banks dries up, as it did during the economic recession in 2008 and 2009, the consequences are sometimes fatal for small companies. Entrepreneurs must be efficient with their working capital and keep external capital needs to a minimum; they need to be self-sufficient and grow within their means. Otherwise, they won't survive.

This chapter describes various financing options for entrepreneurs and identifies potential financing pitfalls and solutions. It also discusses how these issues are influenced by the type of industry and life cycle of the firm and how management should plan accordingly.

Getting Access to Funds—Starting with Internal Sources

Entrepreneurs requiring initial start-up capital, funds used for growth, and working capital generally seek funds from internal sources. This contrasts with managers or owners of large, mature firms that have access to profits from operations as well as funds from external sources. We distinguish internal from external funds because internal funding sources do not require external analysts or investors to independently appraise the worthiness of the capital investments before releasing funds. Moreover, since external investors and lenders do not share the entrepreneur's vision, they may view the potential risk/return trade-off in a different vein and may demand a relatively certain return on their investment after the firm has an established financial track record.

Exhibit 8.1 shows a listing of funding sources and the approximate timing of the firm's usage. In the embryonic stages of the firm's existence, much of the funding comes from the entrepreneur's own pocket. For example, in the beginning, entrepreneurs will consume their personal savings accounts, credit cards, home equity lines, and other assets such as personal computers, fax machines, in-home offices, furniture, and automobiles. Soon after entrepreneurs begin tapping their personal fund sources, they may also solicit funds from relatives, friends, and banks. Entrepreneurs would generally prefer to use other people's money (OPM) rather than their own so that if their personal investment turns sour, they still have a nest egg to feed themselves and their families. The nest egg phenomenon may be particularly acute if the entrepreneur leaves a viable job to pursue

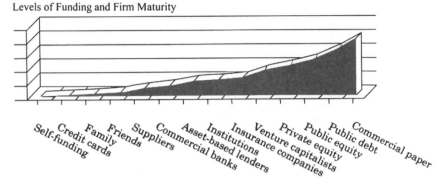

Exhibit 8.1   Sources of Outside Funding

an entrepreneurial dream on a full-time basis. The costs to the entrepreneur in this case include the following:

- The opportunity cost of income from the prior job.
- The forgone interest on the initial investment.
- The potential difficulty of being rehired by a former employer (or others) if the idea does not succeed.

After adding to this the embarrassment of having to beg for a new job while paying off old debts, the prospective entrepreneur quickly realizes that the total cost of engaging in a new venture is very high.

Family and friends may volunteer to fund the entrepreneur's project in the early stages, and often will do so without a formal repayment schedule or specified interest cost. However, the funds are far from free. Total costs, including nonfinancial indirect costs—such as family pressure, internal monitoring, and strained relations—are probably extremely high. Moreover, family and friends make poor financial intermediaries since they have limited financial resources, different repayment expectations, and narrow loan diversification. This will contribute to the entrepreneur's desire to get outside funding from a traditional source as soon as possible. The question is, where can entrepreneurs go before banks will give them money?

Start with Credit Cards and Home Equity Lines

Entrepreneurs who require an immediate infusion of cash often don't have the luxury of time to await the decision of a prospective equity investor or credit lender. Consequently, entrepreneurs are prone to tapping their personal credit cards for business purchases or borrowing against a low-interest-bearing home equity line of credit. According to a Federal Reserve report, at the beginning of 2009, consumers had personal credit outstanding approaching $2,600 billion, with approximately one-third applied to revolving credit (e.g., credit cards).[1] The nonrevolving credit includes personal credit associated with loans for automobiles, vacations, and so on, but does not include home equity lines. This credit, which is derived from commercial banks, finance companies, credit unions, and savings institutions, is for personal consumption. Presumably, some of it has been applied by entrepreneurs for direct business purposes, with the balance enabling the pursuit of entrepreneurial practice. Many banks set up credit cards to be applied for either personal or business use. Moreover, with the proliferation of a "points" system which provides credit towards frequent flier miles or credit towards future purchases, many consumers have economic incentive to maximize their application of credit cards whether for personal or business use.

Home equity lines of credit (HELOC) are another important manner in which consumers provide funding for their businesses. In mid-2004 there was approximately $500 billion in outstanding HELOC, according to the Federal Deposit Insurance Corporation (FDIC). Although the majority of the funds (70 percent) went toward home improvements and debt consolidation, at least 2.5 percent went towards funding small businesses.[2] This means approximately $13 billion of home equity lines of credit were reported to be directly applied to entrepreneurial businesses. Most large banks now accommodate credit card accounts to be used for personal or business use.

Cash Conversion Cycle

One of the most important considerations in setting up a business relates to the timing of when an entrepreneur needs to pay the bills and when the cash is received from customers. The business operating cycle for a traditional manufacturer begins with the purchase of raw materials and ends with the collections from the customer. This includes three key components: the inventory cycle, the accounts receivable cycle, and the accounts payable cycle. The inventory cycle begins with the purchase of the raw materials, includes the work-in-process period, and ends with the sale of the finished goods. The accounts receivable cycle then begins with the sale and concludes with the collection of the receivable. During this operating cycle, the business generally receives some credit from suppliers. This accounts payable cycle begins with the purchase of the raw materials or finished goods, but ends with the payment to the supplier.

The vast majority of organizations, particularly manufacturing operations, experience a gap between the time when they have to pay their suppliers and when they receive payment from their customers. This gap is what is known as the *cash conversion cycle* (CCC). For most companies the credit provided by suppliers ends long before the accounts receivable are paid. This means that as companies grow sales, they need to get external financing to fund working capital needs. This is one of the primary causes of bankruptcy—companies cannot finance operations and need to shut down potentially successful ventures.

In some cases, companies are established in a manner that generates payments from customers before suppliers have to be paid. In this situation, the cash conversion cycle is deemed negative, although from a cash flow perspective it is very positive. Knowing the industry's typical cash conversion cycle before embarking on a new venture is one of the most important considerations that an entrepreneur should examine in the overall financing scheme.

Working Capital—Getting Cash from Receivables and Inventories

The timing of receivables collection and payment of accounts payable are key determinants in whether a firm is cash rich or cash poor. For example, an increase in net working capital (that is, current assets minus current liabilities) does not necessarily translate into an increase in liquidity. One reason for this is that increases in net working capital often result from increases in operating assets, net of increases in operating liabilities. These operating assets, such as accounts receivable or inventory, are usually tied up in operations and are not commonly liquidated prematurely to pay bills. Bills are typically paid with liquid financial assets, such as cash and marketable securities. Thus, only the liquid financial assets can be used to assess a firm's liquidity. Furthermore, corporate insolvency usually results when the firm fails to service debt obligations or callable liabilities in a timely manner. Consequently, corporate liquidity can be estimated fairly accurately by taking the difference between liquid financial assets and callable liabilities. This is referred to as the *net liquid balance*.

Exhibit 8.2 shows how the net liquid balance is actually a part of net working capital. Net working capital is easily calculated in one of two ways:

1. The difference between current assets and current liabilities (as described earlier).
2. The difference between long-term liabilities, including equities, and long-term assets (such as fixed assets).

The first formula is often misinterpreted to be the difference between two liquid components, whereas the second definition suggests that the residual of long-term liabilities minus long-term assets is used to finance current assets, some of which may be liquid. The second definition also enables us to analyze the current assets and liabilities as consisting of both liquid financial/callable components and operating components.

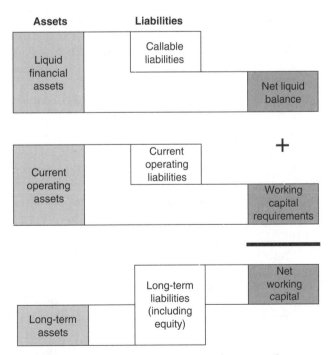

Exhibit 8.2   Integrative Approach to Working Capital Management

Net working capital is actually the sum of working capital requirements. This suggests that only a part of net working capital is liquid. Clearly, as a small firm grows, current operating assets will increase. If current operating liabilities do not increase at the same rate as the increase in current operating assets (which is true when an entrepreneur pays suppliers before receiving payment from customers), then the entrepreneur will find that the firm's net liquid balance will decrease (assuming the firm does not increase its long-term funding arrangements). This may be true even though the firm is generating paper profits. As long as the increase in working capital requirements exceeds the increase in profits, then the firm will find itself reducing its liquidity levels. (*Note*: Profits are included in the long-term liabilities part of Exhibit 8.2 due to increase in stockholders' equity.)

This highlights one of the fundamental weaknesses of the traditional liquidity ratios, such as the current ratio or quick ratio. These ratios include both liquid financial assets and operating assets in their formula. Since operating assets are tied up in operations, inclusion of these assets in a liquidity ratio is not very useful from an ongoing concern perspective. Note the difference between a liquidity perspective and a liquidation perspective. A *liquidation* perspective assumes that in the event of a crisis, assets may be sold off in order to meet financial obligations, while a *liquidity* perspective assumes the firm's financial obligations are met without impairing the viability of future operations. From an ongoing perspective, a new ratio—net liquid balance to total assets—may be more indicative of liquidity than either the current ratio or the quick ratio.

Using Accounts Receivable as Working Capital

Accounts receivable (that is, the money owed to the company as a result of sales made on credit for which payment has not yet been received) are a major element in working capital for most companies. And they are one of the items that gave us reason to assert that working capital is not the same as available cash, and that the timing of short-term flows is vitally important.

If a company is selling a major part of its output on credit and giving 30 days' credit, its accounts receivable will be about equal to sales of 30 days. That is, to one-twelfth of its annual sales, if sales are reasonably stable over the year. And if the company's collection policies are so liberal or ineffective that in practice customers are paying on average, say, 45 days after they are billed, accounts receivable are no less than one-eighth of annual sales. Investment in accounts receivable is a use of funds. The company has to finance the credit it is giving to its customers by allowing its money to be tied up in this way instead of being available for investment in productive uses. Therefore, accounts receivable, like cash, have an opportunity cost.

But a company that does not give credit will obviously lose sales, particularly if its competitors offer generous credit. There is a trade-off to be made between the cost of giving credit and the cost of restricting credit. In other words, there are two possible errors that a firm can make: It can incur the cost of being too conservative (deny credit to a good customer) or risk being too aggressive (grant credit to a poor customer). Most firms choose to exercise caution in granting credit, since the cost of extending credit to a customer who doesn't pay can far exceed the profits lost by not extending credit.

The magnitude of a company's accounts receivable obviously depends upon a number of factors:

- The level and the pattern of sales.
- The breakdown between cash and credit sales.
- The nominal credit terms offered.
- The way these credit terms are enforced through a collection policy.

Each of these factors is discussed in detail in the following sections.

The Sales Pattern

The basis of all receivables and collections is clearly actual net sales (that is, sales sold minus any returns). From actual sales come the assumptions about receipts from future cash sales and collections of future credit sales. These are the key inputs in forecasting cash flow, as discussed later in this chapter.

Techniques for forecasting future sales fall into two broad groups:

1. Techniques that use external or economic information.
2. Techniques based on internal or historical data from the company's own past sales.

Most managers are more familiar with the techniques in the second group than they are with the techniques of economic forecasting. The methods for forecasting from historical data range from the very simple (such as straightforward moving average) to fairly sophisticated models. For instance, variations on exponential smoothing make it possible to take into account both long-term trends in the company's sales and seasonal variations. Simply put, although the more sophisticated techniques are useful, no forecasting method based only on historical sales data is completely satisfactory. You cannot be sure that either total industry sales or the company's share of the sales will be the same as they have been. There are a variety of external factors that an entrepreneur must also consider.

Methods of forecasting environmental change also fall into two broad groups. One group is primarily concerned with forecasting the future performance of the economy as a whole, particularly future levels of the gross national product (GNP) and the national income. These GNP models, as they are called, are highly complex, computer-based models. Their construction may be beyond the capabilities of most entrepreneurs, but their output can readily be purchased. The other group is more concerned with forecasting sales for individual industries and products. One way to do this is to identify economic time series that can be used as leading indicators to signal changes in the variable being forecast. Again, this technique is best used by an experienced economist with a computer. The important point for the entrepreneur is that forecasting techniques are becoming progressively less of an art and more of a science.

Cash versus Credit Sales

The relative proportions of cash sales and credit sales may make an important difference to expected cash flows. Unfortunately, this is a variable over which most entrepreneurs have little control. For example, a company in retail sales can certainly take steps to increase its cash sales, either by banning credit entirely or by offering a discount on cash sales. But a company selling primarily to other corporate organizations—other manufacturing companies, wholesalers, distributors, or retail chains—has few cash sales.

Its best hope is to set its credit terms to encourage prompt payment; but the sales will still be credit sales, not cash sales.

Credit Policies

Credit policies can be summarized into two general questions:

1. To whom should credit be given?
2. How much credit should be given?

But the two questions are closely interconnected. Most potential credit sales need to be evaluated on their own merits, and this is costly and time consuming. In fact, the salaries and overhead of the credit analysts are likely to be the largest single item in the cost of giving credit to customers.

How much freedom a company has in setting the terms on which it will grant credit depends very much on its competitive position. For example, an organization in a monopolistic position has considerably more flexibility than one that faces aggressive competition. But real monopolies are rare. Most companies approach such a position only during very short periods, after they have introduced radically new products and before their competitors have had time to introduce similar products. A company in such a position may be tempted to take advantage of it through product price, but it is unlikely to tighten up its credit policy as well. The advantage will be fairly short-lived, but the damage to customer relations arising from a restriction of credit would continue for a long time.

Nevertheless, economic factors do play an important part in credit policy. The key issue is elasticity of demand for the entrepreneur's product. This assumes that the credit terms offered to customers are a component of the overall price as the customer sees it, and those customers will resist a reduction in credit, just as they will resist a price increase. If demand for a product is inelastic—that is, if an increase in price or restriction in the terms of credit will produce a relatively small drop in demand, with the result that net sales revenues actually increase—then there is some potential flexibility in the terms of sale. Even here, however, it will be the industry as a whole that enjoys this flexibility; individual companies will probably have to accept whatever is general industry practice. If demand for a product is elastic, however, there will be little room to change the terms of the sale, either at company or at industry level.

Finally, an entrepreneur's credit policies may be influenced by the length of the company's order backlog and whether the company is working at full output capacity. A company operating below full capacity or below its optimum output may well be tempted to offer unusually generous credit terms in order to stimulate demand. The key question then will be whether the cost of the additional funds tied up in accounts receivable will be more than offset by the additional sales and reduced operating costs. Alternatively, a company working at full capacity, with its product back-ordered, is in a position to tighten up on its credit policies to reduce its investment in receivables.

Setting Credit Terms

The terms of credit include both the length of time given before payment is due and the discount given for prompt payment. Terms expressed as "2/10, net 30" mean that payment is due within 30 days (from the date of invoice) and that 2 percent may be deducted from the bill if payment is made within 10 days. Some companies set their net terms as payment by the end of the month following the month in which the sale is invoiced. Obviously, this latter policy is considerably more generous than "net 30" and is likely to result in a much larger investment in receivables.

An entrepreneur's failure to take advantage of cash discounts available on its accounts payable may be a very expensive mistake, equivalent to borrowing short-term funds at 36 percent. Therefore, is it an equally serious mistake for a company to offer the same terms to its customers? The answer is that it depends on whether giving a cash discount really does speed up collections, and whether the opportunity cost of the funds that would otherwise have been locked up in receivables justifies the reduction in net sales revenues.

For example, assume that an entrepreneur's terms are 2/10, net 30 and that 25 percent of its customers actually take advantage of this discount. Annual sales are $36 million, of which $9 million are discounted, and the company recognizes profits when the sales are made. The discount cost is, therefore, 2 percent of $9 million, or $180,000. Assuming that 25 percent of the customers pay in 10 days and the rest pay in 30, the average collection period (including both discount and nondiscount sales) is 25 days, yielding an average accounts receivable of $2.5 million, as shown in the following equation:

$$\$36,000,000/(360/25) = \$2,500,000$$

If the company did not give a discount, none of its customers would pay within 10 days, and the average collection period would fall from 25 to 30. In that case average accounts receivable would be $3 million:

$$\$36,000,000/(360/30) = \$3,000,000$$

The question is, then, whether the added return the company makes on the $500,000 by which the discount policy has reduced the average accounts receivable exceeds $180,000, the cost of the discount policy. As this represents a return on investment of more than 36 percent, the answer is probably no.

A change in the net terms, however, is likely to make a greater difference to the average accounts receivable balance than giving or withholding a discount for prompt payment. Even if terms of 2/10, net 30 are given, you may assume that a relatively small percentage of the company's customers will take advantage of the discount. But if the net terms are changed from 30 days to 45, doubtless a high percentage of customers will take advantage of this change. Going back to the previous example and assuming that 25 percent of customers pay within 10 days and the rest at the end of 45 days, the average payment period now becomes approximately 36 days [(10 × 0.25) + (45 × 0.75)], and the average accounts receivable will now be $3.6 million, as shown:

$$\$36,000,000/(360/36) = \$3,600,000$$

This example, however, has assumed that if the net terms are set at 30 or 45 days, everyone who does not take advantage of the discount for prompt payment will pay by the end of the net period. This is unrealistic. Many entrepreneurs and the companies they do business with make a practice of reducing their requirements for funds by paying all their bills late. True, the most commonly offered terms are 2/10, net 30, but a 2008 ProSales survey revealed that the actual experience of U.S. companies is that their average receivables run between 45 and 50 days (and has been increasing during the recession).[3] A company's accounts receivable depend not only on the terms of credit offered, but on how well those terms are enforced through the company's collection policy. Entrepreneurs have another method of reducing overdue accounts and limiting bad debts: setting limits to the credit allowed on individual accounts, or even refusing to give a credit to a customer. One of the most difficult decisions that an entrepreneur has to make as a credit manager is whether a prospective customer is to receive credit.

The evaluation of creditworthiness is slowly evolving from an art to a science, with all sorts of computerized packages used to perform the analysis. However, the two major determinants of the credit decision are the *character* of the individual creditor or management of the creditor firm, and the *capacity* of the firm to repay the loan. In other words, what is the likelihood that management will be willing to pay according to the terms of the agreement, and what is the ability of the firm to repay the loan out of future cash flows? Entrepreneurs will find that the same simple set of guidelines that they use in extending credit to customers will be used by banks extending credit to entrepreneurs. The guidelines are known as the five Cs of credit:

- *Character* refers to the customer's integrity and willingness to repay the financial obligation.
- *Capacity* addresses the borrower's cash flow and ability to repay the debt from ongoing business operations.
- *Capital* is the borrower's financial net worth; consequently, a wealthy borrower may be a desirable customer even if her annual cash flows are relatively low.
- *Collateral* refers to the resale value of the product in the event that repossession becomes necessary.
- *Conditions* refers to national or international economic, industrial, and firm-specific prospects during the time period of the credit.

Although the opportunity costs for accounts receivable may be quite large, the largest current asset balances are usually in inventories. Accordingly, as the entrepreneur's business grows, inventory balances rise, and resulting operating cash flows decline. Consequently, the entrepreneur needs to monitor both accounts receivable and inventories and keep the levels as low as possible without interfering with profitable sales. This is especially true if the entrepreneur has a shortage of capital or credit limitations.

Inventory

Inventory represents the most important current asset of most manufacturing and trading companies. Indeed, for many entrepreneurs, inventories account for an important part of total assets. Yet money invested in inventory does not earn a return. In fact, it costs money to maintain inventories. They must be stored, moved about, insured, and protected from theft and deterioration. Records must be kept, and clerks must be paid to keep those records. In addition, some inventory will be devalued or become a total loss because it deteriorates or becomes obsolete before it can be used or sold. These costs can easily add up to 20 percent or more annually of the inventory value. Since the money tied up in inventory might otherwise be invested profitably, the real costs plus the opportunity costs of carrying inventory may add up to 30 percent, 40 percent, or even more.

As with accounts receivable, the dollar amount of inventory depends on when the entrepreneur chooses to recognize profit: Is it at the time of production or the time of sale? A strong argument can be made for valuing inventories at cost or market, whichever is lower. With inventories, there may be a lot of uncertainty as to how much cash flow will actually be generated, so a conservative approach to valuation is recommended.

Entrepreneurs usually want to keep inventory levels as low as possible. Although they are not likely to be directly interested in the more detailed and lower-level decisions (which are usually made by production or purchasing personnel), they must be able to evaluate and influence overall results. Not only does keeping inventory at a minimum reduce the inventory carrying charges, such as storage costs and insurance, but it also ensures that as little as possible of the entrepreneur's capital is tied up in inventory. But carrying too little inventory also incurs heavy costs. These include:

- The costs of too frequent reordering.
- Loss of quantity discounts.
- Loss of customer goodwill or plant efficiency due to items being unavailable when needed.

Entrepreneurs must be able to weigh these costs against those of carrying excessive inventory in order to be able to determine the optimum inventory level.

The control of investment in inventories is particularly important to the management of working capital. Inventories are likely to represent the entrepreneur's largest current investment, and they are likely to be the least liquid of his current assets. Marketable securities can be turned into cash in a matter of hours, and most accounts receivable will usually be collected within the next 30 days. But three months' supply of inventory will take three months to turn into cash, if forecasts of demand or usage prove to have been accurate. If forecasts prove to have been too optimistic, even more time than this may be required. The alternative—an immediate forced sale—is hardly attractive. Marketable securities can be sold for their market value, and receivables can usually be sold, or factored, for something like 80 percent of their face value. But inventories, other than some raw materials for which a ready market always exists, traditionally sell for little more than 10 percent of their acquisition cost in a forced sale. Thus, controlling a company's investment in inventory is of critical importance to the management of working capital.

Sources of Short-Term Cash—More Payables, Less Receivables

Entrepreneurs usually do not have all the cash they need all the time. Very often, an entrepreneurial firm needs to build up its inventory, thus reducing cash levels. Or an entrepreneur's customers may place unusually large orders, thus increasing accounts receivable financing or reducing company cash levels. This section describes the many ways entrepreneurs obtain additional short-term cash to restore their cash balances to the required levels.

As a rule, entrepreneurs look for short-term cash at the lowest possible rates. If they cannot obtain cash at no cost or at a very small cost, they begin to explore more expensive sources of cash. For example, an entrepreneur faced with a cash shortage might look first to her company's suppliers and her customers. She would look to suppliers because they extend credit to the company by collecting for goods and services after those goods and services are supplied. The entrepreneur can enlarge this credit by paying bills more slowly. The entrepreneur may also obtain additional cash by collecting from her company's customers more quickly.

Cash from Short-Term Bank Loans

Although supplier financing is convenient, it is often cheaper to pursue bank financing if possible. Entrepreneurs faced with a severe cash shortage may also try to convert into cash two of their working capital assets: accounts receivable and inventory. An entrepreneur may pledge her accounts receivable to a finance company in exchange for a loan, or she may sell them to a factoring company for cash. Similarly, an entrepreneur may pledge her inventory (often using a warehousing system) in exchange for a loan.

Cash from Trade Credit

Trade credit is one important and often low-cost source of cash. Nearly all entrepreneurs make use of trade credit to some degree by not paying suppliers immediately for goods and services. Instead, companies bill the entrepreneur, and the entrepreneur pays in 10 days, 30 days, or more. From the time when the supplier first provides the goods or services to the time when the customer finally pays for them, the supplier has, in effect, loaned the entrepreneur money. The sum of all these loans (bills) represents an entrepreneur's trade credit. By paying bills more slowly, an entrepreneur can increase the amount of these loans from his suppliers.

One way an entrepreneur can take more time to pay his bills (or stretch his payables) is to stop taking discounts. For example, if his company normally takes advantage of all prompt-payment discounts, such as 2 percent for payment within 10 days, he can increase his company's cash by passing up the discount and paying the bill in the expected 30 days. Of course, this is an expensive source of cash. If he loses a 2 percent discount and has the use of the funds for 20 more days, he has paid approximately 36 percent interest (annual rate) for using the money.

However, he might argue that, in practice, the interest cost would not really be 36 percent because by forgoing discounts and aggressively stretching payables, the company would not pay the bill in 30 days. Instead, such a company would stretch out this payable as long as possible and perhaps attempt to pay in 60 days. Now, the equivalent interest rate is only about 15 percent (50 days' extra use of the money for 2 percent).

This brings up the subject of late payments. Many entrepreneurs do not consider 30 days (or any other stated terms) a real deadline. Instead, they try to determine the exact point at which further delay of payment will have a penalty. For example, if a company pays too slowly, the supplier may take one of the following actions:

- Require payment in full on future orders.
- Report the company to a credit bureau, which would damage the company's credit rating with all suppliers.
- Bring legal action against the company.

Many cash managers believe, however, that as long as they can pay company bills just before incurring any of these penalties, they maximize their company's cash at little or no cost. The hidden costs of this approach include such risks as damaged reputation, lower credit limit from suppliers, higher prices from suppliers to compensate for delayed payment, and the risk of exceeding the supplier's final deadline and incurring a penalty.

Cash Obtained by Negotiating with Suppliers

If an entrepreneur wants more credit and would like to stretch out her payables, she does not always have to incur the risks previously described. Very often, she can negotiate with her suppliers for more generous credit terms, at least temporarily. If she and her supplier agree on longer credit terms (say 60 or 90 days), she can get the extra trade credits she needs without jeopardizing her supplier relations or credit ratings. It's important to bear in mind that suppliers are trying to build up their businesses and must compete with other suppliers. One way suppliers compete is through credit terms, and that fact can be used to the entrepreneur's advantage. Just as the entrepreneur solicits several price quotes before placing a major order, an entrepreneur should also try to encourage competition among suppliers for credit terms.

Some suppliers use generous terms of trade credit as a form of sales promotion. This is especially likely where a distributor is trying to enter a few geographical areas and is faced with the need to lure customers away from established rivals. In such circumstances, generous credit may well be more effective than an intensive advertising campaign or a high-pressure sales team. The credit may be a simple extension of the discount or net terms, or it may take a modified form such as an inventory loan.

Cash Available Because of Seasonal Business Credit Terms

If the entrepreneur is in a highly seasonal business, such as many types of retailing, he will find large differences in credit terms in different seasons. For example, as a retailer, he might be very short of cash in the fall as he builds up inventory for the Christmas selling season. Many suppliers will understand this and willingly extend their normal 30-day terms.

Furthermore, some suppliers will offer exceedingly generous credit terms in order to smooth out their own manufacturing cycle. Consider a game manufacturer that sells half its annual production in the few months before Christmas. Rather than produce and ship most of the games in the late summer, this manufacturer would much rather spread out its production and shipping schedule over most of the year. To accomplish this, the manufacturer may offer seasonal dating to its retail store customers. Seasonal dating provides longer credit terms on orders placed in off-peak periods. For example, the game manufacturer might offer 120-day terms on May orders, 90-day terms on June orders, and so on. This will encourage customers to order early, and it will allow the game manufacturer to spread out production over more of the year.

Advantages of Trade Credit

Trade credit has two important advantages that justify its extensive use. The first advantage is convenience and ready availability; because it is not negotiated, it requires no great expenditure of executive time and no legal expenses. If a supplier accepts a company as a customer, the usual credit terms are automatically extended even though the maximum line of credit may be set low at first.

The second advantage (which is closely related to the first) is that the credit available from this source automatically grows as the company grows. Accounts payable are known as a spontaneous source of financing. As sales expand, production schedules increase, which in turn means that larger quantities of materials and supplies must be bought. In the absence of limits on credit, the additional credit becomes available automatically simply by placing orders for the extra material. Of course, if the manufacturing process is long and the supplier's payment date is reached before the goods have been sold, some additional source of credit will also be needed. But the amount required will be much less than it would have been if no trade credit had been available.

Cash Obtained by Tightening Up Accounts Receivable Collections

Rapidly growing accounts receivable tie up a company's money and can cause a cash squeeze. However, these same accounts receivable become cash when they are collected. Some techniques, such as lockboxes and wire transfers, enable firms to collect receivables quickly and regularly. However, the question is: How can the rate of collection of receivables be increased temporarily during a cash shortage?

The most effective way to collect receivables quickly is simply to ask for the money. If the entrepreneur just sends a statement every month and shows the amount past due, the customer may not feel a great pressure to pay quickly. But if the entrepreneur asks for the money, either with a handwritten note on the statement of account, a phone call, or a formal letter, the customer will usually pay more quickly. To take an extreme case, a customer receiving several calls a week from an aggressive entrepreneur may pay the bill just to get the entrepreneur to stop bothering him. Of course, these more aggressive collection techniques also have costs, such as loss of customer goodwill, scaring away new customers, loss of old customers to more lenient suppliers, and the generation of industry rumors that the company is short of cash and may be a poor credit risk.

Stretching out accounts payable and collecting accounts receivable more quickly are really two sides of the same issue. Most entrepreneurs attempt to stretch out their bill payments as long as is reasonably possible and to collect their own bills as quickly as competitively possible. The entrepreneur's objective is to maximize company cash, using both techniques, without antagonizing either suppliers or customers so much that his working relationship with them suffers.

Although the fastest way to collect receivables is to ask for the money regularly, the entrepreneur can also change his sales terms to collect cash more quickly. The entrepreneur has several options, including:

1. *Introduce discounts.* A company can initiate a discount for prompt payment (for example, a 2 percent discount for payment within 10 days). Similarly, a company with an existing discount may increase the discount (for example, increase discount from 1 percent to 2 percent).

2. *Reduce credit terms.* If competitively possible, an entrepreneur may require payment in full in 15 days, a deposit when the order is placed, COD orders (in which the customer must pay for goods on delivery), or even full payment with the order. Companies will have difficulty instituting these measures if competitors offer significantly more lenient credit terms.

3. *Emphasize cash sales.* Some entrepreneurs, particularly those selling directly to consumers, may be able to increase their percentage of cash sales.

4. *Accept credit cards.* Sales made on bank credit cards or on travel or entertainment cards are convertible within a couple of days into cash. The credit card companies charge 3 to 7 percent of the amount of the sale for this service.

5. *Impose a penalty for late payment.* Some companies now charge 1.0 or 1.5 percent of the unpaid balance per month as a penalty for late payment. Again, competitive conditions may make this approach unlikely.

Asset-based Lending: Borrowing through Available Collateral

Bankers evaluate a number of criteria in deciding whether to extend credit to a prospective customer. Usually they will apply some combination of the five Cs described earlier, in deciding creditworthiness and the appropriate terms, if credit is extended. Bankers typically provide funding based on the borrower's ability to generate future cash flow and repay the loan. However, bankers will also extend credit based on a customer's existing assets. A consumer's home equity line of credit is based on this concept. Irrespective of the borrower's income stream, a banker might provide credit using the home equity as a source of collateral. Commercial borrowers have the same option. They could use the appreciated value of an owned building or land as collateral for a bank loan or perhaps find some other asset.

The most common assets to use for asset-based lending are the assets with the greatest liquidity or marketability. In this manner, if the bank does have to reclaim the asset in lieu of loan repayment, it wants to ensure that it will have a quick, low-risk path to convert the asset to cash. Land, buildings, and other fixed assets are generally not considered very liquid, so bankers will either seek other assets to use for collateral, or lend only a very conservative percentage of the assets' perceived market value (pledge ratio). Assets that might be considered more liquid, such as high-quality accounts receivables or certain types of product inventory, might be eligible for relatively high pledge ratios. The following is a discussion of asset-based financing with emphasis on accounts receivable and inventory.

Obtaining Bank Loans through Accounts Receivable Financing

One approach an entrepreneur can take to free up working capital funds is to convert his accounts receivable into cash more quickly through aggressive collection techniques. However, when the entrepreneur fears that aggressive collection may offend customers and cause them to take their business to competitors, the entrepreneur may decide to convert his accounts receivable to cash through a financing company. In this form of financing, the entrepreneur can choose between two methods: pledging and factoring. In practice, finance companies or banks offer many variations on these two financing methods.

Pledging

Pledging means using accounts receivable as collateral for a loan from a finance company or bank. The finance company then gives money to the borrower, and as the borrower's customers pay their bills, the borrower repays the loan to the finance company.

With this form of accounts receivable financing, the borrower's customers are not notified that their bills are being used as collateral for a loan. Therefore, pledging is called *nonnotification* financing. Furthermore, if customers do not pay their bills, the borrower (rather than the finance company) must absorb the loss. Thus, if the customer defaults, the lender has the right of recourse to the borrower.

In general, a finance company will not lend the full face value of the accounts receivable pledged. In determining what fraction of the face value of receivables to lend, the finance company considers three factors:

1. The credit rating of the borrower's customers (because bills that may be paid slowly, or not at all, obviously do not make good collateral).

2. The quantity and dollar value of the accounts receivable (because a small number of large-dollar-value receivables is easier to control).

3. The borrower's credit rating (because the finance company prefers having the loan repaid to taking possession of the collateral). Typically, a company can borrow 75 to 90 percent of the face value of its accounts receivable if it has a good credit rating and its customers have excellent credit ratings. Companies with lower credit ratings can generally borrow 60 percent to 75 percent of the face value of their receivables.

Pledging receivables is not a cheap source of credit. Moreover, an additional charge is often made to cover the lender's expenses incurred in appraising credit risks. Therefore, this source of financing is used mostly by smaller companies that have no other source of funds open to them.

Pledging with Notification

Another form of pledging is called *pledging with notification*, in which the borrower instructs its customers to pay their bills directly to the lender (often a bank). As checks from customers arrive, the bank deposits them in a special account and notifies the borrower that money has arrived.

With this approach, the lender controls the receivables more closely and does not have to worry that the borrower may collect pledged accounts receivable and then not notify the lender. The company loses under this system, however, because it must notify its customers that it has pledged its accounts receivable, which can reduce the company's credit rating.

Factoring

Factoring is defined as selling accounts receivable at a discount to a finance company (known as the *factor*). There are many variations of factoring, but the following example covers the main points. With factoring, a company usually transfers the functions of its credit department to the factor. That is, the factor takes over credit checking and collection. If the factor rejects a potential customer as an unacceptable credit risk, the company must either turn down the order or insist on cash payment.

Suppose the W. Buygraves Inc. Company (buyer) orders $10,000 worth of exotic wood and marble from the Saleman Company (seller). The Saleman Company calls its factor to report the order. The factor checks the credit rating of Buygraves and, if all is satisfactory, calls the Saleman Company with an approval. The Saleman Company then ships the goods and sends an invoice to the Buygraves Company. The invoice instructs the Buygraves Company to pay the factor. At the same time, the Saleman Company sends a copy of the invoice to the factor, and the factor sends approximately 85 percent of the invoice amount ($8,500 in this case) to Saleman. The factor must now collect the $10,000 from Buygraves. When the factor actually collects the bill, it may send Saleman a small additional amount of money to recognize collections being higher than original estimates.

The fees that factors charge vary widely. These fees include:

- An interest charge, usually expressed on a daily basis (for the time the bill is outstanding) and equivalent to a 15 to 30 percent annual interest rate.
- A collection fee, usually in the range of an additional 6 to 10 percent annual rate.
- A credit checking charge, either a percentage of the invoice or a flat dollar amount.

The factor keeps a holdback amount (which is not immediately paid to the Saleman Company) to more than cover these various fees and charges, deducts the total from the holdback amount, and sends the remainder to the Saleman Company.

Recourse

Factoring may be with or without recourse. In the previous example, factoring without recourse means that if Buygraves does not pay its bill, the factor must absorb the loss. Factoring with recourse, by contrast, means that if Buygraves does not pay the bill within a prenegotiated time (for example, 90 days), the factor collects from the Saleman Company. Saleman must then try to collect from Buygraves directly.

Naturally, a factor charges extra for factoring without recourse. Typically, a factor adds 6 to 12 percent (on an annual basis) to the interest rate it charges Saleman. For factoring without recourse, factors generally come out ahead because they minimize bad-debt expense by carefully checking each customer's credit. Nevertheless, the Saleman Company might prefer factoring without recourse for two reasons:

1. The Saleman Company does not have to worry that any bills will be returned. In this way, factoring without recourse is a form of insurance.
2. The factor expresses the extra charge for factoring without recourse as part of the daily interest rate. This daily interest rate may look very small.

Most factoring is done with notification. This means that the customer is notified and instructed to pay its bill directly to the factor. Occasionally, factoring is done without notification. In this case, the customer sends his payment either directly to the supplier or to a post office box. In general, factoring is more expensive than pledging. However, factors provide services, such as credit checking and collection, that a company would otherwise have to carry out itself. For a small company, using the factor is often less expensive than providing the services on an internal basis.

Obtaining Loans against Inventory

An entrepreneur's inventory is an asset that can often be used as collateral for a loan. In this way, entrepreneurs can get the cash they need while still retaining access to their inventory. There are four basic ways to use inventory as security for a loan, depending on how closely the lender controls the physical inventory:

1. *Chattel mortgage,* in which specific inventory is used to secure the loan.
2. *Floating (or blanket) lien,* in which the loan is secured by all the borrower's inventory.
3. *Field warehousing,* in which the lender physically separates and guards the pledged inventory right on the borrower's premises.
4. *Public warehousing,* in which the lender transfers the pledged inventory to a separate warehouse.

Each of these methods is discussed in the following sections.

Chattel Mortgage

A chattel (or property) mortgage is a loan secured by specific assets. For example, a borrower might pledge 5,000 new refrigerators as collateral for a loan. To guarantee the lender's position as a secured creditor (in case of bankruptcy), a chattel mortgage must precisely describe the items pledged as collateral. In the case of the refrigerators, the loan agreement would include the serial numbers of the specific refrigerators pledged by the borrower. If the borrower sells some of these refrigerators or receives a new shipment of refrigerators, the chattel mortgage must be rewritten to include these changes specifically.

Because the chattel mortgage describes the collateral so specifically, it offers fairly high security to a lender. Lenders further reduce their risk by lending only a fraction of the estimated market value of the collateral. This fraction depends on how easily the assets can be transported and sold. In the case of refrigerators, which are easy to sell, a borrower might obtain as much as 90 percent of their wholesale cost. But a borrower with a highly specialized inventory, such as bulldozer scoops, might get 50 percent or less of their fair market value because the lender would have difficulty selling the bulldozer scoops to recover the money. Because chattel mortgages describe the collateral so specifically, lenders limit their use to high-value items.

Floating Lien

Instead of naming specific items of inventory to secure a loan, borrowers may pledge all of their inventory. This is a floating, or blanket, lien. Because such an arrangement does not describe specific items of inventory, it does not have to be rewritten each time the borrower sells an item from inventory or receives new items into inventory. However, this flexibility makes it extremely difficult for the lender to maintain the security for the loan. For example, the borrower might sell most of the inventory and not leave enough to secure the loan. For this reason, banks and finance companies will usually lend only a small fraction of the inventory's market value when using a floating lien.

Field Warehousing

Field warehousing was invented to fully protect the lender's security. Under a field warehousing arrangement, the borrower designates a section of the premises, often a room or a specific area of the regular warehouse, for the use of the finance company. The finance company then locks and guards this field warehouse area and stores in it the actual inventory that the borrower is using as collateral. The finance company gives the borrower the agreed-on fraction of the fair market value of the inventory and receives in return a warehouse receipt, which gives the finance company title to the inventory. Companies use field warehousing when the inventory is especially bulky or valuable, such as structural steel, bulk chemicals, or diamonds.

Whenever the borrowing firm needs some of the inventory, it repays part of the loan, and the finance company releases part of the inventory. In this way, the finance company guarantees that there is sufficient collateral at all times to secure the loan.

Public Warehousing

Public warehousing is similar to field warehousing except that the actual inventory is moved to an independent warehouse away from the borrower's plant. As with field warehousing, the finance company releases inventory as the borrower repays the loan. Again, this ensures that the collateral is always sufficient to cover the loan.

There are many variations of warehousing. For example, some bonded warehouses accept checks in payment for loans and then forward these checks to the finance company while releasing the appropriate amount of inventory to the borrower. If such an arrangement is acceptable to all parties, it helps the borrower regain title to the inventory more quickly.

Costs of Warehousing

Warehousing companies collect both a service charge and interest. The service charge is usually a fixed amount plus 1 to 2 percent of the loan itself. This service charge covers the cost of providing field warehousing facilities or of transferring inventory to a public warehouse. In addition, the warehouse company charges interest, usually 10 percent or more. Because of the high fixed costs of setting up a warehousing system, this form of financing is practical only for inventories with value greater than about $500,000.

Obtaining Financing from Customer Prepayments

Some companies are actually financed by their customers. This situation typically occurs on large, complex, long-term projects; it includes defense contractors, building contractors, ship builders, and management consulting firms. These companies typically divide their large projects into a series of stages and require payment as they complete each stage. This significantly reduces the cash these companies require, compared to firms that finance an entire project themselves and receive payment on completion. In some companies, customers pay in advance for everything they buy. Many mail-order operations are financed this way.

Choosing the Right Mix of Short-Term Financing

The entrepreneur attempts to secure the required short-term funds at the lowest cost. The lowest cost usually results from some combination of trade credit, unsecured and secured bank loans, accounts receivable financing, and inventory financing. Though it is virtually impossible to evaluate every possible combination of short-term financing, entrepreneurs can use their experience and subjective opinion to put together a short-term financing package that will have a reasonable cost. At the same time, the entrepreneur must be aware of future requirements and the impact that using certain sources today may have on the availability of short-term funds in the future.

In selecting the best financing package, the entrepreneur should consider the following factors:

- The firm's current situation and requirements.
- The current and future costs of the alternatives.
- The firm's future situation and requirements.

For small firms, the options available may be somewhat limited, and the total short-term financing package may be less important. Conversely, larger firms may be faced with a myriad of possibilities. Clearly, the short-term borrowing decision can become quite complex, but the selection of the right combination can be of significant financial value to the entrepreneur's firm.

Traditional Bank Lending: Short-Term Bank Loans

Beginning with the mortgage crisis and the ensuing global recession, banks curtailed much of their lending to consumers and businesses throughout 2008 and 2009. As a consequence, the U.S. Congress hoped to stimulate banking lending with the $700 billion Troubled Asset Relief Program (TARP) and then later with the Term Asset-Backed Securities Loan Facility (TALF). Both programs were designed with the intent that banks would increase lending to customers. However, irrespective of governmental support, entrepreneurs may be out of luck during troubled times. According to a 2009 report by the Small Business Administration, bank lending to small business has dried up, due in part to a very high failure rate.[4] Entrepreneurs might still be able to get bank credit during periods of economic contraction, but it will not be easy. It will likely require a very detailed plan of repayment along with a strong track record of earnings growth and success.

Generally, an entrepreneur pursues a bank loan after she has fully used her trade credit and collected her receivables as quickly as competitively possible. The most common bank loan is a short-term, unsecured loan made for 90 days. Standard variations include loans made for periods of 30 days to a year and loans requiring collateral. Interest charges on these loans typically vary from the prime rate (the amount a bank charges its largest and most financially strong customers) to about 3 percent above prime.

Very often, an entrepreneur doesn't immediately need money but can forecast that she will have a definite need in, say, six months. The entrepreneur would not want to borrow the required money now and pay unnecessary interest for the next six months. Instead, the entrepreneur would formally apply to its bank for a line of credit, which is an assurance by the bank that, as long as the company remains financially healthy, the bank will lend the company money up to a specified limit whenever the company needs it. Banks usually review a company's credit line each year. A line of credit is not a guarantee that the bank will make a loan in the future. Instead, when the company actually needs the money, the bank will examine the company's current financial statements to make sure that actual results coincide with earlier plans.

Line of Credit

Banks also grant guaranteed lines of credit. Under this arrangement, the bank guarantees to supply funds up to a specified limit, regardless of circumstances. This relieves the company of any worries that money may not be available when it is needed. Banks usually charge extra for this guarantee, typically 1 percent per year on the unused amount of the guaranteed line of credit. For example, if the bank guarantees a credit line of $1 million and the company borrows only $300,000, the company will have to pay a commitment fee of perhaps $7,000 for the $700,000 it did not borrow.

In return for granting lines of credit, banks sometimes require that an entrepreneur maintain a compensating balance (that is, keep a specified amount in her checking account without interest). For example, if an entrepreneur receives a $1 million line of credit with the requirement that she maintain a 15 percent compensating balance, the entrepreneur must keep at least $150,000 in her demand account with that bank all year. The bank, of course, does not have to pay interest on this demand account money; so the use of this money is the bank's compensation for standing ready to grant up to $1 million in loans for a year. Of course, when the bank actually makes loans during the year, it charges the negotiated rate of interest on the loan.

Letter of Credit

A letter of credit, though often confused with a line of credit, is actually much different. A letter of credit or L/C is an irrevocable payment used primarily in international trade between a supplier in one country and a customer in another. The L/C enables foreign parties to transfer payment risk from the customer to a bank, thus reducing the risk of nonpayment. Once the supplier (known as the beneficiary) presents a commercial invoice or bill of lading to his bank, he receives payment sent from the customer's bank. The actual timing and subtle agreements may vary among parties, but essentially, the L/C creates a simple flow of credit between international customers and suppliers through their respective country's banks.

Maturity of Loans

The most common time period, or maturity, for short-term bank loans is 90 days; however, an entrepreneur can negotiate maturities of 30 days to one year. Banks often prefer 90-day maturities, even when the entrepreneur will really need the money for longer than 90 days, because the three-month maturity gives the bank a chance to check the entrepreneur's financial statements regularly. If the entrepreneur's position has deteriorated, the bank may refuse to renew the loan and, therefore, avoid a future loss.

Entrepreneurs, however, prefer maturities that closely match the time they expect to need the money. A longer maturity (rather than a series of short, constantly renewed loans) eliminates the possibility that the bank will refuse to extend a short-term loan because of a temporary weakness in the entrepreneur's operations.

Interest Rates

The rates of interest charged by commercial banks vary in two ways:

1. The general level of interest rates varies over time.
2. At any given time, different rates are charged to different borrowers.

The base rate for most commercial banks traditionally has been the prime rate, which is the rate that commercial banks charge their very best business customers for short-term borrowing. It is the rate that the financial press puts on the front page every time it is changed. Congress and the business community speculate about the prime rate's influence on economic activity because it is the baseline for loan pricing in most loan agreements.

Historically, the prime rate was a baseline for loan pricing; "prime plus two" or "2 percent above prime" was a normal statement of interest rate on many loan contracts. However, as the banking industry has begun to price its loans and services more aggressively, the prime rate is becoming less important. Along with the change in the prime rate, compensating balances (that is, the borrower's agreeing to hold a certain percentage of the amount of the loan in a non-interest-bearing account) are becoming less popular.

The current trend in loan pricing is to price the loan at a rate above the marginal cost of funds as typically reflected by the interest rates on certificates of deposit. The bank then adds an interest rate margin to the cost of funds, and the sum becomes the rate charged to the borrower. This rate changes daily in line with the changes on money market rates offered by the bank. As liability management becomes more of a way of life for bankers, the pricing of loans will become a function of the amount of competition, both domestic and international, that the banker faces in securing lendable funds. As a result of this competition for corporate customers and enhanced competition from the commercial paper market, large, financially stable corporations are often able to borrow at a rate below prime.

Interest represents the price that borrowers pay to the bank for credit over specified periods of time. The amount of interest paid depends on several factors:

- The dollar amount of the loan.
- The length of time involved.
- The nominal annual rate of interest.
- The repayment schedule.
- The method used to calculate the interest.

The various methods used to calculate interest are all variations of the simple interest calculation. Simple interest is calculated on the amount borrowed for the length of time the loan is outstanding. For example, if $1 million is borrowed at 15 percent and repaid in one payment at the end of one year, the simple interest would be $1 million times 0.15, or $150,000.

When the add-in interest method is used, interest is calculated on the full amount of the original principal. The interest amount is immediately added to the original principal, and payments are determined by dividing principal plus interest by the number of payments to be made. When only one payment is involved, this method is identical to simple interest. However, when two or more payments are to be made, the use of this method results in an effective rate of interest that is greater than the nominal rate. In the preceding example, if the $1 million loan were repaid in two six-month installments of $575,000 each, the effective rate is higher than 15 percent because the borrower does not have the use of funds for the entire year.

The bank discount method is commonly used with short-term business loans. Generally, there are no immediate payments, and the life of the loan is usually one year or less.

Interest is calculated on the amount of the loan, and the borrower receives the difference between the amount to be paid back and the amount of interest. In the example, the effective interest rate is 17.6 percent. The interest amount of $150,000 is subtracted from the $1 million, and the borrower has the use of $850,000 for one year. If you divide the interest payment by the amount of money actually used by the borrower ($150,000 divided by $850,000), the effective rate is 17.6 percent.

If the loan were to require a compensating balance of 10 percent, the borrower does not have the use of the entire loan amount; rather, the borrower has use of the loan amount less the compensating balance requirement. The effective rate of interest in this case would be 20 percent—the interest amount of $150,000 divided by the funds available, which is $750,000 ($1,000,000 minus $150,000 interest and minus a compensating balance of $100,000).

The effective interest cost on a revolving credit agreement includes both interest costs and the commitment fee. For example, assume the TBA Corporation has a $1 million revolving credit agreement with a bank. Interest on the borrowed funds is 15 percent per annum. TBA must pay a commitment fee of 1 percent on the unused portion of the credit line. If the firm borrows $500,000, the effective annual interest rate is 16 percent: [(0.15 × $500,000) + (0.01 × $500,000) divided by $500,000].

Because many factors influence the effective rate of a loan, when evaluating borrowing costs, only the effective annual rate should be used as a standard of comparison to ensure that the actual costs of borrowing are used in making the decision.

Collateral

To reduce their risks in making loans, banks may require collateral from entrepreneurs. Collateral may be any asset that has value. If the entrepreneur does not repay the loan, the bank owns the collateral and may sell it to recover the amount of the loan.

Typical collateral includes both specific high-value items owned by the company (such as buildings, computer equipment, or large machinery) and all items of a particular type (such as all raw materials or all inventories). Banks use blanket liens as collateral where individual items are of low value but the collective value of all items is large enough to serve as collateral.

The highest level of risk comes in making loans to small companies, and it is not surprising to find that a high proportion of loans made to small companies—probably 75 percent—are secured. Larger companies present less risk and have stronger bargaining positions; only about 30 percent of loans made to companies in this class are secured.

One aspect of protection that most banks require is key person insurance on the principal officers of the company taking out the loan. Because the repayment of the loan usually depends on the entrepreneur or managers running the company in a profitable manner, if something should happen to the entrepreneur or key managers, there may be some question about the safety of the loan. To avoid this uncertainty, a term insurance policy is taken out for the value of the loan on the life of the entrepreneur or key managers. If the officer or officers die, the proceeds of the policy are paid to the bank in settlement of the loan.

When making loans to very small companies, banks often require that the owners and top managers personally sign for the loan. Then, if the company does not repay the loan, the bank can claim the signer's personal assets, such as houses, automobiles, and stock investments.

Applying for a Bank Loan

To maximize the chances of success in applying for a bank loan, an entrepreneur should maintain good banking relations. Personal visits by the entrepreneur and other senior officers, as well as quarterly delivery of income statements, balance sheets, and cash flow statements, are useful means of sustaining such relations.

The actual process of obtaining bank credit (whether a line of credit or an actual loan) must be conducted on a personal basis with the bank loan officer. The loan officer will be interested in knowing the following information:

- How much money the company needs.
- How the company will use this money.
- How the company will repay the bank.
- When the company will repay the bank.

Entrepreneurs should be able to fully answer these questions and support their answers with past results and realistic forecasts; if so, they stand an improved chance of obtaining the line of credit or loan that they need.

Restrictive Covenants

Bank term loans are negotiated credit, granted after formal negotiations take place between borrower and lender. As part of the terms agreed to in these negotiations, the bank usually seeks to set various restrictions, or covenants, on the borrower's activities during the life of the loan. These restrictions are tailored to the individual borrower's situation and needs; thus, it is difficult to generalize about them. This section introduces some of the more widely used covenants and their implications. All of these covenants are (at least to some degree) negotiable; it is wise for the financial executive to carefully review the loan contract and to attempt to moderate any overly restrictive clause a bank may request.

The restrictive covenants in a loan agreement may be classified as:

- *General provisions.* These are found in most loan agreements and are designed to force the borrower to preserve liquidity and limit cash outflows.
- *Routine provisions.* These are also found in most loan agreements and are normally not subject to modification during the loan period.
- *Specific provisions.* These are used according to the situation and are used to achieve a desired total level of protection.

The following sections describe these restrictions in more detail.

General Provisions

Most common of all general provisions is a requirement relating to the maintenance of working capital. This may simply be a provision that net working capital is to be maintained at or above a specified level. Alternatively, when the company is expected to grow fairly rapidly, the required working capital may be set on an increasing scale. For example, the bank may stipulate that working capital is to be maintained above $500,000 during the first 12 months of the loan, above $600,000 during the second, above $750,000 during the third, and so on. If the borrower's business is highly seasonal, the requirement for working capital may have to be modified to reflect the seasonal variations.

The provision covering working capital is often set in terms of the borrower's current ratio—current assets divided by current liabilities—which must be kept above, for example, 3 or 3.5 to 1. The actual figure is based on the bank's judgment and whatever is considered a safe figure for that particular industry.

Working capital covenants are easy to understand and very widely used. Unfortunately, they are often of rather doubtful value. As discussed in this chapter, a company may have a large net working capital and still be short of cash.

Another widely used covenant is a limit on the borrower's expenditures for capital investment. The bank may have made the loan to provide the borrower with additional working capital and does not wish to see the funds sunk into capital equipment instead. The covenant may take the form of a simple dollar limit on the investment in capital equipment in any period. Alternatively, the borrower is often allowed to invest up to, but not more than, the extent of the current depreciation expense. Such a provision may prove to be a serious restriction to a rapidly growing company. And clearly, any company will find such a covenant damaging if the maximum expenditure is set below the figure needed to maintain productive capacity at an adequate and competitive level.

Most term loan agreements include covenants to prevent the borrower from selling or mortgaging capital assets without the lender's permission. This may be extended to cover current assets other than the normal sale of finished goods, in which case the borrower is prohibited from factoring accounts receivable, selling any part of the raw-material inventory, or assigning inventory to a warehouse finance company without the bank's express permission.

Limitations on additional long-term debt are also common. The borrower is often theoretically forbidden to undertake any long-term debt during the life of the term loan, though in practice the bank usually allows new debt funds to be used in moderation as the company grows. The provision is often extended to prevent the borrower from entering into any long-term leases without the bank's authorization.

One type of covenant that clearly recognizes the importance of cash flows to a growing company is a prohibition of or limit to the payment of cash dividends. Again, if dividends are not completely prohibited, they may be either limited to a set dollar figure or based upon a set percentage of net earnings. The latter approach is obviously the less restrictive.

Routine Provisions

The second category of restrictive covenants includes routine provisions found in most loan agreements that usually are not variable. The loan agreement ordinarily includes the following requirements:

- The borrower must furnish the bank with periodic financial statements and maintain adequate property insurance.

- The borrower agrees not to sell a significant portion of its assets. A provision forbidding the pledging of the borrower's assets is also included in most loan agreements. This provision is often termed a *negative pledge clause*.

- The borrower is restricted from entering into any new leasing agreements that might endanger the ability to pay the loan.

- The borrower is restricted from acquiring other firms unless prior approval has been obtained from the lender.

Specific Provisions

Finally, a number of restrictions relate more to the borrowing company's management than to its financial performance. For example:

- Key executives may be required to sign employment contracts or take out substantial life insurance.
- The bank may require the right to be consulted before any changes are made in the company's top management.
- Some covenants prevent increases in top management salaries or other compensation.

Restrictive covenants are very important in borrowing term loans. If any covenant is breached, the bank has the right to take legal action to recover its loan, probably forcing the company into insolvency. Conversely, it may be argued that the covenants protect the borrowing company as well as the lender, in that their intention is to make it impossible for the borrower to get into serious financial trouble without first infringing on one or more restrictions, thus giving the bank a right to step in and apply a guiding hand. A bank is very reluctant to force any client into liquidation. In the event that restriction is infringed on, however, the bank may use its very powerful bargaining position to demand even tighter restrictions—and some control over the borrower's operations—as the price of continuing the loan.

Equipment Financing

Leasing has become popular in recent years because there has been a trend emphasizing the ability to *use* property over the legal *ownership* of property. Other reasons often mentioned include the sharing of tax benefits between lessors and lessees. But the big incentives for leasing are nontax attributes such as flexibility, a hedge against obsolescence and inflation risk, service and maintenance contracts, convenience, lower costs, and off-balance-sheet financing.

Many entrepreneurs have come to realize that the use of a piece of equipment is more important to the production of income than the possession of a piece of paper conveying title to the equipment. In fact, if people can use equipment for most of its economic life without having the full legal responsibilities, risks, and burdens of ownership, why should they ever desire to own it? Even farmers, who may have traditionally valued land ownership, now readily acknowledge that the use of land is more important than ownership of it. Many farmers and ranchers lease tracts of land to increase production of cattle or crops.

Capital equipment is often financed by intermediate-term funds. These may be straightforward term loans, usually secured by the equipment itself. Both banks and finance companies make equipment loans of this type. The nonbank companies charge considerably higher interest rates; they are used primarily by smaller companies that are unable to qualify for bank term loans.

As with other types of secured loans, the lender will evaluate the quality of the collateral and advance a percentage of the market value. In determining the repayment schedule, the lender ensures that the value of the equipment exceeds the loan balance. In addition, the loan repayment schedule is often made to coincide with the depreciation schedule of the equipment.

One further form of equipment financing that should be considered is the conditional sales contract, which normally covers between two and five years. Under such a contract, the buyer agrees to buy a piece of equipment by installment payments over a period of years. During this time the buyer has the use of the equipment, but the seller retains title to it until the payments are completed. Companies that are unable to find credit from any other source may be able to buy equipment on these terms. The lender's risk is small because the equipment can be repossessed at any time if an installment is missed. Equipment distributors who sell equipment under conditional sales contracts often sell the contract to a bank or finance company, in which case a transaction becomes an interesting combination of equipment financing for the buyer and receivables financing for the seller.

The credit available under a conditional sales contract is less than the full purchase price of the equipment. Typically, the buyer is expected to make an immediate down payment of 25 to 33 percent of the full cash price, and only the balance is financed. The cost of the credit given may be quite high. Equipment that is highly specialized or subject to rapid obsolescence represents a greater risk to the lender than widely used standard equipment, and the interest charged on the sale of such specialized equipment to a small company may exceed 15 to 20 percent.

Obtaining Early Financing from External Sources

It is almost impossible for a brand new company to get a conventional bank loan, because it has no trading history nor does it usually have assets to secure the loan. Even after a young company is up and running it is still difficult to get a bank loan. Many entrepreneurs overlook the possibility of getting an SBA-guaranteed loan from a bank. SBA-guaranteed loans are available to small companies that have sought and been refused conventional financing loans banks. Details of SBA loan programs are in Chapter 9.

Summary

Most start-ups and baby companies do not have as much external funding as the entrepreneurs had hoped to get when they opened their doors for business. The reasons are simply that start-ups and baby businesses do not have a proven track record of operating profitably and generating sufficient cash flow to assure bankers that their loans will be repaid, nor do they usually have enough assets to collateralize significant loans. Thus, conventional bank loans for start-up and baby businesses are rare unless the entrepreneurs have personal assets sufficient to cover the amount of the loans and are willing to put them up as collateral. SBA-guaranteed bank loans are available for start-ups and small businesses that have been refused conventional bank loans, but small business owners have to sign personal guarantees, so they could lose some or all of their personal assets if their businesses fail to repay their loans.

As was pointed out in Chapter 7, most entrepreneurs have no choice but to put some of their own savings into the company and then turn to family and friends for their initial financing. Sometimes they are able to get external financing from angel investors. And in very rare instances, they are able to get it from venture capital firms.

This means that entrepreneurs should operate their businesses as efficiently as possible and optimize internal cash flow by chasing accounts receivable, stretching out payables, and turning over inventory as quickly as possible. Of course, in doing so they must take care not to upset customers and suppliers.

Notes

1. Board of Governors of the Federal Reserve System, "Consumer Credit," Federal Reserve Statistical Release, June 5, 2000, http://www.federalreserve.gov/releases/g19/current/.
2. "LendingTree Survey Finds 2004 the Year of Home Equity Lending," LendingTree Press Release, June 8, 2004, http://www.lendingtree.com/about-us/press-room/news-releases/2004/2004-the-year-of-home-equity/.
3. C. Webb, ed., "ProSales Accounts Receivable Survey," September 24, 2008, http://imgs.ebuild.com/cms/Hanley_Wood_News_Service/2008/55964/ProSales-AR-Survey-080924.pdf
4. Emily Maltby, "Small Biz Loan Failure Rate Hits 12%," CNNMoney.com, February 25, 2009, http://money.cnn.com/2009/02/25/smallbusiness/smallbiz_loan_defaults_soar.smb/index.htm.

9

External Assistance for Start-ups and Small Businesses

Elizabeth J. Gatewood and Carol McLaurin

How This Chapter Fits Into a Typical MBA Curriculum
The material in this chapter is usually introduced after the sections on financing in an entrepreneurship course because it contains valuable information about small business funding that is available from the U.S. government either directly or indirectly through guaranteed loans. It also deals with other forms of external assistance for small businesses such as consulting and sources of information that are available inexpensively or sometimes free.

Who Uses This Material in the Real World—and Why It Is Important
Finding external sources of assistance is time consuming and often frustrating for entrepreneurs; this chapter puts at entrepreneurs' fingertips information on major providers of external support for small business. Any small business owner who has been turned down for a conventional bank loan will benefit from the information and tips in this chapter on how to apply for an SBA-guaranteed bank loan. And high-technology entrepreneurs will benefit from the knowledge that they may well be able to support their product development with SBIR awards, which are described in this chapter.

There is a wealth of external assistance out there that you have probably never heard of. Federal, state, and local governments and nonprofit institutions together offer a bewildering array of helpful resources. This chapter offers a map for the varied terrain of entrepreneurial assistance.

Why You Should Consider External Assistance Programs

External sources of assistance are certainly useful and probably necessary for almost all entrepreneurs, because the successful creation of a start-up company, or the management of a small, growing company, is a highly complex, time-consuming, and difficult process. You may need all the help you can get.

The stereotypical entrepreneur—the so-called rugged individualist who doesn't need help—may still wince at the thought of government assistance. Some entrepreneurs believe that government regulations (especially in the areas of taxation, employee benefits, and environmental controls) may hinder small business. Nevertheless, many agencies of the government are committed to assisting entrepreneurship, usually because of the potential of small businesses to create jobs.

Not all successful companies have required external assistance in their early stages. But many successful entrepreneurs have built their companies with government-guaranteed start-up loans, lucrative government contracts, or government-sponsored advice on business plan development. Prominent examples include Ben & Jerry's, Compaq Computer, Federal Express, Gymboree, Intel, Nike, Outback Steakhouse, Staples, and T.J. Cinnamons. Apple Computer received capital from a Small Business Investment Company (SBIC), which received part of its capital from the U.S. Small Business Association (SBA).

External assistance programs have helped entrepreneurs at all phases of small company growth, in all sectors of industry, at all income levels, of all races, and of both genders. You should consider external assistance programs because they are available either free or inexpensively, and are often effective in delivering useful services. They can also give you a competitive advantage in the difficult and complex project of starting up a new company or building a small company.

External Assistance Available Nationwide to Anyone in the United States

Getting Advice: Business Development Programs

Most small business owners or would-be entrepreneurs begin with a need for business development assistance. This may involve managerial or technical assistance—for example, identifying and accessing relevant business and technical information, or using such information to evaluate new products, business concepts, and business plans. Many turn to the U.S. Small Business Administration.

The U.S. Small Business Administration

The Small Business Administration (SBA, www.sba.gov) is the primary federal agency charged with aiding, counseling, assisting, and protecting the interests of small business, although other federal agencies also provide services to this diverse economic constituency. In 2008, the agency had over 100 offices covering every state, the District of Columbia, Guam, Puerto Rico, and the U.S. Virgin Islands. From its beginnings in 1953 to year 2000, over 20 million small businesses have received direct or indirect help from SBA programs. From 1991 to 2000, the SBA assisted 435,000 small businesses to secure more than $94.6 billion in loans. In 2000 alone, the SBA backed more than $12.3 billion in loans to small businesses. More than $1 billion was made available for disaster loans and more than $40 billion in federal contracts was secured by small businesses with SBA's help.

A small business must meet certain size criteria to be eligible for the SBA's services. These services include not only business development programs carried out by the SBA's Resource Partners (discussed later in this chapter), but also loans, procurement assistance, and international trade assistance. For business development assistance, loans, and other services, the SBA defines eligibility either by employment size or annual revenue criteria that vary by industry and change periodically. In 2008, the criteria were 500 employees or less for most manufacturing and mining industries and $7.0 million in sales for most nonmanufacturing industries. However, exceptions do exist and you should visit www.sba.gov for the most updated size regulations.

The SBA sales and employment size criteria in 2008 were as follows:

- *Services and retailing.* The size standard for most services and retail trade firms to be considered "small" is $7 million in sales. A few industries may go higher, up to $35.5 million.

- *Wholesaling.* Small if number of employees does not exceed 100. Other standards apply for various programs.

- *Manufacturing.* About seventy-five percent of manufacturing industries are considered small if average employment in the preceding four calendar quarters did not exceed 500, including employees of any affiliates. If your employment is between 500 and 1,500, check the size standard for your particular industry to see if you will meet the small size criteria.

- *Construction.* Small if average annual sales for three years preceding application did not exceed $33.5 million, except for specialty contractors, for whom sales may not have exceeded $14 million.

- *Other.* Because there is so much variation in gas, electric, agriculture, finance, insurance, real estate, communications, and transportation, there are no common patterns in size standards.

The SBA has gradually reduced its provision of management and technical assistance to small business firms via its own field representatives. Technical and management assistance is now primarily provided through several innovative partnerships, collectively called the SBA's Resource Partners, described in the next sections of this chapter. The SBA still provides a comprehensive set of useful publications and hosts an extensive web site that details their products and services; provides access to necessary forms, e-newletters, and FAQs; and even includes free online training and courses.

As mentioned, the SBA supports business development efforts through the following Resource Partners:

- The Small Business Development Center (SBDC) program.
- The Service Corps of Retired Executives (SCORE) program.
- Women Business Centers (WBC) program.

Small Business Development Centers

Small Business Development Centers (SBDCs) offer one-stop assistance to small businesses and start-ups by providing a wide variety of information and guidance in central and easily accessible locations. They offer free counseling services and reasonably priced seminars and workshops to new and existing businesses.

SBDC assistance may be divided into two main areas: free one-on-one counseling and inexpensive classroom-style training. Customized counseling services range from informal detailed evaluations of business plans by an industry-experienced counselor to advising growing companies on expansion plans for new territorial or product markets. In 2005 alone, the Small Business Development Center Network provided assistance to nearly 1.25 million clients. Stressing client education, the SBDC program is the federal government's largest and most successful management and technical assistance program for small businesses.

SBDCs sometimes supplement their free counseling services by making referrals on specialized accounting, legal, or technical subjects to professional business services. One SBDC, at the University of Houston, has negotiated a reduced-fee program for these services. The service also offers referrals to potential advisory board members for the small business owner.

SBDC training seminars are usually priced at substantial discounts off commercial rates (for example, $30 to $60 for a four-hour mini-course on how to write a business plan). In addition, many SBDCs offer online tutorials, webinars, and podcasts that can be accessed 24/7 for no cost or low cost. Training seminars are offered by SBDC staff or recognized local experts. Training seminars cover topics such as:

- Strategic planning.
  - Business planning.
- Market analysis and strategy.
  - Marketing to the government.
  - International trade.
  - E-commerce.
- Product feasibility and development.
  - Technology access.
- Organizational analysis.
  - Operations planning
  - Human resource management
- Financial control.
  - Loan assistance.
  - Cash management.
  - Bookkeeping and accounting.

Some SBDCs also feature specialized centers that provide assistance in the following areas:

- Government contracting (procurement).
- International trade (for existing businesses looking for international expansion, or start-ups focused on international trade).
- Technology transfer and product development. Guidance in commercializing new products or services may include advice on royalty agreements, patent research, and new product evaluations.
- Angel investing and private equity funds.

Each SBDC center has full-time and part-time employees and recruits qualified volunteers from professional and trade associations, the legal and banking communities, academia, and chambers of commerce to counsel clients. Many SBDCs also use paid consultants, consulting engineers, and testing laboratories from the private sector to help clients who need specialized expertise.

SBDCs maintain strict client confidentiality. Only counselors directly working with you learn details of your company's operations. All advisers—whether staff, paid consultants, or volunteers—have to sign a conflict-of-interest agreement. This prohibits disclosure of information about any client to any non-SBDC personnel or any other client, solicitation or acceptance of gifts from clients, or investment in SBDC clients.

The SBA provides 50 percent or less of the operating funds for each state SBDC. The matching-fund contributions come from state legislatures, private sector foundations and grants, state and local chambers of commerce, state-chartered economic development corporations, public and private universities, vocational and technical schools, and community colleges. The success of SBDCs is reflected in the increasing tendency of sponsors' contributions to exceed the minimum 50 percent matching share. Unlike the SCORE (described in the next section of this chapter), which is totally funded by the SBA, SBDCs are freer to develop programs and services independently of the SBA.

Where to Find SBDCs

For a local office, look in the Blue Pages under the U.S. Government listing. The Association of Small Business Development Centers (ASBDC) is located at:

8990 Burke Lake Road, Second Floor

Burke, VA 22015

Phone: 703-764-9850

Fax: 703-764-1234

www.asbdc-us.org

SCORE: Counselors to America's Small Business

The Service Corps of Retired Executives (SCORE) provides business information and management help through confidential counseling, training, and workshops. SCORE was founded in 1964 and has more than 11,000 retired and active executives and small business owners who volunteer their professional management expertise to help current and future business owners and managers.

SCORE has assisted 8 million people through its workshops and counseling program since 1964. Its clients have included a wide variety of businesses—for example, consumer retail, graphic arts companies, archaeological consulting firms, and security systems stores—including some well-known names such as Vera Bradley, Jelly Belly Candy Company, and Vermont Teddy Bears.

SCORE is headquartered in Herndon, Virginia, with 389 offices throughout the United States and its territories. Counseling may occur at a SCORE office or at the client's place of business. It is even possible to find a mentor, receive advice, or take courses online. Online courses include more general offerings, such as starting and managing a business, as well as more specific courses on marketing, taxes, advisory boards, and many more topics. Its web site also provides an extensive library of how-to articles. More than 3 million people visited SCORE's web site in 2008.

Where to Find SCORE

The National SCORE Office (NSO) is located at

> 1175 Herndon Parkway, Suite 900
> Herndon, VA 20170
> Phone: (800) 634-0245
> www.score.org

Women's Business Centers

America's 10.6 million women-owned businesses employ 19.1 million people and contribute $2.46 trillion to the economy. SBA provides matching grants to Women's Business Centers across the country. They promote the growth of women-owned businesses through programs that address business training and technical assistance, and provide access to credit and capital, federal contracts, and international trade opportunities. At every stage of developing and expanding a successful business, the WBCs counsel, teach, encourage, and inspire. (See more details in the section "Business Assistance Programs for Women.")

Where to Find SBA Women's Business Centers

To locate a Women's Business Center, go to

> http://www.sba.gov/services/counseling/wbc/index.html

Getting Money: Financial Assistance from the SBA

Debt fuels growth. The entrepreneur promoting a new business venture through a well-prepared business plan and the successful small business proprietor both face the challenge of finding money for start-up operations, for working capital, and for expansion and growth. A variety of institutions respond to these needs.

The SBA's financial assistance programs for small companies and start-ups complement its business development programs. SBA guarantees loans made by lending institutions to small businesses, provides venture capital through its Small Business Investment Company (SBIC) program, and provides loans to nonprofit organizations to fund small loans to small businesses. Many SBA loan programs are targeted to specific groups and needs. Borrowers can use different SBA financial assistance programs simultaneously, up to the SBA's statutory loan guarantee limit of $2 million.

Loan Guarantees

The 7(a) General Loan Guarantee

This is the SBA's principal way of financially promoting small business creation and growth. The 7(a) name refers to a section of the original SBA law. The program represents more than 80 percent of the agency's total loan effort. In fiscal year 2000 the SBA provided guarantees for $12.3 billion in loans to small businesses. SBA does not directly make the loans; 7(a) loans are made by private lenders to small businesses that cannot obtain credit without an SBA guarantee. Not all lenders choose to participate in the program, but most U.S. lenders do.

The maximum loan guarantee is $2 million; however, the average loan amount is $178,000. SBA guarantees range typically from 50 percent up to 90 percent of the amount provided by the commercial bank. Funds can be used for short-term or long-term working capital; to construct, expand, or convert facilities; to purchase machinery, equipment, furniture, fixtures, supplies; to buy land and buildings; for a seasonal line of credit; for inventory; or to purchase a business. In some cases the loan may be used for refinancing certain types of debt. Actual loan maturities are based on the ability to repay, the purpose of the loan proceeds, and the useful life of the assets financed. However, maximum loan maturities have been established: 25 years for real estate, 10 years for equipment, and generally 7 years for working capital.

In order to get a 7(a) loan, borrowers must meet certain eligibility requirements. The first requirement is that the business meets SBA's definition of a small business, which varies by the type of business. Wholesale businesses must not exceed 100 employees; retail and service businesses must not have sales exceeding $21 million; manufacturers must not exceed 500 employees; and construction companies must not have sales of more than $17.5 million.

Repayment ability from the cash flow of the business is a primary consideration in the SBA loan decision process; good character, management capability, collateral, and owner's equity contribution are also important considerations. All owners of 20 percent or more are required to personally guarantee SBA loans. The vast majority of businesses are eligible for financial assistance from the SBA. However, applicant businesses must operate for profit; be engaged in, or propose to do business in the United States or its possessions; have reasonable owner equity to invest; and use alternative financial resources first, including personal assets. It should be noted that some businesses are ineligible for financial assistance—for example, real estate investment firms and pyramid businesses. More details about eligibility criteria can be found on the SBA web site.

A study by Price Waterhouse reported that businesses that got loan guarantees showed higher growth than comparable businesses.[1] Perhaps only companies with very strong business plans and founding teams can pass the screens of a primary lender and the SBA guarantee evaluation.

Pollution Control Loans Program

SBA provides loan guarantees under the 7(a) program to small businesses that are planning, designing, or installing a pollution control facility. The facility must abate, control, prevent, or reduce any form of pollution, including recycling. This program follows the 7(a) guidelines with the following exception: Use of proceeds must be for fixed assets only. The maximum guarantee amount is $1 million. However, if the company has an existing SBA loan guarantee, this amount is reduced by the outstanding guarantee.

Other Loans

The 504 Certified Development Company Loan Program

The CDC program finances fixed assets with long-term, low-interest funds through certified development companies (CDCs). These are nonprofit economic development agencies, certified by the SBA and licensed by the state to operate in designated counties only. There are about 270 CDCs nationwide, each covering a specific geographic area. To be eligible for a CDC loan, a business must be operated for profit and fall within the size standards set by the SBA. Under the 504 Program, the business qualifies as small if it does not have a tangible net worth in excess of $7.5 million and does not have an average net income in excess of $2.5 million after taxes for the preceding two years. Loans cannot be made to businesses engaged in speculation or investment in rental real estate. CDCs consider jobs generated or jobs saved in choosing projects to fund.

Funds can be used for purchasing land or grading and street improvements, parking lots, and landscaping; purchasing, constructing, renovating, or expanding buildings; or buying machinery or long-term equipment. The 504 Program cannot be used for working capital or inventory, consolidating or repaying debt, or refinancing. Collateral and personal guarantees are required. Interest rates are based on 5- and 10-year U.S. Treasury issues plus an increment. Fees are approximately 3 percent of the debenture and may be financed with the loan proceeds. The typical structure for a CDC funding project would include 50 percent conventional bank financing, 40 percent CDC second mortgage, and 10 percent owner's equity. The maximum for 504 loans is up to $1.5 million when meeting job creation goals (one job for $50,000 in debentures), $2 million when meeting public policy goals (see SBA web site and the 504 Loan Program for a list of public policy goals), and up to $4 million for manufacturers at 10- to 20-year maturities.

Disaster Loans

The SBA provides financial assistance to businesses located in disaster areas designated by the President or the SBA administrator. Businesses suffering uninsured property damage or economic losses from the disaster can obtain long-term recovery loans at low interest rates. Property damage to real estate, machinery, equipment, supplies, or inventory is eligible for physical disaster loans of generally up to $1.5 million to nonfarm businesses of all sizes damaged in a disaster. Loans of up to $1.5 million for economic losses, for working capital until normal operations resume after the physical disaster, are available to small businesses and agricultural cooperatives that are not able to access credit elsewhere. Interest rates for physical disaster loans are up to 4 percent; up to 8 percent for business with other sources of credit. Economic injury disaster loans for working capital are up to 4 percent. Terms are negotiated with the borrower with a maximum of 30 years; however, businesses with other credit sources are limited to shorter terms. Businesses damaged by Hurricanes Katrina and Ike and the Midwest floods were beneficiaries of SBA disaster loans.

Micro-Loans

The Micro-Loan Program provides short-term loans of up to $35,000 to small businesses and not-for-profit day care centers. These micro-loans are targeted at women, low-income, and minority entrepreneurs, especially those in areas that have suffered economic downturns. They help entrepreneurs form or expand small, often home-based, enterprises. Individuals should have the skills but not the capital needed to operate a small business. The average loan is $13,000. Funds may be used for working capital, inventory, supplies, furniture, fixtures, machinery, and equipment. The loans cannot be used to pay existing debt or for real estate transactions. Borrowers must demonstrate that they cannot obtain credit from other sources at comparable rates. The maximum term of the loan is six years. Loan terms vary depending upon the size of the loan, the use of the proceeds, the needs of the borrower, and the requirements of the intermediary. The interest rate on these loans typically varies between 8 and 13 percent.

The program is distributed through nonprofit organizations (for example, community service and church groups) with experience in lending and technical assistance. The SBA makes the loan to the nonprofit intermediary, who in turn makes the loan to the small business. The micro-loan program is available in 46 states (excluding Alaska, Rhode Island, Utah, and West Virginia), Washington D.C., and Puerto Rico. To find an intermediary, see the SBA web site and the Micro-Loan Program.

The Surety Bond Guarantee Program

The SBA provides guarantee bonds for qualified small contractors who are unable to obtain surety bonds through regular bonding markets. To be eligible a business must meet certain size standards: For federal prime contracts, revenues must not exceed $13 to $32.5 million, depending upon the type of project (see the SBA web site and the Surety Bond Program for more details); for other contracts annual revenue cannot exceed $7 million.

The SBA guarantees bonds for contracts up to $5 million. The guarantees are for 80 percent or 90 percent, depending on the amount of the contract or the status of the contractor. Approved socially or economically disadvantaged contractors receive a 90 percent guarantee for contracts regardless of the contract size; other contractors receive a 90 percent guarantee for contracts not exceeding $100,000 and an 80 percent guarantee for those over $100,000. The small business pays the SBA a guarantee fee of $7.29 per thousand of the contract amount, and when the bond is issued, it pays the surety company's bond premium.

Small Business Investment Company Program

Small Business Investment Companies (SBICs) are privately owned and managed investment firms that are licensed and regulated by the SBA. They augment their own funds by borrowing at favorable rates with SBA guarantees. They provide equity capital and long-term loans to small businesses. To be eligible, you must qualify as a small business using SBA criteria (see earlier section). In fiscal year 2007, there were 370 SBICs that invested a total of $2.8 billion in 2057 firms; 33 percent of the funds went to companies less than two years old. Some familiar names in the business world have received SBIC funding, including Apple Computer, Compaq Computer, Restoration Hardware, and Outback Steakhouse.

SBA Interest Rate Policy

Interest rates on guaranteed loans are negotiated between borrowers and lenders, although rates cannot be higher than levels set by SBA regulations. Interest rates may be fixed or variable. For fixed rate loans, maturing in less than seven years, rates may not exceed 2.25 percent plus prime; maturing in seven years or more, rates may not exceed 2.75 percent. For loans less than $25,000, the maximum is 4.25 percent and 4.75 percent respectively. For loans between $25,000 and $50,000, the maximums are 3.25 percent and 3.75 percent. In the SBA Express Loan program, lenders may charge up to 6.5 percent over prime rate for loans of $50,000 or less and up to 4.5 percent over the prime rate for loans over $50,000.

Variable rate loans are based on the lowest prime rate or the SBA optional peg rate, which is calculated quarterly and published in the Federal Register. The lender and borrower negotiate the amount that will be added to the base rate. All guaranteed loans require payment of a guarantee fee to the SBA by the lender, which varies with the size and maturity of the loan and typically is passed on to the borrower. Fees range from 0.25 to 3.5 percent, computed on the guaranteed portion of the loan, and can be paid out of the proceeds of the loan. In rare instances, such as the economic recovery efforts during the 2008–2009 recession, loan fees are waived.

How to Apply for an SBA Loan Guarantee

The SBA has the following five general credit requirements:

1. The applicant must be of good character and have a good credit history.
2. The applicant must have experience in business management and demonstrate the commitment necessary for a successful operation.
3. The applicant must have enough funds—including the SBA-guaranteed loan plus personal equity capital—to operate the business on a sound financial basis. If the company is a new business, this means enough cash to fund start-up expenses and sustain expected losses during the early stages of operation.
4. If the company is an existing business, it must have a past earning record and future prospects to show repayment ability.
5. If the company is a new business, the start-up entrepreneurs must provide at least one-third of the total start-up capital needed. Therefore, the loan requested should be no more than twice the value of the owner's equity capital in the business.

Borrowers must fully secure the loan with collateral and provide personal guarantees. The SBA normally takes about two weeks to process a request.

Where to Find the SBA

To reach SBA by Mail:

U.S. Small Business Administration
409 3rd Street SW
Washington, DC 20416

To reach SBA by phone or e-mail:

SBA Answer Desk

Phone: 1-800-U-ASK-SBA (1-800-827-5722)

answerdesk@sba.gov

Answer Desk TTY: (704) 344-6640

Web site: www.sba.gov

For specific information related to financing:

www.sba.gov/services/financialassistance

Finding an SBA-Approved Lender

It is worth your while to identify SBA-preferred lenders in your area because they are empowered to apply an SBA loan guarantee to a loan without consulting the SBA in advance. The benefit of dealing with an SBA-certified lender is that the SBA will normally decide whether to guarantee a bank loan within three days. To find out which lenders are preferred or certified, call your SBA district office.

It is important to find a bank that has a lot of experience with SBA-guaranteed loans. For example, a Massachusetts entrepreneur (looking for information in April 2009) should go to the SBA Massachusetts site, http://www.sba.gov/ma/; then click on "(2009) Lender Ranking" to get a list of banks that granted at least one SBA loan between October 1, 2008, and February 28, 2009. As of April 2009, at the top of the list was Citizens Bank with 52 loans totaling $2.8 million; followed by Sovereign Bank with 37 loans totaling $2.8 million; and Rockland Trust with 22 loans totaling $2.9 million. At the bottom of the rankings are banks that made only one or two loans in the same period. In general, the entrepreneur will have a better chance of getting a loan in a timely manner from a bank that processes lots of SBA loans rather than one that processes only a few. Once the small business owner has selected a bank, she can find out who to contact by clicking on "SBA Lenders" on www.sba.gov/ma.

Boost for SBA Loans during the 2009 Economic Collapse

During much of the 1970s, 1980s, and 1990s, the SBA provided billions of dollars to small business owners and entrepreneurs through the SBA direct and guaranteed loan programs. However, the direct loan program in which the SBA worked in concert with banks or local agencies to provide loans directly to borrowers was strongly curtailed; and in the 2008 and 2009 economic collapse, the flow of SBA-guaranteed lending slowed to a trickle.[2]

Fortunately, SBA programs received a big boost in the American Recovery and Reinvestment Act of 2009 that President Obama signed into law on February 17, 2009. The Act provides for temporary reductions or elimination of fees in the popular SBA 7(a) and 504 programs. The bill instructs the SBA to give borrowers and small banks priority in receiving fee relief. The intent of this provision in the bill is to reduce the cost on the $13.5 billion in long-term bank loans that create or retain as many as 300,000 jobs. Moreover, the temporary increase in SBA guarantee levels allows the SBA, on a case-by-case basis, to temporarily raise the guarantee level up to 90 percent for 7(a) loans through the SBA express program. The U.S. Senate believes the increased guarantee will loosen lending standards among nervous bankers.[3]

Selling to the Government: The Art of Procurement

The federal government is a big customer. It buys $425 billion worth of goods and services every year from U.S. businesses. The government especially encourages small businesses to bid on contracts for some of these needs. In fact, federal agencies are required to target at least 23 percent of all government buying from small businesses. Nearly 98 percent of all procurement contracts are for $25,000 or less, although this comprises only 20 percent of all spending.

Procurement Assistance Programs Sponsored by the SBA

The Small Business Act provides for preferential treatment to be granted to small business concerns in the award of government procurement contracts. The SBA has developed cooperative programs with major government purchasing agencies under which proposed purchases are reviewed by purchasing officials and suitable items are set aside, wholly or partially, for small business bidders. This system of preferences in contract awards is known as *set-asides*. They are aimed at small businesses, disadvantaged small businesses, and small businesses owned by women.

The law also requires large prime government contractors to subcontract work to small businesses. The SBA accordingly develops subcontracting opportunities by negotiating the amounts to be subcontracted to small business concerns by prime contractors undertaking major federal projects.

The SBA operates a Procurement Center Representatives (PCR) program to assist small businesses in obtaining government contracts. Representatives provide counseling and other services to small business owners seeking to do business with the federal government. Services can include:

- Identifying the government agencies that are prospective customers.
- Instructing small businesses about inclusion on bidders' lists.
- Obtaining drawings and specifications for specific contracts.
- Identifying, developing, and marketing small businesses to large prime contractors.
- Assisting small businesses in identifying and obtaining subcontracts.

The SBA also provides surety bonds, whereby it guarantees up to 80 percent (90 percent depending upon the status of the borrower or the size of the contract) of losses incurred under bid, payment, or performance bonds issued to contractors on government contracts valued up to $5 million. The Surety Bond Guarantee Program was described earlier in this chapter.

Doing business with the federal government has the following advantages:

- Variety—the federal government has a wide range of purchasing needs.
- Creditworthiness.
- The potential for long-term contracts.
- Detailed bidding procedures designed to ensure fairness.

Disadvantages include the fact that the competitive nature of the bidding process may reduce profit margins, and its bureaucratic aspects require painstaking attention to involved procedures.

Pursuing Opportunities

It's important to register with the Central Contractor Registration (CCR) database so that government agencies can find your business when they have a contracting opportunity. Agencies can search for companies based on a number of factors including size, product, location, and experience. For more details and to register, go to www.ccr.gov. You should also register with Federal Business Opportunities (FedBizOpps.gov), a comprehensive listing of all government opportunities expected to exceed $25,000. Agencies use this site to communicate their buying needs and preferences to potential contractors. For more information, go to www.fbo.gov.

Programs to Assist Special Groups

The SBA 8(a) Business Development Program offers a broad range of assistance to firms that are owned and controlled at least 51 percent by socially and economically disadvantaged individuals. New regulations permit 8(a) companies to form partnerships and allow federal agencies to streamline the contacting process. New rules make it easier for nonminority firms to participate by proving their social disadvantage. Participation is divided into two phases over nine years: a four-year developmental stage and a five-year transition stage.

More than half of all federal procurement through disadvantaged firms is channeled through the 8(a) program. The SBA has helped thousands of aspiring entrepreneurs over the years to gain a foothold in government contracting. The SBA Mentor-Protégé program enhances the capability of 8(a) participants to compete more successfully for federal government contracts. Mentors provide technical and management assistance, financial assistance in the form of equity investments and/or loans, subcontract support, and assistance in performing prime contracts through joint venture arrangements with 8(a) firms. The new program is offered under SBA's 8(a) Business Development program serving disadvantaged firms. Under SBA's Mentor-Protégé program, protégés can gain the following benefits:

- *Technical and management assistance.* The mentor's expertise, resources, and capabilities are made available to the protégé.

- *Prime contracting.* Mentors can enter into joint-venture arrangements with protégés to compete for government contracts.

- *Financial assistance* in the form of equity or loans. Mentors can own equity interest of up to 40 percent in a protégé firm to help it raise capital.

- *Qualification for other SBA programs.* A protégé can obtain other forms of SBA assistance as the result of its good standing in the Mentor-Protégé program.

The Defense Logistics Agency's Procurement Technical Assistance Program

The Defense Logistics Agency (DLA) supplies the nation's military services and several civilian agencies with the critical resources they need to accomplish their worldwide missions. The DLA provides wide-ranging logistical support for peacetime and wartime operations as well as emergency preparedness and humanitarian missions. Administered by the DLA Office of Small and Disadvantaged Business Utilization, the Procurement Technical Assistance Program (PTAP) supports and extends the DLA's mission of providing the best value logistics support to America's armed forces by acting as a bridge between buyer and supplier, bringing to bear knowledge of both government contracting and the capabilities of an extensive network of contractors to maximize fast, reliable service to the government with better quality and at lower costs.

The PTAP is a cooperative program in which the DLA shares the cost of the services with state and local governments and nonprofit organizations. These services can help business owners and entrepreneurs seeking to sell goods and services to the federal government. They provide the same services for state and local government. The core of the procurement assistance program is counseling. PTAP counselors provide assistance in such areas as:

- Identifying preference eligibility and completing applicable certifications.
- Researching contract award histories.
- Understanding solicitation requirements and terminology.
- Locating specifications and standards.
- Reviewing bids and proposals.
- Assisting in completing mandatory/beneficial registrations.
- Explaining how the government uses electronic transactions.
- Searching government databases to identify opportunities.
- Providing up-to-the-minute information on government procurement processes and procedures.

The Association of Procurement Technical Assistance Centers (APTAC) is a membership organization comprising and supporting Procurement Technical Assistance Centers (PTACs) and the professionals who work for them. APTAC's mission is to support the PTACs in their efforts to provide the very highest levels of government contracting assistance, thereby increasing and improving the supplier base which serves the U.S. armed forces and the government as a whole.

How to Get SBA and PTAC Procurement Help

To reach SBA by Mail:

> U.S. Small Business Administration
> 409 3rd Street SW
> Washington, DC 20416

To reach SBA by phone or e-mail:

> SBA Answer Desk
> 1-800-U-ASK-SBA (1-800-827-5722)
> answerdesk@sba.gov
> Answer Desk TTY: (704) 344-6640
> http://www.sba.gov

To reach the APTAC:

Association of Procurement Technical Assistance Centers (APTAC)
360 Sunset Island Trail
Gallatin, TN 37066
Phone: (615) 268-6644
www.aptac-us.org

Selling Abroad: International Business in the Global Village

Small and medium-size firms account for the majority of growth in new exporters and account for 97 percent of U.S. exporters, but still represent only 30 percent of the total export value of the United States. More than two-thirds of exporters have fewer than 20 employees. According to the SBA, every billion dollars in U.S. exports generates about 25,000 jobs. Because of the importance of small business in export, the SBA, the SBA's Resource Partners, the U.S. Department of Commerce, the U.S. Export-Import Bank, and the Overseas Private Investment Corporation (OPIC) have business development and financial assistance programs to help companies involved in exporting.

The U.S. government's export promotion and finance portal is designed to deliver critical export information and services from across the U.S. government to small and medium-size U.S. companies to begin or expand their exporting business. Federal export assistance is delivered by many U.S. government agencies. According to its web site (www.export.gov), Export.gov brings together resources from across the U.S. government to assist American businesses in planning their international sales strategies and succeeding in today's global marketplace. From market research and trade leads from the U.S. Department of Commerce's Commercial Service to export finance information from Export-Import Bank and the Small Business Administration to agricultural export assistance from USDA, Export.gov helps American exporters navigate the international sales process and avoid pitfalls such as nonpayment and intellectual property misappropriation.

Export Business Development Programs

U.S. Export Assistance Centers

U.S. Export Assistance Centers (USEACs) are located in major cities in the United States. They integrate services provided by the U.S. Small Business Administration, the U.S. Department of Commerce, the Foreign Commercial Service, the Export-Import Bank, and local international trade programs by providing a single location for access.

The USEACs provide one-on-one counseling to firms to assist them in identifying target markets and developing international marketing strategies. They also provide assistance in areas relating to export finance.

In 2009 there were 19 USEACs, located in Atlanta, Baltimore, Boston, Charlotte, Chicago, Cleveland, Dallas, Denver, Detroit, Miami, Minneapolis, Newport Beach, New Orleans, New York, Philadelphia, Portland, Sacramento, Seattle, and St. Louis.

Export Legal Assistance Network

Under an agreement between the SBA and the Federal Bar Association, the Export Legal Assistance Network (ELAN) offers free initial consultations with an experienced international trade attorney on topics ranging from contract negotiation to agent/distributor agreements, export licensing requirements, and credit collection procedures. Visit www.exportlegal.org for more information.

The International Trade Administration

The U.S. Department of Commerce (USDOC) also helps companies expand their international trade capabilities through the International Trade Administration (ITA). ITA operates domestic and overseas programs designed to stimulate the expansion of U.S. exports. Major programs include export counseling and assistance.

Through ITA a U.S. business can tap into a worldwide network of:

- Trade specialists who can provide export counseling on a variety of products and industries.
- Country specialists versed in international economic policies and specific markets.
- Industry specialists who help develop trade promotion programs.
- Import trade specialists who can advise domestic industries with regard to unfair trade practices.

The ITA's U.S. Commercial Service can access a network of export and industry specialists located in 80 countries, 104 U.S. cities, and Commerce Headquarters in Washington, D.C. This network covers 95 percent of the global markets for U.S. goods and services.

The following services are available through your U.S. Commercial Service offices. Some services are offered at no cost and some services have fees associated with them.

Developing Export Expertise

- The *Export Qualifier Program* helps firms evaluate their readiness to export through a computerized diagnostic questionnaire.

Identifying Target Markets

- The *National Trade DataBank* includes over 100,000 trade-related documents, product-specific market research reports, and trade statistics. Information is collected by 17 agencies, updated monthly, and issued on two CD-ROM disks.
- The *Customized Market Analysis* can assess the competitiveness of your product in a specific market. It involves intensive custom research including product-specific interviews or surveys. Although potentially useful, this service may be cost prohibitive for small businesses.

Finding Potential Partners

- The *Agent/Distributor Service* can help you locate up to six foreign representatives who, after looking at your product literature, may be interested in marketing your product.
- *International Company Profile* will help you evaluate potential partners overseas, in terms of reliability, creditworthiness, and standing in the local business community.
- *Commercial News USA* is a catalog of new U.S. products and services sent to 110,000 potential overseas buyers, agents, and distributors.

- The *International Buyer Program* brings delegations of overseas buyers from around the world to your exhibit at participating U.S. trade shows.

- The *Trade Opportunities Program* identifies timely sales leads overseas and provides them to U.S. businesses.

- *Catalog and video/catalog exhibitions* are organized every year for certain industries in selected markets. The Department of Commerce shows U.S. exporter catalogs and videos to potential agents, distributors, and other buyers in each market. Participating exporters often receive up to 50 leads from each exhibition.

- *Trade mission/trade shows* organized with state, local, or private groups help U.S. companies that have representatives visiting their targeted overseas export market to introduce and market their products there.

- *Matchmaker delegations* are introductory missions for firms entering export markets. The Matchmaker program visits more than 15 countries each year. Matchmaker organizers evaluate a product's potential for a market and make introductions to potential buyers or licensees. This program is also for entrepreneurs who are visiting their export market.

- The *Gold Key Service* provides the following services to U.S. businesspeople who are visiting their export market:
  - Market orientation briefings.
  - Specialized market research.
  - Introductions to potential partners.
  - Interpreter for meetings.

Export Financial Assistance

The SBA offers three types of export loan guarantees that protect the lender from default by the exporter. All must be collateralized with U.S.-based assets. For the fiscal year 2008, the SBA guaranteed 3,320 loans to exporters with a value of $1.082 billion that generated export sales of nearly $2.5 billion dollars.

1. *Export Express.* The SBA Export Express program provides exporters and lenders a streamlined method to obtain SBA-backed financing for loans and lines of credit up to $250,000. Lenders use their own credit decision process and loan documentation; exporters get access to their funds faster. The SBA provides an expedited eligibility review and response. Loan proceeds may be used for standby letters of credit, trade shows, marketing materials, lines of credit, real estate and equipment purchases, facilities improvement, and more.

   The maximum Export Express line of credit/loan amount is $250,000. Participating banks receive an 85 percent SBA guaranty on loan amounts up to $150,000 and 75 percent on loan amounts between $150,000 and $250,000.

2. *Export Working Capital Program (EWCP) loans.* These are short-term loan guarantees available to small businesses based in the United States that are at least one year old. Loans provide working capital to acquire inventory, to pay for direct manufacturing costs, to purchase goods and services for export, or to support standby letters of credit. The maximum EWCP line of credit/loan amount is $2 million. Participating banks receive a 90 percent SBA guaranty provided that

the total SBA guaranteed portion to the borrower does not exceed $1.5 million. In those instances where the SBA-guaranteed portion reaches the $1.5 million cap, banks can still get a 90 percent guaranty thanks to a co-guaranty program between SBA and the Export-Import Bank of the United States.

3. *International Trade loans.* These are guaranteed loans through private lenders that help U.S.-based facilities that engage in international trade or are recovering from the effects of import competition. International Trade loan funds may be used for the acquisition, construction, renovation, modernization, improvement, or expansion of long-term fixed assets, or for the refinancing of an existing loan used for these same purposes. The maximum gross amount ($2 million) and SBA-guaranteed amount ($1.5 million) for an International Trade loan is the same as a regular 7(a) loan. In some cases, the SBA will guarantee up to 1.75 million.

The Export-Import Bank of the United States

The Export-Import Bank of the United States (Ex-Im Bank), an independent federal government agency, is the official export credit agency of the United States. Ex-Im Bank assists in financing the export of U.S. goods and services to international markets.

Ex-Im Bank has three export finance programs of interest to small businesses: working capital guarantees, export credit insurance, and guarantees and loans extended to finance the sale of U.S. goods and services abroad. In the past five years, over 6,000 companies were assisted in their export activities by Ex-Im Bank, and over 37 percent of these were small businesses. Visit www.exim.gov for more information.

1. *Working capital guarantees.* This Ex-Im Bank program is very similar to the SBA's Export Working Capital loan guarantees (see previous section). The guarantees cover loans to provide working capital to acquire inventory or pay for direct manufacturing costs, to purchase goods and services for export, or to support standing letters of credit. Guarantees may be for a single transaction or a revolving line of credit. Terms are generally for 12 months and are renewable. Companies need to be based in the United States, have positive net worth, and be in business for at least one year to be eligible for this program. Unlike the SBA, Ex-Im Bank does not require the business to meet the SBA definition of a small business. Ex-Im Bank will guarantee 90 percent of the loan amount and sets no limit on loan size.

2. *Export credit insurance.* Ex-Im Bank offers a variety of insurance policies to protect U.S. exporters from foreign buyers' defaulting on payment because of commercial or political risks. One program, geared for the small exporter, offers a short-term (up to 180 days) policy that covers 95 percent of commercial and political risk. The exporter is required to insure all export credit sales, not just specific sales. The program is open to businesses that have an average annual export credit sales volume of less than $5 million in the previous three years and meet the SBA definition of a small business.

3. *Direct loans and guarantees.* Ex-Im Bank provides direct loans and guarantees of commercial financing to foreign buyers of U.S. capital goods and related services. The loans and guarantees cover up to 100 percent of commercial and political risk. There are no limits on transaction size, and medium- and long-term financing are available.

The Overseas Private Investment Corporation

In general, the Overseas Private Investment Corporation (OPIC) encourages U.S. businesses to invest in developing countries and in newly emerging democracies and free market economies. OPIC offers a number of programs to insure U.S. investment against political violence, expropriation, and currency risks. It also provides medium- to long-term financing through direct loans and loan guarantees for new investments, privatizations, and expansions and modernizations of existing plants by U.S. investors. If investors contribute additional capital for modernization and expansion, acquisitions of existing operations are also eligible. In 2009, there were 150 countries or areas on the OPIC program list.

OPIC's Small Business Center (SBC) offers qualified small businesses, with annual revenues less than $35 million, the opportunity to utilize OPIC's streamlined approval process. SBC Financing offers direct loans from $100,000 to $10 million with terms from 3 to 15 years. Loan guarantees are generally for loans above $10 million.

Political risk insurance is available to U.S. exporters, contractors, and investors and is available for investments in new ventures, expansions of existing enterprises, privatizations, and acquisitions with positive developmental benefits.

Where to Find International Trade Assistance

Contact the U.S. Small Business Administration at

409 3rd Street, SW

Washington, DC 20416

SBA Answer Desk: 1-800-U-ASK-SBA (1-800-827-5722)

www.sba.gov/aboutsba/sbaprograms/internationaltrade/index.html

The Department of Commerce's 800-USA-TRAD is a clearinghouse of international trade sources. For the hearing impaired, the TDD number is 800-TDD- TRAD. You can find Department of Commerce industry and country desk officers at:

U.S. Department of Commerce

International Trade Administration

14th and Constitution Avenue NW

Washington, DC 20230

Phone: (202) 482-2867

www.ita.doc.gov

Contact the Export-Import Bank of the United States at

811 Vermont Avenue NW

Washington, DC 20571

Phone: (202) 565-3946

(continued)

Export Hotline: (800) 565-EXIM

www.exim.gov

Contact the Overseas Private Investment Corporation at

1615 M Street NW
Washington, DC 20527
Phone: (202) 336-8799
www.opic.gov

External Assistance for Special Groups, Locations, and Industries

Business Assistance Programs for Women

Despite the importance of women business owners in our economy, few special support programs are aimed solely at women. This has fueled a debate about whether women need special programs or whether they are better served by accessing business assistance programs aimed at the general population.

All SBA offices have a staff member designated as a Women's Business Ownership Representative, whose duty it is to discuss resources that are available for women and to provide assistance for accessing those resources. One of SBAs partner programs is the Women's Business Center Program, which provides services to potential or current women business owners. The Women's Business Centers, located in most states, support entrepreneurial development among women as a way to achieve economic self-sufficiency, create wealth, and participate in economic development through education, training, mentoring, business development, and financing opportunities. The centers offer counseling and technical training in a variety of topics, including management, marketing, and finance. Although open to all women, the program was developed for women who might not normally use services provided through traditional channels.

Where to Find SBA Help for Women

Office of Women's Business Ownership
Small Business Administration
409 Third Street SW, Sixth Floor
Washington, DC 20416
Phone: (202) 205-6673
owbo@sba.gov
www.sba.gov/aboutsba/sbaprograms/onlinewbc/

Exhibit 9.1   Growth in Minority-Owned Businesses, 1997–2002

	1997	2002	Increase (%)
All	20,821,934	22,974,655	10
White	17,316,796	18,609,599	6
Hispanic	1,119,896	1,573,464	31
Black	823,499	1,197,567	45
Asian	893,590	1,103,587	24
Native American	197,300	201,387	2
Islander	19,370	28,948	49

Assistance Programs for Minority-Owned Businesses

Recent statistics on business ownership from the Bureau of the Census show the changing face of small business in America. (See Exhibit 9.1.) Minority-owned small businesses in America reached 18 percent of the total business population in 2002, or approximately 4.1 million firms. This is a significant increase from the 2 million minority firms in 1992, or 11.6 percent of total firms. The growth rate in minority-owned businesses far exceeds that of non-minority-owned businesses. The overall growth rate for minority-owned business was approximately 35 percent between 1997 and 2002 compared to non-minority-owned growth at 6 percent.

The Minority Business Development Agency (MBDA), an agency of the U.S. Department of Commerce, is the only federal agency specifically created to establish policies and programs to develop the U.S. minority business community. The MBDA sponsors a network of approximately 60 Minority and Indian Business Development Centers (MBDCs/IBDCs), located throughout the country in areas with the largest minority populations. To qualify as a minority business, the business must be 51 percent owned, controlled, and actively managed by minority persons.

The centers cannot make or underwrite loans because the MBDA has no loan-making authority. MBDCs and IBDCs do engage in business development counseling for a fee. The hourly fees depend upon the gross sales of the business. Services typically offered include loan packaging, business planning, marketing, and financial analysis. (Other minority assistance programs are discussed in the section on procurement.)

Where to Find the MBDA

The U.S. Department of Commerce

Minority Business Development Agency

1401 Constitution Avenue NW

Washington, DC 20230

To locate the nearest MBDA office, call 1-888-324-1551, or go to www .mbda.gov.

Business Assistance Programs for Veterans

The SBA has a special mission to help veterans get into business and stay in business. In each local SBA office, there is a staff person designated the Veterans Affairs Officer, specially trained to guide the veteran seeking business assistance. In addition to SBA Resource Partners' normal business development counseling and training courses (which veterans are welcome to attend), the SBA and its resource partners at times conduct special business training conferences for veterans.

For example, during the Iraq war, SCORE has been conducting workshops to teach businesspeople called up by the Reserves how to cope with sudden and long absences from their businesses. SCORE members also mentor family members and others chosen to manage businesses during the reserves' absences. In addition, SBA has created a loan program specifically targeted to veterans. The SBA and its resource partners are also focusing additional efforts on counseling and training to augment this loan initiative.

Patriot Express Pilot Loan Initiative

The SBA's Patriot Express Pilot Loan Initiative was specifically designed for veterans and members of the military community wanting to establish or expand small businesses. Eligible military community members include veterans; service-disabled veterans; active-duty service members eligible for the military's Transition Assistance Program; reservists and National Guard members; current spouses of any of the above; and widowed spouses of service members or veterans who died during service or of a service-connected disability.

The Patriot Express loan is offered by SBA's network of participating lenders nationwide. Loans are available up to $500,000 and qualify for SBA's maximum guaranty of up to 85 percent for loans of $150,000 or less and up to 75 percent for loans over $150,000 up to $500,000. For loans above $350,000, lenders are required to take all available collateral. The Patriot Express loan can be used for most business purposes, including start-up, expansion, equipment purchases, working capital, inventory, or business-occupied real estate purchases. Patriot Express loans feature SBA's lowest interest rates for business loans, generally 2.25 percent to 4.75 percent over prime, depending upon the size and maturity of the loan. Your local SBA district office will have a listing of Patriot Express lenders in your area. The SBA promises the fastest turnarounds for loan approvals for this program.

If you are already a small business, SBA has a number of program offerings that may be of use to you—for example, preparing your business for your deployment, online and other training programs to help you manage your business, assistance in selling to the federal government and private corporations, and even recovery assistance for recovering from natural disasters.

Where to Find SBA Help for Veterans

For your district SBA office, look in the Blue Pages, under the U.S. Government listing headed "U.S. Small Business Administration." Or call the 24-hour SBA answer desk at 1-800-U-ASK-SBA (1-800-827-5722) for your district SBA office. Speak to the Veterans Affairs Officer. For the hearing-impaired, the TDD number is (703) 344-6640. The web site is www.sba.gov.

Business Assistance for Rural and Agricultural Entrepreneurs

Before describing programs for this group, it should be pointed out that *rural* is not synonymous with *agricultural.* Not all rural entrepreneurs are engaged in the traditional rural occupation of agriculture. Consider different potential sources of assistance based on your location *and* your line of business. For example, the U.S. Department of Agriculture offers programs that provide management and technical assistance, guaranteed and other loans, and grants and cooperative agreements in areas not limited to traditional agricultural enterprises.

The Agricultural Extension Service

This is the outreach arm of the Department of Agriculture. Although the Agricultural Extension Service has agents in all land-grant universities and nearly all the nation's 3,150 counties, services of interest to businesses vary dramatically by location. It sometimes provides management and marketing assistance to rural businesses, including agricultural and natural-resource-based enterprises, manufacturers, retail businesses, and service businesses. The services are aimed at increasing the profitability and growth of existing businesses, as well as identifying neglected market segments.

The U.S. Department of Agriculture has a number of loan and grant programs of interest to entrepreneurs and small business owners.

How to Find the Cooperative Extension Service

To find what services are available in your area, look under the Blue Pages (U.S. Government) for "U.S. Department of Agriculture" or the Blue Pages {County) for "County Extension Office."

Rural Business-Cooperative Service (RBS) Business and Industry Guaranteed Loan Program

This program offers loan guarantees similar to the SBA's for businesses located outside any city with a population of 50,000 or more and its immediately adjacent urbanized area. Most loans are made in towns with populations of 25,000 or less. Funds can be used for working capital; land, machinery, and equipment purchases; improvement, construction, or acquisition of fixed assets (including land and buildings); and, in some cases, debt refinancing.

The maximum loan amount is $10 million (with some exceptions this may increase to $25 or $40 million), and the average is slightly over $1 million. A minimum of 10 percent of total capital is required in the form of equity for existing businesses (20 percent for start-ups). The terms are up to 30 years for land and building, 15 years for machinery and equipment, and 7 years for working capital. RBS loan guarantees do not require that you prove your inability to get credit without the guarantee. Interest rates may be fixed or variable and are at competitive banking rates. Collateral is required. A fee of 2 percent of the guaranteed portion of the loan is payable to USDA Rural Development when the guarantee is issued with a 0.25 percent annual renewal fee.

The Rural Energy for America Program Loans and Grants

This program provides financial assistance in the form of loans and grants to agricultural producers and rural small businesses for purchase and installation of renewable energy systems or for energy efficiency improvements, and related projects fees. Combination grants and guaranteed loans can fund up to 50 percent of a project's total eligible costs. Grants can fund up to 25 percent of a project's total eligible costs. Grants are limited to $500,000 for renewable energy projects or $250,000 for energy efficiency improvements. The minimum for grants is $2,500 for renewable energy projects and $1,500 for energy efficiency projects. Guaranteed loans can fund up to 50 percent of a project's total eligible costs—with a minimum of $5,000 and a maximum of $25 million. Terms for loans are 30 years for real estate, 20 years for equipment, and 7 years for working capital. Collateral is required for loans. Borrowers are required to have 15 percent equity for loans of $600,000 or less, 25 percent for loans greater than $600,000.

The Intermediary Relending Program

This program makes loans to nonprofit organizations, which in turn lend funds to small businesses in their service area. The nonprofit organization may provide up to 75 percent of each project's cost up to $150,000. The Intermediary Relending Program (IRP) has the following requirements:

- Projects must create new jobs or retain old jobs.
- Funds must be used in rural areas including cities with 25,000 or fewer people.
- Applicants must have been turned down by at least two other sources before applying for this program.

Funds may be used to start a new business or expand an existing one. The interest rate to the nonprofits is 1 percent for up to 30 years. The nonprofits charge interest at a rate to cover their operating costs, typically around 7 to 9 percent, but that may change with economic conditions.

How to Find Help for Rural and Agricultural Entrepreneurs

Look under the Blue Pages (U.S. Government) for "U.S. Department of Agriculture" or the Blue Pages (County) for "County Extension Office."

U.S. Department of Agriculture
1400 Independence Avenue SW
Washington, DC 20250
www.usda.gov

Business Assistance for Urban Entrepreneurs

The U.S. Department of Housing and Urban Development (HUD) offers a number of programs of interest to entrepreneurs and small business owners.

- *The Community Development Block Grant (CDBG) Program* awards grants annually to eligible metropolitan cities and urban counties. Communities receiving grants are free to develop programs that meet local needs in housing, public works, economic development, public services, acquisition, clearance or redevelopment of real property, or administration and planning concerning urban needs, as long as the activities meet the national objectives of the program. The national objectives are to benefit low- and moderate-income persons, to prevent or eliminate slums or blight, or to meet other urgent community needs. Some communities establish revolving loan pools that may be accessed by private sector businesses that promise to start or expand their business.

- *The Section 108 Loan Guarantee Program* is a source of financing for economic development, housing rehabilitation, public facilities rehab, construction, or installation for the benefit of low- to moderate-income persons, or to aid in the prevention of slums. The Section 108 program allows CDBG grantees to borrow federally guaranteed funds for community development, including lending to private businesses. This program increases the ability of grantees to expand the scale of their operations because they can borrow five times the amount they receive in grants. Over $4 billion in investments were made through the Section 108 funding throughout the 1990s.

- *The Brownfields Economic Development Initiative (BEDI)* is designed to assist cities with the redevelopment of abandoned, idled, and underused industrial and commercial facilities where expansion and redevelopment is burdened by *real or potential* environmental contamination. BEDI grant funds are primarily targeted for use with a particular emphasis upon the redevelopment of *brownfield* sites in economic development projects and the increase of economic opportunities for low- and moderate-income persons as part of the creation or retention of businesses, jobs, and increases in the local tax base. BEDI grant funds are initially made available by HUD to public entities approved for assistance. Such public entities may relend the Section 108 loan proceeds and provide BEDI funds to a business or other entity to carry out an approved economic development project, or the public entity may carry out the eligible project itself.

HUD spent more than $80 billion in the 1990s for community development in urban areas, although not all that amount went to revolving loan funds for private businesses.

Where to Find HUD

Businesses should contact their city or county planners to determine whether a CDBG, Section 108, or Brownfield revolving loan pool exists or could be started for funding their projects. City or county planners should contact HUD (look in the Blue Pages under U.S. Government) for more information.

U.S. Department of Housing and Urban Development

451 7th Street SW

Washington, DC 20410

Phone: 202-708-1112

TTY: 202-708-1455

www.hud.gov

Business Assistance for Entrepreneurs in Distressed Areas

The U.S. Department of Commerce, Economic Development Administration's (EDA) mission is to generate jobs, help retain existing jobs, and stimulate industrial and commercial growth in economically distressed areas of the United States. EDA assistance is available to urban (and rural) areas experiencing high unemployment, low income, or other severe economic distress, including recovering from the economic impacts of natural disasters such as hurricanes, the closure of military installations and other federal facilities, changing trade patterns, and the depletion of natural resources. To be eligible for funding, the community must demonstrate very high unemployment or very low per capita income. The funding to the community must be used for planning or implementing economic rebuilding. Some communities have chosen, as part of their rebuilding efforts, to establish revolving loan pools. The funds are then available for targeted small business start-ups and expansions, business and job retention projects, and the redevelopment of blighted land and vacant facilities.

For More Information about the Economic Development Administration

Businesses should contact their city or county planners to determine whether an EDA revolving loan pool exists or could be started for funding their projects. City or county planners should contact EDA for more information.

To locate a regional office near you, see www.eda.gov.

Engineering and Technical Assistance

According to the SBA, U.S. small businesses in the twentieth century invented the airplane, the aerosol can, double-knit fabric, the heart valve, the optical scanner, the pacemaker, the personal computer, the soft contact lens, and the zipper. Although building a better mousetrap may not automatically trigger a stampede to your door, technological innovation is a valuable competitive advantage.

Recognizing this, a variety of federal initiatives promote technological innovation. Unfortunately, these federal technological assistance programs are somewhat fragmented, the result of many different initiatives over many years.

The federal government provides both business development programs and financial assistance programs. Development programs for technology-oriented businesses include the following:

- Small Business Development Centers.
- Manufacturing Extension Partnership Program.
- The Federal Laboratory Consortium for Technology Transfer.
- NASA Regional Technology Transfer Centers.
- National Technology Transfer Center.
- The National Technical Information Service.
- Federal Research in Progress Database.

Financial assistance programs for technologically oriented businesses include:

- The Small Business Innovation Research Program.
- The Small Business Technology Transfer Program.
- Technology Innovations Program.
- Inventions and Innovations.

Small Business Development Centers

Small Business Development Centers (SBDCs) provide technical services to start-ups and small businesses. These services provide assistance in product licensing or small business formation based on new product development. Several SBDCs around the nation provide innovation assessments designed to determine a new product idea's potential for commercialization.

More than 80 percent of SBDCs provide assistance to small businesses developing Small Business Innovation Research proposals (discussed in the next section). All SBDCs provide links to federal, state, and local sources of technology and technical information.

For More Information about SBDCs

For a local office, look in the Blue Pages under the U.S. Government listing. The Association of Small Business Development Centers (ASBDC) is located at:

8990 Burke Lake Road, Second Floor

Burke, VA 22015

Phone: 703-764-9850

Fax: 703-764-1234

www.asbdc-us.org

Manufacturing Extension Partnership

Manufacturing Extension Partnership (MEP) centers are nonprofit, university- or state-based organizations, which receive one-third of their operational funding from the National Institute of Science and Technology (NIST), with a matching two-thirds realized from state funds, other regional partners, and revenue from fees paid by manufacturers for the services they receive. State and federal funding for the centers makes it possible for these organizations to reach even the smallest firms. MEP provides knowledgeable manufacturing and business expertise through local centers and by tapping into the linked national MEP network.

In 2008, there were 59 centers in 393 locations in all 50 states and Puerto Rico. Services vary depending upon the local client base and regional needs. In 2007, MEP clients reported $5.6 billion in new sales and $1.44 billion in cost savings. In general, centers provide in-depth assessments of manufacturing and technology needs, assistance in selecting appropriate technologies and processes, and plans for integrating these technologies into company operations.

For More Information about MEP Centers

Manufacturing Extension Partnership

100 Bureau Drive, Stop 4800

Gaithersburg, MD 20899-3460

Phone: (301) 975-5020

Fax: (301)963-6556

www.mep.nist.gov

The Federal Laboratory Consortium for Technology Transfer

Each year, federal research and development laboratories receive billions in R&D investment. Federal laboratories may enter into agreements with individuals or companies to conduct cooperative research. The U.S. government also holds thousands of patents available for licensing. The key to entrepreneurial success may be deciding how to access these resources given the number of federal laboratories and the complexity of their technological resources.

The Federal Laboratory Consortium for Technology Transfer (FLC) is the nationwide network of federal laboratories that provides the forum to develop strategies and opportunities for linking laboratory mission technologies and expertise with the marketplace. The Consortium creates an environment that adds value to and supports the technology transfer efforts of its members and potential partners. The FLC develops and tests transfer methods, addresses barriers to the process, provides training, highlights grassroots transfer efforts, and emphasizes national initiatives where technology transfer has a role. For the public and private sectors, the FLC brings laboratories together with potential users of government-developed technologies. This is in part accomplished by the FLC's Technology Locator network and regional and national meetings. The FLC's activities include:

- Promoting and facilitating the full range of technical cooperation between the federal laboratories and America's large and small businesses, academia, state and local governments, and federal agencies.

- Providing direct services to member laboratories and agencies in support of their technology transfer efforts.

- Enhancing efforts that couple federal laboratories with American industry and small businesses to strengthen the nation's economic competitiveness.

- Stimulating acceptance by the U.S. private and public sectors of the federal laboratory system and technology transfer as valuable assets.

- Collaborating with local, state, regional, and national organizations that promote technical cooperation.

- Serving as an interagency forum to develop and strengthen nationwide technology transfer in support of national policy.

For More Information about the FLC

FLC Management Support Office

950 North Kings Hwy, Suite 208

Cherry Hill, NJ 08034

Phone: 856-667-7727

Fax: 856-667-8009

www.federallabs.org

NASA Regional Technology Transfer Centers

The NASA Regional Technology Transfer Centers' (RTTCs) mission is to transfer and assist in the commercialization of NASA and other federal technology. RTTC consultants assist in the identification, evaluation, acquisition, and adaptation of technology to meet specific business needs. The centers, divided along geographic boundaries, each rely on an affiliate network to provide direct and timely service to companies and other organizations. The RTTCs help companies locate, access, acquire, and use technologies and expertise within federal laboratories, state programs, and private industry.

For More Information

To contact your RTTC, call 800-472-6785 or visit www.usrttc.org.

National Technology Transfer Center

The National Technology Transfer Center (NTTC) helps businesses access NASA and other federal technology resources by matching specific needs of the business with the appropriate NASA or federal resource. The NTTC will search NASA and federal databases and will expedite communication with NASA or federal laboratory experts who may assist with solutions. The NTTC works closely with the Federal Lab Consortium, the NASA Regional Technology Transfer Centers, and other organizations interested in technology transfer for commercialization purposes.

The NTTC also operates a national electronic bulletin board service for the public and private sectors. The free service includes announcement of new technologies, answering of questions on technical problems, and notices of technology transfer conferences and meetings. The bulletin board also includes a number of searchable databases.

For More Information on the NTTC

National Technology Transfer Center

Wheeling Jesuit University

316 Washington Avenue

Wheeling, WV 26003

Phone: (800) 678-6882

Fax: (304) 243-2523

www.nttc.edu

The National Technical Information Service

The National Technical Information Service (NTIS) serves as the largest central resource for government-funded scientific, technical, engineering, and business-related information available today. For more than 60 years NTIS has provided businesses, universities, and the public timely access to approximately 3 million publications covering over 350 subject areas.

For More Information on NTIS

Office of Customer Services

National Technical Information Service

5285 Port Royal Road

Springfield, VA 22161

Phone: (888) 584-8332 or (803) 605-6050

www.ntis.gov

Federal Research in Progress Database

The Federal Research in Progress (FEDRIP) database provides access to information about ongoing federally funded projects in the fields of the physical sciences, engineering, and life sciences. The ongoing research announced in FEDRIP is an important component to the technology transfer process in the United States. In 2008 it included over 190,000 preliminary, ongoing, or final project reports. Each FEDRIP entry includes title, principal investigator, performing and sponsoring organization, detailed abstract, project objectives, and sometimes intermediate findings and funding amount. The summaries provide up-to-date research progress in specific technical areas before technical reports or journal articles are published. Updates to the database are done monthly.

For More Information on FEDRIP

To subscribe:

NTIS Subscriptions Department

5285 Port Royal Road

Springfield, VA 22161

Phone: (800) 363-2068

http://grc.ntis.gov/fedrip.htm

The Small Business Innovation Research Program

Many high-technology companies started up with a government research and development (R&D) grant or contract. If your company has the ability to do technological R&D and has the interest and ability to commercialize that product or service that you develop, you should consider applying to the Small Business Innovation Research (SBIR) program. The SBIR program is a multi-agency federal research and development program coordinated through, but not managed by, the SBA. The SBIR program began in 1982 with the enactment of the Small Business Innovation Development Act. The SBIR program aims to fund scientifically sound research proposals that will, if successful, meet the missions of the participating federal agencies and have strong commercial potential. SBIR's primary objectives are to:

- Increase small firm participation in federal R&D.
- Foster commercial applications from applied federal research.
- Encourage innovation for public benefit.

The SBIR program involves a competitive three-phase award system that provides qualified small business concerns with opportunities to propose innovative studies that meet the specific R&D needs of the various agencies of the federal government:

- Phase 1: SBIR awardees receive up to $100,000 to evaluate the scientific merit and technical feasibility of an idea. The period of performance normally does not exceed six months. Only Phase 1 awardees are eligible for consideration in Phase 2.

- Phase 2: Awardees receive up to $750,000 to develop prototypes, finalize products, and further expand on the research results of Phase 1. The period of performance normally does not exceed two years.

- Phase 3: Firms try to commercialize the results of Phase 2. Despite its classification as Phase 3, this stage requires the use of private or non-SBIR federal funding. No SBIR funds are utilized in Phase 3. However, Phase 3 may involve production contracts with a federal agency for future use by the federal government.

From the start of the SBIR program in 1982 through fiscal year 2007, the participating federal agencies made almost 100,000 competitive awards totaling $22.4 billion to qualified small business concerns. Many firms of 10 or fewer employees have won funding for their proposals. In fiscal year 2007 small businesses successfully competed for approximately 3,900 Phase I and 1,600 Phase 2 awards under the SBIR program. These awards in total were worth over $2 billion.

The Small Business Technology Transfer Program

The Small Business Technology Transfer (STTR) program encourages the fostering of partnerships between small businesses and nonprofit research institutions (in many cases universities). The five largest federal agencies, as determined by their extramural R&D budget, are required by STTR to set aside 0.3 percent of their R&D budget for awards to small business/nonprofit research institution partnerships. Participating agencies are the Department of Defense, Department of Energy, Health and Human Services, National Aeronautics and Space Administration, and National Science Foundation.

The STTR, like the SBIR program, involves a competitive three-phase award system.

- Phase 1: STTR awardees receive up to $100,000 for the exploration of the scientific, technical, and commercial feasibility of an idea or technology. The period of performance is approximately one year. Only Phase 1 awardees are eligible for Phase 2 awards.
- Phase 2: Awardees receive up to $500,000 to expand R&D results and commercial potential. The period of performance is a maximum of two years.
- Phase 3: Firms try to commercialize the results from Phase 2. No STTR funds are available for Phase 3; however, awardees may pursue other federal agency funding.

To be eligible for STTR funding, the business must be for-profit; must be at least 51 percent owned and controlled by individuals who are citizens of, or lawfully admitted permanent residents of, the United States; and, including affiliates, may not have more than 500 employees. The non-profit research institution must be located in the United States. The principal researcher, unlike in the SBIR program, does not have to be an employee of the business.

Exhibit 9.2 provides a summary of these aspects of SBIR and STTR.

How to Apply for an SBIR or STTR Award

Although the SBA sponsors various SBIR/STTR conferences and seminars in every state, the agency does not distribute copies of SBIR or STTR solicitations. The participating federal agencies responsible for generating SBIR and STTR topics and conferring awards release their own solicitation announcements. However, the SBA collects solicitation information from participating agencies and publishes it quarterly in its electronic Pre-Solicitation Announcement (PSA). PSAs provide the following information:

- The research topics of current interest to each participating agency.
- The opening and closing dates of each solicitation.
- Whom to contact for a copy of the agency solicitation.

	SBIR	STTR
Phase I Level of Effort	Minimum of two-thirds of the effort must be performed by small business.	Minimum of 40 percent of the effort must be performed by small business.
	Maximum of one-third of the effort may be performed by consultants and/or subcontractors.	Minimum of 30 percent of the effort must be performed by a nonprofit research institution.
Phase II Level of Effort	Minimum of 50 percent of the effort must be performed by small business.	(Same as Phase I)
	Maximum of 50 percent of the effort may be performed by consultants and/or subcontractors.	(Same as Phase I)
Subcontractors	May have subcontractors involved.	Must have non-profit research institute involved as subcontractor.
Project Duration	Phase I—approximately six months	Phase I—Approximately one year.
	Phase II—2 years	Phase II—2 years
Maximum Award Amount	Phase I—$100,000	Phase I—$100,000
	Phase II—$750,000	Phase II—$750,000
Number of Agencies Participating	Ten	Five
Principal Investigator	Must be employed with small business.	May be employed with either small business or nonprofit research institution. (This requirement varies among agencies.)

Exhibit 9.2   SBIR and STTR Facts

For More Information about SBIR and STTR Awards

U.S. Small Business Administration

Office of Technology

409 Third Street SW

Washington, DC 20416

Phone: (202) 205-6450

http://www.sba.gov/sbir

TECH-Net

TECH-Net is an electronic portal of resources and information for and about technology-based small businesses. It contains a database of SBIR and STTR awardees. It is a free service for those seeking small business partners, small business contractors and subcontractors, research partners, manufacturing centers, and investors. Businesses profiled on the TECH-Net system can be searched by location, company name, phase, agency, award year, and more. To visit the TECH-Net database, go to www.sba.gov and type "tech-net" into the search box.

Technology Innovation Program

The National Institute of Standards and Technology supports the Technology Innovation Program (TIP). Created in 2007 as part of the America COMPETES Act, TIP was established to support, promote, and accelerate innovation in the United States through high-risk, high-reward research areas of critical national need. TIP defines high-risk, high-reward as research that (a) has the potential for yielding transformational results with far-ranging implications; (b) addresses critical national needs that support, promote, and accelerate innovation in the United States and is within NIST's areas of technical competence; and (c) is too novel or spans too diverse a range of disciplines to fare well in the traditional peer-review process. The program will fund small and medium-size businesses, universities, and research consortia on a competitive, cost-share basis for research on potentially revolutionary technologies.

TIP can fund single company projects for up to $3 million over three years, contingent to the rules on matching funds. TIP will fund no more than 50 percent of total projects costs, and its funds may be used only for so-called direct costs, not indirect costs (such as overhead), profits, or management fees. No TIP funding may go to a large company.

How to Find TIP

Proposals must be submitted to specifically dated solicitations. To get your name on the mailing list for solicitation announcements, contact:

> National Institute of Standards and Technology
>
> Technology Innovation Program
>
> 100 Bureau Drive, Stop 4701
>
> Administration Building 101, Room A407
>
> Gaithersburg, MD 20899-4701
>
> Phone: (888) TIP-NIST or (888) 847-6478
>
> www.nist.gov/tip

Inventions and Innovations Program

Inventions and Innovation (I&I), part of the U.S. Department of Energy's Technology Innovation Program (TIP), provides grants to independent inventors and small companies with sound ideas for energy efficiency technologies. I&I was established in 1976 as the Energy Related Inventions Program (ERIP). The program received initial funding of $1,500,000 and through 2000 received cumulative funding of $116,838,000. More than 25 percent of I&I grantees have been successful in entering the marketplace.

I&I supports energy efficiency and renewable energy technology development in focus areas that align with the Department of Energy related programs, including biomass;

building technologies; vehicle technologies; geothermal technologies; hydrogen, fuel cells, and infrastructure technologies; industrial technologies; solar energy; weatherization; and wind and hydropower technologies. Once or twice each year, I&I solicits proposals from engineers, scientists, and small businesses. These solicitations can attract from 400 to 500 proposals each, and result in 20 to 30 awards. The awards are given at two levels: up to $50,000 for technologies in early stage development and up to $250,000 for technologies approaching the point of prototype. Cost-share is strongly encouraged.

In addition to competitively awarded financial assistance, I&I provides awardees with business planning assistance and networking resources. For grantees who demonstrate a commitment to commercializing their technology, I&I also funds a market assessment and offers business strategy assistance. I&I recently launched Energy TechNet, a web site that offers information tools and valuable network resources for the entrepreneur. Finally, awardees have the option of working with a private organization of past successful grantees that will mentor or otherwise aid new entrepreneurs graduating from I&I. Since I&I's inception, over 34,000 proposals have been submitted, resulting in over 900 projects selected for financial and commercialization assistance.

How to Find I&I

U.S. Department of Energy – Inventions and Innovation

1000 Independence Avenue S

Washington, DC 20585-0121

Phone: (877) 337-3463

www1.eere.energy.gov/inventions/energytechnet

External Assistance Available Primarily to State and Local Residents

State Resources

State, local, and regional development agencies imitate, support, and expand federal efforts to help start-ups and small businesses. Like the federal agencies, their services target business development, start-up and small business financing, procurement, and international trade. Their clients include women, minorities, entrepreneurial ventures in rural or depressed areas, and technologically oriented start-ups.

Your first stop should be your state department of commerce, a useful starting place for finding other resources, such as those national programs described in this chapter, and other state-, regional-, and local-sponsored management assistance and financial support programs. This management and technical assistance may range from business planning to licensing, helping firms locate capital, and finding state and federal procurement opportunities. They typically offer state certification programs for businesses owned by minorities and women.

Local Resources

Chambers of Commerce

These are city-based groupings of local businesses that often provide assistance for firms wishing to relocate or start operations in the city. Chambers often provide information packages on local regulations and taxes. They also work closely with economic development organizations to lobby the city government for more favorable business conditions. They have traditionally provided a setting for business leaders, including entrepreneurs, to network and discuss common problems.

Incubators

Incubators nurture fledgling firms that share services and equipment and occupy building space at a reduced rate. Nationwide there are about 1,100 incubators, more than double what existed 10 years ago. Businesses graduating from incubators have an 87 percent success rate, which is higher than the average success rate.[4] In addition to low-cost shelter and services, one of the biggest benefits provided by incubators is the support and counsel provided by a network of business assistant professionals.

Where to Find Incubators

National Business Incubation Association

20 E. Circle Drive, #37198

Athens, OH 45701

Phone: 740-593-4331

www.nbia.org

University Libraries

Although they have no direct charter to assist start-ups, many university business libraries, particularly those at public universities, are dedicated to serving the information needs of business. They offer reasonably priced information services, including:

- Photocopies or book loans.
- Government publications.
- Company reports—annual or 10K.
- Scientific or technical information.
- Business management information.
- Market or product studies.
- Reviews of computer hardware or software.
- Tax or legal information searches.
- Patent and trademark searches.
- Technical standards and specifications.
- Consumer profiles and census data.

- Corporate financial information.
- Mailing labels.
- Other search help.

Public Libraries

The business sections of city-funded public libraries also provide useful resources.

Summary

This chapter describes a number of federal, state, and local resources that are available for entrepreneurs and small business owners to start, improve, and grow their businesses. Although it may not always be easy to find the information you need to identify the best programs for your situation, it can be worth the effort to search web sites and make phone calls to the most likely organizations with programs to assist you. You might start with the Small Business Development Center in your area as they have information about various federal, state, and local programs and can answer your questions or refer you to the appropriate contact. One thing to keep in mind is that programs change. Agencies regularly eliminate or modify existing programs or add new programs, so it is worthwhile to check back on a regular basis.

Downloadable Resources for this chapter available at www.wiley.com/go/portablembainentrepreneurship

Where to Find SBDC's

Notes

1. A. L. Riding and G. Haines, Jr., "Loan Guaranties: Costs of Default and Benefits to Small Firms," *Journal of Business Venturing* 16, no. 6 (2001): 595–612.
2. Stacy Cowley, "Message to Obama: Send Loans Fast," CNNMoney.com, November 16, 2008, http://money.cnn.com/2008/11/14/smallbusiness/loans_needed_asap.smb/index.htm?postversion=2008111608.
3. "Senate Sends Economic Recovery Package with Key Small Business Assistance to President's Desk," U.S. Senate Committee on Small Business & Entrepreneurship press release, February 13, 2009, http://sbc.senate.gov/press/record.cfm?id=308318&.
4. University of Michigan, National Business Incubation Association, Ohio University, and Southern Technology Council, *Business Incubation Works: The Results of the Impact of Incubator Investments Study* (Athens, OH: NBIA Publications, 1997).

10

Legal and Tax Issues

Richard Mandel

How This Chapter Fits Into a Typical MBA Curriculum
The legal issues and concepts discussed in this chapter are often encountered in a basic business law course in MBA programs, although, sadly, more and more MBA programs are dispensing with such courses. The tax concepts discussed in this chapter will often turn up in a separate course in federal taxation. Alternatively, some enlightened MBA programs contain electives with names such as Entrepreneurial Law, which normally will cover virtually all the concepts included in this chapter.

Who Uses This Material in the Real World—And Why It Is Important
The material in this chapter is not meant to be used by entrepreneurs as a substitute for consultation with legal and tax professionals. Yet anyone who has dealt with lawyers and accountants will most likely agree that the quality (and cost) of that experience depends largely on the client's ability to ask the right questions and understand the advice received. This chapter is designed to give the entrepreneur much of the basic knowledge and context necessary to efficiently employ those professionals in the establishment and operation of a successful business.

The Entrepreneurs

Jake and Cori worked in the Operations department of a large movie studio, so they were acutely aware of a revolutionary development about to take place in the industry. In fact, they were somewhat surprised it had not happened earlier. Up until now, whenever a movie was finished and ready for distribution to theaters all over the world, the studio had engaged in the extremely expensive process of making hundreds of copies of the film to be distributed to exhibitors and run on their projectors. The cost of making these copies was significant, as was the cost of shipping these heavy and bulky packages and ensuring their security from theft and piracy. It had recently been announced that most of the large movie studios were planning to abandon this practice and distribute their movies as digital computer files.

At least part of the reason this change in distribution method had not already taken place was the strong objections of the exhibitors. Similar to the conversion from silent to sound movies, this development would require theatres to replace all their current projection systems with costly new digital systems. Such systems were becoming available from a few overseas manufacturers at relatively steep prices. Jake and Cori believed that the distribution of such systems to the exhibitors represented another potentially significant source of revenue for the movie studios, but their idea had thus far fallen upon deaf ears. The studios were not interested in branching out into the purchase, resale, and financing of equipment.

But Jake and Cori were undeterred. If their studio wasn't interested, they were certain they could make this idea a success as an independent business. They knew that in addition to their own limited resources they would need significant bank and investor financing to purchase inventory and establish a distribution network. Fortunately, they had run the idea by a few potential investors and already received some encouragement. Through their own jobs, Jake and Cori were familiar with the overseas manufacturers of digital equipment and knew they were looking for distribution in the States. And the two entrepreneurs were friendly with a number of their fellow studio employees who dealt with the exhibitors on a regular basis. Immensely excited about the upside potential of their idea, Cori and Jake prepared to submit their resignations to the studio.

Leaving Your Present Position

Many enthusiastic entrepreneurs are so excited about where they are going that they forget to consider where they have been. Many are surprised to learn that there may be serious limitations imposed upon their freedom of action arising out of their former employment. Some of these limitations may be the result of agreements signed by the entrepreneur while employed in her former position. Others may be imposed as a matter of law without any agreement or even knowledge on the part of the employee.

Corporate Opportunity

The corporate opportunity doctrine is an outgrowth of the traditional obligation of loyalty owed by an agent to a principal. In its most common form, it prohibits an officer or director of a corporation, a partner in partnership, or persons in similar positions from identifying a business opportunity which would be valuable to his company and using that information for his own benefit or the benefit of a competitor.

Thus, a corporate director who discovers that one of the corporation's competitors may shortly be put on the market cannot raise money and purchase the competitive company himself. In order to discharge his legal obligation to the corporation of which he is a director, he would be required to disclose the opportunity to his board of directors and allow the board to decide (without his participation) whether the corporation will make the purchase. Only after the corporation has been fully informed and decided not to take advantage of the opportunity may the director use that information for himself. Even then, as the new owner of a competitor, he would be required to resign from his position with the other business.

The scope of this duty of loyalty is normally adjusted by the law to reflect the individual's position within the business. While the president and members of the board may be required to turn over knowledge of all opportunities that may be in any way related to the business of the company, lower-level employees probably have such an obligation only with regard to opportunities that are directly relevant to their positions. Thus, arguably, a sales manager may be required to inform her company of any sales opportunities she may encounter that are relevant to the company's products. She may not be required to inform the company of a potential business acquisition.

Cori and Jake should consider the corporate opportunity doctrine since the opportunity to distribute and finance digital projection equipment is at least indirectly relevant to the operations of a movie studio. Yet it is probably the case that both Cori and Jake have positions low enough in the company hierarchy that their responsibilities in regard to corporate opportunities are very limited. After all, they are not charged with the responsibility to decide how the exhibitors will obtain the new equipment. In fact, they have already presented this potential opportunity to their employer and have been met with indifference. They would be well advised to retain copies of any e-mails or other correspondence they generated in this regard.

Recruitment of Fellow Employees

As Jake and Cori delved more deeply into their dream, they began to identify certain fellow employees who might wish to join their company sometime down the road. This, too, can in some circumstances be problematic.

Another aspect of the duty of loyalty owed by an employee to an employer is the legal requirement that the employee not knowingly take action designed to harm the employer's business. This is, perhaps, pure common sense. After all, the employee is collecting a paycheck to perform tasks that advance the employer's interests. We would not expect the law to countenance a paid salesperson's regularly recommending that customers patronize a competitor, nor would we expect the law to endorse an engineer's giving his best ideas to another company. Similarly, courts have held that it is a breach of the duty of loyalty to solicit and induce fellow employees to leave their jobs.

Once again, the likelihood that a court would enforce this obligation against an employee depends to some extent on the nature of the employee's activities and her position in the company. Neither Jake nor Cori need fear reprisals for their having convinced each other to leave. Nor would there be much likelihood of liability if they convinced another employee to leave with them, especially if these conversations took place after working hours. However, if either of them worked in the Human Resources department where their job descriptions would include recruiting and retention of employees, or if either were the vice president of the division for which the employees worked, this same activity might well expose them to liability. Further, if their plan included the wholesale resignations of a relatively large number of employees, such that the company's ability to continue to efficiently function might be compromised, a court might be more likely to intervene with injunctive or other relief. This would be especially true if the defendants' job descriptions included maintaining the efficient operation of the departments they were involved in destroying.

Proprietary Information

Another potential complication arising out of the present employment of Cori and Jake involves the possible use by them of information or technology belonging to their former employer. Such information need not be subject to formal patent or copyright protection to be protected from such use. Any information that the company has successfully kept confidential, and which is not otherwise known to outsiders, is likely to be protected by law as a trade secret. Such information may include inventions and technology, but may also include such other valuable information as customer lists, pricing strategies, and unique operating methods.

In this case, if Cori is aware of the technical specifications of a digital projection system only as a result of her job responsibilities, that information might well belong to the company and be unavailable to Cori and Jake for their new enterprise. Or if their current employer had compiled an extensive list of exhibitors known only to the company, Cori and Jake might be prohibited from marketing to that list. Of course, it is not enough for a concept or list to be developed by or for the company; the information must be unique and unknown to the industry at large, and the company must have taken steps to keep it that way. Thus, the company should label any physical manifestations of the information as "confidential," and should restrict its distribution to those who have either a legal or contractual obligation to keep such information private. If, however, the company had deliberately or carelessly allowed the distribution of the information to outsiders, or if the information is generally known within the industry (as is probably true in this case), the company has likely lost the right to restrict its use.

Many companies require their employees to sign agreements that specifically spell out the employees' obligation to protect trade secrets. This has led some employees to believe that such an obligation must only attach to those who have signed such an agreement, leaving the remaining employees free to make whatever use of their employers' information they may choose. This is a misconception, however. The obligation to respect an employer's trade secrets and keep them confidential is imposed by law and is not dependent upon contract. Furthermore, that obligation continues after the employment relationship has been terminated, for whatever reason, and continues indefinitely until the information makes its way into the public domain by other means.

Employers who require a confidentiality agreement from their employees are generally not misinformed about the general applicability of the law; they normally require the agreement as a method of making sure that their employees are aware of their responsibilities in this regard. After all, if an employee, under a mistaken belief about his rights, releases proprietary information to the outside, it is small comfort to the employer that it may have the right to sue said employee for damages. And requiring employees to sign such agreements can be used as evidence that the employer has taken reasonable steps to keep its information confidential, thus making the information more likely to be deemed a trade secret.

Fortunately for Cori and Jake, they appear to have merely identified a need that is known generally to the industry. And the list of potential buyers is quite generally available. On this set of facts, it is extremely doubtful that this new enterprise will make use of any information that legally belongs to their former employer.

Noncompetition

Somewhat related to the obligation not to disclose proprietary information is the obligation not to compete with one's employer. Like most of the obligations discussed already, this obligation is derived from the fiduciary relationship between employer and employee, specifically the duty of loyalty. How can one justify accepting a paycheck from one's employer while one is simultaneously establishing, working for, or financing a competing business?

The law imposes this duty not to compete upon all employees, officers, directors, partners, and so on, while their association with the employer remains in effect. Unlike the obligation to protect proprietary information, however, this obligation does not extend to the period after the termination of the relationship. To accomplish such an extension of the obligation, the employer must obtain the contractual promise of the employee. Thus, in the absence of a contract, as soon as Jake and Cori quit their present jobs (but not before), they are free to go into direct competition with their former employer, so long as in doing so they do not make use of any of the employer's proprietary information.

Since in Jake and Cori's case there is no indication that they have signed a noncompetition agreement, they would need only to resign from their current positions before taking any affirmative steps to establish a competitive enterprise. After their resignations, they would be under no further noncompetitive restrictions. In this case, in fact, it is probable that Cori and Jake's new business would not be deemed competitive with their present employer at all. Thus they may be able to begin this business at night and on weekends while remaining employed by their present employer, so long as the time devoted to the new business does not detract from their obligation to devote their full business time to their present job. (Further information on employment agreements is in Chapter 11.)

Choosing an Attorney and Accountant

There is a natural reluctance to incur what are perceived as unnecessary expenses when beginning a new venture, and many people perceive engaging an attorney and accountant as just such expenses. However, as may already be evident from the preceding discussion, the earlier these professionals can be consulted, the more likely it is that the business will avoid costly mistakes. If an ounce of prevention is usually worth a pound of cure, there is no context in which that is truer than in avoiding early legal, accounting, or tax mistakes so as to avoid paying to clean them up later on.

The choice of an appropriate attorney is complicated by the fact that American law does not officially recognize legal specialties. Thus, in virtually all states, there is only one form of licensing; and once licensed, an attorney can practice in all areas of the law. In practice, however, the American legal profession has become highly specialized, with many attorneys confining their practices to one or two areas of expertise. Thus, most patent attorneys do very little else; and most good litigation attorneys concentrate on litigating. Few very good corporate attorneys know their way around a courtroom. Just as these legal areas are practiced mainly by specialists, the representation of start-ups and small businesses has become a specialty as well.

Jake and Cori would do well to ask any prospective attorney to describe her experience in representing small businesses and to supply some clients as references. The local generalist may not be sufficiently aware of the many technical matters identified in this chapter and elsewhere in this volume. Also, an attorney experienced in the problems of start-ups will be familiar with the unique cash flow problems of such ventures. A business may never have a greater need for legal services in comparison with its ability to pay than at the outset. The attorney may be willing to work out installment payments or other arrangements to avoid postponing essential early planning.

Unfortunately, during the Internet bubble of the late 1990s, many attorneys practicing in this area adopted a policy of accepting equity in the new business as part of the fee arrangement. Interestingly, many such attorneys did not lower their fees in exchange for equity, but justified taking equity as the price of accepting the risk that their fee might not be paid if the business did not succeed. Such an arrangement led, in some cases, to dangerous conflicts of interest, as legal advice affected the value of the company's stock. For example, can one be confident of an attorney's advice regarding the suitability of the company for a public offering, when such an offering would have the effect of creating a market for the same attorney's stock? After the Internet bubble burst, many law firms understandably discontinued the practice of taking equity as fees. Even if such arrangements were still offered, however, Jake and Cori may wish to avoid such an arrangement if possible.

Many of the same considerations inform the choice of an accountant. Although the level of expertise in the national and international firms is unmatched, most of them have little experience with start-ups such as that proposed by Jake and Cori since their fee structures are inappropriate for the size of such businesses. Many local firms have all the skills necessary to serve the start-up and can be sensitive to the cash flow issues mentioned earlier.

It is important to engage the accountant as early as possible so she can establish the information management systems and recommend the computer software which will get the company's records off on the right track. This gives the entrepreneur the tools necessary to gauge the success of his efforts against budget before it is too late to adapt, and avoids the expensive and frustrating task of reconstructing the company's results from fragmented and missing records at the end of the year.

Choice of Legal Form

Forms Available

One of the first issues Cori, Jake, and their professional advisers will confront, after weaving their way through the thicket of issues associated with leaving their current jobs, is what legal form they should choose to operate their new venture. Many choices are available.

The most basic business form, and the one that will result unless an entrepreneur chooses otherwise, is the *sole proprietorship*. This is a business owned and operated by one owner who is in total control. No new legal entity is created; the individual entrepreneur just goes into business, either alone or with employees, but without any co-owners. This is the simplest of entities but will not be attractive to Cori and Jake unless one of them chooses to forgo ownership and act only as an employee.

The default mode for Jake and Cori is the *general partnership*. This is the legal form that results when two or more persons go into business for profit, as co-owners, sharing profits and losses. Since Jake and Cori clearly contemplate sharing ownership and control, they will find themselves in a partnership unless they affirmatively choose otherwise.

Another choice available to our entrepreneurs is the *corporation*. This form is created by state government, as a routine matter, upon the entrepreneurs' filing an application and paying a fee. It is a separate legal entity, with legal existence apart from its owners, the stockholders. Cori and Jake might well choose to form a corporation, allocating its stock initially between them.

A variation of the corporate choice is the so-called *subchapter S* or *small business corporation*. If a corporation passes a number of tests, it may elect to be treated as such. However, it is essential to understand that such election affects only the tax status of the corporation. In all other respects, a subchapter S corporation is indistinguishable from all other corporations.

Another variation of the corporate form is the so-called *professional corporation*. This type of corporation is typically available only to businesses that intend to render professional services, such as medical or legal practices, accountants, architects, social workers, and the like. It was originally created primarily to allow these professionals to take advantage of certain tax opportunities available only to corporations, without granting them the limited liability afforded by normal business corporations. Over time, however, many of the tax advantages formerly available only to corporations have been extended to sole proprietorships and partnerships, and some of the limited liability formerly associated with business corporations has been extended to professional corporations. Thus, the differences between these forms have narrowed considerably. In any case, Jake and Cori will not be practicing a profession, so this business form will not be available to them.

Related to the professional corporation is the *limited liability partnership* (LLP), an entity that has become widely available over the last 20 years or so. The limited liability partnership is a general partnership that has elected, by filing documents with the state and paying a fee, to grant limited liability to its partners. This entity is thought to differ from other forms of limited liability entity in two ways: (1) as in a general partnership, all partners owe strict fiduciary obligations to each other; and (2) laws prohibiting mandatory retirement ages for employees may not apply to partners (as opposed to employees). These differences tend to appeal to those groups of practicing professionals who used to operate as general partnerships when there was no available way to limit personal exposure. Thus, law firms, accounting firms, and the like tend to elect this business form, but it is not widely used by other businesses, such as the one planned by Jake and Cori.

Another possible legal form is a hybrid of the corporate and partnership forms, known as the *limited partnership*. Such a business would have one or more general partners who would conduct the business and take on personal risk, and one or more limited partners who would act as passive investors (similar to stockholders with no other interest in the business). Since both Jake and Cori intend to be actively involved in the business, neither would qualify as a limited partner. And as it is difficult to find many managers who would be willing to take on personal exposure for the risks of the business, this form of entity has over time faded to only a few niche uses. One finds limited partnerships in use by a number of venture capital and hedge funds, and in recent years they have come into use as an estate planning technique, but they are no longer attractive to most businesses.

An increasingly popular form of business entity is the *limited liability company* (LLC). These entities are owned by *members*, who either manage the business themselves or appoint *managers* (either outsiders or a subset of the members) to run it for them. All members and managers have the benefit of limited liability (as they would in a corporation) and, in most cases, are taxed similarly to a subchapter S corporation without having to conform to the S corporation restrictions described later in this chapter.

A summary of the available business forms should not omit the possibility of the *not-for-profit* (or *nonprofit*) entity. Typically, such a business will take the form of a corporation or trust, and elect not-for-profit status as a tax matter. Although many start-ups do not make a profit, not-for-profit status is available only to certain types of activities, such as churches, educational institutions, social welfare organizations, industry associations, and the like. If an organization so qualifies, its income is exempt from taxation (as long as it doesn't stray from its exempt purpose), and if certain additional tests are met, contributions to it may be tax deductible. Since Cori and Jake plan to operate their business as a profit-making venture, distributing profits to themselves and investors, we need not further explore this option.

Faced with all these choices, a budding entrepreneur will want to compare these various business forms on a number of measures relevant to the needs of his business. Both the attorney and the accountant for the business can be extremely helpful at this stage. Although these forms may be compared on an almost endless list of factors, those normally most relevant include control issues, exposure to personal liability, tax factors, and administrative costs. These issues are discussed in detail in the following sections, and Exhibit 10.1 provides an overview of the issues and how they play out in each business form.

Control

The sole proprietorship is the simplest and most direct on the subject of control. Since there is only one principal in the business, he wields total control over all issues. However, that option is not available to Jake and Cori.

The simplest option that is available to them would be the general partnership. In that mode, control is divided among the principals in accordance with their partnership agreement. Although a written agreement is normally not legally required, this and many other issues that arise in a partnership argue for a written agreement to encourage specificity. The parties may decide that all decisions must be made by unanimous vote, or they may adopt a majority standard (making their angel investor the swing vote). More likely, they may require unanimity for a stated group of significant decisions, and allow a majority vote on others. In addition, Cori and Jake may delegate authority for certain types of decisions to one or both of the active partners.

Regardless of how this power is allocated in the partnership agreement, however, third parties are allowed to rely on the authority of any partner to bind the partnership to contracts relevant to the ordinary course of the partnership's business. Thus, no matter what may have been agreed among them, each of the partners will have a free hand with third parties, subject only to the consequences of his breaching his agreement with the others. This is also true for the consequences of torts committed by any partner acting in the course of partnership business.

All the preceding statements apply equally to the limited liability partnership (since it is merely a general partnership that has elected liability protection), a form of business not likely to appeal to Jake and Cori, as previously explained. The looseness of these rules in general partnerships may well also be enough to discourage Cori and Jake from choosing the general partnership option.

A corporation, whether professional or business, and regardless of whether it has elected subchapter S status, is controlled by three levels of authority. Broadly speaking, the stockholders vote, in proportion to the number of shares owned, on the election of the board of directors, sale or dissolution of the business, and amendments to the corporation's charter. In virtually all cases, these decisions are made either by the majority or two-thirds of the votes cast. Thus, if Jake, Cori, and an investor each owned one-third of the issued stock, Jake and Cori (if they voted together) could elect the entire board and sell the business over the objections of the investor. Unless agreed otherwise, the investor would not even be entitled to a minority position on the board. He would, however, be the swing vote should Cori and Jake ever disagree, perhaps prompting them to consider nonvoting stock or some similar device for the investor.

The board of directors, in turn, makes all the long-term and significant policy decisions for the business, as well as electing the officers of the corporation. Votes are virtually

Exhibit 10.1   Comparison of Various Business Forms

	Control	Liability	Taxation	Administrative Obligations
Sole proprietorship	Owner has complete control	Unlimited personal liability	Not a separate taxable entity	Only those applicable to all businesses
Partnership	Partners share control	Joint and several unlimited personal liability	Not a separate taxable entity	Only those applicable to all businesses
Corporation	Control distributed among shareholders, directors, and officers	Limited personal liability	Separate taxable entity unless subchapter S election	Some additional
Limited partnership	General partners control, limited partners do not	General partners: joint and several unlimited personal liability; limited partners: limited personal liability	Not a separate entity unless affirmatively chosen	Some additional
Limited liability company	Members share control or appoint managers	Limited personal liability	Not a separate entity unless affirmatively chosen	Some additional

always decided by majority. The officers, consisting of a president, treasurer, and secretary at a minimum, run the day-to-day business of the corporation and, as such, are the only level of authority that can bind the corporation by contract or in tort. In this case, one would expect either Jake or Cori to be president and the other, perhaps, to be executive vice president and treasurer. Other commonly used titles are chief executive officer, chief operating officer, chief financial officer, vice president, and so on. We might also expect that Cori and Jake would convince investors not to insist upon titles, thus eliminating their power to deal with third parties on the corporation's behalf.

The limited partnership (not likely a viable option for Jake and Cori, as previously explained) concentrates all control in the general partners, who exercise that control as set forth in the limited partnership agreement (just as such control is allocated in a general partnership agreement). Limited partners have virtually no control, unless the limited partnership agreement has granted them some influence over significant issues such as sale of the business or dissolution. Only the general partners have the apparent authority to bind the partnership in contract or tort with third parties. Since the limited partnership is required to file the names of its general partners with the state, third parties are deemed to know that limited partners (whose names do not appear) cannot have such authority.

The limited liability company can be operated much like a general partnership. All members can share in control to the extent set forth in their agreement, known in most states as an *operating agreement*. However, members may choose to appoint one or more managers to control most of the day-to-day operations of the business. In the case of Cori, Jake, and their investors, we might expect the members to appoint Cori and Jake as managers to avoid giving the investors the obligation and authority to deal with outsiders on behalf of the business.

Based upon control issues alone, therefore, Jake and Cori would likely be leaning away from a general partnership and toward the limited partnership, limited liability company, or corporation. Their decision will, however, be greatly affected by considerations of personal liability.

Personal Liability

Should the business incur current liabilities beyond its ability to pay, must the individual owners of the business make up the difference? If so, this could easily result in personal bankruptcy for the owners on top of the loss of their business. And this unhappy result need not occur only as a result of poor management or bad business conditions. It could just as easily be brought about by an uninsured tort claim from a buyer of the product or a victim of a delivery person's careless driving.

In both the partnership and the sole proprietorship, the business is not recognized as a legal entity separate from its owners. Thus the debts of the business are ultimately the debts of the owners if the business cannot pay. This unlimited liability is enough to recommend avoidance of these forms for virtually any business, with the exception perhaps of the one-person consulting firm, all of whose liability will be the direct result of the wrongdoing of its owner in any case.

If this unlimited liability is uncomfortable for Cori and Jake, imagine what it would mean to an investor. Such a person no doubt has significant assets to lose and will likely have only limited control over the business decisions that may generate liability. This is made even worse by the fact that all partnership liabilities are considered joint and several obligations of all partners. Thus, the investor will be responsible for full payment of all partnership liabilities if Cori and Jake have no significant assets of their own.

Investors can gain solace from the fact that in trading away their influence over the operation of the business in a limited partnership, they are granted limited liability for its debts. Thus, if the limited partnership cannot meet its obligations, an investor will lose his investment, but his personal assets will not be exposed to partnership creditors except to the extent, if any, that he may have made promises of future investment.

However, the limited partnership does not afford this protection to the general partners. They retain unlimited exposure. Jake and Cori may believe they can afford to take this risk, especially if they have no significant assets. Yet even if that is so today, it may not be the case at the time liability is incurred, and absent personal bankruptcy, judgments remain collectible for a long period of time.

The solution to all this lies in the corporation and the limited liability company, both of which afford limited liability to all owners. None of the owners of our enterprise would have personal liability for its debts. If the business ultimately becomes insolvent, its creditors will look only to business assets for payment; any shortfall will be absorbed by the unfortunate creditors. Such protection is also afforded to the owners of a limited liability partnership, for those specialized enterprises who may choose to employ that form of entity.

This solution is not quite as all-encompassing as it sounds. To begin with, creditors know these rules equally as well as the entrepreneurs. Thus, large or sophisticated creditors, such as banks and other financial institutions, will insist upon personal guarantees from the owners of the business before extending credit. In addition, the law has developed a number of theories that allow creditors to pierce the corporate veil and go after the owners of a failed corporation or LLC under certain conditions. Generally, these fall into one of two general categories.

The first of these covers businesses that were initially underfunded or thinly capitalized. A business should start out with a combination of capital and liability insurance adequate to cover the claims to which it might normally expect to be exposed. As long as the capital was there at the outset and has not been depleted by dividends or other distributions to owners, causing insolvency, the protection of the separate entity survives even after the capital has been depleted by unsuccessful operation.

The second situation that may result in the piercing of the corporate (or LLC) veil is the failure of the owners to treat the corporation or limited liability company as an entity separate from themselves. This may be manifested by the entrepreneurs acting in one or more of the following ways:

- Failing to use *Inc.,Corp., LLC,* or a similar legal indicator when dealing with third parties.
- Commingling business and personal assets either in a personal bank account or by allowing unreimbursed personal use of corporate assets.
- Failing to keep business and legal records and hold regular directors, stockholders, or members meetings.

After all, why should creditors be required to respect the difference between the business and its owners when the owners themselves have not?

Assuming, however, that Jake and Cori will avoid conduct that would expose them to such personal liability, both the corporate and limited liability company forms should look rather attractive to them. No significant business decision should be made, however, without a look at the tax consequences.

Taxation

Once again, the simplest of the business forms to understand in regard to taxation is the sole proprietorship. The financial results of the business are calculated, and the profit or loss appears on the tax return of the sole owner. She can eliminate much of the profit by taking it out of the business as salary, but that has no tax effect as it simply increases taxable wages in the exact amount that it lowers profit. The tax rate applied to any profit would be the maximum marginal rate to which the taxpayer is exposed by the combination of this profit and all her other taxable income. If there is a loss, the results of the business act as a sort of tax shelter on the owner's return by offsetting an equal amount of other taxable income, if any.

As one might expect, the partnership acts in a manner very similar to the sole proprietorship. Since a partnership is not recognized as a separate legal entity, it pays no taxes itself (although in many cases it is required to file an informational tax return). Its profit or loss is reported by its partners on their personal returns. This includes any profit retained by the partnership and not distributed to the partners (resulting in so-called *phantom income*). The only complication is allocating the percentage of this profit or loss to be reported by each partner. This is normally determined by the allocations of profit and loss set forth in the partnership agreement by the partners themselves, so long as that allocation reflects a substantial economic reality.

The limited partnership is taxed in exactly the same way as the partnership, with profit and loss allocated among *all* partners, both general and limited, in accordance with the limited partnership agreement. Since the business contemplated by Cori and Jake is likely to lose money at the outset, the tax sheltering aspects of both the partnership and limited partnership may be attractive to investors who surely have other sources of income they would like to shelter.

Of the two, the limited partnership would be preferable, since by accepting limited partner status, the investors can have their tax shelter without being exposed to personal liability. They may be tempted to request that the agreement allocate 99 percent of the losses to the investors, since they likely need the shelter more than Cori and Jake do. However, unless investors contribute 99 percent of the capital and will receive a similar percentage of profit, such an allocation might run afoul of the "substantial economic reality" test without careful, professional tax planning.

Further obstacles to an investor's taking advantage of the possible tax shelter of early losses are presented by the passive loss and basis rules of the Internal Revenue Code. Simply stated, if an investor is not "materially participating" in the business (which would by definition be the case if he were a limited partner), any losses distributable to him from the business could be used to offset income generated only by other passive activities (such as investments in other limited partnerships). The losses could not shelter income from salaries, interest, or dividends from traditional portfolio investments. Furthermore, in no event can an owner use as a tax shelter losses that exceed his basis in his investment (normally the amount invested).

Were the business to be organized as a corporation, Jake and Cori would doubtless be warned about the bugaboo of *double taxation*. This fear results from the fact that a corporation *is* recognized as a separate legal entity for tax purposes, and thus pays a separate corporate level of income tax. Double taxation arises when the corporation makes a profit, pays tax on it, and distributes the remainder to its stockholders as a dividend. The stockholders must then pay income tax on the dividend, resulting in the same money being taxed twice (although at a reduced dividend rate the second time).

The same would be true if the corporation paid tax on its profit and then retained the remainder for operations. When the corporation or any of its stock is eventually sold, the increased value caused by that retention of earnings would be taxed to the selling stockholders as capital gain.

In reality, however, double taxation is more a myth to the small business than a legitimate fear. In fact, in most cases, it presents an opportunity for significant economic savings. To begin with, most small corporations lower or even eliminate their profit by increasing deductible salaries and bonuses for their owners. This can be done up to the point at which the compensation of these individuals is deemed "unreasonable" by the Internal Revenue Service. If profit is eliminated in this way, the owners will have removed their money from the corporation and will pay only their own individual income tax on it.

Conversely, if it is necessary to retain some of these earnings, the corporation will normally pay income tax at a *lower* rate than the stockholders would have, since tax will be imposed at the lowest marginal corporate rate, rather than at the stockholders' highest rate. When the corporation is later sold, the stockholders will be taxed at favorable capital gain rates and the corporation will have had the use of the money in the meantime to create greater value. Thus, it is the rare small corporation that will actually pay the much feared double tax.

Furthermore, if the corporation meets certain eligibility requirements, it can elect, under subchapter S of the Internal Revenue Code, to be taxed essentially as if it were a partnership. Whatever profit or loss it may generate will appear on the tax returns of the stockholders in proportion to the shares of stock they own, and the corporation will file only an informational return. To take advantage of this option, the corporation must have 100 or fewer stockholders, all of whom must be individuals (with some exceptions) and either resident aliens or citizens of the United States. The corporation can have only one class of stock (with the exception of classes based solely on differing voting rights) and is ineligible to participate in most multiple-entity corporate structures. Note that despite being commonly referred to as "small business corporations," there is no size limit on subchapter S eligibility.

The subchapter S election can be very useful in a number of circumstances. For example, if the business is expected to be profitable, and investors insist upon a share of those profits, Jake and Cori could not otherwise avoid double taxation by increasing salaries and bonuses. Since an investor performs no services for the business, any compensation paid to him would automatically be deemed "unreasonable." But under subchapter S, since there is no corporate tax, a dividend to the stockholders would only be taxed at the stockholder level.

If the business were to become extremely successful, Cori and Jake could reap the rewards without fear that their salaries might be attacked as "unreasonable," since, again, there are no corporate compensation deductions to disallow. An early subchapter S election can also avoid double tax should the corporation eventually sell all its assets and distribute the proceeds to the stockholders in liquidation.

Furthermore, if the business is expecting losses in the short term, the investors might be able to use their share of the losses (determined by percentage of stock) as a shelter (subject to the passive loss and basis considerations described earlier). Even Jake and Cori could use their share of losses against the salary from their former jobs in the earlier part of the year or against income earned by their spouses if they filed joint returns. However, as mentioned earlier, this advantage will be limited to the amount of their investment in the business, which is likely to be quite small. And Cori and Jake will find that a subchapter S election (and, for that matter, use of a limited liability company or limited liability partnership, all three of which are often referred to as *pass-through entities*) will make it difficult for them to receive tax-free employee benefits.

Having considered all of these factors, at this point Cori and Jake might wish to form a corporation, elect subchapter S treatment, and arrange their affairs such that when third parties invest in the business, such investors could make as much use of short-term losses as could be supported by the "substantial economic reality" and "passive loss" rules. However, since profits and losses in an S corporation must be allocated in accordance with stock ownership, and only one class of stock is allowed, any disproportionate allocation of losses to the investors would have to be accompanied by a disproportionate allocation to them of later profits. More creative allocations of profit, loss, and control could be accomplished in a general or limited partnership, but one or more of the owners would have to accept exposure to unlimited liability in those entities.

Limited liability companies were designed to solve exactly this problem. If structured carefully, they afford the limited liability and pass-through tax treatment of the S corporation, while avoiding the S corporation's restrictive eligibility requirements. Freed from these restrictions, limited liability companies can make use of creative allocations of profit, loss, and control that would constitute prohibited multiple classes of stock in the S corporation context. However, since limited liability companies (as well as limited partnerships and limited liability partnerships) are required to calculate their income and loss in accordance with partnership tax rules (as opposed to S corporations, which use corporate tax rules), there may be some negative effects from this choice. For example, certain tax-free methods of selling the company may not be available to a limited liability company. However, in some circumstances involving significant company borrowings, partnership tax rules may allow greater losses to pass through to those owners who are eligible to make use of them.

At this point in the analysis, Jake and Cori are probably still not sure of the solution. The limited liability company appears attractive since it shields all its owners from personal liability, and as managers, it might give them a measure of control of the company apart from the investors. The limited liability company would also allow them to allocate the maximum amount of short-term loss available under applicable tax rules to their investors, recognizing that Jake and Cori's small initial investment would make any such losses useless to them. However, the investors may also have little ability to use these losses due to their lack of material participation in the business. Worse yet, the investors would certainly not be enthusiastic at the notion of phantom income when the company's financial performance turns positive and earnings are retained to fuel growth. Perhaps a further investigation of the tax implications of initial investment will lead Cori and Jake to an answer.

Initial Investment of the Founders

Left to their own devices, Jake and Cori would likely arrange the issuance of their equity in the business for no tangible investment whatsoever. After all, they intend to look to investors for working capital in the short run, and their investment will be the services they intend to perform for the business in the future.

Historically, in the context of a corporation, such a plan would have run afoul of some rather anachronistic corporate legal restraints which required the consideration for stock issuances to take the form of present property or cash and to at least equal the par value of the stock issued. These rules have been eroded over the years, however, by a number of different developments such as no-par-value stock. These problems are minimized in limited liability companies and their cousins, such as limited partnerships and limited liability partnerships. In these business forms, tangible investments are merely reflected as credits to the member or partner's capital account, while service contributors normally are given no such credit.

Of more practical concern than these problems, however, is the fact that any property (including stock or membership interests) transferred to an employee in exchange for the employee's services is considered taxable income under the Internal Revenue Code. Thus, even if it were possible to issue Cori and Jake corporate stock in exchange for future services under corporate law, they would face an unexpected tax liability as a result.

The solution to all this in the corporate context may be to require Jake and Cori to reach into their limited resources and contribute some minimal cash amount to the corporation in exchange for their stock. So long as the cash amount exceeds the par value (which will be minimal or nonexistent), this would avoid the corporate and tax problems associated with issuance for future services. In the LLC or partnership context, the Internal Revenue Service will, in most cases, value the ownership interest granted to the partner or member as equivalent to the amount credited to the capital account. Thus, as long as a noncontributing owner's capital account begins at zero and grows only to the extent of future profits, there will be no current taxation at the time of issuance. However, as already noted, if Cori and Jake's minimal investment was the full extent of the business' initial capitalization, the limited liability protection (the so-called corporate veil) might well be in danger.

Of course, Cori and Jake will have no reason to fear exposure to personal liability on this account, since at approximately the same time that they will be making their minimal investment, the investors will be putting in the real money. Yet the participation of the investors may, in the corporate context, expose Cori and Jake to a danger they may believe they have successfully avoided. Since the investors will be paying substantially more for their stock than will Cori and Jake, the Internal Revenue Service will likely take the position that they are being afforded the opportunity for a bargain purchase in exchange for the services they are providing to their company. Thus, once again, Jake and Cori may be facing an unexpected income tax on the difference between the per-share price of the investors' stock and the price of theirs.

One way to solve this problem would be to postpone the investors' contribution until a time sufficiently remote from the date of Jake and Cori's investment that an argument can be made for an increase in the value of the corporation's stock. Aside from the essentially fictional nature of this approach, Cori and Jake probably cannot wait that long. In order to solve this problem in the corporate context, the parties must design a vehicle for the investors that is sufficiently different from Cori and Jake's interest so as to justify the higher price. As has previously been mentioned, this is taken care of in the LLC or partnership context by the difference in capital accounts. But the corporate context is a bit more complicated.

It may seem immediately advisable to create some sort of senior security for the investors, such as preferred stock with a liquidation preference of approximately the amount invested. In fact, assuming for a moment that the initial plan was to split the common stock equally among the parties, the investors would probably insist on such a security, since otherwise Jake and Cori could immediately after formation dissolve the corporation and walk away with two-thirds of the investors' money. The investors might also insist that their stock share in the company's growth in addition to having a preference upon liquidation, but this could be accommodated either by allowing the preferred stock to participate in profits remaining for distribution after dividend and liquidation preferences have been paid, or by providing for a right to convert the preferred stock to common stock at a fixed conversion price.

Demonstrating the sometimes frustrating interrelated character of tax and corporate law, however, the issuance of preferred stock would render a corporation ineligible for subchapter S status, as it would then have more than one class of stock. The LLC and its cousins are not bound by any such restriction.

Another solution to this problem could lie in the utilization of debt securities. If the investors pay for their stock the same price per share as was paid by Cori and Jake and inject the remainder of the investment in the form of a loan, Cori and Jake will not face taxable compensation income and the business will retain the opportunity to benefit from subchapter S, if desired.

Investment as debt also affords the investors the potential for future nontaxable distributions from the company in the form of debt repayment, and they also gain priority as creditors should the corporation be forced to liquidate. All the while, the investors protect participation in growth through the additional ownership of equity.

As with all benefits, it is possible to get too much of a good thing. Too high a ratio of debt to equity may expose all the owners to the accusation of thin capitalization, resulting in the piercing of the corporate (or LLC) veil. And abusively high debt/equity ratios or failure to respect debt formalities and repayment schedules might induce the Internal Revenue to reclassify the debt as equity, thus imposing many of the adverse tax results described earlier.

How does all of this inform the choice of entity, then? The investors' aversion to the LLC and other pass-through forms of entity has already been described. Essentially, the pass-through form exposes the investors to potential phantom income if the company does well, while failing to provide practical use of losses on their returns if the company loses money. By contrast, preferred stock in a C corporation provides the liquidation, dividend, participation, and conversion privileges that the investors desire without the risk of phantom income. And from Cori and Jake's point of view, issuance of preferred stock to their investors has the benefit of solving their potential income tax problems without saddling them with restrictive repayment schedules or the risk of unintended personal liability. The parties will likely agree on the C corporation as the best choice of entity in this case.

Administrative Obligations

Certain administrative obligations will be required no matter which business form Cori and Jake choose. For example, upon entering business, they should obtain an Internal Revenue Service federal identification number for their business. This will facilitate interaction with the federal government, including the filing of tax returns (real or informational) and the withholding of income and payroll taxes.

On the state level, the business should obtain a sales and use tax registration number, both to facilitate reporting and collection of such taxes and to qualify for exemption from such taxes when it purchases items for resale. A nonprofit entity has 18 months to file for and secure nonprofit status from the Internal Revenue Service. Furthermore, as earlier described, all business entities will incur a certain amount of additional accounting expense, specifically for the calculation and reporting of taxable profit and loss.

Corporations, limited liability companies, limited liability partnerships, and limited partnerships, however, bring some additional administrative burden and expense. All four must file an annual report with the state government in addition to their tax return. This document usually reports only the business's current address, officers, directors, managers, general partners, and similar information, but is accompanied by an annual maintenance fee. The fee, in addition to any income tax that the state may levy, must be paid to avoid eventual involuntary dissolution by the state.

In addition, corporations are sometimes formed under the laws of one state while operating in another. In particular, the state of Delaware has acquired the reputation of having a corporate law that is particularly sympathetic to management in dealing with stockholders, as well as having been thoroughly interpreted by its long history of complex corporate litigation. Although these are questionable advantages in the context of a small business (where management and stockholders are generally the same people), Delaware does offer the slight advantage of providing a method of calculating its fees that does not penalize a corporation for having a large number of authorized shares. This allows a corporation whose compensation strategy includes stock grants or stock options to use much larger numbers of shares in these grants, creating a psychological appearance of generosity which may not mathematically exist. Even corporations that have not adopted such a strategy often form in Delaware merely to share in an appearance of sophistication.

In all such cases, the corporation must not only pay initial and maintenance fees to the state of Delaware (or whichever state is chosen for formation) along with the costs of maintaining an address for service of process there, but must also pay initial and annual maintenance fees to qualify to do business in each state in which it actually operates. Many large, national concerns pay these fees in virtually all 50 states. Although Cori and Jake could avoid these fees by operating as a partnership, it is likely they will conclude that the advantages of the corporate or limited liability forms are worth the price. They would likely be well advised, however, to form their entity in the same state as their operations in order to avoid duplicate fees. Reincorporation in Delaware can always occur in the future, generally just preceding a public offering.

Choosing a Name

The choice of a name for a business may seem at first to be a matter of personal taste, without many legal ramifications. However, since a business's name is ultimately the repository of its goodwill, care must be taken to choose a name that will not be confused with the name of another business. If such care is not exercised, the entrepreneur may discover sometime in the future that she has expended considerable money and effort enhancing the goodwill of another entity. Worse yet, she may be about to be sued for infringement of another's rights. These same considerations apply if the entrepreneur expects to use names for her products or services which are different from her company name.

Even apart from these concerns, an entrepreneur choosing to operate in the corporate, limited liability company, limited liability partnership, or limited partnership forms must clear her choice of name with the state of organization. Although partnerships and sole proprietorships need not do so, corporations, limited liability companies, limited liability partnerships, and limited partnerships obtain their existence by filing charters with the state. As part of this process, each state will check to see if the name chosen by the potential new entity is "confusingly similar" to the name used by any other entity currently registered with that state. This includes entities formed under that state's laws and also foreign entities qualified to do business there. Some states will also deny the use of a name they deem misleading, even if is not similar to the name of another entity.

Once Cori and Jake have chosen a name for their business and product, and elected the level of protection with which they are comfortable, they can turn their attention to the initial funding of their enterprise. (Further information on protecting corporate names and trade and service marks is in Chapter 11.)

Stockholder and Operating Agreements

The results of the negotiations among Cori, Jake, and their investors regarding their respective investments would normally be memorialized in an operating agreement in the case of an LLC and a combination of a Stock Purchase Agreement, Charter Amendments and Stockholders' Agreement in the case of a corporation. In the unlikely event that this business were to be organized as a partnership or limited partnership, very similar provisions allocating equity interests and rights to distributions of profit and cash flow would appear in a Partnership Agreement. In all these cases, however, the parties would be well advised to go beyond these subjects and reach written agreement on a number of other potentially thorny issues at the outset of their relationship.

Negotiating Employment Terms

As an example of such an issue, Jake and Cori should reach agreement with the investors as to the extent of their commitment to provide services and the level of compensation for doing so. It would be very unusual for persons in the position of Jake and Cori to forego compensation solely to share the profits of the business with their investor. For one thing, what would they be living on in the interim? For another, the profits of the business are properly conceived of as the amount left over after payment of the expenses of the business (including reasonable compensation to its employees). Thus, Cori and Jake should negotiate employment terms into the operating or stockholders agreement, setting forth their responsibilities, titles, compensation, and related issues.

This is especially important in this case, since each of the stockholders will likely hold only a minority interest in the corporation (depending upon the voting rights given to the preferred stock). Both Jake and Cori will wish to forestall the possibility that the investors might ally with one of them and employ a majority of the shares to remove the other as a director, officer, or employee of the company. Given the lack of any market for the shares of this corporation, such a move would essentially destroy any value the shares had for the holder in the short run.

Although a concise description of each party's obligations and rewards is still advisable to avoid dispute, the negative scenario just drawn would be illegal in a partnership (in the absence of serious misconduct by the party being removed) since the majority partners would be violating the fiduciary duty of loyalty imposed upon each partner toward the others under partnership law. Although no such duty formally exists among stockholders in a corporation, many states (not including Delaware) have imported the fiduciary duties of partners to the relationship among the founders of a closely held corporation. Similar doctrines may be developed for LLCs. Thus, in many states, were Cori to be removed without cause from her employment and corporate positions by Jake and the investors, she would have effective legal recourse even in the absence of a stockholder agreement.

Disposition of Equity Interests

As for other items that might be covered in the agreement among Cori, Jake, and the investors, many such agreements address the disposition of equity held by the owners under certain circumstances.

Transfer to Third Parties

To begin with, it is probably not contemplated by any of these persons that their stock will be freely transferable, such that they may have new partners imposed upon them by a selling stockholder. Although sale of stock in a close corporation or LLC is made rather difficult by federal and state securities regulation and the lack of any market for the shares, transfers are still possible under the correct circumstances. To avoid that possibility, stockholder and operating agreements frequently require that any owner wishing to transfer equity to a third party must first offer it to the company and/or the other owners, who may purchase the equity, often at the lower of a formula price or the amount being offered by the third party.

Disposition of Equity on the Owner's Death

Stockholder and operating agreements should also address the disposition of each owner's equity upon death. Again, it is unlikely that each owner would be comfortable allowing the deceased owner's stock to fall into the hands of the deceased's spouse, children, or other heirs, although this may be more acceptable in the case of a pure investor. Moreover, should the business succeed over time, each owner's equity may well be worth a significant amount upon death. If so, the Internal Revenue Service and many state governments will wish to impose an estate tax based upon the equity's value, regardless of the fact that it is an illiquid asset. Under such circumstances, the owner's estate may wish to have the assurance that some or all of such equity will be converted to cash so the tax may be paid. If the agreement forbids free transfer of the equity during the person's lifetime and requires that the equity be redeemed at death for a reasonable price, the agreement may well be accepted for tax purposes as a persuasive indication of the equity's value, thus also avoiding an expensive and time-consuming valuation controversy.

Any redemption provision at the death of the owner, especially one which is mandatory at the instance of the estate, immediately raises the question of the availability of funds.

Exhibit 10.2 Comparison of Stock Redemption Agreement and Stock Cross-purchase Agreement

	Effect on Tax Basis	Effect on Alternative Minimum Tax	Need for Adequate Corporate Surplus
Redemption agreement	No stepped-up basis	Risk of accumulated current earnings preference for larger C corporations	Need adequate surplus
Cross-purchase agreement	Stepped-up basis	No risk	Surplus is irrelevant

Just when the business may be reeling from the effects of the loss of one of its most valuable employees, it may be expected to scrape together enough cash to buy out the deceased's ownership. To avoid this disastrous result, many of these arrangements are funded by life insurance policies on the lives of the owners. This would be in addition to any key person insurance held by the business for the purpose of recovering from the effects of the loss. In structuring such an arrangement, however, the parties should be aware of two quite different models.

The first and most traditional model is referred to as a *redemption agreement*. Under such agreement, the business owns the policies and is obligated to purchase the equity upon death. The second model is referred to as a *cross-purchase agreement* and provides for each owner to own insurance on the others and to buy a proportional amount of the deceased's equity. Exhibit 10.2 illustrates the primary differences between the two forms of agreement.

The latter arrangement raises some serious mechanical problems, but may be quite advantageous if these problems can be overcome. To begin with, the cross-purchase agreement becomes quite complicated if there are more than a few stockholders, since each stockholder must own and maintain a policy on each of the others. There must be a mechanism (such as a form of trust or escrow agreement) to ensure that all these policies are kept in force and that the proceeds are actually used for their intended purpose. In addition, if the ages of the stockholders are materially different, certain owners will be paying higher premiums than others. One might ignore this difference on the basis that those who pay most are also most likely to benefit from this arrangement since their insured is likely to die first. Otherwise, one might attempt to equalize the impact of the premiums by adjusting the parties' compensation from the company.

If these complications can be overcome, however, the cross-purchase agreement provides some significant benefits over the redemption agreement. Take for example, a company in which each of three owners own one-third of the stock. If one of them were to die and the corporation purchased his stock, the remaining two would each own 50 percent of the corporation's stock, but their cost basis for a later sale would remain at the minimal consideration originally paid for their stock. In a cross-purchase arrangement, the remaining two would purchase the deceased owner's stock directly. This would still result in 50-50 ownership, but their cost basis for later sale would equal their original investment plus the amount of the insurance proceeds used to purchase the deceased owner's stock. Upon later sale of their stock or the company as a whole, the capital gains tax would be significantly lowered.

Another benefit of the cross-purchase agreement derives from the fact that although the receipt of life insurance proceeds is exempt from income taxation, it can result in a tax preference item for a C corporation. This would expose the corporation to the alternative minimum tax. This tax preference item does not apply to individuals, and is thus avoided by adopting the cross-purchase model. It can also be avoided by LLCs, S corporations, and certain smaller C corporations.

Lastly, the cross-purchase model eliminates the possibility that the company may not have sufficient retained earnings or surplus to fund a buyout upon the death of an owner. It would be highly ironic if the owner's life insurance merely funded an earnings deficit to the benefit of creditors and could not be used to buy his equity.

Disposition of Equity Upon Termination of Employment

Stockholder and operating agreements normally also address disposition of equity upon events other than death. Repurchase of equity upon termination of employment can be very important for all parties. The former employee whose equity no longer represents an opportunity for employment would like the opportunity to cash in her investment. The company and other owners may resent the presence of an inactive owner who can capitalize on their later efforts. Thus, both operating and stockholders agreements will normally provide for repurchase of the interest of a stockholder or member who is no longer actively employed by the company. This, of course, applies only to stockholders or members whose efforts on behalf of the company were the basis of their participation in the first place. Such provisions would not apply to Jake and Cori's investors, for example, since their participation was based entirely upon their investment.

This portion of the agreement presents a number of additional problems peculiar to the employee-owner. For example, the company cannot obtain insurance to cover an obligation to purchase equity upon termination of employment. Thus, it may encounter an obligation to purchase the equity of the former employee at a time when its cash position will not support such a purchase. Furthermore, in addition to the requirement of adequate surplus, courts uniformly prohibit repurchases that would render the company insolvent. Common solutions to these problems involve committing the company to an installment purchase of the affected equity over a period of years (with appropriate interest and security) or a commitment by the remaining owners to make the purchase personally if the company is unable to do so for any reason.

Furthermore, these agreements frequently impose penalties upon the premature termination of a stockholder or member's employment. In our example, the investors are relying upon the efforts of Jake and Cori in making this investment, and Jake and Cori are each relying upon the other's efforts when entering this risky situation. Should either Cori or Jake be entitled to a buyout at full fair market value if he or she simply decides to walk away from the venture? Often, these agreements contain so-called *vesting* provisions, which require a specified period of service before repurchase will be made at full value. As an example, such a vesting provision might state that unless Jake had stayed with the venture for a year, all his equity would be forfeited upon his departure. After a year, one-quarter of his equity would be repurchased for full value, but the rest would be forfeited. Another 25 percent would vest at the end of each ensuing year.

Such provisions, in addition to providing incentive to remain with the company, have complicated tax implications as well. As earlier discussed, if an employee receives equity for less than fair market value, the discount would be considered taxable compensation. The Internal Revenue Code provides that compensation income with regard to unvested equity is not taxed until the stock is vested. But at that time, the amount of income is measured by the difference between the price paid for the equity and its value *at the time of vesting*. The only way to avoid this result is to file an election to pay the tax on the compensation income measured at the time of the purchase of the equity, even though the equity is not then vested.

For Jake and Cori, this provision acts as a trap. Although they have arranged the initial investments of the parties such that there is no compensation income at the time they purchased their stock, if it is not then fully vested, their taxable income will be measured at the end of each future year as portions of the stock vest. Thus, they must file the election to have their income measured at the time of purchase in order to avoid a tax disaster, even though there is then no income to measure. And contrary to what they might think, that election must be filed within 30 days of their receipt of the stock, not at the end of the year.

Some agreements go beyond vesting provisions and give incentive to their founders by providing further penalties for owners who leave voluntarily or are terminated for cause. Thus, the agreement applicable to Cori and Jake might provide that vested equity is repurchased for full fair market value if they are terminated involuntarily (including as a result of disability or death), but for only half of fair market value if they leave for any other reason. Of course, involuntary termination without cause is a somewhat remote possibility due to the expansion of the concept of fiduciary loyalty mentioned earlier.

Distributions of Company Profits

Stockholder and operating agreements may also include numerous other provisions peculiar to the facts and circumstances of the particular business. Thus, pass-through entities often provide for mandatory distributions of profit to the members or stockholders at least in the amount of the tax obligation each will incur as a result of the profits of the business. Other agreements might include provisions to resolve voting deadlocks between owners, since otherwise, a 50-50 split of voting stock might paralyze the company. Various types of arbitration provisions might be employed to avoid this problem.

Redemption Provisions

Further, some stockholder or operating agreements provide investors with the right to demand repurchase of their equity at some predetermined formula price at a designated future time, so they will not be forever locked into a minority investment in a closely held company. Conversely, some such agreements provide the company with the right to repurchase such equity at a predetermined price (usually involving a premium) should the capital no longer be needed. Other agreements protect investors against being left behind if the founders sell their equity to third parties. The presence or absence of all these provisions depends, of course, on the relative negotiating strengths of the parties.

Legal and Tax Issues in Hiring Employees

From the beginning of this venture, Jake and Cori have known that if they were successful, they would soon have to hire employees for the marketing and sales functions. Thus, they need to consider some of the issues raised by the presence of employees.

Employees as Agents of the Company

To begin with, it should be understood that employees are agents of the company and, as such, are governed by many of the agency rules which already affect the relationships of partners to a partnership and officers to a corporation. Thus, employees have the previously described duty of loyalty to the company and obligations not to compete, to respect confidentiality, and to account for their activities.

Yet Cori and Jake are probably more interested in the potential of their employees to affect the business's relationships with third parties, such as customers and suppliers. Here the rules of agency require that a distinction be drawn between obligations based upon contractual liability and those resulting from noncontractual relationships such as tort actions. Exhibit 10.3 provides an overview of these relationships.

Employees are authorized to bind their employers to contracts with third parties if such actions have either been expressly or impliedly authorized. Thus, if Jake and Cori hire a sales manager and inform her that she has the authority to close any sale up to $50,000, she may wield that authority without further consultation with her principals. She also has the implied authority to do whatever is necessary to close such deals (such as sign a purchase order in the company's name, arrange delivery, and perhaps even alter some of the company's standard warranty terms).

However, the employee has authority that often extends beyond that expressly or impliedly given her. To illustrate this, suppose Jake and Cori's sales manager decides to close a sale for $100,000. This goes beyond her express authority and is not within her

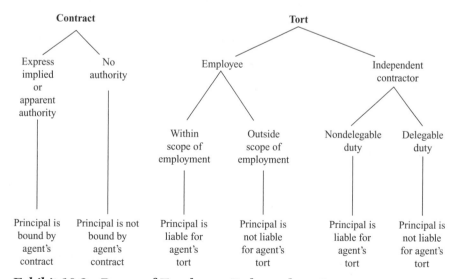

Exhibit 10.3   Power of Employees/Independent Contractors to Create Contractual and Tort Liability for Principals

implied authority since it was expressly prohibited. Yet, from the point of view of the customer, the company's sales manager appears to have the authority to close all sales transactions.

Unless the customer has been informed of the limitation imposed upon the employee, he has no reason to think that anything is wrong. The law vindicates the customer in this situation by providing that the employee has apparent authority to conclude contracts within the scope of authority she appears to have due to actions of her employer. Since she was put into that position by her employer, and the employer has not informed the customer of the limits imposed upon the employee, the employer is bound by the employee's actions.

Outside of the contract arena, the employee's power to bind the employer is based upon similar considerations. The employer, under the doctrine of *respondent superior* (or *vicarious liability*), is responsible for any actions of the employee occurring within the scope of her employment. Thus, if the sales manager causes a traffic accident on her way to a sales call, the employer is responsible for damages. This imposition of liability is not in any way based upon the employer's fault. It is liability without fault imposed as a result of the economic judgment that employers are better able to spread losses among customers and insurance companies. Consistent with this approach, employers are normally not liable for the tort or criminal actions of employees outside the scope of their employment, such as actions occurring after hours or while the employee is pursuing his own interests. Furthermore, employers are normally not liable for the torts or criminal actions of agents who are not employees (so-called *independent contractors*) since they are more likely to be able to spread these costs among their own customers and insurers.

However, employers should not take this as an invitation to avoid all liability by wholesale hiring of independent contractors. To begin with, the labeling of a potential employee as an independent contractor is not necessarily binding upon the courts. They will look to the level of control exerted by the employer and other related factors to make this determination. In addition, many activities of employers are considered nondelegable (such as disposal of hazardous waste). Employers cannot escape the consequences of such activities by hiding behind independent contractors.

Similarly, it should be clearly understood that one's status as an employee (or, for that matter, as an independent contractor) does not relieve him of responsibility for tortious or criminal acts. Notwithstanding any liability of the employer, the agent is always still jointly responsible for his own wrongful acts.

Employment Discrimination

In addition to the preceding common-law considerations, there are, of course, a number of statutory rules of law which govern the employer-employee relationship. Perhaps the most well-known of these are the laws prohibiting employment discrimination. These laws, which include Title VII of the Civil Rights Act of 1964, the Age Discrimination in Employment Act, and laws protecting disabled and pregnant employees, collectively prohibit employment discrimination on the basis of sex, race, national origin, religion, age, and disability. Interestingly, they do not yet prohibit discrimination on the basis of sexual orientation, although a number of state and local laws do.

Prohibited discrimination can occur not only in hiring, but also in promotion, firing, and conditions of employment. In fact, sexual discrimination has been found in cases of sexual harassment unconnected to hiring, promotion, or firing, but which simply created a so-called "hostile environment" for the employee.

These statutes are exceptions to the age-old common-law concept of employment at will, which allowed employers to hire and fire at their whim, for any reason or no reason at all. This rule is still in force in situations not covered by discrimination laws and, of course, not involving employment contracts. Notwithstanding that rule, however, courts in many states have carved out exceptions to employment at will for reasons of public policy, such as cases involving employees fired for refusing to perform illegal acts, or employees fired in bad faith to avoid paying commissions or other earned compensation to the employee. Furthermore, courts in some states have been willing to discover employment contracts hidden in employee manuals or personnel communications which employers may not have thought legally binding.

Other Employment Statutes

When they begin taking on employees other than themselves, Jake and Cori will begin to encounter a variety of other statutes which regulate the employment relationship and the workplace itself. For example, the Employee Retirement Income Security Act (ERISA) and the Internal Revenue Code closely regulate the form and amounts of any pension, profit-sharing, 401(k), or welfare plans that they may wish to maintain, generally denying favorable tax treatment for plans that discriminate in favor of owners and highly paid employees. They will also find that the Occupational Safety and Health Administration (OSHA) and the regulations adopted under the OSH Act closely regulate safety and health conditions in the workplace, imposing heavy fines for violations. The Fair Labor Standards Act provides minimum wages and overtime pay for employees in nonexempt (generally nonexecutive) positions, as well as prohibiting child labor and other practices.

The business will find itself contributing to the Social Security system and an unemployment compensation fund for each of its employees, as well as withholding social security and income taxes from its employees' wages. With regard to unemployment compensation, the amount of their contribution may depend upon the number of employees laid off over the years, motivating Cori and Jake to contest claims from employees who may have left voluntarily or been fired for cause.

In addition, the corporation will probably be required to carry workers compensation insurance to cover claims under that system. Although the premiums may seem burdensome, workers compensation was, at the outset, a welcome compromise between the interests of employers and employees. In exchange for avoiding the costs and uncertainties of litigation, employees were assured payment for job-related injuries but lost the opportunity to sue for increased amounts based upon pain, suffering, and punitive damages. Employers gave up many common-law defenses that formerly could be used against employees, but could now avoid disastrously high jury judgments formerly available under common law.

Employment Agreements

In addition to the common-law and statutory considerations common to the hiring of all employees, the hiring of persons for professional positions presents its own set of issues. Such persons are likely to demand employment agreements and a piece of the action in some form.

The attraction of employment agreements comes, in the main, from their protection against firing without cause. Thus, a major item of negotiation will likely be the length of the contract. Although one might think that the downside of such a provision to the employee is a commitment to stay with a company she may learn to dislike, courts have universally held that an employee cannot be forced to work for an employer against her will. Any contrary ruling would, it has been said, amount to a form of slavery! Thus, an employment contract is essentially a one-way street. The employee is promised employment for a period of time, with accompanying salary, bonus, and incentive provisions; but she can leave the company at any time without consequence (unless legally enforceable consequences are specifically provided). As a result, Jake and Cori would be well advised to avoid employment agreements whenever possible, and, if forced to grant one, at least obtain some accompanying benefit for the company.

Such benefit usually comes in the form of the noncompetition and proprietary information covenants discussed at the beginning of this chapter. For example, an employee may promise, in exchange for a two-year employment agreement, not to work in the projection equipment industry for a year after the termination of his employment. Yet, as mentioned earlier in the context of Jake and Cori's former employment, proprietary information obligations exist quite apart from any employee agreement and it is quite possible that courts would refuse to enforce noncompetition provisions against the employee.

Equity Sharing

In addition to demands for job security, higher-level employees will frequently ask for participation in the company's success. This can be easily accomplished by a grant of stock, but Cori and Jake would be well advised to resist such a demand since that might well upset the corporate balance of power and expectations of economic return among the major stockholders. These demands can often be satisfied by an incentive bonus plan tied to the success of the company or, more effectively, to the accomplishment of individual goals set for the employee.

If this is unacceptable to the employee, her return could be tied to the fortunes of the company by the use of phantom stock or stock appreciation rights (or similar devices in the context of an LLC) which simulate the effect of equity without involving actual equity ownership. These plans grant the employee bonuses equal to any distributions that would have been made to her if she had owned a certain number of shares, while additionally rewarding her through payment of any increase in value such shares would have experienced. However, even this type of plan might not be acceptable to an employee with significant negotiating leverage, since it does not give her voting rights. In addition, since the employee does not actually own stock or a membership interest (a capital asset), she cannot report the increase in value as capital gain at lower federal income tax rates. Thus, in certain cases it may be necessary to grant the employee stock in some form.

As previously mentioned, a direct grant of stock to an employee is considered a taxable event. The employee pays income tax on the difference between the value of the stock and the amount she paid for it, if any. However, as previously described, the imposition of tax can be postponed if the stock is forfeitable—for example, upon the employee's leaving the employ of the company before the passage of a designated period of time. No doubt Cori and Jake would condition the grant of stock to any employee on her remaining employed for a substantial period, so this rule would apply.

The negative side of this rule, of course, is that when the stock is finally vested, the taxable income is measured by the difference between the amount paid, if any, and the value of the stock *at the time of vesting*. Worse yet, this tax will be payable before the employee has received any cash with respect to this transaction. Cash will be available upon sale of the stock, but typically, the employee will not wish to sell at this time, and there will be no market for stock in a closely held corporation in any case.

Stock Options

The issuance of stock options is often thought of as a solution to this problem. The employee is given the right to purchase stock in the corporation at a fixed price for a significant period of time. Similar devices can be constructed with regard to membership interests in an LLC. Thus, without investing any money, the employee can watch the value of this right increase as the value of the stock increases relative to the amount she would have to pay to purchase it. This right would be much less valuable, of course, if the grant of the option to the employee were a taxable event, but, unless the option is transferable and there is a recognized market for it (extremely unlikely in a closely held company), the grant of the option is not taxable.

Unfortunately, however, when the employee ultimately exercises the option and purchases the stock, the Internal Revenue Code requires recognition of income in the amount of the difference between the amount paid and the value of the stock at that time. Again, this occurs at a time when the employee has received no cash and likely has little desire or ability to sell.

Recognizing this problem, Congress has provided more favorable tax treatment for an employee stock option which meets a number of requirements (although this treatment is, unfortunately, available only in the context of corporations). Some of these requirements are as follows:

- The incentive stock options (ISOs) must be issued pursuant to a stock option plan approved by the corporation's stockholders.
- The exercise price must be the fair market value of the stock at the time of issuance.
- Each option cannot last more than 10 years, and no more than $100,000 of exercise price may become initially exercisable in any one year.
- Perhaps most significantly, the employee must hold on to any stock purchased pursuant to the option for the longer of one year after exercise or two years after the grant of the option.

If these requirements are met, unless she is subject to the alternative minimum tax, the employee is not taxed until she actually sells the stock acquired under the option (and has cash to pay tax). The income is then taxed at favorable long-term capital gain rates.

The corporation can still require the employee to sell such shares back to the corporation upon termination of employment. From the corporation's point of view, the only drawback is that the corporation loses any deduction that would otherwise be available for compensation paid to employees. Jake and Cori may find this plan to be an attractive way to grant the requested incentive to their key employees.

Exhibit 10.4 compares these various methods of sharing equity with employees.

Exhibit 10.4 Comparison of Equity Sharing Methods (Downloadable)
Copyright © 2010 by William D. Bygrave and Andrew Zacharakis. To
download this form for your personal use, please visit
www.wiley.com/go/portablembainentrepreneurship.

Equity Grant	Date of Grant	Risk Removed	Sale of Equity
Vested equity	Ordinary income	Not applicable	Capital gain
Risk of forfeiture	No income	Ordinary income	Capital gain
Risk of forfeiture Sec. 83(B) election	Ordinary income	No income	Capital gain
Stock Options	**Date of Grant**	**Date of Exercise**	**Sale of Stock**
Nonqualified stock option with readily ascertainable value	Ordinary income	No income	Capital gain
Nonqualified stock option with no ascertainable value	No income	Ordinary income	Capital gain
Incentive stock option (ISO)	No income	No income	Capital gain

Insurance

The expenses associated with beginning a business are not inconsiderable. The fees demanded by the state and the costs associated with retaining attorneys and accountants have already been described. As employees are added to the organization, Social Security, unemployment compensation, and other costs increase. As previously mentioned, workers compensation insurance is required by many states. But such insurance is not the only insurance that may be advisable to obtain.

Property Insurance

To begin with, Jake and Cori should consider property insurance for any equipment or inventory that they may have on hand. In fact, should they ever obtain a loan for their business, the lender will likely take inventory and equipment as collateral and insist that it be insured (with the proceeds payable to the lender).

Liability Insurance

Cori and Jake should also consider purchasing liability insurance to cover claims against their business for product liability and other possible tort claims. As mentioned before, the presence of such insurance often mitigates against claims of undercapitalization by plaintiffs attempting to pierce the corporate veil. And although the corporate veil protects Cori and Jake's personal assets against such claims, they no doubt share the hope that someday soon their business will have its own considerable net worth to protect. Automobile liability insurance is required by many states as a condition to registration of a car. And the dangers of tort liability caused by employees has been highlighted earlier.

Key Person Life Insurance

The advisability of life insurance to cover stock redemptions under cross-purchase or redemption agreements has previously been discussed. Yet such is not the only role for life insurance in a business. Consider what would occur upon Jake's untimely death. Not only may Cori or the corporation be required to repurchase his stock, but the operations of the corporation would likely grind to a standstill while it searched for someone to replace Jake. If the corporation owned additional life insurance on Jake's life (known as *key person* insurance), it would have funds to tide it over during this business slowdown as well as money to apply to the search for and compensation of Jake's successor.

Business Interruption Insurance

Similar in effect is so-called business interruption insurance which, in many cases of catastrophic business shutdown, will replace some of the company's cash flow. Such a policy is usually quite expensive, however, and may not be within the reach of a typical start-up.

Group Life, Disability, and Health Insurance for Employees

As the company grows and adds employees, there will be increasing demand for insurance as employee benefits. Many corporations provide group life insurance and/or group disability insurance for its employees. The latter can be very helpful in avoiding the moral dilemma caused by an employee who is too sick to work. Cutting off his salary may seem unthinkable; but paying another full salary for a long-term replacement may be too much for the company to afford. Purchasing a policy with a significant deductible (such as 90 to 180 days) may solve this problem at very reasonable cost. Furthermore, in many industries it has become routine to expect the employer to provide health insurance as an employee benefit. Here, too, recent changes in the tax law may make more affordable, high-deductible policies an appropriate choice.

These three group policies (life, disability, and health) may be provided to employees tax-free while the corporation may deduct the costs of premiums. The only exceptions to this favorable tax result are for partners in partnerships, members of LLCs, or significant shareholders of subchapter S corporations, all of whom must report these benefits as taxable income (although they may receive a corresponding deduction for a portion of the health insurance premiums). Thus, one additional positive aspect of the choice of a C corporation for Cori and Jake is that any group life, disability, or health insurance provided to them by the corporation would be free of income tax.

Raising Money

Thoughts of future hirings will inevitably bring Cori and Jake to consideration of another of the challenges they anticipated. Raising money from their potential investors (as well as probable future rounds of investors) involves another set of complex legal issues.

Loans

Although it is an unlikely source of funding for a start-up venture, at some point in the business's life cycle it may seek debt financing from a commercial bank or other institutional lender. Although these institutions are notoriously loath to make loans to start-up companies, such a loan may be possible when sufficient revenues, collateral, and/or guarantees are available. Such a loan may take the form of a term note, a line of credit, or some sort of revolving credit plan, depending upon the circumstances. One thing that will almost certainly be the case, however, is that the lender will insist upon security for the loan.

Security Interests

At a minimum, this security will consist of an interest in all of the borrower's assets. In Cori and Jake's case, that will mean the lender will perfect a security interest under Article 9 of the Uniform Commercial Code (UCC) on the company's machinery and equipment (computers, filing cabinets, desks, etc.), inventory (digital projection equipment, etc.), accounts receivable, and all intangible property (copyrights, patents, service marks, and trade secrets relating to their business). Notice of such security interest will be filed under the UCC wherever appropriate to perfect this interest such that no future potential lender or purchaser will be misled.

Under the provisions of the UCC, such filing will perfect the lender's security interest on any new machinery or equipment purchased after the loan is made unless such new items are purchased on credit and a security interest is granted to the seller or lender. Later arising accounts receivable will be covered as well. All new inventory will be covered by the security interest, while any inventory sold to customers in the ordinary course of business will be automatically freed from the security interest. Furthermore, the security interest will automatically cover any further amounts advanced by the lender to the company in the future.

If the loan ultimately goes into default, the lender may take possession of the collateral and arrange its sale. The proceeds are then applied to the costs of repossession and sale and the amount unpaid under the loan. Any additional amounts would be turned over to any lower-priority secured creditor and then ultimately to the borrower.

Although such a security interest might seem sufficient to provide adequate security to the lender, most lenders will further insist upon guarantees from additional parties. In some cases, guarantees from governmental agencies such as the Small Business Administration may be available. However, in almost every case, the lender will insist upon personal guarantees from the major stockholders of the borrower. In our case, this will certainly include Jake and Cori, but most likely will exempt their investors. In many cases, the lender further demands that such guarantees be backed by collateral interests in the private property of the guaranteeing stockholders, such as mortgages on their residences.

As noted earlier, these personal guarantees circumvent the limited liability that entrepreneurs hope to achieve through the use of the corporate or LLC forms. The abandonment of this protection is unavoidable, however, and only extends to the particular lender. The stockholders or members remain protected against other trade creditors and tort plaintiffs.

Tax Effects

As a matter of strategy, the form in which a guarantee is given can have serious negative tax effects if insufficient care is given to structuring the loan transaction. As an example, if Cori and Jake were to approach a small, local bank, they might find the bank uncomfortable lending to a corporation under any circumstances. Under these facts, the two stockholders may choose to borrow the money personally and invest the proceeds in the corporation themselves. Repayment of the loan would then be made by the stockholders out of the company's profits distributed to them. As a result of this arrangement, however, the stockholders would be receiving taxable distributions from the corporation (either in the form of salary or dividends) but would receive no compensating deduction for the repayment of a personal loan.

A better result would be reached if they could convince the bank to lend to the corporation and take personal guarantees. Then the corporation could repay the loan directly (deducting the interest as a business expense) and the money would never pass through the hands of the stockholders. Alternatively (but with some additional risk), the stockholders could borrow directly from the bank but grant it a second mortgage on their residences as collateral, thereby potentially rendering the interest deductible for them as mortgage interest.

Ironically, if the corporation were to elect subchapter S treatment, strategy considerations may point in the opposite direction. Since the motivation for such a choice would likely have been the desire to have corporate losses appear on the personal returns of the stockholders, they would be concerned that the amount of loss they may use is limited to their tax basis in their subchapter S investment. Such basis consists (in S corporations) only of the amount paid for their stock, plus any amount they lend directly to the corporation. For S corporations (but not, for the most part, LLCs), if the corporation were to borrow from the bank, and the stockholders were merely to guarantee the loan, the amount of the loan would not increase their basis (and thus their allowable loss). Were they to personally borrow the money from the bank and lend it to the corporation, their basis would be increased. Of course, in either event, the amount of loss each stockholder can use may also be limited, in the case of a passive investor, by the passive loss rules discussed earlier.

Legal Issues in the Sale of Securities to Investors

As an alternative to institutional lending, Cori and Jake plan to turn to an outside investor. Although it will be difficult to attract venture capitalists to such a small start-up, other sources of capital in the form of friends and family or local professionals and other individuals or entities with an interest in ground-floor investing may be available. Having chosen to take this route, it is crucial that they purge themselves of two common misconceptions.

Although most businesspeople are aware of the fact that both federal and state law regulates the offer and sale of securities, many believe that these statutes apply only to the offerings of large corporations. Small companies, they believe, are exempt from these acts. Unfortunately, this is one of the dangerous misconceptions held by many persons in the position of Cori and Jake. In fact, these laws (specifically the federal Securities Act of 1933, the federal Securities Exchange Act of 1934, and state so-called blue-sky statutes) apply to all issuers and their principals.

Further, even those businesspeople who are aware of the reach of these acts believe that they only apply to issuers of equity securities, mainly stock. This, too, is a misconception. All these statutes apply to issuers of *securities*, not just stock. Securities include, in addition to stock, most debt (other than very short-term loans or loans for very specific purposes such as real estate mortgages), options, warrants, LLC membership interests, and any other form of investment in which the investor buys into a common enterprise and relies upon the efforts of others for the investment's success. Thus, such disparate items as orange groves, Hawaiian condominiums, and even worms have been held to be regulated securities under the circumstances of their respective cases.

The wide scope of these statutes led some to assert that they include the offering of franchise opportunities as well as stocks, bonds, and so on. Those offering franchises argued in return that the success of a franchisee was not normally determined solely by the efforts of the franchisor, but required significant effort on the part of the franchisee. This debate was rendered moot, however, by the adoption by the Federal Trade Commission of regulations requiring disclosure by franchisors of virtually the same range of information that would have been required under a securities registration statement. Many states have enacted similar franchise registration laws, requiring dual federal and state registration in most franchise offerings. (Further discussion of franchising can be found in Chapter 14.)

In general, then, the securities laws prohibit the offering of securities to the public without prior (and very expensive) registration with an appropriate government authority such as the federal Securities and Exchange Commission. They also punish fraudulent activities in connection with such offerings, including not only affirmatively false statements, but mere nondisclosure of material facts about the investment. Due to the complex and expensive nature of registration, these laws provide exceptions to the registration requirement in specific circumstances, but even these offerings are subject to the antifraud provisions of the laws. Thus, the challenge to our two entrepreneurs is to identify provisions in the securities laws which will offer them an exemption from registration, understanding that they must still provide sufficient disclosure to potential investors (in the form of either a so-called *offering circular* or, in appropriate circumstances, unlimited opportunity to perform due diligence) to avoid antifraud liability.

One such exemption contained in the Securities Act of 1933 is the so-called intrastate offering exemption. Based upon the general principle that the federal government can constitutionally regulate only *interstate* commerce, the statute necessarily exempts offerings that are purely local. However, the scope of this exemption is relatively narrow. Not only must all persons who purchase the securities be resident in one state, all offerees must be resident there as well. Furthermore, the company offering the securities must be incorporated under the laws of that state (disqualifying many Delaware corporations) and have most of its assets and do most of its business there. Due to these restrictions, this exemption may be useful only in the case of the smallest of offerings. Besides, the exemption only excuses the offering from registration with the Securities and Exchange Commission. The state's securities laws may still require expensive and time-consuming state registration.

The more popular exemption from registration under the federal act is the so-called *private placement* exemption, which excuses from registration any transactions "not involving a public offering." The SEC has relied in part upon this exemption to issue regulations designed to facilitate the raising of capital by small businesses in small offerings. Thus, as of this writing, Regulation D under the Act exempts from registration any offering of under $1 million of securities. Above that amount, the regulation requires increasing levels of disclosure (still short of full registration, however) and limits the number of offerees to 35 plus an unlimited number of so-called *accredited* investors. For these purposes, accredited investors are certain institutions, as well as individuals with net worth or annual income at levels that argue a need for less protection. Even apart from the regulation, however, issuers can argue under the statute that offerings made only to relatively sophisticated investors with prior relationships to the issuer, qualify as transactions "not involving a public offering."

Of course, exemption from registration under the federal act does not grant exemption under state acts. In fact, offerings made to investors in a number of states require attention to the blue-sky statutes of each such state. Fortunately, however, federal law has preempted state regulation in offerings beyond a certain size, and even in the absence of preemption, virtually all state statutes contain similar exemptions for private placements, typically exempting offerings to 25 or fewer persons.

Thus, Jake and Cori will likely be able to seek out the investment they will ultimately need without the necessity of registering with either the federal or state governments. However, it cannot be overemphasized that they remain subject to the antifraud provisions of these acts. Thus, they will be well advised to seek professional assistance in identifying the applicable statutory exemptions, drawing up a comprehensive offering circular for their offering if appropriate, and disclosing all that an investor would need to know about their company to make an intelligent investment decision. (Further discussion of informal investment and venture capital is contained in Chapter 7.)

Conclusion

Considering all the legal and tax pitfalls described in this chapter, one is tempted to ask whether Cori, Jake, or any other entrepreneur would choose to go down the road of the start-up if she were fully aware of all the complications potentially lying in wait. Surely this would be an overreaction. Yet not to be aware of these matters is to consciously choose to play the game without knowing the rules. These issues are there whether one chooses to prepare for them or not. Surely, Jake and Cori are much more likely to succeed in their venture for having taken the time to become aware of the legal and tax issues facing the entrepreneur.

Downloadable Resources for this chapter available at www.wiley.com/go/portablembainentrepreneurship

Comparison of Equity Sharing Methods

11

Intellectual Property

Kirk Teska and Joseph S. Iandiorio

How This Chapter Fits into a Typical MBA Curriculum

Businesses of all kinds rely heavily on intellectual property. Patents are often the life blood of high-tech companies. But even non-high-tech service providers can find themselves accused of patent infringement. Trademarks are key to restaurants, stores, and other high- and low-tech businesses as well as businesses that might someday franchise. Domain name disputes are now commonplace. Since software is now everywhere and since copyrights and trade secrets protect software, all business managers need to have a working knowledge of the copyright and trade secret laws.

MBA students learn about management concepts in general and, in particular, project management and quality assurance. Intellectual property (IP), too, must be managed. Investors will not be happy with managers who fail to protect what can be protected. Financial officers will not be happy if money is wasted. And no one wants to incur the costs and uncertainties associated with being sued over someone else's IP rights.

It is not enough in today's information economy and in this flat world to merely understand the difference between patents, trade and service marks, copyrights, and trade secrets: Savvy managers must think about strategic IP.

Who Uses This Material in the Real World—and Why It Is Important

It used to be that chief technology officers in high-tech companies primarily dealt with patents. The marketing department of a company would deal with trademarks. Threats of potential IP litigation went to a CEO or in-house attorney. But things have changed.

Even small Internet-based retailers began getting sued for patent infringement. In the 1990s, I attended an appellate court hearing regarding a patent infringement lawsuit brought against a sole proprietor, a local florist. The patent involved flower holders. Companies also began getting sued over domain names, ad words, and hyperlinks.

The cumulative effect of the proliferation of IP across the board affecting businesses of all kinds means a manager who is not IP savvy is a liability instead of an asset.

So the answer to the question "Who needs to understand IP?" is everyone in every business.

> In a survey we conducted, nearly 90 percent of venture capital firms in New England ranked IP as important or extremely important in making an investment decision.

The Basics: What Is Protectable and How Should It Be Protected?

When a new idea is conceived or a new product or service is planned, one of the first questions that arise is: Can I protect this? Can I keep competitors from copying this? There are very practical reasons for protecting a new idea. Investors are loath to put money into a venture that cannot establish a unique niche. Stockholders will challenge a corporation's investment of its resources in an idea that can be easily copied once it is introduced to the market. All the time, effort, and money invested in perfecting a product or service, as well as advertising and promoting it, may be wasted if imitators can enter the market on your heels with a product or service just like yours. Moreover, the imitators can cut prices because they have not incurred the start-up expenses you had to endure to bring the idea from conception to a mass-producible, reliable, and appealing product or service. The next question is: Does my new product or service infringe the IP rights of anyone else? Only by understanding the basics of IP can these questions be answered.

Once it has been determined that a new idea, product, or service is eligible for one or more forms of IP protection—a patent, trade secret, trademark, or copyright—the rights should be secured as quickly as the budget allows. Each form of protection is obtained in a different manner and provides a different set of rights. But a single product can involve different forms of protection. For example, consider a typical modern product—a microprocessor-based handheld device. It bears the name of the manufacturer and a brand name and is accompanied by a user's manual. What is protectable, and how should you protect it? Where might others have IP which must be considered? The following sections provide information to help answer these questions pertaining to the various forms of IP protection.

Patents

Patents are often a necessary, but not a sufficient, condition precedent to business success. Although there are actually three different kinds of patents, *utility patents* are the kind commonly considered when one seeks to protect an invention. Think utility patent whenever you think "better, cheaper, faster." But don't confuse *invention* in the patent sense with "eureka" type ideas. Many patents are combinations of well-known components. Consider the following examples.

In one case a patent allegedly protected the notion of a document scanner equipped with a universal serial bus (USB) port. A USB is simply a connection between a computer and a peripheral device such as a scanner. The USB connection transfers data between the two and also allows the scanner to be powered from the computer. That way, with a USB connection, you don't have to plug the scanner into an electrical wall socket. Indeed, the scanner can even be powered by the computer's battery in the case of a portable computer. The inventors of this particular patent didn't invent either USB or the scanner. But when they decided to put the two together, they won a patent.

Consider also Aerogel. Aerogel is listed in the *Guinness Book of World Records* as the world's lightest substance. A block of Aerogel as big as you weighs less than a pound but can support a small car. Recently, numerous companies have been patenting new uses for Aerogel—as insulation, in fuel cells, and as building structures, just to give a few examples. Engineers at those companies didn't invent Aerogel—a Stanford University researcher discovered it in the early 1930s. Still, the Patent Office might grant patents for new uses of Aerogel.

Utility Patents

Technically speaking, utility patents cover these classes of inventions:

- *Chemical inventions* include new compounds, new methods of making old or new compounds, new methods of using old or new compounds, and new combinations of old compounds. Assays, biological materials and methods, drugs, foodstuffs, drug therapy, plastics, petroleum derivatives, synthetic materials, adhesives, pesticides, fertilizers, and feeds are all protectable.

- *General/mechanical inventions* include everything from gears and engines to tweezers and propellers, from zippers to Jacque Cousteau's scuba regulator. For example, complex textile-weaving machines, space capsule locks and seals, and diaper pins are all protectable.

- *Electrical inventions* include everything from lasers to light switches, from the smallest circuit details to overall system architectural concepts.

Computer software is also patentable in various forms:

- Application programs, such as the software that runs in a computer used to control a chemical-processing plant or a rubber-molding machine, are patentable.

- Software for running a cash management account at a brokerage house or bank is patentable.

- The microcode in a ROM that embodies the entire inventive notion of a new tachometer is patentable.

- Internal or operations programs that direct the handling of data in the computer's own operations are patentable.

> A common misconception is that software, Internet-based business ideas, and so-called *business methods* are not patentable. The truth is software has long been patentable. And, in 1998, the high patent court put to bed the notion that business methods were an exception to patentable subject matter when Signature Financial Group's patent for a mutual fund administration system was upheld as valid. Another well-known example is Amazon's "One-Click" Internet shopping patent (No. 5,960,411), litigated in 1999 against Barnes & Noble. Beware, though: In 2008 a new court decision made it more difficult to procure business method patents.

Obtaining a Utility Patent

So there is no rule that patents cover only remarkable inventions. Instead, the basic requirement for a utility patent is that the idea be different in some way from what came before. Most importantly, patent protection can be broad: The owner of the patent has the right to exclude others from making, using, and selling, offering for sale, or importing the patented invention during the term of the patent. And the term of a patent is fairly long.

The patenting effort begins when the inventor or inventors conceive the invention. Typically a registered patent attorney on the inventor's behalf prepares a patent application and files it in the U.S. Patent and Trademark Office. From the date that the application is filed there is a "patent pending." There are no real legal rights associated with "patent pending" status. Full protection only applies if and when the Patent Office agrees that the invention is patentable and issues the patent. But with the "patent pending" designation, a would-be competitor doesn't always know exactly what will be patented or when, and thus may proceed with caution in making the decision to offer the same or a similar product.

The *timing* of the filing of the patent application is critical. In the United States, a patent application must be filed within one year of the first public disclosure, public use, sale, or even offer for sale of the product, or the filing will be barred and the opportunity to obtain a patent forever lost. This is known as the one-year period of grace. This may change in the future to a system in which there is no period of grace (the application must be filed before any of the activities just listed), to conform with the laws of most other countries. Even now, if patent protection is desirable in foreign countries, a patent application must be filed in the United States before any public activity occurs.

A sale more than a year before the application will generally bar a patent even if the invention is embedded so deeply within a larger system that it could not ever be discovered. If the device containing the invention is sold, that is enough. The idea is that an inventor should be given only one year in which to file his patent application after he has begun to commercially exploit or to attempt to commercially exploit his invention. Thus, for an invention embodied in a production machine installed in a locked, secure room, the one-year period for filing a patent application begins the first time a device produced by that machine is sold, even though the machine may never be known to or seen by anyone other than the inventor. And it is not just an actual sale that triggers the one-year period: An offer for sale is sometimes enough, even if the sale is never consummated.

Criteria for Obtaining a Utility Patent

A patent application is not a form to be filled out. Instead, each patent application is unique, although the form of each patent contains the same three basic sections:

1. Drawings showing an embodiment of the invention.
2. A written description of the invention referring to the drawings, akin to an engineering specification.
3. One or more claims—hybrid legal and technical language that captures the invention in words.

The definition of the patented invention, the protected property, is not what is disclosed in the drawings or specification portion of the application; this is only a description of one or more specific versions of the invention. Instead, the coverage of the patent is defined by the third part of the application, the legal claims. In commercial real estate, the three most important things are location, location, and location. In patents, the three most important things are the claims, the claims, and the claims.

To qualify for a patent, the claims must describe something both novel and unobvious. *Novelty* is a relatively easy standard to define: if a single earlier patent, publication, or product shows the entire claimed invention, the invention is not new and no patent will issue. *Obviousness* is somewhat more difficult to grasp and, worse, the test for obviousness is fairly subjective: Are the differences between the invention and all prior knowledge (including patents, publications, and products) such that the invention would have been obvious to a person having ordinary skill in the art? If so, the invention is not patentable even if it is novel. The U.S. Supreme Court has found that a combination of two devices where, in the combination, each device functions as intended, is obvious and not patentable.

Obviousness is a somewhat subjective determination, but many ideas have ultimately been deemed patentable even though they were originally rejected as obvious by an Examiner of the United States Patent and Trademark Office. In one notable case, Anita Dembiczak came up with the idea of a plastic leaf bag configured to look like a giant Halloween style pumpkin when stuffed with leaves. The United States Patent and Trademark Office essentially concluded that since leaf bags were well known and pumpkins drawn on paper lunch sacks were also well known, the idea of a pumpkin leaf bag was obvious and therefore not patentable. Not so, said the Court of Appeals for the Federal Circuit: The Patent Office failed to prove there was any motivation to combine the idea of a Halloween pumpkin with a leaf bag. As a result, the patent for the leaf bag pumpkin was issued. Obviousness rejections are to be expected from the Patent Office.

The meanings of *novelty* and *unobvious* in the area of patentability can be better understood with an example. Suppose a person is struggling to screw a wood screw into hard wood, and he realizes that the problem is that he cannot supply enough twisting force with the blade of the screwdriver in the slot in the head of the screw. So he gets the bright idea of making the slot a little deeper, so that the screwdriver blade can bite a little deeper and confront more surface area of the slot, thus applying more force to turn the screw. This is a good idea, but it creates another problem. The deeper slot extends much closer to the sides of the screw head. There is less support, and fatigue lines develop, which eventually cause the screw head to crack. The inventor then gets the idea to use a new screwdriver with two shorter, crossed blades, which will give increased surface area contact with two crossed slots in the head of the screw.

But a problem still exists. Although the twin blades do not require such deep slots, there are now twice as many slots, and the screw head is seriously weakened. Now the inventor sees another path: Keep the double-blade configuration, but chop off the corners, so that the slots need not extend out so close to the edge of the new screw head.

The result: he has invented the Phillips head screwdriver, for use with a Phillips head screw. Certainly the invention is novel: No one else had made that design before. It is also unobvious and thus patentable. The addition of the second blade and elimination of the corners has resulted in a wholly new screwdriver concept. The concept is patentable.

Now suppose another party, seeing the patent issued on this double-blade Phillips head, comes up with an improvement of her own. Her invention is to use three crossed blades (cutting the head of the screw into six equal areas), with their corners removed. This design may not be patentable. Certainly it is novel, but is it obvious? Perhaps. Once the first inventor has originated the idea of increasing the number of blades and eliminating corners, it may be obvious to simply add more blades. Even so, patents are still regularly issued today for new screw heads and even more mundane items such as the shape of the arbor hole in a circular saw blade.

Drafting the Patent Claims

Once it is decided that a patentable invention exists, it must be protected by properly drafted patent *claims*. It is the claims that the U.S. Patent and Trademark Office examiner analyzes and accepts or rejects in considering the issuance of the patent; it is the claims that determine if someone has infringed a patent; and it is the claims that define the patented property.

Claims are clearly, then, the most important part of a patent. It is no good to have claims that cover the invention and yet do not protect your product or process from being copied by competitors. Does this sound contradictory? Study the following example and you will understand.

Suppose an entrepreneur meets with a patent attorney and shows the attorney a new invention for carrying beverages on the slopes while skiing. The invention eliminates the risk of smashing glass, denting metal, or squashing a wineskin, and it also eliminates the need to carry any extra equipment: It's a hollow ski pole. The ski pole has a shaft, a chamber, and a handle. The handle has a threaded hole opening into the hollow shaft. Partway down the inside of the hollow shaft is a plastic liner that creates a chamber for holding liquid. The plastic liner is sealed to the shaft. The chamber is closed by a threaded plug. The entrepreneur wants to patent this invention and so he assists the patent attorney in writing a description of the ski pole. They write the following claim:

A hollow ski pole for carrying liquids, comprising:

a hollow shaft;

a plastic liner inside the shaft to define a chamber for containing liquid;

a handle on the shaft;

a threaded hole in the handle which opens into the chamber; and

a threaded plug for sealing the threaded hole.

The patent application is filed. The U.S. Patent and Trademark Office examines the application and three years later issues the patent with that claim. The total cost to the entrepreneur is around $12,000. The inventor is happy: The claim describes exactly what the entrepreneur markets and sells. But not for long, because a competitor comes out with a similar hollow ski pole that doesn't use a liner. The competitor simply welds a piece of metal across the inside of the shaft to make a sealed chamber. The competitor has avoided infringing the patent because there is no liner, which was one of the requirements of the patented claim. Still another competitor replaces the threaded plug with an upscale mahogany cork. Again the patent is not infringed because there is no threaded plug as required by the claim. Patent claims list requirements, and a competitor who can sell a competing product without meeting *all* the claim requirements doesn't infringe the patent.

This problem can be avoided by exploring the various ways in which the product can be built before the patent application is filed. This may require input from sales, marketing, engineering, and production people as well as the inventor. After a thorough study, a better claim might emerge as follows:

A hollow ski pole for carrying liquids, comprising:

a hollow shaft;

a chamber in the hollow shaft for containing a liquid;

a handle on the shaft having a hole opening into the chamber; and

a closure for the hole in the handle.

Now the liner and a threaded plug are not explicitly required. This claim, then, would likely be good enough to keep competitors at bay. There is a limit to how broadly the claim can be worded, however. Eventually, if the claim becomes broader and broader, and does not specify the ski pole or hollow shaft, it may apply to a bottle or a pot with a cover, and the patent will not be obtainable—it is not new. Careful claim drafting is thus critical.

If you don't remember anything else about patents, remember this: It's the claims that matter. Remember, too, that patents are expensive but for engineering, ideas, innovations, basic science, and improvements, patents are generally the only viable way to protect a company's market share.

Provisional Patent Applications

A relatively new type of patent application, referred to as a *provisional*, is now available. People like provisionals because they don't have to include patent claims—indeed, a technical or scientific paper, specification, or report can be filed as a provisional. Be careful though. In one case, a product embodying an invention was sold in the spring of 1996, a provisional application was filed in the spring of 1997 for the product, and a full patent application was filed in the fall of 1997. But the provisional failed to adequately describe the invention actually claimed in the full patent application. The result? The patent was held invalid because the provisional failed to provide the necessary disclosure. When the patent owner sued a competitor for patent infringement, a court found the resulting patent claims contained detailed information not present in the provisional patent application. As a result, the patent was invalidated and the competitor was free to use the patented invention.

Provisionals have found favor because they are typically less expensive than full patent applications and allow companies to advertise "patent pending." In 2002, over 80,000 provisional patent applications were filed. But, as the preceding case proves, provisionals are only as good as the details they contain.

Design Patents

Another type of patent is the design patent. Hockey uniforms, ladies' dresses, computer housings, automobile bodies, buildings, shoes, and game boards are all protectable with design patents. But this type of patent covers only the ornamental *appearance* of the product, not the idea, underlying concept, or functionality of the product. What you see is what you get. Design patents are generally less expensive than utility patents but typically also offer far less protection.

Managing Patent Costs

Patents are expensive: Plan on spending between $8,000 and $15,000 to prepare and file a patent application and between $4,000 and $6,000 to prosecute the patent application. *Prosecution* is what occurs in the two to three years following filing of the application as you attempt to convince the Patent Office that the invention is worthy of a patent in the face of inevitable rejections. Foreign patents can cost $5,000 to $10,000 in filing fees alone per country.

But you have to put these costs in perspective. Consider the price of a mold for a plastic part, for example, or the cost of a marketing study undertaken by a consultant. Because of the potential value of a patent, the cost is often well worth it. If, for example, Gillette's patent for the three-bladed Mach3 razor can really be used to stop all competitors from introducing razors with three or more blades, the cost of the Gillette patent and even the cost of patent litigation (typically $1 million or more) is well worth the protection afforded, especially given the enormous cost of Gillette's advertising campaigns surrounding the Mach3 razor.

However, some patents may not have enough potential value to provide a return on the investment. Consider a patent for Aerogel used as an insulative liner in deep-sea oil well piping. If other insulating materials work just or almost as well, the patent might not be worth the cost—unless it is worth something to advertise "the only deep-sea oil well piping with Aerogel!"

The problem is, at the time the patenting decision must be made, the value of the patent might be hard to measure. Large companies, then, regularly file for numerous patents and have a yearly IP budget in the millions of dollars. Emerging companies cannot typically afford those costs and thus must be particularly adept at planning and managing patents and other IP, all the while remembering the deadlines involved and also that the value of a given patent is measured by its claims.

Finally, don't forget to check to make sure your new product or service doesn't infringe someone else's patent. In our survey of venture capitalists, 63 percent had experienced IP lawsuits against companies they had funded.

Strategic Patenting

Patents, like every other company asset, need to be managed. Much has been written about *strategic patenting*. Numerous service providers now offer "patent mapping" services and market "comprehensive patent analysis platforms." What exactly is strategic patenting, though?

The basic notion evolved from a combination of the fairly old idea of patent management, studies that proved some patents were basically worthless, strategies that realized the best protection for a given product involved not one but many patents (a so-called *patent fence*), the idea of *defensive* patents (and *patent truces*), the fairly new ability to more easily search out existing patents and even published patent applications (and to present the search results in colorful charts and maps), and, to a certain degree, patents being asserted against even non-high-tech companies and service providers. Companies also began to realize that their patent portfolios could be used to generate money even if, and maybe especially when, a given patent was not being used. A patent hidden in the attic might be worth something and could be sold or licensed—even to a competitor.

Today, it is not acceptable for corporate management to fail to understand what it has by way of patent protection. Indeed, management is expected to maximize a return on patent expenditures.

But strategic patenting is really nothing new and is actually quite simple. Patents need to be viewed as a project and project management techniques employed. A plan is put into motion now to provide protection where you need it in the future, in contrast to an ad-hoc patenting effort.

The starting place is the company's existing patents both in the United States and in foreign countries. What do they protect? What did they cost? How much will it cost to maintain the portfolio? Consider a commercial handheld electronic product called the "jpod" (but do not use that name for your own product). Suppose there is one U.S. patent issued, two pending, and a series of foreign patent applications for each U.S. filing. A simple management spreadsheet might look like Exhibit 11.1.

Project jpod

Entry 1 reveals that the basic functionality of the jpod is fairly well protected and the cost to pursue foreign patents is reasonable given the scope of the U.S. patent. But entry 2

Exhibit 11.1 Patent Management Spreadsheet (Downloadable) Copyright © 2010 by William D. Bygrave and Andrew Zacharakis. To download this form for your personal use, please visit www.wiley.com/go/portablembainentrepreneurship.

	Patent No.	Status	Covers	Cost to Date	Cost to Pursue/ Maintain (U.S.)	Cost to Pursue/ Maintain (Foreign)
1.	7,214,229	Issued	Overall Functionality	$12,328	$8,265	$30,298
2.	60/250,936	Pending	User Interface	$16,291	$15,391	$60,351
3.	60/635,891	Pending	Next Generation Functionality	$8,641	$18,250	$60,451

is troublesome. A lot of money has been spent, the patent would only cover the user interface of the product, but no patent has yet issued. Maybe the idea of protecting the user interface in foreign countries should be abandoned given the trouble experienced in securing even a U.S. patent. Maybe even the U.S. patent should be scrapped. Or suppose the user interface has changed and money is being spent on patent protection for something the company doesn't even use anymore. If that's the case, can the patent rights be licensed to someone else to recoup the patent expenditures so far? Entry 3 can be evaluated in a similar manner.

This fairly simple patent map may also reveal something important via entries that are *not* present. Suppose engineering has touted a particular circuit in the jpod—let's call it a new power management circuit that lets the product run longer on a set of batteries. Why aren't there any entries on the spreadsheet for patents covering this circuit? Did we forget to protect it? Can we still protect it? What else are the engineers working on right now? Do we have a patent protection plan for all aspects of the next-generation product? Are any of the other patents in the portfolio not being used offensively or defensively? Can we make money from them? The main point is that management needs to know what it has (and does not have).

The second step is to analyze what others have or are at least pursuing. It is relatively easy to search out the patents and pending published patent applications of competitors. You can even track whether your own patents (for example, entry 1 in this spreadsheet) have been cited in later patents by others. An analysis of those patents might be revealing.

Suppose it turns out that someone else is seeking a series of patents regarding a technology clearly adapted for the jpod. That would be nice to know. Services are even available that electronically notify you regarding new patent applications meeting your predefined criteria. Some patent owners regularly keep track of the patenting efforts of competitors. Other key questions: Are there basic patents predating ours covering jpod-like products? Are they still valid? If not, are there any previously patented features we can now incorporate in our product? For still valid patents: Are the patent owners litigious? Are we infringing?

The third step involves predicting the future. Where is the market heading? Will our patents protect us there? Are there spaces where we should be inventing? Who is suing whom and what ideas should we stay away from? When will our patents expire and how will we then protect against knockoffs?

Strategic patenting, then, is simply the confluence of patent law (what can be patented and how) and project management with quality assurance ideas mixed in. That being said, no single strategy fits all companies: What works for IBM does not necessarily work for a life sciences start-up. And all of these concepts apply, to a certain extent, to other species of intellectual property: trade and service marks, copyrights, trade secrets, licensing programs, and the like. All the IP must be managed.

Probably the worst result is the expenditure of money for an analysis documented in numerous colorful reports and maps, presented to management at a series of meetings, and then filed away and forgotten—kind of like talking about ISO compliance for years and hiring ISO consultants, but never quite implementing it. Patent mapping services provide lots of data, but it is up to management to analyze the data and then act on the analysis.

Patent Glossary

Defensive patent—a patent procured to prevent anyone else from patenting the same idea, or to use to establish a patent truce.

Patent alignment—ensuring a company's patents are aligned with the company's business objectives.

Patent fence—numerous patents surrounding a product to protect it.

Patent map—also called *IP landscape*. Definitions vary, but usually these terms refer to a graphical interactive description of patents held by a particular company or covering a particular technology.

Patent scoring—the idea that certain metrics can be used to determine the value of a particular patent.

Patent thicket—the situation that occurs when the development of a given technology would almost certainly infringe several patents held by others.

Patent truce—the idea that Company A with lots of patents will never sue Company B, also with lots of patents, and vice versa because of the threat of retaliation.

Rembrandts in the attic—forgotten patents held by a company that may have value apart from defensive or offensive use.

White space—areas where patents might be possible. *Dark space* is where other companies hold patents.

Trade Secrets

One benefit of trade secrets is they can protect things a patent cannot. A *trade secret* is defined as knowledge, which may include business knowledge or technical knowledge, that is kept secret for the purpose of gaining an advantage in business over one's competitors. Customer lists, sources of supply of scarce material, or sources of supply with faster delivery or lower prices may be trade secrets. Such knowledge is not generally patentable. Certainly, secret processes, formulas, recipes, techniques, manufacturing know-how, advertising schemes, marketing programs, and business plans are all protectable.

Another benefit of trade secrets is there is no high standard of invention to meet as there is with a patent. If the idea is new in this context, if it is secret with respect to a particular industry or product, then it can be protected as a trade secret. Also, unlike patents, trademarks, and copyrights, there is no formal government procedure for obtaining trade secret protection. Protection is established by the nature of the secret and the effort to keep it secret.

Finally, a trade secret can be protected eternally against disclosure by all those who have received it in confidence and all who would obtain it by theft for as long as the knowledge or information is kept secret.

The key disadvantage of trade secrets compared with patents is that there is no protection against discovery by fair means, such as accidental disclosure, independent inventions, and reverse engineering. Many important inventions, such as the laser and the airplane, were developed more or less simultaneously by different persons. Trade secret protection would not permit the first inventor to prevent the second and subsequent inventors from exploiting the invention as a patent would. Also, it is generally difficult to keep secret anything sold to consumers.

The distinction between patents and trade secrets is illustrated in a case in which a woman who designed a novel key holder immediately filed a patent application. It was a simple design and could be easily copied. While the patent was still pending, she licensed it to a manufacturer for a 5 percent royalty, with the agreement that if the patent didn't issue in five years, the royalty would drop to 2.5 percent. The patent never issued, and the royalty was dropped to 2.5 percent. Over the next 14 years, on sales of $7 million, the manufacturer's edge eroded as others freely copied the design. The manufacturer repudiated the royalty contract on the grounds that it required payment forever for the small jump that the manufacturer got on its competitors, whereas the patent, had it issued, would have allowed only 17 years of exclusivity. The court held in favor of the inventor. The ruling allowed the inventor to receive 2.5 percent royalty for as long as the manufacturer continued to sell the key holder. Had the patent issued, royalties would have lasted only 17 years!

But don't be misled into thinking trade secrets are a fallback position to patents or that trade secrets are free protection. Consider the feature of the Windows program that allows you to open two files at the same time, display them on the screen, and drag content from one into the other. Nice feature, but it cannot be a trade secret. Why? Because you and everyone else can see the feature in operation every time you use it. Microsoft even advertises the feature. It's not a secret. Any competitor of Windows can write code that involves the same functionality. Microsoft's exact code that carries out that functionality is secret, to be sure, but even it is not free protection when you consider the overhead costs Microsoft incurs to ensure the code is always kept under wraps and the costs incurred to make sure Microsoft's numerous employees and consultants are subject to secrecy agreements.

Software law is really a collection of many different federal and state laws: patent law broadly protecting the functionality of the software; copyright law protecting the code itself and, to a limited extent, the structure of the code; trademark law protecting the commercial name given the software; trade secret law (in some cases); contract law for licenses associated with the software (click wrap licenses, shrink wrap licenses, user agreements, development agreements, and other software agreements); tort law (you'll want to disclaim warranties in all licenses); and even criminal law. The Digital Millennium Copyright Act further defines what is and what is not permissible in the area of reverse engineering and breaking access protection schemes implemented in software.

Many companies use both approaches, filing a patent application and during its pendency keeping the invention secret. When the patent is ready to issue, the company reevaluates its position. If the competition is close, they let the patent issue. If not, the patent application is allowed to go abandoned and trade secret protection is relied on. But following a change in law, patent applications are now published 18 months after their earliest filing date, voiding trade secret protection unless active steps are taken to prevent publication, such as agreement not to file an application for the invention in any foreign country.

Despite the problems with trade secrets, certain trade secrets have been appraised at many millions of dollars, and some are virtually priceless. For example, the formula for Coca-Cola is one of the best-kept trade secrets in the world. Known as "Merchandise 7X," it has been tightly guarded since it was invented over 100 years ago. It is known by only two persons within the Coca-Cola Company and is kept in a security vault at the Trust Company Bank in Atlanta, Georgia, which can be opened only by a resolution from the company's board of directors. The company refuses to allow the identities of those who know the formula to be disclosed or to allow them to fly in the same airplane at the same time. The company elected to forgo producing Coca-Cola in India, a potential market of 550 million people, because the Indian government requires the company to disclose the secret formula as a condition for doing business there. While some of the mystique surrounding the Coca-Cola formula may be marketing hype, it is beyond dispute that the company possesses trade secrets that are carefully safeguarded and are extremely valuable.

Secrecy is essential to establishing trade secret rights; without it there is no trade secret property. There are four primary steps for ensuring secrecy:

1. Negotiate confidential disclosure agreements with all employees, agents, consultants, suppliers, and anyone else who will be exposed to the secret information. The agreement should bind them not to use or disclose the information without permission.

2. Take security precautions to keep third parties from entering the premises where the trade secrets are used. Sturdy locks, perimeter fences, guards, badges, visitor sign-in books, escorts, and designated off-limits areas are just some of the ways that a trade secret owner can exercise control over the area containing the secrets.

3. Stamp specific documents containing the trade secrets with a confidentiality legend and keep them in a secure place with limited access, such as a safe or locked drawer or cabinet.

4. Make sure all employees, consultants, and others who are concerned with, have access to, or have knowledge about the trade secrets understand that they are trade secrets, and make sure they recognize the value to the company of this information and the requirement for secrecy.

Trade secret owners rarely do all of these things, but enough must be done so that a person who misappropriates the secrets cannot reasonably excuse his conduct by saying that he didn't know or that no precautions were ever taken to indicate that something was a trade secret. This is important because, unlike patents, trade secret protection provides no deed to the property.

Since there is no formal protection procedure, the necessary steps for establishing trade secrets are often not taken seriously until a lawsuit is brought by the owner against one who has misappropriated them. In each specific case the owner must show that the precautions taken were adequate. Those precautions, in turn, can incur significant overhead costs, especially as the number of secrets, employees, and consultants grow.

Trade secret misappropriation cases generally fall into one of two classes: Someone who has a confidential relationship with the owner violates the duty of confidentiality, or someone under no duty of confidentiality uses improper means to discover the secret.

Trade secret theft issues frequently arise with respect to the conduct of ex-employees. Certainly, a good employee will learn a lot about the business during his employment. And some of that learning he will take with him as experience when he leaves. That cannot be prevented. The question is, did he just come smart and leave smarter, or did he take certain information that was exclusively the company's?

For example, in one case a company that had been making widgets for the government for many years did not get its annual contract renewal. When the company questioned the loss of the contract, it was explained that a competitor was supplying widgets of equal quality at a lower price. Upon investigation, the company determined that the competitor was located in the same town, that the competitor's widgets were uncannily identical in every dimension, and that the competitor was owned by an ex-employee of the company who had left over a year before. Amicable approaches failed, and a lawsuit was instituted during which the company discovered that the ex-employee had copied their detailed engineering drawings to make the widgets. This eliminated all engineering and design costs and enabled the competitor to sell the widgets to the government at a much lower price.

But the ex-employee had not stolen anything. It seems the man knew that every year his ex-employer reissued important engineering drawings that had become torn and tattered or that needed updating, and threw out the old ones. The ex-employee testified that while driving by one day, he saw the old drawings sticking out of the dumpster. He drove in, took them out of the dumpster, put the ones he wanted in his car, and chucked the rest back in the dumpster. That's how he got a widget with identical dimensions. The court held him liable for misappropriation of trade secrets. He had trespassed to obtain the drawings, and he had learned of the ex-employer's practice of disposing of old drawings while an employee with a duty of confidentiality to the company. The court granted an injunction preventing the ex-employee from selling widgets for a period of months equal to the jump he got by not having to develop his own engineering drawings.

But what if the ex-employee had not trespassed to obtain the drawings from the trash? What if he had waited for the trash collector to remove them and then asked if he could look over the trash? Or what if he had gone to the dump and picked the drawings out of the mud? When does the owner part with ownership of trade secret materials dumped in the trash?

In summary, trade secrets can be valuable but they are not a form of free protection, nor is protection available for secrets which can be discovered. Still, in a survey, venture capitalists ranked trade secrets at least as important as patents when making an investment decision in a start-up company.

Trademarks

Trademarks are the stuff of marketing and advertising. Technically speaking, trademark protection is obtainable for any word, symbol, or combination thereof that is used on goods to indicate their source. Any word—even a common word such as *look*, *life*, or *apple*—can become a trademark, so long as the word is not used descriptively. *Apple* for fruit salad might not be protectable, but Apple for computers certainly is and so, too, is Apple for a record company.

Common forms such as geometric shapes (circles, triangles, squares), natural shapes (trees, animals, humans), combinations of shapes, or colors may also be protected. Even the single color pink has been protected as a trademark for building insulation. Three-dimensional shapes such as bottle and container shapes and building features (for example, McDonald's golden arches) can serve as trademarks.

> **If a name is too descriptive, it cannot be registered and may freely be used as is or in a slightly modified form by competitors. The more descriptive the mark, the less advertising required to inform consumers what the product is for. But, such a mark enjoys a much lower level of protection. On the other hand, a highly protectable arbitrary mark (Exxon®, Kodak®) requires significant expenditures in advertising dollars in order to inform consumers as to what the product or service associated with the mark actually is. Pick trademarks which are suggestive enough to adequately inform consumers but which are not too descriptive. Examples of marks held to be too descriptive include "Beer Nuts," "Chap-Stick," "Vision Center" (for an optical clinic), "Professional Portfolio System" (stock valuations), "5 Minute" (glue which sets in five minutes), "Body Soap" (body shampoo), "Consumer Electronics Monthly," "Light Beer," and "Shredded Wheat." The trademark Windows® itself has more than once been the subject of legal action wherein evidence existed that "windows" was descriptive before Microsoft adopted it.**

While people generally only speak of *trademarks*, that term also encompasses other types of marks. A trademark is for products. A *service mark* is a word or symbol or combination used in connection with the offering and provision of services. Blue Cross/Blue Shield, Prudential Insurance, and McDonald's are service marks for health insurance services, general insurance services, and restaurant services, respectively. *McDonald's* is both a service mark (fast-food restaurant services) and a trademark (the McDonald's brand Big Mac hamburger).

If you use any such name or feature to identify and distinguish your products, then think trademark protection. Ownership of a trademark allows you to exclude others from using a similar mark on similar goods that would be likely to confuse consumers as to the source of the goods. This right applies for the duration of ownership of the mark, which is as long as the owner uses the mark.

Trademarks can be more valuable to some companies than patents and trade secrets combined. Consider the sudden appearance and abrupt increase in the worth of trademarks such as Cuisinart, Haagen-Dazs, and Ben & Jerry's. Consider also the increased value that a trademark name such as IBM, Microsoft, or GE brings to even a brand-new product. But don't be misled—trademark and service marks protect the *names* of products and services, not the products and services themselves.

A trademark, unlike a patent, can be established without any formal governmental procedure. Ownership of a trademark is acquired simply by being the first to use the mark on the goods sold in commerce. And it remains the owner's property as long as the owner keeps using it. And keep using it you must, for nonuse for a period of three years or more may constitute abandonment.

The mark should not be too descriptive of the goods on which it is used, and it is best to select a mark that is arbitrary and fanciful with respect to the goods. This is because every company, including a competitor, has the right to use a descriptive term to refer to its goods. One case illustrates the limits associated with a trademark, especially if it is too descriptive. For years, a company operated a tourist service in Boston called Boston Duck Tours. Tourists were taken around the streets of Boston in amphibious vehicles and then into the water at the end of the tour. It was a good business until another company calling itself Super Duck Tours began offering the same service. There was even evidence in the case that people confused the two services. But the court found *Duck Tours* was highly descriptive, generic in fact, and thus Super Duck Tours was not an infringement of Boston Duck Tours, any more than Super Pizza would be an infringement of Boston Pizza.

A trademark owner should also take care to prevent a good mark from becoming generic, as happened to Aspirin, Cellophane, Linoleum, and other product names. Thus, it is not proper to refer to, for example, a xerox. The correct form of description is a Xerox brand photocopier.

It is wise to research a proposed new mark to be sure that the mark is clear before it is used—that is, to verify that no one else is already using or has registered the same or a similar mark on the same or similar products. It is confusing to customers and expensive to change a mark and undertake the costs of all new printing, advertising, and promotional materials when you later discover that your mark had previously been used by another. Moreover, in a due diligence study, either at the time of an investment in an entrepreneurial company, when a public offering is made, or during a sale or merger, you can be sure a trademark search will be conducted. It would be unfortunate, for example, if you've been incorporated in one state for five years under a company name used earlier by another company in another state. Also, if foreign markets are to be exploited, make sure your mark does not mean something unintended in a foreign language.

Registering a Mark

Although trademarks don't have to be registered, there are significant benefits associated with registration that make it worthwhile. Registration may be made in individual states, or a federal registration may be obtained. A state registration applies only in the particular state that granted the registration and requires only use of the mark in that state. A federal registration applies to all 50 states, but to qualify, the mark must be used in interstate commerce—commerce between two states. A distinct advantage of federal registration is that even if a mark is used initially only locally, say in New England, federal protection can be established in all 50 states. Without a federal registration, you may later be blocked from using your mark in other states if a later user of the same mark, without knowledge of your use of the mark, federally registers it.

Also, an application can be filed to register a mark that is not yet in use. After the U.S. Patent and Trademark Office examines the application and determines that the mark is registerable, the applicant is required to show actual use within six months.

The six-month period can be extended if good cause is shown for the nonuse. Nevertheless, before registration, even before actual use, the mere filing of the application establishes greater rights over others who actually used it earlier but did not file an application for registration.

A typical search and registration costs between $1,000 and $3,000 per mark. Given these fairly low costs, entrepreneurial companies regularly seek federal registration for all trade and service marks. A search is conducted to increase the odds that the registration will be successful, since the Trademark Office primarily evaluates two things: Is the mark too descriptive or it is too similar to another already registered mark? If the answer to both these questions is no, the registration typically issues about a year after the trademark application is filed.

Ownership of a Mark

Care must be taken with trademark properties. A trademark cannot simply be sold by itself or transferred like a desk or car, or a patent or copyright. A trademark must be sold together with the business or goodwill associated with the mark, or the mark will be abandoned. Further, if a mark is licensed for use with a product or service, provisions must be made for quality control of that product or service. That is, the trademark owner must require the licensee to maintain specific quality levels for products or services with which the mark is used. And the owner must actually exercise that control through periodic inspection, testing, or other monitoring that will ensure that the licensee's product quality is up to a prescribed level.

Ownership of a mark can be an important business decision. When Cuisinart started selling its food processors, it promoted them vigorously under the trademark Cuisinart. A good part of the business's success was due to the fact that the machines were sturdily made by a quality-conscious French company, Robot Coupe, who had been making the machines for many years before they became popular among U.S. consumers under the mark Cuisinart. When price competition reared its head, Cuisinart found cheaper sources. Robot Coupe owned no patents and had no other protection. When Cuisinart began selling brand X under the name Cuisinart, a wild fight ensued through the courts and across the pages of major newspapers in the United States, but to no avail. The whole market had been created under the name Cuisinart, and Cuisinart had the right to apply its name to any machine made anywhere by anyone it chose. Robot Coupe, whose machine had helped create the demand for food processors, was left holding its chopper.

Copyright

Copyrights cover all manner of writings, and the term *writings* is very broadly interpreted. It includes books, advertisements, brochures, spec sheets, catalogs, manuals, parts lists, promotional materials, packaging and decorative graphics, jewelry, fabric designs, photographs, pictures, film and video presentations, audio recordings, architectural designs, and software.

Exact copying is not always required in order to engage in infringement. For example, one can infringe a book without copying every word; the theme may be protected even though upon successive generalizations the theme will devolve to one of seven nonprotectable basic plots. This is apparent in the software area, where using the teachings of a book to write a program has resulted in copyright infringement of the book by the computer program. In another case, a program was infringed by another program even though the second program was written in an entirely different language and for an entirely different computer.

Copyright then, can sometimes be a good source of protection, but be careful: Copyright doesn't generally protect engineering, inventions, marketing or advertising ideas, or business plans. The good news is that a copyright registration is easy to obtain, protection lasts a long time, and it is inexpensive (typically less that $500). But unless your business is related to some form of the arts (music, movies, books, photography, etc) or software, copyright usually only offers very limited protection because ideas and functionality are not generally protected by copyright.

Registering a Copyright

Copyright registration is not compulsory, but it, too, bestows a few valuable benefits. If the copyright owner has registered the copyright, special damages can be recovered. This can be a real advantage in copyright cases where actual damages can be difficult and expensive to prove or actual damages are limited.

Registration simply requires filling out the proper form and mailing it to the Copyright Office with the proper fee and copies of the work to be registered. The Copyright Office doesn't really check to make sure the material is copyrightable: Provided the form is filled out correctly, the copyright office will stamp it and you have a registration.

Summing Up

Now consider the question posed at the beginning of this chapter: What parts of a handheld microprocessor-based product are protectable, and how can they be protected? The circuitry, the programming of the microprocessor, as well as the overall architecture and functionality of the product, could be protected by patents. All of the other software resident in the device could be protected by patent, too. That same software and the screen displays could be protected by copyright. The user's manual for the product could also be protected by copyright. The company name and the product name could be trademarks. The business and marketing studies and plans surrounding the product's introduction could be trade secrets—at least until the product is formally released. Sources of supply, customer lists, and ideas for later versions of the product could also be trade secrets. The table in Exhibit 11.2 summarizes a few key aspects of the different avenues of IP protection.

International Protection for Intellectual Property

Obtaining protection for patents, trademarks, and copyrights in the United States alone is no longer sufficient in the modern arena of international competition and global markets. International protection often needs to be extensive and can be quite expensive, but there are ways to reduce and postpone the expense in some cases. Protection must be considered in countries where you intend to market the new product or where competitors may be poised to manufacture your product.

A patent in one country does not protect the product in any other country: A novel product or method must be protected by a separate patent in each country. In addition, different countries have different conditions that must be met, or no patent protection can

Exhibit 11.2   Summary of IP Protection Methods

	Patents	Trade Secrets	Trademarks	Copyright
Subject Matter	Inventions, improvements and innovation (i.e., new products, features, functionality)	Only that which can be kept secret	Names of companies, their products and services	Works of authorship (i.e., the arts and software)
Cost	Expensive, $10–20K per patent per country	Depends on the volume of those secrets and the number of employees and consultants—definitely not free	Moderate, $1–3K per mark	Inexpensive, less than $500
Government Review	Yes—extensive and mandatory	No	Yes—moderate and optional but a good idea	Yes—but it is a rubber stamp.
Term of Protection	20 years from filing	Potentially forever—as long as the secret is kept secret	Potentially forever as long as the mark is used	Long time—100 years
How Long to Achieve Protection	A fairly long time: 3–5 years	Immediate	Immediate when the mark is used; registration takes about a year.	Immediate and registration takes only about a month.
Pros	Can provide very broad protection even when an infringer didn't know about your patent.	No government review; protects things not protectable by patents.	Cost is moderate and the odds of achieving a registration can be determined beforehand.	Inexpensive and immediate
Cons	Value is commensurate with the claims; high level of government scrutiny; strict time requirements.	Cannot be used if the "secret" really isn't. Others have the right to discover the secret on their own. Reverse engineering is legal.	Only protects names, not the products or the services themselves.	Outside of software and the arts, copyright usually doesn't offer extensive protection.

be obtained. The first and most important restriction is the *time* within which you must file an application to obtain a patent in a country or else *forever lose your right to do so*.

Patent Filing Deadlines

Not all countries are the same with respect to filing deadlines. For example, as previously noted, in the United States an inventor may still file an application to obtain a patent on an invention up to one year after the product has become public through a publication or public use of the product, or the sale or offer for sale of the product. This one-year period is known as the *period of grace*.

There is no period of grace in any other country. And each country has a slightly different view of what constitutes making an invention public. In Japan, for example, public use before the filing of an application bars a patent only if the public use occurred within Japan, but in France any public knowledge of the invention anywhere bars the patent.

Thus, whereas the United States allows a business *one full year* to test-market its new product, most other countries require that the patent application be filed *before any public disclosure*—that is, before the owner can begin to determine whether the new product will be even a modest success. And meeting this requirement is not inexpensive, especially when the U.S. dollar is down against the currencies of other major countries.

How to Extend Patent Filing Deadlines

However, there are ways around having to file immediately in all foreign countries. If you file in the United States and then file in another country within one year of the date on which you filed in the United States, the U.S. filing date applies as the filing date for that country. In this way, by filing one application for the invention in the United States, you can preserve your initial U.S. filing date for up to one year. This means that you can file an application in the United States, and then immediately make the invention public through advertising, published articles, and sales. If within one year the product appears to be a success, you can then file in selected foreign countries, even though the prior public use of the invention would ordinarily bar your filing in those countries. You can even delay up to 20 or even 30 months before the costs of filing in individual countries are incurred.

By filing a special Patent Cooperation Treaty (PCT) patent application in a specially designated PCT office within one year of your U.S. filing, and by designating certain countries, you can preserve your right to file in those countries without further expense for 20 or 30 months after the U.S. filing date. That will provide additional time for test-marketing the product. This does introduce the extra cost of the PCT application filing, but if you are considering filing in, say, six or more countries, the extra PCT filing may be well worth the cost for three reasons:

1. It delays the outflow of cash that you may not presently have or may require for other urgent needs.

2. It provides for a uniform examination of the patent application.

3. If the product proves insufficiently successful, you can decide not to file in any of the countries designated under the PCT and save the cost of all six national application filings.

Another cost-saving feature of international patent practice is the European Patent Convention (EPC), which is compatible with a PCT filing and which enables you to file a single European patent application and designate any one or more of the European countries in which you wish the patent to issue.

There are a number of international treaties that affect trademark rights and copyrights as well. A European trademark registration, for example, is now available, known as a Community Trade Mark (CTM), wherein a single registration will cover the entire European Union: With the benefit of a single filing, plenary protection is provided. However, there are certain drawbacks. For example, a single user in any country of the Union could block registration everywhere, and cost considerations make a CTM filing uneconomical generally unless trademarks are sought in at least three countries. Registration is also now possible simultaneously in the United States and other foreign countries via a treaty known as the Madrid Protocol.

Licensing and Technology Transfer

Let's now take yet another look at our handheld microprocessor-based product. We filed two U.S. patent applications last week and we did it before anything was made public about the product. The product introduction will occur in a few weeks. We now have nearly a year to file our foreign PCT patent application at a cost of between $3,000 and $5,000. It will then be a year and a half after that before we have to file in the specific countries at a cost of between $3,000 and $10,000 per country. But it is not too late to begin planning now. Where will we sell the product? Where will our competitors be located? Also, do we need trademark registrations in any of these countries?

Large and small businesses regularly *license out* their intellectual property and also *license in* the intellectual property of others. A license is simply a special form of contract or agreement that sets forth each party's future rights and obligations. It is a contract in which the subject matter is technology or intellectual property. Each party promises to do or pay something in return for the other party doing or paying something. Contracts that deal with the transfer of technology or, more broadly, intellectual property—patents, trade secrets, know-how, copyrights, and trademarks—are generally referred to as licenses. The licensed property can be anything from the right to use Mickey Mouse on a T-shirt or to make copies of the movie *Star Wars*, to the right to operate under the McDonald's name, to manufacture or sell a patented product (such as our handheld microprocessor-based product), or to reproduce, use, or sell a piece of software. Software licenses are just one of the many types of licenses. The basic considerations are the same as for any other license, but specific clauses and language are tailored to the software environment.

Sometimes the so-called boilerplate provisions of a license or other technology agreement can come back to haunt one or both of the parties. One court held that the contractual language "jurisdiction for any and all disputes arising out of or in connection with this agreement is California" was *permissive* rather than mandatory, allowing the defaulting company

(continued)

> to file suit in a location remote from the licensor. In other cases, courts have found inconsistencies between various boilerplate provisions placing important contractual rights in jeopardy. Even the contractual boilerplate is important and should be carefully thought out and drafted.

Common Concerns and Clauses

The term *license* is typically used to refer to a number of different types of contracts involving intellectual property, including primarily an assignment, an exclusive license, and a nonexclusive license. This broad reference is used in this section.

An *assignment* actually is an outright sale of the property. Title passes from the owner, the *assignor*, to the buyer, the *assignee*.

A license is more like a rental or lease. The owner of the property, the *licensor*, retains ownership; the buyer, the *licensee*, receives the right to use under the property, be it a patent, trade secret, know-how, copyright, or trademark. An *exclusive license* gives the licensee the sole and exclusive right to operate under the property to the exclusion of everyone else, sometimes even the licensor. A *nonexclusive license*, in contrast, permits the licensee to operate under the licensed property but without any guarantee of exclusivity. The licensor can try to find more licensees and license them, there may be others who are already licensed, and the licensor can also operate under the property.

By definition, an assignment is exclusive since the assignee acquires full right and title to the property. Many licensees prefer an assignment or exclusive license because they want a clear playing field with no competitors in order to maximize their revenue from the property and justify the license cost. Licensees, though, generally pay more for an exclusive versus a nonexclusive license.

Besides the nonexclusive versus exclusive consideration in licensing, there are a lot of other considerations and possibilities in a license. Only a few are listed here.

- Can the licensee sublicense or transfer the license?
- How long does the license last?
- What happens if there is a dispute concerning the license? Where and how is it settled?
- Are there any guarantees or warranties?
- What happens if improvements are made by the licensee to the property licensed?
- What happens if either the licensee or licensor goes bankrupt?

No consideration in a license, however, is more important than defining the property being licensed.

Defining the Property Being Licensed

Great care must be exercised to clearly define the property being licensed. For example, consider the following questions:

- Is it more than one patent, just one patent, or only a part of one patent?
- Is it just the trademark, or the entire corporate image—names, advertising, and promotional scheme and graphics?

- If it concerns copyright, does it cover just the right to copy a book or other printed material in the same print form, or does it include any of the following rights?
  - Translation into another language.
  - Adaptation for stage, screen, or video.
  - Merchandising its characters and events on T-shirts and toys.
- If it involves know-how or trade secrets, where are they defined?

Licensees must be sure that they are getting what they want and need. And a licensor must make clear the limits of the grant. In a software license, if the grant is only to use the software, not to modify it or merge it with other software, that must be expressly stated.

Limitations on Licenses

A license may have numerous, different limitations, including time, the unit quantity, and the dollar value of products or services sold. The license can also be limited geographically. Field-of-use limitations are quite common, too. This type of limitation restricts the licensee to exploit the licensed property only in a designated field or market.

Assigning Value to a License

Perhaps the most universal concern in negotiating a license is, how do you assign a dollar value to intellectual property? First, determine what it *cost* to acquire or build that property. For example, all of the following are hard costs that go into creating a property:

- The research and development cost involved in coming up with a new invention.
- The design cost of coming up with a new trademark or copyrighted work.
- The cost of commercializing the invention.
- The cost of advertising and promoting the trademark or copyrighted work.
- Incidental costs, such as legal costs, engineering costs, and accounting costs.

Second, determine how this intellectual property affects the profitability of the product or the business. Can you charge more because the product has a famous name or because of the new features the invention has bestowed on the product? Can your costs be cut because of the new technology of the invention? If so, determine dollar values for those figures.

You might also determine how much the intellectual property increases gross revenues by opening new markets or by acquiring a greater percentage of established markets. All of these figures can be converted into dollar amounts for valuation.

Royalty Rates

A typical royalty rate for a nonexclusive license to a patent, trade secret, or know-how is universally stated to be 5 percent, but that rule is breached as often as it is honored. Nonexclusive license royalty rates in patent licenses can be 10 percent, 20 percent, 25 percent, or even higher. And exclusive license royalty rates tend to be higher because the licensee receives total exclusivity and the licensor is at risk if the licensee does not perform. Exclusive licensors generally demand initial payments for the same reason. In determining a reasonable royalty as a damage award in an infringement suit, courts have considered the following factors:

- The remaining life of the patent.
- The advantages and unique characteristics of the patented device over other, prior devices.
- Evidence of substantial customer preference for products made under the patent.
- Lack of acceptable noninfringing substitutes.
- The extent of the infringer's use of the patent.
- The alleged profit the infringer made that is credited to the patent.

Negotiating License Agreements

In any commercial agreement in which the consideration promised by one party to the other is a percentage of profits or receipts or is a royalty on goods sold, there is nearly always an implied promise of diligent, careful performance and good faith. But licensors generally seek some way to ensure that the licensee will use its best efforts to exploit the property and maximize the licensor's income. One approach is simply to add a clause in which the licensee promises to use its "best efforts." Another approach is to compel certain achievements by the licensee. The license may require a minimum investment in promotion and development of the property, which may be expressed in dollars, human labor hours, or even specific stated goals of performance or sales. Or the simpler approach of a minimum royalty can be employed: The licensee pays a certain minimum dollar amount in running royalties annually, whether or not the licensee's sales actually support those royalties—not a pleasant condition for the licensee but one that provides a lot of peace of mind for the licensor.

Perhaps the best assurance of performance is a competent, enthusiastic licensee. A little preliminary investigation of the licensee (in terms of net worth, credit rating, experience, reputation, manufacturing/sales capability, and prior successes/failures) can assuage a lot of fears and eliminate risky licensees. A *reverter clause*, which evicts the licensee and returns control to the licensor in the event of unmet goals, is the ultimate protection. Often the licensor's greatest concern is that the licensee might now or later sell one or more competing products, leading to a plain conflict of interest. A *noncompetition clause* can prevent this, but antitrust dangers are raised by such clauses, and licensees do not like this constraint on their freedom. Other approaches are safer, such as specified minimum performance levels.

Confidential disclosure clauses are necessary in nearly all license agreements, especially those involving trade secrets, know-how, and patent applications. Such clauses are necessary to protect not only the property that is the subject of the license, but also all of the technical, business, financial, marketing, and other information the parties will learn about each other during the license term, and even during negotiations before the license is executed.

The Internet

Internet activity is placing new pressures on intellectual property practice. Uploading and downloading of copyrighted material on the Internet can be copyright infringement.

Copyright infringement has also been found in some cases against bulletin board operators and administrators who have received and stored such material.

Domain names are taking on some of the characteristics of trademarks. Further, there have been some instances where a party has incorporated a well-known name or mark of another in his own domain name, resulting in infringement. There is now a domain name dispute resolution system offering trademark owners a less expensive alternative to court when pursuing cyber squatters.

Web pages can be fraught with IP issues. Google, for example, was sued by Geico because when a user typed in "Geico" using the Google search engine, Geico's competitors were listed as sponsors. Ad words, spyware, pop-up ads, links, and other features of web sites are regularly litigated but often without predictable results. Dual-use software—software that both has legitimate purposes and can also be used to download or traffic in protected content—can also raise IP issues. Licensing via the Internet using so-called *click wrap* agreements can also be problematic if not undertaken in accordance with general contract law precepts. Finally, the dust has yet to settle on the question of whether a company located in one state can be sued in a distant state merely on account of the company's web site.

IP Agreements

Frequently, when a person thinks of protecting a new idea or product, the thoughts turn to patents, trade secrets, and copyrights. But the game can be won or lost long before one has the opportunity to establish one of those forms of protection. That is why a fundamental form of protection—confidential disclosure agreements, employment contracts, and consultant contracts—is so important. Whether or not an idea or product is protectable by an exclusive statutory right such as a patent or copyright, there still is a need at an early stage, before such protection can be obtained, to *keep the basic information confidential* in order to prevent public use or disclosure, which can result in the loss of rights and inspire others to seek statutory rights before you.

Confidential disclosure agreements, employment agreements, and consultant agreements have some things in common. They define the obligations of the parties during the critical early stages of development of a new concept, product, or process. They are usually overlooked until it's too late, after the relationship is well under way and a problem has arisen. One of the worst things that can happen in due diligence is to discover that a programmer hired by the company as an independent consultant never signed over his copyright in and to the company's flagship product. For proper protection of the business, there must be agreements with employees, consultants, and in some cases suppliers and customers to keep secret all important information of the business and to assign to the business all rights to that information.

It is commonly thought that only technical information can be protected. This is not so. All of the following can be protectable information:

- Ideas for new products or product lines.
- A new advertising or marketing program.
- A new trademark idea.
- The identity of a critical supplier.
- A refinancing plan.

And all of these can be even more valuable than the technical matters when it comes to establishing an edge over the competition and gaining a greater market share.

Employment contracts, consultant contracts, and confidential disclosure agreements all should be in writing and signed before the relationship begins, before any work is done, before any critical information is exposed, and before any money changes hands. A business must not be in such a rush to get on with the project that it ends up without full ownership of the very thing it paid for. And the employees, consultants, or other parties must not be so anxious to get the work that they fail to understand clearly at the outset what they are giving up in undertaking this relationship. Different jurisdictions have different rules—especially with respect to employees. Thus, it's best to have a local attorney draft or at least review your agreements to make sure they are not thrown out by a judge.

Transfer of Employee Rights to Company Innovations

One of the most important clauses in an employment contract is the agreement by the employee to transfer to the company the entire right, title, and interest in and to all ideas, innovations, and creations. These include designs, developments, inventions, improvements, trade secrets, discoveries, writings, and other works, including software, databases, and other computer-related products and processes. The transfer is required whether or not these items are patentable or copyrightable. They should be assigned to the company if they were made, conceived, or first reduced to practice by the employee. This obligation should hold whether the employee was working alone or with others and whether or not the work was done during normal working hours or on the company premises. So long as the work is within the scope of the company's business, research, or investigation or it resulted from or is suggested by any of the work performed for the company, its ownership is required to be assigned to the company.

Be careful if employees use so-called *open source* code. Such code is indeed open but it's not free. Often, the originator of the code requires that any patents relating to products containing any open source code in it be freely licensed to all. In due diligence, one question that might be asked of your company is, was any open source code used in your products? Expect a frown from the investors if the answer is yes.

This clause should not seek to compel transfer of ownership for everything an employee does, even if it has no relation to the company's business. For example, an engineer employed to design phased array radar for an electronics company may invent a new horseshoe or write a book on the history of steeplechase racing. An attempt to compel assignment of ownership of such works under an employment agreement could be seen as overreaching and unenforceable. The same may be true of a clause that seeks to vest in the employer ownership of inventions, innovations, or other works made for a period of time after employment ends or before employment begins.

Ancillary to this transfer or assignment clause is the agreement of the employee to promptly disclose the inventions, innovations, and works to the company or to any person designated by the company, and to assist in obtaining protection for the company, including patents and copyrights in all countries designated by the company. The employee at this point also agrees to execute:

- Patent applications and copyright applications.
- Assignments of issued patents and copyright registrations.
- Any other documents necessary to perfect the various properties and vest their ownership clearly in the company.

If these activities are called for after the employee has left the company, she is still obligated to comply but must be paid for time and expenses.

Noncompetition Clauses

A closely related notion is a *noncompetition* provision whereby the employee agrees not to compete during his employment with the company and for some period after leaving the company's employ. This is a more sensitive area. It may be perfectly understandable that a company does not want its key salesperson, an officer, a manager, or the head of marketing or engineering to move to a new job with a competitor and have the inside track on his ex-employer's best customers, new product plans, manufacturing techniques, or new marketing program. But the courts do not like to prevent a person from earning a livelihood. Courts do not compel a lifelong radar engineer, for example, to turn down a job with a competitor in the same field and instead take a job designing cellular phones.

However, the higher up and more important a person is in the operation of the company, the greater is the probability that that person will be prevented from competing if the employment agreement provides for it. Officers, directors, founders, majority stockholders, and other key personnel have had such provisions enforced against them, but even then the scope of the exclusion must be fair and reasonable in terms of both time and geography. A few months, a year, or even two years could be acceptable, depending on how fast the technology and market is moving. Worldwide exclusion might be acceptable for a salesperson who sells transport planes. In the restaurant business, a few miles might be all that is necessary. A contract that seeks to extend the exclusion beyond what's fair will not be enforced. In general, courts will heavily scrutinize noncompete agreements.

One way to ensure that an ex-employee does not compete is to allow the company to employ the person on a consultant basis over some designated period of time. In this way the employee's involvement in critical information areas can gradually be phased out, so that by the time the employee is free to go to a competitor there is no longer a threat to the company, and at the same time the employee has been fairly compensated.

Bear in mind, however, that even if ex-employees are free to compete, they are not free to take with them (in their memories or in recorded form) any trade secrets or any information confidential or proprietary to the company or to use it or disclose it in any way. To reinforce this, the employment contract should provide that the employee will not, during employment by the company or at any time thereafter, disclose to others or use for her own benefit or for the benefit of others any trade secrets or any confidential or proprietary information pertaining to any businesses of the company—technical, commercial, financial, sales, marketing, or otherwise. The restriction could also protect such information pertaining to the business of any of the company's clients, customers, consultants, licensees, affiliates, and the like.

Along with this, the employment contract should provide that all documents, records, models, electronic storage devices, prototypes, and other tangible items representing or embodying company property or information are the sole and exclusive property of the company and must be surrendered to the company no later than the termination of employment, or at any earlier time upon request of the company. This is an important provision for both the employer and employee to understand. In some states, the law imposes serious criminal sanctions and fines for the removal of tangible trade secret property.

Courts in different jurisdictions take different approaches to noncompetes. In New Hampshire, for example, an ex-employee cannot be prohibited from soliciting *all* the employers' customers. Instead, solicitation is prohibited only as to the customers with whom the ex-employee had contact during his employ. Massachusetts, in contrast, may uphold noncompete agreements that prohibit solicitation of all the company's customers irrespective of whether the ex-employee had contact with them. That being said, Massachusetts courts have completely invalidated noncompetes when, for example, the employee changed jobs within the company and was not required to execute a new noncompete.

Preventing Employee Raiding

Another potential area of conflict is *employee raiding*, the hiring away of employees by an ex-employee who is now employed by a competitor or who has founded a competing business. This is a particularly sensitive situation when the ex-employee holds a position of high trust and confidence and was looked up to by the employees she is now attempting to hire. And it is particularly damaging when the employees being seduced are critical to operations because of either their expertise or their sheer numbers. In all circumstances such an outflow of employees is threatening because of the potential loss to a competitor of trade secrets and know-how. This can be addressed by a clause prohibiting an employee, during her employment period and for some period thereafter, from hiring away fellow employees for another competing enterprise.

Employee Ownership of Copyright

One of the most hazardous areas of ownership involves the title to copyrights. If a copyrighted work is created or authored by an employee, the company automatically owns the copyright. But the employee must be a bona fide employee. That is, there must be all the trappings of regular employment. If a dispute arises over ownership between the company and the author, the courts will seek to determine whether the author was really an employee. Was this person provided a full work week, benefits, withholdings, unemployment insurance, worker's compensation, and an office or workspace? If the author was anything less than a full employee, the copyright for the work belongs to the person. It does not belong to the company!

This means that if the company hires a part-time employee, a consultant, a friend, or a moonlighter, that person may end up owning the copyright for the work. Thus, when the nonemployee completes the software system that will revolutionize the industry and bring income cascading to the enterprise, the nonemployee, not the company, will own the copyright. The company will own the embodiment of the system that the nonemployee developed for the company, but the nonemployee will own the right to reproduce, copy, and sell the system over and over again. It has happened. A company that spent hundreds of thousands of dollars to develop a software system owned the finished product but not the copyright in the product. The nonemployee owned the copyright and had the right to reproduce the product without limit and sell it to those who most desired it—typically the company's competitors and customers.

This is a chilling scenario but one that is easy to avoid with a little forethought. The solution is easy: Simply get it in writing. Before any work starts, payment changes hands, or plans are revealed, *have the proposed author sign a written agreement* specifying that, whether or not the author is subsequently held to be an employee or a nonemployee, all right, title, and interest in any copyrightable material is assigned to the company. The lack of such a clear understanding in writing can wreck great dreams, ruin friendships and partnerships, and hamstring businesses to the point of insolvency while the parties fight over who owns the bunny rabbit, the book, the software, the poster, or the videotape on how to be a successful entrepreneur.

Rights of Prior Employees

There is another issue to consider under employment contracts. When a new employee is to be hired, obtain a copy of the employment contract with the previous employer or the last few employers to determine whether this employee is free to work for this company now, in the capacity the employee seeks. Prior employers have rights, too, that can conflict, rightly or wrongly, with the employee's new employment.

Consultant Contracts

Consultant contracts should contain provisions similar to those in an employment contract, along with some additional provisions. A consultant agreement should clearly define the task for which the consultant is hired—for example, to research a new area; analyze or solve a problem; design or redesign a product; set up a production line; or assist in marketing, sales, management, technical, or financial matters. This is important to show:

- Why the consultant was hired.
- What the consultant is expected to do.
- What the consultant may be exposed to in the way of company trade secrets and confidential and proprietary information.
- What the consultant is expected to assign to the company in the way of innovations, inventions, patents, and copyrights.

A company hiring a consultant wants to own the result of whatever the consultant was hired to do, just as in the case of an employee. But a consultant's stock in trade is the expertise and ability to solve problems swiftly and elegantly in a specific subject area. Sharp lines must be drawn as to what the consultant will and will not assign, to give both parties peace of mind.

Consulting relationships by their nature can expose each of the parties to a great deal of the other party's trade secrets and confidential and proprietary information. The company can protect itself with clear identification of the pertinent information and by employing the usual safeguards for trade secrets. It also must limit disclosure to the consultant to what is necessary to do the job, and also limit the consultant's freedom to use the information in work for others and to disseminate the information. Consultants must protect themselves in the same way to prevent the company from misappropriating the consultant's special knowledge, problem-solving approaches, and analytical techniques.

An often overlooked area is the ownership of notes, memos, and failed avenues of investigation. False starts and failures can be as important as the solution, especially to competitors. Related to this is the question of the ownership of the raw data. Raw data may be extremely valuable in its own right but also may be used to easily reconstruct the end result of the consultant's work, such as a market survey.

Confidential Disclosure Agreements

Whenever an idea, information, an invention, or any knowledge of peculiar value is to be revealed, a *confidential disclosure agreement* (aka *nondisclosure agreement*) should be signed by the receiving party to protect the disclosing party. The disclosure may be necessary for any of the following reasons:

- To interest a manufacturer in taking a license to make and sell a new product.
- To hire a consultant to advise in a certain area.
- To permit a supplier to give an accurate bid.
- To allow a customer to determine whether or not it wants a product or wants a product modified.

Disclosure agreements are important not only to protect the knowledge or information itself, but also to preserve valuable related rights such as *domestic and foreign patent rights*. These agreements should be short and to the point.

Basically, the recipient should agree to keep confidential all information disclosed. Information is defined as all trade secrets and all proprietary and confidential information, whether tangible or intangible, oral or written, and of whatever nature (for example, technical, sales, marketing, advertising, promotional, merchandising, financial, or commercial).

The recipient should agree to receive all such information in confidence and not to use or disclose the information without the express written consent of the discloser. It should be made clear that no secrecy obligation is incurred for any information proven to be in the public domain.

The receiver should be limited to disclosing the information only to those of its employees who need to know in order to carry out the purposes of the agreement and who have obligations of secrecy and confidentiality to the receiver. Further, the receiver should agree that all of its employees to whom any information is communicated are obligated under written employment agreements to keep the information secret. The receiver should also represent that it will exercise the same standard of care in safeguarding this information as it does for its own, and in no event less than a reasonable standard of care. This latter phrase is necessary because some businesses have no standard of care or a very sloppy attitude toward even their own important information.

Provision should be made for the return of all tangible embodiments of the confidentially disclosed information, including drawings, blueprints, designs, parameters of design, monographs, specifications, flow charts, sketches, descriptions, and data. A provision could also be included preventing the receiving party from entering a competing business or introducing a competing product or service in the area of the disclosed information. Often a time limit is requested by the receiver, after which the receiver is free to disclose or use the information. Such a time period could extend from a few months to a number of years, depending on the life cycle of the information, tendency to copy, competitive lead time, and other factors present in a particular industry. Strong, clear language should be used to establish that no license or any other right, express or implied, to the information is given by the agreement.

While such confidential disclosure agreements between the discloser and receiver are the ideal, they are not always obtainable. The receiver may argue that no such agreement is necessary, saying in effect, "Trust me." Or the receiver may flatly refuse on the grounds that it is against its policy. Some large corporations turn the tables and demand that their own standard *nonconfidential* disclosure agreement be signed before the disclosure of any information.

Under a nonconfidential disclosure agreement, often referred to as *idea submission agreements*, the discloser gives up all rights to the information except as covered by a U.S. patent or copyright. Outside of those protections the receiver is free to use, disclose, or do whatever it wishes with the information. This is not due simply to arrogance or orneriness. A large corporation has many departments and divisions where research and development of new ideas is occurring unknown to other areas of the corporation. In addition, in a number of cases courts have held corporations liable for misappropriation of ideas and information when no written agreement existed, and even where a nonconfidential disclosure agreement purported to free the receiver from any restriction against dissemination and use of the idea.

If no agreement can be reached or if the nonconfidential disclosure agreement counteroffer occurs, the discloser must decide whether to keep the idea under the mattress or take a chance on the honesty of the receiver; however, in such a case it is wise to reduce the initial disclosure to a minimum to cut the losses should a careless or unscrupulous receiver make public or misappropriate the idea.

A middle ground that courts have recognized is an implied confidential relationship evidenced by the actions of the parties. In one case a letter soliciting a receiver's interest in a particular field and indicating that the matter was confidential, resulted in a face-to-face meeting between the discloser and receiver, where the full idea was revealed. Later, when the receiver came out with a product using the idea, the discloser sued and won. The letter set up a confidential relationship which the receiver did not reject, but rather accepted by meeting with the discloser and accepting the idea without any comment or exclusion. The letter was not signed by the receiver, but it bound the company nevertheless under the totality of the circumstances.

These basic forms of protection—employment contracts, consultant contracts, and confidential disclosure agreements—need not be complex or lengthy, but they are essential at the earliest stages of idea generation to protect and preserve for the business some of its most valuable and critical property.

A Final Summation

Consider now again our hypothetical handheld microprocessor-based product. Suppose we need a supply agreement for the microprocessor itself; a consultant to write the software; and a manufacturing house to deliver the main circuit board to us for final assembly. A license to a patent covering a component we want to incorporate in the product is required, and we also need a web site designer to develop our web site which will advertise the product for sale. Confidentiality concerns probably exist with respect to all the resulting agreements, as do ownership and noncompetition issues.

Time passes and the product is an unqualified success. Have any of our ex-employees, suppliers, consultants, or vendors begun competing unfairly? With our own IP—patents, copyrights, trademarks, and trade secrets—in place, we have a good chance at protecting our market share. And with our written agreements clearly spelling out the ownership, noncompetition, and confidentiality issues, we further protect our valuable IP.

Or did we rely on the wrong form of IP protection, forget to address IP ownership issues and/or the IP of others? Did our provisional patent application lack sufficient details? Did we fail to meet a deadline imposed by law, cut out certain types of protection because of budget constraints, or fail to conduct the necessary searches to make sure, for example, our trademark was clear? Now, not only might the people we once trusted compete, but others, too, might start eroding our market share or, worse, levy a charge of IP infringement against us.

One premise of this book is that entrepreneurship can be taught. The stewardship of intellectual property, too, being synonymous with entrepreneurship, can be learned. Intellectual property doesn't guarantee product sales or the success of a new service, but without IP protection, the entrepreneur has little chance of fending off the inevitable competition. And, as we have learned, some forms of IP protection have deadlines. Manage your IP from the beginning and later everything will be easier.

Downloadable Resources for this chapter available at www.wiley.com/go/portablembainentrepreneurship

Patent Management Spreadsheet

12

Selling in an Entrepreneurial Context

Mark P. Rice and H. David Hennessey

How This Chapter Fits into a Typical MBA Curriculum
The topic of selling doesn't fit into the typical MBA curriculum—but it should. Sometimes it gets mentioned in a marketing course, but faculty typically see marketing as a legitimate academic subject whereas selling is a skill to be learned on the job. Occasionally it is taught as an elective by an alumnus of the business school who has the ear of the dean, who believes that selling is a critically important skill for any MBA who aspires to management. (Deans hear regularly and loudly from employers and alumni that selling is a critical skill for any MBA graduate.) Occasionally a sales course is taught by regular faculty. If they teach it well and the course receives positive reviews from students, course enrollment is sustained year after year.

Who Uses This Material in the Real World—and Why It Is Important
In every corner of every enterprise—for profit or not-for-profit, business or nonbusiness, large or small—selling is a fact of life. It's going on inside the enterprise, and between the enterprise and external entities. An engineer is trying to sell his project idea to his manager, seeking funding, use of facilities and equipment, and other employees to be assigned to her project team. An accountant in the budget office is trying to sell a manager on complying with the reporting guidelines, tracking expenses in a systematic manner, and meeting the quarterly report submission deadline. The finance professional is trying to sell a rating agency on raising the firm's bond rating. A young professional in the marketing department is trying to sell the business unit manager on altering the mix of marketing methodologies and on allocating a larger portion of the marketing budget to search-engine optimization. A software engineer in the IT department is trying to sell her boss on abandoning the decades-old legacy software that is consuming the staff with software maintenance and moving to a more productive platform. And of course, salespeople are meeting with current and potential customers, communicating their value propositions and trying to win orders. Selling gets people talking about the pros and cons of various alternatives as a precursor to making a decision and to agreeing to a path forward. Sales is the human activity that reduces the resistance at every boundary in every value chain and in every value network between supplier and customer.

Introduction

This chapter explores how selling fits into the portfolio of knowledge, skills, and attitudes necessary for entrepreneurial success. We start by exploring a mindset for success in selling—consultative selling or value selling—and then discuss how to make that mindset operational. We end the chapter with a discussion of the skill sets that can be developed through practice over time.

All too often entrepreneurs fall into the better mousetrap trap mythology. The statement attributed to Ralph Waldo Emerson goes as follows:

> If a man can write a better book, preach a better sermon, or make a better mousetrap than his neighbor, though he build his house in the woods, the world will make a beaten path to his door.

It is commonly accepted business wisdom that this concept misses the importance of sales and marketing. The first author of this chapter served as the director of a technology business incubator for five years, and interacted with a significant number of brilliant engineers and scientists who lived the Emerson quote. They were developing innovative technologies with little appreciation for the difficulty of getting customers to write a check. The accompanying box tells one of their sad tales.

Better Mousetrap Case Study

One entrepreneurial team—composed of two mechanical engineers and one software engineer—wrote an excellent business plan for the development of an automated system for circuit board testing and repair. Until that time, all of the elements of the production process for circuit boards had been automated with the exception of test and repair. As a result, circuit boards that failed the testing process piled up in the corner, awaiting human attention. The founders of the new venture had deep experience working in a previous venture involved in computer integrated modular manufacturing, which itself was a spinoff of a world-class automation company.

During the incubator admissions review process, the incubator director commented to the team: "I believe there is a good chance that you will be able to complete prototype development in three months, as you project in your plan, but I'm more skeptical about the prospects for ramping up sales to $1 million per year by the end of the first year." The company was admitted to the incubator, and sure enough, finished the prototype within three months. At the one-year mark, the company had to shut down—as it had not yet made a sale and had run out of cash. In the debrief, a member of the founding team commented to the incubator director: "We heard you when you told us that selling our system might prove to be more difficult than we anticipated in our business plan, but we had no idea what you were talking about. We didn't understand that getting customers to buy our system would be so difficult."

Mindset for Successful Selling: Good Selling versus Bad Selling

When someone is asked what comes to mind when he hears the term *salesperson* (or salesman or saleswoman), typical responses include "pressure," "manipulation," "won't take no for an answer," "revulsion," "sleazy," and "slimy." Why do people have these negative reactions? They feel that salespeople have tried to manipulate them into buying something they don't want or need, or that doesn't really fulfill their wants or needs, all for the purpose of meeting the salesperson's need to make quota. The typical consumer has over the years had numerous—and too often negative—interactions with automobile, time-share, appliance, telemarketing, real estate, and insurance salespeople, many of whom are not professionally trained or skillful in relationship or consultative selling. Hence, many consumers have a poor perception of salespeople because they have been repeatedly subjected to bad sales practices.

Bad selling can also take the form of nonselling. If the buyer really needs to buy what the seller has to offer in order to acquire a product or service that is essential for the buyer's success, then the seller has a responsibility to help the buyer through the buying process—ideally professionally, efficiently, and painlessly.

The classic *nonseller* is the typical sales clerk in a store's clothing section of a department store. When the shopper wanders in and starts looking around, the sales clerk will approach and ask: "Can I help you?" The buyer, trying to avoid being bothered by a bad seller, states: "No, I'm just looking." Typically the sales clerk walks away, instead of saying: "Perhaps I can help you determine whether we have what you are looking for? If yes, then you can decide whether you are interested in buying it today. Since I know what we have in stock, I've been able to help many other shoppers save time during their search process. If you are willing to share with me what you are looking for, I promise to help you through your search process and, if you prefer, leave you alone in your decision-making process." Most shoppers—whether just browsing or absolutely sure about their purpose in shopping—would be so stunned by this very different and very professional approach that they would happily engage the sales clerk in looking for a positive outcome.

This chapter focuses on *consultative* selling—a concept and philosophy widely espoused in books on the topic of selling (see the Additional Resources at the end of this chapter for a short list of some of the books that advocate this perspective on the selling process). If the right decision for a prospective customer is to buy your product or service, then you have a professional responsibility to help that individual reach that decision. Conversely, if your product or service really isn't a good fit with his needs, then you have a responsibility to help the individual recognize that and help him pursue an alternative. *Value* selling is a relationship-building process through which the salesperson communicates the potential value of a product/service to prospective customers. The prospective customer returns value to the salesperson by carefully considering the value proposition;

engaging with the salesperson in the decision-making process; and, ultimately, if the product fits the customer's needs, then buying it.

Those who excel in consultative selling will actually serve their customers as *buying consultants*. A highly skillful consultative salesperson will help the customer through the customer's own buying process, helping ensure that the buyer makes a wise decision, even if it's to purchase a competitor's offering. This approach establishes trust—leading the buyer to come back to the consultative salesperson later when there is a good fit between the buyer's needs and the salesperson's offerings, and to refer other buyers to the trustworthy, professional, and skillful consultative salesperson.

Linking the Entrepreneurial Mindset and Selling

An individual who has a well-developed entrepreneurial mindset focuses on two activities: (1) recognizing and assessing opportunity; and (2) proactive, passionate, persistent, and professional pursuit of the opportunity. In an entrepreneurial context, *opportunity* is defined by the extent to which there is a good fit between a need in the marketplace and the entrepreneur's offering. Typically the need in the marketplace is currently unmet or underserved, or in some cases may be created by a new and innovative offering by the entrepreneur that changes the basis of competition in an industry. Most often the entrepreneur's offering takes the form of a product or service. The concept of opportunity is essentially the same in a sales context. The seller seeks to identify and assess customer needs, and if there is a good fit between the customer needs and the seller's offerings, then the seller pursues the opportunity for a win-win. The customer wins by making the purchase and the seller wins by making the sale.

Establishing trust is important in entrepreneurial selling. The entrepreneur—particularly during start-up and early growth—has no track record (nor established brand) to reduce the perceived risk on the part of the buyer. Any failure to perform in the best interests of the potential customer dramatically decreases the probability that the customer will take on the risk of purchasing an unknown and untried offering, and increases the probability that the customer will take the safe route and go with a proven supplier.

Trust is important in all of the relationships the entrepreneur seeks to establish. Entrepreneurs do not always have all the resources they need in order to pursue their opportunities. Hence entrepreneurs need to be skillful in resource acquisition—which means they are constantly selling someone on their dreams in order to get access to resources for free, at a discount, or on a temporary, marginal-cost basis. In addition to potential customers, they are selling potential co-founders, key employees, advisers, service providers, landlords, suppliers, investors—and often spouses or significant others. If the entrepreneur is pursuing aggressive growth, the various buyers and the entrepreneur's value proposition are constantly in a state of flux.

Starting with an entrepreneurial mindset, the entrepreneur engages in consultative selling, in order to build trust and to efficiently and effectively determine whether the entrepreneur's offering is a good fit with the buyer's need. However in most cases the first salesperson in an entrepreneurial venture is the founder, who often has deep understanding (and enthusiasm) for a wonderful product, service, or technology. Often the driven entrepreneur will focus 100 percent on the new product, service, or technology without ever asking prospective customers about their needs. Consultative selling focuses the seller's effort on engaging with the buyer in a process of determining the ideal value proposition (or perhaps a set of alternative and equally acceptable value propositions) from the buyer's perspective. Although the salesperson rarely has the freedom to ignore his firm's own selling process, efficiency and effectiveness will improve to the extent that the seller can adapt and align the selling process to the buyer's purchasing process.

Aligning the Buying and Selling Processes

The ultimate role of the salesperson is to help the buyer make a purchase decision. The pathway to that outcome typically does not follow the steps the salesperson has learned to implement in the selling process, but rather the steps the buyer will follow in the buying process. Hence, the salesperson will utilize whatever is useful in the selling process in order to engage professionally and proactively in the buyer's buying process. The successful salesperson will do whatever is necessary, appropriate, and useful in assisting customers through the process they use to buy products or services. Exhibit 12.1 documents the relationship between a typical buying process and a typical selling process.[1] The activities identified in the exhibit are frequently iterative, rather than linear, but ultimately must reach closing and post-close follow-up if the selling/buying process is to be successful. If the sales process is truncated quickly and efficiently because it is determined that there is not a good fit between customer needs and seller's offerings, that outcome can be viewed as a success as well.

The seller might execute all the steps in the selling process in outstanding fashion and yet not make the sale. However, if the buyer does everything required in his company's buying process in order to make the purchase—even if the seller does not complete all the tasks in the selling process—then the purchase/sale can be closed. Hence, the seller will increase the probability of making a sale by doing everything possible to help the buyer move through the buyer's buying process. This idea goes far beyond addressing

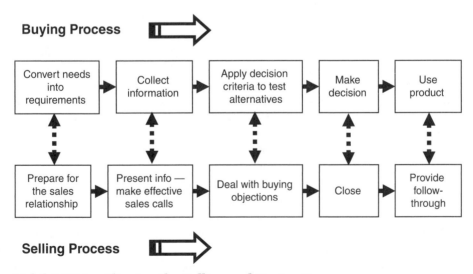

Exhibit 12.1   Aligning the Selling and Buying Processes

the purchase specifications propagated by a buyer's purchasing department. It starts with the idea that the seller will achieve desired sales results only if the seller's product or service enables the buyer to achieve business results, such as increasing market share to grow revenue, increasing profitability, increasing customer satisfaction, and so forth. This requires the seller to engage in a much more comprehensive approach in preparing for the sale.

Finding, Assessing, and Preparing to Pursue Sales Opportunities

The primary reason that companies buy products or services is to improve performance—as measured by increased sales, increased profitability, lower costs, improved utilization of assets, and so forth. The buyer (in the role of seller in the value chain) looks at what its customer needs in order to be successful, and even further to help its customers understand the needs of their customers. This deep understanding of the downstream participant(s) in its value chain, as well as knowledge of what is available from its potential suppliers, enables the buyer to develop products/services to meet its customers' needs, and further to define initial requirements and specifications for products/services that it will outsource to suppliers. Meanwhile the seller is studying the needs of the potential buyers for its goods and services—starting with a search for and identification of a set of competitors (an industry) with unmet or underserved needs that the seller might be able to meet. When an attractive industry is indentified, then the seller begins identifying and assessing individual potential buyers, a process referred to as *prospecting*.

For a salesperson starting out in an established organization, there already exists a customer base and a sales history. The primary focus of this salesperson may be on doing more of the same and doing it better. However, the salesperson in an entrepreneurial context needs to build the sales pipeline and a customer base, which often means displacing established suppliers. The entrepreneurial firm needs to determine how it can differentiate itself from current suppliers or substitutes—in ways that matter to the buyer. To determine which potential customers may have the greatest motivation to consider the offerings of a new entrant into the marketplace, the entrepreneur needs to develop deep understanding of (1) the overall environment in which the industry operates; (2) the characteristics of the industry; and (3) the characteristics of each individual firm competing in that industry.

Understanding the Environmental Context

Entrepreneurs often pursue opportunities in markets that are dynamic, rather than settled with well-established customers and suppliers and well-established routines. These markets may be undergoing rapid change as a result of disruptions in the context in which they operate. The disruptions may be precipitated by (1) government action, such as changing regulations in health care or fuel efficiency; (2) rapid change or discontinuities in the economy; (3) environmental changes, such as global warming, hurricanes, or earthquakes; (4) geopolitical crises, like war in the Middle East; (5) decrease in availability of basic inputs, like energy, water, and raw materials; (6) breakthrough innovations driven by new scientific discoveries, such as the Internet, mapping the human genome, nanotechnologies, stem cell research, and so forth. Entrepreneurs and entrepreneurial salespeople can get buried in the details of start-up and survival, and lose sight of the forest while focusing on the trees. In order to understand trends and anticipate change, some percentage of total bandwidth needs to be reserved for maintaining a perspective of the big picture.

In addition to understanding the competitive landscape in the salesperson's own industry, it is important to understand the overall context in which the customers operate. The process of identifying and assessing the factors and trends in the external context that may drive decision-making by customers (including buying decisions) is called *environmental analysis*. One commonly used framework for environmental analysis—often referred to as P.E.S.T.—is based on four components of context:

1. **P**olitical and legal factors and trends.
2. **E**conomic factors and trends.
3. **S**ocial and cultural factors and trends.
4. **T**echnological factors and trends.

In order for the salesperson to keep abreast of changes in the customer's environmental context and industry (as discussed in the next section), it is useful to review industry publications, attend trade shows, subscribe to relevant online newsletters, join industry blogs, view security analysts' reports, and build a professional network. For example, if the salesperson's company has developed a new device to track underground water leakage in pipes, it may be useful to read *Engineering News Record*, a magazine that targets engineers; or to attend the American Water Works Association annual conference; or to subscribe to the National Rural Water Association newsletter. Given the very large potential federal investment in state and local infrastructure, the salesperson may want to contact his senator or representatives in Washington to determine what funding may be available to find and repair water leaks in municipal water systems.

Keeping up-to-date with the customer's environment will enable the salesperson to identify pressure points which may force an industry to change. For example, the U.S. Congress recently approved a higher education law that requires college campuses to have a certain type of security devices to protect students. This new law may force colleges and universities to replace current door-locking systems, which could present a significant selling opportunity for companies who manufacture advanced security technologies.

Understanding the Customer's Industry

Understanding customers requires the salesperson to develop a deep understanding of the industry in which they operate. The industry view is based on gaining insights from analyzing an entire industry. With this different, more comprehensive, and more coherent view of an entire industry, a rich set of insights can be gained that deal with the dynamics of an industry, eventually leading to an understanding of the basic requirements that must be addressed by all competitors. These basic requirements, called key success factors (KSFs), are essential building blocks for developing a sophisticated understanding of competitive strategies being adopted within the set of competitors. This understanding of the KSFs is a prerequisite for figuring out the strategy of each target customer and determining the value that the salesperson can create for each customer.

The basic building block of understanding an industry is the macro business system. It includes all industry participants connected in a successive chain of value-adding units, starting from raw materials and moving downstream to original equipment manufacturer (OEM) customers, wholesalers, retailers, and customers or end users. It may also include complementers that are not directly part of the value chain but who are a part of the overall system. In many situations the value chain also includes a recycling stage.

Just as in macro economics, where *macro* denotes the study of the behavior of the economy as a whole, the term *macro business systems* applies to an entire industry with all the relevant participants represented in the value-added stream, both up- and downstream, from the point of view of any particular participant in the value chain. The number of different stages present in a macro business system depends on the prevalent industry structure and the extent to which one finds freestanding activities among independent firms. For any stage in a macro value chain represented by a significant number of independent entities, a separate stage or participant category needs to be considered for analysis.

A standard (and simplified) model of a business system consists of raw material suppliers, manufacturers, distributors, and customers/end users. Although it is helpful to illustrate the concept of the business system in a simple version, reality is such that most industries are more complex and will require the analyst to think more creatively about the value-creating flow. The standard business system view is appropriate for firms supplying components or raw materials that become part of their global account's own products.

Once the salesperson has assembled the necessary data to lay out the industry macro business system for a potential customer, the next step is to extract the key lessons from the analysis. To be successful in consultative selling, a salesperson needs to learn a client's requirements for success in a given industry. The salesperson needs to crack the code of the industry, which contains the key success factors, or basic competitive requirements to succeed. The industry *code* is the behavior required from a company participating in the value chain (or network) in order to assure long-term success. The code must be followed to achieve profitability and success. Implied in this language is the understanding that violating the industry code would endanger the profitability of a business.

To be useful, the code needs to contain an industry's *imperatives*, which are a collection of musts, or things a company must do. They are different from mere *core competencies*, which describe what a company does well. Imperatives are important for a company to know, because they must be observed for long-term success. Also included in the industry code are the key success factors, which are the basic competitive requirements that an industry participant needs to master for long-term success. Typically, KSFs describe basic actions, or industry behaviors, that winning companies must master. We categorize KSFs into *qualifiers,* which determine if a participant is able to play in an industry, and *differentiators*, which are KSFs that can set players apart from others. All industry participants need to comply with the qualifiers, but only some players may perform on the basis of differentiators.

For an industry code to be of value, it must answer some important questions that relate to the competitive behavior in an industry. Following is a list of some typical imperatives that are part of a code, but each industry is likely to have aspects that may be unique. Here are some of the more frequently cited elements of an industry code.

- *Must segments* are segments in which a competitor needs to be present in order to be a major player. Must segments are important because of their relative size, their above-average profitability, or their growth and technical development. Once must segments have been identified, every leading player should be in those sectors.

- *Minimum amount of market coverage* to reach strategic goals is also a strategic conclusion that comes from understanding the industry code. For example, a company might need to have access to, say, 60 percent of the total market opportunity to be a leader. It may be able to achieve its strategic objective with less (or might need more), but it needs to have determined this factor in the industry code.

- *Critical mass*, a frequently cited notion in many industries, can also be of prime importance. Described as the minimum size required to be competitive, or successful, critical mass is difficult to assess because the definition is not apparent. Critical mass may occur around a company's entire volume, or may be more relevant if assessed by segment, country or geographic unit, key function (such as minimum R&D budget), or another part of a company's business. Again, a deep understanding and appreciation of the industry's relevant critical mass comes from the analysis mentioned earlier.

- *Required level of integration* can be important in some industries. The industry code may require different levels of integration for a firm to be successful. *Forward integration* deals with the ownership or control of the downstream part of the industry. *Backward integration* deals with the upstream aspects of ownership or control. Understanding the relevant amount of integration and its impact on industry profitability is an important part of sizing up the industry.

- *Required focus*, or restrictions on selected activities, can be an important part of the industry code in most industries. The important job of the analyst is to figure out where firms should focus. Focus dimensions might include integration levels, range of products, range of segments, geographic spread, range of technologies, and so forth.

- *Strategic dilemmas* can be expressed as critical questions that face company senior executives and cause them to lose sleep at night. One of the frequently asked questions when dealing with global account teams is how a team may develop a deep understanding of the client's strategic dilemmas. Those dilemmas that are already widely recognized, expressed in a company's annual report, or learned by the seller from discussions with the client are not perceived by the client to be as impressive and as valuable as those obtained independently by the entrepreneur/seller. If an account team wants to do more than read up on an industry, uncovering the answers to a few critical questions that reflect strategic dilemmas will help shape a proprietary view of the client's industry.

Reviewing the industry's development and assessing the strategic dilemmas faced by industry participants could contribute to developing a proprietary view of the client's industry and the challenges facing the client. Dilemmas manifest themselves through choices or decisions to be made—determining which forks in the road to take. Dilemmas could be centered on forward or backward integration, segment focus, bundles of segments, mastering of single or multiple technologies, and so on.

Salespeople need to look beyond the firm or individual normally identified as their *customer*, to firms that are one or more steps downstream in the business system. A thorough analysis requires moving all the way downstream, sometimes including multiple stages in the business system, to include all downstream industry participants. Equally important, a comprehensive perspective of the business system involves a look at any upstream participants of a firm's industry.

Understanding the Client's Strategy

Building on the foundation of deep understanding of the customer's context and industry, the salesperson also needs to develop a deep understanding of each customer's requirements and strategy, in order to better understand how the salesperson's products and/or services may be able to create value for the customer.

Assessing the company's competitiveness may start with an understanding of its strategic position compared to that of directly competing firms. Common ways of assessing position are determining industry rankings or market share in either unit volume or sales. While being aware of rankings can be useful, it's also important to be cognizant of the fact that a company may not compete in all sectors of a given industry.

An understanding of the customer's industry and competitive landscape may reveal strategic dilemmas the customer faces. Strategic dilemmas are similar to forks in the road: A decision has to be made as to which fork to take, but it is not always clear which one. In any industry, companies face such choices, or dilemmas, where a decision appears to be required in the form of a choice, but it is not always apparent how to resolve the dilemma.

The entrepreneurial salesperson should look out for major strategic dilemmas confronting players in an industry. The strategic dilemmas will often drive a firm's strategy to win. Working with many firms, we have found that customers place a premium on salespeople who understand their problems and strategic issues. Demonstrating knowledge of a client firm's strategic dilemmas is a proxy for customer orientation or closeness to a client's business. Such perceived closeness builds credibility and opens the door to more business. Beyond providing credibility with the customer, this kind of close relationship also reveals additional opportunities for the salesperson's firm to deliver value to the customer, and hence to develop additional sales opportunities.

One useful framework for assessing a customer's strategy suggests that a company should seek to be the market leader in operational excellence (enabling lowest cost), should strive for product leadership (requiring a commitment to innovation), or should focus on establishing customer intimacy, while being at least average in the remaining two disciplines.[2] Understanding the customer's strategy enables the salesperson to customize the offering and to deliver it in a way that maximizes value to the customer.

Data Sources for Developing a Deep Understanding of Context, Industry, and Customer

Naturally, good data sources will be of substantial help. For most consultative salespeople, it is essential to engage in a process of gathering and analyzing data that will create a foundation for deep understanding of the overall environment in which the customer operates, the industry in which the customer competes, and the customer's competitive strategy. This may appear to the salesperson to be a somewhat daunting task and a distraction from getting out there and selling. However, the consultative salesperson cannot provide significant and differentiated value to the customer without this understanding. In today's freewheeling and information-rich environment, an amazing amount of data is openly available at no or low cost—readily accessible to the person who makes an effort.

Throughout the previous sections, we have noted potential sources of data and will provide here only a limited list.

- Investor analyst reports, particularly those sections that cover the industry of a target company, not just the company itself.
- Publicly available information on industries through daily newspapers, weekly magazines, industry trade journals, other journals accessible through Web-based search engines, and so forth.
- Government-issued information, or reports issued by semipublic agencies.
- Reports prepared by independent research organizations, usually for a fee.
- Trade shows.
- General Web-based information, although the user must be careful to confirm its reliability.

Data Sources for Developing a Deep Understanding of the Target Client

- Investor analyst reports, particularly those parts that focus on the target client. (We suggest using several analysts, not just one, and being sensitive to potential bias.)
- Publicly available information on specific competitors within industries—through daily newspapers, weekly magazines, industry trade journals, other journals accessible through Web-based search engines, and so forth.
- Target company publications, including annual reports, SEC filings, web sites, and press releases.
- General Web-based information, although the user must be careful to confirm its reliability.
- Communications with the client via e-mail, mail, telephone, or in person meetings.
- The salesperson's customer service department.

Developing a Compelling Value Proposition

Delivering superior value is the essence of a successful selling process. The value offered should be superior to competing alternatives and should create a specific, measurable, and favorable result for the customer. Ultimately, the value the customer seeks is improved business performance. Buying a particular product or service is simply the means to that end. The customer recognizes the current, unsatisfactory state, and envisions a future, more satisfactory state. The purchase of the seller's product or service creates value by enabling the customer to move from the current state to the future state.[3] An in-depth understanding of the customer's needs will enhance the potential for discovering and delivering superior value, compared with that achieved by current or other potential suppliers.

A benchmark study of 58 firms determined that clients are willing to pay for four broad categories of value: technology, processes, administrative services that reduce costs, and sales and marketing support.[4] The examples that follow are of established brand-name companies (most often the subjects of business cases), but the principles are equally applicable to entrepreneurial ventures, particularly because they often have to compete against established incumbent suppliers.

Customers highly value technology that is core to their business results but not within their capabilities to produce. For example, Occidental Chemical has developed a portfolio of high-technology, value-added services such as technical support, logistics, product management, and R&D which their customers highly value.

Customers value processes that improve productivity by improving quality, reducing overhead, and producing measurable savings. For example, Marriott has developed a process to train travel agents on their bookings, product knowledge, service knowledge, and consultative skills, which better serves the customers who in turn may opt to stay at a Marriott property. This process improves the individual travel agent's productivity, as well as the entire agency's profitability.

Customers value administrative services that reduce costs and improve profit. For example, Boise Cascade Office Products developed an information system that allows customers to review pricing, delivery, service, and remedial action independently at any time.

Sales and marketing support that leads to increased sales is also valued by customers. For example, AC Delco has an advertising campaign that supports a strong brand, which, combined with other retail support, boosts sales growth for its customers.

Another useful framework for creating a value proposition is embodied in the concept of a *resulting experience* for the buyer—the events that the customer experiences as a result of using and interacting with the supplying firm's products, services, and actions.[5] A *resulting experience* is:

- An event, or sequence of events, physical and/or emotional, that happens in the customer's life because of doing what some supplier business proposes.
- The end-result consequence of this event for the customer.
- An experience that is superior, equal, or inferior in comparison to a customer's alternative experience.
- The value for the customer of this relative consequence.
- Specific and measurable: One can objectively determine if the customer experienced the events, consequences, and value compared to alternatives.

In developing the value proposition, it is helpful to have complete understanding of the level of problems the customer is facing and the potential for a superior resulting experience that addresses one or more of those problems. Delivering the value proposition to a customer is a dynamic and continually changing endeavor. In order for the nature of the relationship between buyer and supplier to change from one focusing on transactions to one that focuses on a strategic relationship, the original value proposition must change—and in fact shift toward creating significantly more value that contributes to the customer's success in ways that can be measured by the customer. Any change in the value proposition will also change its delivery.

The successful delivery of a value proposition is rooted in the supplier company's ability to constantly communicate the value it is creating for the client company and to engage the client company in providing feedback. Effective communication enables a forum in which both companies can improve the value proposition. The value proposition delivery system starts with the strategy of both the supplying company and the client company. The value proposition should include a time frame (for both implementation and delivery), the intended customer (a specific group within the client company or the client's customers), customer alternatives, and the intended resulting experience the client company should receive as a result of the supplier's offering.

Delivery of the value proposition requires putting the understanding of the process of developing the value proposition into action. Delivering the value proposition means turning the abstract concepts behind the value proposition into tangible products, services, and, most importantly, relationships that are mutually profitable in the long term. Providing a product or a service is the most obvious way the supplier delivers on the value proposition, which starts with engaging with the customer in the buying process, closing on the purchase, and supporting the customer's use of the product/service as a vehicle to achieve an intended business result. The product/service vehicle is tailored to meet the unique intended needs of the client company. Since successful selling is as much about relationships as it is about products and services, the value proposition needs to recognize this, thus making it a product/service/relationship vehicle.

Communication is the means through which a client company understands the value proposition and, if it is superior to competitive offerings, accepts and adopts it. Communications can take the form of advertising, presentations, packaging, or newsletters, but the most compelling communication is carried out through the direct salesperson-buyer relationship. The salesperson should be continuously communicating the value proposition to the client company. The 3M case study in the accompanying box illustrates the process of delivering the value proposition.[6]

3M

A 3M salesperson was assigned to manage the relationship with the IBM Storage business unit, which produces giant magnetic resistive heads (GMR heads) for computer hard drives. After a number of months of interviewing, listening, and planning, the salesperson began to understand how IBM Storage fit into IBM's overall marketing strategy and observed some of the challenges IBM faced in manufacturing GMR heads. Through meetings with IBM's Operations and R&D staff, the salesperson learned that one of IBM Storage's major business problems was a manufacturing process that was extremely sensitive to electrostatic discharge (ESD), which causes product loss and increased costs. Knowing that 3M had proprietary technology that could help address IBM Storage's ESD problem, the salesperson worked with his technical group and IBM to solve the problem. Through these efforts, 3M significantly reduced IBM Storage's GMR product loss, which translated into an annual savings of several million dollars for IBM. Because of that success, whenever IBM Storage had a problem, it sought out 3M's salesperson to see if 3M's resources could help. 3M found itself modifying some of its existing products or combining existing technologies to create new products to support IBM's needs.

The process of understanding a customer's environment, industry, and strategy to win in that industry is complex and demanding. However, done well, it provides a foundation for determining how to create value for a customer, which a salesperson must then convert into a compelling value proposition, and finally communicate and deliver to the customer.

Pursuing Sales Opportunities[7]

In the previous sections we discussed how the salesperson can go about building a deep understanding of the environment, the industry, and the target customer(s) and with that understanding can proceed to develop a compelling value proposition. Clearly that understanding and that value proposition can and should be modified and improved based on interactions with the customer. A complement to this process is prospecting for potential clients whose needs profiles align well with the seller's value proposition.

One of the objectives of developing deep understanding of the salesperson's customer is determining who can and will be involved in the buying process—including gatekeepers, decision influencers, decision approvers, and decision makers. The value proposition may very well be different for the different categories and levels of players in the buying process and will likely need to be customized to create maximum value for each player. For example, a design engineer may be most concerned about the match between the features of a component product and the overall design of an assembly or system. A manufacturing manager charged with integrating the component into an assembly may be concerned about ease of installation, training requirements, ability to use existing production equipment, and time of delivery. The vice president of operations may be interested in the impact of the integration of the new component on manufacturing cycle time, process yields, and reliability of supply. The CFO may be concerned about the impact on profitability. In addition to profitability, the CEO may want to hear about how the new component will enable product or process innovation that will differentiate the company's products from competitors or even enable a new line of business. Whether the salesperson starts with a gatekeeper, a senior decision maker, or anywhere in between, the focus needs to be on the value that matters to that individual.

Cold Calls versus Warm Calls

At some point, the salesperson needs to initiate first contact. Generally, a *cold call* —reaching out via letter, phone, or e-mail to a customer contact with whom the salesperson has no prior relationship and no reference to a trusted intermediary—is the least effective method of getting an appointment. Hence, it is typically worth the investment of time and energy to try to identify an individual within the company with whom the salesperson has some connection and who might be willing to serve as an advocate (or at least as a facilitator), increasing the probability that the salesperson will get an audience with a decision maker. Alternatively, the salesperson might reach out to an individual outside the target company who has a potentially useful contact within the target company and who would be willing to serve as an intermediary. Networking and relationship building are an important part of the salesperson's skill set—perhaps even more so in the entrepreneurship context, as the entrepreneur often has little or no track record to stand on. Hence, tapping trust relationships derived from prior experience can be critical for success in making initial sales calls and sales.

In some cases, there is no way for the seller to create a warm call and hence he must resort to a cold call. That often starts with a gatekeeper—an individual who stands between the seller and the person with whom the seller would like an appointment—who may be an administrative assistant, an appointments secretary, or a lower-level employee. The professional consultative salesperson treats gatekeepers with professionalism, courtesy, and respect, as they can choose to open doors—or not.

In order to create value for the customer via consultative selling (i.e., serving as a buying consultant), the seller needs to establish a relationship with one or more individuals in the company who are gatekeepers, decision influencers, and decision makers. Generally this is best done person-to-person, although telephone dialogue is often an important part of the communications process, and in some cases is the primary or only medium of communication. Mail or e-mail can support the process, but generally will not create sufficient impact by itself for consultative selling.

Precall Planning

Preparation is a major determinant of sales success. Understanding the context and industry of your customer, as well as the value chain and the customer's strategy to be successful in that environment, establishes the foundation upon which the salesperson and his product/services can create value for the customer. It is also important to research the person whom the salesperson will be meeting. Where did the individual go to school? Where was the individual previously employed? What was the individual's hometown? To what organizations do they belong? And what other special interests does the individual have? This research on the person's background can reveal common interests and experiences, and hence can support a natural human-to-human conversation that can start to build common ground and a mutually beneficial relationship.

Before initiating contact, the salesperson should develop a precall planning list, which should include some or all of the following.

- A written sales call objective.
- A list of needs analysis questions to ask.
- Something tangible to show—a prototype, a chart, a picture of the product/service in use by others.
- A list of benefits that could be important to customers.
- An analysis of the customer's investment return—in other words, quantification of the financial benefits of the benefits of the product/service.
- An analysis of points of difference vis-à-vis competitors.
- A list of typical or likely concerns and objections that the customer might raise.
- Strategies for handling/resolving each potential objection or concern.
- Description of possible alternative scenarios for reaching agreement on a sale (closing strategies).
- A list of individuals with whom the salesperson will try to connect, including an assessment of whether each individual is a gatekeeper, influencer, decision approver, or decision maker.

Before initiating contact, the salesperson should conduct one or more trial-run practice sessions with a colleague, which will help the salesperson focus on sales call objectives, develop the discipline to use the contact's time wisely, and inspire some alternative approaches for the initial interaction.

Facilitating the Buying Process by Establishing Common Ground

When initial contact is made, the salesperson should engage first in trying to develop a relationship. This practice is called *establishing common ground*. It signals that the salesperson is genuinely interested in the buyer as a human being, rather than just a vehicle through which a transaction is to be made. It doesn't have to take a lot of time but it gets a conversation started. Generally, finding common ground starts with asking open questions, active listening, and observation—three of the most important skills of a successful salesperson.

In the best of all worlds, the open questions can be derived from the seller's due diligence about the company and the individual being contacted, and hence reflect the seller's understanding of what is personally or professionally important to the buyer. For example, if the buyer is a sports fan, the seller might ask about a local sports team. If the buyer and seller graduated from the same university, the seller might ask about the buyer's perspective on something going on at their shared alma mater. If the seller has been referred to the buyer by a mutual acquaintance, the seller might ask about the history of the buyer's relationship with that individual. If the buyer is engaged in a major new initiative at the company that has received press coverage, the seller might make mention of the story and ask about the progress of the initiative. If the salesperson notices a six-sigma award plaque or a picture of the buyer at a groundbreaking ceremony, the salesperson might ask questions about them, which in turn may reveal additional insights into the buyer. From the seller's perspective, the exchange should result in a sense of sharing related to something of mutual importance.

Seeking an Exchange of Value

If the seller has done a thorough job of precall due diligence and preparation, it may be possible for the seller to explain to the customer why the seller's product or service is a perfect fit with the needs of the buyer. However, it is much more useful to engage the customer in a discussion of the customer's needs. This approach not only serves to confirm (or adjust) the findings from the seller's due diligence efforts, which are seldom 100 percent on target, but it also demonstrates to the buyer that the seller values and wants to hear the buyer's perspective.

With this input from the buyer, the seller can begin to explore the extent to which the seller's product/service is actually a good fit with the customer's needs. If there appears to be a good fit, then the outcome of the initial interaction is a shared understanding that the buyer may be able to gain value through the seller's offerings and the seller may be able to gain value through the revenue received, connections to future business, and even connections to other business with other potential customers in the buyer's network. However far the initial conversation progresses, if there appears to be a valid reason to continue the dialogue, the seller should establish the next step. Of course, if it becomes clear that there is not a good fit between the seller's offering and the customer's need, then the seller should acknowledge that and offer information or advice that could help the customer identify an alternative supplier. In addition, the seller should ask for referrals to others in the buyer's network who might value the seller's offering and also for the opportunity to reengage at some point in the future.

Handling Rejection

No matter how prepared the seller is or how on target is the seller's value proposition, buyers will have reservations or concerns, which are referred to as *objections*. It is common for new salespeople to view objections as a form of rejection. In fact, as the buyer raises concerns, it shows that he is thinking about purchasing the salesperson's product or service and has identified areas of concern where the product or service may not align properly with customer needs. Recognizing and understanding these misalignments gives the salesperson an opportunity to better understand the customer's needs and address their concerns and issues.

There are many possible reasons for the buyer to raise concerns. Maybe there is insufficient motivation for the buyer to consider switching suppliers. Perhaps the buyer is consumed with other, more important priorities. Maybe the buyer is just having a bad day—for personal or professional reasons. Although it's possible that there is a personality clash between seller and buyer, usually the rejection by the buyer is not a rejection of the seller, but rather of the seller's offering or request for a meeting. Sometimes the rejection only applies to the present and not to the long term.

The seller should handle the rejection professionally and gracefully, and solicit feedback from the buyer regarding the reasons for the rejection. This can provide useful input for determining whether future contact might be welcome and useful, and if so, how the salesperson can be more on target next time. If the seller determines that the probability of fit and a future sale is low, the salesperson should consider this a positive outcome, as it has become clear early in the process that investing additional time and resources in pursuing the sale with this particular buyer has a low probability of providing a good return on investment.

The seller should look at every rejection as an opportunity for continuing education and analyze each rejection for what it can teach about the seller's offering, the marketplace, customer needs, and about the sales approach. In this way, every rejection helps the seller fine-tune his sales skills and increases the probability of future success.

As mentioned earlier, it is possible that there is a personality clash—or incompatibility of styles—between buyer and seller. Sellers can't change who they are, but skillful sellers are able to assess the buyer's style and adapt their own style appropriately. This can be another sign of respect and professional accommodation that the seller shows the buyer, an appropriate method for establishing a more productive interaction, and a way to ensure that the focus of the interaction can be on the potential for mutual value exchange rather than on the nature of the interaction. Naturally the style may adjust as the relationship between buyer and seller matures over time. If the seller can't sufficiently adapt to the buyer's style and tension remains, it is appropriate to transfer the account to another seller.

Dealing with Objections

An inexperienced or incompetent salesperson fears objections, seeing them as the buyer's rejection of the offering or, worse yet, of the salesperson. No one who is offering something to another likes to hear the word *no*. However, the experienced and competent salesperson recognizes no as a signal, either that it's time to move on and avoid investing additional time and effort in a process that is unlikely to yield the desired outcome—a win-win for both buyer and seller—or that the buyer still has issues that must be resolved before the no becomes a yes. It is common sense generally in sales that the person who gets the most nos also gets the most yeses. Therefore the competent salesperson welcomes objections. Objections indicate that the customer is considering purchasing from the seller but is not yet ready to reach agreement. Objections reveal what must be resolved before the buyer and seller can close the sale.

An experienced salesperson has engaged in the buying process with many buyers and, chances are, has already heard most or all possible objections. For example, prospective buyers might object to the seller's offering because of its cost, quality, some particular performance feature, the product warranty, the service plan, time lag for delivery, or simply because they are satisfied with their current vendor relationships. The competent salesperson has already worked through typical objections with multiple buyers and has developed alternative approaches to resolving them. In fact, an important asset for the consultative salesperson seeking to serve the buyer as a buying consultant is the experience with other buyers in resolving objections, challenges, problems, and issues that are getting in the way of coming to closure.

The salesperson should be proactive in uncovering objections, as objections can't be resolved until they are identified. However, the salesperson may end up wasting time in addressing objections that are actually smokescreens. It is important to identify real objections—all of them—before investing time and energy in finding solutions. This requires skill in asking probing questions and carefully listening to the buyer's responses. To draw out a buyer's real objections, the salesperson should ask open questions to probe around the edges of a buyer's initial objection, and listen attentively, taking notes where helpful. By asking the buyer how the seller can be helpful in resolving the objection, the seller may be handed the best solution.

When the buyer is reticent and uncomfortable in stating a specific objection, the seller may offer objections he has heard from other buyers, as a way of encouraging the prospect to voice his own objections. The best way to do this will be to offer the objection in the form of a question. For example: "Some of my customers have expressed concern about the sixty-day lag time between order and delivery. Will that be an issue for you?" Or, "For some of my customers the cost of our system has not been an issue, but concerns over reliability have been paramount. For those customers, our enhanced service program has been important for overcoming that concern. Would minimizing unscheduled downtime be an important issue for you, and if so, would our more frequent periodic routine maintenance program be of value to your company?"

A classic response to an objection—commonly referred to as the "feel, felt, found, close," goes something like the following: "I understand how you *feel* (i.e., frustrated or uncomfortable or perhaps convinced that you can't proceed because of this unresolved issue). Many of my other customers have *felt* the same way. What we've *found* is that we can work together to resolve this issue in order to determine whether there is a good fit between your need and our offering, and if so, to reach a positive outcome for both of us." In this way the seller has acknowledged and validated the concern expressed by the buyer and defuses any tension that may have arisen as a result of the objection, and hence the initial rejection by the buyer of the seller's offering. Further, the seller gives the buyer confidence that there are ways to address the stated concern.

This approach illustrates one way that a seller can help a buyer deal with an emotional objection. It is common for one or more influencers or decision makers to get emotional during the buying process. They may be facing a variety of internal pressures and naturally want to make a good decision. In fact, their jobs may be on the line. The seller needs to avoid ratcheting up the emotional situation by directly (and emotionally) reacting to the objection, but instead needs to retain his composure and seek to defuse it. Sometimes just acknowledging the buyer's frustration with "I understand how you feel" helps calm emotions, after which the seller can say something like: "Can we consider together how we might be able to resolve your concerns?"

A natural follow-on question to a statement by the seller acknowledging the buyer's objection is as follows: "If we can find a satisfactory solution to your concern, is there anything else standing in the way of us moving ahead?" If the answer from the buyer is no, then the seller knows what has to be done to move the sale forward. If the answer from the buyer is yes, then the seller has the opportunity to identify and clarify additional issues that must be resolved. This is also a way that the seller can test and assess whether the stated objections are smokescreens and can assemble a list of genuine objections.

Once the salesperson is reasonably confident that there is agreement with the buyer on the objections that must be addressed, the salesperson can proceed to engage the buyer in exploring the pluses and minuses of alternative solutions. In some cases, there are objections that cannot be resolved to the satisfaction of the buyer. In those situations, the seller needs to review with the buyer the pluses and minuses of proceeding with the seller's offer. Ideally, the pluses will outweigh the minuses, even including the objection that cannot be fully resolved. However, the seller may need to be willing to negotiate some terms of the deal in order to make the offering sufficiently attractive to the buyer and to craft a win-win solution. The seller will likely be experienced with potential trade-offs and be able to give something extra of value to the buyer in order to get something that will advance the sale. The perspective adopted by successful consultative salespeople toward objections is demonstrated in the following excerpt from the book *Rainmakers*.[8]

> Rainmakers welcome customer objections because they know objections are simply the way customers express their desires. The Rainmaker knows that when the customer says, "Your price is too high," the customer's goal is to get the proper value for the money invested. The objection tells the Rainmaker that the customer does not yet have enough information to make a positive buying decision.
>
> The Rainmaker always turns a customer objection into a mutual—customer/Rainmaker—objective. The Rainmaker, in question form, restates the customer's objection as an objective. To illustrate: The customer says, "Your delivery time is too long." The Rainmaker responds, "So our objective is to get you the product when you want it, correct?"

The Closing Process

The inexperienced and incompetent salesperson never asks for the order out of fear of hearing the word no. Instead, the salesperson just waits—hoping that the buyer will reach the decision to buy and will ask: "Would it be okay with you if I purchased your product or service at whatever price and under whatever terms you deem appropriate?" Ironically, the buyer is expecting the salesperson to ask for the order and, if the salesperson doesn't ask for it, then the buyer wonders what hidden issue the salesperson is avoiding raising.

When is the right time to close? The easy answer is: when all objections have been resolved. But in truth, the salesperson should be asking closing questions throughout the buying process. These are called *trial closes*—they are the salesperson's way of checking whether the buying process is still on track, what issues the buyer still needs to get resolved before moving ahead, and the comfort level of the buyer. The salesperson is testing how far along the buyer is in the due diligence process and the readiness of the buyer to buy, and is looking for both buying signals and indicators from the buyer regarding remaining issues to be resolved. Remember, the primary purpose of the salesperson is to help the buyer through the buying process.

Even at the beginning of the buying process, a closing question could take the following form: "Based on your knowledge about our product, how do you see the product fitting your needs?" If the buyer states that he still has a lot to learn and isn't sure there is a fit, then the salesperson knows that there's still a lot of work ahead—but at least the buyer has signaled that he is engaging in the due diligence process. If the buyer states that the due diligence he has conducted prior to meeting with the salesperson and the recommendations he has received about the product indicates that there is a relatively good fit, then the salesperson knows that it's time to ask the classic closing question: "What do we still need to resolve before we can proceed with your purchase?" That question is even easier to ask when the buyer is a current customer who is happy with the product.

The skillful salesperson learns to read verbal and nonverbal clues from the client as buying signals—or, alternatively, nonbuying signals that indicate the buyer's concerns or resistance. If the salesperson is uncertain about the signals coming from the buyer, then making trial closes allows the salesperson to check on the buyers' sense of forward momentum and/or resistance or uncertainty. Also, buyers often reveal the set of assumptions they're working under when they use the future tense; hence, sellers should listen for the future tense in clients' statements as well as in their questions.

For example, the salesperson might ask: "When would you need to install the product in order to meet your schedule for completing your production line?" The buyer might respond: "If we select your product, we will need it by the end of March." This signals that the buyer is seriously considering the purchase of the salesperson's product. An even stronger buying signal would take the following form: "When we complete our purchase process, we will be installing your product no later than the end of March." Note that this is an example of the use of the future tense. The buyer is saying "when," not "if"—indicating the intention to buy the salesperson's product.

Old-fashioned and often counterproductive approaches to closing involve pressure tactics. The incompetent salesperson is taught to ask for the order and then to be silent. The idea is to crank up the pressure on the buyer to make a decision. The mantra is, "He who speaks first, loses"—as if this is a contest to see whether the buyer can resist the salesperson's pressure tactics; if the buyer capitulates, he loses the contest, rather than winning as a result of making the right decision about a purchase that he needs to make.

The skillful, professional consultative salesperson wants the buyer to make the right decision and to succeed. If the consultative salesperson has helped the buyer navigate through the buying process, if all issues and objections have been resolved, and if it's clear that the salesperson's product is the best option for the buyer, then there should be no doubt, uncertainty, or sense of pressure. Instead, the buyer should feel relieved that the decision is clear and feel ready to reach agreement with the salesperson. At this point, it should be easy and comfortable for the salesperson to ask the final closing question—final because it should produce the response from the buyer, "Yes, I'm ready to move ahead with the purchase order."

Structuring the purchase correctly is important for building a long-term relationship. Since the seller may have worked through purchase agreements with multiple buyers, the seller may have a higher level of sophistication than the buyer regarding the variables and the pluses and minuses of various purchase options. Hence the seller should protect the buyer by making sure the purchase is structured in a way that protects the buyer's interests. This is the best approach to building and sustaining trust, which in turn establishes the foundation for future orders and a positive long-term relationship.

As long as the seller is convinced that the buyer is best served by purchasing the seller's product or service, then the appropriate approach by the seller is to be professionally persistent (not *pushy*, but professionally persistent). The seller should approach the end of the buying process—the close—in a spirit of partnership with the buyer, moving forward with confidence and a positive attitude, and assuming that the sale is going to take place. This approach reassures the buyer that it is appropriate to continue moving forward through the buying process in order to determine whether the purchase makes sense.

In selling in the entrepreneurial context, the offer may be technologically advanced and the buyer may be less knowledgeable than the seller; less confident about executing the buying process effectively; and concerned about making mistakes in the buying process and making the wrong buying decision, and hence being subject to criticism by a superior or even termination for poor performance. The job of the consultative salesperson (buying consultant) is to use professional skills, knowledge, and attitudes to help the buyer through the buying process to the optimal outcome.

Follow-Through and Customer Service

The inexperienced and incompetent salesperson thinks the job is done when the purchase order is signed—failing to remember a cardinal rule of sales: The easiest sale is a repeat sale to a satisfied customer. The skillful and professional consultative salesperson knows that investing time and energy in ensuring follow-through and attentive customer service will generate a highly attractive return on investment, as customer service and support help lay the groundwork for future sales.

Follow-through starts with making sure that the customer receives the product or service in a timely manner, and that the billing is done appropriately. Likewise, if the seller's firm has agreed to provide training or assistance with installation, the salesperson follows up to make sure those services are provided to the satisfaction of the buyer. Naturally, the salesperson needs to be responsive to buyer contacts—answering questions, taking care of requests, and handling issues before they become problems. In addition, periodically the salesperson should follow up with the buyers to ensure continuing satisfaction with the product or service, doing this with the frequency established by the preference of the customer. The salesperson should keep a log of customer service calls as part of tracking and management of the account. With this level of professional attention, the salesperson is also in a good position to stay abreast of needs for additional products and services; to be aware of changing customer needs; to meet new employees in the buyer's company who may be gatekeepers, influencers, and decision makers for future buying processes;

to participate in shaping the specifications and timing of future purchase orders; and to ask for references to others in the buyer's network who might value what the seller has to offer.

Typically, others from the seller's company will be involved in providing customer service—trainers, installers, service technicians, the billing department, and so forth. Hence the salesperson needs to be a team player within his own company in order to service accounts successfully, and therefore needs to work diligently to build cordial, professional relationships with the other people in the company who provide sales support.

In some cases the salesperson's product or service will be incorporated into a more comprehensive product or service, which the buyer's firm then sells to another customer downstream in the value chain. The salesperson should be prepared to help the buyer *sell through* to the buyer's customer and to support that sale as well.

Occasionally the salesperson may be caught between the buyer and his own customer support network. Perhaps the buyer is being unreasonable in seeking support that goes beyond the purchase contract, or perhaps the buyer has failed to properly install, use, or maintain the seller's product, resulting in a performance problem, and the buyer may attempt to transfer responsibility for dealing with the problem back to the seller's customer support personnel. The salesperson should confront the situation diplomatically and professionally—in a manner that fits the operating style of the client, seeking a mutually satisfactory solution, and thereby enhancing the long-term relationship with the customer.

Sometimes—regardless of whether buyer or seller has responsibility for resolving an issue with the seller's product or service—the salesperson is confronted by an angry customer. Skill in negotiating is a valuable asset for the salesperson in this situation. Rather than being defensive or argumentative, the salesperson should patiently allow the customer to vent the anger and frustration; confirm the complaint and what the customer would like to see happen to resolve the issue; determine what the seller's firm can do to help; communicate that clearly to the customer; and then execute the commitment to resolve the complaint. In reality, effectively dealing with client complaints is an opportunity to build trust, confidence, and customer loyalty.

Developing Sales Skills

It's not enough to have comprehensive knowledge about the selling and buying processes. The salesperson also needs skill that only comes with practice and experience. Naturally there are skills associated with each element of the selling/buying process. Preparing for the sales relationship requires skill in data gathering and analysis in order to develop a deep understanding of the environmental context, the industry, the strategy of each competitor within a target industry, and the individuals within each target company who may play a role in the buying process. In addition, building a pipeline starts with developing a list of attractive potential targets (in sales parlance, *generating sales leads*). Networking can be a particularly important skill for engaging in this activity. Throughout the segments of the sales process—identified earlier as making sales calls, handling objections, and closing—asking questions and listening are critically important, as are negotiations, creative problem solving, and presentation skills. Throughout the entire engagement with a potential customer, process management, time management, and information management are also important skills.

The value of being skillful at asking questions effectively and listening is often un-recognized or underestimated. Too often salespeople believe that the key is successful presentation of the features and benefits of the product or service. Note that the focus here is on the seller, not on the buyer. There is no doubt that the salesperson has to be prepared to present a compelling value proposition, but it is much easier to do so if the seller first fully understands the buyer's objectives and buying process, and is thereby able to align the value proposition and the selling process to the buyer's objectives and buying process, respectively. Being skillful at asking questions and listening requires that the seller totally owns the knowledge about the buyer and about the seller's offering. That permits the seller to focus on the buyer—with the confidence that the right words (information) will flow out of the seller's mouth at the right time without much thinking on the part of the salesperson. This provides the freedom and the mental bandwidth for the salesperson to:

- Absorb fully what the buyer is communicating—verbally and non-verbally.
- Truly hear those messages with all their complexities and subtleties.
- Acknowledge those messages—and affirm the buyer.
- Confirm and enhance the seller's understanding of the buyer's needs and objectives.
- Explore and document the buying process, including influencers, approvers, and decision makers.
- Uncover all the buyer's issues, concerns, and objections that must be addressed.
- Offer appropriate responses and follow-up questions to encourage and sustain con-tinuing communication from the buyer.
- When appropriate, provide information that addresses the buyer's information needs.
- Keep the engagement going forward to closure, or until it's clear that the process should be terminated.

Highly competent and professional salespeople are able—relatively quickly and easily—to establish trust with the buyer and a shared commitment to achieving a mutu-ally beneficial outcome from the buying process. In a sense, they develop a resonance with their buyers and become partners in achieving a win-win. Naturally, this resonance, a constructive working relationship, and these positive results are easier to achieve with highly competent, professional, and experienced buyers—and may be difficult or even impossible to achieve with inexperienced, distrustful, unskillful, incompetent buyers who lack confidence. Of course, competent and professional salespeople will avoid buyers with whom they have a low probability of establishing a constructive relationship.

How does the salesperson develop these skills? Learning about them and practicing them in training programs (whether internally sponsored or provided by an external sales training organization) are important first steps, but it's also important to continue refreshing those skills through periodic retraining. Training programs are important, but on-the-job training is the only way to fully develop the skill set of a highly competent salesperson.

Many people entering sales never achieve competence in selling skills because they have too little success in the early stages of their developmental process; they become discouraged, and they quit before they become skillful—and successful. Hence, in the early going it makes sense for the novice salesperson to ask for support and guidance from sales managers and/or veteran salespeople in order to get through the challenging and often frustrating awkward front end of the developmental process. In addition, selecting initial target customers who may be tolerant of a novice salesperson is a good strategy. If the novice salesperson is direct, honest, and focused on helping the buyer (rather than making the sale), it may even be possible to engage buyers as developmental partners.

The good news is that it doesn't take too much experience to become relatively competent and professional, even if a high level of competence and peak performance requires significantly more time and experience.

Revisiting the Motivation for Consultative Selling

Above all else, consultative selling maximizes the opportunity for buyer and seller to create value for each other and for others in the business ecosystem in which they participate. The highly effective consultative salesperson will likely know as much or more about the customer's environmental context, industry, and competitive strategy as the does the customer. Through superior understanding and skill, the consultative salesperson will create and deliver a superior value proposition and product/service/relationship offering. For the entrepreneurial venture, this approach will provide the best opportunity to displace established incumbent suppliers and competing new entrants. Through an effective partnering relationship with the customer as the customer's buying consultant, the entrepreneur can overcome the liability of newness and capture the early adopters, thereby building a foundation for survival, growth, and success.

Additional Resources

For those interested in learning more, please refer to the following resources.

Hanan, Mack. *Consultative Selling Advanced Sixth Edition: The Hanan Formula for High-Margin Sales at High Levels*. American Management Association, 1999.

Heiman, Stephen, and Diane Sanchez. *The New Conceptual Selling*. New York: Warner Books, 1999.

Stinnett, Bill. *Selling Results!: The Innovative System for Maximizing Sales by Helping Your Customers Achieve Their Business Goals*. McGraw-Hill Professional, 2006.

Notes

1. The model for the selling process is drawn from *Inc.* magazine's *Real Selling* (1992 videotape series). The videotapes have been used by the authors for the past six years in their course entitled "Business Development through Professional Selling."
2. Michael Treacy and Fred Wiersema, *The Discipline of Market Leaders* (Perseus Books Group, 1997).
3. Bill Stinnett, *Selling Results!: The Innovative System for Maximizing Sales by Helping Your Customers Achieve Their Business Goals* (McGraw-Hill Professional: 2006).

4. National Account Management Association (NAMA), *NAM/GAM Benchmark Consortium: National Account Benchmarking* (Chicago, IL: National Account Management Association and HR Chally Group Consortium, 1997).

5. Michael J. Lanning, *Delivering Profitable Value* (Perseus Books, 2000).

6. Joseph P. Sperry, "Giant Companies, Small Details: 3M and IBM Co-creating Value at All Levels," *Velocity* quarter 3 (2000): 16–17.

7. *Inc.* magazine, *Real Selling* videotape series (Inc., 1992). The lessons offered in these videotapes and the teaching materials developed to complement them are the primary source for this section.

8. Jeffrey J. Fox, *How to Become a Rainmaker* (St. Martin's Press, 2001).

13

Beyond Start-up: Developing and Sustaining the Growing Organization

Donna Kelley and Edward Marram

How This Chapter Fits into a Typical MBA Curriculum

This chapter can be used for courses on entrepreneurship and managing growth in an MBA curriculum. For entrepreneurship courses, the topic of managing growth can come later in the semester, after the students have studied the process of identifying opportunities and starting a business. As we describe later and illustrate in Exhibit 13.4, growth can be positioned as a stage in the life cycle of a venture. While an entrepreneurship course concentrates on the challenges and requirements of starting a business, it's important for students to understand the growth phase. Actions and decisions made early on will affect businesses in their growth stages. In addition, students need to recognize the need for adapting their focus once these ventures experience initial success.

This chapter can also be used to design a course specifically focused on managing growth. Some MBA students may start companies or join new ventures that, if successful, will encounter the particular challenges of growth. Students may also join companies already in their growth stages. While it is most useful to study growth after taking an entrepreneurship course, students may elect to specifically study this phase of a business. This chapter may also be used in a strategy or management course, where the particular nature of this organizational life cycle phase can be viewed from a strategic or managerial perspective.

Who Uses This Material in the Real World—and Why It Is Important

The material in this chapter is most useful for entrepreneurs who have started companies and wish to build a company that can function optimally as it enters its growth phase. This chapter can also be used in companies that are currently growing, and where efforts have already been made to develop the organizational aspects of their businesses. The model of the four domains (organization, leadership, strategy, and resource) can serve as a check on these efforts—to assess the changes that have already been made and identify any gaps still needing to be addressed. It is critical to think of the four domains as functioning best when in balance. If one or more domains are weak, it will be difficult for the organization to operate effectively. For example, an entrepreneur could institute control systems, but these will not provide their full value if there are not qualified managers in place to oversee them. Entrepreneurs can assess the strength of each domain, determining which areas warrant attention.

This chapter can also be useful for managers joining an entrepreneurial firm that is entering its growth phase. A growing organization will have different challenges than those of a start-up or mature organization. Managers joining a growth-stage company may have considerable business and industry experience acquired from more established organizations. The information in this chapter can help these managers understand the specific nature of the environment they will be entering and the issues needing to be addressed. Finally, firms already passing through growth may find this material useful for conducting periodic health checks on their organizations. Given the impact of internal and external shifts on a company over time, and new challenges on the horizon, it can be worthwhile to re-assess the effectiveness of the organization, leadership, strategy, and resources, and perhaps determine the appropriateness of the firm's current and future growth trajectory.

The Growth Challenge

Many businesses are started each year. According to the Global Entrepreneurship Monitor (GEM), there are over thirty million entrepreneurs in the United States.[1] Yet few of these entrepreneurs, about 15 percent, anticipate adding 20 or more employees over the next five years. We typically assume that growth is good, and that entrepreneurs should generally pursue rapid expansion of their businesses. But the reality is that growth is rare. It can bring greater revenues, which should result in higher profits and value for the firm. But it also complicates matters, bringing higher complexity to the management role and increasing the risk of failure. Conversely, *not* growing can be equally risky if the firm loses its competitive edge over time. The entrepreneur must carefully consider whether growth is the best path for the venture, and if so, how much—and how—the firm should grow.

The Growth Decision: External Factors

Much of a venture's growth capacity relies on external factors, which are typically not under the entrepreneur's control. The economic environment, for example, can affect the supply of funding. It can also impact the market for an entrepreneur's product or services. During the economic downturn starting in 2008, nearly every industry experienced a shrinking in revenues and profits as consumers, particularly those experiencing or fearing job loss, reduced their spending. Yet industry response to this economic shift was not uniform. IBIS World reported negative growth for book stores, restaurants, and tourism in 2008, while retirement communities, child care, and health fitness clubs showed no or very little growth. Industries with higher growth included biotechnology, video games, and telecommunications networking equipment.[2]

Because economic cycles do not affect industries equally, it is important to be aware of differences in sensitivity to the economic situation. For example, when times are tough, travel and restaurant businesses typically see fewer customers spending their discretionary dollars on entertainment. In these types of industries, entrepreneurs must deal with the higher vulnerability of their businesses to the ups and downs of the economy.

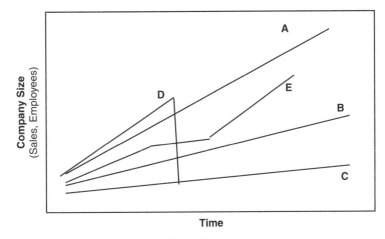

Exhibit 13.1   Levels of Growth

They may see brisk business during good times, but their investments in the future may be at risk if an economic downturn is on the horizon. It is important to remember, however, that creative entrepreneurs can find opportunities to leverage what others may consider impossible conditions. It is therefore possible to grow businesses, even in difficult times. Still, performance can be affected by choice of industry, so it's worthwhile to understand how this can factor into one's growth ambitions.

Exhibit 13.1 shows three levels of growth potential. The steep line (A) is representative of a technology-intensive or emerging industry—for example, the biotechnology, video game, or telecommunication equipment businesses mentioned earlier. These industries show rapid growth, but also high volatility due to quick changes in markets and competition. There may be frequent turnover in firms, with many new firms starting up, but also a fair number failing. Entrepreneurs competing in these types of industries are often in a grow-or-die situation. In order to compete for a significant period of time, they need to keep growing and changing. They may have achieved great initial success with their product or service, but this advantage can be quickly diluted by shifts in customer needs or the introduction of better products or services by competitors.

The middle line (B) shows moderate growth. Businesses based around sports/athletics and education, for example, are not typically fast-growing firms. But they can achieve steady growth in markets where consumers are willing to spend on education or buy the latest sports equipment. Entrepreneurs can make a range of choices relative to their growth ambitions. They can focus on niche markets, providing new products and services to keep their customers happy, perhaps seeing their offerings and markets evolve over time. Or they can seek a higher level of growth by moving into new markets, expanding their geographic reach, or adding new businesses to their portfolio. To stay competitive, though, they need some level of differentiation or a focus on a niche market, particularly when a few large and powerful players dominate the industry.

In the low-growth industries (A), firms will need to improve to survive, but it's not likely they will achieve a high rate of growth for long periods. In those industries with numerous small players, like dry cleaning, health clubs, or child care, there is little differentiation and much local competition. Firms may operate as lifestyle businesses, offering comfortable salaries for the owners. In mature industries dominated by a few major players, like insurance and retail, small, new firms will face challenges competing in environments with saturated competition, slow demand growth, and low profitability. As Steffens et al. indicate, most young companies are me-too imitators in mature industries. They have lower productivity than that of large and established firms who have cost advantages and efficient routines. However, they are not held back by the large firms' rigid routines and cultures, bureaucratic structures, and risk-averse employees, customers, or investors.[3] Entrepreneurs therefore have advantages as well as challenges in mature industries. They will need to be creative and ambitious to break out of the pack.

The influence of industry can be summed up by this quote from Scott Shane, an author and professor of entrepreneurial studies:

> I think the biggest myth entrepreneurs have is that the growth and performance of their start-ups depends more on their entrepreneurial talent than on the businesses they choose . . . . The industry a person picks to start a business has a huge effect on the odds that it will grow. If you go back 20 years or so, about 4 percent of all the start-ups in the computer and office equipment industry made the Inc. 500, 0.005 percent of start-ups in the hotel and motel industries made that list, and 0.007 percent of start-ups in eating and drinking establishments. So that means the odds that you make the Inc. 500 were 840 times higher if you started a computer company than if you started a hotel or motel.[4]

As lines D and E show, the key to growth can also lie in determining the appropriate level of growth for a company over time. Line D illustrates how one can grow fast and crash just as quickly, while line E shows a slowing of growth to allow an organization to catch up before it can proceed again on its growth path. The key is to evaluate and plan the organization's growth path over time, ensuring the organization is well positioned to achieve its potential. Next we discuss the internal aspects that factor in the growth decision.

The Growth Decision: Internal Factors

While the external environment can impact a venture's growth potential, internal, firm-level factors invariably weigh in. Some key factors are summarized in Exhibit 13.2 for the three different growth levels. A low-growth firm is typically oriented toward paying a salary to the owners. Moderate growth requires a broader outlook on the business, in terms of either the region served or the product/service offering. High-growth firms are typically in high-potential industries and rely on knowledge and/or capital investment.

In seeking a higher level of growth, entrepreneurs will need to rely on capable managers. In the pursuit of high growth, this likely means professional leadership teams with entrepreneurs in more specialized roles suited to their expertise and interests, such as marketing or technology. Entrepreneurs need to balance the potential for the business with their own personal considerations. To pursue growth they must delegate responsibilities to others, work as a member of an effective leadership team, and in some cases, step aside and let others make key decisions.

Strategy becomes more complex with greater growth aspirations. At the same time, even lifestyle firms aren't exempt from strategic considerations. They can often exist in highly competitive local markets with seemingly me-too businesses. Yet they can't rely solely on cost competition; that will only serve to hurt all competitors. They need to constantly seek new ways to stand out, providing an offering that continues to satisfy their customers. They need to pay attention to changes on the horizon in markets, technology,

Exhibit 13.2   Growth Considerations at Three Levels

	Low Growth	Moderate Growth	High Growth
Type of Business	Local, lifestyle	Regional or focused business	Knowledge-based in high-potential industry
Organization	Basic systems emphasizing efficiency. Reporting to entrepreneur.	Delegating responsibility areas. Budgets and control systems.	Sophisticated control systems. Formal management practices. Decentralized management.
Leadership	Founder	Founder with managers	Professional management
Strategy	Anticipate and adjust to changes in external environment.	Focused on exploiting and renewing source of differentiation, recognizing new opportunities.	Portfolio of investments ranging from extending current advantage to exploring potential breakthroughs.
Resources	Retained earnings; credit cards; loans from family, friends, and local banks.	Asset-based lending, equity (angels).	Equity: angel, venture capital, investment banks, with exit strategy (sale, IPO)

and competition. In these types of businesses, this responsibility will likely fall on the entrepreneur.

For moderate growth, a team approach will generally be more viable, since managers in particular areas can contribute their insights into future opportunities. A two-pronged approach is needed, where, first, the current source of advantage is effectively leveraged, in order to provide a return on investment from the current business. The current business will also need to be periodically renewed to keep the firm competitive. Second, the firm will need to maintain a search for new opportunities. Typically, the moderate growth firm doesn't have the resources to risk investing in high-potential breakthroughs, unless the current business is threatened and needs to be transformed, or if leadership determines that such a big bet is worth the risk. But there are peripheral moves one can make with additional products or services, and moves into new markets. Throughout this process, the entrepreneur will need to carefully define the business to provide a central logic for growth.

For high growth, strategy will become much more sophisticated, with a focus on a portfolio of investments: from lower-risk, lower-cost extensions of the current businesses to riskier bets on potential big wins. Strategy is defined broadly enough to accommodate experimentation and can be seen as a moving target, adjusting over time to changing conditions and successful venturing into new areas. These firms will need to take care that their resources are invested ambitiously but carefully in businesses that not only exhibit high market potential but are feasible and logical for the organization to pursue.

Growth also requires different financing considerations, as outlined in Exhibit 13.2. While lower growth can be financed through operations and smaller loans, more ambitious growth requires risk capital. In addition, higher growth increases organizational complexity, requiring advanced structure and systems. We talk more about these considerations later in this chapter. We now turn to personal considerations that can influence growth.

The Growth Decision: Personal Factors

Entrepreneurs may base their growth decisions on the potential of the business. That is, they may seek growth because they believe their ventures can be highly successful. Yet their plans for growth will impact them personally. They may need to make a choice between growing and controlling their ventures. As Noam Wasserman indicates, founders can't be both rich and a king. They need to figure out which matters more. He studied 212 public companies founded in the late 1990s and early 2000s. By the time the companies went public, only 25 percent were still led by their founders. He explains that high-potential businesses require more outside equity, which accelerates the replacement of the founder.[5]

Founders may be confident they can make their businesses successful with themselves at the helm. In order to reduce reliance on outside investors, they may dial down their financing strategies, using retained earnings instead of debt, or preferring debt to equity. Yet, despite a promising start, these entrepreneurs may not have the ability to rapidly scale up operations with greater volume and complexity. Their tendency to make decisions in a way that preserves their own control, rather than optimizing the venture's potential, can become increasingly problematic. Entrepreneurs should therefore balance their aspirations with their ability and willingness to lead. They may trade off some growth potential in order to have greater control over their ventures or when they perceive that the returns do not justify the requirements and effort.

Other personal motives may play a key role in the growth decision. One study found that a desire for independence—to run one's own show—diminishes growth intentions and decreases growth. Alternatively, a motivation for achieving financial success was associated with higher growth intentions and actual growth.[6] But other studies show that wealth attainment is not the most significant driver for an entrepreneur, compared with the promise of challenge, innovation, and independence.[7] Entrepreneurs are often concerned with workload and control, or the sacrifice they may need to make relative to quality or level of service.[8] Per Davidsson found that when firms reach a size of five to nine employees, the deterrents appear to outweigh the motivators in the decision to pursue further growth.[9]

Besides the decision to maintain or grow a venture, entrepreneurs may alternatively decide to sell their businesses. Accompanying these decisions are personal choices for the entrepreneur. Exhibit 13.3 presents post-start-up options for an entrepreneurial business. Each option presents at least two alternatives for the founder.

If a new venture is successful in generating sales, entrepreneurs can reap capital gains by finding a suitable buyer. Selling the business can also provide resources to grow the opportunity. If the entrepreneur decides to sell the business, she may stay with the acquiring company, or leave and either seek other employment or start another company. The first situation is perhaps the most common; the entrepreneur sells to reap a capital gain, but stays on with the organization for several years to help in the transition. The

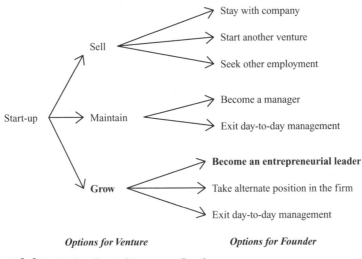

Exhibit 13.3   Post-Start-up Options

buyer typically wants the entrepreneur to stay in order to reduce risk and to ensure that valuable human assets do not leave the organization.

A typical acquisition might give the entrepreneur one-third of the price in cash, one-third in the acquiring company's stock (that is vested over the term of an employment contract), and one-third in an earn-out that is tied to the performance of the acquired company. If the acquired company meets certain milestones, the entrepreneur earns the full amount of the earn-out. If it falters, the entrepreneur's earn-out is at risk. Thus, the entrepreneur has an incentive to work hard after the acquisition takes place. When selling a business, there are often contractual agreements to consider, like restrictions on the founders' activities if they exit—for example, noncompete clauses that place limitations on their next venture. Acquirers will most certainly prohibit the sellers from starting a new, directly competing business.

When maintaining a business, the entrepreneur is faced with two basic choices. He can continue to lead the organization or he can exit day-to-day operations. Many entrepreneurs choose to operate lifestyle businesses that pay enough salary for the owner to have a comfortable lifestyle, with less risk and complexity. These firms could be sold at some point, but the main objective for the entrepreneur is to maintain, rather than sell or grow, the business.

Because this chapter is about managing growth, it works from the perspective of a company that is currently growing and is led by an entrepreneur who has chosen to sustain a growing organization, rather than sell it or maintain a lifestyle business. We focus on the founder as CEO, although most of the concepts are equally relevant in situations where founders are replaced. In addition, we concentrate on entrepreneurship after the start-up phase, assuming entrepreneurs have achieved success with their initial opportunity. Decisions made in the start-up stage are important, however, as the next section demonstrates. This chapter can also serve as a guide for an organization with its initial growth years already behind it—either as it anticipates new future growth, or as it recognizes the need to align the organization with an already accelerated growth trajectory. The lessons here are very specific, but broadly applicable.

There are two primary concerns relative to growth. The first lies in creating a professional organization that is capable of effectively managing its growing operations. The second sets the stage for future growth. The entrepreneur needs to build an organization that can execute its entrepreneurial ambitions while positioning it for continued entrepreneurship. The organization needs to have the capacity for sustaining its growth and avoiding decline in its maturity.

We next review the key stages of growth, to provide a context for understanding a venture's growth phase, as well as what happens before and after this focal point.

Growth Stages

Many researchers have explained the nature of new firm growth using stage models. As Exhibit 13.4 illustrates, an entrepreneurial firm typically passes through a sequence of stages, each with its own particular characteristics and challenges.

During the start-up stage, the business opportunity is taking shape, but significant sales have not yet been made. The founders are acquiring resources and organizing initial operations—and they do everything. These critical early tasks are covered in other chapters of the *Portable MBA*. As previously mentioned, this chapter is concerned with how entrepreneurs operate once they've started and, we assume, the companies have reached a point of initial success with their opportunity. However, it is important to remember that some actions in the start-up stage can influence the decisions and challenges encountered in the growth stages. For example, the entrepreneur should address, as early as possible, considerations about ownership structure, agreements covering disputes or exits of founders, the hiring of key management, the recruitment of advisers, and intellectual property protection.

In addition, decisions made about the pursuit of growth versus profitability in a firm's start-up stage can impact the firm's future viability. A study of 3,500 small Australian firms by Steffens et al. indicates that long-term above-average profitability is more likely

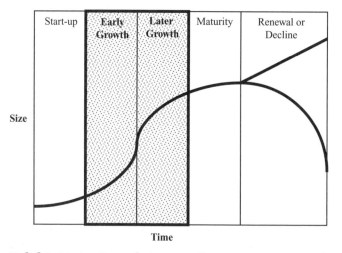

Exhibit 13.4   Growth Stages of an Entrepreneurial Firm

achieved by focusing first on profitability, and then striving for growth.[10] Even simultaneous high growth in sales and profitability (in terms of return on assets) tends to be short-lived. These authors caution that a blind pursuit of growth, with the assumption that profitability can be built later, is misguided. New firms need to carefully consider how to develop both growth and profitability over time.

At the other end of the growth stage model, in the mature stage and beyond, a business must deal with conditions of a well-established organization. Systems and structures can become entrenched and the culture can impede efforts to grow further, leading to decline. However, if the company is able to periodically renew itself, or undertake transformation efforts when needed, it will continue to prosper. Additionally, entering a significant new business may require a redesign of the organization, new leadership, or different systems. The more mature company may therefore find itself revisiting the challenges encountered during its earlier years. It may need to occasionally revert back to a growth-stage mentality to prepare itself for future expansion.

Exhibit 13.4 shows two growth stages, differentiating between a venture's early and later growth. The early phase begins as the company's growth is starting to ramp up, then accelerates to a rapid rate. The later phase starts during accelerated growth, which then levels off as the company becomes more established. This distinction is important because the problems facing a company at an early stage of growth are different from those it faces in later stages. The decisions and solutions will therefore change. By knowing where the organization stands in the life cycle, an entrepreneur can tell which problems are normal and which require special attention. For example, while an entrepreneur needs to focus the company's strategy during early growth, she will need to look toward expansion in later growth stages.

The primary task for an entrepreneurial firm in its growth phase is to ensure the organization can sustain growth into this mature stage. To do so it needs to create a professional organization that is both responsive to external change and entrepreneurial enough to continually create new businesses through innovative thinking. Obviously, it is far better to plan for growth than to allow problems to fester into a crisis. But the combination of expanding sales and limited resources often compels the organization to sacrifice planning in favor of getting product out the door. Entrepreneurs can exacerbate the situation if they continue to chase all the interesting opportunities that have surfaced since their initial success. In addition, they may not have the skills or interest in the organization-building aspects of the business. They may be more comfortable making sales or developing new products. As a result, they may hire technologists or marketing people before bringing in someone with organizational and business skills.

But if left untended, growth will eventually overwhelm the organization. In order to survive and continue to grow over the long term, the entrepreneur will need to pay attention to the requirements necessary for effectively managing growth. By understanding the nature and requirements for growth, the entrepreneur should be better positioned to anticipate and prepare for this, rather than being forced to react under extreme conditions, where damage will need to be undone.

While entrepreneurial skills are critical during the venture's early stages, these skills will soon need to be balanced with managerial skills to prepare the firm for growth. At the same time, the organization will need to retain its entrepreneurial spirit as it grows. Young firms have advantages over older firms in their ability to recognize innovative opportunities and bring them to market quickly. They need to also tap these opportunities to their fullest potential by scaling them up, improving on them, and perhaps also producing complementary products or services. Concurrently, they will need to explore novel opportunities that can create future business prospects. As customer needs change, technologies advance, and competitors offer new alternatives, the advantages of existing businesses fade. Entrepreneurs cannot allow their organizations to lose the flexibility and innovativeness that made them great in the first place. They will therefore need to find a way to both exploit their current advantage and seek new future growth paths.

Four Domains for Managing Growth

In managing growth, there are several key areas of concern for entrepreneurs. A number of studies have revealed particular characteristics and actions associated with successful growth in entrepreneurial firms:[11]

1. *Founder characteristics:* high commitment, proactive.
2. *Founder skills:* higher education, strong technical and industry skills.
3. *Leadership:* clear organizational vision, team-based organizational design, attention to the human resource function.
4. *Organization's image:* focus on reputation and quality.
5. *Organizational planning for growth:* culture, processes, structure.
6. *Strategy:* effective differentiation, focus on new technologies and market expansion, with more distant customers.
7. *Financing:* adequate capitalization with a wider range of financing sources.

Assuming entrepreneurs have the commitment and ability to grow their ventures, or can recruit others with needed capabilities, we can focus our attention on a few elements entrepreneurs must address in the growth phase of their businesses. In this chapter, we describe four domains: the leadership domain, the organizational domain, the strategic domain, and the financial domain. These four domains are illustrated in Exhibit 13.5 and covered in detail in this chapter. Before we move to this discussion, however, there are several key points to consider.

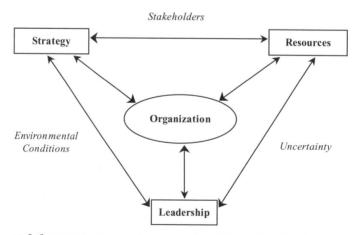

Exhibit 13.5   Four Domains for Managing Growth

First, the organization will need to address the needs of its stakeholders. Stakeholders are those who have a stake in the venture's success, like investors, customers, suppliers, and employees. As a new venture grows, it accumulates a range of insiders and outsiders who become increasingly dependent on the firm and exert heavy influence on its decisions. Second, environmental conditions, such as economic cycles, the regulatory environment, or technological change can impact a venture's viability and success. And finally, it's important to recognize the many sources of uncertainty that can affect the organization. Many events cannot always be predicted, such as a competitor introducing a superior product soon after launch, or customers adopting a product much more slowly than anticipated. The growing organization will therefore need to manage these four domains amid conditions over which it has little control.

Exhibit 13.6 shows the challenges associated with the four domains outlined in Exhibit 13.5, and the key imperatives that need to be addressed at a venture's early and later growth stages. In early growth, entrepreneurs will need to develop basic controls and simple budgets and metrics. They will need to start delegating and developing/hiring managers. Strategy will likely need considerable focus, particularly when resources are limited.

In later growth, it will become increasingly necessary to bring in professional management and a board of directors. Systems and controls will need greater sophistication and formality, to ensure that they can manage an ever more complex and expanding organization. Efficient operations, however, will need to be balanced with entrepreneurial capabilities. Strategy will include not just building on existing businesses, but also exploring new arenas for the longer term. While firms are likely to seek growth capital to finance future expansion, they should not forget how to maintain a bootstrap mentality and manage cash to generate internal growth resources.

We next describe, in greater detail, the growth challenges and key imperatives for each of the four domains.

Organization

The growth model has the organization at its core. The organization depends on the other components in the model: leadership, strategy, and resources. But it has the most direct link to execution and the ability for the organization to generate and maintain profitability. A start-up is commonly loosely managed, with few controls, very little performance assessment, and a lack of responsibility for outcomes. It often puts an emphasis on sales over profits. For example, chasing new customers can take priority over considering whether this can be done profitably. With only so many hours in the day and so many days in a week, it is hard to step back, develop and implement new processes, hire and train people, and insure everything functions adequately. Yet it is essential to creating an organization that can continue to thrive and grow.

The entrepreneur and managers may see signs that the organization needs attention: frequent inventory outages, overdue collections, diminishing cash flows, and delivery restrictions by suppliers. Uncontrolled growth can lead to poor coordination between activities such as sales and inventory planning. Without an adequate system of controls, the company can't optimize its decision making and prevent the waste of resources. Therefore, the most critical first task in transitioning beyond start-up is to create an efficient operation. This will eventually need to coexist with efforts to sustain an entrepreneurial organization, but the firm will first need to catch the organization up to its

Exhibit 13.6   Challenges and Key Imperatives in Four Domains for Managing Growth

	Early Growth		Later Growth	
	Challenges	Key Imperatives	Challenges	Key Imperatives
Organization	Emphasis on sales over profits. Reactive orientation (fighting fires). Rapid growth overwhelms operations. Inadequate systems and planning leads to inefficiency, poor control, and quality problems. Informal communication and processes create confusion and lack of accountability.	Develop basic systems to manage cash and control receivables, inventory, and payables. Develop simple budgets and metrics to track performance and expenditures.	Organization outgrows initial systems and planning structure. Difficulties with coordination and control as decentralization increases.	Upgrade and formalize systems for control and planning for the longer term/future—before they are needed. Proactive planning replaces reactive approach. Maintain balance between control and creativity; ensure processes don't constrain innovation.
Leadership	Company outgrows entrepreneur's abilities. Entrepreneur unable to delegate. Internally promoted managers often lack adequate skills.	Start the process of delegating responsibility to others. Promote/hire functional managers/supervisory level managers. Invest in management training.	Management lacks the managerial sophistication required for the increasing size and complexity of a growing organization. Inadequate communication throughout organization. Tensions between professional management and entrepreneur, between new and old managers and employees.	Recruit key professional management talent. Build fully functioning board of directors. Ensure leadership team shares in strategic planning and preserves entrepreneurial capability. Create decentralized reporting structure.

Strategy	Tendency to overcommit, pursue many diverse opportunities. Lack of clear strategy for how the venture competes.	Develop a focused strategy that leverages the company's unique value. Maintain the consistency of this strategy with all company activities, such as product development, marketing, operations.	Original opportunity domain may provide fewer opportunities for growth. Competitive pressures and changes in the market may threaten current businesses.	Establish competitive uniqueness and move beyond one-product orientation. Expand into the periphery with products and markets. Also, develop strategy for future that provides new momentum and long-run effectiveness. Anticipate/respond to changes in industry/market environment.
Resources	Financial and human resources constrained as rapidly expanding sales requires more people and financing. Generalized skills increasingly incapable of handling increased complexity.	Get profitability and cash flow in check. Tap early financing sources. Hire people with specialized expertise. Protect intellectual property.	Insufficient resources for growth.	Maintain bootstrap mentality. Manage cash for internal growth resources. Secure growth financing.

burgeoning growth. Then it can set the stage for creating new sources of growth in the future. As the firm grows, it will need to upgrade its planning, coordination, and control systems to effectively handle the increasingly complex and decentralized operations.

The key objectives for a control system should be to manage current assets and liabilities: cash, inventory, receivables, and payables. In addition, the company should develop measurement systems to track the effectiveness of its control systems and assess financial performance, both of which can be used in decision making and to improve practices. These can be basic to start, with ongoing attention to adapting and upgrading them to more sophisticated and formal systems as the company continues to grow.

Managing Current Assets and Liabilities

The cash cycle shows the amount of time that passes between cash outlays and cash inflows during the company's sales process. It also shows the relationship between three key ratios: days in payables, days in inventory, and days sales are outstanding. It can be used to evaluate the management of current asset/liabilities and to develop better controls, which can conserve resources and improve operational efficiency. (Material in this section builds on information on working capital presented in Chapter 8.) Exhibit 13.7 illustrates a typical cash cycle.

As this figure illustrates, the cash conversion period extends from the time of cash outlay (to suppliers) to cash inflow (from customers). Looking at this diagram, we can image how an increase in sales would actually decrease cash inflows in the short term. The company would need to borrow money to cover the costs associated with this increase in sales until cash comes in 98 days later. In the meantime, as additional sales are made, the company would need to cover these costs. When cash finally comes in, the company would likely need that cash for more inventory! Another problem revealed in this analysis is the length of time it takes to pay suppliers. If typical payment terms are 30 days, and the company, on average, is paying in 53 days, the company may be testing its relationship with suppliers. This could lead suppliers to postpone shipments of additional product until past invoices are paid, or, in the worst case, lead them to refuse to do business with the company.

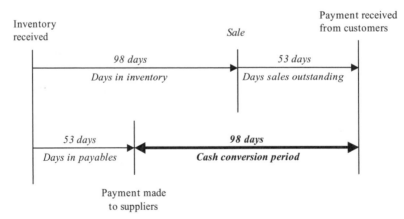

Exhibit 13.7   Cash Conversion Period

The easy solution would be to borrow from a bank or other debt source, preferably a revolving line of credit that allows the company to draw funds as needed and pay them back when cash is received. These short-term loans are designed to cover shortfalls such as this. Borrowing can get expensive, though, so why not think about reducing the average cash conversion period? This is much more difficult but instills a sense of resource parsimony that boosts a company's efficiency. Looking at Exhibit 13.7, just reducing days in inventory (through inventory control) or the number of days sales are outstanding (through an accounts receivable policy) would reduce the cash conversion period.

An accounts receivable policy has to weigh the desire for cash as soon as possible with the need to maximize revenue by offering attractive payment terms. A typical way of obtaining early payments from customers is to offer them discounts for paying early. But the most important impact on accounts receivable involves something often lacking in the entrepreneurial firm: constant attention to a collections policy that both ensures on-time payment and reduces losses due to uncollectible accounts. An accounts receivable policy should include:

- When communication is made relative to account balances or payment reminders.
- When/how contact is made for past due accounts.
- When/how collection efforts are undertaken.

Inventory controls need to balance both the threat of stock-outs and the threat of overstocks. Stock-outs can mean lost sales. Overstocks not only tie up cash until the items are sold, but carry the risk of total loss due to obsolescence, theft, damage, or spoilage. Monitoring sales levels, understanding seasonality, and estimating life-cycle trends can help improve inventory management. Accounts payable policies should allow for payment as late as possible, while managing payables in a way that maintains good relationships with vendors. Vendors may have required stricter payment terms when the firm was just starting. As the company grows, it may be able to negotiate for more favorable payment terms.

Performance Measures

In order to detect inefficiencies or a need for policy changes in the company's cash management practices, the company can identify a set of metrics that can track and reveal trends in receivables, inventory, and payables. As reviewed earlier, this can include the number of days it takes on average to collect receivables, turn over inventory, and make payments to suppliers. Controls also need to monitor spending and evaluate performance in different areas. A growing firm's selling and administrative costs often expand rapidly with its escalation in sales. This is often justified because marketing is needed to generate sales, and administrative overhead is needed to support the burgeoning organization. Yet these areas need to be monitored to determine effectiveness and detect overspending. For example, certain advertising approaches may be more effective than others, or they may work in one region but not another.

As the company begins to sell more and more products or services into multiple markets, it is useful to analyze performance in different product or market segments. Entrepreneurs need to understand what each product costs and whether a profit is truly being made. All the costs going into each product are those, both variable and fixed, that would disappear if the product were discontinued. After these are covered, the remainder contributes toward company overhead and generating profits. The same analysis can be done to examine geographic regions or markets. The firm can therefore slice its business up in multiple ways. Depending on the nature of the company's business, one or more particular approaches will work better. The end goal is not to collect a lot of data but to assemble and analyze information in a manner that is most beneficial for evaluation and decision making.

The company should also track the level and effectiveness of its expenditures. When a company is rapidly growing, there seems to be an endless need for staff, administrative expenditures, marketing, and so forth. This may all be necessary, but the firm needs to be aware of changes in these expenditures to determine if they are consistent with the company's strategy and objectives, and whether they are truly contributing to a more effective operation. Expenditures can be examined as a percentage of sales or other measures, such as number of customers or employees. Extraordinary changes should have a logical explanation. In addition, they should be matched with outcomes. Did an increase in marketing in a region lead to greater sales there? Did R&D investments lead to a higher number or more innovative products?

Performance metrics can aid companies in their decisions about investments and expenditures. Performance measurements in an early stage company are designed less for evaluation of actual outcomes against a plan, as they would be in a more stable, established organization. Instead, they are targeted toward entrepreneurial decision making. As the company's operations expand, managers can develop metrics to help them answer questions such as the following:

- Which products or regions generate the highest revenues and margins?
- Which customers or customer groups are reliable accounts (make timely payments, are at low risk of default)?
- How effective are our expenditures in areas such as marketing and sales, and does this differ across markets?

The first control system in early growth should be relatively simple. The organization should be able to get it up and running and train people how to use it quickly and easily. With simple systems, there is less that can go wrong, and as employees and managers get accustomed to these practices, the systems can later be upgraded to handle a larger and more complex organization. In addition, the systems can be implemented stepwise—for example, starting with components having the greatest gap between actual and desired performance, or those that are easiest to put in place and therefore able to make a quick impact.

In summary, an effective control system should include the following:

- Accounts receivables and collections policies.
- An inventory management system.
- Accounts payables policies.
- Assessment of performance and expenditures.
- Metrics to track trends in cash, receivables, inventory, payables, expenditures, and performance.

How does a company determine what's good or bad when examining key metrics? For some financial ratios, published sources can provide industry averages for comparison. Entrepreneurial firms, however, often adopt policies differing from more stable, established firms, such as the need to spend on marketing while building brand awareness. It may be more useful to look at trends in metrics over time—for example, an increase in the collection period for receivables could indicate a relaxing in collection efforts, or an increase in inventory turns could indicate a greater risk of stock-outs. Shifts in metrics may reflect prior policy changes, but other than that, significant changes should be accompanied by a search for causes and an examination of the need for adjustment in policy.

The company can also develop simple budgeting practices to estimate cash and inventory needs, schedule production, determine staffing requirements, and set sales and profitability goals. The controller of a successful baked goods company comments on his company's budgeting practices:

> Since 2000 our systems have been getting more precise every quarter. We break out sales by division on a weekly basis—what we budget, what we forecast, what we actually produced, and what we did in the prior period. We update those forecasts on a monthly basis and those are the numbers the production manager works with.[12]

These controls, metrics, and budgets should be upgraded and more formalized as the company moves toward later growth. But more importantly, they should evolve to provide the best information possible, to aid the company's decision-making processes. The value they provide should more than justify the time and effort spent to develop and maintain them. In addition, performance measures should be as simple and inexpensive to track as possible, while providing information leading to better decision making.

Managing the Pace of Growth

Managers, particularly those seeking high growth, must recognize that controls need to be a step ahead of growth—sophisticated enough to handle the growing firm at the next level. The more rapidly growing the firm, the quicker this will happen, and in greater magnitude. At times it may be better to slow the pursuit of new growth to give the company room to improve its operations. This can get the organization under control and prepare it to proceed along a faster growth path. Joel Kolen, president of Empress International Ltd., a seafood distributor, emphasizes that "By taking a break from growth and putting in controls such as those at a large company, an entrepreneur can ease the growth transition and ensure that the qualities that helped build the company don't get lost in the rush to fill new orders."[13]

It's better that a decision to slow down growth is anticipated and planned, rather than an after-the-fact reaction. If reactive, it could lead to a greater drop in revenues and profit, and perhaps damage the company's relationships or reputation. If the company is able to recover from this, it will take much longer. Going back to Exhibit 13.1, ventures attempting to grow too fast can collapse in failure, as line D illustrated. By contrast, as line E exhibits, a slowing of growth may be a smart choice, allowing the organization to reset itself for future growth. Consequently, it's important to continually assess the company's current growth trajectory and the organization's readiness for managing this in the most optimal manner.

This discussion of growth and operations warrants one additional point. When there are severe economic downturns, the firm may need to curtail growth, just as many did when the 2008 recession hit. Although industry-specific downturns may require a change in strategy, an economic recession is widespread enough to cause firms to retrench and ensure that the cash situation can hold until times are better. Survival is the primary concern for most in these circumstances.

Nevertheless, while shocks such as recessions cause firms to think short-term, they also need to think of the long-term consequences of cutting back. Firms don't want to emerge from a recession with obsolete products, or reduce marketing so much that building back awareness is near impossible. Entrepreneurs need to think carefully about where they are making cuts. A recession can, in fact, be the best time to invest in new businesses. The iPod was hatched during the 2001 slump, and mainstay products like Miracle Whip, Kraft Macaroni and Cheese, and nylon were launched during the Great Depression. Proactive entrepreneurs may indeed find growth opportunities amid difficult conditions, so investments in the future can be a smart move in tough times.

With all this talk about efficiency and controls, it's hard to imagine how anything entrepreneurial can happen. That is sadly the case with many companies. A history of success creates preferences for recreating the past, rather than building toward the future. Efficiency in current operations often does not accommodate new initiatives, like those requiring different sales channels or different value chain partners. How, then, can a well-run organization maintain the ability to create new businesses? It's primarily a combination of the three remaining domains: how leadership develops people, views and manages its strategy, and obtains and allocates resources.

Leadership

Exhibit 13.8 summarizes some key differences between entrepreneurs, managers, and entrepreneurial leaders. While the entrepreneur has the inspiration and vision to create a business out of an opportunity, a manager is skilled at organizing and planning. The entrepreneurial leader, however, plays a distinct role in sustaining a growing organization. He must ensure that the organization's culture, structure, and systems are conducive not only to efficient operations but also to continued entrepreneurship. He needs to ensure that the organization builds and leverages distinct capabilities—for example, in specific technology areas or through a network of relationships with value chain players. Over time, these capabilities can be improved and combined with other new capabilities either through in-house development or in partnership with others. As a leader, he articulates the company's vision, and ensures that organization members are both empowered and supported to effectively achieve this vision.

Starting the Delegation Process

For the entrepreneur who has successfully led the venture through its start-up phase, it becomes critical to ensure effective management is in place while simultaneously ensuring that the organization can preserve the entrepreneurial spirit it was founded on. This requires both assuming a changing role and sharing some of the tasks with others. At the beginning, however, the entrepreneur typically starts out doing everything. She answers phones, ships product, designs advertisements: in essence, performing just about all the activities needed to ensure the organization gets product sold and out the door. But

Exhibit 13.8 The Entrepreneur versus Manager versus Entrepreneurial Leader

Entrepreneur	Manager	Entrepreneurial Leader
Locates new ideas.	Maintains current operations.	Leverages core business while exploring new opportunities.
Starts a business.	Implements the business.	Starts businesses within an ongoing organization.
Is opportunity driven.	Is resource driven.	Is capability and opportunity driven. Leverages capabilities and builds new ones to expand opportunity domain.
Establishes and implements a vision.	Plans, organizes, staffs, controls.	Establishes a vision and empowers others to carry it out.
Builds an organization around the opportunity.	Enhances efficiency of organization.	Maintains entrepreneurial ability as organization grows. Ensures culture, structure, systems are conducive to entrepreneurship; removes barriers.
Leads and inspires others.	Supervises and monitors others.	Develops and guides entrepreneurial individuals; bridges between individuals and groups with diverse expertise and orientation.
Orchestrates change in the competitive environment.	Maintains consistency and predictability.	Orchestrates change in both the organizational and competitive environment.

sometime in early growth the organization will outgrow her ability to keep up. She will have neither the time nor the expertise to deal with the range of challenges a burgeoning business presents. She will need to make an early start in delegating responsibilities to others in the organization. The process of delegation is mapped out in Exhibit 13.9.

As Exhibit 13.9 shows, the entrepreneur starts out assigning specific tasks to others. As delegation proceeds, the entrepreneur passes responsibility for achieving objectives to specialists, then managers, without needing to understand or know about the underlying mechanics. Then the setting of objectives moves to others: experienced managers and teams close to the activity. This process enables the entrepreneur to spend less time on the day-to-day details of everything and focus on what she does best, while leaving decisions to those most qualified to make them. At the same time, the entrepreneur needs to oversee execution; this can be done by providing guidance to managers and using metrics to evaluate progress. But the entrepreneur may need to be available to step in when necessary, particularly when initiatives are met with resistance.

Delegation, while necessary for surviving the entrepreneurial growth phase, is typically difficult for the entrepreneur to accomplish. She may continue to attempt to do everything herself, but she's increasingly unable to do so. Faced with these challenges, the entrepreneur may revert back to what she does best; ignoring tasks she has neither the comfort nor ability to deal with. A technical entrepreneur may retreat to developing

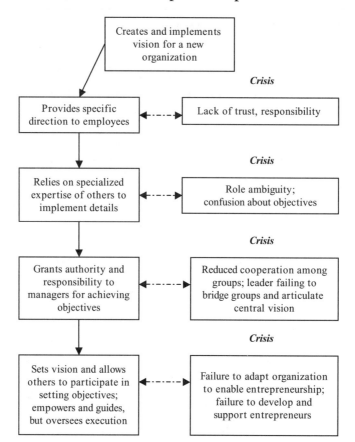

Exhibit 13.9   Transition from Entrepreneur to Entrepreneurial Leader

new products, for example, while ignoring the company's lateness in paying its bills. Employees may not have a problem with the lack of delegation. They may prefer that the entrepreneur make decisions, which they can then carry out. In so doing, they don't need to take responsibility for outcomes. It's not the entrepreneur doing what she does best that's the problem—it's having no one pay attention to the company's most critical concerns.

Conversely, in allowing employees to take responsibility for decisions, the entrepreneur needs to let them make mistakes and learn from them—circumstances neither the employees nor the entrepreneur may feel comfortable with. The entrepreneur cannot continue to be the central decision maker, however, when the volume of decisions mushrooms and she becomes increasingly less qualified to provide direction in many areas. As the entrepreneur delegates, she will need to put managers in place who can be responsible for executing in specialized areas. Then, in her leadership role, she must develop the ability to inspire people with a range of expertise to organize, communicate, collaborate—and be creative in both running an efficient operation and pursuing entrepreneurial ideas.

First-Level Management

In early growth, the first set of supervisors can come from within. In some sense, they deserve to be promoted because they have been with the company since its early days and have contributed to its success. They were willing to chip in whenever and wherever needed and they have worked closely with the entrepreneur, and therefore understand the vision and purpose of the organization. They may have the respect of their peers.

The entrepreneur will need to assess whether these people have the potential to become managers, however, and whether they can develop their abilities through training and experience. There are a few things the entrepreneur should do: (1) Set expectations up front, including setting personal performance goals; (2) provide coaching, mentoring, and training; and (3) periodically assess behavior and performance. It is terribly important to realize that developing managers takes time. If the venture is late in forming its management structure and therefore playing catch-up, if internal and external conditions are rapidly changing, or if the learning gap between current employees and needed management is too wide, then allowing managers to learn on the job is too risky. The entrepreneur will need to hire from the outside. This will more likely happen with higher-growth firms.

Hiring from the outside has its own hazards, though. Employees, particularly those who have been there from the beginning, may not respect outsiders who lack the shared experiences gained through the organization's history. The entrepreneur will need to first act as a broker between the employees and management during this transition. This includes advising the new manager and recognizing the cooperation and contributions of employees. The latter can mean acknowledging accomplishments through personal contact or making these visible around the organization. In addition, the entrepreneur (and managers) can ensure that employees have a satisfactory career path by promoting them and moving them into jobs in which they increasingly feel engaged and challenged.

Where possible, the entrepreneur can employ a mix of externally hired managers and internally promoted managers. Again, the entrepreneur will need to broker between these internal and external managers during the transition, which can be done by setting expectations, through advising and coaching, and by monitoring behavior. By obtaining cooperation among internal and external managers, the entrepreneur is more likely to build a cohesive organization. The entrepreneur also needs to reinforce the authority of these new managers, whether they originate from the inside or outside. For example, employees who have always gone directly to the entrepreneur need to be routed to their managers.

From Delegation to Decentralization

What starts as a process of delegation in early growth evolves into a decentralized reporting structure as the organization approaches later growth. As functions become more specialized and the product and service offering broadens, responsibility and decision making are best left to those with the expertise and day-to-day involvement in specific areas.

A decentralized structure can also aid communication flow throughout the organization. In the early days, everyone works closely with the entrepreneur. It is easy to understand his vision and the organization's objectives. These may not even need to be openly expressed. As the growing organization changes and becomes more complex, however, communication becomes a challenge, leading to confusion about direction and purpose. A consistent message needs to emanate from the management team throughout the organization.

The founder of a growing information technology services firm designed his company's office space with an open concept to allow for clear and easy communication. Critical metrics for sales were projected on a large wall for all to see. Other walls were covered with motivational posters, challenge goals, and descriptions of fun incentives. Everyone worked to beat well-defined milestones, and achievements and recognition were posted and publicized throughout the company. This charged the atmosphere with a sense of mission and purpose. As this example shows, it is important to constantly communicate the organization's goals, and reinforce these with both motivational targets and rewards.[14]

Professional Management and Boards

In later growth, the organization needs to ensure it has a leadership team in place: professional managers who share in the organization's strategic planning process and have the capability to balance the need for efficient operations with the benefits of maintaining its entrepreneurial edge. Once the organization has created control systems, a management structure, and a strategic focus, it needs to look toward its future. This job becomes increasingly complex and requires those with experience and track records. Employees who have been promoted into managerial positions are not likely to be qualified for the organization's top levels, particularly in high-growth firms. Consequently, professional management will most likely come from experienced outsiders.

With the introduction of a leadership team, the organization itself becomes more professional. This is a major change, even more so than the shift from start-up to early growth. Some employees will make this transition, but others may leave. The practices put in place to integrate managers and employees and insiders and outsiders during early growth will be critical to the successful introduction of a professional management team.

A well-assembled board of directors can provide alternative perspectives and depth and breadth of experience to the growing firm. The board should include experts from outside the firm; they can provide critical input to the strategic planning process. What's important for the firm is a proactive, rather than reactive, approach to extending and building the firm's value. The composition of the company's board of directors will typically need to undergo changes as the firm emerges from its start-up phase. Initially, the board may be informal—occupied by those unlikely to have high-level experience, but able to provide support to the entrepreneur in her early endeavors. In early growth, boards typically evolve to include those able to provide operational guidance—for example, retired bankers, investors, and lawyers.

As the company professionalizes, the board should be more useful for strategic purposes, with members having a broader and visionary view of the market and industry—for example, other CEOs, industry experts, and senior executives in related businesses. While many investors require representation on the board of directors, it is advisable to avoid stakeholders who can control the firm for their benefit through board positions, such as suppliers, customers, and the company's lenders.

The skill and experience of the company's leadership and board of directors can be supplemented with the skill and experience of advisory boards and consultants. For example, the company may assemble a group of technology experts from universities, government labs, and corporations to examine industry technological trends. Or it may bring in a marketing consulting firm to determine tactics for expanding into overseas markets.

Strategy

While a start-up is concentrated around shaping an opportunity and bringing it to life, the growing organization needs to make strategic sense of the opportunities it pursues. Otherwise, it can end up chasing many disparate ideas and building too few core strengths that it can leverage across this diverse assortment of businesses. A strategic focus in early growth helps guide the firm through the maze of possibilities that materialize once it experiences initial success. Here, the company should define its core focus—what it can do distinctly well—and develop capabilities around this. Its limited resources and time should be spent close to this core.

As the organization grows, its leadership needs to continually shape and redefine its strategic arena in a way that guides decisions on how it competes in its industry and creates value for its targeted markets. An organization defines this arena through a balance of the unique abilities it is building and insights into how it can differentiate itself in its competitive environment. Once defined, this focus guides strategic decision making—in particular, which opportunities it pursues in expanding its business.

It is important, however, to pay attention to new developments in the industry and market environment. This may determine where a company should best focus its strategic efforts at specific points in time. For instance, the company may emphasize a current product to gain maximum returns before competition comes in. Or it may seek new ground if the market is becoming crowded by large competitors or if a technological foundation is becoming obsolete.

In later growth, the company has established its competitive uniqueness and can now leverage this, while training a strategic eye on the future. It may continue to extend its advantage in its current position—for example, by upgrading its products. Over time, however, opportunities will eventually diminish in a particular product space, and the company will need to combine incremental extensions with expansion into the periphery. A company may create a next-generation product that includes improvements and new features for existing customers, while exploring new products and new markets. At some point, however, it may experience stagnating growth in its core business, but see little opportunity for expansion into the periphery. It may need to make drastic shifts in its business. Acquisitions can provide inroads into new businesses for a company, but there needs to be an underlying logic to this undertaking. The central precept is the connection to the company's unique capabilities.

Growing organizations should therefore select opportunities, not simply because they appear attractive. They should have some particular ability to pursue them better than competitors can. At the same time, they should not restrict themselves solely to opportunities that are close to their current capabilities and businesses. Expansion opportunities will stretch these capabilities, and the company may choose to build new competence over time. The firm can define its strategy more broadly, to allow for experimentation, yet build on its core strengths.

For example, LoJack Corporation has long positioned itself as a leader in tracking and recovering stolen automobiles. Its growth ambitions, however, are driven by a broader strategy: to be the premier worldwide provider of wireless tracking and recovery systems for mobile assets. This guides new business efforts that can leverage their technology and logistics capabilities to track other items of high value that move. This can include people—Alzheimer's patients, for example. It can involve assets like cargo in the trucking business. LoJack's broad, yet coherent, definition of its strategy allows it to think beyond automobiles toward new markets, such as in the medical and transportation businesses.

Expansion beyond the periphery needs to be done carefully, however, particularly for small firms with limited resources. The company can experiment or partner to reduce risk. It can adopt an options logic, where exploratory resources are spread across multiple business options with the expectation that a few as-yet-unknown opportunities will warrant more substantial commitments. The company can also stage its investments, similar to venture capital investing, where a minimum amount is invested in a new business opportunity, and further investment is tied to the achievement of milestones or the reduction of uncertainty. These practices minimize impact on the organization until more is known.

The one uncertainty entrepreneurs can count on, however, is change. The company will need to anticipate, respond to, and even sometimes drive change. Richard Osborne examined 26 privately held firms, all of which experienced initial success. Six of these firms were able to sustain growth beyond the entrepreneurial phase, while the rest saw their growth stalled. Factors such as inadequate resources, poor managerial capabilities of the entrepreneur, and bureaucracy were minor factors in the growth stall, according to this research. The main factor was the inability to perceive and respond to changing opportunities and conditions in their environment.[15]

As the company grows, its strategic planning efforts will benefit from the input of others inside and outside the company with critical knowledge that can influence the company's direction. Customers, particularly lead users, can provide information about market needs. Specialist employees who are close to markets and technologies can identify future opportunities. The firm can institute a function that gathers and monitors outside information and examines external trends and opportunities. The growing company therefore needs to be responsive to impending environmental shifts, maintaining the ability to transform its strategy in a way that establishes a new source of uniqueness in a changed environment.

Resources

Resources at startup include capital and people. Financial capital allows the firm to finance operations, invest in fixed assets, and hire employees. The most critical human resource will lie within the founder or founding team. As the company grows, it builds intangible assets. These refer to such resources as the proprietary knowledge underlying the firm's products and services and the skills of the organization's people. The entrepreneur should have addressed intellectual property considerations early on, before early growth—even before starting the business. But this should also be an ongoing process requiring continual legal advice and subsequent actions to protect technologies, processes, and creative work through trade secrets, copyrights, trademarks, and patents. These intangible assets can be the key foundation underlying the company's long-term success. This also requires capital and continued investment in people.

Obtaining Financial Resources for the Growing Company

Efforts to internally finance growth go hand in hand with controls. By improving its cash flow, the growing company can better avoid a crisis of being out of cash and at the mercy of reluctant or expensive lenders or investors. The company may even be able to self-finance some of its future growth, reducing reliance on more costly sources of funding. The key lesson is this: A bootstrap mentality does not apply just to starting a company; it is a lasting orientation that maximizes returns through resource parsimony.

Shortening operating cash cycles and increasing margins are therefore vital for conserving cash. They essentially represent costless financing. The rapidly growing organization, however, will likely need to tap additional sources to finance its growth. Not only will financing be needed to support accelerating sales, but new policies, such as granting customer payment terms or taking on bulk orders, as well as investments in new products or services, will create a drain on cash.

Despite its success and future prospects, however, a company early in its growth cycle may have only certain options available. For example, a bank would not typically extend credit to a firm with little operating history and fluctuating sales. But a supplier who is motivated to make a sale and gain a loyal, growing customer might. After a company has been established for a year, a bank might be willing to loan monies against a portion of its receivables, the founders' good credit, or with signed guarantees, perhaps requiring loan covenants to maintain certain numbers or ratios.

Thinking in terms of stages can therefore be useful when financing growth. Sources closed to the firm earlier in its life may open up later. For that reason, it is worthwhile to undertake periodic surveys of the firm's current financing options, and consider any changes that may open up new and cheaper financing sources. In this respect, the firm may recognize new opportunities for refinancing at lower rates.

Sources of financing for early growth include:

- Investment from key management.
- Founder loans.
- Family and friends.
- Angel investors.
- Loans on assets, such as receivables, inventory, and equipment.
- Equipment leases.
- Credit cards.

As the company moves into later growth and undertakes expansion efforts, such as selling internationally or launching new products or services, financing will need to come from sources more appropriate for higher-risk and longer-term investment. Banks typically will not loan substantial funds, unsecured, for riskier expansion efforts that won't generate returns for quite some time. The firm will likely need to rely on equity sources. In seeking this type of capital, though, an oft-repeated cautionary note is in order. Investors can exert control over the enterprise, which is particularly problematic when their goals conflict with that of the entrepreneurs, as Phil Diamond found out.[16]

Diamond founded and ran an East Coast–based direct-response advertising business, which was financed in part by a $2.5 million venture capital (VC) investment. The

VCs wanted to prepare the firm for sale to a larger advertising firm. So they replaced Diamond with a CEO who had reputation and experience in corporate advertising and, the VCs believed, a style that would appeal to potential buyers. Soon after the new CEO came on board, it was clear to Diamond and others in the organization that the CEO would completely disrupt what had taken years to build. While employees were at first looking forward to learning from the CEO and benefiting from his relationships with important prospective customers, they soon realized he was only concerned with "fixing" the company for sale. His choice not to relocate from Chicago was one sign he perceived this as a temporary assignment. Diamond, seeing his company as more than a financial investment, eventually got his company back and paid off the VCs. His management team stayed with him and the company thrived. While this story has a happy ending, the critical lesson to be learned is that it's important for entrepreneurs to ensure that their goals align with investors' goals—before the investment is made.

Entrepreneurs can explore a number of ways to finance future growth, besides traditional debt and equity. A company can look to strategic partners who may provide more favorable financing terms. The company may also decide to expand by franchising. The risks of these financing modes must be taken into consideration. For example, potential customers who compete with a firm's strategic partner may view a relationship with the firm as too risky because the partner has some control over the firm, or has greater access to information that could unfavorably impact the customer. Resource needs are also determined by a firm's range of value chain activities. Reducing activities to those considered core to the business and achieving better coordination throughout the chain can reduce resource requirements and risk.

Human Resources

Starting in early growth, the entrepreneur will need to develop or hire people with specialized skills. Generalist skills are important at start-up: Everyone should be able to pitch in and help with shipping, inventory control, marketing, and so forth. It is more important for the lean team to maintain the flexibility and broad skills needed to accomplish a lot with a little. As volume increases and the business becomes more complex, it becomes harder to maintain efficiency and effectiveness with generalist skills. The entrepreneur will need to hire specialists in areas such as marketing, inventory management, accounting and finance, and logistics.

The most common people mistakes an entrepreneurial firm makes are preparing its people inadequately and maintaining the wrong people as the organization grows. As the need for specialists and managers arises, the tasks expected of some employees may exceed their abilities, and the entrepreneur may need to place them in other roles, or even fire them if necessary. Other employees may be able to rise up to the challenges presented and assume these new functions and responsibilities. The process of adapting to these new roles takes time, however. The company will often need to do some hiring from the outside.

The second tier of employees, beyond the founding group, is often said to be more like nine-to-fivers. While the original employees would pitch in and do what's needed, staying late if necessary, the new hires tend to view working there as a job. But in most companies, there are entrepreneurs in the mix. While it is often thought that ideas come from anywhere or that anyone can be creative if given a chance, the reality is that some people don't have the stomach for ambiguity and risk. And in many companies, the entrepreneur remains the sole entrepreneurial engine. Our research on corporate entrepreneurship suggests the organization's leaders need to:

- Identify those exhibiting passion for entrepreneurship.
- Develop their ability to work under conditions of high ambiguity.
- Ensure that they have the inclination and credibility to convince others in the organization to contribute and commit to their projects.
- Facilitate, support, and guide their efforts while also providing them with sufficient freedom and empowerment.
- Recognize their contribution to the company's innovation and growth ambitions.
- View failure as a risk associated with entrepreneurship, and an opportunity for learning, therefore ensuring that well-intentioned failures are not punished.

We suspect these practices are also critical in smaller organizations. One study, for example, reports that human resource practices involving training and development distinguish high-growth firms from more slowly growing ones.[17] One of the most critical actions a growing organization's leaders can take is to identify, develop, and support entrepreneurial individuals. In so doing, they ensure that the ability to pursue new opportunities can outlast any one person and is truly an organizational capability.

Conclusions

As an entrepreneurial firm moves beyond its founding days, it will need to address the challenges and requirements of growth. It is imperative for the entrepreneur to understand and anticipate the challenges associated with building and managing a growing organization at different stages. The key task lies in preparing this organization to execute effectively at each point, as well as setting the stage for a healthy future.

A firm's capacity for growth is influenced by external conditions and personal considerations. The firm may be in an industry with low growth potential. To achieve a higher rate of growth will take considerable effort and creativity. At the same time, competing in a high-growth industry often requires a high-growth orientation to respond and stay competitive in a rapidly changing environment. Entrepreneurs can assess their own capacities for growth, and this should be done in conjunction with external realities. Whatever their growth aspirations, however, all entrepreneurs need to pay attention to building their organizations to handle their expanding operations and position their ventures for the longer term.

Working from the perspective of the owner/manager of a growing organization, we have identified four domains entrepreneurs must address in their company's growth stages. The organizational domain includes controls and performance assessment, which can be simple at first, becoming increasingly more sophisticated as the organization expands. The leadership domain involves a process of delegating, developing/hiring managers, and building a leadership team. For the strategic domain, the firm can start with a strategic focus that enables it to create a core foundation of capabilities that can be leveraged in existing and peripheral markets, and then build the ability to explore newer areas for the future. The resource domain recognizes that financing sources may change as the organization grows, but stresses the nonfinancial considerations that should factor into these decisions. In addition, internal sources of financing and a bootstrap mentality will be just as critical as the firm expands. The resource domain also includes the development of the company's human resources.

Amid these organization-building efforts, entrepreneurs need to maintain a connection to the firm's entrepreneurial roots, even as it becomes more professional and efficient. Growing companies struggle, not just with such concerns as having fewer resources than big companies and coordinating an increasingly bigger and more complex business; they must also work to prevent the organization from becoming a bureaucracy that inhibits entrepreneurship. They must continually foster entrepreneurial actions even at times when this is their biggest challenge. They have to consciously work on preserving and maintaining their entrepreneurial spirit; and if lost, they have to rejuvenate the company and rekindle entrepreneurship before it's too late.

Notes

1. Bosma, Niels, Acs, Zoltan, Autio, Erkko, Coduras, Alicia, and Levie, Jonathan. (2008). Global Entrepreneurship Monitor 2008 Executive Report. London: Global Entrepreneurship Research Association.
2. www.IBISWorld.com/industry.
3. Paul Steffens, Per Davidsson, and Jason Fitzsimmons, "Performance Configurations over Time: Implications for Growth and Profit-Oriented Strategies," *Entrepreneurship: Theory and Practice* 33, no. 1 (2009): 125–148.
4. John Tozzi, "The Entrepreneurship Myth," *BusinessWeek Online,* January 24, 2008.
5. Noam Wasserman, "The Founder's Dilemma," *Harvard Business Review* 86, no. 2 (2008): 102–109.
6. Gavin Cassar, "Money, Money, Money? A Longitudinal Investigation of Entrepreneur Career Reasons, Growth Preferences, and Achieved Growth," *Entrepreneurship and Regional Development* 19 (2007): 89–107.
7. Raphael Amit, Kenneth R. MacCrimmon, Charlene Zietsma, and John M. Oesc, "Does Money Matter? Wealth Attainment as the Motive for Initiating Growth-Oriented Technology Ventures," *Journal of Business Venturing* 16 (2000): 119–143.
8. Jennifer Cliff, "Does One Size Fit All? Exploring the Relationship Between Attitudes Toward Growth, Gender, and Business Size," *Journal of Business Venturing* 13 (1998): 523–542.
9. Per Davidsson, "Entrepreneurship—and After? A Study of Growth Willingness in Small Firms," *Journal of Business Venturing* 4 (1989): 211–226.
10. Steffens et al., "Performance Configurations over Time."
11. J. Robert Baum, Edwin A. Locke, and Ken G. Smith, "A Multidimensional Model of Venture Growth," *Academy of Management Journal* 44 (2) (2001): 292–303; Lisa K. Gundry and Harold P. Welsch, "The Ambitious Entrepreneur: High Growth Strategies of Women-Owned Enterprises," *Journal of Business Venturing* 16 (2001): 453–470; Lars Kolvereid, "Growth Aspirations Among Norwegian Entrepreneurs," *Journal of Business Venturing* 7 (1992), 209–222; Y. K. Shin, "The Traits and Leadership Styles of CEOs in Korean Companies, *International Studies of Management and Organization* 28, no. 4 (1999): 40–48.
12. Carl Hedberg, Edward P. Marram, and Glenn Kaplus, *Dancing Deer Baking Company,* Babson College Case Study (Babson Park, MA: Babson College, 2006).
13. Joel Kolen and Susan Biddle Jaffe, "Knowing When to Take a Breather: Controlling Company Growth," *Nation's Business* 83 (11): 6.

14. Carl Hedberg and Edward P. Marram, *Everon IT,* Babson College Case Study (Babson Park, MA: Babson College, 2008).

15. Richard L. Osborne, "Second Phase Entrepreneurship: Breaking Through the Growth Wall," *Business Horizons* 37, no. 1 (1994).

16. Entrepreneur's name changed from actual.

17. Osborne, "Second Phase Entrepreneurship."

14

Franchising

Steve Spinelli

How This Chapter Fits into a Typical MBA Curriculum

In the United States, franchising is the dominant retail business form. In 2009, almost 900,000 franchised outlets had total sales over $1 trillion, accounting for 35 percent of all retail sales.[1] Total value chain output might be as much as $2.3 trillion and 21 million jobs.[2] There are another 80,000 franchised outlets internationally. Public franchise companies dominate fast- and fast-casual food and the automotive segments. Franchisee companies are increasingly becoming multiple outlet operators. That dominant position is a double-edged sword. The economic downturn will certainly affect franchising, especially in the automotive arena. Some speculate that fast food might continue to do well. However, 2009 or 2010 may mark the first time in a generation that franchise units shrink. The sheer size and economic impact of what is called franchising demands investigation.

MBA students study franchising as a business model and growth strategy. People interested in entrepreneurship and new venture creation study franchising because owning and operating a franchise is a means to reduce risk. The franchisee is investing in a proven business model with some level of brand equity. Franchising can be a stand-alone course or a special topic within other entrepreneurship courses such as new venture creation.

Who Uses This Material in the Real World—and Why It Is Important

As already noted, anybody involved in franchising would find this chapter valuable. Whether a person is considering franchising a business concept that they have developed (franchisor) as part of their growth strategy or the person is contemplating buying a single or multiple franchise units (franchisee), this chapter will provide the grounding the person needs to make a strong decision.

What Is Franchising?

Over the years franchising has been much maligned as anything from a pyramid scheme to just another form of employment. Robert T. Justis, Professor of Franchising at the University of Nebraska, defines franchising in general as "a business opportunity by which the owner, producer, or distributor (franchisor) of a service or trademarked product grants exclusive rights to an individual (franchisee) for the local distribution of the product or service, and in return receives a payment or royalty and conformance to quality standards."

> *Franchising* is a business opportunity by which the owner, producer, or distributor (franchisor) of a service or trademarked product grants exclusive rights to an individual (franchisee) for the local distribution of the product or service, and in return receives a payment or royalty and conformance to quality standards.

There are two general forms of franchising: product franchising and business format franchising. A *product franchise* consists of a branded product offered for sale in another otherwise branded business. An example would be selling Westinghouse dishwashers in Zack's Home Appliance. *Business format franchising* is defined as a contractual, ongoing business relationship between a franchisor and franchisee. The business format concept includes a marketing plan, documented and enforced procedures, process assistance, and business development and innovation. Business format franchising is an overall method of doing business and is a more complex relationship than franchising solely for the purpose of product distribution. The relationship in a business format franchise must be as dynamic as the marketplace to survive. This chapter focuses on the business format franchise.

Historical Background

Most business practitioners and students have heard about the McDonald's story and its founder, Ray Kroc. Although their contribution to franchising is monumental, the history of franchising begins much earlier.

The extensive pub network in the United Kingdom may be the oldest franchise system in the world. During the Roman occupation of Britain, the major supplier of food, drink, and accommodations for the traveler was the Church. Religious tenets of the time dictated that two days' food and lodging be supplied free to any traveler. Abuses of these privileges resulted in the growth of commercial enterprises around 740–750 AD.

By 957 King Edgar decided there were too many alehouses and decreed a limit of one per village. As a part of that decree some common standards were instituted. The business format required a standard measure, limited quantities, and a prohibition of sales to priests.[3] A monitoring system was established and fines levied against violators. Franchising was born.

The population steadily grew, and evolving consumer and economic realities forced consolidation of the industry. The national brewers recognized a need to secure market share. Publicans grappled with the difficulty of keeping pace with fast moving events and the ever-increasing demands of various kinds. More and more pub owners allied with brewers. By the early nineteenth century, half of all alehouses were tied by some form of agreement. The House of Commons Committee on Public Breweries in 1818 noted that tied houses were "of much higher order" than free houses.[4] Franchising was here to stay.

It can be logically argued that Christopher Columbus was awarded franchise development rights for the new world by Queen Isabella of Spain in 1492. The franchise companies listed in Exhibit 14.1 have helped shape the retail landscape of the United States, creating brands that others have emulated.

Exhibit 14.1   Franchise Milestones

Rexall Drugs	1902
Western Auto	1909
Howard Johnson	1925
McDonald's	1955
Kentucky Fried Chicken	1955
International House of Pancakes (IHOP)	1959
Subway	1965
UPS Stores	1980

The most common categories of franchises (listed alphabetically) include both broad and specific applications:

- Automotive
- Business services
- Children's businesses
- Financial services
- Food
- Home improvement
- Hotels and motels
- Information technology services
- Maintenance
- Personal care
- Pet businesses
- Recreation
- Retail
- Services
- Training

Franchising in the United States began in the 1840s. Two distinct types of franchises have developed. The first, *product franchising,* was created by makers of complex durable goods who found existing wholesalers either unwilling or unable to market their products. These manufacturers built their own distribution systems and created franchise systems as alternatives to the high cost of company-owned outlets. The second type, *business format franchising,* was created in the 1950s when it became evident that the outlet itself could be a vehicle for entrepreneurial activity.

A franchise system can be a combination of franchisor-operated outlets and franchisee-operated outlets or only franchisee-operated outlets. The percentage of franchised versus company-owned outlets varies greatly among franchises. Dunkin' Donuts has historically operated very few company-owned restaurants. McDonald's owns about 21 percent of system restaurants. Eighty-seven percent of the outlets in U.S. franchise systems are operated by franchisees.[5] Types of businesses generally included in business format franchising are restaurants, food and nonfood retailing, and business services.

The flowering of the Internet spawned a new array of franchised service companies. Midas and Dunkin' Donuts are two examples of business format franchises. A consumer electronics retailer of Sony would be a product franchise.

Becoming a Franchisee versus Starting a Stand-alone Business

The keys to success in a franchise are the same as for any other business. The difference is that the array of factors responsible for a franchise's success is tried and true, and there is a proven ability to transfer this system of excellence to varied and dispersed locations. Therefore, the franchise model is predicated on the assumption that value has been developed through the careful operation, testing, and documentation of a commercially viable idea. Given that this has been accomplished (which your own due diligence must verify), the initial success of the system lies in the ability of the franchisor to communicate this system to qualified franchisees. The long-term success of the system is uniquely tied to the franchisor's ability to receive and assimilate process feedback from the franchisees and use this feedback to modify the system.

The choice of becoming a franchisee or starting a stand-alone business hinges on your answers to two important questions:

1. Is risk sufficiently mitigated by the trademark value, operating system, economies of scale, and support process of the franchise to justify a sharing of equity with the franchisor (vis-à-vis the franchise fee and royalty payments)?

2. Is my personality and management style amenable to sharing decision-making responsibilities in my business with the franchisor and other franchisees?

For those who need to quantify the choice between a franchise and a stand-alone business, I offer the following equation:

$$\text{Franchise fee} + \text{PV of royalty} = \text{PV of the increased net income from the value of the franchise trademark}$$

Where

PV   is the present value of a sum of money. (For an explanation of PV, see Chapter 7 and the Glossary.)

If your analysis reveals this equation to be true, or if it is an inequality and the right-hand side of the equation is greater than the left-hand side, the franchise decision is appropriate. However, this formula is more art than science. The key is estimating how much more business you'll do because you have a recognizable brand instead of a new entry.

Much of this chapter focuses on the quantity and quality of the services and systems that a franchise offers. The choice of a franchise versus stand-alone start-up is a question of due diligence, of evaluating the competitive advantages offered by the franchise. Those advantages must exist in sufficient quantity to justify the cost in franchise fees, royalties, and management encumbrances.

Due diligence should start with the contract between the franchisee and franchisor.

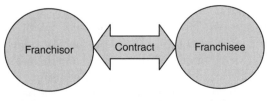

Exhibit 14.2 Traditional View of the Franchise Relationship

The Franchise Contract

The most refined franchise relationship develops into a partnership between the franchisor and the franchisee, and among the franchisees. However, a contract is necessary to ensure an understanding between the parties of their rights and obligations and the associated costs. In franchising, this contract is usually called a *license agreement* or a *franchise contract* (see Exhibit 14.2). Because of the degree of regulation of franchising in the United States, the license agreement has become the definitive statement if litigation occurs.

In a mature franchise the trade name and trademark are the most valuable assets owned by the franchisor. In the business format franchise, the documented operating system is integral to the trade name and trademark. Together they are responsible for the market value of the franchise. In some cases, building specifications, equipment design, and secret formulas or recipes may be important parts of the franchisor's assets. (For example, the Colonel adamantly believed his "secret recipe" was integral to the product and image of Kentucky Fried Chicken.) Some assets may be patented or copyrighted.

Consideration of franchising by a company or due diligence by a franchise prospect requires an intimate understanding of the license agreement. Franchising is a legal specialization, and some firms concentrate their entire practice in this field. An attorney's review of the license agreement is a necessary cost of franchising. As a part of the legal review, the attorney should prepare a lay-language brief of the license agreement. In the development or review of a license agreement, business issues will be woven into the legalese. The more practical the detail in the license agreement, the better the chance for a healthy long-term relationship. However, implementing the license agreement will require the franchisor to incur monitoring costs, which must be considered along with other costs of the relationship such as litigation expense and quality concerns.

This chapter uses the license agreement, or franchise contract, as a guide to the due diligence process. Understanding the terms of the license agreement is an integral part of the risk management process vital to all franchise endeavors. The following sections highlight the normal operating parameters in a franchise contract with special attention to the pitfalls. Remember, proper evaluation of the franchise opportunity rests in assessing the value and cost of the franchise in relation to expected profits from going it alone.

Services Provided by the Franchisor

This section of the contract is invariably briefer than that detailing the franchisee obligations. However, a few key references will be sufficient to indicate the franchisor's positive intent and obligation. The services provided by the franchisor are separated into initial and continuing services. The type of business will heavily influence the services the franchisor supplies. As a rule of thumb, the prospective franchisee should discount any personal knowledge or experience in the industry and then ask the question, will the magnitude of the initial services establish the franchisee business in a manner appropriate to efficient operation on the day of opening and beyond?

Real Estate Development

Because many business format franchises include a real estate ingredient, site selection and construction specification and supervision are extremely important. Adages such as "Location, location, location," "Just around the corner from success," and "A 'B' site will get you an 'F' in profitability" are not exaggerations. The real estate on which an outlet is located is often both the point of sale and the physical foundation for the service delivery system. It usually cannot be changed without severe economic stress. Most franchisors will approve the location, but not all will actually search for a site. Even fewer will take *responsibility* for finding a site.

The key aspects of site location include a thorough understanding of the primary target audience (PTA), your most likely customer, and the propensity of the PTA to patronize your franchise under varying environmental conditions. An important part of the franchisor's value lies in the accumulation and processing of data from the operating units. Although the franchisor cannot and should not give out information regarding specific stores, compilations with analysis are usually available. This is how the PTA information is gathered. If it is the franchisee's responsibility to locate a site, there must be clearly documented processes linking the PTA to the location specifics. General location parameters include cost, population, traffic volume, traffic patterns, visibility, zoning and permits, and ingress and egress; each of these factors is discussed in the following sections.

Cost

Lodging franchises require the largest initial investment and ongoing expenses (ranging from $4 to $6 million), followed by full-service restaurants (from $700,000 to $3.5 million), fast-food restaurants (from $250,000 to $2 million), and auto repair (from $200,000 to $800,000). Mobile and home-based business franchises make up the most affordable category. Much of the variance is in the real estate. In fact, real estate often accounts for the majority of the capital required to open a franchise. Even a long-established retail venture that decides to franchise must perform a thorough analysis of the site characteristics to reveal location standards for successful expansion. Because real estate is so important to most franchises, the occupancy cost should be constantly reevaluated in your financial model. Changing demographics and infrastructure and growth into varying regions might drastically affect your ability to be profitable.

Contact a large commercial real estate broker and review your site specification needs. Gather examples of recently sold or leased property with comparable specifications. Do the property or occupancy costs correlate with the franchisor guidelines for operating a profitable outlet? This process should also be followed by the franchisor, especially when expansion into new geographic territories is contemplated. Even if purchase prices are the same, lease terms and conditions can vary over time and among regions. Make sure that the capitalization (cap) rates used in calculating lease cost are comparable. The cap rate is the percentage return the landlord can expect her property to yield on the value of the asset (in this case, land and building) that is being leased. The term of a lease, the amount of time the lessee contractually holds the property, should match the term of the license agreement.

Population

How many targeted customers—not members of the general population—in how wide a market area is prescribed by the franchisor? For example, Service-Master lawn care tracks dual-income homes in its trade areas. Cross-reference the minimum PTA number with the franchisor pro forma market share and sales projection:

Three-mile radius

Population 50,000; PTA 20,000.

Market share of 10 percent.

$$2,000 \text{ PTA} \times 3 \text{ visits per year} = 6,000 \text{ customers}$$
$$\text{Franchisor's sales projections}/6,000 = \text{Average ticket price}$$

Create a spreadsheet analysis ramping up volume to track these sample numbers. Are your projections reasonable and in line with the numbers projected by the franchisor? Will existing outlets' performance validate these projections?

Traffic Volume

Volume is quoted as pedestrians or vehicles per day. Many franchisors will prescribe a minimum volume, usually quoted on a 12- or 24-hour basis. Take note of the outlets the franchisor has singled out or the outlets of franchisees who have expressed satisfaction with their sales volume. Most state departments of motor vehicles, registry, or public works have traffic flow information.

Traffic Patterns

The more sophisticated franchisors analyze day parts and weigh traffic patterns appropriately. Corner location, the homeward-bound versus work-bound side of the road, and speed of traffic are but a few of the critical issues related to traffic patterns. A donut or coffee franchise may require the work-bound side of the road, as customers are less likely to stop for morning coffee if they must cross traffic when rushing to their jobs. This is an example of the fine distinction between a marginal return and a substantial return—or worse, the difference between failure and success.

Visibility

Visibility is especially important for products bought on impulse. When it is noon and you are hungry, you may act on impulse in reaction to a fast-food sign. Finding a preschool (a growing area of franchising) is probably a more considered choice and not an impulse purchase.

Visibility is a three-pronged issue, including the elements of sign, building, and property entrance. At the top speed of the vehicles traveling the road of the proposed location (not to be confused with the posted speed), how many feet and seconds pass from the first view of each of these criteria to the entrance of the site? Is there sufficient time from the initial sighting of the location variable for a driver to comfortably turn into the location? A location that provides adequate turning time with respect to all three visibility variables has the highest ranking in this area.

Seasonality has an impact on visibility. A site as viewed in the winter may yield dramatically different results from the same site in the spring, with trees in full leaf.

Zoning and Permits

The cost and time requirements relating to zoning can vary dramatically from state to state and among local municipalities. Often a land use attorney is required for the process, as well as architects, surveyors, civil engineers, and traffic specialists. Increasingly, environmental impact studies are mandated by state regulation. Estimate the cost of these professionals as a part of due diligence.

Usually the franchisee is required to bear these costs up front. If the franchisor bears the costs, they are often capitalized in the real estate development expense and will be reflected in the outlet rent. In particularly complicated zoning affairs the cost may inflate the project well beyond the ultimate market value and potentially beyond the occupancy cost projected in the franchisor's financial pro forma.

Ingress and Egress

This is real estate jargon for entrance to and exit from the site. Checkers drive-in restaurant, launched in 1986, requires most site plans to have two drive-through windows in the flow of ingress and egress. Planning boards frequently modify a site plan even at the last minute. A quick change in entrance and exit layout can dramatically alter site acquisition criteria.

Summing Up: Don't Ignore Location Success Factors

If franchising is the vehicle chosen by a currently operating firm for expansion, it is critical to match the existing location success factors to the business format developed for sale to a franchisee. To neglect this is a fatal flaw, especially if the franchisee is responsible for finding the new location. It is extremely difficult to overcome location flaws and often impossible to change them.

In rapidly growing franchise systems there is a greater propensity to compromise on the development of individual stores in a rush to gain market share. Often the decision to franchise is made as a result of the desire to grow quickly. This cannot be allowed to dominate good business practice if long-term stability is to be achieved.

It is mutually beneficial to the franchisor and franchisee to have franchisor professionals provide detailed input in the real estate development. Some franchises typically locate in a mall—T-Shirts Plus, for example. The same attention to location and demographic issues applies. A successful outlet will yield profit for the franchisee and capital for expansion. The franchisor will gain larger royalty payments. If the franchise is operated poorly and it ultimately fails, the franchisor can turn over the unit quickly, operate it as a company store, or sell the property to an unrelated third party only if the real estate has been carefully acquired and developed.

Investing in the real estate is a separate business venture from the franchise for both the franchisor and the franchisee. In evaluating the franchise opportunity, calculate the occupancy cost on a market *rental rate*. This can be done by multiplying the market square footage rental cost by the size of the proposed project. Alternatively, use the *market lease factor*—7.0 percent in a recessionary market (almost everywhere in 2009),

12 percent in an expansive market (New York)—applied to the total project cost. The market lease factor is the rate the landlord will charge based on the current demand in the marketplace.

A franchisor who wishes to be the realty holder or lessor will need to negotiate the rental relationship. Some franchisors use what is called *percentage rent* to calculate the occupancy cost for the franchisee. There are a number of methods to implement percentage rents. The simplest is to charge a constant percentage of gross sales. This can be beneficial in the start-up phase but can result in above-market rents for the exceptionally performing location. This is particularly true for businesses with rapidly escalating costs and pricing, and can result in squeezed franchisee margins. This rental formula may seem attractive at the outset but could become burdensome. The variations in the use of percentage rents are limitless. Other methods include charging base rent, a minimum amount each month plus a smaller amount of top-line sales, or an amount slightly less than market rent plus a percentage of top-line sales over the projected break-even sales volume. Some franchisors will offer a variety of options; some will not. The franchisee should negotiate the options as a result of pro forma analysis and in congruence with risk mentality.

Established expertise in interpreting crucial real estate variables is included as part of the franchise purchase. Therefore, the franchisee must be sufficiently convinced that the necessary expertise is in place, available, and utilized.

Construction Specification and Supervision

Upon preliminary qualification of the site, the franchisor should integrate its construction department into the process. The franchisor usually has a standard set of blueprints. Most states require modification to meet state building code with the stamp of an architect from that state. Further modification may be required by local municipalities. Some franchisors modify plans even to the local level, but most do not. The level of sophistication of the model plans will greatly impact modification cost and efficiency. Very general plans leave much room for architectural inventiveness, resulting in diminished standardization, loss of efficiency, and reduced market value of the real estate.

Beyond the physical blueprints, the franchisor may provide construction supervision. Bidding contracts, draw approvals, construction monitoring, and final punch list are the categories of construction supervision. Beware of the franchisor who controls the construction process without independent bidding. There is nothing wrong with construction as a profit center if it also accrues benefits to the franchisee. This is best monitored through the marketplace of contractors. The franchisee should be involved in the construction process even if it is totally supervised by the franchisor. The franchise operator will understand the building better and live with it in greater harmony. Minor examples of building aspects the operator must be familiar with include the heating, ventilation, and air conditioning, and basement sump pump operation.

Training

Training is a vital initial service and is also helpful on a continuing basis. The license agreement must define the *specific* form in which this franchisor responsibility will be carried out. It should extend significantly beyond a manual and the classroom. Training will vary with the specifics of the franchise but invariably should include organized and monitored on-the-job experience. Well-established and stable franchise systems require operational experience in the system for as long as a year prior to the purchase of a franchise. However, this is not the norm. Once the franchise is operational, the franchisee may be expected to do much or all of the on-site training. Manuals, testing, training aids such as videos, and certification processes are often provided by the franchisor.

As discussed previously, the trade name and mark are the most valuable assets in a franchise system. This is the result of delivery of the product on a consistent basis to consumers who acknowledge the value through paying a price that includes a profit margin. A poor training regimen will inevitably dilute the standardized, consistent delivery of the product and reduce trade name value.

New thinking and practices involving Web 2.0, creating multiple routes and directions of communication via the Internet, are driving new models and levels of dynamic training content generation, systems synergy, best practice evolution, and community adoption. This is especially helpful in franchising. A great franchise has communications infrastructure that provides franchisees with findings of research and development and a clear view toward implementing innovation. Knowledge sharing in franchising is the foundation of competitive positioning and consistent brand building.

Preopening Support

The foundation of the support services program is the level and sophistication of preopening support. Preopening support is a concentrated, multifunctional program to launch the new franchise. Inventory and equipment purchase and setup, staff hiring and training, and start-up marketing are key variables. Built upon a sound location program, preparedness at launch can create the momentum for success. The franchisor who has the expertise in place to provide sophisticated start-up assistance likely has the capability to provide the contractually required continuing services. A poor opening experience is an ominous sign concerning the quality of the franchise.

Continuing Services

Many license agreements define royalties as payment for the use of intellectual property. However, the continuity of the franchise relationship often rests on the cost/value rationalization of the royalty payment by the franchisee to the franchisor. Not only must the franchisor create a marketplace basket of services, but in the provision of services the system must be sustained and nurtured.

The actions of each franchisee affect the value of the trademark and thus the value of each individual franchise. The actions of the franchisor also affect franchise value. Both parties are necessarily interdependent and have a vested interest in actively supporting the system. A franchise agreement that acknowledges and addresses this interdependence is advantageous. The franchisee's performance is somewhat dependent on the quantity and quality of franchisor support. Conversely, the degree of franchisor support is usually inversely related to franchisee performance; more attention is usually provided to the underperforming franchisee. Although this is a reasonable response to a threat to trademark value, balance in the application of franchisor resources is a key ingredient for success.

Performance and Standards Monitoring

By developing an array of statistical and financial monitoring devices, the franchisor can identify both the exceptional performer and the potential failure. Application of resources against identified problems maintains a stable system. Operational systems or marketing programs are often changed in a franchise system because of the exceptional performer. The best franchise systems not only compile data but analyze and efficiently distribute the information to franchisees for feedback. Does the contract provide for this informational conduit role?

Field Support

The license agreement should provide for scheduled visits to the franchisee's place of business with prescribed objectives. An efficient agenda might include performance review, field training, facilities inspection, local marketing review, and operations audit. The reality is that some franchisors use their field role as a diplomatic or pejorative exercise. The greater the substance of the field function, the easier it is for the franchisee to justify the royalty cost. Additionally, in a litigious environment a well-documented field support program will mute franchisee claims.

One means of understanding the franchisor's field support motive is to investigate the manner in which the field support personnel are compensated. If field staff are paid commensurate with franchisee performance and ultimate profitability, then politics will play a diminished role. Warning signals are bonuses for growth in the number of stores versus individual store sales growth, and pay or bonus for franchisee product usage. Tying arrangements will be discussed later. However, the field support system is a part of the practical application of the influence strategy the franchisor has chosen.

Operational Research and Development

Economies of scale in research and development are a principal benefit in franchising. These economies are best achieved through the centralized, monitored, and standardized franchisor. Research of a franchise should track operations-level changes in franchised stores over a period of two to four years. How are changes in the system encouraged, cultivated, harvested, and communicated? A practical mechanism should be referred to or specifically outlined in the license agreement.

This is a difficult and delicate area for the franchisor. The franchisor must ensure standardization but also must encourage change. This paradox is resolved by realizing that change will occur but must be managed. Franchising provides the mechanism for the efficient management of change. Customer needs, the legal environment, competition, and most of all the entrepreneurial fervor of franchisees will stretch the envelope of standardization. Recognizing this, the franchise must provide rules in the license agreement for optimizing efforts in the search for betterment of the system. In franchise systems where the franchisor does not operate a number of company-owned stores, the existing franchise body or representative group should play a part in reviewing and approving issues of product or operational change. These kinds of changes are sometimes covered in the marketing services section of the license agreement.

Marketing, Advertising, and Promotion

This is one of the most sensitive areas in the ongoing franchise relationship. Marketing imprints the trade name and mark in the mind of the consumer. If delivery of the product validates the marketing message, the value of the franchise is enhanced. Unit growth increases budgets and spreads marketing costs, optimizing the marketing program for the system.

There are a number of mechanisms to fund and implement a marketing program. Typically, a national advertising fund is controlled by the franchisor. Each franchisee contributes a percentage of top-line sales. The franchisor then produces materials (television, radio, and newspaper ads; direct mail pieces; and point-of-sale materials) and, depending on the size of the fund, buys media time or space. As it is virtually impossible to allocate these services on an exactly equal basis among franchisees, the license agreement may specify the use of "best efforts" to approximate equal treatment, or some such language. "Best efforts" invariably leave some franchisees with a little more and others with a little less advertising. Over time, this should balance but must be carefully monitored.

The second level of marketing, advertising, and promotion in franchising is regional. This is often structured on the basis of an *area of dominant influence* (ADI). All the stores in a given ADI—Greater Hartford, Connecticut, for example—would contribute a percentage of top-line sales to the ADI advertising cooperative. The cooperative's primary function is usually to buy media using franchisor-supplied or -approved advertising and to coordinate regional promotions. If the franchise has a regional advertising cooperative requirement in the license agreement, it should also have standardized ADI cooperative bylaws. These bylaws will outline such things as voting rights and define expenditure parameters. A single-store franchisee can be disadvantaged in a poorly organized cooperative. Conversely, a major contributor to the cooperative may find voting rights disproportionately low.

The final level of advertising is typically dubbed local advertising or local store marketing. At this level the franchisee is contractually required to make direct expenditures on advertising. There is a wide spectrum of permissible advertising expenditures, depending on the franchisor guidelines. However, the license agreement will probably not be specific. Franchisors will try to maintain discretion on this issue for maximum flexibility in the marketplace. Company-owned stores should have advertising requirements equal to those for the franchised units to avoid franchisor free-riding. Historical behavior is the best gauge of reasonableness.

It is important that the franchisor monitor and enforce marketing expenditures. A customer leaving one ADI and entering another will have been affected by the advertising of adjacent regions. Additionally, an individual franchisee can free-ride on system advertising, if franchisors don't monitor expenditures. The result is underinvestment in advertising and therefore marketing impressions lost to the system. The marketing leverage inherent in franchising is thus suboptimized.

Product Purchase Provision

In many franchise systems, a major benefit is bulk buying and inventory control. There are a number of ways to account for this in a license agreement. Most franchisors will not be bound to best-price requirements. Changing markets, competitors, and U.S. antitrust laws make it impossible for the franchisor to ensure this. The franchise should employ a standard of best efforts or good faith to acquire both national and regional product contracts.

Depending on the nature of the product, regional deals might make more sense than national ones. Regional contracts may provide greater advantages to the franchisee because of shipping weight and cost or service needs. The clever franchisor will recognize this. When this is true and the franchisor doesn't act, the franchisees will fill the void.

The monthly ADI meeting then becomes an expanded forum. The results of such ad hoc organizations can be reduced control of quality and expansion of franchisee associations outside the confines of the license agreement. Advanced activity of this nature can fractionalize a franchise system or even render the franchisor effectively obsolete. In some cases the franchisor and franchisee-operated buying co-ops peaceably coexist, acting as competitors and lowering the costs to the operator. However, dual buying co-ops usually reduce economies of scale and dilute system resources, as well as providing fertile ground for conflict.

For purposes of quality control, the franchisor will reserve the right to publish a product specifications list. The list will very clearly establish the quality standards of raw materials or goods used in the operation. From those specifications a subsequent list of approved suppliers is generated. This list can evolve into a franchise *tying arrangement*, which occurs when the business format franchise license agreement binds the franchisee to the purchase of a specifically branded product. This varies from the product specifications list because brand, not product content, is the qualifying specification. The important question here is whether the tying arrangement of franchise and product create an enhancement for the franchisee in the marketplace. If so, then are arm's-length controls in place to ensure that pricing, netted from the enhanced value, will yield positive results? This is impossible to quantify exactly. However, if the tying arrangement is specified in the license agreement, the prospective franchise owner is advised to make a judgment before purchasing the franchise. A franchisor should make a clear distinction of value or abandon the tying arrangement.

Less overt tying arrangements occur when the license agreement calls for an approved suppliers list that ultimately lists only one supplier. If adding suppliers to the list is nearly impossible, there is a de facto tying arrangement. Another tying arrangement occurs when the product specification is written so that only one brand can possibly qualify. A franchisor should disclose any remuneration gained by the franchisor or its officers, directly or indirectly, from product purchase in the franchise system. The market value enhancement test is again proof of a credible arrangement.

The Operations Manual

The business format is documented in a manual or series of manuals. The fact that it is documented should be noted in the license agreement. The operations manual is the heart of the franchise asset, as it delineates the manner in which the trade name and mark are to be delivered to the customer. The franchise purchase should be made on the basis of the business's effectiveness in the marketplace. However, to remain viable, the operations manual must be a dynamic instrument. In 1984 Ray Kroc said, "I don't know what we'll be serving in the year 2000, but I know we'll be serving more of it than anybody else."

The research and development previously discussed must be documented in the operations manual before being implemented. The method of change is crucial to the health of the system, again emphasizing the delicate line between standardization and change. Some license agreements will contain a clause stating that the franchisee must adhere to the operations system as outlined in the "current operations manual," which may change from time to time. Given that the system should change to maintain a competitive advantage, the franchisee must be comfortable that this change will take place for valid commercial reasons and be willing to live with less personal control of the operational techniques.

Specialist Support

The franchisor's organizational design must be congruent with franchisee support needs. If real estate is a system variable, there must be sufficient real estate expertise in the franchisor organization to meet the demand created by the sale of franchises. This should occur in all management disciplines.

Territorial Rights

It is very difficult to establish a protected geographic area that is fair to both the franchisee and the franchisor. Demographics are a constantly evolving factor, and hence the true market area will inevitably change. A territory suitable for one site today may support three sites tomorrow because of a road change or mall development. The newer the franchise system, the more pronounced the problem.

If likely market penetration cannot be judged, then how can geography or customers be allocated? On the sale of a single franchise the address is sometimes the only protected territory. This allows the franchisor to ensure that the market is fully developed, but it provides little protection for the franchisee. When the individual outlet reaches a preestablished market share (measured by sales dollars, customers, or units of output), the franchisor will conclude that customer demand is not being fully met. Its concern is that unfilled customer needs create an opportunity for competition. Because of the market leader's advertising and promotion, a copycat operation can propel its start-up through the leader's market exposure. Indeed, this is a viable market strategy for some franchisors. Fast-food operators have been known to purposefully locate directly adjacent to the market leader.

One way to handle this problem is to formalize the criteria for market share in an individual location to give the operator the opportunity for a return commensurate with existing franchisees. Penetration within the agreed band of market share for a given period of time triggers the creation of another location for development. The franchisee in the first location has the right of first refusal of the second location. This right may be qualified based on balance sheet and operational standards. This solution allows for the full exploitation of the marketplace, with the performing franchisee having an equally exciting upside.

Related to the territorial issue is the *relocation clause*. This item may be separate or contained within the exclusive territory clause or the operations clause. It may give the franchisor the right to compel a franchisee to relocate the business under specific economic or demographic conditions. Typically, a relocation clause is not found in a franchise contract when the franchisee is required to make a real estate investment.

European franchising has considerably different legal considerations. If the franchise company is large enough to affect trade between nations, the European Community competition laws may come into effect. These laws were established to regulate contracts or practices that may be anticompetitive. Exclusive territory agreements are generally barred in the EC. However, block exemptions can be granted, and a properly structured franchise exclusive territory will likely qualify for this exemption.

Term of the Agreement

Generally, the franchise relationship is established on a long-term basis. A 15- or 20-year agreement is normal, but some can be as short as 5 years. The key is renewal rights. If the terms of the agreement have been met, the franchisee may reasonably expect the relationship to continue. In some states the renewal right is legislated, and in others there is legal precedent for court-enforced renewal.

A franchise prospect should be wary of an agreement that does not address renewal. It may be an indicator that the franchisor is predisposed not to grant renewals. Legally enforced renewal will be expensive, or the franchisor may impose substantial renewal fees as a condition for continuing the relationship. Many franchise systems do not have a long history, and renewal is not an easily researched issue. Therefore, it should always be contractually stipulated.

Sale of the Business

A good franchisor spends considerable time establishing the basis for choosing franchisees. It is understandable that they want to have some control over who their partners will be. The franchisee is motivated by the ownership of a business and accruing the benefits of that ownership and, at the end of the experience, a capital gain. All issues regarding control of the sale of the existing franchisee company should be covered in the license agreement. Additionally, the procedure by which the controls are implemented must be clearly defined.

Three other clauses will affect the franchisee's ability to sell the business.

1. *Right of first refusal.* Some license agreements give the franchisor this right. If so, the price should be equal to or a premium of the bona fide third-party offer. A right of first refusal will typically hinder a sale. The prospective buyer may not be willing to spend time or money on a deal that might be pulled out from under him by the franchisor—hence the premium requirement.

2. *Buyout formula.* At the beginning of the franchise relationship the franchisor has an advantage in understanding the ultimate value of a successful franchisee company. Franchisors have been known to set a buyout formula in the license agreement.

3. *License agreement.* Some agreements call for the buyer of an existing franchise to sign the "then current form of license agreement." Of course, the new franchisee has no way of knowing what future changes will be incorporated, and the franchisee is not bound to modify his license. Therefore, the value of the franchisee company in the marketplace can be significantly altered by a unilateral decision of the franchisor. The value will, of course, be diminished if the new form of agreement changes the fee structure, institutes tying arrangements, or modifies the protected territory or term.

Owner-Operator Clause

This clause requires that the franchised outlet be under the direct supervision of the licensee. This clause has ebbed and flowed in importance over time. Initially it was established to avoid absentee ownership and assure that the franchisee would be the owner-operator. This becomes more problematic if the single unit operator becomes more sophisticated and ambitious and wants to own multiple units. The specific history of the franchise establishes precedent regarding the owner-operator clause and its implications for multiple unit operations.

Death or Incapacity of the Franchisee

Most license agreements are signed personally. This generally means that the franchisee must devote all or a majority of her professional life to operating the franchise. Also, the economics of the relationship are guaranteed by the individual(s) who signs the license agreement. Usually, the personal attention of the franchisee is impossible to monitor. However, upon death or disability the franchisee or his estate may be forced into an uneconomic sale of the company or even the loss of the franchise rights. The proper stipulation is for the franchisor to render short-term assistance in operating the franchise (for a fee) until it is sold or transferred to a qualified heir.

Arbitration

The cost of litigation is often too high for a single-outlet operator to bear. The franchisor will sometimes exclude an arbitration clause because it may afford a small franchisee the opportunity to air a grievance and receive redress she otherwise might not be granted. Conversely, such a clause reduces the likelihood of petty arguments. Arbitration is done in private proceedings with an issue judged by an individual who usually has special knowledge of the subject in dispute. Arbitration can be binding or nonbinding. It is usually to the advantage of the smaller franchisee but is gaining support among franchisors also.

License Agreement Termination

Issues of default must be specifically delineated in this section. Important is a reasonable right to remedy a default, provided the breaches are not recurring. Termination means that the franchisee must cease using the trade name and mark, and other property rights of the franchisor. Practically, this means taking down the sign, changing the name of the operation, and returning all manuals and marketing and promotional materials.

In some cases, the franchisor will tie the property lease to the license agreement. Termination of one can mean voiding of the other. This tie can occur even when the franchisor does not own the property vis-à-vis an assignment and assumption agreement. This agreement is signed as an addendum to the lease and states that the termination of the license agreement triggers the right, but not obligation, of the franchisor to assume the franchisee's position in a lease. The lessor must be a party to the assignment for it to be valid.

Exhibit 14.3 is a checklist that helps franchisees and franchisors think through the agreement. Exhibit 14.4 provides an expanded view of the franchise relationship.[6] In this view, noncontractual components of the relationship are very important. At the center of decision making are the needs of the customer and the ability of the system, or business format, to meet those needs.

Exhibit 14.5 provides a summary of the basic responsibilities of the franchisor and the franchisee.

Exhibit 14.3 License Agreement Key Provision Impact Analysis (Downloadable) Copyright © 2010 by William D. Bygrave and Andrew Zacharakis. To download this form for your personal use, please visit www.wiley.com/go/portablembainentrepreneurship.

License Agreement Item	Impact	Marketplace Signal
Term: Details the length of the contract between the franchisor and franchisee in years.	This defines the number of years used in the calculation of the PDV of the income stream.	Longer = positive
Renewal: This defines the ability of the franchisee to add additional years to the license agreement.	This increases the number of years of potential income stream.	Renewal = positive
Franchise Fee: The one-time up-front fee the franchisee pays the franchisor when the license agreement is signed.	Impacts the initial investment and signals relative quality of the franchise.	Higher = positive
Royalty: This is a percentage of the outlet revenue that is paid to the franchisor throughout the term of the license agreement.	Establishes the linkage between the success of the franchisee and the franchisor.	Higher = positive
Marketing Fee: This is usually a percentage of revenue (sometimes a flat fee) that the franchisee must commit to marketing expenditures.	Signals the firm's commitment to building the brand and driving economies of scale in marketing.	Higher = positive
Supply Requirements: Outlines the rights and responsibilities of the franchisee in purchasing the cost of goods component of the end user product.	Some franchisors attempt to make money by selling goods to their franchisees. Others act as a negotiating agent for the franchisee to obtain national contracts. This section of the license agreement is key to understanding the potential for economies of scale in supply.	National contracts with third party vendors = positive

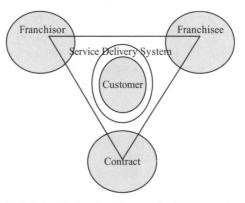

**Exhibit 14.4   An Expanded View of
the Franchise Relationship**

Noncontractual Considerations of Buying a Franchise

Virtually all franchises are dynamic operations responding to changes in both the market-place and within franchisor and franchisee organizations. These changes can be better understood or even anticipated if you have a keen understanding of the financial information provided by classic finance documentation.

Exhibit 14.5   The Generic Franchise Service Delivery System

Transaction	Franchisor	Franchisee
Site criteria	Define	Local market application
Site acquisition	Advise	Execute
Zoning and permitting	Advise	Execute
Construction	Blueprints	Local government approvals
	Standardized contract and pert chart	Local bids from contractors
	Management support	Day-to-day management of the contractor relationship
Equipment purchase	National contract	Timing and installation and payment
Building or leasehold improvement	Site plan	Local execution
Inventory purchase	National contract	Local management and purchase
Employee training	Franchisee and founding employees training	Ongoing training and training for new/replacement employees
Grand opening advertising	Design	Design execution and local promotion
Ongoing advertising	Creative development and national advertising brand support	Local media purchase and promotional execution

Financial Analysis

The dream of entrepreneurship can become a nightmare if your financial well-being is threatened. An advantage of franchising is a track record that can be scrutinized. The prospect can and should make an in-depth analysis of the offered franchise. The franchisor is wise to package the offering in a manner that assists this due diligence. The franchisor who demonstrates a keen financial understanding gains a pricing advantage in the franchise sales marketplace, attracts a more sophisticated franchisee, and offers the franchisee an advantage in the capital marketplace.

U.S. law requires franchisors to disclose pertinent details of the offer. However, franchisor earning claims regarding the performance of outlets are optional. The federal requirement is fulfilled through the Uniform Franchise Offering Circular (UFOC), which is filed with the Federal Trade Commission and is a matter of public record. The UFOC must be given to the franchisee the sooner of 10 days prior to the franchisor's accepting a fee or the first personal meeting. Many states have similar but usually more stringent disclosure requirements.

A vast majority of franchisors adhere to disclosure laws. A franchise search that reveals the slightest deviation from FTC or state rules should be abandoned. The disclosure will have pro forma financials based on actual franchisee experience. These are not designed to apply to any individual investment; they are an average of the composite operations. Assuredly, the new operator will find variances in the actual statements from the disclosure pro forma financial projections. The next sections focus on the areas of likely variance.

Estimating Start-up Cost/Initial Investment

If there is a real estate component to the franchise, it is often treated as a lease or rental and not included in the start-up calculation. If owning the real estate is a part of the franchisee's strategic plan, it must be accounted for separately from the franchise investment. The basics included in this section are leasehold improvements, furniture and fixtures, machinery and equipment, and tools. Even so-called turnkey arrangements will have some start-up expense associated with the leasehold interest. Equipment can sometimes be leased also. This is especially true in restaurant franchises.

Low initial investment may dramatically affect operating expenses. A lease is simply a way to leverage your start-up cost. Start-up losses should be funded in the initial capitalization but are not always included in the disclosure. Assume a worst-case scenario. Even in franchising, undercapitalization is a major reason for failure.

Calculating Profit and Loss/Income Statement

All the numbers should be adjusted by the prospective franchisee to reflect the realities of the area where their operation is planned. For example, New York City will be more expensive to operate in than Pocatello, Idaho, but income will probably be higher also. Decisions about owner's compensation should be incorporated into the pro forma statements (or into the cash-flow projections, discussed later). The disclosure will typically show the average manager's compensation, and not any remuneration to the franchisee. The franchisor will assume the franchisee is the manager. If the ownership of the franchised company is spread over more than one individual, the issue of compensation is best answered up front.

Remember the discussion of lease versus buy. If leasing is the leverage decision, its costs should be incorporated here. Also, a disclosure pro forma may not include interest payments. The franchisor takes the position that capitalization methods vary so dramatically as to render an average impractical.

Another item sometimes neglected in pro forma projections is depreciation and amortization. These noncash items represent the cost to the business of the decreasing value of fixed assets. Understanding depreciation and amortization will allow for better pricing decisions and more accurate calculation of profit margins.

Pro forma income statements are often annualized. The ramping up of sales and the accrual of expenses on a *monthly* basis will prove invaluable in the first year of operation. Many financial institutions require 36 months of pro forma statements. Although some franchisors will generate or help generate the additional monthly projections, many will reasonably avoid this out of fear of misleading a franchisee and incurring some liability. What a franchisee sees as help in the start-up may be remembered as a promise years later, especially in a courtroom setting.

Constructing a Balance Sheet

The long-term health of a franchisee company can be significantly aided by constructing a strong opening balance sheet. Too often small businesses focus solely on the income statement and ignore the balance sheet. Business format franchises are heavily weighted in the service and particularly retail segments of the economy. Strong understanding of working capital management in a retail environment, depending on the business, can mean advantageous supplier terms along with cash payments from customers. This may provide you with significant short-term leverage. As with the income statement, franchising gives you the unique opportunity to use pertinent historical data in the balance sheet to lay a sound foundation in your company through proper capitalization.

There is a whole series of financial ratios that should be constructed for the ideally positioned franchisee company. In general, everyone should be aware of liquidity, capital, debt, and trade ratios as they apply to the franchisee requirements. In theory, liquidity is measured to assess a company's ability to generate operating capital or meet sudden credit demands. The lever of optimal liquidity varies dramatically by industry. Franchising allows you to know the details and risks prior to start-up, and the astute franchisor will make this analysis readily available.

The Initial Investment section of the UFOC, modified for your specific needs, will define your capital requirement but will not specify the form of capital. Use historical numbers from the franchisor to generate stability ratios to help answer this question. This is particularly important if there is a tying arrangement in the franchise, even if the arrangement is informal. Also, when the franchisor is a key supplier, inventory estimates will be very precise. However, conflicts of interest by the franchisor should be carefully avoided, such as excessive start-up inventory requirements.

Cash-Flow Projections

Happiness is a positive cash flow no matter what commercial vehicle you choose. However, profitability does not equate to positive cash flow; a profitable business can suffocate and fail due to insufficient cash flow. Cash-flow projections should also be done on a 36-month basis to match the income statement and balance sheet pro forma. Often omitted in the franchisor's cash-flow projections will be the prospect's franchise search cost, professional consultant expense, and the site search and acquisition costs. Failure to consider these will strangle cash flow even before start-up.

Financing a Franchise

Financing requirements for a franchise are no different than for any other business start-up. Acquisition or alteration of business premises, fittings and fixtures, machinery and equipment, and working capital are all included in the list. Cash flow shortages due to business cycle may be added later. The advantage of franchise financing is the added variable of the franchisee. The franchisor packages a proven product and business methods. The franchisee is a partner in the deal who brings additional capital and entrepreneurial commitment. This should provide greater comfort to the financing institution. Properly exhibiting the transferability of the success factors is the principle function of the loan request. Existing operations that are profitable make access to a lender's ear easier.

A franchisor will systematically meet with large banks to help build confidence in the concept and clear initial hurdles for franchisees. Structuring a debt proposal should utilize much of the due diligence included in the franchise search. In general, the franchise system and the outlets operating in it should be presented both as an integrated organization and as a stand-alone operation. This will promote the franchisee as one who is independently capable of success but whose prospects are dramatically enhanced by being a part of a system. A banker will likely define the long run as the amount of time debt is outstanding. If the successful operation of the franchise system exceeds the term of the loan, the lender will have a higher comfort level.

From the franchisee's perspective, a franchise is a risk management tool. The increased prospects for success will allow for a more secure loan for the bank. Examples of the franchise system's changing to meet the demands of the marketplace will be helpful in projecting future success. The franchisor's organizational chart and support role are appropriate material to review with a banker. It gives depth to the not-as-yet-operating franchisee organization, an advantage the solo start-up doesn't have. Pressing the franchise advantage at start-up might yield a more competitive loan and more serviceable debt, compounding the advantage over the nonfranchised competitor. Even with these advantages, the personal commitment of the franchisee in the form of cash invested in the business is inevitably required. The financial analysis done in the investigative stage will be helpful in the search for capital. For the purposes of securing debt, add the proposed loan and subsequent debt service to the projections.

The terms in the loan will vary by specific business, franchisor strength, franchisee strength, and general economic conditions. Loans for the substantiated initial investment can run as high as 80 percent, but 50 percent to 67 percent is more likely. Machinery and equipment will have a three- to seven-year term with a corresponding amortization. The franchisor can help boost the loan-to-value ratio if a market for used machinery and equipment can be demonstrated. Real estate will likely have a three- to five-year term with a 15- to 20-year amortization. A few franchisors will provide some financing, and a few more will assist in placing debt. However, a franchisor should not be expected to be a vehicle for acquiring capital.

A problem the franchisor must be cognizant of is franchisee underinvestment. Many franchisees are required to invest a substantial portion of their wealth in the franchise. Theoretically, this could result in a burdensome risk perspective that might cause the franchisee to pass on a favorable opportunity. Franchisee underinvestment is interwoven with the issue of protected territory and expansion rights. Some franchisors include expansion requirements where rights are given. This is especially true when a geographic territory is sold to a franchisee. Often a development schedule is agreed on in advance. Failure of the franchisee to build out the territory under the terms of the agreement (sometimes called an *area development agreement*) results in loss of the exclusivity.

Multiple Outlet Ownership

Almost 90 percent of all franchisees in the United States own a single outlet of a franchise. But some franchisees have developed large companies. A company based in Kansas developed Pizza Hut franchises all over the country and became a publicly traded company. Many Midas franchisees have 10 or more stores. One of the more intriguing aspects of franchising is that you can become a franchisee and still have significant growth potential.

An individual franchisee grows either organically, one or two stores at a time as success in each unit builds, or by purchasing a larger geographic territory with a specified unit growth objective. Let's discuss the latter. Buying a defined market entails projecting the maximum number of potential stores and negotiating a build-out schedule with the franchisor. The conclusions of this negotiation will be memorialized in an area development agreement (ADA). Fast-growing Panera Bread employs the area development agreement as its main vehicle for adding new restaurants.

An ADA usually grants the franchisee an exclusive right to develop and own outlets in a defined geographic space for a specified period of time. The total number of outlets to be developed and the timing of that development are also specified. The franchisee keeps exclusivity only if the development schedule is met. The advantages to the franchisee are a higher degree of freedom in site selection, bigger upside potential, and usually a reduced per-outlet franchise fee. The disadvantages are higher capitalization requirements, bigger up-front payments, and pressure to develop new stores that might make you take your eye off of your operating responsibilities.

For the franchisor, an ADA provides higher up-front cash to help fund early capitalization needs and enhances the pace of growth. The downside is that the cash can only be booked as revenue when each outlet is developed, and larger franchisees tend to wield more power in a franchise relationship than do individual outlet owners. Also, it can be more difficult to dislodge an underperforming ADA than it would be a single outlet license.

A Brief Note on International Franchising

The Southland Ice Company opened its first convenience store in 1927 and called it a Tote'm. In 1946 the company changed its store name to 7-Eleven to reflect its operating hours. The company entered franchising in 1964, signed its first United States area licensing agreement in 1968, and signed the first international licensing agreement with Mexico in 1971. In 1991 Southland Corporation, the quintessential American company, was purchased by its Japanese franchisee. In 2003 almost 80 percent of 7-Eleven's 24,400 stores are located outside of the United States.

Because franchising is a vehicle for growth, many franchisors ask, why stop at U.S. national borders? International franchising has taken on new meaning in the past 10 years. Before 1990, U.S. franchise presence abroad meant a McDonald's in Tokyo or one next to the Spanish Steps in Rome. However, even as early as the 1970s, several European-based franchises existed, such as Dyno Rod and Prontaprint. A 1995 report by Arthur Andersen showed that two-thirds of all U.S. franchisors who decided to expand abroad did so based on first contact from a prospective foreign franchisee.[7] By 2003, thousands of U.S. franchises in food, retail, and services had moved into emerging markets around the globe.

However, the complexities of the franchise relationship increase significantly outside U.S. borders and are beyond the scope of this chapter. I recommend starting with a basic understanding of foreign laws that govern franchising. Exhibit 14.6 provides a checklist that can help you gauge the attractiveness of international franchising.

One useful document that summarizes the existing franchise-specific laws in various countries is available for free download from a company called Franchise Consulting. Visit the International Franchise Association web site www.franchise.org for information regarding country-specific laws and profiles.

Exhibit 14.6   Checklist for International Financing (Downloadable) Copyright © 2010 by William D. Bygrave and Andrew Zacharakis. To download this form for your personal use, please visit www.wiley.com/go/portablembainentrepreneurship.

1. Is the country's legal and regulatory environment for franchising:
   Prohibitive
   Restrictive
   Conducive

2. Are import rules and customs procedures:
   Prohibitive
   Restrictive
   Conducive

3. For franchising, are tax rates:
   Prohibitive
   Restrictive
   Conducive

4. Are the costs and availability of labor:
   Prohibitive
   Restrictive
   Conducive

5. Is the purchasing power of the population:
   Prohibitive
   Restrictive
   Conducive

6. Is the economic and political stability of the country:
   Prohibitive
   Restrictive
   Conducive

7. The franchises currently operating in the country suggest that overall it is:
   Prohibitive
   Restrictive
   Conducive

8. The effect of differences in language for the franchise is:
   Prohibitive
   Restrictive
   Conducive

9. The effect of cultural differences on the franchise is:
   Prohibitive
   Restrictive
   Conducive

How Selling a Franchise Is Regulated

The United States has an extensive statutory regulatory system governing franchising. In essence, the sale of a franchise is subject to the same scrutiny as the sale of a security. On the federal level, the government mandates extensive disclosure through the Uniform Franchise Offering Circular (UFOC), developed by the American Securities Administrators Organization. The document must include a copy of the license agreement, an area development agreement if applicable, and a laundry list of standard disclosure items.

Details of the costs and ongoing payments and product tying arrangements follow. Typically, the document opens with a narrative description of the franchise. The franchisor must also list details concerning litigation; bankruptcy; and store transfer, acquisition, and termination. There is also a summary of the franchisee's responsibilities and the services provided by the franchisor. There is usually a pro forma compilation of financial statements taken from franchise operating histories. If the UFOC does not present financial information, any statement about the economics of the franchise by the franchisor must be disclosed to the prospective franchisee in an *earnings claim document*. If the claims are made in a public fashion, such as in the newspaper, then the earnings claim document is required regardless of UFOC content and use.

The franchisor is required to file the UFOC with the Federal Trade Commission (FTC). Any change to the license agreement or any executory document must be filed at least five days prior to signing. The prospective franchisee is asked to sign a receipt for the UFOC, which the franchisor keeps on file. Although the FTC dictates disclosure requirements, it does not editorialize or approve the quality of the content.

A number of state governments have passed legislation specific to franchising that also requires a disclosure document. Financial and termination disclosure is often more extensive than under federal requirements. Franchisors face a morass of complicated laws and must be mindful of the legal costs when contemplating a national expansion program.

Limitations of Franchising

The franchisor must recognize that equity in the business is being sold when a franchise is sold. Rapid growth and a highly motivated management team are born, but a partner, not an employee, is created. That partner, the franchisee, will risk time, energy, and capital and will expect a return. Because of the long-term nature of the license agreement, the franchisor is bound to this partnership for many years. Anyone who considers expansion through franchising must understand that the benefits of a system must endure the test of time.

Sources of Conflict

As a part of understanding the implications of franchising, one should note the potential sources of conflict in the relationship. As discussed, the franchisor builds a prototype operation, completes system documentation, establishes support overhead, complies with regulatory requirements, and then sells the first franchise. Typically, a large amount of capital has been used before any franchise fees or royalties are received. Therefore, a high percentage of the franchisor's costs are necessarily fixed. As the system of franchisees and outlets grows, the franchisor's costs are spread over an increasing base. The average cost to the franchisor for providing services per franchisee decreases as the number of outlets increases.

On the revenue side, the franchisor is motivated to maximize system sales. The franchisor's continuing income is derived from franchisee royalty payments, a percentage of top-line outlet sales paid to the franchisor. System growth in terms of the number of outlets and individual outlet sales results in higher franchisor revenue applied against lower per-unit support costs.

The franchisee, conversely, aspires to achieve optimal unit sales (not necessarily maximum sales) to maximize profit. An important aspect of optimal sales is the optimal number of outlets in the market (again, not necessarily the maximum). The franchisee's operating model has more variable expense than the franchisor's. The implication is that there may be sensitive discussion in the areas of pricing, promotion, and the development of outlets. The potential for conflict is exacerbated by the phenomenon of larger, more sophisticated franchisees. With today's heightened level of competition in the marketplace, franchisees are necessarily more educated, with more capital, entrepreneurial drive, and organizational skills, and are capable of building fully integrated companies.

Inefficient Investment

Especially in single-outlet franchise systems, the franchisee is investing a high proportion of personal wealth in the venture. This is opposed to the large operation, where one additional store does not consume a majority of ownership capital. Therefore, such a franchisee might be excessively risk-averse when facing a large capital outlay. The investment might be forgone, creating an opportunity for the competition or simply suboptimizing the system potential.

Conclusion

Franchising might best be described as the combination of a unique association of corporate organizations and a unique form of raising capital. For franchising to work best, the franchisor and franchisee goals must be congruent. The relationship must be highly interactive and dynamic. Although the license agreement is the focal point of franchising, if it is strictly interpreted, the probability of conflict being resolved through litigation is heightened. The franchise system that understands that interdependence is a reality has a higher probability of optimizing return. That interdependence and the inherent economies of scale in franchising lend themselves to significant utilization of the Internet and intranet. The web of branded entrepreneurs in a franchise system can now communicate better among themselves and with partners in the value chain such as suppliers. The potential for wealth creation in franchising now seems even better.

Downloadable Resources for this chapter available at www.wiley.com/go/portablembainentrepreneurship

License Agreement Key Provision Impact Analysis
Checklist for International Franchising

Notes

1. International Franchise Association Press Release, "IFA Urges Government to Improve Marketplace for Small Business Loans," December 23, 2008.
2. *Economic Impact of Franchised Businesses*, vol. 2, PricewaterhouseCoopers, March 2008.
3. King Edgar's measurement standard for ale was two pegs in a beer stein; one halfway up the container for half a pint and one at the top to show a full pint. Pouring someone a half pint was "knocking 'em down a peg."
4. Ibid.
5. S. Spinelli, Jr., "A Multivariate Analysis of Conflict in the Franchisee–Franchisor Relationship" (PhD diss., Imperial College, University of London, 1995).
6. This view is well documented by franchise consultant D. R. Widder.
7. International Franchise Association, http://www.franchise.org/industrysecondary.aspx?id=40514.

15

Social Entrepreneurship[*]

Heidi M. Neck

How This Chapter Fits into a Typical MBA Curriculum

Graduates of MBA programs around the world are entering environments of unprecedented change and instability. Social problems, including environmental problems, are creating opportunity spaces for entrepreneurial activity that can create both economic and social value. More and more business students entering post graduate programs are searching for meaning and a path that connects their own values to the world of business. For many this path is social entrepreneurship—participating in the entrepreneurship process to contribute to the solution set of the globe's most pressing problems. MBA students with traditional entrepreneurial skills combined with a greater sense of purpose are poised to build mission-based businesses for a better world. However, social entrepreneurship is misunderstood and there are as many definitions of it as there are social entrepreneurs. Understanding the territory of social entrepreneurship, the various types of social ventures, and available sources of capital is important for any practicing or aspiring social entrepreneur.

Who Uses This Material in the Real World—and Why It Is Important

Any opportunity-obsessed entrepreneur reading these pages will likely come away with a new, mission-driven idea that has the potential to change the world. And this chapter paves the way for potential discoveries by defining the landscape of social entrepreneurship, discussing the challenges facing the globe, and sharing the stories of social entrepreneurs who have acted on opportunities and are building scalable, high-growth social ventures—regardless of profit orientation. From low-income markets at the base of the pyramid to emerging technologies for more efficient alternative energy sources, a social entrepreneur is seeing and preserving the future with heart and mind.

I've been in several venues recently where I listened to presenters speak about today's apex of power. Throughout the centuries the power has shifted from religion to states or governments and now business. This evolution is depicted by the assembly of great churches, synagogues, and temples; then taking rise to palaces, castles, gilded state buildings, and enormous statues of political figures; and lastly to city skylines and sports complexes named in honor of banks, beer, soda, pet stores, and telecommunication giants—just to name a few.

[*]Portions of this chapter are reproduced with permission from Neck, H.M. (2008) Chapter 7: Opportunities for Social Entrepreneurship. In J. Timmons & S. Spinelli *New Venture Creation, 8th edition*. Boston, McGraw-Hill.

But perhaps the power is shifting a bit once again. Not completely away from business but rather a shift to using the power of business to effect positive systemic change. We are also witnessing the power of the human race—a global gathering that is demanding empathy, compassion, and action to not only solve major issues facing the globe today but to also preserve and protect what we have for future generations.

What Is Social Entrepreneurship?

Social entrepreneurship has become a global movement—a movement with a goal to effect positive social change. On the surface we know social entrepreneurship is a good thing, but upon further study it becomes quite apparent that social entrepreneurship is a complicated phenomenon and difficult to define. The effect leads to a perception of nebulous boundaries. Such ill-defined boundaries have led some to argue that *all* entrepreneurship is social or that any differences between social and the more traditional, commercial entrepreneurship are neither well articulated nor understood. Some view social entrepreneurship purely as a form of entrepreneurship in nonprofit sectors. For example, a pundit in a large foundation questioned if social entrepreneurs can even become economic entrepreneurs.[1] Such either/or thinking is creating false boundaries that lead to a perception that entrepreneurs have to choose between social and economic impact. As you will see from examples in this chapter, the reality is that social entrepreneurs can do both. Social entrepreneurship encompasses for-profit and not-for-profit ventures.

As with any emerging area of intellectual and practical significance, it is important to have a guiding definition for the purpose of shared understanding and discussion. A guiding definition does not, however, imply a unifying definition. Social entrepreneurship, in theory and in practice, lacks a unifying, agreed upon definition. Exhibit 15.1 offers a few of the most popular definitions. These definitions share a common theme: their method and execution are very entrepreneurial in thinking and action, while their mission and purpose are driven by social need and benefit.

Recently I was speaking to an audience of approximately 50 (academics, consultants, entrepreneurs, students), all interested in social entrepreneurship education. I asked each participant to write their definition of social entrepreneurship on an index card. Naturally, I received 50 very unique definitions, but there were identifiable patterns or commonalities across all submitted definitions. Participants wrote about identifying opportunities, creating systemic social change, developing sustainable solutions to social problems, and generating economic and social returns. My personal favorite referred to social entrepreneurship as using principles of entrepreneurship to create economically sustainable social value. Jeff Stamp, assistant professor at the University of North Dakota, offered a very thought-provoking perspective. He wrote, "All ventures require investment; all ventures require return. The social question is who pays and what is the return horizon. The decision is a social value decision." This question of value for what purpose and to whom is important to the practice of social entrepreneurship.

Further exacerbating the confusion around what is or is not a social entrepreneurship is the concept of sustainability. Sustainability, also difficult to define, is most commonly associated with limiting the amount of harm inflicted by humans to the planet to preserve the quality of life for future generations. Stuart Hart, in his compelling book *Capitalism at the Crossroads* (New Jersey: Wharton School Publishing, 2007), listed 40 different buzzwords from the sustainability literature. Some examples on the list are *greening*,

Exhibit 15.1 Popular Definitions of Social Entrepreneurship (or Social Entrepreneur)

Definition	Author
Social entrepreneurs play the role of change agents in the social sector by (a) adopting a mission to create and sustain social value (not just private value); (b) recognizing and relentlessly pursuing new opportunities to serve that mission; (c) engaging in a process of continuous innovation, adaptation, and learning; (d) acting boldly without being limited by resources currently in hand; and (e) exhibiting heightened accountability to the constituencies served and for the outcomes created.	Greg Dees, 1998[a]
A process involving the innovative use and combination of resources to pursue opportunities to catalyze social change and/or address social needs.	Johanna Mair and Ignasi Marti, 2006[b]
Innovative, social value–creating activity that can occur within or across the nonprofit, business, or government sectors.	James Austin, Howard Stevenson, and Jane Wei-Skillern, 2006[c]
A process that includes the identification of a specific social problem and a specific solution (or set of solutions) to address it; the evaluation of the social impact, the business model, and the sustainability of the venture; and the creation of a social mission-oriented for-profit or a business-oriented nonprofit entity that pursues the double (or triple) bottom line.	Jeffrey Robinson, 2006[d]
Social entrepreneurship is (a) about applying practical, innovative, and sustainable approaches to benefit society in general, with an emphasis on those who are marginalized and poor; (b) a term that captures a unique approach to economic and social problems, an approach that cuts across sectors and disciplines; (c) grounded in certain values and processes that are common to each social entrepreneur.	The Schwab Foundation for Social Entrepreneurship[e]

[a.] "The Meaning of 'Social Entrepreneurship,'" http://www.caseatduke.org/documents/dees_SE.pdf, p. 4

[b.] "Social Entrepreneurship Research: A Source of Explanation, Prediction, and Delight," *Journal of World Business* 41:37.

[c.] "Social and Commercial Entrepreneurship: Same, Different, Both?" *Entrepreneurship Theory and Practice*, January, p. 2.

[d.] "Navigating Social and Institutional Barriers to Market: How Social Entrepreneurs Identify and Evaluate Opportunities," in J. Mair, J. Robinson, and K. Hockerts, *Social Entrepreneurship*, (New York: Palgrave MacMillan, 2006), 95.

[e.] http://www.schwabfound.org/sf/SocialEntrepreneurs/Whatisasocialentrepreneur/index.htm.

corporate social responsibility, life-cycle management, waste reduction, clean technology, eco-efficiency, civic entrepreneurship, corporate citizenship, cradle-to-grave, triple bottom line, base of pyramid, and *community capitalism.* To my surprise the moniker *social entrepreneurship* did not make it onto the list, but Hall admitted in his prose that the list was not exhaustive. What is perhaps most important is an understanding that the world today is requiring a different type of entrepreneurship. As Al Gore, former vice president of the United States, noted in the Foreword of *Capitalism at the Crossroads*:

> There are, of course, limits to the ability of traditional businesses to deal with sustainability challenges by themselves. Now, more than ever, our societies need new models to address systemic, long-term challenges like the climate crisis, poverty, pandemics, water scarcity, and demographic shifts. This will involve more business and government innovation, social entrepreneurship, public-private partnerships, and more effective civil society participation.[2]

A single and definitive view of social entrepreneurship is not necessarily important. What is most important is an understanding of the key differentiating factors between social entrepreneurship and traditional entrepreneurship, while also realizing that there is not just one type of social entrepreneurship. For the purposes of this chapter the concept of social entrepreneurship requires a dual focus: the *source* of opportunity and the *social value* generated from acting on the opportunity. More specifically, social entrepreneurs act on opportunities stemming from problems related to *people* and problems related to the *planet*—regardless of profit orientation. In other words, social entrepreneurship seeks creative and valuable solutions to such issues as education, poverty, health care, global warming, global water shortages, and energy—just to name a few.

The overall process of entrepreneurship, however, remains the same regardless of entrepreneurial venture type. Bill Drayton is the CEO and Founder of Ashoka, which is a global (and the most well-known) association of social entrepreneurs. He is often quoted as saying, "Social entrepreneurs are not content just to give a fish, or teach how to fish. They will not rest until they have revolutionized the fishing industry." Again, it's challenging to identify the differences that allow researchers and practitioners alike to create a new practice, a new field, called social entrepreneurship. This chapter focuses on the subtle nuances that separate the types of entrepreneurship and why social entrepreneurship is gaining unprecedented popularity among MBA students today.

Types of Social Entrepreneurship

The shaded area of Exhibit 15.2 depicts the territory of social entrepreneurship. The primary difference between traditional entrepreneurship and social entrepreneurship is the intended mission. Social entrepreneurs develop ventures with a mission to solve a pressing social problem. Social problems are most typically associated with such sectors as health care, education, poverty, environment, waste, water, and energy. We will address these opportunity sectors shortly. What is important now is to acquire an understanding of language, territory, and definitions of social entrepreneurship.

Social purpose ventures (Exhibit 15.2, quadrant 1) are founded on the premise that a social problem will be solved, yet the venture is for-profit and the impact on the market is typically seen as economic. Consider the example of a company called BigBelly Solar that was founded by Jim Poss in 2003, while earning his MBA from Babson College.

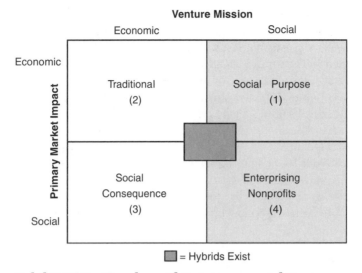

Venture Mission

 = Hybrids Exist

Exhibit 15.2 Typology of Entrepreneurial Ventures

Source: H. M. Neck, C. Brush, and E. Allen, "The Landscape of
Social Entrepreneurship," *Business Horizons* 52 (2009): 13–19.

The core product is a solar-powered trash compactor designed to replace traditional trash receptacles in such areas as city streets, urban parks, amusement parks, beaches, ski resorts, and other similar venues. Jim is a great example of a social entrepreneur starting a social purpose venture. He founded the company on the premise of building an enterprise that would help solve environmental problems. At the same time, the economic impact of the BigBelly solar trash compactor is driving sales and the growth of his company. According to Jim Poss:

> The problem at large is that there are 180,000 garbage trucks in the United States that burn over a billion gallons of diesel fuel every year. These are heavy particulates—cancer-causing, asthma-causing pollutants. Obviously greenhouse gases are being emitted. Those 180,000 garbage trucks also cost about $50 billion a year. So [waste companies] are pouring a lot of money into a system that is incredibly inefficient. The [trash] pickup frequency is driven by the container—the receptacle capacity. So when it's full you have to make a garbage truck trip. We use technology [in the receptacle] to reduce the pickup frequency by about a factor of five.[3]

Jim considers himself a social entrepreneur. He started studying the environment in 1992 and he found the problems and potential consequences of human action alarming. In Jim's eyes, starting a business was the best way to tackle some of the world's environmental problems. Social ventures like this one are mission-driven and economically sustainable. Remember, Jim's mission is social—help the environment—but he recognizes the importance of sustainable business economics: "If you have a business that can sustain itself economically and do something environmentally beneficial, then it can be on its own growth path without the need for fundraising every year to sustain a nonprofit."[4]

BigBelly Solar is attracting a lot of attention because the company is green. Would a cordless trash compactor garner so much attention from investors and the press if it lacked the alternative energy focus? Probably not, and other companies are also capitalizing on the positive image of being green. TerraCycle sells plant food made of worm excrement that is sold in recycled plastic bottles. Visit your local Home Depot for a sample! Founded by Tom Szaky and Jon Beyer in 2001, the company's novel and somewhat quirky product has generated a significant amount of publicity—free marketing. Szaky and Beyer self-identify as eco-capitalists and sought to build a business that was sustainable economically, environmentally friendly, and socially responsible.

Pretend you are at a dinner with a group of friends. You tell the BigBelly Solar story and the TerraCycle story. Then you ask the questions. Let's also assume for the sake of argument that your friends are familiar with the typology presented in Exhibit 15.2. Are these companies traditional ventures or social purpose ventures? Is Jim a social entrepreneur? What about Tim and Jon? It's likely that an interesting debate will ensue and comments similar to the following will contribute to the dialogue.

> "Jim has a history of being concerned about the environment. This is why he started the business, so that makes him a social entrepreneur."
>
> "No way! The 'green' thing is all marketing to attract customers and investors. BigBelly Solar is a traditional venture."
>
> "TerraCycle is just a small business using recycled materials and worm poop—seems like a bunch of liberals having fun, so they are definitely social entrepreneurs."
>
> "BigBelly Solar and TerraCycle have to earn a profit to stay alive. They have employees and investors. Even if they have social motives the economic motive will win in the end. This is the nature of capitalism."
>
> "I'm not sure how to answer your questions at this juncture. Furthermore, I'm not sure it matters. Jim Poss is doing something positive for the environment, as are Tom Szaky and Jon Beyer. Does it matter that they are making money at the same time?"

Welcome to the gray areas of social entrepreneurship that are conflicting students, practitioners, and academics. Social purpose ventures, like most organizations, are rooted in the founder's mission and purpose. The deeper meaning is not always articulated in company press kits, annual reports, or web sites. If you sit down with Jim Poss, he would tell you that he *only* wanted to start an environmental company. Skim through TerraCycle's web site and you learn that Tom and Jon were disenchanted with how people do business and wanted to show the world that there could be a company that is both environmentally and economically sustainable. It is these nuances—understanding the motivations and intentions of the social entrepreneur—that help us conclude that BigBelly Solar and TerraCycle are in fact social purpose ventures.

Enterprising Nonprofits

Exacerbating the confusion about "what is social entrepreneurship" is a preconceived notion that all entrepreneurship taking place in social sectors is reserved for nonprofit organizations. As just illustrated with the Jim Poss story, not all social entrepreneurs start a nonprofit. Furthermore, not all nonprofits are entrepreneurial. This is why the term *enterprising nonprofits* is used in quadrant 4 in Exhibit 15.2. Enterprising nonprofits represent a form of social entrepreneurship. In addition to their social mission, the impact on the market is social because the profit motive exists only to channel operating monies to the organization. Whereas social ventures may distribute profit to owners, enterprising nonprofits by law may not.

Exhibit 15.3   **Number of Nonprofit Organizations in the United States, 1996 and 2006**

	1996		2006		
	Number of Organizations	Percent of All Organizations	Number of Organizations	Percent of All Organizations	Percent Change
All Nonprofit Organization	1,084,939	100.00%	1,478,194	100.00%	36.20%
501(c)(3) Public Charities	535,930	49.40%	904,313	61.20%	68.70%
501(c)(3) Public Foundations	58,774	5.40%	109,852	7.40%	86.90%
Other 501(c) Nonprofit Organizations	490,235	45.20%	464,029	31.40%	−5.30%

Source: National Center for Charitable Statistics.

One can argue that any nonprofit start-up is entrepreneurial. Agreed. Consistent with MBA curricula and research in entrepreneurship, however, the scaling and sustainability of new ventures is incredibly important to the economy (as it is with for-profit ventures) and to systemic change (as with nonprofit organizations). It is not enough, from both an economic and social perspective, to simply start a venture; it must be scalable and sustainable. It is with longevity, innovation, and an eye towards growth that significant impact can be made. Starting any organization is an entrepreneurial act, but this does not imply that entrepreneurship continues to flourish. Entrepreneurship is a process, and without attention given to the process, entrepreneurship ceases inside an organization. Over 100 new nonprofit organizations are started in the United States every day. Out of those that remain active an astounding 91 percent fail to exceed $1 million in revenues.[5] Today, assets totaling more than $3 trillion are under nonprofit management, yet average revenue is $915,000. There is growing evidence that nonprofits can benefit from a more entrepreneurial and enterprising mindset. See Exhibits 15.3 and 15.4 for aggregate and state statistics.

There are two types of enterprising nonprofits. The first type utilizes earned-income activities (e.g., selling products or services) to generate a significant portion of total revenue. In many ways enterprising nonprofits are applying the principles of entrepreneurship to generate revenue to sustain their mission-driven organizations. The second type has a focus on growth and economic sustainability. Such an enterprising nonprofit may incorporate outside investment, in the form of venture philanthropy, to significantly scale the organization for better impact toward systemic social change. Just as a social venture may receive value-added venture capital or angel investment, an enterprising nonprofit may receive venture philanthropy funding, which is different from grant funding or donations. Venture philanthropy is a blend of financial assistance with a high level of professional engagement by the funder. The funding concept is addressed later in this chapter.

KickStart International is an example of an enterprising nonprofit using earned-income activities and venture philanthropy. Martin Fisher and Nick Moon founded KickStart in 1991 with a mission to end poverty in sub-Saharan Africa. They started in Kenya and today have offices in Tanzania and Mali. Though Martin and Nick have introduced many technologies related to irrigation, oil processing, and building, their greatest success to date is with their micro-irrigation pump known as the MoneyMaker. This low-cost irrigation system has helped rural farmers in Kenya to increase their crop production by a factor of 10, which allowed the farmers to produce crops not only for family survival

Exhibit 15.4   Number of Nonprofit Organizations by State (2006)

	Number of Organizations	Revenue (millions)	Total Assets (millions)		Number of Organizations	Revenue (millions)	Total Assets (millions)
Alabama	17,547	9,445	23,237	Montana	8,939	3,736	7,824
Alaska	4,845	2,778	5,278	Nebraska	12,186	8,985	17,686
Arizona	19,216	19,144	32,055	Nevada	7,118	4,464	13,099
Arkansas	11,709	11,300	12,620	New Hampshire	7,074	7,435	20,521
California	147,732	146,487	374,460	New Jersey	39,377	41,989	85,963
Colorado	25,652	18,132	45,239	New Mexico	9,692	5,278	11,334
Connecticut	19,006	27,570	81,271	New York	94,232	175,814	334,135
Delaware	4,984	4,178	18,293	North Carolina	39,043	36,716	94,202
District of Columbia	14,568	35,600	56,984	North Dakota	5,266	3,251	5,573
Florida	65,714	60,871	116,801	Ohio	58,002	65,152	129,309
Georgia	33,051	32,953	71,771	Oklahoma	17,784	11,119	28,387
Hawaii	7,107	6,177	16,992	Oregon	20,637	57,410	59,790
Idaho	6,888	2,700	7,127	Pennsylvania	60,858	83,724	168,323
Illinois	59,861	69,078	176,814	Rhode Island	5,928	8,658	19,057
Indiana	32,498	30,052	73,456	South Carolina	19,352	9,877	21,009
Iowa	26,493	15,383	36,024	South Dakota	5,892	4,860	9,887
Kansas	16,139	10,972	20,775	Tennessee	27,261	22,741	52,629
Kentucky	16,583	17,074	28,327	Texas	91,578	67,243	157,072
Louisiana	18,023	10,467	18,602	Utah	8,095	6,111	11,077
Maine	8,277	8,581	13,842	Vermont	5,331	3,520	7,033
Maryland	29,666	36,410	87,385	Virginia	36,450	39,873	104,721
Massachusetts	35,890	82,281	199,874	Washington	32,967	36,243	100,310
Michigan	44,770	52,663	104,177	West Virginia	9,553	6,433	10,135
Minnesota	30,423	37,133	71,909	Wisconsin	31,417	31,486	67,173
Mississippi	10,681	8,153	15,338	Wyoming	4,081	1,532	3,834
Missouri	33,848	30,024	65,574	**Total**	1,399,284	1,529,255	3,314,308

Source: National Center for Charitable Statistics.

but for profitable return. Their metrics supporting success are inspiring. By late 2008, KickStart featured the following statistics on their web site:[6]

- Number of pumps sold: 105,627.
- Number of enterprises created: 70,769.
- Number of people who have moved out of poverty: 338,284.
- The pumps generate $77 million per year in new profits and wages.
- Farmers earn $17 for each dollar spent.
- More than 50 percent of the pumps are managed by women entrepreneurs.
- Over 400 retailers are selling the pumps throughout Kenya, Tanzania, and Mali.

Winners of the *Fast Company* Social Capitalist awards for 2007 and 2008, KickStart and its enterprising ways are making great strides to deliver on their mission of fighting poverty.

Another enterprising nonprofit, Building Impact, has an aggressive growth plan. The idea is simple: Make access to civic engagement easy for the average person. This Boston-based organization is working to increase civic engagement and philanthropy, building by building—literally! Building Impact delivers community engagement opportunities, such as volunteer events and donation drives, right to office buildings and residential apartment buildings. The organization harnesses the collective energy of individuals and companies living and working within these buildings, and generates resources such as volunteers, mentors, and donated items to benefit over 20 nonprofit partners in greater Boston. It currently serves 45 buildings across greater Boston. This building-centric approach to increasing civic engagement earned Building Impact the Social Innovator's Award in 2007, granted by the Social Innovation Forum each year.

The business model is based on an earned-income stream and contributions. Building Impact partners with real estate companies who pay a licensing fee, adding Building Impact as a tenant amenity for their tenant companies or residents. Approximately 50 percent of total revenue is earned through these building fees while the remainder comes from more traditional channels such as foundations, grants, and individual contributors. Key to Building Impact's early success is volunteer ambassadors. Each Building Impact building has "ambassadors" from each company in the building. Once a month ambassadors receive an e-mail promoting upcoming events for the month and the ambassadors forward the e-mail internally to co-workers. This shared ownership, or co-creation of community impact, is an integral part of its strategy.

Growth is both aggressive and strategic. Building Impact has seen average annual growth in excess of 80 percent and anticipates revenues (earned income and contributions) to exceed $560,000 in 2009. The company served 12 buildings in 2005 and expects to serve 60 or more in 2009. The Building Impact strategy revolves around three primary activities: volunteer events, donation drives, and "Connect" events. Volunteer events bring building residents together for local events in the community such as serving meals to the homeless or working at a local Boys and Girls Club. Donation drives, such as clothing drives, blood drives, or toy drives, happen inside or right outside Building Impact buildings. Finally, Connect events bring building residents together in a more social setting but for a charitable purposes. A Connect event could be a book club night featuring books about social responsibility, or a poker night in an apartment building where proceeds are collected for charity.

The opportunity for Building Impact emerged in 2003. Research indicated that Massachusetts was ranked 41 out of 50 in civic engagement. Specifically in Boston, many residents of the city felt that their work (time and place) prevented them from being more involved, there was a lack of information with how to get involved, and individuals did not feel welcome when they did participate in a volunteer event.[7] Enter Building Impact—bringing welcoming civic engagement to your door.

Enterprising nonprofits tend to act more entrepreneurially. A study was conducted by the Yale School of Management–The Goldman Sachs Foundation Partnership on Nonprofit Ventures, to better understand how and why enterprising nonprofits pursue earned-income activities.[8] Of the 519 nonprofit organizations participating in the study, 42 percent were operating earned-income ventures, 5 percent had tried but with little success, and 53 percent had never tried to pursue any type of revenue-generating activity beyond fund-raising, grant writing, and other traditional methods. The study asked nonprofit participants what *entrepreneurial* means in the nonprofit world, and the results were not much different from what I would expect a classroom of MBA students at Babson College to say (Exhibit 15.5). Additionally, the key findings are evidence that enterprising nonprofits are a force generating systemic change through entrepreneurial action. In general, nonprofits pursuing earned-income activities[9]:

- Had more employees. Fifty-five percent of the enterprising nonprofits had 100 or more employees, compared to 36 percent that had never participated in any type of venturing activity.

- Believe they are more entrepreneurial. Seventy-seven percent of the enterprising nonprofits characterized themselves as entrepreneurship, compared to 46 percent that had never participated in any type of venturing activity.

- Typically do not wait for complete financing before starting a business.

- Have budgets of $5 to $25 million. This is an important figure because the majority of nonprofits in the United States never exceed a budget of $1 million.

- Do so to fund other programs (66 percent), become self-sustaining (52 percent), or diversify revenue streams (51 percent). Other reasons included job creation and building community.

- Have a strong desire to see their ventures grow and replicate, but only 55 percent had actually written a business plan. However, 56 percent said they would find help writing a business plan valuable.

Hybrid Models of Social Entrepreneurship

There are many types of ventures within the domain of social entrepreneurship that do not fit nicely into quadrants 1 or 4 in Exhibit 15.2. As a matter of fact there are probably more hybrid arrangements than social ventures or enterprising nonprofits combined. In a recent survey, 2,200 entrepreneurs were asked about the primary goals of their business.[10] Entrepreneurs chose one from the following four options:

- For-profit, primarily achieving economics goals.
- For-profit, primarily achieving social goals.
- For-profit, equally emphasizing social and economic goals.
- Not for profit, serving a social mission.

Exhibit 15.5   The Meaning of *Entrepreneurial* for Nonprofit Organizations

- Increasing earned revenue and profit.
- Agile.
- Looking for resources and opportunities.
- Crafting deals.
- Responding to market demand and opportunities.
- Creating an environment for new ideas and strategies.
- Challenging the status quo, familiar paradigms, and established beliefs.
- Constantly redefining customers.
- Developing and testing new products and services.
- Redefining business in response to actual and anticipated developments.
- Implementing "outside the box" strategies.
- Innovative.
- Risk-taking.
- Creating, collaborating, and synthesizing.
- Inventing new ways to do business.
- Nontraditional.
- Operating in a fast, flexible, and focused manner.
- Seeking nontraditional funding/capitalization.
- Creating new models for the sector.
- Moving quickly to new challenges.
- Applying private sector thinking and ideals to operations and activities.
- Forming strategic partnerships.
- Designing and developing programs that reach out beyond traditional constituencies and supporters.
- Cutting edge.

Source: Cynthia W. Massarsky and Samantha L. Beinhecker, "Enterprising Nonprofits: Revenue Generation in the Nonprofit Sector," Yale School of Management–The Goldman Sachs Foundation Partnership on Nonprofit Ventures, 2002, p. 6.

How do you think 2,200 random entrepreneurs in the United States, not necessarily classified as social entrepreneurs, responded to this question? The majority of the entrepreneurs (71 percent) were traditional enterprisers (quadrant 2). They identified as having a for-profit venture with purely economic goals. Another 5 percent classified their venture as for-profit with a purely social purpose—similar to Jim Poss and his BigBelly solar trash compactor, previously discussed. Only 5 percent of the entrepreneurs surveyed identified themselves as not-for-profit. Most interesting were the 19 percent of entrepreneurs who claimed to be for-profit with social and economic goals. These findings begin to show evidence that new ways of organizing are emerging—a dual purpose organization with missions that equally emphasize economic and social goals.

Scojo Vision, an eyewear company, is an example of a hybrid model. Founded in New York by two entrepreneurs, Scott Berrie and Jordan Kassalow, the company employed a mission that addressed economic and social needs. In addition to their stylish lines of eyewear, they created a program that brought eye care and affordable reading glasses to rural areas of Latin America and India. The program trained women entrepreneurs to build businesses by selling inexpensive reading glasses to workers who depend on their vision for their livelihood, such as tailors, textile workers, and weavers. In 2008, Scott and Jordan sold Scojo Vision but continue to lead the foundation under a new name, VisionSpring, with the same mission.[11]

Recently a new classification of organization has emerged called *for-benefit*. A growing army of volunteers and interested social entrepreneurs are participating in a community called the Fourth Sector Project.[12] The fourth sector emerges from a rather unchanged historical classification of types of business that have served either the private or public sectors, but not both. There are for-profit entities, nonprofit (non-governmental) social organizations, and government. The Fourth Sector Project seeks to recognize a new model, the for-benefit model, as sectors begin to blur.

Hybrid models are not examples of *corporate social responsibility*—a term that is growing in popularity both in theory and in practice. Corporate social responsibility (CSR) emphasizes doing good and serving communities while still making a profit. You may be saying, "Well, this certainly sounds like a hybrid model of social entrepreneurship!" Revisit Exhibit 15.2 and recall that the primary difference between social and the more traditional, commercial views of entrepreneurship is the intended mission. The primary mission of both social ventures and enterprising nonprofits is social regardless of market impact. The hybrid model *equally* emphasizes social and economic goals. CSR activities align best with "Social Consequence" ventures as seen in quadrant 3 of Exhibit 15.2—mission is economic with a social, but not central, connection. Exhibit 15.6 summarizes the primary differences between CSR and social entrepreneurship.

Corporations with CSR practices impact communities in which they operate and other stakeholders in many ways, but CSR is not the core component of their business model. For example, the Dow Chemical Company donates Styrofoam to Habitat for Humanity for new home insulation. Starbucks builds relationships with local farmers, pays fair market prices, and extends credit so local farmers can grow their coffee bean businesses. Anheuser-Busch commercials encourage consumers to drink responsibly to prevent abuse and drunk driving. In 2005, Wal-Mart announced lofty long-term goals to show their support for the environment. These goals stated that Wal-Mart would work to be supplied by 100 percent renewable energy, create zero waste, and sell environmentally friendly products.

Such CSR examples are numerous and growing, and many large corporations are making a positive impact on the world. Some companies have created CSR job

Exhibit 15.6 Corporate Social Responsibility versus Social Entrepreneurship

Corporate Social Responsibility	Social Entrepreneurship
Peripheral to mission	Core to mission
Side show	Main event
A department	The entire organization
Seeks to reduce harm	Measures social impact
Feel and look good	Do good
Stakeholder is the observer	Stakeholder is the customer
Consequence driven	Purpose driven
Image motivated	Opportunity motivated

functions. For example, the Walt Disney Company has a corporate responsibility department led by a senior manager of corporate responsibility. Similar positions can be found at other companies such as Gap and American Express. But CSR is a support function. These companies were not founded on missions to solve the world's most pressing social problems. CSR activities benefit many but are not considered part of the domain of social entrepreneurship. CSR is simply good business practice that is necessary in today's environment wrought with business scandals, unethical practices, and lack of individual and corporate accountability. Every MBA should understand CSR as one of the most important components of leadership and management, but it has little to do with venture creation based on identifying and acting on opportunities that solve or contribute to the solution of some of the world's greatest social problems.

Wicked Problems and Opportunity Spaces

Opportunities in social sectors and environmental issues are included here, and are driven by large, very complex problems. Perhaps we can be so bold as to call social problems *wicked problems*. In the early 1970s the notion of wicked problems emerged out of the complexity of resolving issues related to urban and governmental planning; wicked problems were contrasted with tame problems.[13] In other words, the linear and traditional approaches to solving tame problems were being used on social issues with little success. Further observation indicated that the problems were ill-defined, so the perception of what the problem actually is, perhaps, was not the actual problem but the symptom of another problem. As such, wicked problems became characterized as malign, viscous, tricky, and aggressive.[14] An examination of the characteristics of a wicked problem (Exhibit 15.7) reveals the considerable challenges facing social entrepreneurs.

**Exhibit 15.7 Wicked versus Tame Problems (Downloadable) Copyright ©
2010 by William D. Bygrave and Andrew Zacharakis. To download this form
for your personal use, please visit
www.wiley.com/go/portablembainentrepreneurship.**

Characteristics of Wicked Problems	Characteristics of Tame Problems
You don't understand the problem until you have developed a solution.	Has a well-defined and stable problem statement.
Wicked problems have no stopping rule.	Has a definite stopping point: when a solution is reached.
Solutions to wicked problems are not right or wrong.	Has a solution that can be objectively evaluated as right or wrong.
Every wicked problem is unique and novel.	Belongs to a class of similar problems that are all solved in a similar way.
Every solution to a wicked problem is a one-shot operation.	Has solutions that can be easily tried and abandoned.
Wicked problems have no given alternative solutions—infinite set.	Comes with a limited set of alternative solutions.

Source: Jeff Conklin, *Dialogue Mapping: Building Shared Understanding of Wicked Problems* (New York: John Wiley & Sons, 2006), Chapter 1.

As an example, let's consider the aging of the world's population as a significant social problem—a wicked problem—that will continue to gain prominence as baby boomers continue to retire. Between 2010 and 2020 we will see, for the first time in history, the number of people over 65 outnumbering children under 5.[15] Given advances in health care, specifically disease control, humans are living longer. In 1903, for example, 15 percent of white females lived to the age of approximately 80, but today close to 70 percent of white females live to be 80 years old.[16]

Our aging world population creates significant challenges for society. Pensions and retirement incomes will need to last longer. Health care costs are likely to increase. The service economy will capture an increasing percentage of the GDP as the elderly require more assistance from services as opposed to products. Also consider that the workforce (taxpayers) pays for the social benefits of the elderly. As the population ages there are fewer taxpayers supporting the growing number of nonworking retirees.

But in addition to these tangible issues are the intangibles such as the emotional and physical sides of aging. The aging of the population creates challenges socially and economically, yet there are also issues related to human rights:

> Young people burn countertops with hot pans, forget appointments, and write overdrafts on their checking accounts. But when the old do these same things, they experience double jeopardy. Their mistakes are not viewed as accidents but rather as loss of functioning. Such mistakes have implications for their freedom.[17]

As with many such issues, this massive societal challenge represents a growing opportunity space for alert social entrepreneurs. Let's consider one aspect of this issue using the characteristics of wicked problems as the backdrop. The elderly want to maintain their independence as long as possible, and so for many the move to an assisted living facility or nursing home is the last and least desired option. Furthermore, as the population ages and baby boomers enter their declining years, the availability of quality assisted living facilities will be sparse. A solution may be to create the next generation of smart homes that allow the elderly to stay in their own home yet reap the benefits and security of assisted living. Let's assume the technology is in place and retrofitting existing homes is possible. Is this a good solution? On the surface yes, but consider other challenges.

- The elderly are not comfortable with technology
- They do not earn money to pay for the smart features.
- Staying in their own home requires assistance to hospitals in cases of emergency, so more elderly at home means a potential stretch for the U.S. 911 emergency response system.
- Cities and towns may be expected to create services to serve a larger elderly population, and these services are paid for through increased property taxes.

The list could go on, but the point is that sometimes we do not understand the whole problem until the solution is developed (characteristic 1 of wicked problems). But let's continue with the idea of a smart home for the elderly. How much independence should be built into the home? What are the trade-offs of being able to use both floors of a two-story home versus just the bottom floor? Does the entire home need to be smart?

Wicked problems do not have a predetermined stopping rule (characteristic 2), so the social entrepreneur is forced to make rational choices based on a rigorous evaluation of trade-offs. The social entrepreneur must face the fact that a wicked problem is never fully solved or the solution is not likely to meet all expectations—also known as *satisficing* behavior. As wicked problem characteristic 3 states, there are no right or wrong solutions. If the smart home is built, there will be criticism of the choices you made or did not make. Each choice brings you down a different path, but any path is not necessarily right or wrong.

Independent living for the elderly is a unique social problem (characteristic 4)—and interpretation of the dilemma is in the eye of the beholder. The problem in this example affects not only the elderly person but also many other stakeholders. Potential solutions to wicked problems are known to have consequences over an extended period of time. The smart home may be a good idea for the elderly person wanting to maintain her independence, but consider the amount of work involved in retrofitting a home. What systems need to be installed? What changes to the home structure are anticipated? Finally, for the beneficiary, how difficult will it be to sell an "elder smart" home on the market, and would it be easy to take the "smartness" out of the home upon the death of the independent elder? Perhaps there are many other consequences of making a home smart in this context, but for a wicked problem only time can tell.

Elderly independence is just one aspect of the overarching social problem that we will encounter as the population ages. There are innumerable possibilities, and wicked problem theory tells us that there is not a finite solution set (characteristic 6). Perhaps some see this as a limitation, but social entrepreneurs see an ocean of possibilities and opportunities.

The aging of the population (nationally and internationally) is but one of many wicked problems that are being addressed by social entrepreneurs. To get a better understanding of the social challenges facing the planet, the United Nations' "Millennium Development Goals" is a good starting point. The goals were developed in 2000 in a historically significant event where world leaders came together to address the world's most pressing social issues. The gathering resulted in the United Nations Millennium Declaration, an inspiring document when you consider the collaboration required across nations and leaders. According to United Nations Secretary-General Kofi Annan, the eight goals (see Exhibit 15.8), with a target achievement date of 2015,

> . . .form a blueprint agreed by all the word's countries and all the world's leading development institutions—a set of simple but powerful objectives that every man and woman in the street, from New York to Nairobi to New Delhi, can easily support and understand. Since their adoption, the Goals have galvanized unprecedented efforts to meet the needs of the world's poorest.[18]

Although these goals represent the UN's view of our most pressing social problems, the opportunity spaces for social entrepreneurs (in for-profit and nonprofit areas) are vast and promising.

The Copenhagen Consensus is yet another organization tracking major social problems as well as identifying the best solutions. The Copenhagen Consensus brought together some of the world's preeminent economists to research and identify solutions to what they deemed to be the top 10 challenges. The challenges identified in 2008 were air pollution,

Exhibit 15.8   United Nations Millennium Development Goals

1. Eradicate extreme poverty and hunger.
2. Achieve universal primary education.
3. Promote gender equality and empower women.
4. Reduce child mortality.
5. Improve maternal health.
6. Combat HIV/AIDS, malaria, and other diseases.
7. Ensure environmental sustainability.
8. Develop a global partnership for development.

Source: The Millennium Development Goals Report 2005
(http://www.un.org/millenniumgoals/background.html).

conflicts, diseases, education, global warming, hunger and malnutrition, sanitation and water, subsidies and trade barriers, terrorism, and women and development. For each of these major problems, experts have submitted best practice papers that outline the most viable solutions.[19] Examples of solutions include micronutrient supplements for malnourished children, multipurpose dams in Africa to attack the clean water crisis, and bio-sand filters for home water treatment.

Both the UN Millennium Development Goals and the Copenhagen Consensus have identified some challenges designed to meet the needs of those at the base of the pyramid.[20] The *base of the pyramid* is defined as the four billion extremely poor people around the world with less than $1,500 annual per capita income—those living on just over $4 per day. Not only does the base of the pyramid represent two-thirds of the world's population, some have argued that it represents significant untapped markets.[21] KickStart, the enterprising nonprofit, is an excellent example of a company reaching and earning revenue from those living at the base of the pyramid. The goal in reaching those living at the base is both economically and socially driven—sell to the poor in order to enrich their lives.

Another example is Cemex, one of the top producers of cement in the world. Cemex reached an untapped market at the base of the pyramid in Mexico through a special program called Patrimonio Hoy (translated, it means "property today"). The market identified was poor rural Mexicans who spent 10 or more years building their homes in a very piecemeal, do-it-yourself fashion as cash and materials became available. Through the Patrimonio Hoy program, home owners could finance the cost of materials over a 70-week period. By paying $1,000 over 70 weeks, homeowners purchased materials delivered at phased intervals as well as services from architects and inspectors. Homes were built faster and cheaper than ever before. It has been reported that Cemex has distributed approximately $42 million in supplies to residents participating in Patrimonio Hoy. The loan repayment rate (required on-time payments) is 99.2 percent, and over 10,000 homes have been built.[22]

The simplicity of entrepreneurship applied to wicked problems creates a powerful force for humankind. An opportunity is simply the positive view of a problem or challenge. Entrepreneurs are opportunity creators and problem solvers. Social entrepreneurs are mission-driven individuals building businesses for a better world. What opportunities can you identify in these spaces?

Capital Markets for Social Entrepreneurs

Not unlike more traditional entrepreneurial ventures, resource acquisition is critical to the success of social purpose ventures, enterprising nonprofits, and even hybrid forms. Most social entrepreneurs will admit that access to capital is a burgeoning challenge as more and more social ventures emerge, especially with high growth aspirations and visions of international scalability. Bootstrapping is prevalent among passionate social entrepreneurs who are often quiet in their approach as they struggle to build sustainable business models.

Two sources of capital have emerged for social entrepreneurs. On the for-profit side, social venture capital (SVC) has emerged as subset of the traditional venture capital market. SVCs seek to invest in for-profit ventures not only for financial return but also for social and/or environmental return—also known as the *double bottom line* or *triple bottom line*. Research out of Columbia University estimated that $2.6 billion is under management in the double bottom line private equity market.[23]

Within the social venture capital territory there are primarily three different funds. First, there is the *focused* fund. For example, Expansion Capital Partners, with offices in San Francisco and New York, invests solely in expansion stage clean technology businesses related to energy, water, transportation, and manufacturing. Similarly, Commons Capital, operating outside of Boston, invests in early stage companies operating in one of four areas of social concern—education, health care, energy, and the environment. Both companies explicitly promote the environmental and/or social focus of their funds.

The second type of fund is the *community* fund, and its purpose is typically economic development and job creation in impoverished areas. CEI Ventures, headquartered in Portland, Maine, invests in businesses operating in underserved markets. Each company in the CEI portfolio is required to hire employees with low-income backgrounds from the community in which the business is operating.

The third type of fund is what has been referred to as *VC with a conscience*.[24] These funds stipulate that a certain percentage of the fund will be invested in socially responsible businesses related to their target investment areas. For example, Solstice Capital operates offices in Boston, Massachusetts, and Tucson, Arizona. They invest 50 percent of their fund in information technology and the remaining 50 percent is invested in socially responsible companies. According to their web site, "Socially responsive investments can generate superior venture capital returns and make a positive contribution to the natural and social environments."[25]

For nonprofits, a popular source of funding has emerged called *venture philanthropy* that provides value-added funding for nonprofit organizations to increase their potential for social impact. Though the origin of venture philanthropy has been attributed to John D. Rockefeller III in 1969 as he spoke before Congress in support of tax reform, the modern-day version looks more like venture capital but with a social return on investment.[26] There are various definitions, but the European Venture Philanthropy Association (EVPA) adopted several tenets that are similar across all definitions of venture philanthropy—both in Europe and the United States, where the concept is gaining in popularity (see Exhibit 15.9).

New Profit Inc., based in Cambridge, Massachusetts, exemplifies venture philanthropy using venture capital methodology. With 25 full-time employees, New Profit has a venture fund that has invested in 20 nonprofit organizations, with plans to grow its total portfolio

Exhibit 15.9   Accepted Principles of Venture Philanthropy from the European Venture Philanthropy Association

Characteristic	Description
High engagement	Venture philanthropists have a close, hands-on relationship with the social entrepreneurs and ventures they support, driving innovative and scalable models of social change. Some may take board seats on these organizations, and all are far more intimately involved at strategic and operational levels than are traditional nonprofit funders.
Multiyear support	Venture philanthropists provide substantial and sustained financial support to a limited number of organizations. Support typically lasts at least three to five years, with an objective of helping the organization to become financially self-sustaining by the end of the funding period.
Tailored financing	As in venture capital, venture philanthropists take an investment approach to determine the most appropriate financing for each organization. Depending on their own missions and the ventures they choose to support, venture philanthropists can operate across the spectrum of investment returns.
Organizational capacity-building	Venture philanthropists focus on building the operational capacity and long-term viability of the organizations in their portfolios, rather than funding individual projects or programs. They recognize the importance of funding core operating costs to help organizations achieve greater social impact and operational efficiency.
Nonfinancial support	In addition to financial support, venture philanthropists provide value-added services such as strategic planning, marketing and communications, executive coaching, human resource advice, and access to other networks and potential funders.
Performance measurement	Venture philanthropy investment is performance-based, placing emphasis on good business planning, measurable outcomes, achievement of milestones, and high levels of financial accountability and management competence.

Source: Rob John, "Venture Philanthropy: The Evolution of High Engagement Philanthropy in Europe" (working paper, Oxford Said Business School, Skoll Center for Entrepreneurship, 2006).

to 50 organizations by 2012. Average investment in each organization is $1 million over a four-year period. However, New Profit tends to stay with organizations longer than four years in order to achieve sustainability and desired scale. In addition to providing growth capital financing, portfolio organizations receive strategic support from a New Profit portfolio manager and New Profit's signature partner, Monitor Group—a global advisory and financial services firm. Monitor Group, through a collaborative and unprecedented

Exhibit 15.10   New Profit Doubles a $1 Investment

$ 1.00	Financial capital donated to New Profit portfolio organization
− 0.00	New Profit expense or management fee (overhead and operating costs are covered by New Profit's board of directors)
+ 0.48	Value of New Profit portfolio manager
+ 0.50	Value of Monitor Group services donated
$1.98	Total investment to New Profit portfolio organization

Source: New Profit collateral materials, 2008.

partnership, provides New Profit portfolio organizations with pro-bono consulting as well as providing New Profit with additional operating resources. It is estimated that since 1999 Monitor Group has provided New Profit and its portfolio organizations with more than $30 million in pro-bono services.

Given the value-added investment capability of New Profit, this venture philanthropy organization is able to double the impact of each investment dollar from donors, as illustrated in Exhibit 15.10. Thus, donors (or investors) of New Profit know that for every $1 they invest, the nonprofit portfolio organization actually receives $1.98 due to services, support, and intellectual capital delivered by the New Profit team in conjunction with Monitor Group.

New Profit has significantly increased the social impact of many nonprofit organizations across various sectors, including education, workforce development, and health care, among other areas. To date (1997–2007), the New Profit portfolio as a whole boasts an impressive 44 percent compound annual growth rate for revenue and a 49 percent compound annual growth in lives touched. In 1999, New Profit portfolio organizations touched approximately 3,000 lives, and by 2007 this number had jumped to more than 700,000.[27] The innovative approach of venture philanthropists such as New Profit illustrates the power of entrepreneurial principles to scale nonprofit organizations to achieve unparalleled social reach.

Social venture capitalists and venture philanthropists are significantly contributing to the growth and impact of social ventures and enterprising nonprofits, but another category of social financing has gained global celebrity: *microfinance*. Microfinance, the banking practice of issuing very small loans to low-income and poor clients for entrepreneurial activities, became a global movement since Muhammad Yunus, founder of the Grameen Bank, was award the Nobel Peace Prize in 2006.

Muhammad Yunus is the banker to the poor. He revolutionized the banking industry in the late 1970s when he started offering micro-loans with no collateral to the poorest of poor in Bangladesh. Over 25 years later he and his Grameen Bank were introduced to the mainstream as recipients of the Nobel Peace Prize for their contributions to social and economic development by breaking the cycle of poverty through micro-credit.

The idea is simple yet powerful. Borrowers are organized into groups of five, but not all members can borrow at once. Two borrowers may receive a micro-loan at one time but it is not until these two borrowers begin to pay back the principal plus interest that the other members become eligible for their own loans. The average interest rate is 16 percent and the repayment rate is an unprecedented 98 percent, which is attributed to group pressure, empowerment, and motivation. The loans are tiny—typically enough to buy a goat, tools, or a small piece of machinery that can be used to produce new sources of income.

The Grameen Bank was founded by Yunus with the following objectives:

- Extend banking facilities to poor men and women.
- Eliminate the exploitation of the poor by money lenders.
- Create opportunities for self-employment for the vast multitude of unemployed people in rural Bangladesh.
- Bring the disadvantaged, mostly women from the poorest households, within the fold of an organizational format that they can understand and manage by themselves.
- Reverse the age-old vicious circle of low income, low saving, and low investment, into the virtuous circle of low income, injection of credit, investment, more income, more savings, more investment, more income.

The Grameen Bank has served 7.87 million borrowers, of which 97 percent are women. The Bank operates 2,556 branches and employs 23,445 people. Since 1983, the Grameen Bank has disbursed over $8 billion to the poorest of poor and has been profitable every year except 1983, 1991, and 1992. According to Yunus, "This is not charity. This is business—business with a social objective, which is to help people get out of poverty."[28] Not only is the Grameen Bank a source of capital for social entrepreneurs but it is also a *social purpose* organization (Exhibit 15.2).

Social Entrepreneurs and Their Stakeholders

As previously discussed, social entrepreneurship seeks to solve wicked problems, and such problems cannot be solved in isolation. The environment to solve social problems requires a spirit of collaboration and an understanding of how value is generated for multiple stakeholder groups external to the organization. Stakeholders may include the community, investors, foundations, benefactors, government, customers, suppliers, manufacturers, or, in the case of the Grameen Bank, villagers—anyone who affects or is affected by the organization and plays a role in helping or hindering an organization in achieving its objectives.[29]

An experienced social entrepreneur understands how to assess stakeholder importance and work to generate value for each stakeholder to ensure venture success. The current momentum around social entrepreneurship is exciting, but the sustainability of "doing good" can only be achieved if it delivers some type of value for those most involved. In other words, social ventures must deliver value for key stakeholders. What the value is and to whom will vary, but it is important that the social entrepreneur understand the interaction between and among stakeholders as well as the potential value derived from being associated with the venture.

Think back to the Jim Poss example at the beginning of the chapter. Jim must understand the value proposition with regard to each of his stakeholders. In a municipality, for example, the company responsible for waste management needs to see money saved by reducing the frequency of trash pickups. Jim must show the mayor of the city that the Big Belly supports greening initiatives. For city planners, Jim can address space-saving and aesthetic features. But what about labor unions? What if reducing the number of trash pickups leads to a reduction in the number of trucks needed, which would then lead to a reduction in the number of drivers needed? With every social innovation there is likely to be a down side, and the social entrepreneur needs to consider not only the value derived but also the value loss to various stakeholder groups, and assess consequences as well as identify alternative sources of value for those feeling disenfranchised. One of the primary questions underlying stakeholder theory is what is at stake and for whom? This is an important point. Even social entrepreneurs must assess the risk inherent in their new ventures—including social risk.

Understanding stakeholders, how they are connected, and to what degree is not an easy task. Some stakeholders are more important to the undertaking than others, depending on context and timing. Researchers of stakeholder theory have identified three primary attributes of stakeholders.[30] The first attribute is *power*, broadly defined as the person in a position to hinder or help even in the face of resistance. For example, a social entrepreneur trying to get new legislation passed to support green initiatives in his state may not get far if his local legislator does not see green projects as a top priority when budgets are tight. Here the legislator has authority to prevent the social entrepreneur from achieving organizational objectives.

The second attribute is *legitimacy*. If something or someone is labeled legitimate then it is socially accepted, expected, and somewhat trusted. Max Weber, touted as one of the most influential thinkers of the twentieth century, who brought bureaucracy to the forefront as a rational and efficient way of organizing, stated that power in conjunction with legitimacy creates authority. Authority, however, is not a separate attribute of stakeholders but only exists when the combination of power and legitimacy is present.

Finally, the third attribute of stakeholders is *urgency*. Are there stakeholders calling for immediate and pressing action? The basic premise is that the number of attributes held by a stakeholder is positively and directly related to the salience of that stakeholder. So a stakeholder may have power or legitimacy or authority or a combination of the three. Taking into consideration all possible combinations, there are seven different types of stakeholders, as depicted in Exhibit 15.11.[31]

Dormant stakeholders have power, but without legitimacy or a sense of urgency they will not likely have a direct and significant connection to the organization. These are the sleepers; they should be watched but are not a priority for action and value generation. *Discretionary* stakeholders, in the corporate strategy literature, are associated with corporate social responsibility because they are most likely to contribute to society with socially acceptable principles and values.[32] Within the world of social entrepreneurship, discretionary stakeholders are allies. Establishing and maintaining relationships with discretionary stakeholders is important but not difficult because these stakeholders represent the fan club. The third, single-attribute stakeholder is the *demanding* stakeholder. Demanding stakeholders are the elephant in the room—always there and obtrusive but not dangerous or incredibly salient. Without associated power or legitimacy or both, the demanding stakeholder can make a lot of noise but may not be able to force or prevent action.

The saliency of a stakeholder increases when attributes are combined. *Dominant* stakeholders matter to the social entrepreneur. These stakeholders have legitimacy and power, which indicates a high level of authority. *Dependent* stakeholders are the passionate individuals connected to the organization or cause. They may not have significant influence but their advocacy is contagious and will likely attract dominant stakeholders to

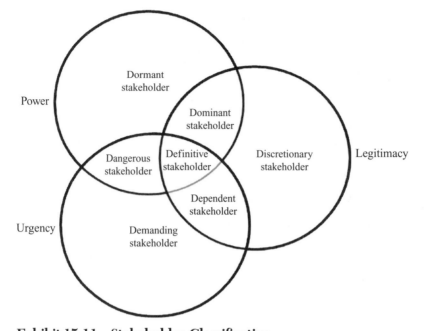

Exhibit 15.11   Stakeholder Classification

Source: R. Mitchell, B. Agle, and D. Wood, "Toward a Theory of Stakeholder Identification and Salience: Defining the Principle of Who and What Really Counts," *Academy of Management Review* 22(4) (1997): 874.

the organization. *Dangerous* stakeholders are, in fact, dangerous! Social issues are often emotional issues, and firm stances are made either for or against a solution. Exercising power and urgency in favor of the social entrepreneur is great social capital, but when it is exercised *against* the social entrepreneurs, significant challenges may emerge.

Finally, the most salient of all stakeholders are the *definitive* stakeholders. Definitive stakeholders possess all three attributes—power, legitimacy, urgency—and are likely to play an integral role in the organization or be closely connected to the organization. What is important for the social entrepreneur to monitor is when dominant, dependent, or dangerous stakeholders become definitive.

Stakeholders for social entrepreneurs, unlike stakeholders for large corporations, represent the network of resources, support, mentorship, advocacy, and policy makers. Social entrepreneurs are committed, passionate, and build powerful networks through various social entrepreneurship–focused organizations. There is something unique about like-minded entrepreneurs and investors coming together to address world problems and understanding that their solutions, or a lack thereof, will change the world forever. But communities of stakeholders are emerging everywhere to share best practices, learn, create, and collaborate to build and grow ventures for a better world. Social Venture Network, Investors Circle, Echoing Green, Ashoka, Net Impact, and Social Enterprise Alliance are just a few places to start connecting to and learning about stakeholders. Bill Drayton, founder of Ashoka, believes "The inertia of our experience pulls us into conventional directions. We must engage in group entrepreneurship to collaborate and become far more than the sum of the parts." Stakeholders are vital to group entrepreneurship.

Concluding Thoughts: Change Agent Now or Later?

Bank of America commissioned a report on philanthropy which found that entrepreneurs, on average, give 25 percent more to charitable causes compared to other types of wealthy donors.[33] Any entrepreneur should be quite proud of this statistic!

Or perhaps not. Of course the spirit of giving among entrepreneurs should be recognized and applauded, but is such giving sufficient? The story of a successful entrepreneur building a company, creating personal wealth, and *then* making significant charitable contributions is commonplace and represents a significant portion of total philanthropy. Mark Albion, co-founder of Net Impact and author of *More Than Money*, identified two types of MBA students: conflicted achievers and passionate strivers. *Conflicted achievers* are those who pursue a less-than-satisfying path in order to acquire the resources to do what they really want to do later in life. *Passionate strivers*, by contrast, seek immediate satisfaction through meaningful work. Albion states, and I agree, that both paths are fine as long as one does not get stuck.

Social entrepreneurs, like the passionate strivers, do not wait to give back. Social entrepreneurs build businesses where economic value and societal contribution are two sides of the same coin. They identify opportunities to solve problems related to education, health care, poverty, energy, water, and the environment—just to name a few. They are cause fighters and change agents using the fundamental principles of entrepreneurship to promote positive change and permanent impact. Social entrepreneurs are creating the future.

Downloadable Resources for this chapter available at www.wiley.com/go/portablembainentrepreneurship

Wicked versus Tame Problems

Resources for Social Entrepreneurs

Ashoka (www.ashoka.org).   Ashoka is a global association of social entrepreneurs. The web site provides a wealth of information and resources for social entrepreneurs working in primarily nonprofit sectors. Ashoka both connects and funds social entrepreneurs in the citizen sector.

Echoing Green (www.echoinggreen.org).   Echoing Green invests in and supports social entrepreneurs launching and operating bold, high-impact social ventures.

Envirolink (www.envirolink.org).   Envirolink is an online portal for environmental resources including research, job postings, government resources, and events.

Global Social Venture Competition (www.gsvc.org).   The Global Social Venture Competition is the oldest and largest student-led business plan competition. The annual grand prize is $25,000 and the Competition has awarded over $250,000 since its inception in 1999.

Investor's Circle (www.investorscircle.net).   Investors Circle is a group of formal and informal investors that invests patient capital in ventures that focus on building a sustainable economy.

Lewis Institute (www.babson.edu/lewis).   The Lewis Institute of Babson College strives to contribute to the solution of the world's problems through cutting-edge education, thought leadership, and entrepreneurship.

Net Impact (www.netimpact.org).   Net Impact is an international organization with graduate, undergraduate, and professional chapters. The organization brings together an extensive network of individuals who seek to positively change the world through business.

Root Cause (www.rootcause.org).   Root Cause supports social innovators and social investors through uniting and networking public, private, and nonprofit sectors. The web site provides knowledge resources and how-to resources on everything from business plan writing to measuring social impact.

Schwab Foundation for Social Entrepreneurship (www.schwabfound.org).   The Schwab Foundation is a networking and support organization for leading social entrepreneurs hand-selected to join a prestigious network. Each year 20 to 30 social entrepreneurs enter the network through the annual Social Entrepreneur of the Year competition.

Skoll Foundation (www.skollfoundation.org).   The Skoll Foundation invests in and connects social entrepreneurs working for systemic change in areas of tolerance and human rights, health, environmental sustainability, economic and social equity, institutional responsibility, and peace and security.

Social Edge (www.socialedge.org).   Social Edge is a global online community of social entrepreneurs, built for social entrepreneurs by social entrepreneurs, where community members share resources, knowledge, and networks.

Social Enterprise Alliance (www.se-alliance.org).   The Social Enterprise Alliance brings together multiple stakeholder groups connected to social enterprise, including nonprofits, social purpose businesses, funders, investors, and consultants. Its annual conference, the Social Enterprise Summit, is one of the largest conferences serving social entrepreneurship today.

Social Fusion (www.socialfusion.org).   Social Fusion is an incubator for nonprofit and for-profit social ventures. The organization provides a menu of services and programs to help entrepreneurs start and build sustainable businesses.

Social Innovation Forum (www.socialinnovationforum.org).   The Social Innovation Forum connects social innovators to social impact investors in order to accelerate the creation of enduring solutions to social problems.

Social Venture Network (www.svn.org).   The mission of Social Venture Network is "to inspire a community of business and social leaders to build a just economy and sustainable planet." The organization hosts two annual conferences that bring together an extensive network of social entrepreneurs and others who support business as a way to change to the world.

William James Foundation (www.williamjamesfoundation.org).   The William James Foundation offers support to mission-driven businesses through socially responsible business plan competitions, speaker series, co-sponsored events, and fiscal assistance.

Notes

1. Nicole Wallace, "Social Entrepreneurs Challenged to Become 'Economic Entrepreneurs,'" *Chronicle of Philanthropy,* April 23, 2007, http://www.philanthropy.com/free/update/2007/04/2007042301.htm.

2. S. Hart, Foreword to *Capitalism at the Crossroads* (New Jersey: Wharton School Publishing, 2007), xxv.

3. Interview with Jim Poss at Babson College on November 28, 2007.

4. Ibid.

5. Presentation by Dannielle Boudreau, Director of Investor Relations for New Profit Inc., Cambridge, MA, April 11, 2009 at Babson College.

6. http://www.kickstart.org/what-we-do/impact/.

7. The Boston Foundation, "Social Capital in Boston: Findings from the Social Capital Community Benchmark Survey," 2001.

8. Cynthia W. Massarsky and Samantha L. Beinhecker, "Enterprising Nonprofits: Revenue Generation in the Nonprofit Sector," Yale School of Management–The Goldman Sachs Foundation Partnership on Nonprofit Ventures, 2002.

9. Ibid., 5–12.

10. Questions related to social entrepreneurship were included in the Global Entrepreneurship Monitor survey for the United States sponsored by Babson College. Social entrepreneurship results are included in Heidi Neck, Candida Brush, and Elaine Allen, "Exploring Social Entrepreneurship Activity in the United States: For Profit Ventures Generating Social and Economic Value" (working paper, Babson College, 2007).

11. http://www.visionspring.org/about/our-story.php.

12. See http://www.fourthsector.net/ for more information.

13. Horst Rittel and Melvin Webber, "Dilemmas in a General Theory of Planning," *Policy Sciences* 4 (1973): 155–169.

14. Ibid., 60.

15. United Nations Department of Economic and Social Affairs, Population Division. *World Population Prospects: The 2004 Revision.* New York: United Nations, 2005.

16. Ibid.

17. Mary Pipher, "Society Fears the Aging Process," in Laura Egendorf, ed., *Opposing Viewpoints: An Aging Population* (Greenhaven Press, 2002).

18. Kofi Annan, The Millennium Development Goals Report 2005, p. 3, http://www.unfpa.org/icpd/docs/mdgrept2005.pdf.

19. http://www.copenhagenconsensus.com/Default.aspx?ID=1168.

20. *Base of the pyramid* and *bottom of the pyramid* have both been used in the literature. C. K. Prahalad popularized the term in his book *Fortune at the Bottom of the Pyramid* (New Jersey: Wharton Business School Publishing, 2006). Prior to the book's publication, C. K. Prahalad and Stuart Hall co-authored an article by the same name in *Strategy + Business* in 2002. Stuart Hall changed the word *bottom* to *base* in his book *Capitalism at the Crossroads* (New Jersey: Wharton Business School Publishing, 2007). Hall noted in a chapter note, "At the suggestion of my UNC colleague Ted London, we changed the name from 'Bottom' to 'Base' of the Pyramid to remove any hint that those on the lower end of the income scale are in any way inferior to those at the high end of the income scale" (p. 137).

21. Both C. K. Prahalad and Stuart Hall have written extensively on markets and the base of the pyramid. See C. K. Prahalad, *Fortune at the Bottom of the Pyramid* (New Jersey: Wharton Business School Publishing, 2006); S. Hall, *Capitalism at the Crossroads* (New

Jersey: Wharton Business School Publishing, 2007); C. K. Prahalad and S. Hall, "Fortune at the Bottom of the Pyramid," *Strategy + Business* 26 (2002): 1–14.

22. Ricardo Sandoval, "Block by Block: How One of the World's Largest Companies Builds Loyalty among Mexico's Poor," *Stanford Social Innovation Review* 3, no. 2 (2005): 34–37.

23. Catherine Clark, *RISE Capital Market Report: The Double Bottom Line Private Equity Landscape in 2002–2003*, Columbia Business School, 2003.

24. Ibid.

25. http://www.solcap.com/approach.

26. Rob John, "Venture Philanthropy: The Evolution of High Engagement Philanthropy in Europe" (working paper, Skoll Center for Entrepreneurship, Oxford Saïd Business School, 2006).

27. http://www.newprofit.com/impact_results.asp.

28. Grameen Bank at a Glance, June 2009, http://www.grameen-info.org/index.php?option= com_content&task=view&id=26&Itemid=175.

29. This definition of *stakeholder* represents the most classic approach to stakeholder theory. See E. Freeman, *Strategic Management: A Stakeholder Approach* (Boston: Pitman, 1984), 47. For an intellectual review of stakeholder theory see R. Mitchell, B. Agle, and D. Wood, "Toward a Theory of Stakeholder Identification and Salience: Defining the Principle of Who and What Really Counts," *Academy of Management Review* 22, no. 4 (1997): 853–886.

30. R. Mitchell, B. Agle, and D. Wood, "Toward a Theory of Stakeholder Identification and Salience: Defining the Principle of Who and What Really Counts," *Academy of Management Review* 22, no. 4 (1997): 853–886.

31. Ibid.

32. Ibid.

33. Caroline Preston, "Entrepreneurs Are Among Most-Generous Wealthy, Report Finds," *Chronicle of Philanthropy* 20, no. 5 (2007).

Glossary

Accounts payable A liability created by purchasing on a credit basis; it represents the amount owed to a supplier or vendor by the company.

Accounts receivable An asset that is created by a sale on a credit basis; it represents the amount owed to the company by the customer.

Accredited investor Under the Securities Act of 1933, a company that offers or sells its securities must register the securities with the Securities and Exchange Commission (SEC) or find an exemption from the registration requirements. The Act provides companies with a number of exemptions. For some of the exemptions, such as rules 505 and 506 of Regulation D, a company may sell its securities to what are known as *accredited investors*.

The federal securities laws define the term *accredited investor* in Rule 501 of Regulation D as: (1) a bank, insurance company, registered investment company, business development company, or small business investment company; an employee benefit plan, within the meaning of the Employee Retirement Income Security Act (ERISA), if a bank, insurance company, or registered investment adviser makes the investment decisions, or if the plan has total assets in excess of $5 million; (2) a charitable organization, corporation, or partnership with assets exceeding $5 million; (3) a director, executive officer, or general partner of the company selling the securities; (4) a business in which all the equity owners are accredited investors; (5) a natural person who has individual net worth, or joint net worth with the person's spouse, that exceeds $1 million at the time of the purchase; (6) a natural person with income exceeding $200,000 in each of the two most recent years or joint income with a spouse exceeding $300,000 for those years and a reasonable expectation of the same income level in the current year; or (7) a trust with assets in excess of $5 million, not formed to acquire the securities offered, whose purchases a sophisticated person makes.

Accumulated depreciation The sum of all depreciation expense recorded to date; it is subtracted from the cost of the asset in order to derive the asset's net book value.

Acquisition Acquiring control of a *corporation*, called a *target*, by *stock* purchase or exchange, either hostile or friendly; also called *takeover*.

Agency theory A branch of economics dealing with the behavior of principals (for example, owners) and their agents (for example, managers).

Alert ideas Ideas that are created in a spontaneous, less calculated manner.

American Stock Exchange (Amex) Stock exchange located in New York, listings companies that are generally smaller and younger than those on the much larger New York Stock Exchange (NYSE).

Amortization A noncash expense that reduces the value of an intangible asset.

Ancillary goods Goods that provide extra or supplementary income but are not the company's primary product or source of revenues.

Angel An individual who invests in private companies. The term *business angel* is sometimes reserved for sophisticated angel investors who invest sizeable sums in private companies. See *invisible venture capital* and *informal investor*.

Antidilution (of ownership) The right of an investor to maintain the same percentage ownership of a company's common stock in the event that the company issues more stock. See *dilution*.

Approver (decision-making) A person in the prospect organization who has the power and budgetary authority to agree to a sales proposal. Also known as the *decision maker*.

Arbitration A process by which a disagreement is resolved by impartial individuals (arbitrators) in order to avoid costly and lengthy litigation.

Asked The price level at which sellers offer securities to buyers.

Asset Resources that are owned by a business, will provide future benefits, and can be measured.

Asset acquisition Means of effecting a buyout by purchase of certain desired assets rather than shares of the target company.

Asset utilization Value of the revenues that a company generates for each dollar invested in assets.

Audited financial statements A company's financial statements prepared and certified by a certified public accounting (CPA) firm that is totally independent of the company.

Augmented product The set of attributes peripherally related to the core product or service.

Average lifetime value of a customer See *customer lifetime value*.

Balance sheet Summary statement of a company's financial position at a given point in time. It summarizes the accounting value of the assets, liabilities, preferred stock, common stock, and retained earnings. Assets = Liabilities + Preferred stock + Common stock + Retained earnings. See *pro forma statements*.

Basis point One one-hundredth of a percent (0.01%), typically used in expressing yield differentials:

$$7.50\% - 7.15\% = 0.35\%, \quad \text{or} \quad 35 \text{ basis points}$$

See *yield*.

Bear A person who expects prices to fall.

Bear market A period of generally falling prices and pessimistic attitudes.

Best efforts offering The underwriter makes its best efforts to sell as much as it can of the shares at the offering price. Hence, unlike a firm commitment offering, the company offering its shares is not guaranteed a definite amount of money by the underwriter.

Beta customer Customers who purchase a prototype or unfinished form of a product.

Beta site An unfinished web site that is open to the public.

Bid The price level at which buyers offer to acquire securities from sellers.

Big Board See *New York Stock Exchange*.

Blue sky Refers to laws that safeguard investors from being misled by unscrupulous promoters of companies with little or no substance.

Book value (of an asset) The accounting or book value of an asset as shown on a balance sheet is the cost of the asset minus its accumulated depreciation. It is not necessarily identical to its market value.

Book value (of a company) The common stock equity shown on the balance sheet. It is equal to total assets minus liabilities and preferred stock (synonymous with *net worth* and *owners' equity*).

Bootstrap To build a business out of nothing with minimum outside capital.

Bottom line Business slang for net income or profits—which is found on the bottom line of the income statement.

Brand awareness The customer's ability to recognize and recall the brand when provided a cue.

Brand equity The value of the brand itself.

Brand image How customers perceive the brand.

Brand recognition Customer awareness of a certain brand, company, or product.

Break-even point The sales volume at which a company's net sales revenue just equals its costs. A commonly used approximate formula for the break-even point is:

$$\text{Sales revenue} = \text{Total fixed costs/Gross margin}.$$

Bridging finance Short-term finance that is expected to be repaid relatively quickly. It usually bridges a short-term financing need. For example, it provides cash needed before an expected stock flotation.

Burn rate The negative real-time cash flow from a company's operations, usually computed monthly.

Business format franchise An arrangement where the franchisor grants a license to the franchisee to use business systems prescribed by the franchisor and associated with the franchisor's trademark. In return for strict adherence to methods and controls of the franchisor's system, the franchisor provides significant assistance, a marketing plan or system to the franchisee. Also known as a *package franchise*.

Business model The way in which a business makes a profit. As an example, here is IBM's definition of its business model: "IBM sells services, hardware, and software. These offerings are bolstered by IBM's research and development capabilities. If a customer requires financing, IBM can provide that, too." Southwest Airlines' business model is to provide inexpensive fares by keeping costs low through being more efficient than its major competitors.

Business plan A document prepared by entrepreneurs, possibly in conjunction with their professional advisers, detailing the past, present, and intended future of the company. It contains a thorough analysis of the managerial, physical, labor, product, and financial resources of the company, plus the background of the company, its previous trading record, and its market position. The business plan contains detailed profit, balance sheet, and cash flow projections for two years ahead, and less detailed information for the ensuing three years. The business plan crystallizes and focuses the management team's ideas. It explains their strategies, sets objectives, and is used to monitor their subsequent performance.

Buyback A corporation's repurchase of stock that it has previously issued; for example, a company's buying its stock back from a venture capital firm that has previously been issued stock in return for money invested in the company.

Call A contract allowing the issuer of a security to buy back that security from the purchaser at an agreed-upon price during a specific period of time.

Capability Ability and capacity of an organization expressed in terms of its human resources (number, quality, skills, etc), physical and material resources, financial resources, information resources, and intellectual resources (copyrights, patents, etc.).

Capital expense/expenditure Outlay charged to a long-term asset account. A capital expense either adds a fixed asset unit or increases the value of an existing fixed asset. An example is a new motor for a truck. A capital expense appears in full on the income statement the moment it is contracted for work. Also known as *CAPEX*.

Capital gain The amount by which the selling price of an asset (for example, common stock) exceeds the seller's initial purchase price.

Capitalization rate The discount rate K used to determine the present value of a stream of future earnings.

$$PV = (\text{Normalized earnings after taxes})/(K/100)$$

where PV is the present value of the firm and K is the firm's cost of capital.

Carried interest A venture capital firm's share of the profit earned by a fund. In the United States, the carried interest (*carry*) is typically 20 percent of the profit after investors' principal has been repaid.

Cash An asset that represents the amount of a firm's available cash and funds on deposit at a bank in checking accounts and savings accounts.

Cash flow The difference between the company's cash receipts and its cash payments in a given period.

Cash flow statement A summary of a company's cash flow over a period of time. See *pro forma statements*.

Channel conflict Situations where differing objectives and ownership rights between channel partners leads to true disharmony in the distribution channel.

Channel coverage The manner in which a corporation decides to distribute its product. The three types of coverage are intensive, selective, and exclusive.

Channel of distribution The route a product takes as it moves from producer to end user.

Channel partner A company that partners with a manufacturer or producer to market and sell the manufacturer's products or services.

Channel power The ability of one channel member to influence another.

Chattel mortgage A lien on specifically identified property (assets other than real estate) backing a loan.

Collateral An asset pledged as security for a loan.

Commodity goods A good or service whose wide availability typically leads to smaller profit margins and diminishes the importance of factors (as brand name) other than price.

Common-sized income statement An income statement where line items are expressed as percentages of total revenue rather than dollar amounts.

Common stock Shares of ownership, or equity, in a corporation.

Communications mix (marketing) The particular combination of marketing tools that work together to communicate the marketer's message, to achieve the marketer's objectives, and to satisfy the target market. Also known as the *marketing communications mix*.

Comparable A company in the same or similar industry, and/or at the same or similar stage of development, to which a start-up can compare itself regarding various key operating ratios and valuation metrics. Comparables are useful for planning start-up costs and common operating ratios by providing entrepreneurs examples of the financial performance experienced by established companies in the same or similar lines of business. Comparables are also used to derive valuations of private and public companies.

Compensating balance A bank requires a customer to maintain a certain level of demand deposits that do not bear interest. The interest forgone by the customer on that compensating balance recompenses the bank for services provided, credit lines, and loans.

Competency A key ability or strength that an organization has acquired that differentiates it from others, gives it competitive advantage, and contributes to its long-term success.

Competitive benchmarking A continuous process of comparing a firm's practices and performance measures with that of its most successful competitor(s).

Competitive pricing A pricing strategy whereby a company or organization sets a price comparable to competitive products.

Complementer A product, service, or company that provides a product or service that complements another product (e.g., spaghetti and spaghetti sauce).

Conceptual Age A theory developed by Daniel Pink which describes the current age as one that requires both right- (creative) and left- (noncreative) brain thinking in order to develop talent that technology cannot replace.

Consultative selling A concept and philosophy where the salesperson has a responsibility to identify consumer needs, help the potential customer recognize whether the product or service fulfills a customer need, and, if not, help them pursue an alternative. A highly skillful consultative salesperson will help the customer through the customer's own buying process—helping ensure that the buyer makes a wise decision, even if it is to purchase a competitor's offering.

Conversion ratio The number of shares of common stock that may be received in exchange for each share of a convertible security.

Convertible debt A loan that can be exchanged for equity.

Convertible security Preferred stock that is convertible into common stock according to a specified ratio at the security holder's option.

Core competency A key ability or strength that an organization has acquired that differentiates it from others, gives it competitive advantage, and contributes to its long-term success.

Core customer A company or product's primary target audience. See *primary target audience*.

Core product The essential good or service that a company produces.

Corporate entrepreneurship A process whereby employees and managers of a large existing company identify and take advantage of new opportunities.

Corporate social responsibility A form of corporate self-regulation whereby a company would monitor and adhere to legal, ethical, and international norms while embracing the responsibility of the impact of its activities on the environment and on various stakeholders.

Corporation A business form that is an entity legally separate from its owners. Its important features include limited liability, easy transfer of ownership, and unlimited life.

Cost-based pricing A pricing strategy where products and services are priced based on cost to develop plus a predetermined amount or margin. See *cost-plus pricing*.

Cost of capital The required rate of return of various types of financing. The overall cost of capital is a weighted average of the individual required rates of returns (costs).

Cost of customer acquisition Cost associated with the acquisition of a new customer.

Cost of debt capital The interest rate charged by a company's lenders.

Cost of equity capital The rate of return on investment required by the company's common shareholders (colloquially called the *hurdle rate*).

Cost of goods sold The direct cost of the product sold. For a retail business, the cost of all goods sold in a given period equals the inventory at the beginning of the period plus the cost of goods purchased during that period, minus the inventory at the end of the period.

Cost of preferred stock The rate of return on investment required by the company's preferred shareholders.

Cost-plus pricing A pricing strategy where products and services are priced based on cost to develop plus a predetermined amount or margin.

Cost structure The expenses that a company incurs when manufacturing a product or service.

Couponing Distribution or redemption of coupons.

Covenant A restriction on a borrower imposed by a lender. For example, it could be a requirement placed on a company to achieve and maintain specified targets such as levels of cash flow, balance sheet ratios, or specified capital expenditure levels in order to retain financing facilities.

Creativity A product or response will be judged as creative to the extent that (1) it is both a novel and appropriate, useful, correct, or valuable response to the task at hand; and (2) the task is heuristic rather than algorithmic.

Cumulative dividend provision A requirement that unpaid dividends on preferred stock accumulate and have to be paid before a dividend is paid on common stock.

Current ratio Current assets/current liabilities. This ratio indicates a company's ability to cover its current liabilities with its current assets.

Customer base The buyers of a company's product or services. Also known as a company's *target market*.

Customer intimacy A strategy of competitive advantage where a company focuses on providing superior customer service and support.

Customer lifetime value (CLV) A formula that calculates the dollar value associated with the long-term relationship of any given customer, revealing how much a customer relationship is worth over a given period of time.

Customer orientation A corporate or entrepreneurial outlook that involves understanding the market and future trends.

Customer relationship management (CRM) A system that is designed to help companies compile and manage data about their customers.

Customer segment (market segment) A subgroup of a market sharing one or more characteristics.

Customer value proposition The difference between total customer benefits and total customer costs.

Deal flow The rate at which new investment propositions come to funding institutions.

Debt financing Financing provided to a company by debt providers. Unlike equity financing, debt financing does not buy ownership in the company. However, the company is expected to pay back any debt financing and interest expenses.

Debt providers Organizations that specialize in providing debt funding to businesses (e.g., banks).

Debt service Payments of principal and interest required on a debt over a given period.

Deep pockets Refers to an investor who has substantial financial resources.

Default The nonperformance of a stated obligation (e.g., nonpayment by the issuer of interest or principal on a bond) or the nonperformance of a covenant.

Deferred payment A debt that has been incurred and will be repaid at some future date.

Demographics Statistical characteristics of human populations (such as age, income, sex) used to identify markets.

Depreciation The systematic allocation of the cost of an asset over a period of time for financial reporting and tax purposes. Depreciation is a noncash expense that reduces the value of an asset as a result of wear and tear, age, or obsolescence. Because it is a noncash expense, depreciation lowers the company's reported earnings while increasing free cash flow.

Differentiation strategy A marketing strategy where a company distinguishes the differences of its products from competitive products on a nonprice basis. Product differentiation can be a source of competitive advantage.

Differentiators Key success factors that set one company, product, or brand apart from other competing companies, products, or brands.

Dilution (of ownership) This happens when a new stock issue results in a decrease in the preissue owners' percentage of the common stock.

Direct marketing The practice of delivering promotional messages directly to potential customers on an individual basis as opposed to through the use of a mass medium.

Discounted cash flow (DCF) Methods of evaluating investments by adjusting the cash flows for the time value of money. In the decision to invest in a project, all future cash flows expected from that investment are discounted back to their present value at the time the investment is made. The discount rate is whatever rate of return the investor requires. In theory, if the present value of the future cash flows is greater than the money being invested, the investment should be made. See *discount rate, internal rate of return, net present value*, and *present value*.

Discount rate (capitalization rate) Rate of return used to convert future values to present values. See *capitalization rate, internal rate of return*, and *rate of return*.

Disintermediation The act of cutting intermediaries out of traditional distribution channels by selling direct to consumers.

Distribution channel A chain of intermediaries that a firm's product must go through in order to reach the customer. Also known as *channel*. See *multichannel distribution strategy* and *common distribution strategy*.

Distribution strategy An organization's plan for moving products through intermediaries and to final customers.

Dividends paid Cash dividends paid to shareholders.

Doriot, General Georges Founder of American Research and Development Corporation in 1946, which started the modern venture capital industry; Harvard Business School professor; and one of the creators of INSEAD.

Double jeopardy The case where an entrepreneur's main source of income and most of his net worth depend on his business.

Due diligence The process of investigation by investors into a potential investee's management team, resources, and trading performance. This includes rigorous testing of the business plan assumptions and the verification of material facts (such as existing accounts).

Dun & Bradstreet (D&B) The biggest credit-reporting agency in the United States.

Early growth One of the four stages of a company's growth cycle. The four stages are start-up, growth, maturity, and decline. (See also *start-up*.)

Early stage financing This category includes seed stage, start-up stage, and first-stage financing.

Earned-income stream Income earned through the sale of products or services.

Earning-capitalization valuation This values a company by capitalizing its earnings:

$$\text{Company value} = \text{Net Income/Capitalization Rate.}$$

Earnings This is synonymous with income and profit.

Earnings before interest and taxes (EBIT) See *operating income*.

Earnings before interest, taxes, depreciation, and amortization (EBITDA) Often referred to as *cash flow*. It removes noncash charges, such as depreciation and amortization, to get a cleaner view of the cash-flow-generating ability of a company.

Earnings per share (EPS) A company's net income divided by the number of common shares issued and outstanding.

Economy of scale Reduction in cost per unit resulting from increased production, realized through operational efficiencies.

Elasticity of demand The percentage change in the quantity of a good demanded divided by the percentage change in the price of that good. When the elasticity is greater than 1, the demand is said to be elastic, and when it is less than 1, it is inelastic. In the short term, the demand for nonessential goods (for example, airline travel) is usually elastic, and the demand for essentials (for example, electricity) is usually inelastic.

Emerging market A new and growing market or industry.

Employment agreement An agreement whereby senior managers contract to remain with the company for a specified period. For the investing institutions, such an agreement provides some measure of security that the company's performance will not be adversely affected by the unexpected departure of key managers.

Employee stock ownership plan (ESOP) A trust established to acquire shares in a company for subsequent allocation to employees over a period of time. Several possibilities are available for structuring the operation of an ESOP. Essentially, either the company makes payments to the trust, which the trust uses to purchase shares; or the trust, having previously borrowed to acquire shares, may use the payments from the company to repay loans. The latter form is referred to as a *leveraged ESOP* and may be used as a means of providing part of the funding required to effect a buyout. A particular advantage of an ESOP is the possibility of tax relief for the contributions made by the company to the trust and on the cost of borrowing in those cases where the trust purchases shares in advance.

Entrepreneurial mindset An individual who has a well-developed entrepreneurial mindset focuses on two activities: (1) recognizing and assessing opportunity; and (2) proactive, passionate, persistent, and professional pursuit of the opportunity.

Entrepreneurship The practice of starting new organizations or revitalizing mature organizations in response to identified opportunities.

Environmental analysis The process of identifying and assessing the factors and trends in the external context that may drive decision making (including buying decisions) by customers.

Equity Interest or ownership in a business. See *owner's equity*.

Equity investors People (e.g., angels) or institutions (e.g., venture capitalists) who invest capital in return for ownership (equity) of the company.

Equity kicker (or warrant) An option or instrument linked to the provision of other types of funding, particularly mezzanine finance, which enables the provider to obtain an equity stake and hence a share in capital gains. In this way, providers of subordinated debt can be compensated for the higher risk they incur.

Exit The means by which investors in a company realize all or part of their investment. (Also known as *harvest*.)

Expansion financing Working capital for the initial expansion of a company that is producing and shipping products and has growing accounts receivable and inventories.

Factoring A means of enhancing the cash flow of a business. A factoring company pays to the firm a certain proportion of the value of the firm's trade debts and then receives the cash as the trade debtors settle their accounts. Invoice discounting is a similar procedure.

Filing Documents, including the prospectus, filed with the SEC for approval before an IPO.

Financials (financial statements) Summary reports that demonstrate how a firm has used its funds and its current financial position. The three basic financial statements are *income statement*, *balance sheet*, and *cash flow statement*. Also known as *financial statements*.

Financing flows Cash flows generated by debt and equity financing.

Finder A person or firm that attempts to raise funding for a private company.

Firm commitment offering The underwriter guarantees to raise a certain amount of money for the company and other selling stockholders at the IPO.

First-round financing The first investment made by external investors.

First-stage financing Financing to initiate full manufacturing and sales.

Five Cs of credit The five crucial elements for obtaining credit are character (borrower's integrity), capacity (sufficient cash flow to service the debt), capital (borrower's net worth), collateral (assets to secure the debt), and conditions (of the borrowing company, its industry, and the general economy).

Fixed and floating charges Claims on assets pledged as security for debt. Fixed charges cover specific fixed assets, and floating charges relate to all or part of a company's assets.

Fixed expense Expenses or costs that do not change with sales volume.

Floating lien A general lien against a group of assets, such as accounts receivable or inventory, without the assets being specifically identified.

Flotation A method of raising equity financing by selling shares on a stock market, and often allowing management and institutions to realize some of their investment at the same time. See *initial public offering*.

Foreign direct investment Under this strategy, companies set up a physical presence in the countries of interest, whether that is a sales office, retail outlets, production facilities, or something else.

Four Fs Founders, family, friends, and foolhardy persons who invest in a person's private business—generally a start-up. See *informal investor* and *angel*.

Four Ps of marketing Product, price, place, and promotion.

Fragmented industry An industry in which no single firm or company has a large share of the market.

Franchise (franchising) An organizational form in which a firm (the franchisor) with a market-tested business package centered on a product or service enters into a continuing contractual relationship with franchisees operating under the franchisor's trade name to produce or market goods or services according to a format specified by the franchisor.

Franchise fee Fee paid by the franchisee to the franchisor to acquire the franchise.

Franchisee The person or entity who purchases the rights to open a franchise.

Franchisor The entity or person who owns the rights or license of the business. The franchisor grants the license of permission to franchise to the franchisee.

Free cash flow Cash flow in excess of that required to fund all projects that have a positive net present value when discounted at the relevant cost of capital. Conflicts of interest between shareholders and managers may arise when the organization generates free cash flow. Shareholders may desire higher dividends, but managers may wish to invest in projects providing a return below the cost of capital. See *cost of capital* and *net present value*.

Frequency The number of times a target market member is exposed to an ad campaign during a certain period.

Fulfillment Services provided by a company that handles warehousing, picking, and delivery of product to the end consumer on behalf of the fulfillment company's clients.

Future value The value at a future date of a present amount of money.

$$FV_t = PV \times (1 + K/100)^t$$

Where
FV   is the future value
PV   is the present value

K   is the percentage annual rate of return

t   is the number of years.

For example, an investment of $100,000 must have a future value of $384,160 after four years to produce a rate of return of 40 percent, which is the kind of return that an investor in an early stage company expects to earn. (See *net present value, present value,* and *rate of return.*)

Gearing British term of leverage. See *leverage.*

Global Entrepreneurship Monitor (GEM) An annual study of entrepreneurial activity within different countries.

Going concern This assumes that the company will continue as an operating business as opposed to going out of business and liquidating its assets.

Golden handcuffs A combination of rewards and penalties given to key managers to dissuade them from leaving the company. Examples are high salaries, paid on a deferred basis while employment is maintained, and stock options.

Goodwill The difference between the purchase price of a company and the net value of its assets purchased.

Gross domestic product (GDP) The total dollar value of all goods and services produced by citizens of a country.

Gross margin/profit Difference between net sales (revenue) and cost of goods sold. Profit is expressed as an amount of money while margin is expressed as a percentage of sales.

Gross national product (GNP) The value of all the goods and services produced in an economy, plus the value of the goods and services imported, less the goods and services exported.

Guarantee An undertaking to prove that a debt or obligation of another will be paid or performed. It may relate either to a specific debt or to a series of transactions, such as a guarantee of a bank overdraft. For example, entrepreneurs are often required to provide personal guarantees for loans borrowed by their companies.

Guerrilla marketing Marketing activities that are nontraditional, unconventional, and grass-roots.

Harvest The realization of the value of an investment. See *exit.*

High-potential venture A company started with the intent of growing quickly to annual sales of at least $30–50 million in five years. It has the potential to have a firm-commitment IPO.

Hurdle rate The minimum rate of return that is acceptable to investors. See *return on investment.*

Improvement ideas Enhancements to existing products that lack a high degree of novelty (this does not mean zero novelty). See *innovation.*

Income statement A summary of a company's revenues, expenses, and profits over a specified period of time. See *pro forma statements.*

Inelastic demand The lack of change in the quantity demanded of a product in response to a change in price. Inelasticity is measured on a scale of 0 to 1. A product with inelastic demand will experience minimal changes in demand in response to a change in price.

Influencer A person in the prospect organization who has the power to influence and persuade a decision maker. Influencers will generally be decision makers for relatively low-value sales. There is usually more than one influencer in any prospect organization relevant to a particular sale, and large organizations will have several influencers.

Informal investor An individual who puts money into a private company—usually a start-up or a small business. Informal investments range from micro-loans from family members to sizable equity purchases by sophisticated business angels.

Initial public offering (IPO) The process by which a company raises money, and gets listed, on a stock market. See *flotation*.

Innovation The process of converting knowledge and ideas to develop new products, services, and/or strategies.

INSEAD The European Institute of Business Administration located in Fontainebleau, France.

Integrated marketing communications A complementary set of decisions, actions, and initiatives that potentially enhance the positive impact of the individual Ps (product, price, place, and promotion) when properly designed and orchestrated.

Interest cover The extent to which periodic interest commitments on borrowings are exceeded by periodic profits. It is the ratio of profits before the deduction of interest and taxes to interest payments. The ratio may also be expressed as the cash flow from operations divided by the amount of interest payable.

Interest expense Interest charged from obtaining debt financing.

Internal rate of return (IRR) The discount rate that equates the present value of the future net cash flows from an investment with the project's cash outflows. It is a means of expressing the percentage rate of return projected on a proposed investment. For an investment in a company, the calculation takes account of cash invested, cash receipts from dividend payments and redemptions, percentage equity held, expected date of payments, realization of the investment and capitalization at that point, and possible further financing requirements. The calculation will frequently be quoted in a range depending on sensitivity analysis. See *discount rate, present value, future value*, and *rate of return*.

Inventory Finished goods, work in process of manufacture, and raw materials owned by a company.

Investment The outlay of money usually for income or profit.

Investment bank A financial institution engaged in the issue of new securities, including management and underwriting of issues as well as securities trading and distribution.

Investment flows Cash flows associated with purchase and sales of both fixed assets and business interests.

Invisible venture capital (informal venture capital) Venture capital supplied by wealthy individuals (angels), as opposed to *visible* venture capital, which is supplied by formal venture capital firms that make up the organized venture capital industry.

Junior debt Loan ranking after senior debt or secured debt for payment in the event of a default.

Junk bonds A variety of high-yield, unsecured bonds tradable on a secondary market and not considered to be of investment quality by credit rating agencies. High yield normally indicates higher risk.

Key person insurance Additional security provided to financial backers of a company through the purchase of insurance on the lives of key managers who are seen as crucial to the future of the company. Should one or more of those key executives die prematurely, the financial backers would receive the insurance payment.

Key success factors (KSF) The attributes that influence where the customer spends money.

Lead investor In syndicated deals, normally the investor who originates, structures, and subsequently plays the major monitoring role.

Learning curve The rate at which a new skill or subject is learned.

Lemons and plums Bad deals and good deals, respectively.

Leverage The amount of debt in a company's financing structure, which may be expressed as a percentage of the total financing or as a ratio of debt to equity. The various quasi-equity (preference-type shares) and quasi-debt (mezzanine debt) instruments used to fund later stage companies means that great care is required in calculating and interpreting leverage or gearing ratios.

Leveraged buyout (LBO) Acquisition of a company by an investor group, an investor, or an investment/LBO partnership, with a significant amount of debt (usually at least 70 percent of the total capitalization) and with plans to repay the debt with funds generated from the acquired company's operations or from asset sales. LBOs are frequently financed in part with junk bonds.

Liability Obligations and debt that a company must pay in the future.

License agreement A contract between the franchisor and franchisee. Also known as a *franchise contract*.

Lien A legal claim on certain assets that are used to secure a loan.

Limited liability company A company owned by "members," who either manage the business themselves or appoint "managers" to run it for them. All members and managers have the benefit of limited liability and, in most cases, are taxed in the same way as a subchapter S corporation without having to conform to the S corporation restrictions.

Line of credit (with a bank) An arrangement between a bank and a customer, specifying the maximum amount of unsecured debt the customer can owe the bank at a given point in time.

Line of credit (with a vendor) A limit set by the seller on the amount that a purchaser can buy on credit.

Liquidation value (of an asset) The amount of money that can be realized from the sale of an asset sold separately from its operating organization.

Liquidation value (of a company) The market value of the assets of a company that is liquidating minus the liabilities that must be paid.

Liquidity The ability of an asset to be converted to cash as quickly as possible and without any price discount.

Listing Acceptance of a security for trading on an organized stock exchange. Hence, a stock traded on the New York Stock Exchange is said to be listed on the NYSE.

Living dead Venture capital jargon for a company that has no prospect of being harvested with a public offering or an acquisition; hence, the venture capital form cannot realize its investment in the company.

Loan note A form of vendor finance or deferred payment. The purchaser (borrower) may agree to make payments to the holder of the loan note at specified future dates. The holder may be able to obtain cash at an earlier date by selling at a discount to a financing institution that will collect on maturity.

Lockup period An interval during which an investment may not be sold. In the case of an *IPO*, employees may not sell their *shares* for a period of time determined by the *underwriter* and usually lasting 180 days.

Locus of control The perception of the factors responsible for the outcome of an event. An individual with an internal locus of control believes his actions caused the outcome. Conversely, an individual with an external locus of control believes the outcome was determined by outside forces.

Low-cost strategy A marketing or penetration strategy where a company prices its products low in relation to competitive prices. See *penetration pricing strategy*.

Management buy-in (MBI) The transfer of ownership of an entity to a new set of owners in which new managers coming into the entity are a significant element.

Management buyout (MBO) The transfer of ownership of an entity to a new set of owners in which the existing management and employees are a significant element.

Marginal cost The increase in costs to a company to produce one more unit of output.

Market A subgroup of a population determined by shared characteristics and product/service needs. A market can be divided into segments through the use of demographic and psychographic characteristics.

Market capitalization The total value, at market prices, of the securities in issue for a company, a stock market, or a sector of a stock market, calculated by multiplying the number of shares issued by the market price per share.

Market-comparable valuation The value of a private company based on the valuation of similar public companies.

Market demand pricing A pricing strategy where products and services are priced based upon current market prices.

Market forecasting Total level of demand for a product, across all brands, expected to result from a particular marketing effort by the competitors in the market. Environmental trends not under the control of the marketers, such as social trends or economic changes, can greatly impact the accuracy of the market forecast.

Marketing The activity, set of institutions, and processes for creating, communicating, delivering, and exchanging offerings that have value for customers, clients, partners, and society at large.

Marketing communications Coordinated promotional messages delivered through one or more channels such as print, radio, television, direct mail, and personal selling.

Marketing strategy An organizational function and a set of processes for creating, communicating, and delivering value to customers and for managing customer relationships in ways that benefit the organization and its stakeholders.

Market penetration A measure of the percentage or potential percentage of the market that a product or company is able to capture, expressed in terms of total sales or turnover. Market penetration is often used to measure the level of success a new product or service has achieved.

Market research The collection and analysis of any reliable information that improves managerial decisions.

Market segment A subgroup of a market sharing one or more characteristics. See *market*.

Market share The percentage of total sales volume in a market held by a company, brand or product.

Market value The price at which buyers and sellers trade the item in an open market.

Mezzanine financing Strictly, any form of financing instrument between ordinary shares and senior debt. The forms range from senior mezzanine debt, which may simply carry an interest rate above that for senior secured debt, to junior mezzanine debt, which may carry rights to subscribe for equity but no regular interest payment.

Microfinance The provision of small loans (also referred to as microcredit) to poor people to help them engage in productive activities or grow very small businesses. Microfinance may also include a broader range of services such as credit, savings, and insurance.

Middle-market company A company that has sales revenue of $5–20 million and modest growth. In contrast to a high-potential company, it does not have the potential to float an IPO, but it may be a candidate for an acquisition, LBO, MBI, MBO, or ESOP.

Milestone A significant point in development. Milestones are mostly used in business as benchmarks to gauge progress.

Mind-mapping A visual, nonlinear depiction of data using hierarchies, associations, categories, colors, symbols, and pictures.

Multichannel distribution strategy A distribution strategy that utilizes multiple channels to reach the customer (such as retail and online).

Multiple The amount of money realized from the sale of an investment divided by the amount of money originally invested.

Murphy's Law "What can go wrong, will go wrong." An unexpected setback will happen at the most inconvenient moment.

National Association of Securities Dealers (NASD) Organization for brokers and dealers in NASDAQ stocks.

National Association of Securities Dealers Automated Quotation (NASDAQ) An electronic system set up by NASD for trading stocks.

Net income (net earnings, net profit) A company's final income after all expenses and taxes have been deducted from all revenues. Also known as the *bottom line*.

Net income margin Net income as a percentage of net sales revenue. In a typical year an average U.S. company has a net income margin of about 5 percent.

Net liquid value Liquid financial assets minus callable liabilities.

Net present value The present value of an investment's future net cash flows minus the initial investment. In theory, if the net present value is greater than 0, an investment should be made. For example, an investor is asked to invest $100,000 in a company that is expanding. He expects a rate of return of 30 percent. The company offers to pay him back $300,000 after four years. The present value of $300,000 at a rate of return of 30 percent is $105,038. Thus, the net present value of the investment is $5,038, so the investment should be made. See *free cash flow, future value, present value,* and *rate of return.*

Net profit See *net income.*

Net worth See *book value.*

New York Stock Exchange (NYSE) The largest stock exchange in the world, located in New York. Also known as the Big Board.

Nonprofit An organization chartered for other than profit-making activities.

Offering circular See *prospectus.*

Operating cash flows Cash flows directly generated by a company's operations. The cash flow from operating activity equals net income plus depreciation minus increase in accounts receivable minus increase in inventories plus increase in accounts payable plus increase in accruals. See *financing flows* and *investment flows.*

Operating expense/costs The usual customary costs that a company incurs to support its main business activities.

Operating income Earnings (profit) before deduction of interest payments and income taxes, abbreviated to EBIT. It measures a company's earning power from its ongoing operations. It is of particular concern to a company's lenders, such as banks, because operating income demonstrates the ability of a company to earn sufficient income to pay the interest on its debt. See *times interest earned.*

Operational excellence A strategy of competitive advantage where a company focuses on the quality and efficiency of processes and operations.

Opportunity analysis The identification and evaluation of potential business opportunities coupled with an assessment of the organization's ability to exploit them.

Organization chart A diagram illustrating the structure of an organization and positions within the organization.

Out of cash (OOC) A common problem with entrepreneurial companies. The OOC time period is cash on hand divided by the burn rate.

Outsourcing Outsourcing allows businesses to handle key attributes of their products while handing over the responsibility for development and manufacturing to a subcontractor.

Overhead costs Costs that are not directly tied to a specific client (such as a company's monthly electrical expense).

Over the counter (OTC) Refers to stocks, debt securities, and other financial instruments that trade via a dealer network as opposed to on a centralized exchange.

Owners' equity Common stock plus retained earnings. (See *book value* of a company.)

Paid-in capital Par value per share times the number of shares issued. Additional paid-in capital is the price paid in excess of par value times the number of shares issued.

Pain point A potential customer's problem that a business can relieve with its product or service.

Partnership Legal form of a business in which two or more persons are co-owners, sharing profits and losses.

Par value Nominal price placed on a share of common stock.

Penetration pricing strategy A low-cost pricing strategy that seeks to maximize market penetration for a new product.

Piggyback registration rights The right to register unregistered stock in the event of a company having a public stock offering.

Pledging The use of a company's accounts receivable as security (collateral) for a short-term loan.

Pop (first day) Percentage increase in the price of a stock at the end of the first day's trading over the initial offering price.

Portfolio Collection of investments. For example, the portfolio of a venture capital fund comprises all its investments.

Positioning An organization's efforts to influence consumer perception of a brand of product relative to the perception of competing brands or products.

Positioning map A tool used by marketers to visually depict consumer perceptions of brands and their perceived attributes. Also known as a perceptual map.

Post-money valuation The value of a company immediately after a round of additional money has been invested.

Pratt's Guide to Venture Capital Sources Annual sourcebook for the venture capital industry.

Preemptive rights The rights of shareholders to maintain their percentage ownership of a company by purchasing a proportionate number of shares of any new issue of common stock. See *antidilution, dilution,* and *pro-rata interest.*

Preference shares A class of shares that incorporate the right to a fixed dividend and usually a prior claim on assets in preference to ordinary shares, in the event of a liquidation. Cumulative preference shares provide an entitlement to a cumulative dividend if in any year the preference dividend is unpaid due to insufficient profits being earned. Preference shares are usually redeemable at specific dates.

Preliminary prospectus The initial document published by an *underwriter* of a *new issue* of *stock* to be given to prospective investors. It is understood that the document will be modified significantly before the *final prospectus* is published; also called a *red herring.*

Premoney valuation The value of a company's equity before additional money is invested.

Prepayment A payment on a loan made prior to the original due date.

Present value (PV) The current value of a given future cash flow stream, FVt, after t years, discounted at a rate of return of K% is $PV = FV_t /(1 + K/100)^t$. For example, if an investor expects a rate of return of 60 percent on an investment in a seed stage company, and she believes that her investment will be worth $750,000 after five years, then the present value of her investment is $71,526. (See *discount rate, future value, net present value, present value*, and *rate of return*.)

Present value of future cash flows (valuation) Today's value of a future payment, or stream of payments, discounted at some appropriate compound interest, or discount, rate; also called *time value of money*. The present value of a company is the present value of the future free cash flows plus the residual (terminal) value of the firm:

$$PV = \sum_{t=1}^{N} \frac{(FCF_t)}{(1 + K)^t} + \frac{RV_N}{(1 + K)^N}$$

Where
K   is the cost of capital
FCF_t is the free cash flow in year t
N   is the number of years
RV_N is the residual value in year N.

Free Cash Flow

= Operating income

− Interest

− Taxes on operating income

+ Depreciation and other noncash charges

− Increase in net working capital

− Capital expenditures (replacement and growth)

− Principal repayments

Price discrimination The practice of selling the same product to different buyers at different prices. Certain forms of price discrimination may violate antitrust laws while other forms (such as buying wholesale) are common practice by many organizations.

Price-earnings ratio (P/E ratio) The ratio of the market value of a firm's equity to its after-tax profits (may be calculated from price per share and earnings per share).

Price promotion A sales promotion based on a price discount offer. Trade promotions are price discounts that are offered to distribution channel intermediaries, while consumer promotions are price discounts offered to the end consumer.

Price-sensitive consumers Customers who exhibit an elastic demand curve.

Price skimming A strategy through which the producer of a uniquely new item obtains high profits from buyers for whom the new product is a must-have item. Once profits have been skimmed from that segment of the market, the producer drops the price and skims the next tier of interested customers.

Primary data Market data that is collected specifically for a particular purpose through surveys, focus groups, or experiments.

Primary research Research that collects market data through surveys, focus groups, or experiments.

Primary target audience (PTA) A group of potential customers identified by demographic and psychographic data that will be the focus of the company's early marketing and sales efforts.

Prime rate Short-term interest rate charged by a bank to its largest, most creditworthy customers.

Private placement The direct sales of securities to a small number of investors.

Pro-rata interest The right granted the investor to maintain the same percentage ownership in the event of future financings. See *antidilution* and *dilution*.

Product differentiation The process of developing or incorporating attributes that a product's intended consumers perceive to be different (in relation to competing products) and desirable.

Product diffusion curve A model that demonstrates the rate of adoption of a new product by various groups of consumers. The various groups in the product diffusion curve are (1) innovators, (2) early adopters, (3) early majority, (4) late majority, and (5) laggards.

Product franchise An arrangement where the franchisee sells goods that are produced, controlled, or directed by the franchisor (which bears the franchisor's trademark).

Product leadership A strategy of competitive advantage where a company focuses on product innovation and being the innovative leader of the industry.

Product life cycle The four major stages a product passes through: introduction, growth, maturity, and decline.

Product line extension The practice of adding depth to an existing product line by introducing new products in the same product category and under the same brand; product line extensions give customers greater choice and help to protect the firm from a flanking attack by a competitor.

Product mix The variety of product lines that a company produces. Product mix usually refers to the length (the number of products in the product line), breadth (the number of product lines that a company offers), depth (the different varieties of product in the product line), and consistency (the relationship between products in their final destination) of product lines.

Profit Synonymous with income and earnings.

Profit margin Net revenues minus cost of goods sold.

Pro forma statements Projected financial statements: income and cash-flow statements and balance sheets. For a start-up company, it is usual to make pro forma statements monthly for the first two years and annually for the next three years.

Prospecting The search for potential customers of buyers.

Prospectus A document giving a description of a securities issue, including a complete statement of the terms of the issue and a description of the issuer, as well as its historical financial statements. Also referred to as an *offering circular*. See *red herring*.

Psychographics Information that categorizes customers based upon their personality, psychological traits, lifestyles, values, and social membership.

Public relations (PR) The business of inducing the public to have understanding for and goodwill toward a person, firm, or institution.

Pull strategy A marketing communication strategy that focuses on creating end user demand to pull the product through the channel. Pull strategies are aimed at the end user of the distribution channel.

Push strategy A marketing communication strategy that uses tools such as trade promotions, trade shows, and personal selling to distributors or other channel members (retailers, etc.) to push a product through to the end user. Push strategies are aimed at the intermediaries of a distribution channel.

Put A contract allowing the holder to sell a given number of securities back to the issuer of the contract at a fixed price for a given period of time.

Rate of return The annual return on an investment. If a sum of money PV_0 is invested and after t years that investment is worth FV_t, the return on investment:

$$K = \left[(FV_t/PV_0)^{1/t} - 1\right] \times 100\%$$

For example, if $100 is invested originally, and one year later $108 is paid back to the investor, the annual rate of return is 8 percent.

Reach The percentage of a company's target market that is exposed to an ad campaign within a certain time period.

Realization See *exit*.

Redeemable shares Shares that may be redeemable at the option of the company or the shareholder or both.

Red herring Preliminary prospectus circulated by underwriters to gauge investor interest in a planned offering. A legend in red ink on its cover indicates that the registration has not yet become effective and is still being reviewed by the SEC.

Registration statement A carefully worded and organized document, including a prospectus, filed with the SEC before an IPO.

Regulation D Under the Securities Act of 1933, all offers to sell securities must either be registered with the SEC or meet an exemption. Regulation D contains three rules (Rules 504, 505, and 506) offering exemptions from registration requirements, allowing smaller companies to offer and sell securities without having to register the securities with the SEC.

Relationship orientation A corporate or entrepreneurial outlook that focuses on creating structural and emotional ties with all stakeholders.

Resource acquisition The process of identifying, sourcing, and acquiring funding for endeavors.

Resulting experience The events that the customer experiences as a result of using and interacting with the supplying firm's products, services, and actions.

Retained earnings The part of net income retained in the company and not distributed to stockholders.

Return on investment The annual income that an investment earns.

Revenue Net sales; the monies earned through sales of a product before cost of goods sold and other expenses are subtracted.

Revenue drivers Elements within a business model that can be influenced to increase revenue, such as price, quantity sold, awareness of product, availability, and so forth.

Road show A series of meetings with potential investors and *brokers*, conducted by a company and its *underwriter* prior to a *securities offering*, especially an *IPO*.

Royalty A payment made for the use of property, especially a patent, copyrighted work, franchise, or natural resource. The amount is usually a percentage of revenues obtained through its use.

Running returns Periodic returns, such as interest and dividends, from an investment (in contrast to a one-time capital gain).

Sales cycle The time and/or process between first contact with the customer and when the sale is made. Sales cycle times and processes vary enormously depending on the company, type of business (product/service), the effectiveness of the sales process, the market, and the particular situation applying to the customer at the time of the inquiry.

Sales funnel Describes the pattern, plan, or actual achievement of conversion of prospects into sales, pre-enquiry, and then through the sales cycle; so called because it includes the conversion ratio at each stage of the sales cycle, which has a funneling effect.

Sales pipeline A linear equivalent of the sales funnel principle. Prospects need to be fed into the pipeline in order to drop out of the other end as sales. The length of the pipeline is the sales cycle time, which depends on business type, market situation, and the effectiveness of the sales process.

Sales promotion A range of techniques used to stimulate sales of a product, achieved through contests, demonstrations, discounts, point-of-sale displays, merchandising, and special offers. There are three primary types of sales promotion: consumer promotions, trade promotions, and sales force promotions. All types of sales promotions are either price or nonprice promotions.

SBA Small Business Administration.

SBDC Small Business Development Centers (supported by the SBA).

SBI Small Business Institutes, run by universities and colleges with SBA support.

SBIC Small Business Investment Companies.

SBIR Small Business Innovation Research Program.

Scalability (business) The potential for a business or an aspect of a business to continue to function effectively as its size increases.

Schumpeter, Joesph A. Moravian-born economist whose book *The Theory of Economic Development*, written in Vienna in 1912, introduced the modern theory of entrepreneurship, in which the entrepreneur plays the central role in economic development by destroying the static equilibrium of the existing economy. Excellent modern examples are the roles played by Steve Jobs, Bill Gates, and Dan Bricklin in creating the microcomputer industry in the late 1970s. By the beginning of the 1990s, microcomputers (personal computers) were the principal force shaping the computer industry, and the old companies manufacturing mainframe and minicomputers, which dominated the computer industry until the mid-1980s, were in distress, ranging from outright bankruptcy to record-breaking losses.

SCORE Service Core of Retired Executives, sponsored by the SBA to provide consulting to small businesses.

Search ideas Ideas that are created in a deliberate and purposeful manner.

Secondary data Market data that is gathered from already published sources, like an industry association study or census reports.

Secondary offering The sale of stock by an issuer or underwriter after a company's securities have already begun trading publicly.

Secondary research Research that is conducted by collecting market data from already published sources, like an industry association study or census report.

Secondary target audience (STA) A group of potential customers identified by demographic and psychographic data that will be a secondary or alternate focus of the company's early marketing and sales efforts. See *primary target audience*.

Second-round financing The introduction of further funding by the original investors or new investors to enable the company to grow or deal with unexpected problems. Each round of financing tends to cover the next period of growth.

Securities and Exchange Commission (SEC) Regulatory body for investor protection in the United States, created by the Securities Exchange Act of 1934. The supervision of dealers is delegated to the self-regulatory bodies of the stock exchanges and NASD under the provisions of the Maloney Act of 1938.

Seed financing A relatively small amount of money provided to prove a concept; it may involve product development and market research but rarely involves the initial marketing of a product.

Segmentation A process whereby a market is divided into subgroups based on shared characteristics.

Sensitivity analysis Examination of how the projected performance of the business varies with changes in the key assumptions on which the forecasts are based.

Short-term security Generally an obligation maturing in less than one year.

Social entrepreneurship The process of seeking creative and valuable solutions to such issues as education, poverty, health care, global warming, global water shortages, and energy (to name a few).

Social venture capital (SVC) A subset of the traditional venture capital market that seeks to invest in for-profit ventures for financial return and also social and/or environmental return—also known as the double bottom line or triple bottom line. Within SVC there are three different funds: (1) focused funds, which focus on particular technology, fields, and stages of companies; (2) community funds, which focus on businesses that operate in underserved markets; and (3) VCs with a conscience, which stipulate that a certain percentage of the fund will be invested in socially responsible businesses related to their target investment areas.

Sole proprietorship A business structure in which an individual and his company are considered a single entity for tax and liability purposes.

Stakeholder A person or group organization that, directly or indirectly, affects or is affected by an organization's actions.

Start-up financing Funding provided to companies for use in product development and initial marketing. Companies may be in the process of being organized or may have been in business a short time (one year or less), but have not sold their product commercially. Generally, such firms have assembled the key management, prepared a business plan, made market studies, and completed other preliminary tasks.

Statement of cash flows A financial statement showing a firm's cash inflows and outflows for a specific period, classified into operating, investing, and financing categories.

Stock option plan A plan designed to motivate employees, especially key ones, by placing a proportion of the common stock of the company under option at a fixed price to defined employees. The option may then be exercised by the employees at a future date. Stock options are often introduced as part of the remuneration package of senior executives.

Stock-out A situation where the demand or requirement for an item cannot be fulfilled from current (on-hand) inventory.

Strategy The art of developing and employing an elaborate and systematic plan in order to reach a goal.

Subchapter S corporation A small business corporation in which the owners personally pay the corporation's income taxes.

Subordinated debt Loans that may be unsecured or, more commonly, secured by secondary charges and that rank after senior debt for repayment in the event of default. Also referred to as junior debt or mezzanine debt.

Substitute Different goods that, at least partially, satisfy the same needs of the consumers and therefore can be used to replace one another.

Supplier A company that supplies parts or services to another company. Also known as a *vendor*.

Sustainability (business) The quality of careful, efficient, and prudent use of natural, fiscal, and human resources over the long term with minimal waste and accounting for all monetary and nonmonetary costs.

Sweat equity Equity acquired by the management team at favorable terms reflecting the value to the business of the managers' past and future efforts.

Syndicate A group of investors who act together when investing in a company.

Targeting A process whereby the attractiveness of various segments of the market is compared and the most attractive is selected, which becomes the target segment, also called the *target market*.

Target market A specific group of consumers at which a company aims its products and services.

Term loan Debt originally scheduled to be repaid in more than one year, but usually in 10 years or less.

Term sheet Summary of the principal conditions for a proposed investment by a venture capital firm in a company.

Tertiary target audience (TTA) A group of potential customers identified by demographic and psychographic data that will be the focus of the company's later marketing and sales efforts. See *primary target audience*.

Times interest earned Earnings before interest and taxes, divided by interest (EBIT/I). The higher this ratio, the more secure the loan on which interest is paid. It is a basic measure of the creditworthiness of a company.

Trademark A distinctive name, symbol, motto, or design that legally identifies a company or its products and services.

Trade name The name which a business trades under for business purposes. Also known as a business name.

Trade sale The sale of a business to another company, often but not always in a similar line of business.

Triggering event An incident that prompts a person to take steps to start a new venture.

Undercapitalization A situation in which a business lacks sufficient capital to perform normal business activities.

Underwrite An arrangement under which investment banks each agree to buy a certain amount of securities of a new issue on a given date and at a given price, thereby assuring the issuer of the full proceeds of the financing.

Underwriter An institution engaged in the business of underwriting securities issues.

Underwriting fee The share of the gross spread of a new issue accruing to members of the underwriting group after the expenses of the issue have been paid.

Unsecured loans Debt that is not backed by a pledge of specific assets.

Valuation (of a company) The market value of a company. See *market capitalization*.

Value-added (by investors) Many venture capital firms claim that they add more than money to investee companies. They call it value-added, which includes strategic advice on such matters as hiring key employees, marketing, production, control, and financing.

Value-based pricing Pricing method based on the perceived worth of a product's benefits to its intended customers.

Value chain An interlinking of value-added activities that converts inputs into outputs, which adds to the company's bottom line and helps create a competitive advantage.

Value proposition The value of a business's products and services to its customers.

Value selling A relationship-building process through which the salesperson communicates the potential value of a product/service to prospective customers.

Variable costs   Costs that change with changes in sales volume.

Vendor   A seller of goods.

Vendor financing   A loan from one company to another which is used to buy goods from the company providing the loan.

Venture capitalist   A financial institution specializing in the provision of equity and other forms of long-term capital to enterprises, usually to firms with a limited track record but with the expectation of substantial growth. The venture capitalist may provide both funding and varying degrees of managerial and technical expertise. Venture capital has traditionally been associated with start-ups; however, venture capitalists have increasingly participated in later-stage projects.

Venture philanthropy   A field of philanthropic activity where private equity and venture capital business models are applied to the nonprofit and charitable sectors.

Vesting period   The time period before shares are owned unconditionally by an employee who is sold stock with the stipulation that he must continue to work for the company selling him the shares. If his employment terminates before the end of that period, the company has the right to buy back the shares at the same price at which it originally sold them to him.

Visible venture capital (formal venture capital)   The organized venture capital industry consisting of formal firms, in contrast to invisible venture capital or informal venture capital.

Vulture capital   A derogatory term for venture capital.

Waiver   Consent granted by an investor or lender to permit an investor or borrower to be in default on a covenant.

Warrant   An option to purchase common stock at a specified price. See *equity kicker*.

Warranty   A statement of fact or opinion concerning the condition of a company. The inclusion of warranties in an investment agreement gives the investor a claim against the company if it subsequently becomes apparent that the company's condition was not as stated at the time of the investment.

Window of opportunity   A period of time in which an opportunity is more viable.

Working capital   A financial metric that is a measure of current assets of a business that exceed its liabilities and can be applied to its operations.

Yield   Annualized rate of return on a security.

Index